Unit 4

Teacher's Edition

NATIONAL GEOGRAPHIC

Reach for Reading

COMMON CORE PROGRAM

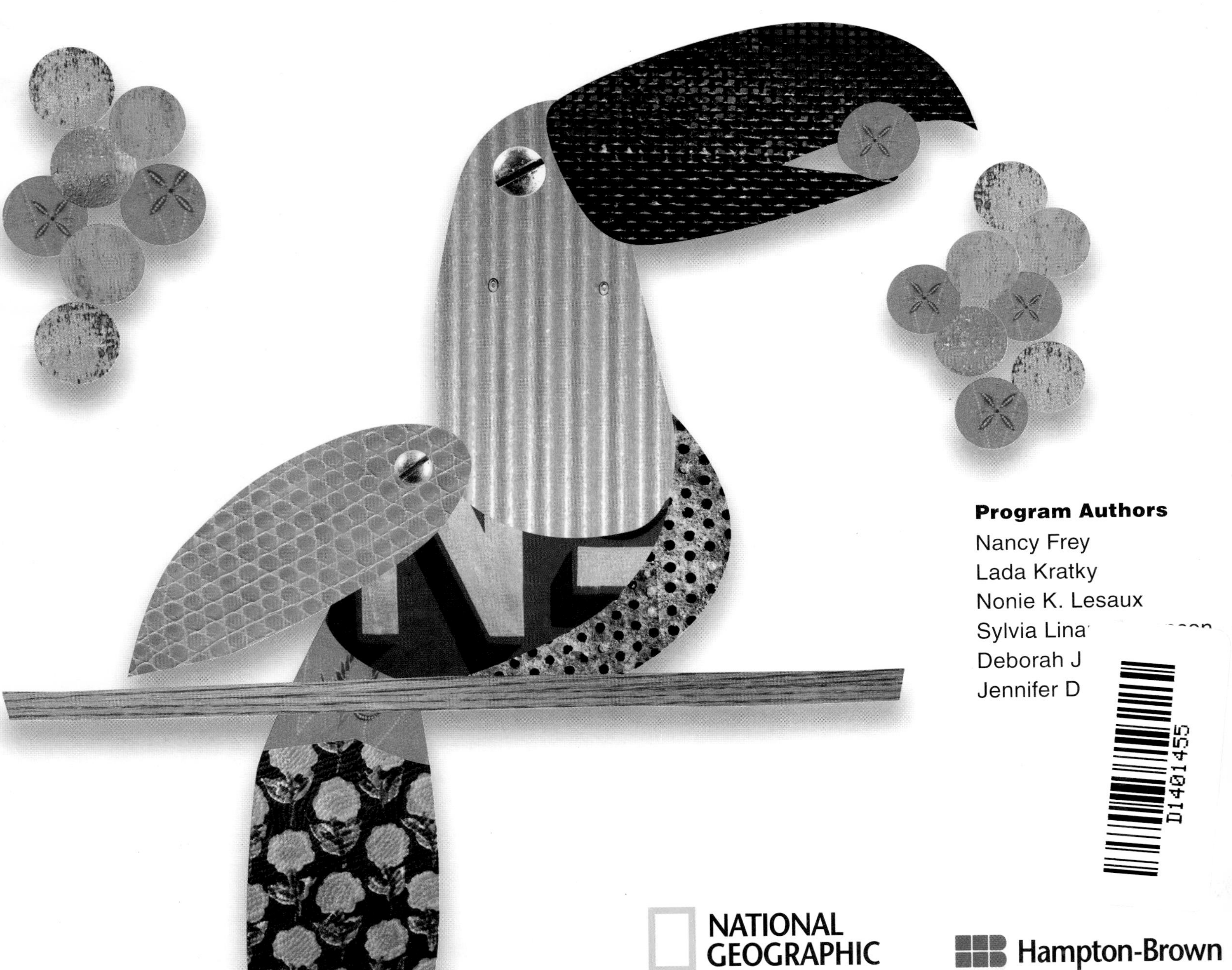

Program Authors

Nancy Frey

Lada Kratky

Nonie K. Lesaux

Sylvia Lina

Deborah J

Jennifer D

NATIONAL GEOGRAPHIC

Hampton-Brown

Meet the Artist

Joel Sotelo grew up in Tijuana, Mexico and began coming to the United States with his mother as a young child. He now lives in San Diego where he works as an artist and designer. Sotelo loves to travel and integrates elements of many countries and cultures into his art.

Acknowledgments
Grateful acknowledgment is given to the authors, artists, photographers, museums, publishers, and agents for permission to reprint copyrighted material. Every effort has been made to secure the appropriate permission. If any omissions have been made or if corrections are required, please contact the Publisher.

Lexile®, Lexile Framework® and the Lexile® logo are trademarks of MetaMetrics, Inc., and are registered in the United States and abroad.

Cover Design and Art Direction: Visual Asylum

Cover Illustration: Joel Sotelo

Illustration Credits: All PM and RT illustrations by National Geographic Learning; A4.6, A4.19 National Geographic Learning.

Photographic Credits: IFC (tl) Design Pics Inc./Alamy, (cl) Blend Images/ Alamy, (bl) Washington Post/Getty Images, (tr) ZSSD/Minden Pictures, (cr) Glow Images/Getty Images, (br) Paul Nicklen/National Geographic Images Collection; T207h, T233h, T2339p, T259f (bl) flab/Alamy; T207c (c) Corbis; T207r (tl) Philip and Karen Smith/Jupiterimages; T208 (br) Corbis; T233d, T239l Bruce Dale/National Geographic Stock; T239r (tl) Jupiterimages; T259b (c) Rich Carey/Shutterstock; A4.41 (tl) Jacek Chabraszewski/Shutterstock, (tc) paulaphoto/Shutterstock, (tr) Andy Dean Photography/Shutterstock.

Acknowledgments and credits continued on page Ack1.

Visit National Geographic Learning online at www.NGSP.com

Visit our corporate website at www.cengage.com

Printed in the USA.

RR Donnelley, Menasha, WI

ISBN: 978-07362-96557

B

12 13 14 15 16 17 18 19 20 21

10 9 8 7 6 5 4 3 2

Let's Work Together

BIG QUESTION

What's the best way to get things done?

READING SKILLS

RESOURCES

Classroom Management

Whole Group Time

TEACHER	STUDENTS

▪ Introduce Anthology
▪ Conduct Reading Lessons
▪ Teach Daily Language Arts
  ▪ Daily Spelling & Word Work
  ▪ Daily Grammar
  ▪ Daily Writing Skills
▪ Differentiate Instruction
▪ Guide Writing Projects
▪ Assess Progress
	▪ Read and Respond to Fiction and Nonfiction
	▪ Build Content Knowledge
	▪ Develop Reading Skills
	▪ Engage in Language Arts Activities
	▪ Collaborate on Writing Projects
	▪ Complete Assessments

Small Group Reading Time

TEACHER	STUDENTS
▪ Introduce Books ▪ Conduct Mini Lessons ▪ Monitor Small Group Reading ▪ Guide Discussion ▪ Assess Progress	▪ Read and Discuss Books ▪ Extend Content Knowledge ▪ Apply Reading Skills ▪ Connect and Compare Texts ▪ Demonstrate Comprehension

Learning Station Time

TEACHER	STUDENTS
▪ Suggest Books for Independent Reading ▪ Introduce Learning Stations ▪ Meet with Small Groups or Individuals for Intervention, Reteaching, or Acceleration ▪ Guide and Redirect as Needed	▪ Read Independently ▪ Complete Learning Station Activities ▪ Meet for Intervention, Reteaching, or Acceleration ▪ Work on Assigned Skills Practice

Let's Work Together

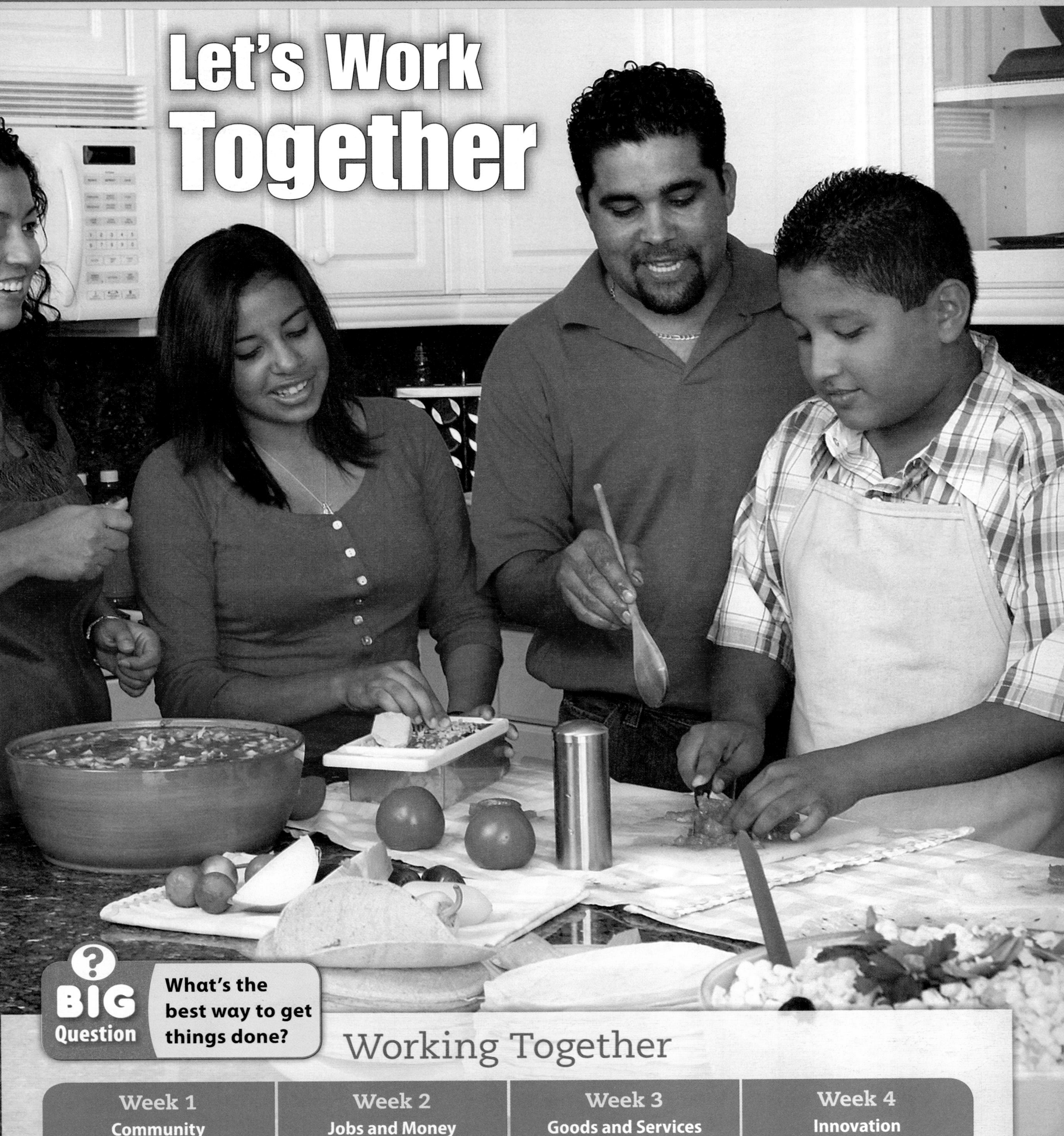

BIG Question What's the best way to get things done?

Working Together

Week 1	Week 2	Week 3	Week 4
Community	Jobs and Money	Goods and Services	Innovation

Program Resources

WHOLE GROUP TIME

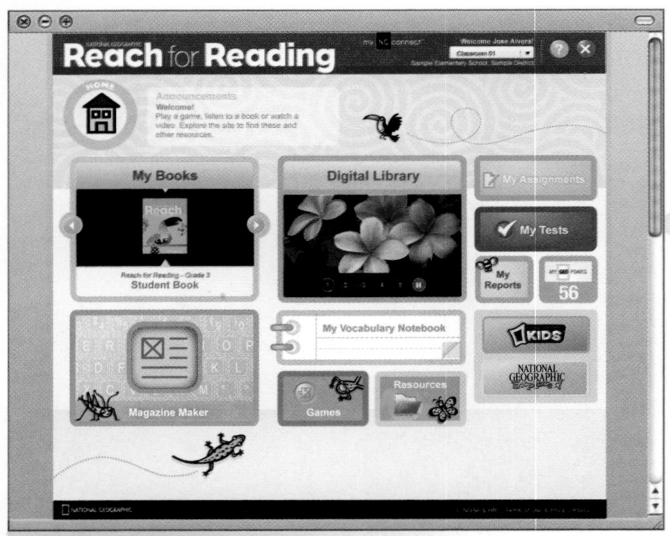
NGReach.com

Student Technology
- Student eEdition
- Digital Library
- Build Background Video
- Other Student Resources

Student eEdition

Build Background Video

Anthology

Interactive Whiteboard

Mark-Up Models 4.1, 4.2

SMALL GROUP READING TIME

Fiction Books

Nonfiction Books

Explorer Books

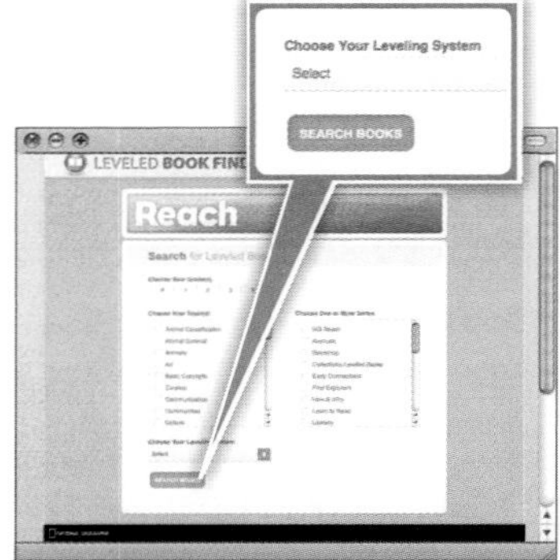
Leveled Book Finder

Small Group Reading Masters
SG4.1–SG4.32

LEARNING STATION TIME

NGReach.com

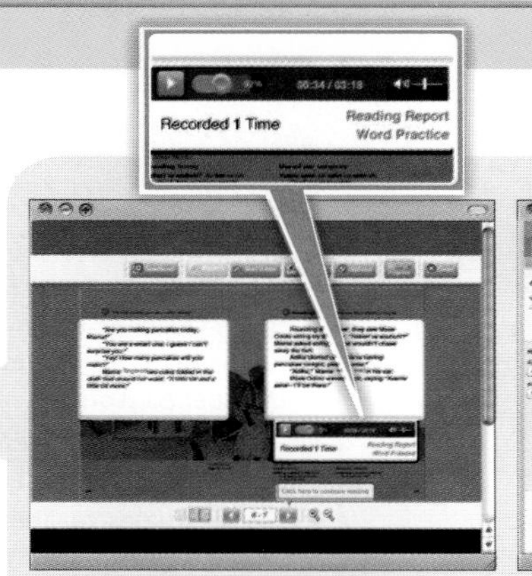

Comprehension Coach

Digital Library

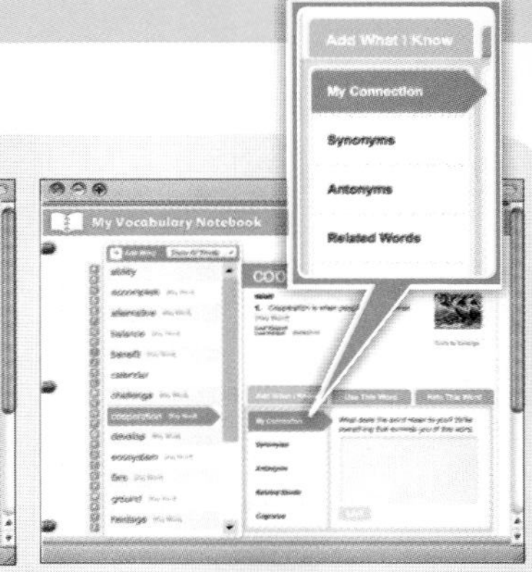

My Vocabulary Notebook

Student Technology
- My Assignments
- My Vocabulary Notebook
- Vocabulary Games
- Comprehension Coach
- Read with Me MP3s
- Fluency MP3s
- Practice Masters
- Teamwork Activities
- Other Student Resources

Practice Book
PM4.1–PM4.32

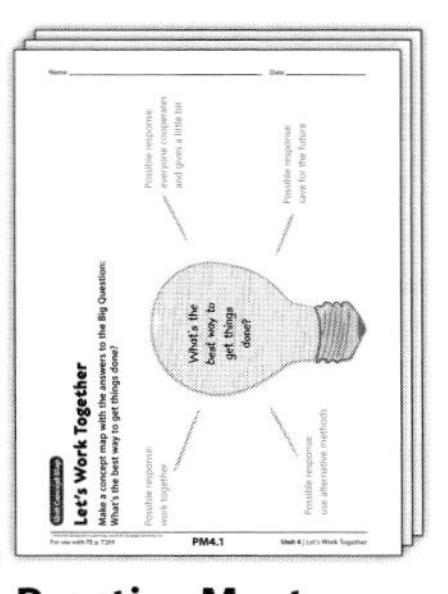
Practice Masters
PM4.1–PM4.32

Teamwork Activities

ESL Kit

Reach into Phonics Kit

PLANNING RESOURCES

NGReach.com

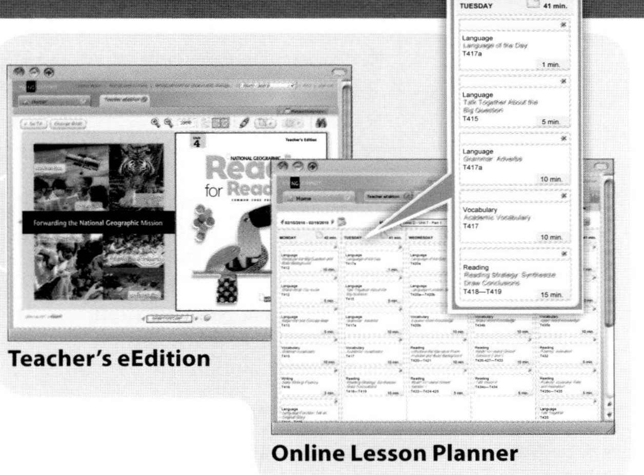

Teacher's eEdition

Online Lesson Planner

Teacher Technology
- Student and Teacher eEditions
- Lesson Planner
- eVisuals 4.1–4.36
- Family Newsletter 4 (in seven languages)
- Teamwork Activities Teacher's Guides
- Test-Taking Strategies Teacher's Guide
- Professional Development
- Other Teacher Resources

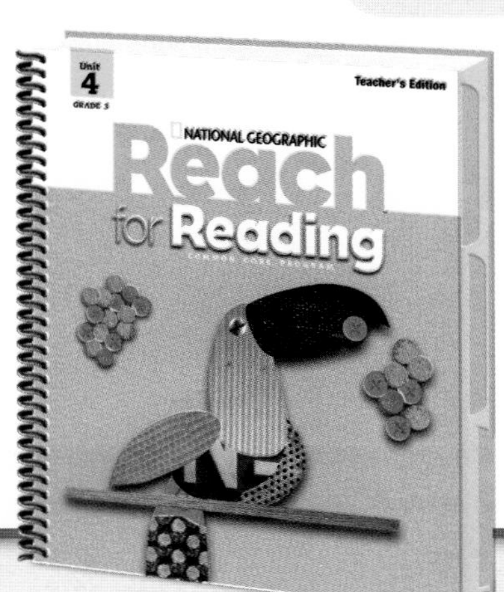

Teacher's Edition
- Whole Group Lessons
- Practice Masters
- Small Group Reading
- Assessment and Reteaching Masters

ASSESSMENT & RETEACHING

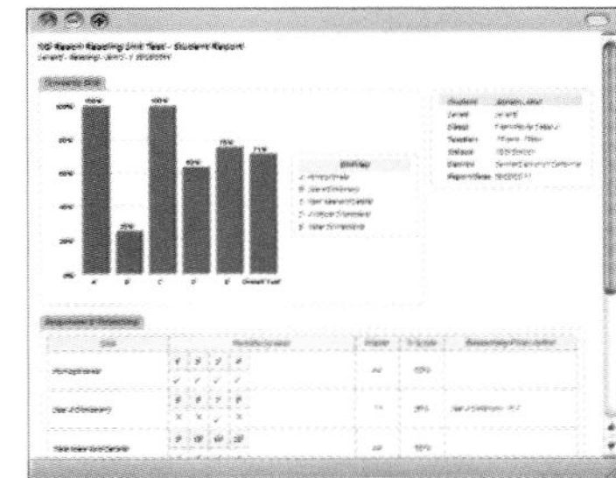
eAssessment™

ExamView®

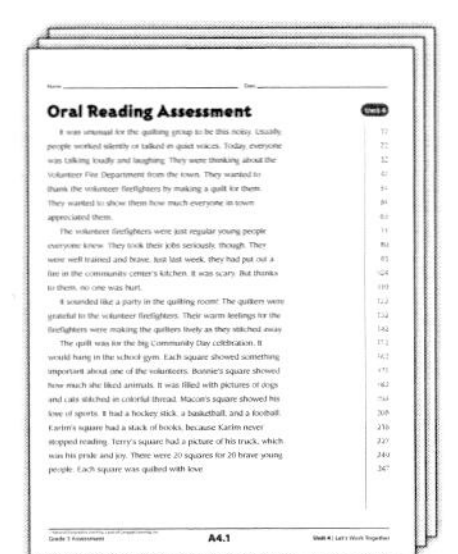

Assessment Masters
A4.1–A4.44

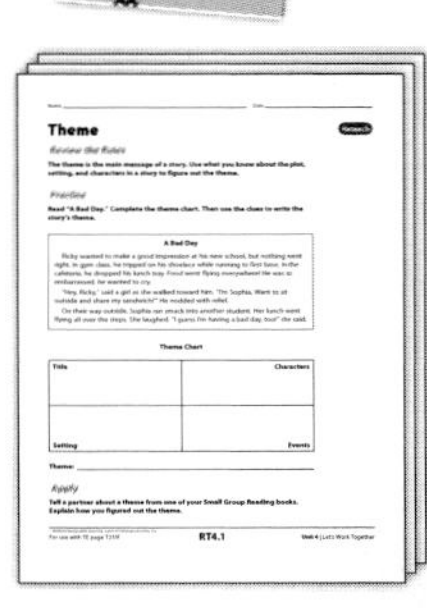

Reteaching Masters
RT4.1–RT4.14

Unit 4 Skills at a Glance

BL = BELOW LEVEL OL = ON LEVEL
BL = BELOW LEVEL AL = ABOVE LEVEL ☑ = TESTED SKILL

Introduce Unit 4	BUILD BACKGROUND VIDEO ▪ INTRODUCE THE BIG QUESTION		
	WHOLE GROUP TIME		
	Speaking and Listening	**Language and Vocabulary**	**Reading**
Week 1 eEdition	Express Needs, Wants, and Feelings Recount an Experience	☑ Daily Spelling and Word Work: Words with Long *a*: *ai*, *ay* and Commonly Misspelled Words ☑ Daily Grammar: Present-Tense Verbs, Action Verbs, Subject-Verb Agreement ☑ Social Studies Vocabulary **advertisement buyer market money pay seller** ☑ Academic Vocabulary **accomplish cooperation determine paraphrase plenty purpose reward theme**	Read and Comprehend Realistic Fiction ☑ Determine Theme ☑ Learn to Determine Importance ☑ Fluency: Practice Intonation, Accuracy, and Rate
Week 2 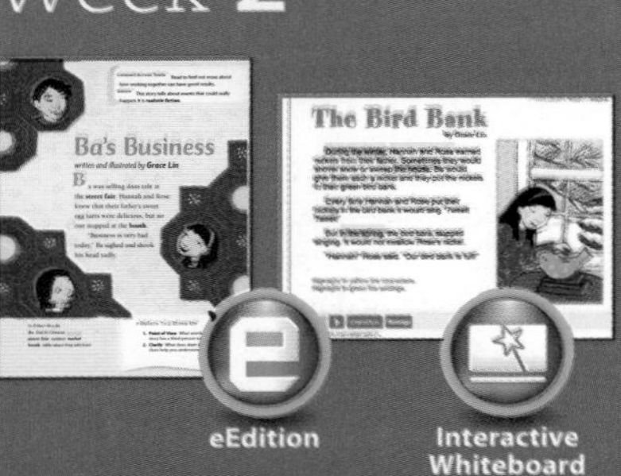 eEdition Interactive Whiteboard	Discuss Story Elements Relate Readings to the Big Question	☑ Daily Spelling and Word Work: Words with Long *e*: *ee, ea*; Long *o*: *oa, ow*; and Commonly Misspelled Words ☑ Daily Grammar: Subject-Verb Agreement, Present-Tense Action Verbs ☑ Prefixes	Read and Comprehend Realistic Fiction ☑ Describe Story Elements ☑ Determine Importance Read and Comprehend Short Stories ☑ Compare Story Elements ☑ Compare Themes ☑ Fluency: Practice Expression, Accuracy, and Rate
Week 3  eEdition	Persuade Make an Argument	☑ Daily Spelling and Word Work: Verbs Ending in *-ed* and Commonly Misspelled Words ☑ Daily Grammar: Helping Verbs, Forms of *Do* ☑ Social Studies Vocabulary **agriculture crop farmer field harvest plow** ☑ Academic Vocabulary **alternative conservation evidence future method opinion summarize sustain**	Read and Comprehend a Persuasive Article ☑ Identify Opinions and Evidence ☑ Learn to Determine Importance ☑ Fluency: Practice Phrasing, Accuracy, and Rate
Week 4 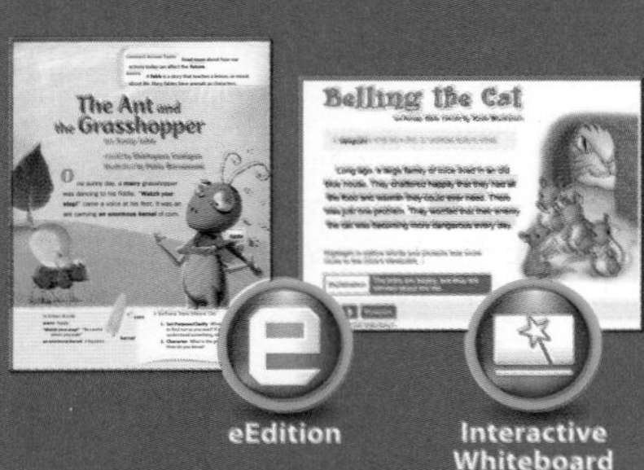 eEdition Interactive Whiteboard	Retell a Story Relate Readings to the Big Question	☑ Daily Spelling and Word Work: Verbs Ending in *-ing* and Commonly Misspelled Words ☑ Daily Grammar: Forms of *be* and *have* ☑ Classify Words	Read and Comprehend a Fable ☑ Determine Author's Purpose ☑ Determine Importance ☑ Distinguish Viewpoint Compare Viewpoints ☑ Fluency: Practice Phrasing, Accuracy, and Rate
Unit 4 Wrap-Up	ANSWER THE BIG QUESTION ▪ UNIT PROJECTS		

What's the best way to get things done?

Writing	SMALL GROUP READING TIME	LEARNING STATION TIME	ASSESSMENT & RETEACHING
Power Writing Write About Theme Write About Important Details Write About Characters Writer's Craft Write About It ☑ Daily Writing Skills: Establish and Follow a Purpose ☑ Writing Project: Write an Opinion Paragraph	☐ *Our Human Footprint* BL *The Runaway Rice Cake* BL *Under the Lemon Moon* OL *Four Feet, Two Sandals* AL *Sadako and the Thousand Paper Cranes*	**Speaking and Listening** Record a Retelling; Flamingo Video **Language and Vocabulary** Games; My Vocabulary Notebook **Writing** Identify the Narrator; Write a Comparison **Cross-Curricular** Model an Assembly Line; Assembly Line History **Reading and Intervention** Comprehension Coach; Read About Kenya; Phonics; ESL Kit	☑ Determine Theme ☑ Determine Importance ☑ Fluency: Intonation, Accuracy, and Rate ☑ Social Studies and Academic Vocabulary ☑ Spelling: Words with Long *a: ai, ay* and Commonly Misspelled Words ☑ Grammar: Present-Tense and Action Verbs ☑ Writing: Establish and Follow a Purpose ☑ Writing Trait: Fluency
Power Writing Write About Story Elements Write About a Character's Actions Write to Reinforce Grammar Write to Compare Story Elements Write to Compare Themes ☑ Daily Writing Skills: Introduce Characters ☑ Writing Project: Write Realistic Fiction	☐ *Dogs at Work* BL *Grandpa's Corner Store* BL *Uncle Willie and the Soup Kitchen* OL *Pitching In For Eubie* AL *My Rows and Piles of Coins*	**Speaking and Listening** Build a Team; Tell a True Story **Language and Vocabulary** Games; My Vocabulary Notebook **Writing** Add Your Ad; Write a Letter **Cross-Curricular** Egg Tart Profits; Working Together **Reading and Intervention** Author Study; Read a Blog Post; Phonics; ESL Kit	☑ Describe Story Elements ☑ Determine Importance ☑ Fluency: Expression, Accuracy, and Rate ☑ Prefixes ☑ Spelling: Words with Long *e, o* and Commonly Misspelled Words ☑ Grammar: Subject-Verb Agreement and Present-Tense Action Verbs ☑ Writing: Introduce Characters ☑ Writing Trait: Voice
Power Writing Write and Support an Opinion Write a Summary Write About Viewpoint Write About It ☑ Daily Writing Skills: Evaluate Information ☑ Research Project: Research Conservation	☐ *Working Hand in Hand* BL *Making Water Clean* BL *Farmers: Then and Now* OL *A Weed Is a Flower* AL *Ryan and Jimmy: And the Well In Africa That Brought Them Together*	**Speaking and Listening** Scenes of Cooperation; Spatulatta **Language and Vocabulary** Games; My Vocabulary Notebook **Writing** Sustainable Farming?; Write a Paragraph **Cross-Curricular** Test Your Soil; Make Your Own 5X5 Pattern **Reading and Intervention** Comprehension Coach; Read More About Brazil; Phonics; ESL Kit	☑ Identify Opinions and Evidence ☑ Determine Importance ☑ Fluency: Phrasing, Accuracy, and Rate ☑ Social Studies and Academic Vocabulary ☑ Spelling: Verbs Ending in *-ed* and Commonly Misspelled Words ☑ Grammar: Helping Verbs and Forms of *do* ☑ Writing: Evaluate Information
Power Writing Write for a Purpose Explain the Moral Write to Reinforce Grammar Write About Viewpoint Write About the Moral ☑ Daily Writing Skills: Link Opinions and Reasons ☑ Writing Project: Write a Persuasive Essay	☐ *First Flight* BL *All Aboard!: Elijah McCoy's Steam Engine* BL *Levi Strauss and the Blue Jeans* OL *Marvelous Mattie: How Margaret E. Knight Became an Inventor* AL *Boy Who Invented TV: The Story of Philo Farnsworth*	**Speaking and Listening** Class Project; Discuss a Video **Language and Vocabulary** Games; My Vocabulary Notebook **Writing** Teamwork; Write an Opinion **Cross-Curricular** What and Why?; Write a Response **Reading and Intervention** Read a Fable Aloud; Read a Blog; Phonics; ESL Kit	☑ Determine Author's Purpose ☑ Determine Importance ☑ Fluency: Phrasing, Accuracy, and Rate ☑ Classify Words ☑ Spelling: Verbs Ending in *-ing* and Commonly Misspelled Words ☑ Grammar: Forms of be and have ☑ Writing: Link Opinions and Reasons ☑ Writing Trait: Ideas

Week 1 Planner

Online Lesson Planner
NGReach.com

☑ = TESTED

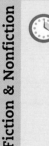

	Day 1	Day 2
WHOLE GROUP TIME (Anthology)	**Listen and Comprehend**	**Read and Comprehend**
Speaking and Listening  5–10 minutes	**Social Studies Background** CC.3.SL.2 Introduce the Big Question; Preview Unit Projects T208–T209 **Academic Talk** CC.3.SL.1; CC.3.SL.1.d Express Needs, Wants, and Feelings T210	**Academic Talk** CC.3.SL.4 Recount an Experience T212a
Language and Vocabulary  15–25 minutes	**Daily Spelling and Word Work** CC.3.Rfou.3; CC.3.Rfou.3.c; CC.3.L.2; CC.3.L.2.e; CC.3.L.2.f ☑ Words with Long *a: ai, ay* and Commonly Misspelled Words T207m **Daily Grammar** CC.3.L.1; CC.3.L.1.a, e, f; CC.3.L.2 ☑ Present-Tense Verbs T207o **Social Studies Vocabulary** CC.3.L.6 ☑ Learn Key Words T210 **advertisement** **buyer** **market** **money** **pay** **seller**	**Daily Spelling and Word Work** CC.3.Rfou.3; CC.3.Rfou.3.c; CC.3.L.2; CC.3.L.4.d ☑ Practice T207m **Daily Grammar** CC.3.L.1; CC.3.L.1.a, e; CC.3.L.2 ☑ Action Verbs T207o **Academic Vocabulary** CC.3.L.4; CC.3.L.6 ☑ Learn More Key Words T212a **accomplish** **cooperation** **determine** **paraphrase** **plenty** **purpose** **theme** **plenty**
Reading  20–40 minutes	**Reading** Read Aloud: Realistic Fiction T211a **Comprehension** CC.3.Rlit.2 ☑ Determine Theme T211a **Fluency** CC.3.Rfou.4 ☑ Model Intonation T211a	**Reading** CC.3.Rfou.4.a Read a Personal Narrative T214 **Comprehension** CC.3.Rfou.4.a ☑ Determine Importance T214 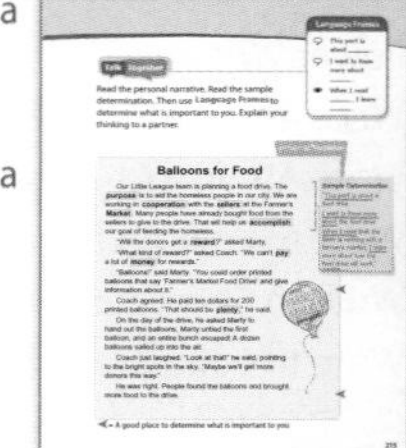 **Fluency** CC.3.Rfou.4 ☑ Practice Intonation T214
Writing  15–45 minutes	**Power Writing** T210 CC.3.W.10 **Daily Writing Skills** CC.3.W.10 ☑ Establish and Follow a Purpose T207q **Writing** CC.3.W.10 Write About Theme T212 **Writing Project: Opinion Paragraph** CC.3.W.1 ☑ Study a Model T233a	**Power Writing** T212a CC.3.W.10 **Daily Writing Skills** CC.3.W.10 ☑ Establish and Follow a Purpose T207q **Writing** CC.3.W.10 Write About Important Details T214 **Writing Project: Opinion Paragraph** CC.3.W.1; CC.3.W.1.b; CC.3.W.5; CC.3.W.10 ☑ Prewrite T233b
SMALL GROUP READING TIME (Fiction & Nonfiction)  20 minutes	**Read Social Studies Articles** **Vocabulary** CC.3.L.6 Learn Social Studies Vocabulary SG4 **Reading** CC.3.Rinf.7; CC.3.Rinf.10 Use Visuals SG4 Build Comprehension SG5 	**Read Fiction Books** **Vocabulary** CC.3.L.6 Learn Story Words SG6–SG7 **Reading** CC.3.Rlit.2; CC.3.Rfou.4.a Introduce SG6–SG7 Read and Integrate Ideas SG8–SG9 ☑ Theme SG8–SG9 ☑ Determine Importance SG8–SG9 

LEARNING STATION TIME/DAILY PHONICS INTERVENTION

 20 minutes

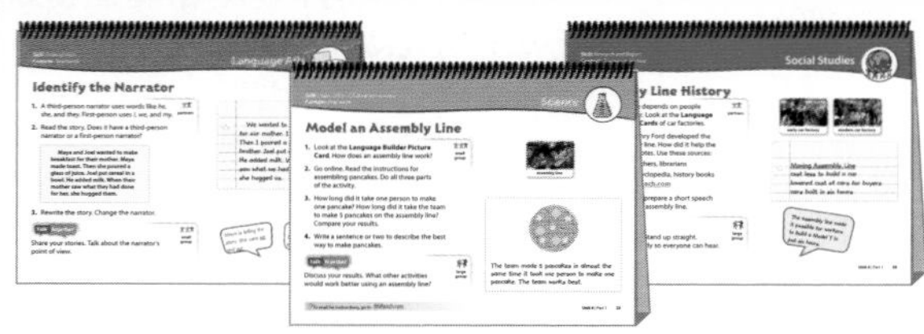

Speaking and Listening T207i CC.3.SL.2; CC.3.SL.4; CC.3.SL.5
Language and Vocabulary T207i CC.3.L.6
Writing T207i CC.3.W.10
Cross-Curricular T207j CC.3.W.2; CC.3.W.7; CC.3.SL.4
Reading and Intervention T207j; SG68 CC.3.Rlit.10; CC.3.Rinf.10; CC.3.Rfou.3; CC.3.Rfou.4.b
Daily Phonics Intervention T207k–T207l CC.3.Rfou.3; CC.3.Rfou.3.d; CC.3.L.2.e; CC.3.L.2.f

BIG Question What's the best way to get things done?

Day 3

Read and Comprehend

Academic Talk CC.3.SL.1
Preview and Predict T216

Daily Spelling and Word Work CC.3.Rfou.3; CC.3.Rfou.3.c; CC.3.L.2.f
☑ Practice T207n

Daily Grammar CC.3.L.1; CC.3.L.1.a; CC.3.L.1.e; CC.3.L.1.f; CC.3.L.2
☑ Subject-Verb Agreement T207p

Vocabulary Practice CC.3.L.6
☑ Expand Word Knowledge T216

Reading CC.3.Rlit.10
Read a Village Tale T217–T222

Comprehension CC.3.Rlit.2, 3, 6
☑ Theme T222
☑ Determine Importance T218–219
Analyze Characters T222

Fluency CC.3.Rfou.4; CC.3.Rfou.4.b
☑ Practice Intonation, Accuracy, and Rate T218–219

Power Writing T216 CC.3.W.10

Daily Writing Skills CC.3.W.10
☑ Establish and Follow a Purpose T207r

Writing CC.3.W.10
Write About Characters T223

Writing Project: Opinion Paragraph CC.3.W.1; CC.3.W.1.b; CC.3.W.5; CC.3.W.10
☑ Draft T233b

Read Fiction Books

Vocabulary CC.3.L.6
Expand Vocabulary Through Wide Reading SG6–SG9

Reading CC.3.Rlit.10; CC.3.Rlit.2; CC.3.Rfou.4.a
Read and Integrate Ideas SG8–SG9
☑ Theme SG8–SG9
☑ Determine Importance SG8–SG9

Day 4

Read and Comprehend

Academic Talk CC.3.SL.1
Summarize Reading T224

Daily Spelling and Word Work CC.3.L.2; .3.L.2.e; CC.3.L.4.d; CC.3.Rfou.3
☑ Practice T207n

Daily Grammar CC.3.W.5; CC.3.L.1; CC.3.L.1.e; CC.3.L.1.f; CC.3.L.2
☑ Grammar and Writing T207p

Vocabulary Practice CC.3.L.6
☑ Share Word Knowledge T224

Reading CC.3.Rlit.10
Read a Village Tale T225–T231

Comprehension CC.3.Rlit.2, 3, 6
☑ Theme T227
☑ Determine Importance T230
Determine Viewpoint T226

Fluency CC.3.Rfou.4.b
☑ Practice Intonation, Accuracy, and Rate T225

Power Writing T224 CC.3.W.10

Daily Writing Skills CC.3.W.10
☑ Establish and Follow a Purpose T207r

Writing CC.3.W.3.b
Writer's Craft T231a

Writing Project: Opinion Paragraph CC.3.W.1; CC.3.W.1.b; CC.3.W.5; CC.3.W.10; CC.3.L.1; CC.3.L.1.d; CC.3.L.3
☑ Revise/Edit and Proofread T233c–T233d

Read Fiction Books

Vocabulary CC.3.L.6
Expand Vocabulary Through Wide Reading SG6–SG9

Reading CC.3.Rlit.10; CC.3.Rlit.2; CC.3.Rfou.4.a
Read and Integrate Ideas SG8–SG9
☑ Theme SG8–SG9
☑ Determine Importance SG8–SG9

Day 5

Review and Apply

Academic Talk CC.3.SL.1; CC.3.SL.1.a; CC.3.L.4
Talk About "Mama Panya's Pancakes" T232

Daily Grammar CC.3.L.1; CC.3.L.1.a; CC.3.L.1.e; CC.3.L.1.f; CC.3.L.2
☑ Review T207p

Vocabulary Review CC.3.L.4, 6
☑ Apply Word Knowledge T231b

Reading CC.3.Rlit.10
Reread a Village Tale T217–T231

Comprehension CC.3.Rlit.2; CC.3.Rlit.3; CC.3.Rlit.5; CC.3.Rlit.10
☑ Determine Theme T232a

Fluency CC.3.Rfou.4.b
☑ Check Intonation, Accuracy, and Rate T233

Power Writing T231b CC.3.W.10

Daily Writing Skills CC.3.W.10
☑ Establish and Follow a Purpose T207r

Writing CC.3.W.10
Write About "Mama Panya's Pancakes" T232

Writing Project: Opinion Paragraph
☑ Publish and Present T233d

Read Fiction Books

Vocabulary CC.3.L.6
Expand Vocabulary Through Wide Reading SG6–SG9

Reading CC.3.Rlit.2; CC.3.Rfou.4.a; CC.3.SL.1.a
Connect Across Texts SG9

Writing CC.3.W.10
Choose a Writing Option SG8–SG9

ASSESSMENT & RETEACHING

Assessment and Reteaching T233e–T233f

☑ Reading Comprehension Test A4.4–A4.5 CC.3.Rlit.2
☑ Reading Strategy Assessment SG4.30–SG4.31 CC.3.Rfou.4.a
☑ Oral Reading Assessment A4.1–A4.3 CC.3.Rfou.4
☑ Vocabulary Test A4.6–A4.7 CC.3.L.6
☑ Spelling Test: Words with Long *a*: *ai*, *ay* and Commonly Misspelled Words T207m CC.3.Rfou.3; CC.3.Rfou.3.c; CC.3.L.2; CC.3.L.2.e; CC.3.L.2.f
☑ Writing, Revising, and Editing Test A4.8–A4.9 CC.3.L.1.e; CC.3.L.1.f
Reteaching Masters RT4.1–RT4.3

Speaking and Listening

Option 1: Record a Retelling

"Then we got the kite out of the tree."

MATERIALS

computer or audio-recording equipment

Display the activity prompt:

> Think of a story you know where people cooperate to achieve a goal. Record yourself retelling the story, using descriptive details where you can. Then, give your recording to a partner, and listen to your partner's recording.

Tell a Story	CC.3.SL.4
Create Audio Recordings	CC.3.SL.5

Option 2: Flamingo Video

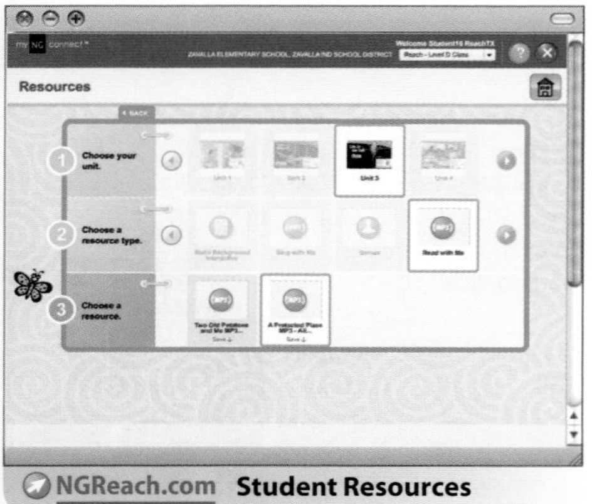

NGReach.com **Student Resources**

Go to Resources > Unit 4 > Learning Stations > Week 1 > Flamingos in Kenya

Have student pairs watch the video and identify the main idea, then discuss details that support it.

Determine the Main Ideas and Supporting Details of Information Presented Visually and Orally in Diverse Media	CC.3.SL.2

Language and Vocabulary

Key Words

accomplish · advertisement · buyer · cooperation determine · market · money · paraphrase · pay plenty · purpose · reward · seller · theme

Option 1: Vocabulary Games

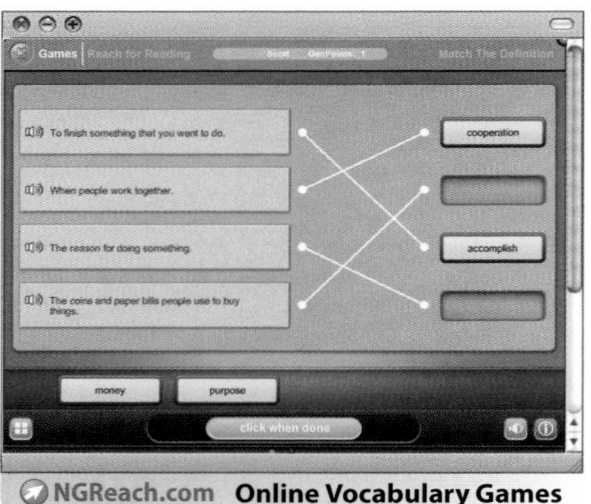

NGReach.com **Online Vocabulary Games**

Acquire and Use Conversational, General Academic, and Domain-Specific Words	CC.3.L.6

Option 2: My Vocabulary Notebook

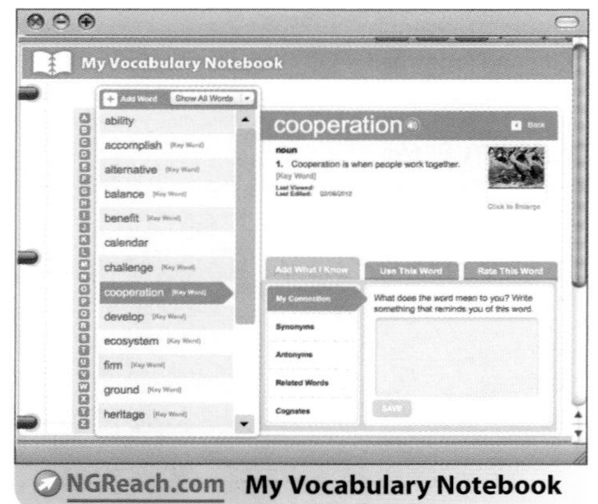

NGReach.com **My Vocabulary Notebook**

Have students expand their word knowledge.

- Under Add What I Know > Synonyms, have students add any synonyms they know for the word.
- Under Use This Word > Restate the Definition, have students define each word in their own words.

Acquire and Use Conversational, General Academic, and Domain-Specific Words	CC.3.L.6

Writing

Option 1: Identify the Narrator

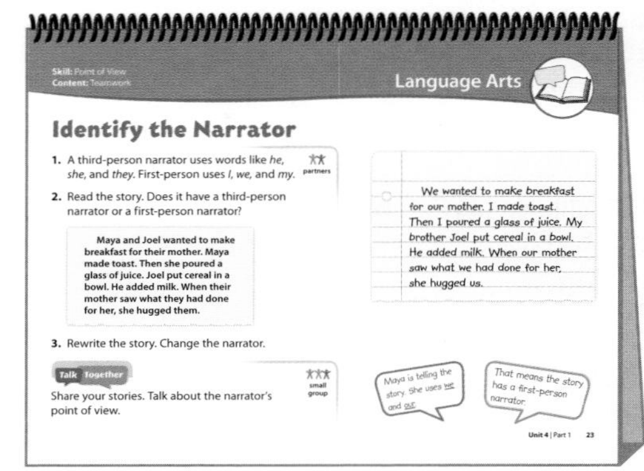

PROGRAM RESOURCES

Language and Literacy Teamwork Activities: Card 23

Teacher's Guide on NGReach.com

Write Over Shorter Time for Specific Tasks	CC.3.W.10

Option 2: Write a Comparison

Display the writing prompt:

> Choose an illustration from "Mama Panya's Pancakes" that shows an activity the family is doing together. Think of how your family does that same activity and write a short paragraph comparing your family's activity with the activity shown in the book.

Write Over Shorter Time for Specific Tasks	CC.3.W.10

= one student = two students = three or more students

Cross-Curricular

Option 1: Model an Assembly Line

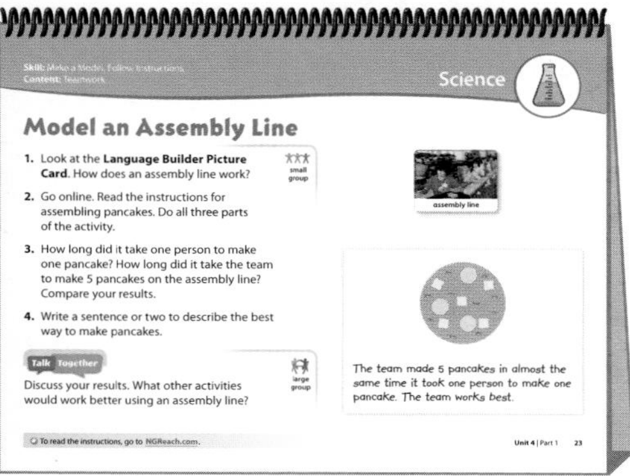

PROGRAM RESOURCES & MATERIALS

Cross-Curricular Teamwork Activities: Card 23

Digital Library: Language Builder Picture Card D43

Teacher's Guide on NGReach.com

Student Resources Directory

rulers • beige, white, yellow, red, and orange construction paper • scissors • glue sticks stopwatches or clock

Write Informative/Explanatory Text to Convey Information	CC.3.W.2
Conduct Research	CC.3.W.7

Option 2: Assembly Line History

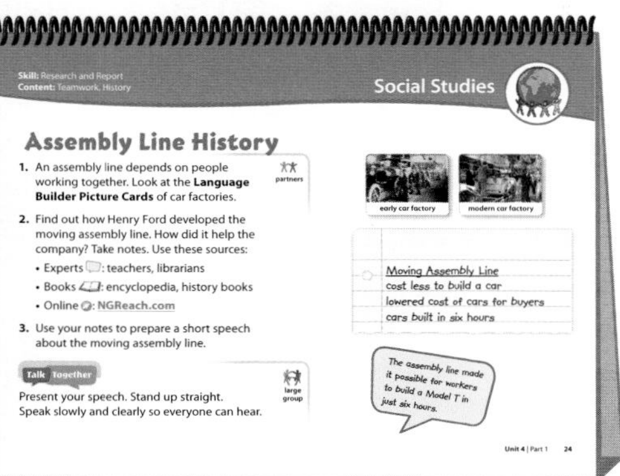

PROGRAM RESOURCES & MATERIALS

Cross-Curricular Teamwork Activities: Card 24

Digital Library Images: Language Builder Picture Cards D44, D45

Teacher's Guide on NGReach.com

Student Resources Directory

encyclopedia • history books • ball or beanbag

Write Informative/Explanatory Text to Examine a Topic	CC.3.W.2
Report on a Topic	CC.3.SL.4

Reading

Option 1: Comprehension Coach

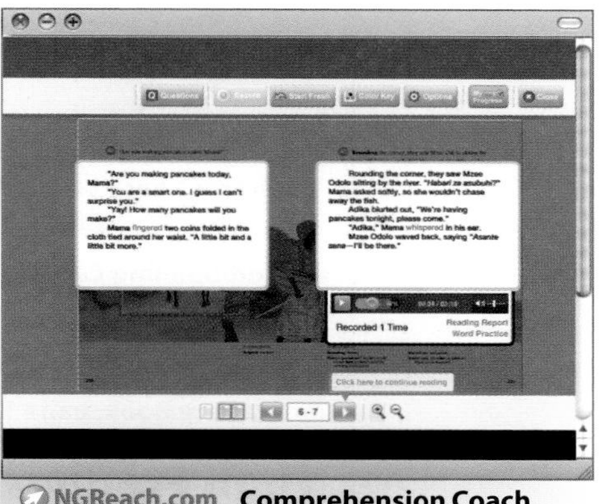

NGReach.com **Comprehension Coach**

Read and Comprehend Literature	CC.3.Rlit.10
Read Orally with Accuracy and Appropriate Rate on Successive Readings	CC.3.Rfou.4.b

Option 2: Read About Kenya

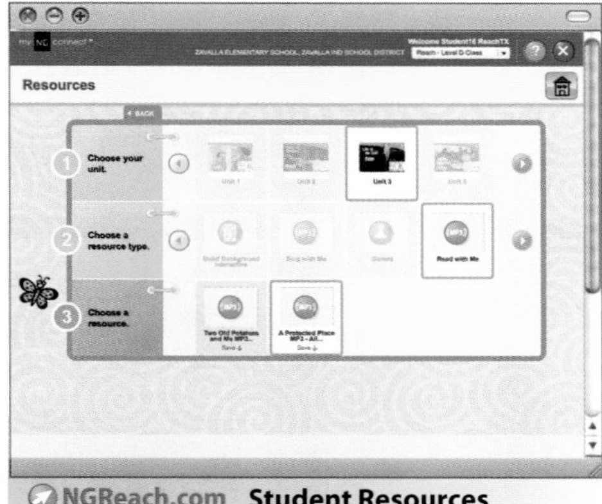

NGReach.com **Student Resources**

Students read a short online article about the land and people of Kenya. Have students go to Resources > Unit 4 > Learning Stations > Week 1 > Kenya Facts.

Then have students list three important facts they learned about Kenya.

Read and Comprehend Informational Text	CC.3.Rinf.10

Intervention

Phonics Games

NGReach.com **Online Phonics Games**

Apply Phonics and Word Analysis Skills	CC.4.Rfou.3

For Reteaching Masters, see pages RT4.1–RT4.3.

Additional Resources

ESL Kit

ESL Teacher's Edition pages T208–T233

Week 1 Daily Phonics Intervention

OBJECTIVES

Thematic Connection: Community

Recognize High Frequency Words

Develop Phonological Awareness: Isolate Sounds

Associate Sounds and Spellings /ā/*ai, ay*; /ē/*ee, ea*; /ō/*oa, ow*

Blend Sounds to Decode Words

Teach Day 1

PROGRAM RESOURCES

High Frequency Words:
Teaching Master 13
Sound/Spelling Card 35
Word Builder: Transparency 41
Decodable Passage: *Far Away*
Practice Book, page 110

Reach into Phonics
Lesson 46, page T78
Lesson 48, pages T80–T81

High Frequency Words

Follow Lesson 46 to present High Frequency Words:

places	important	world	always	or

Long Vowel /ā/*ai, ay*

Follow Lesson 48. Use **Reading Routine 1** and **Sound/Spelling Card 35** to teach sounds and spellings /ā/*ai, ay*. Guide students through **Transparency 41**. Use **Reading Routine 3** to guide students as they read Decodable text.

*For **Reading Routine 1**, see Reach into Phonics, page vi.*
*For **Reading Routine 3**, see Reach into Phonics, page ix.*

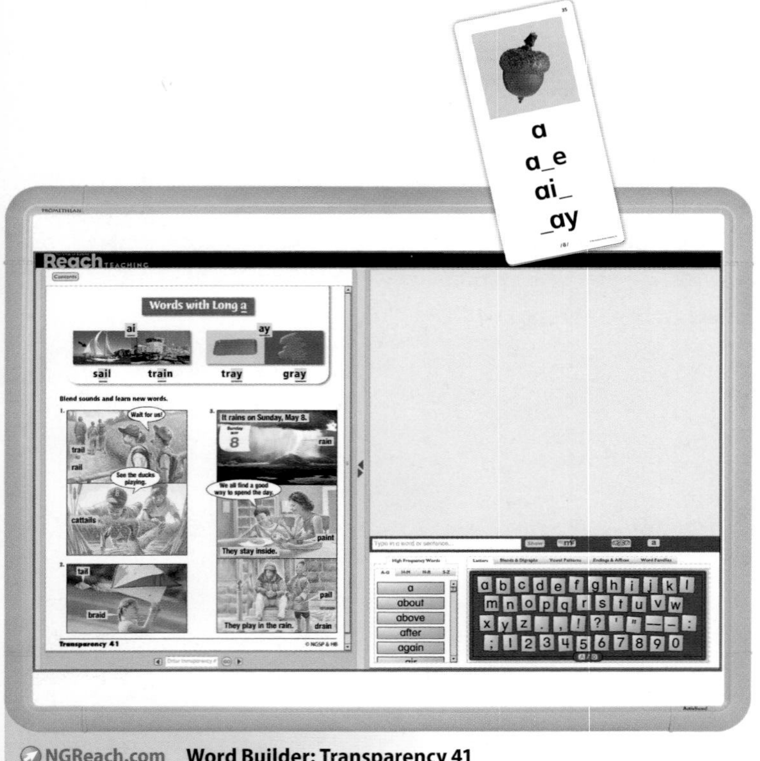

NGReach.com **Word Builder: Transparency 41**

Teach Day 2

PROGRAM RESOURCES

High Frequency Words:
Teaching Master 14
Sound/Spelling Cards 32, 33
Word Builder: Transparency 42
Decodable Passage: *Six Tips Before You Leave*
Practice Book, page 111

Reach into Phonics
Lesson 47, page T79
Lesson 49, pages T82–T83

High Frequency Words

Follow Lesson 47 to present High Frequency Words:

river	through	once	water	below

Long Vowels /ē/*ee, ea*; /ō/*oa, ow*

Follow Lesson 49. Use **Reading Routine 1** and **Sound/Spelling Cards 32** and **33** to teach sounds and spellings /ē/*ee, ea* and /ō/*oa, ow*. Guide students through **Transparency 42**. Use **Reading Routine 3** to guide students as they read Decodable text.

*For **Reading Routine 1**, see Reach into Phonics, page vi.*
*For **Reading Routine 3**, see Reach into Phonics, page ix.*

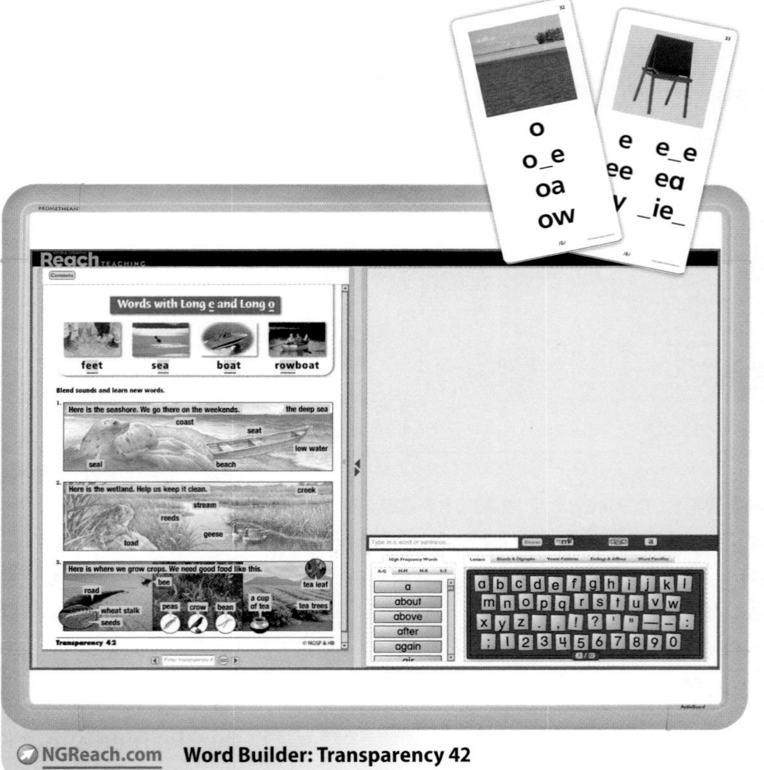

NGReach.com **Word Builder: Transparency 42**

= one student = two students = three or more students

Words with Long *a*, *e*, and *o*

COMMON CORE STANDARDS

Apply Phonics Skills	CC.3.Rfou.3
Use Conventional Spelling	CC.3.L.2.e
Use Spelling Patterns and Generalizations	CC.3.L.2.f
Read Grade-Appropriate Irregularly Spelled Words	CC.3.Rfou.3.d

Word Scramble Day 3  Option 1

MATERIALS

index cards, 15 per student • timer

Prepare

- Have each partner complete a set of cards by writing the vowel spellings *ai, ay, ee, ea, oa, ow,* and the consonants *b, d, h, l, m, n, r, s,* and *t,* each on a separate card.

Play a Game

- Set a timer for 5 minutes. Partner 1 arranges the letter cards into a word with a long vowel sound and reads the word. Partner 2 confirms the long vowel sound and writes the word. Words that do not have a long vowel sound, like *head* or *been*, should not be written down.
- The partners continue to make, read, and write words until time is up. At the end of 5 minutes, Partner 2 reads all the words.
- Have partners switch roles and repeat. The player that makes up the most words wins.

Name the Spelling Day 3  Option 2

MATERIALS

index cards, 12 per pair of students

Prepare

- Have pairs of students collaborate to write each word from the word bank below on a separate card. Then have them place the cards face down in a pile.

stay	seal	toad	tray	speak	loan
stain	feel	tow	trail	speech	low

Play a Game

- Player 1 picks and displays a card. Then, Player 1 identifies the vowel sound, the long vowel spelling, and pronounces the word.
- Player 2 decides if Player 1 has identified the long vowel sound and spelling correctly. If so, Player 1 keeps the card. If not, the card goes back in the pile.
- Play ends after all of the words have been identified correctly. The partner with the most cards wins.

Hop and Read Day 4 

MATERIALS

masking tape • large index cards, 10 per pair of students • markers

Prepare

- Have partners work together to write each High Frequency Word from the word bank on separate cards.
- Have partners use tape to make a hopscotch grid on the classroom floor. Tell students to tape a word card in each box of the hopscotch grid.

places	important	world	always	or
river	through	once	water	below

Play a Game

- Have Player 1 toss a marker inside the first box and then hop through the boxes reading each word, skipping the box the marker is on. Player 1 turns around, hops back, and picks up the marker. Have Player 2 repeat the process.
- The first player to complete the hopscotch grid with the marker on each box wins the game.

Make a Match Day 5 

PROGRAM RESOURCES

Sound/Spelling Cards 32, 33, 35

MATERIALS

index cards, 16 per pair of students • timer

Prepare

- Have partners work together to write each word from the word bank below on a separate card.
- Have partners place the 16 word cards face down.
- Set out **Sound/Spelling Cards 32, 33,** and **35**.

boat	ray	grain	green	gray	train	real	rail
beat	row	groan	beet	grow	treat	stay	stow

Play a Game

- Set a timer for five minutes. Have Partner 1 draw a card and read it aloud.
- Have Partner 2 identify the **Sound/Spelling Card** that has the same sound and also select the correct spelling. Have Partner 1 award one point for each word that is identified correctly. Continue until time is called.
- Have partners switch roles and repeat. The player with the most points wins.

OBJECTIVES

Thematic Connection: Community

- ☑ **Spell Words with Long *a: ai, ay***
- ☑ **Use Commonly Misspelled Words Correctly**

SUGGESTED PACING

DAY 1	Spelling Pretest
DAY 2–4	Daily Practice Options
DAY 5	Spelling Test

Spelling Pretest Day 1

Spelling Test Day 5

Spelling Words

Use these words and sentences for the weekly Spelling Pretest and Spelling Test.

Words with Long *a: ai, ay*	
1. daydream	I was so bored that I started to ***daydream*** about playing baseball in my neighborhood.
2. exclaim	When you ***exclaim***, you say something in an excited or surprised voice.
3. failure	Lightning caused an electrical ***failure*** in our community.
4. gains	When people work together, everyone ***gains*** from helping each other.
5. mainly	I help others ***mainly*** for the good feeling it gives me.
6. painful ✓	When I sprained my ankle at the block party, it was so ***painful*** that I almost cried.
7. payment ✓	Mom sends money each month to make a ***payment*** for the water we use.
8. playful ✓	We watched a ***playful*** kitten bat around a ball of yarn at the animal shelter.
9. raising	The scout troop is working together, ***raising*** money to pay for a trip to a nearby city.
10. saint ✓	Our very helpful neighbor is a ***saint*** in our community.
11. straight ✓	The teacher used a ruler to draw a ***straight*** line.
12. stray	My neighbors put out bowls of food and water for the ***stray*** cats that have no homes.
13. unpaid ✓	A volunteer is an ***unpaid*** person who works for free.
14. vain	My **vain** sister always brags about how pretty she is.
15. x-ray ✓	An **x-ray** of my arm shows where I broke my bone.
Watch-Out Words	
16. lay	You can ***lay*** your soccer equipment on the floor.
17. lie	Then ***lie*** down and rest after the game.
18. plane	My Dad took a ***plane*** to do some volunteer work.
19. plain	The airport food was ***plain*** and tasteless.

Long *a: ai* Day 2 — Option 1

MATERIALS

index cards, 11 per pair of students • scissors

Teach

Display the word *exclaim*; circle *ai*, and pronounce the word. Explain: *The vowel combination* ai *usually makes the long* a *sound.*

Prepare

s a i n t

- Arrange students in pairs and have partners collaborate to print each *ai* spelling word on a separate index card, leaving spaces between the letters for cutting.
- Have students cut apart each word into separate letters, mix the letters up, but keep the letters for each word in one letter group.

Play a Game

- Have each partner choose 5 or 6 letter groups and unscramble the letters to make spelling words.
- Have partners check each other's spelling, then exchange stacks and form spelling words again.
- The partner who correctly forms the most spelling words is the winner.

Apply Phonics Skills	CC.3.Rfou.3
Decode Multisyllabic Words	CC.3.Rfou.3.c

Write a Skit Day 2 — Option 2

Write Dialogue

- Have small groups collaborate to write a short skit using at least two Watch-Out Words and as many other spelling words as they can.
- Have students consult a dictionary as necessary to see that they have used each word correctly, and tell students to underline each spelling word.

> Vain Princess: I think I will lie down by this pond for a nap.
> Playful Frog: I exclaim, there's a princess at my pond!
> Vain Princess: Am I having a daydream? Is that a frog raising his head out of the water and looking straight at me?
> Playful Frog: It is painful to be as plain as I am. I'm a failure.

- If time allows, have groups practice their skits and perform them either for the class or in small groups.

Demonstrate Command of Spelling	CC.3.L.2
Use Glossaries and Dictionaries	CC.3.L.4.d

= one student   = two students   = three or more students

Long *a: ay* Day 3 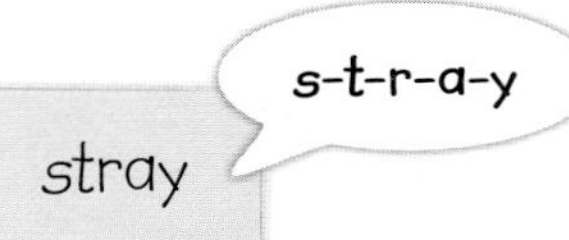 Option 1

MATERIALS
index cards, 19 per pair of students

Teach
Display *playful*; circle *ay*, and pronounce the word. Explain: *The vowel combination* ay, *like* ai, *usually makes the long* a *sound.*

Prepare
Have student pairs write each of the first 15 spelling words, plus the Watch-Out Words *lay* and *plain*, on a separate card. Then have them write each of these phrases on a separate card: *a as in pain/a as in pay.*

Play a Game
- Have one partner take the two phrase cards and the other partner take the 17 word cards.
- The partner with the word cards reads a word, without showing it to his or her partner. The other partner holds up the appropriate phrase card, says the phrase, and spells the word.
- When one partner has spelled all the words, have partners switch roles and repeat the activity.

stray — s-t-r-a-y

Apply Phonics Skills	CC.3.Rfou.3
Use Spelling Patterns and Generalizations	CC.3.L.2.f

Word Scramble Day 3  Option 2

MATERIALS
index cards, 5–7 per student • dictionary, one per pair of students • timer • scissors

Prepare
- Form groups of three. Have each student print 5–7 spelling words on index cards with space between syllables for cutting. Tell students to consult a dictionary to confirm syllable breaks.
- Have students cut the multisyllabic words into syllables and one-syllable words into letters.

Play a Game
- Have students mix up all their letters and syllables and give them to another person in the group.
- Give students five minutes to unscramble and put together as many words as possible.
- Have students award themselves one point for each word they complete. After five minutes, the player with the most points wins.
- Have students switch sets of letters and syllables with another partner and play again.

Decode Multisyllabic Words	CC.3.Rfou.3.c

Trace Letter Shapes Day 4  Option 1

MATERIALS
Highlighters, one per student

Prepare
Have students neatly print three or more words that give them trouble on separate sheets of paper. Tell them to print the letters and words far apart.

Practice
- Have students use a highlighter to outline each letter in the first word.
- Tell students to close their eyes and visualize the shape of the whole word.
- Next, have students study the word again, then turn the paper over, and write the word on the back.
- Students repeat the process until they can spell each word correctly.
- Have them repeat the routine for each difficult word.

Apply Word Analysis Skills	CC.3.Rfou.3
Use Conventional Spelling	CC.3.L.2.e

Use a Dictionary Day 4  Option 2

MATERIALS
index cards, 10 per team • dictionaries, 2 per team

Prepare
- Form two teams and give each team 10 of the spelling words. Have each team collaborate to write each of its spelling words on a separate card. One word will be used twice.
- Tell team members to look up each word in a dictionary and write the definition on the back of the card.

Play a Game
- Join the teams back together and place all 20 cards on a table with the definitions visible.
- Have teams take turns picking a card, reading the definition, and spelling the word that goes with it.
- Tell team members to check one another's spelling. If a student names and spells a word correctly, his or her team keeps the card. If not, the card goes back.
- Play continues until all words have been spelled correctly. The team with more cards at the end wins.

raising — lifting or increasing

Demonstrate Command of Spelling	CC.3.L.2
Use Glossaries and Dictionaries	CC.3.L.4.d

Week 1 Daily Grammar

OBJECTIVES

Thematic Connection: Community

- ☑ **Grammar: Use Present-Tense Verbs**
- ☑ **Grammar: Use Action Verbs**
- ☑ **Grammar: Use Subject-Verb Agreement:** ***he, she, it***

Day 1

PROGRAM RESOURCES

Present-Tense Verbs: eVisual 4.2

MATERIALS

index cards, 12 per pair of students

Teach the Rules

Use the suggestion on page T212 to introduce present-tense verbs. Then introduce verb tense: *An action can happen in the present, past, or future. The verb tense tells when the action happens. The present tense tells about an action that is happening now or that happens all the time.*

Present-Tense Verbs

• If the subject tells about one other person or thing, add **-s** to an **action verb**.	Pablo **cooks** soup. It **tastes** wonderful. He **invites** the neighbors.
• For other subjects, do not add **-s**.	Neighbors **bring** bread. We **eat** everything!

NGReach.com **Present-Tense Verbs: eVisual 4.2**

Play a Game

Have partners collaborate to print each of the words below on a separate card. Then explain the game:

- *Set the subject cards and verb cards face down in separate stacks.*
- *Choose one card from each stack and use them in a sentence. If the subject and verb agree, keep the cards. If not, put them back.*
- *Take turns until no more cards remain in the stacks.*

he	Maria	friends	eat	sit	tell
she	neighbors	we	clap	bring	walk

Differentiate

Below Level

ISSUE Students are not sure when to add *-s* to the verb.

STRATEGY Have students first tell if the subject is about one person or more than one person. Tell them to add *-s* to the verb only if the subject is about one person.

Day 2

PROGRAM RESOURCES

Action Verbs: eVisual 4.7

Teach the Rules

Use the suggestion on page T215 to review action verbs. Then use **eVisual 4.7** to reinforce the concept.

Action Verbs

• Most verbs are **action verbs**. An action verb tells what the subject does.	We **gather** canned and boxed foods. Dad **takes** them to the food drive.

NGReach.com **Action Verbs: eVisual 4.7**

Generate Sentences

Have students generate sentences using present-tense action verbs.

- *Write a sentence about a neighbor. Use the present tense of an action verb in the third position.*
- *Write a sentence about a group that helps out in your community. Use the present tense of an action verb in the fourth position.*
- *Write a sentence about something you do to help others. Use a present-tense action verb in the second position.*

For ***Writing Routine 3****, see page BP49.*

Differentiate

SN Special Needs

ISSUE Students do not understand what the phrase *in the* ____ *position* means.

STRATEGY Have students follow the first sentence of the prompt to dictate two or more sentences that fit the topic. For example:

- My neighbor plays a trumpet.
- My neighbor helps us all the time.

Write the sentences as students dictate, then write a number under each word of each sentence. Explain that the word with the number three beneath it is the word in the third position. Have students copy the sentence that has the word in the correct position.

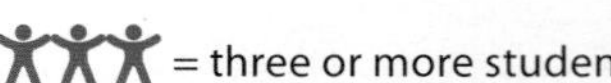

= one student = two students = three or more students

Present-Tense Verbs, Action Verbs Subject-Verb Agreement

COMMON CORE STANDARDS

Edit Writing	CC.3.W.5	Form and Use Verb Tenses	CC.3.L.1.e
Demonstrate Command of Grammar	CC.3.L.1	Ensure Subject-Verb Agreement	CC.3.L.1.f
Explain the Function of Verbs	CC.3.L.1.a	Demonstrate Command of Spelling	CC.3.L.2

Day 3

PROGRAM RESOURCES

Subject-Verb Agreement: eVisual 4.8

Game: Practice Master PM4.3

MATERIALS

index cards, 6 per pair of students

markers, one per pair

Teach the Rules

Use the suggestion on page T222 to review subject-verb agreement. Then use **eVisual 4.8** to teach more about subject-verb agreement with present-tense action verbs.

Subject-Verb Agreement

• To show the present tense for the subject **he**, **she**, or **it**, add **-s** to the end of most action verbs.	He **skips** ahead. She **flips** a pancake. It **sizzles** in the pan.
• If a verb ends in **x, ch, sh, ss,** or **z**, add **-es**.	He **fetches** water. She **mixes** things. He **wishes** for more.

NGReach.com **Subject-Verb Agreement: eVisual 4.8**

Play a Game

Distribute **Practice Master PM4.3** and have partners follow directions to play the game.

Name ____________ Date ________

Grammar: Game

Everyone Is Present

Directions:

1. Make two pronoun cards for each pronoun: *he, she,* and *it.*
2. Shuffle the six cards and stack them face down.
3. Take turns drawing a card and tossing a marker onto a square.
4. Form a sentence using the word from the card and the verb your marker lands on. Write a sentence using the pronoun and the verb. For example: "It stretches."
5. Award yourself one point for using the correct present tense of the verb and one point for spelling it correctly.
6. Put the pronoun card at the bottom of the stack.
7. After eight turns each, the player with more points wins.

hums	fetches	gathers
leaves	waves	taps
misses	rushes	cheers
skips	chases	stretches
pours	visits	mixes

© National Geographic Learning, a part of Cengage Learning, Inc.
For use with TE p. T207p PM4.3 Unit 4 | Let's Work Together

NGReach.com **Practice Master PM4.3**

Differentiate

EL English Learners

ISSUE Students are not sure when to add *-es* to a verb.

STRATEGY Provide a chart of the five verb endings, and examples for students to use.

x	fix	+ -es
ch	stretch	+ -es

Day 4

PROGRAM RESOURCES

Grammar and Writing: Practice Master PM4.4

Grammar and Writing

Distribute **Practice Master PM4.4**. Have students use editing and proofreading marks to correct errors with present-tense action verbs and subject-verb agreement.

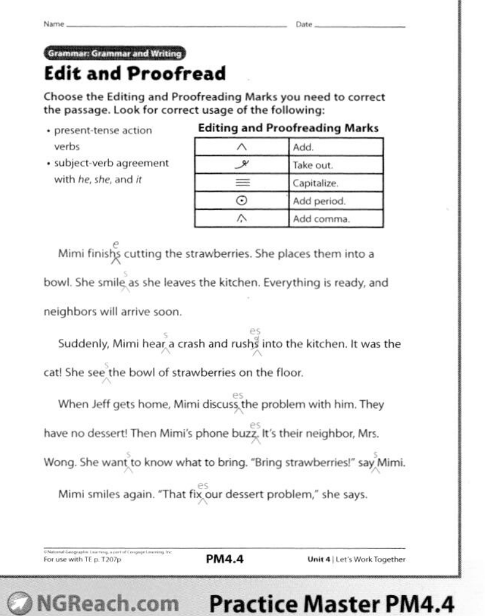
Name ____________ Date ________

Grammar: Grammar and Writing

Edit and Proofread

Choose the Editing and Proofreading Marks you need to correct the passage. Look for correct usage of the following:

- present-tense action verbs
- subject-verb agreement with *he, she,* and *it*

Editing and Proofreading Marks

^	Add.
⌒	Take out.
≡	Capitalize.
⊙	Add period.
^,	Add comma.

Mimi finishs cutting the strawberries. She places them into a bowl. She smile as she leaves the kitchen. Everything is ready, and neighbors will arrive soon.

Suddenly, Mimi hear a crash and rushs into the kitchen. It was the cat! She see the bowl of strawberries on the floor.

When Jeff gets home, Mimi discuss the problem with him. They have no dessert! Then Mimi's phone buzz. It's their neighbor, Mrs. Wong. She want to know what to bring. "Bring strawberries!" say Mimi.

Mimi smiles again. "That fix our dessert problem," she says.

© National Geographic Learning, a part of Cengage Learning, Inc.
For use with TE p. T207p PM4.4 Unit 4 | Let's Work Together

NGReach.com **Practice Master PM4.4**

Day 5

PROGRAM RESOURCES

Writing, Revising, and Editing Test: Assessment Masters A4.8–A4.9

MATERIALS

timer

Review and Assess

Copy and display the chart and have small groups copy it.

Challenge groups to write as many present-tense action verbs as they can in two minutes. Then have each group member choose one verb for *he*, one for *she*, and one for *it* and write a sentence for each. Have students share sentences within the group and check one another's work.

Present-tense Action Verbs	
-s	-es
sings	catches

☑ Administer the **Writing, Revising, and Editing Test**.

Week 1 Daily Writing Skills

OBJECTIVES

Thematic Connection: Community

☑ **Establish and Follow a Purpose**

COMMON CORE STANDARDS

Write Over Shorter Time for Specific Purposes — CC.3.W.10

Introduce Purpose — Day 1

PROGRAM RESOURCES

Author's Purpose and Samples Chart: eVisual 4.3

Persuasive Text: eVisual 4.4

Teach the Skill

Display **eVisual 4.3** and explain: *Every author has a purpose for writing. It may be to entertain, to persuade, to inform or explain, or to express.*

Author's Purpose	Sample Types of Writing
To inform or explain	news story, research report, magazine article
To entertain	short story, novel, poem, play, comic strip
To persuade	movie review, letter to the editor, advertisement
To express	e-mail, thank-you note, journal entry, blog

NGReach.com **Author's Purpose Chart: eVisual 4.3**

INTERACTIVE WHITEBOARD TIP: Circle key words in types of writing.

Explain the purpose of each form and discuss examples of each. Then display and read aloud **eVisual 4.4**.

Persuasive Text

I think the school should put a stop sign in the school parking lot. Every morning, parents drive their kids to school. The parking lot is filled with moving cars. Many times, drivers aren't looking out for students walking across the parking lot. This makes the parking lot very dangerous. We need a stop sign in the parking lot to help protect students!

NGReach.com **Persuasive Text: eVisual 4.4**

INTERACTIVE WHITEBOARD TIP: Highlight the opinion and underline evidence.

Explain that in persuasive text the author's purpose is to convince readers to think or act a certain way. Point out that the author states an opinion in the first sentence. The author then supports the opinion with evidence. (parking lot filled with moving cars; drivers aren't looking out for students)

Write to Persuade — Day 2 — Option 1

Introduce

Arrange students in pairs. Tell partners to imagine they are going to write a persuasive paragraph in which they give an opinion. Provide students with the following topics:

sack lunches vs. cafeteria lunches
inside play vs. outside play

Practice

Have students work together to choose an opinion (sack lunch or cafeteria lunch, inside play or outside play) that they can support with evidence (reasons, facts, examples, and/or experiences).

Have partners create an opinion chart like the following:

Opinion: I think playing outside is better than playing inside.
Evidence: When I play outside, I run around and get exercise.

Have partners share their opinion charts with another pair. Then have the group decide if the writers of the charts gave enough evidence to persuade others of their opinion. Have them discuss ways to provide more evidence for the opinion.

Write to Entertain — Day 2 — Option 2

Introduce

Copy and display the following paragraph. Explain that the writer's purpose was to inform.

On Saturday, Abe and I tried to build a doghouse. Abe and I worked together to put up the walls. We used nails to attach the roof. However, we did not read the directions carefully. When we were finished, the doghouse had no entrance.

Practice

Arrange students in small groups. Have groups work together to rewrite the paragraph to entertain. As they write, remind students that their purpose is to entertain their audience.

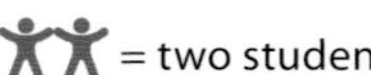

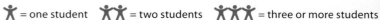

= one student = two students = three or more students

SUGGESTED PACING

DAY 1 Teach the Skill
DAY 2–4 Daily Practice Options
DAY 5 Review and Assess

Entertain and Express Day 3 Option 1

PROGRAM RESOURCES

Digital Library: Language Builder Picture Card D48

Introduce

Arrange students in groups of four and display **Language Builder Picture Card D48** of the children making a sand castle. Explain that one pair will write a paragraph to entertain and the other pair will write to express.

Practice

If needed, provide students with ideas. Students writing to entertain might write a story about how everything went wrong when their characters were building a sand castle. Students writing to express might write a journal entry about how it felt to be at the beach, building a sand castle.

When both groups have finished writing, have partners read their paragraphs to one another and discuss the differences.

Inform and Persuade Day 3  Option 2

PROGRAM RESOURCES

Digital Library: Language Builder Picture Card D48

Introduce

Form groups of four and display **Language Builder Picture Card D48** of the children making a sand castle. Explain that one pair will write a paragraph to inform or explain and the other pair will write to persuade.

Practice

If needed, suggest ideas. Partners writing to inform might describe how to build a sand castle. Partners writing to persuade may write an advertisement for sand castle tools, or state and support the opinion that building sand castles builds creativity.

Have partners read their writing to each other and discuss how they accomplished their purpose.

Follow a Purpose Day 4

MATERIALS

timer

Introduce

Arrange students in four groups. Tell students that each group will write about the same topic: helping in the cafeteria. However, each group will write for a different purpose: to inform or explain, to persuade, to entertain, or to express. Assign a purpose to each group.

Copy, display, and explain the following FATP Chart:

Form: persuasive paragraph
Audience: classmates
Topic: helping in the cafeteria
Purpose: persuade students that they should help clean tables in the cafeteria

Practice

Have each group copy the FATP chart. Give them three minutes to complete the chart for a one-paragraph written work that would accomplish the group's purpose.

Then provide eight minutes for each group to write the assigned paragraph. Remind groups that their purpose must be clear. Have a reader from each group read their paragraph aloud.

Review and Assess Day 5

PROGRAM RESOURCES

Writing, Revising, and Editing Test: Assessment Masters A4.8–A4.9

Review the Skill

Arrange students in small groups and have groups work together to recreate a chart like **eVisual 4.3**, on Day 1. Arrange students in mixed groups so that students who worked on Option 1 activities work with students who worked on Option 2 activities.

Tell students to include, in the right-hand column, the names of pieces written over the course of the week. Suggest that they also include names of **Anthology** selections and categories, such as research reports and journal entries.

☑ Administer the **Writing, Revising, and Editing Test**.

OBJECTIVES

Thematic Connection: Community

Preview Content

PROGRAM RESOURCES

PRINT & TECHNOLOGY

Family Newsletter 4

Unit Concept Map: Practice Master PM4.1

TECHNOLOGY ONLY

Unit 4 Build Background Video

MATERIALS

markers or colored pencils

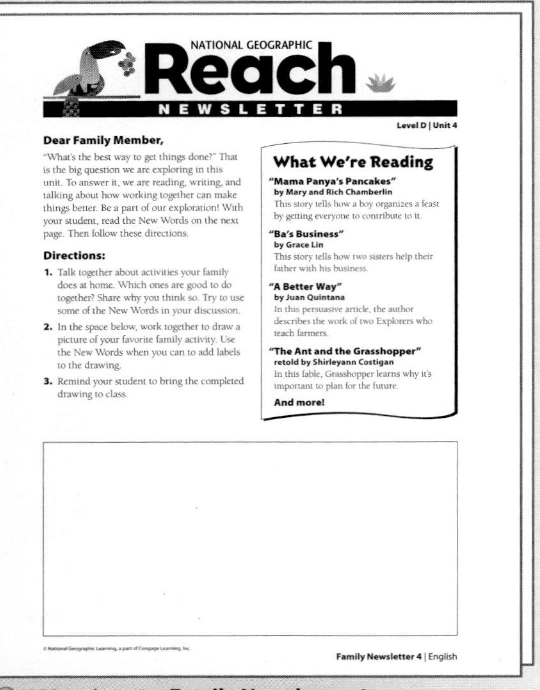

NATIONAL GEOGRAPHIC **Reach** NEWSLETTER

Level D | Unit 4

Dear Family Member,

"What's the best way to get things done?" That is the big question we are exploring in this unit. To answer it, we are reading, writing, and talking about how working together can make things better. Be a part of our exploration! With your student, read the New Words on the next page. Then follow these directions.

Directions:

1. Talk together about activities your family does at home. Which ones are good to do together? Share why you think so. Try to use some of the New Words in your discussion.
2. In the space below, work together to draw a picture of your favorite family activity. Use the New Words when you can to add labels to the drawing.
3. Remind your student to bring the completed drawing to class.

What We're Reading

"Mama Panya's Pancakes"
by Mary and Rich Chamberlin
This story tells how a boy organizes a feast by getting everyone to contribute to it.

"Ba's Business"
by Grace Lin
This story tells how two sisters help their father with his business.

"A Better Way"
by Juan Quintana
In this persuasive article, the author describes the work of two Explorers who teach farmers.

"The Ant and the Grasshopper"
retold by Shirleyann Costigan
In this fable, Grasshopper learns why it's important to plan for the future.

And more!

Family Newsletter 4 | English

NGReach.com **Family Newsletter 4** in seven languages

WARM-UP

Point to the photo on pages 208–209. Ask: *How are the people in the photograph working together? What are the **rewards** of working together?*

Social Studies Background

1 Big Question **Anthology** page 208

Have a volunteer read aloud the Big Question. Tell students they will read about ways people work together. Distribute **Family Newsletter 4**.

2 Share What You Know **Anthology** page 209

Activate prior knowledge: *When have you worked with a group to do something?* Display **Student eEdition** page 209, review the instructions, and distribute materials. Display students' drawings. Have volunteers choose a picture and pantomime the job. Ask classmates to join the pantomime or to guess the job.

3 Build Background Video

Set a purpose for viewing the video: *Watch the video to find out about ways people work together.* Play the video and invite students to take notes. After viewing, ask: *How can people benefit by working together? What can happen if they don't?*

Mini Lesson

Analyze Audio and Images

Explain: *The words and images in a video work together to tell about the most important ideas.*

NGReach.com **Build Background Video**

Stop the video at 0:36. Think aloud:

- *We hear, "It is much easier to complete a big project if you can divide it up into smaller parts." That's the main idea of this segment.*
- *Next, the video shows kids carrying wood while other kids prepare to build with it. Those images and details go with the audio to support the main idea.*

Replay sections of the video, pausing to have groups note main ideas and supporting details from the audio and visuals.

Then ask: *How is the information in a video like information found in a newspaper or Web site? What makes a video different?*

COMMON CORE STANDARDS

Speaking and Listening

Determine the Main Ideas and Supporting Details of Information Presented Visually in Diverse Media CC.3.SL.2

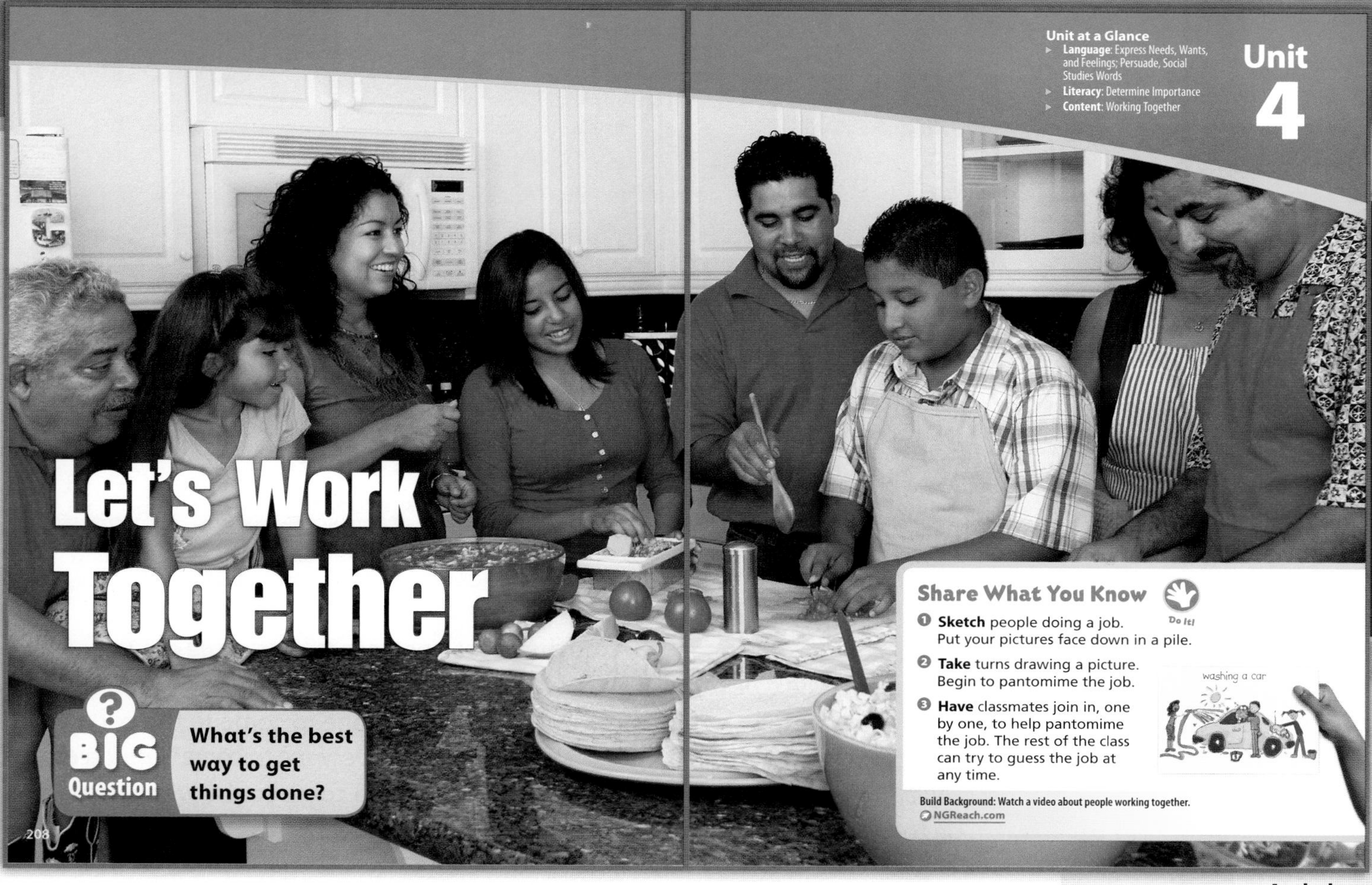

Unit at a Glance
Language: Express Needs, Wants, and Feelings; Persuade, Social Studies Words
Literacy: Determine Importance
Content: Working Together
Unit 4
Let's Work Together
BIG Question
What's the best way to get things done?
Share What You Know
Do It!
1 Sketch people doing a job. Put your pictures face down in a pile.
2 Take turns drawing a picture. Begin to pantomime the job.
3 Have classmates join in, one by one, to help pantomime the job. The rest of the class can try to guess the job at any time.
washing a car
Build Background: Watch a video about people working together.
NGReach.com
208

STUDENT TECHNOLOGY

- Student eEdition
- Video
- Resources

NGReach.com

Anthology
pages 208–209

Unit Projects

4 Introduce the Unit Concept Map

Review the Big Question. As students flip through the unit, prompt predictions: *What do you think you will learn about working together?* Responses should cite examples from the unit. Have pairs compare pages they find interesting.

Display the unit concept map using **Student eEdition** page 272, or provide a bulletin-board version. Explain: *As you go through this unit, you will organize your answers to the Big Question on a concept map.*

work together
everyone cooperates and gives a little bit
What's the best way to get things done?
use alternative methods
save for the future

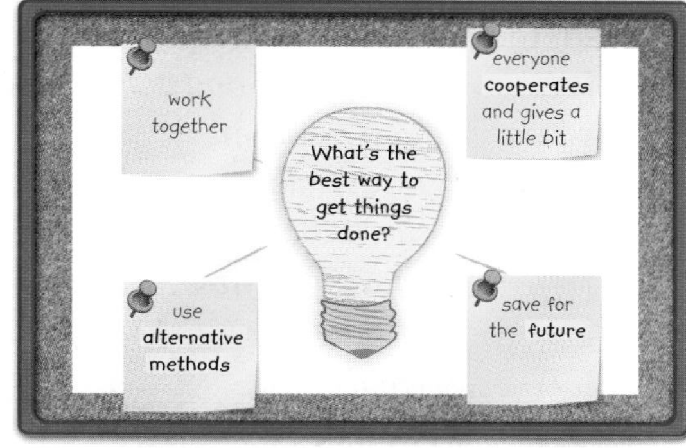

Concept Map

Distribute **Practice Master PM4.1** and model how to fill in a concept map. Ask: *What ideas can we add from the video?* (Possible responses: Some jobs go faster when you work with friends. Sometimes it's easier to divide a big project into smaller parts. Working together, people can find better ways to do things.)

5 Preview Unit Projects

Point out the projects using **Student eEdition** page 273. Have students read the project options so they can think about which one they will choose: write a skit, be a reporter, do a chore together, or write a letter.

Weekly Writing

Gather students' writing throughout the week:

- ✓ Daily Writing Skills Practice (T207q–T207r)
- ✓ Power Writing (T210, T212a, T216, T224, T231b)
- ✓ Writing (T212, T214–215, T223, T231a, T232)
- ✓ Writing Project (T233a–T233d)

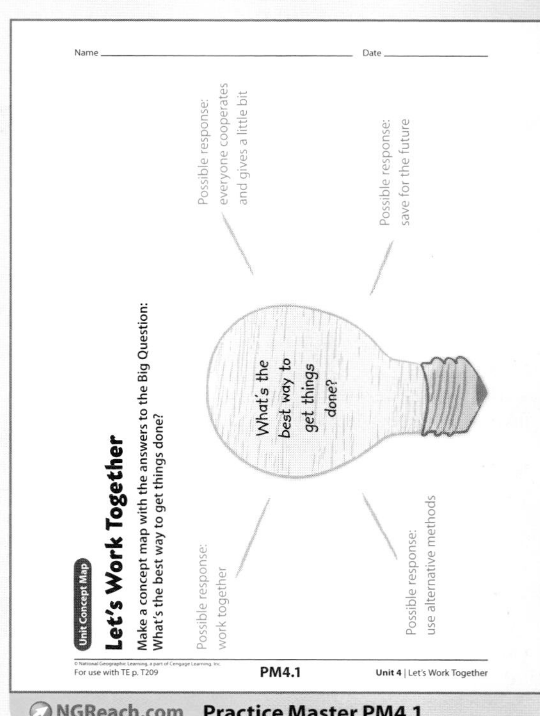

Name ______ Date ______

Unit Concept Map

Let's Work Together

Make a concept map with the answers to the Big Question: What's the best way to get things done?

What's the best way to get things done?

Possible response: everyone cooperates and gives a little bit

Possible response: save for the future

Possible response: work together

Possible response: use alternative methods

© National Geographic Learning, a part of Cengage Learning, Inc.
For use with TE p. T209

PM4.1

Unit 4 | Let's Work Together

NGReach.com **Practice Master PM4.1**

Listen and Comprehend

Realistic Fiction

OBJECTIVES

Thematic Connection: Community

- ☑ **Use Domain-Specific Words**
- ☑ **Determine Theme**

PROGRAM RESOURCES

PRINT & TECHNOLOGY

Family Newsletter 4

Unit Concept Map: Practice Master PM4.1

Theme Chart: Practice Master PM4.2

TECHNOLOGY ONLY

Sing with Me MP3

Digital Library: Key Word Images

My Vocabulary Notebook

Read Aloud: eVisual 4.1

MATERIALS

timer

Power Writing

Have students write as much as they can as well as they can in one minute about the word *money*.

For ***Writing Routine 1****, see page BP47.*

COMMON CORE STANDARDS

Reading	
Determine the Central Message	CC.3.Rlit.2
Read with Fluency to Support Comprehension	CC.3.Rfou.4
Writing	
Write Over Shorter Time for Specific Purposes	CC.3.W.10
Speaking and Listening	
Discuss Topics, Expressing Ideas Clearly	CC.3.SL.1
Explain Ideas and Understanding	CC.3.SL.1.d
Language and Vocabulary	
Acquire and Use General Academic and Domain-Specific Words	CC.3.L.6

Academic Talk

1 Express Needs, Wants, and Feelings **Anthology** page 210

Read aloud the introduction and play the **Sing with Me Language Song**: "Everyone Helps." Explain: *When you discuss a topic, you can express your needs, wants, and feelings. To make sure that your ideas are clear, you should:*

- *use words that clearly describe what you mean*
- *give examples and details that tell more about the topic*
- *explain your ideas, reasons, and understanding*
- *recount experiences that help others better understand your ideas.*

Think aloud: *In the song, I know exactly what Noah needs because he gives examples of the type of help he needs: help with the flowers and balloons.* Point out that Noah doesn't clearly state why he wants everyone to come to the party. Ask: *How could Noah express more clearly why he wants everyone to come? What reason could he give?* (Possible response: I want everyone to come so the whole team can be together.)

Have partners express their needs, wants, and feelings about a class activity, such as a field trip or group project. Remind students to explain their ideas and understanding in a clear way by using descriptive words, giving examples, and recounting experiences. Have partners share their ideas with the class.

Social Studies Vocabulary

2 Key Words ☑ **Anthology** page 211

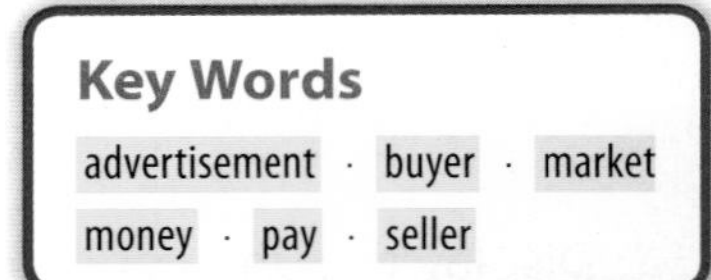

Explain and model using **Vocabulary Routine 1** and the picture on **Student eEdition** page 211 to learn the Key Words.

- ***Pronounce the word*** *and point to the picture:* ***advertisement***.
- ***Rate the word.*** *Hold up your fingers to show how well you know the word. (1=very well; 2=a little; 3=not at all) Tell what you know about this word.*
- ***Define the word:*** *An* ***advertisement*** *tells people about something that is for sale.*
- ***Elaborate:*** *Relate words to knowledge and experience: I saw an* ***advertisement*** *for a new cereal on T.V.*

For ***Vocabulary Routine 1****, see page BP34.*

For more images of the Key Words, use the ***Digital Library****.*

Have partners take turns repeating the routine for each word using page 211. Have each student add the words to **My Vocabulary Notebook**.

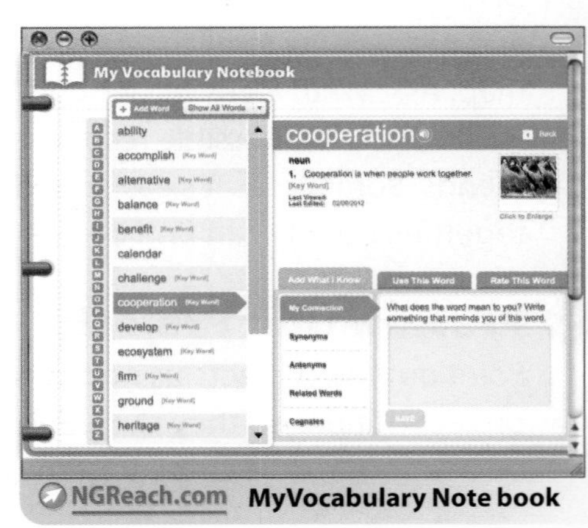

NGReach.com **MyVocabulary Note book**

See **Differentiate**

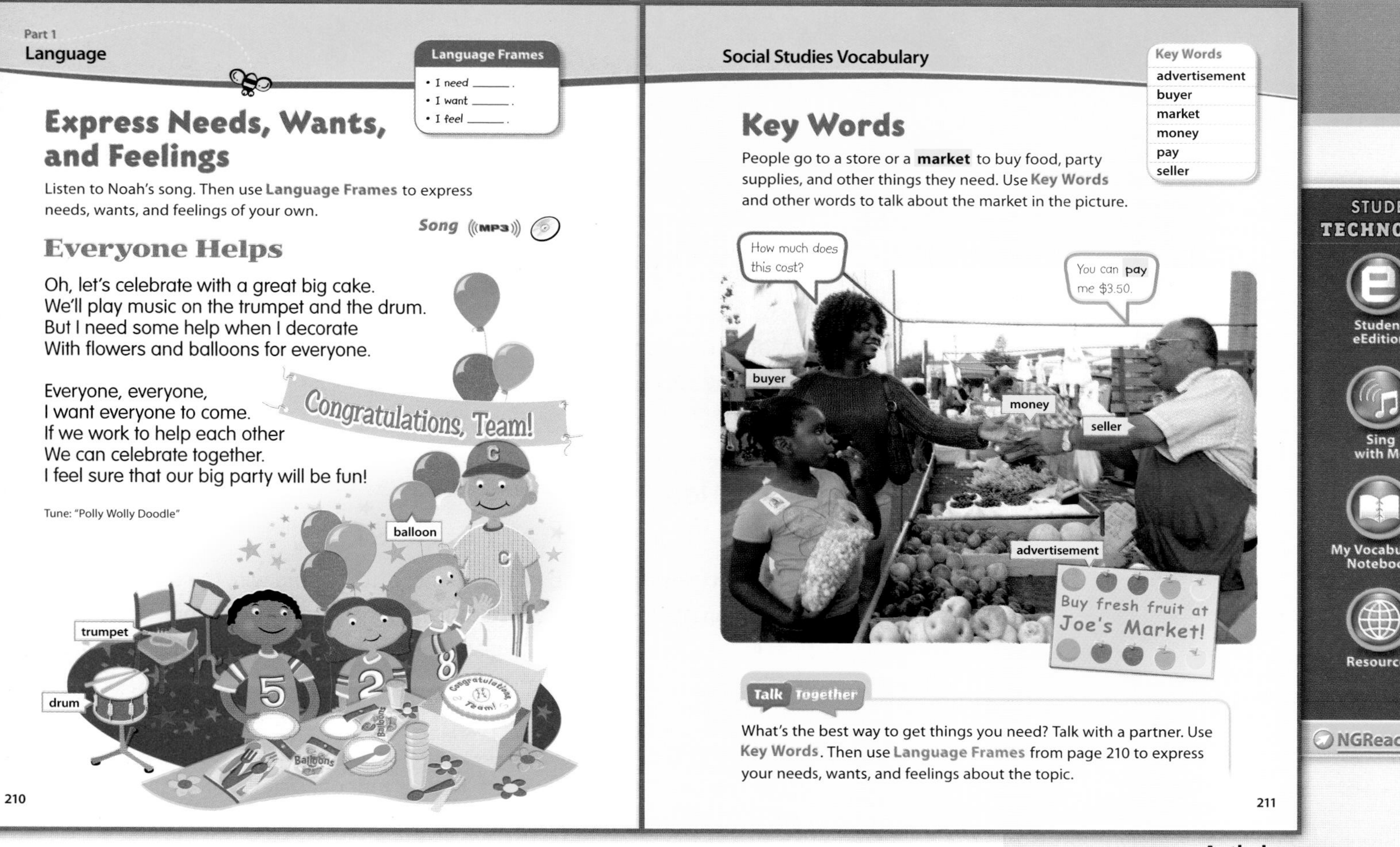

Part 1
Language

Language Frames
- I need ____.
- I want ____.
- I feel ____.

Express Needs, Wants, and Feelings

Listen to Noah's song. Then use **Language Frames** to express needs, wants, and feelings of your own.

Song ((MP3))

Everyone Helps

Oh, let's celebrate with a great big cake.
We'll play music on the trumpet and the drum.
But I need some help when I decorate
With flowers and balloons for everyone.

Everyone, everyone,
I want everyone to come.
If we work to help each other
We can celebrate together.
I feel sure that our big party will be fun!

Tune: "Polly Wolly Doodle"

210

Social Studies Vocabulary

Key Words
advertisement
buyer
market
money
pay
seller

Key Words

People go to a store or a **market** to buy food, party supplies, and other things they need. Use **Key Words** and other words to talk about the market in the picture.

Talk Together

What's the best way to get things you need? Talk with a partner. Use **Key Words**. Then use **Language Frames** from page 210 to express your needs, wants, and feelings about the topic.

211

STUDENT TECHNOLOGY
- Student eEdition
- Sing with Me
- My Vocabulary Notebook
- Resources

NGReach.com

Anthology
pages 210–211

3 Talk Together **Anthology** page 211

Read aloud the directions on page 211 and have partners brainstorm a list of things they need for home, school, or play. Model a response, such as: *When I see an **advertisement** for something I need, I go to the **market** and **pay** for it with the **money** I have earned.*

Check & Reteach

OBJECTIVE: Use Domain-Specific Words ☑

As students express needs, wants, and feelings, listen for correct usage of the Key Words. If students use words incorrectly, provide sentence frames for them to complete orally, such as:

- *Someone who **pays** **money** for something is called a ____.* (**buyer**)
- *Someone who has things that people can buy is called a ____.* (**seller**)
- *A ____ is a place where people can go to buy and sell food.* (**market**)

Differentiate

EL English Learners

ISSUE Students do not understand definitions.

STRATEGY Provide translations of the Key Words. Access **Family Newsletter 4** for translations in seven languages. Use a cognate for Spanish speakers:

market/mercado

BL Below Level

ISSUE Students have difficulty relating the Key Words to experiences.

STRATEGY Have students imagine they are a person in the photo on page 211. They can use one or more of the Key Words to tell what the person does. (Possible response: I am a **buyer**. I **pay** the **seller** with **money**.)

Word Map

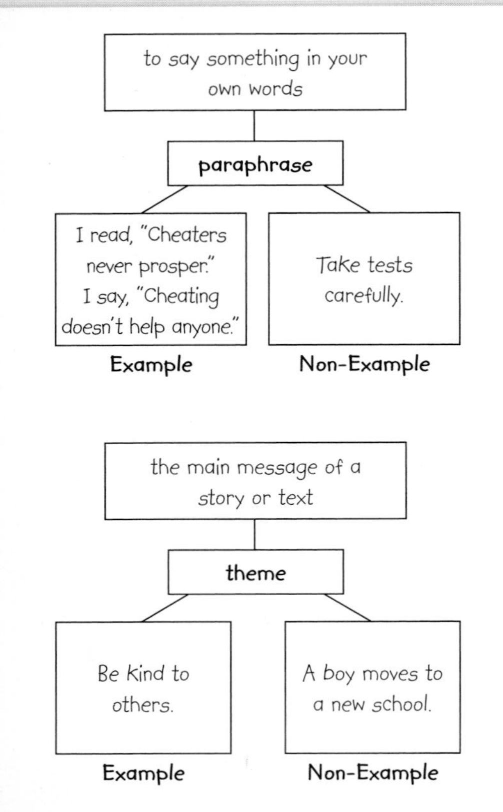

Fluency

Model Intonation Explain the concept: *Fluent readers raise and lower their voices as they read. When you read a statement, your voice rises at the beginning, and then falls at the end. When you read an exclamation, your voice gets louder and shows excitement.* Model intonation with sentences from "An Extra Guest." Then have students practice intonation by reading aloud the song lyrics on **Anthology** page 210.

Comprehension

4 Theme  Anthology page 212

Use Word Maps to teach the terms ***paraphrase*** and ***theme***. Read aloud the information at the top of page 212. Then display **eVisual 4.1** and read aloud "An Extra Guest."

Read Aloud

Realistic Fiction

An Extra Guest

Noah's team wins the championship game! After the big win, the coach plans a huge celebration. He sees an **advertisement** for a party supply store, so he goes there first. At the store, he chooses a giant banner that says "Congratulations, Team!" Then he buys bright balloons. Later, the coach goes to the **market** and **pays** for a great big cake.

On the day of the party, Noah can't wait to celebrate his team's amazing victory. The decorations and cake look fantastic. Noah's younger sister, Marty, goes to the party with him. She wants to join in the fun, but she isn't sure if she is welcome.

Noah tells Marty that she should celebrate with the team. He adds a chair to the table to make space for her. Noah's teammates smile at Marty and thank her for cheering at every game. The coach says, "Welcome, Marty!" and lets her choose her own balloon. Before long, Marty is smiling and joining the big celebration.

NGReach.com **Read Aloud: eVisual 4.1**

INTERACTIVE WHITEBOARD TIP: Circle the characters and underline important events.

5 Map and Talk Anthology page 212

Review plot, setting, and characters. Then have students read how to make a theme chart. Discuss how the clues in the chart support the theme. Then have students review "An Extra Guest" to find more clues that support the theme.

6 Talk Together Anthology page 212

Have one partner tell a story while the other partner uses **Practice Master PM4.2** to create a theme chart. Then have partners trade roles and take turns paraphrasing each other's theme statements.

Check & Reteach

OBJECTIVE: Determine Theme

After students complete their theme charts, ask: *What is the theme of your partner's story? What clues from the story helped you figure out the theme?*

If students have difficulty identifying the theme, ask: *What does the title tell you? What can you learn from the setting and main events of the story?* Then guide students to combine their clues to find the main message of their partners' story.

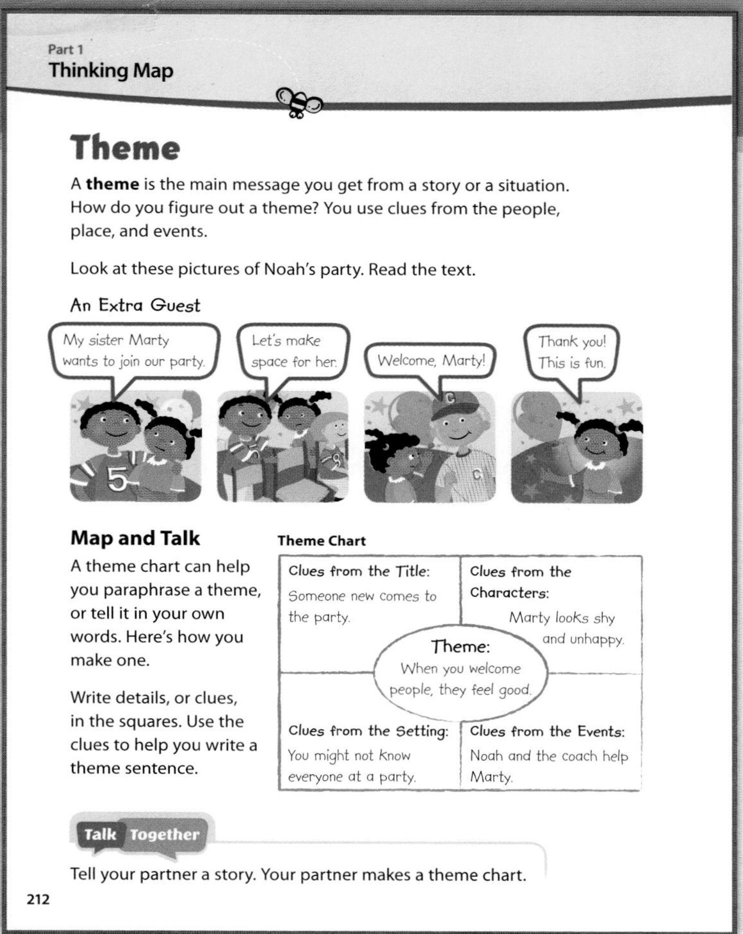
Part 1
Thinking Map

Theme

A **theme** is the main message you get from a story or a situation. How do you figure out a theme? You use clues from the people, place, and events.

Look at these pictures of Noah's party. Read the text.

An Extra Guest

Map and Talk

A theme chart can help you paraphrase a theme, or tell it in your own words. Here's how you make one.

Write details, or clues, in the squares. Use the clues to help you write a theme sentence.

Theme Chart

Clues from the Title: Someone new comes to the party.	Clues from the Characters: Marty looks shy and unhappy.
Clues from the Setting: You might not know everyone at a party.	Clues from the Events: Noah and the coach help Marty.

Theme: When you welcome people, they feel good.

Talk Together

Tell your partner a story. Your partner makes a theme chart.

212

Anthology page 212

Writing

7 Write About Theme

Introduce: *Now you will write a paragraph that explains the **theme** of the story your partner told.* Model how the begin the writing process with "An Extra Guest."

Think Aloud	Write
First, I write about a clue in the title.	Someone new comes to the party.
Next, I write about a clue in the setting.	At the party, there are many people.

*For **Writing Routine 2**, see page BP48.*

To complete the model, have volunteers identify more clues from the theme chart on **Anthology** page 212. Be sure to end the model by writing the theme.

Have students use their charts to write about the theme of their partner's story. After sharing paragraphs, students can add them to the Weekly Writing folders.

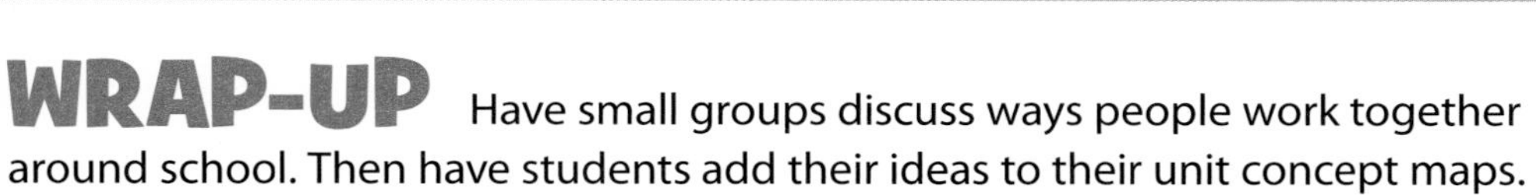

WRAP-UP Have small groups discuss ways people work together around school. Then have students add their ideas to their unit concept maps.

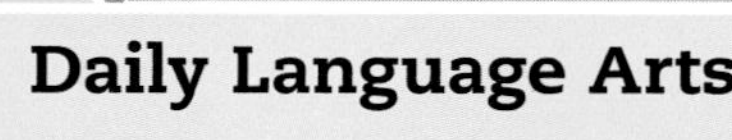

Daily Language Arts

Daily Spelling and Word Work ☑

Pretest page T207m

Daily Grammar ☑

Point to the verb *wins* in the first paragraph of the **Read Aloud**, and explain that it refers to an action that is happening right now. Then use page T207o to teach about present-tense verbs.

Daily Writing Skills ☑

Point out that the purpose of the Read Aloud "An Extra Guest" is to entertain. Then use page T207q to teach about author's purpose.

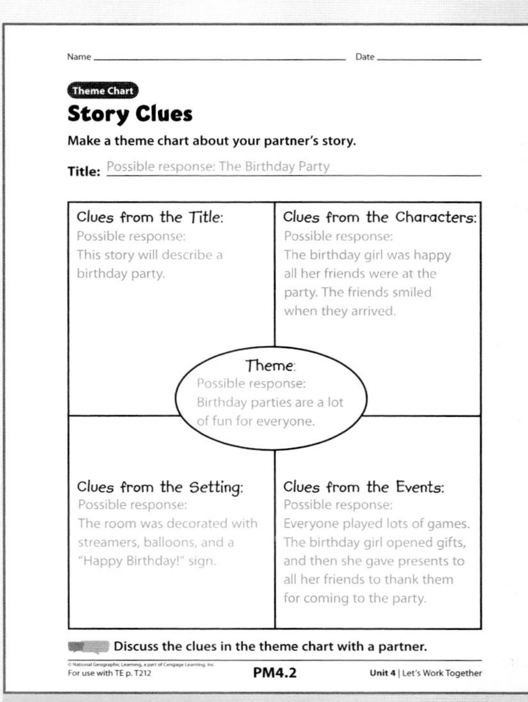
Name ______ Date ______

Theme Chart

Story Clues

Make a theme chart about your partner's story.

Title: Possible response: The Birthday Party

Clues from the Title: Possible response: This story will describe a birthday party.	Clues from the Characters: Possible response: The birthday girl was happy all her friends were at the party. The friends smiled when they arrived.
Clues from the Setting: Possible response: The room was decorated with streamers, balloons, and a "Happy Birthday!" sign.	Clues from the Events: Possible response: Everyone played lots of games. The birthday girl opened gifts, and then she gave presents to all her friends to thank them for coming to the party.

Theme: Possible response: Birthday parties are a lot of fun for everyone.

Discuss the clues in the theme chart with a partner.

For use with TE p. T212 PM4.2 Unit 4 | Let's Work Together

NGReach.com **Practice Master PM4.2**

OBJECTIVES

Thematic Connection: Community

☑ Use Academic Words

☑ Determine Importance

PROGRAM RESOURCES

PRINT & TECHNOLOGY

Family Newsletter 4

TECHNOLOGY ONLY

Digital Library: Key Word Images

My Vocabulary Notebook

MATERIALS

timer • self-stick notes

Power Writing

Have students write as much as they can as well as they can in one minute about the word *market*.

*For **Writing Routine 1**, see page BP47.*

COMMON CORE STANDARDS

Reading	
Read with Fluency to Support Comprehension	CC.3.Rfou.4
Read with Purpose and Understanding	CC.3.Rfou.4.a
Writing	
Write Over Shorter Time for Specific Tasks	CC.3.W.10
Speaking and Listening	
Recount an Experience	CC.3.SL.4
Language and Vocabulary	
Determine Meaning of Words and Phrases	CC.3.L.4
Acquire and Use General Academic Words	CC.3.L.6

WARM-UP

Ask: *How do people in your community work together to help others?* Have students list and discuss community or charity events that they know.

Academic Talk

1 Recount an Experience

Review: *When you recount an experience, you tell about a past event in order, including only relevant facts and descriptive details. When you speak, it's important to pronounce words clearly. Don't speak too slowly or too quickly.*

Model recounting an experience, using a clear voice and a steady pace: *Yesterday, I saw an **advertisement** in the newspaper for color pencils. The **seller's** price was much lower than the prices at other stores. I saved a lot of **money** by paying the lower price.* Explain how the details in the model are relevant to the topic. Point out how you spoke clearly and at an understandable pace.

Then have students recount a time they shopped for something. Divide students into pairs and use a **Three-Step Interview:**

- Student A interviews Student B about a shopping experience. Student B recounts the experience, using Key Words to describe the relevant facts and details.
- Student A and Student B reverse roles.
- Student A tells the group about Student B's experience. Then Student B tells the group about Student A.

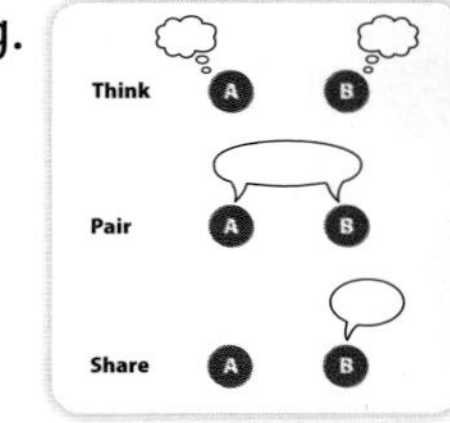

Three-Step Interview

*For **Three-Step Interview**, see page BP46.*

Academic Vocabulary

2 More Key Words ☑ Anthology page 213

Say: *Let's learn some more words to help us communicate effectively.* Model using **Vocabulary Routine 1** and images in the **Student eEdition** to learn Key Words.

Key Words

accomplish · cooperation
plenty · purpose · reward

- ***Pronounce the word*** *and point to its picture:* ***cooperation***.
- ***Rate the word.*** *Hold up your fingers to show how well you know the word (1 = very well; 2 = a little; 3 = not at all). Tell what you know about this word.*
- ***Define the word: Cooperation*** *is when people work together.*
- ***Elaborate.*** *It takes **cooperation** to get a group project done.*

*For **Vocabulary Routine 1**, see page BP34.*

*For more images of the Key Words, use the **Digital Library**.*

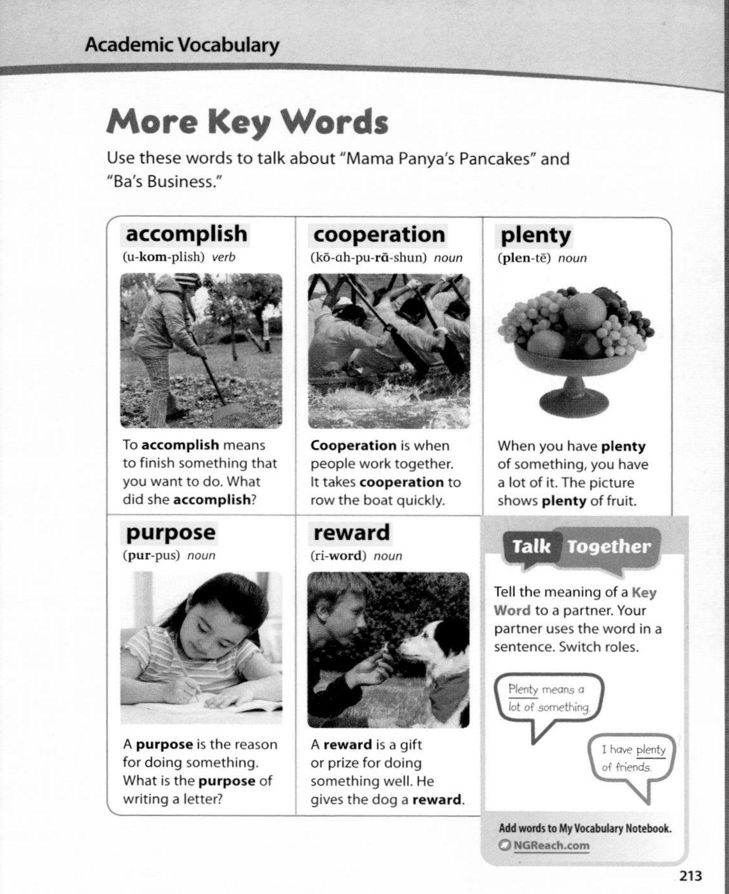
Academic Vocabulary
More Key Words
Use these words to talk about "Mama Panya's Pancakes" and "Ba's Business."
accomplish
(u-kom-plish) verb
To accomplish means to finish something that you want to do. What did she accomplish?
cooperation
(kō-ah-pu-rā-shun) noun
Cooperation is when people work together. It takes cooperation to row the boat quickly.
plenty
(plen-tē) noun
When you have plenty of something, you have a lot of it. The picture shows plenty of fruit.
purpose
(pur-pus) noun
A purpose is the reason for doing something. What is the purpose of writing a letter?
reward
(ri-word) noun
A reward is a gift or prize for doing something well. He gives the dog a reward.
Talk Together
Tell the meaning of a Key Word to a partner. Your partner uses the word in a sentence. Switch roles.
Plenty means a lot of something.
I have plenty of friends.
Add words to My Vocabulary Notebook.
NGReach.com
213

STUDENT TECHNOLOGY
Student eEdition
My Vocabulary Notebook
Resources
NGReach.com

Anthology page 213

Have partners take turns repeating the routine for each word using page 213. Have each student add the words to **My Vocabulary Notebook**.

See **Differentiate**

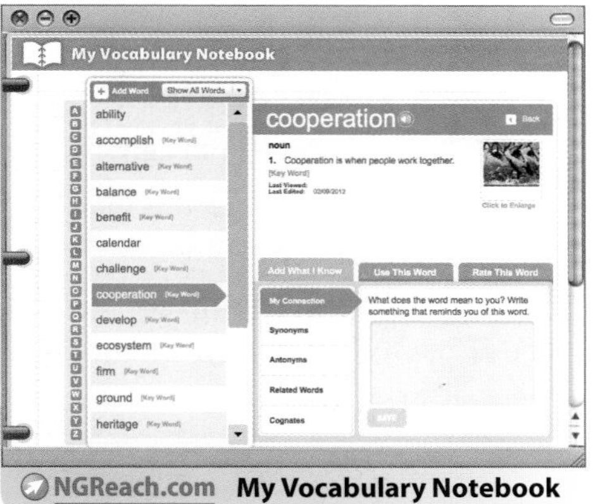
My Vocabulary Notebook
cooperation
Cooperation is when people work together.

NGReach.com **My Vocabulary Notebook**

3 Talk Together **Anthology** page 213

Read aloud the instructions. Have partners take turns telling the meanings of Key Words and using them in sentences. Ask volunteers to share a sentence with the class.

Check & Reteach

OBJECTIVE: Use Academic Words ☑

As students share their sentences, listen for correct usage of the Key Words.

If students use words incorrectly, ask questions about the words, for example:

- *If you have trouble doing something alone, what might you need to get it done?* (**cooperation**)
- *If you win a race, what might you get?* (a **reward**)
- *If you have enough of something, what do you have?* (**plenty**)

Best Practices

Group Strategically When students practice the vocabulary words, use word knowledge ratings from step 2 of the vocabulary routine to pair students who have different levels of word knowledge.

Differentiate

EL English Learners

ISSUE Students do not understand definitions.

STRATEGY Provide translations of the Key Words. Access **Family Newsletter 4** for translations in seven languages. Use a cognate for Spanish speakers:

cooperation/cooperación

BL Below Level

ISSUE Students have difficulty remembering the definitions.

STRATEGY Have students write each definition on a self-stick note. Then have students choose a word, read its definition aloud, and then create a sentence using the word.

Word Map

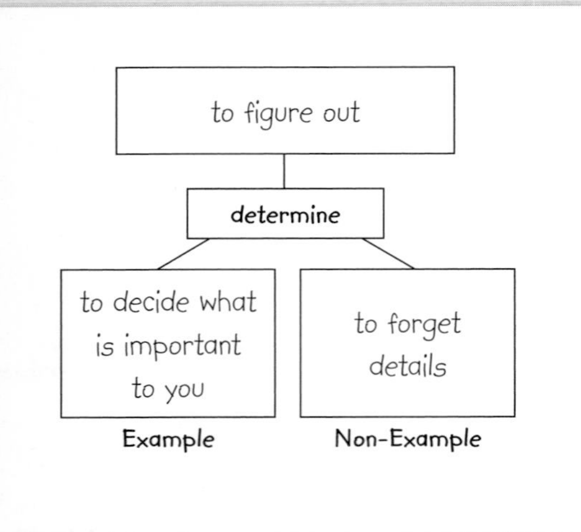

Fluency

Practice Intonation As partners read aloud the personal narrative "Balloons for Food," circulate and listen for correct intonation.

Daily Language Arts

Daily Spelling and Word Work ☑
Practice page T207m

Daily Grammar ☑
Display the illustration on **Anthology** page 214 and say: *The team puts boxes in the truck*. Explain that the word *puts* tells what the team is doing. Then use page T207o to teach action verbs.

Daily Writing Skills ☑
Point out that the purpose of "Balloons for Food" on **Anthology** page 215, is to inform. Then use page T207q to practice writing for different purposes.

Comprehension

4 Learn to Determine Importance ☑ **Anthology** pages 214–215

Use a Word Map to teach the term ***determine***, Then project **Student eEdition** page 214 and read aloud the introduction. Explain: *When you decide what details you want to remember, you* ***determine*** *importance.* Read aloud the How-to chart and then model how to determine important details in the picture:

- *This part is about a food drive.*
- *I want to know more about what happens at a food drive.*
- *When I see kids working together to put food in boxes, I learn that a food drive takes* ***cooperation***.

5 Talk Together **Anthology** page 215

Read aloud the instructions on page 215. Then have partners whisper read the first paragraph of the personal narrative and the sample determination. Ask: *How does* ***determining*** *importance help you understand the story?* (Possible response: As I read, I can look for details about what I think is important.)

Have partners read the rest of "Balloons for Food," pausing to determine importance. Remind students to focus on their purpose and look for details that tell what they want to know. Circulate and monitor their conversations.

Check & Reteach

OBJECTIVE: Determine Importance ☑

As students discuss "Balloons for Food," listen to make sure that they determine importance correctly.

If students have difficulty, have them reread the personal narrative and pause at the first red arrow. Ask: *What do you want to know about the food drive? That is your* ***purpose*** *for reading. As you read on, look for details that tell you more about what you want to know.*

Writing

6 Write About Important Details

Introduce: *Now we are going to write a paragraph about the important details you found in "Balloons for Food."* Model the process:

Think Aloud	Write
First, I write about a detail that I ***determined*** *was important.*	Noah's team uses balloons as an **advertisement** for the food drive.
Then I explain why the detail is important to the story.	This detail is important because I was wondering how the team would spread the news about the food drive.

For ***Writing Routine 2****, see page BP48.*

Learn to Determine Importance

Look at the picture. Which parts mean the most to you? When you figure out what is important to you, you **determine importance**.

FOOD DRIVE TODAY

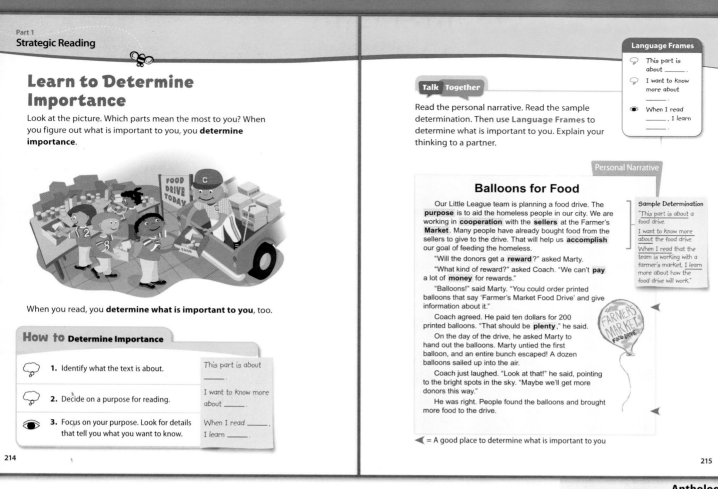

When you read, you **determine what is important to you**, too.

How to Determine Importance

1. Identify what the text is about.	This part is about ____.
2. Decide on a purpose for reading.	I want to know more about ____.
3. Focus on your purpose. Look for details that tell you what you want to know.	When I read ____, I learn ____.

214

Talk Together

Read the personal narrative. Read the sample determination. Then use **Language Frames** to determine what is important to you. Explain your thinking to a partner.

Language Frames

- This part is about ____.
- I want to know more about ____.
- When I read ____, I learn ____.

Personal Narrative

Balloons for Food

Our Little League team is planning a food drive. The **purpose** is to aid the homeless people in our city. We are working in **cooperation** with the **sellers** at the Farmer's **Market**. Many people have already bought food from the sellers to give to the drive. That will help us **accomplish** our goal of feeding the homeless.

"Will the donors get a **reward**?" asked Marty.

"What kind of reward?" asked Coach. "We can't **pay** a lot of **money** for rewards."

"Balloons!" said Marty. "You could order printed balloons that say 'Farmer's Market Food Drive' and give information about it."

Coach agreed. He paid ten dollars for 200 printed balloons. "That should be **plenty**," he said.

On the day of the drive, he asked Marty to hand out the balloons. Marty untied the first balloon, and an entire bunch escaped! A dozen balloons sailed up into the air.

Coach just laughed. "Look at that!" he said, pointing to the bright spots in the sky. "Maybe we'll get more donors this way."

He was right. People found the balloons and brought more food to the drive.

FARMER'S MARKET FOOD DRIVE

Sample Determination

"This part is about a food drive.

I want to know more about the food drive.

When I read that the team is working with a farmer's market, I learn more about how the food drive will work."

◄ = A good place to determine what is important to you

215

Anthology
pages 214–215

Have students write a paragraph about a detail they considered important in the personal narrative "Balloons for Food." Remind them that the first sentence should state which detail they think is important. The remaining sentences should give reasons that support and explain why the detail is important to the reader and the story.

Have students add their paragraphs to their Weekly Writing folders.

See **Differentiate**

WRAP-UP Remind students that they have read about how Noah's Little League team planned a food drive. Have partners brainstorm other ways Noah's Little League team could help the community.

Differentiate

EL English Learners

ISSUE Students have difficulty writing about details.

STRATEGY Provide sentence frames to structure students' paragraphs: In the story ____. This detail is important to me because I wanted to find out ____. The detail is an important part of the story because it ____.

Day 3 Read and Comprehend

Realistic Fiction

OBJECTIVES

Thematic Connection: Community

- ☑ **Determine Theme**
- ☑ **Determine Importance**

PROGRAM RESOURCES

TECHNOLOGY ONLY

My Vocabulary Notebook

Read with Me: Selection Recordings: MP3 or CD1 Track 19

MATERIALS

timer • map of Africa

Power Writing

Have students write as much as they can as well as they can in one minute about the word *purpose.*

*For **Writing Routine 1**, see page BP47.*

COMMON CORE STANDARDS

Reading	
Determine the Central Message	CC.3.Rlit.2
Describe Characters and Explain Characters' Responses	CC.3.Rlit.3
Distinguish Points of View	CC.3.Rlit.6
Read and Comprehend Literature	CC.3.Rlit.10
Read with Fluency to Support Comprehension	CC.3.Rfou.4
Read Orally with Accuracy and Appropriate Rate on Successive Readings	CC.3.Rfou.4.b
Writing	
Write Over Shorter Time for Specific Audiences	CC.3.W.10
Speaking and Listening	
Discuss Texts, Building on Others' Ideas and Expressing Ideas Clearly	CC.3.SL.1
Language and Vocabulary	
Acquire and Use General Academic and Domain-Specific Words	CC.3.L.6

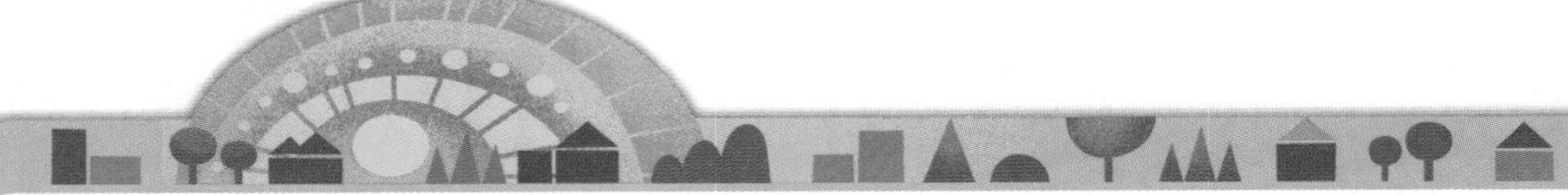

WARM-UP

Have students think about family celebrations or other occasions on which many people gather to eat a meal. Ask volunteers to share their experiences.

Vocabulary Practice

1 Expand Word Knowledge ☑

Students will practice Key Words by creating Three-Quarter Books. Use **Vocabulary Routine 2** to model how to make an organizer for the word ***plenty***.

- Write the word.
- Draw a picture.
- Add a definition.
- Add a context sentence inside.

*For **Vocabulary Routine 2**, see page BP35.*

Key Words

accomplish · advertisement · buyer
cooperation · determine · market
money · paraphrase · pay · plenty
purpose · reward · seller · theme

Assign a Key Word to each set of partners. After students complete their organizers, have them add the context sentences to **My Vocabulary Notebook**. Display the organizers in the classroom.

Academic Talk

2 Preview and Predict

REVIEW Remind students that one way they can preview a text is to look at the illustrations and make predictions about them. Model: *On pages 216–217, I see **plenty** of people around a fire. After I read the title and see someone cooking over the fire, I predict the people will make pancakes together.* Have volunteers build on your ideas as they discuss the text and make their own predictions.

Display Key Words: *accomplish, cooperation, money, plenty,* and *purpose*. Have students use a **Think, Pair, Share** to make predictions about the selection."

- Students preview the illustrations on **Anthology** pages 218–223 independently.
- Students form pairs to share their predictions. They should use Key Words and convey their ideas precisely as they build on each other's ideas.
- Individuals share their questions and predictions with a student from another pair.

Think A B
Pair A B
Share A B

Think, Pair, Share

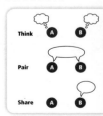

*For **Think, Pair, Share**, see page BP46.*

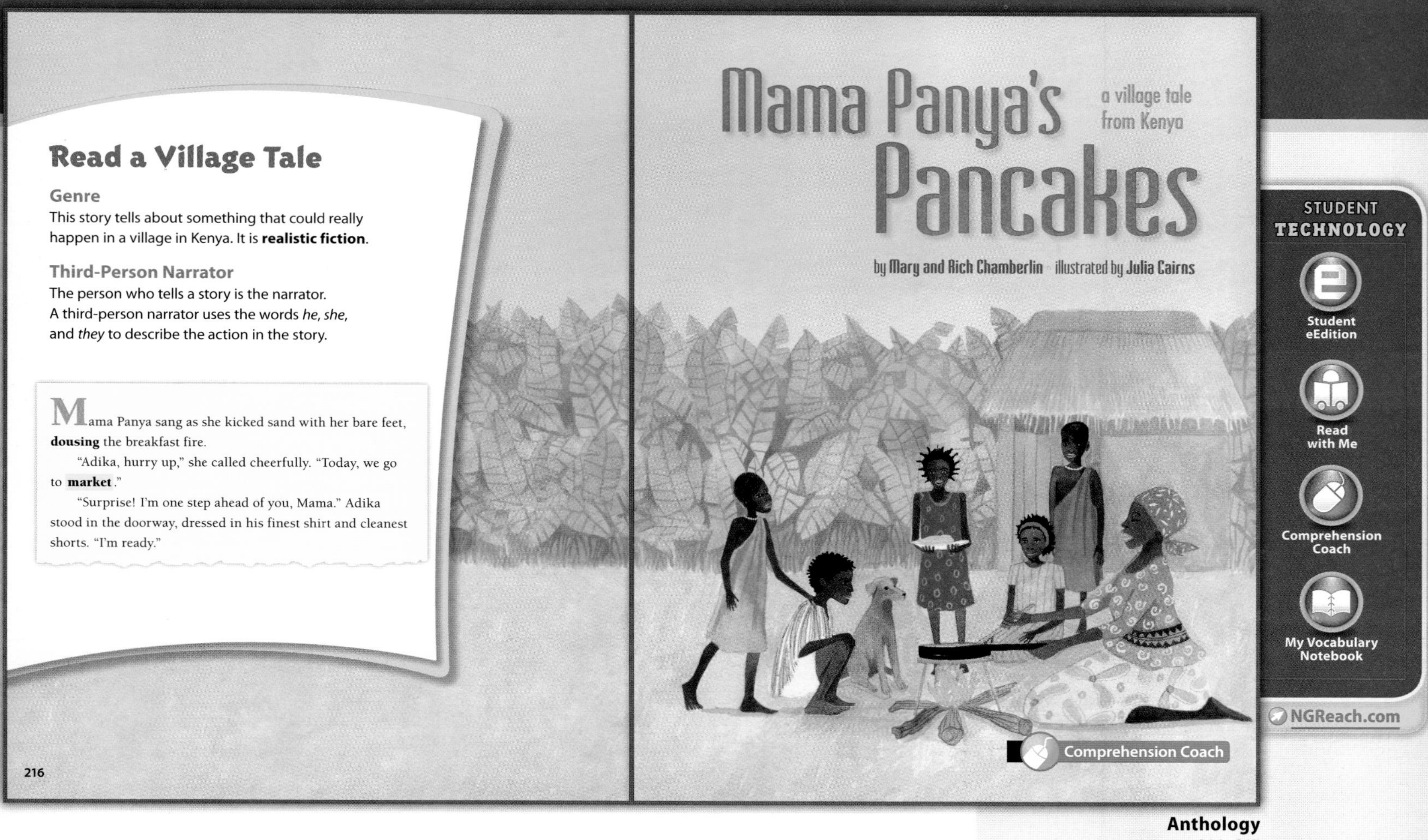
Read a Village Tale

Genre

This story tells about something that could really happen in a village in Kenya. It is **realistic fiction**.

Third-Person Narrator

The person who tells a story is the narrator. A third-person narrator uses the words *he, she,* and *they* to describe the action in the story.

Mama Panya sang as she kicked sand with her bare feet, **dousing** the breakfast fire.

"Adika, hurry up," she called cheerfully. "Today, we go to **market**."

"Surprise! I'm one step ahead of you, Mama." Adika stood in the doorway, dressed in his finest shirt and cleanest shorts. "I'm ready."

216

Mama Panya's Pancakes

a village tale from Kenya

by Mary and Rich Chamberlin illustrated by Julia Cairns

Anthology
pages 216–217

Reading

3 Read a Village Tale **Anthology** pages 216–217

GENRE Have a volunteer read aloud the definition of realistic fiction. Elaborate: *The characters are not real, but they seem like real people. The events could really happen.*

THIRD-PERSON NARRATOR Ask a volunteer to read aloud the definition of a third-person narrator. Elaborate: *A third-person narrator is not a character in the story. The narrator tells how all the characters feel and what they do.*

SOCIAL STUDIES BACKGROUND Share information to build background:

- *This story takes place in a small village in the country of Kenya.* Display a map of Africa and point to Kenya on the eastern coast.
- *People in small villages often walk to* ***markets*** *to* ***buy*** *goods and visit one another.*

Have students read pages 218–223. See **Differentiate**

Best Practices

Model Academic Language If the Academic Talk discussions reflect too much informal talk, model an academic conversation with or between two students. Then have students echo the model to role-play academic discussions in small groups.

Differentiate

BL Below Level

FRONTLOAD Preview and discuss the illustrations. Then read aloud the story and use the questions to build comprehension.

OL On Level

READ TOGETHER Partners take turns whisper reading the story together. Use the questions to build comprehension.

AL Above Level

READ INDEPENDENTLY As students read silently, have them note clues that help determine theme. Use the questions to build comprehension.

Day **3**

1 ▸ Set a Purpose
Find out what happens when Mama Panya and her son go to buy food.

Mama Panya sang as she kicked sand with her bare feet, **dousing** the breakfast fire.

"Adika, hurry up," she called cheerfully. "Today, we go to **market**."

"Surprise! I'm one step ahead of you, Mama." Adika stood in the doorway, dressed in his finest shirt and cleanest shorts. "I'm ready."

Now Mama Panya had to hurry.

In Other Words
dousing putting out

218

After **storing** her pots, gathering her bag and slipping her feet into her sandals, Mama Panya called, "I'm ready too, Adika. Where are you?"

"Here I am, Mama—two steps ahead of you." He sat under the baobab tree, Mama Panya's walking stick in hand.

"Why, yes you are." She **accepted** the stick and led them down the road.

"What will you get at the market, Mama?"

"Oh, a little bit and a little bit more."   

In Other Words
storing putting away
accepted took

219

Anthology
pages 218–219

Fluency

Practice Intonation As students read, monitor their intonation, accuracy, and rate.

Read and Build Comprehension

1 Set a Purpose Have a student read aloud the purpose statement. Discuss what might happen when Mama Panya and Adika go to buy food.

2 Determine Importance ☑ *What happens on pages 218–219? What do you want to learn more about?* (Possible response: This part is about Adika and Mama getting ready to go to the **market**. I want to know more about what they will buy. When I read that Adika asks what Mama will get, I learn that Mama wants it to be a surprise.)

3 Analyze Setting *What is the setting of the story?* (a small village in Kenya) *As you read, think about how the setting is important to the* ***theme****, or message, of the story.*

Differentiate

SN Special Needs

ISSUE Students do not see the importance of identifying story elements.

STRATEGY Review the story elements identified in the selection. Remind students that story elements are clues to a story's theme, which is determined at the end of the story.

AL Above Level

ISSUE Students do not use newly acquired vocabulary.

STRATEGY Challenge students to use at least one content, academic, or classroom vocabulary word in each response. Ask: *How can you rephrase your response to use some of the Key Words?*

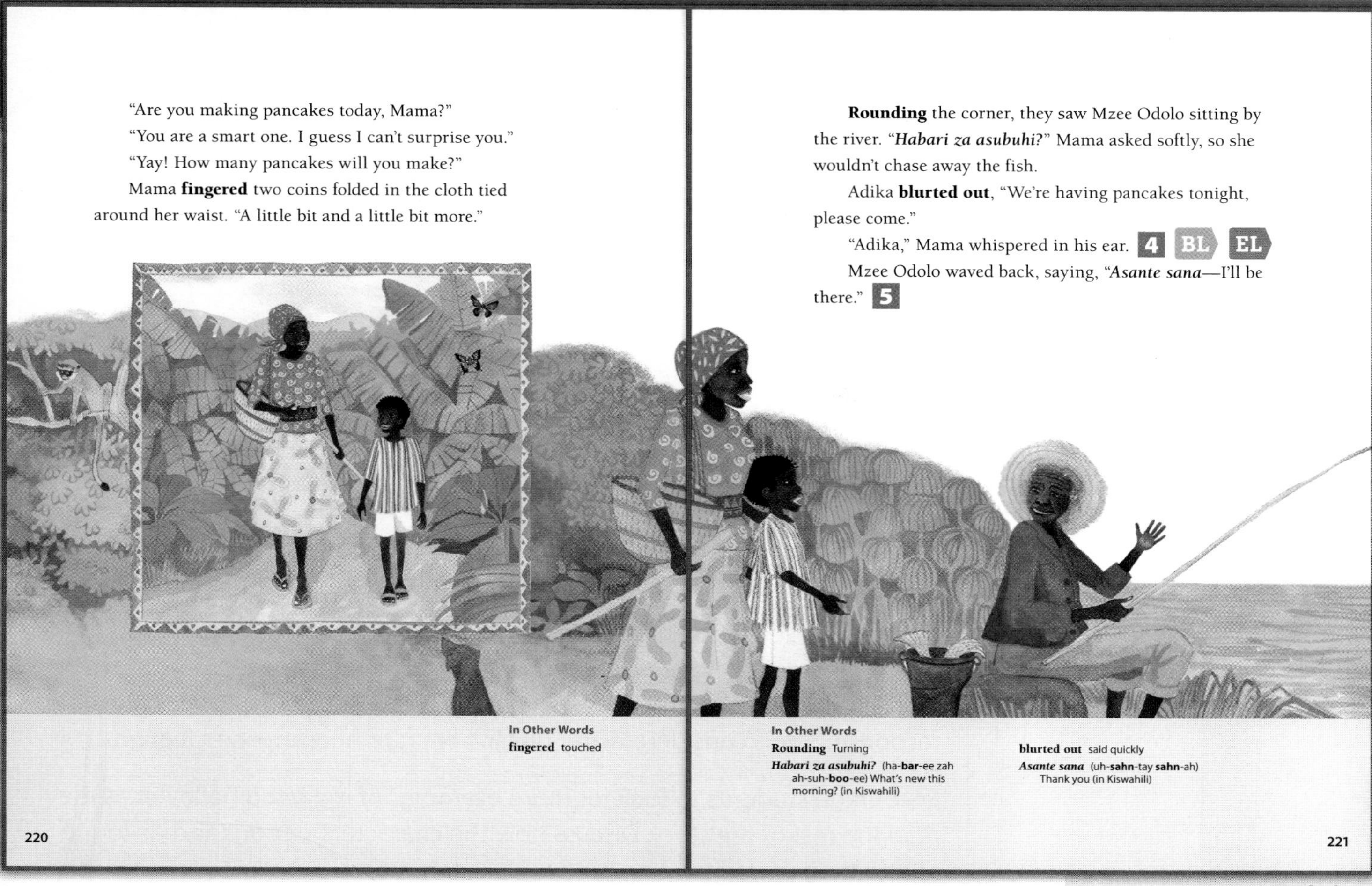

"Are you making pancakes today, Mama?"

"You are a smart one. I guess I can't surprise you."

"Yay! How many pancakes will you make?"

Mama **fingered** two coins folded in the cloth tied around her waist. "A little bit and a little bit more."

In Other Words
fingered touched

220

Rounding the corner, they saw Mzee Odolo sitting by the river. "***Habari za asubuhi?***" Mama asked softly, so she wouldn't chase away the fish.

Adika **blurted out**, "We're having pancakes tonight, please come."

"Adika," Mama whispered in his ear. **4** BL EL

Mzee Odolo waved back, saying, "*Asante sana*—I'll be there." **5**

In Other Words
Rounding Turning
Habari za asubuhi? (ha-**bar**-ee zah ah-suh-**boo**-ee) What's new this morning? (in Kiswahili)
blurted out said quickly
Asante sana (uh-**sahn**-tay **sahn**-ah) Thank you (in Kiswahili)

221

Anthology
pages 220–221

4 **Clarify Meaning** *What do you think Mama means by "a little bit and a little bit more?"* (Possible response: I read that Adika asks Mama if she's making pancakes. Mama probably means that she will buy a few small ingredients for pancakes at the **market**.)

5 **Draw Conclusions** *Why does Mama whisper in Adika's ear after he invites Mzee Odolo for pancakes?* (Possible response: I read that Mama speaks softly so she won't chase away the fish. I also read that Adika blurts out his words. I connect the ideas and conclude that Adika is being too loud, and Mama wants him to speak more quietly.)

Differentiate

BL Below Level

ISSUE Students have difficulty synthesizing story details to draw a conclusion about Mama's motives in question 5.

STRATEGY Review Mama's character and actions in the story. Then ask: *Why do people usually whisper?* (to keep an area quiet, to tell a secret) *Which of these reasons matches the details you read about Mama in the text?* Explain that students can put together details they read in the text to make a guess about Mama's actions.

EL English Learners

ISSUE Students lack language proficiency to explain characters' motives.

STRATEGY Prompt with forced-choice questions, such as: *Why does Mama whisper in Adika's ear? Does she want Adika to be quieter or does she want to tell him something?*

Mini Lesson

Analyze Characters

Explain: *We learn about characters by what they say and do in a story. If a character does the same thing many times, that can be a clue about what the character is like, too.*

Reread pages 221 to 223 and have students summarize Adika's behavior. Ask: *What does Adika keep doing?* (inviting people to eat pancakes) *What does this tell you about Adika?* (Possible response: He is welcoming and generous.)

To check understanding, have students identify repeated behavior for Mama Panya. Ask: *What does Mama do each time Adika invites someone to dinner?* (She says nothing.) Ask: *What does this tell you about Mama?* (Possible response: She is considerate and doesn't want to hurt anyone's feelings.)

Encourage students to look for more examples of repeated behavior as they read the rest of the story. Discuss how the characters' actions and dialogue add to their understanding of the characters' traits.

Daily Language Arts

Daily Spelling and Word Work ☑
Practice page T207n

Daily Grammar ☑
Display the illustration on **Anthology** page 221 and say: *Mzee Odolo sits by the river.* Then use page T207p to teach about subject-verb agreement.

Daily Writing Skills ☑
Explain that the purpose of the **Anthology** story *Mama Panya's Pancakes* is to entertain. Then use page T207r to practice writing for different purposes.

Read and Build Comprehension

1 **Analyze Character's Feelings** *On page 223, what does Mama do when Adika invites more friends?* (She frowns.) *What does this detail tell you about how Mama feels?* (She is worried about having enough supplies to make pancakes for everyone.)

2 **Determine Theme** ☑ *What are the most important details about the setting and characters so far?* (Possible response: Adika's village is filled with kind friends and neighbors. Adika is generous. Mama is worried about having enough.) Remind students to keep gathering clues that will help them determine the theme at the end of the story.

Check & Reteach

OBJECTIVE: Determine Theme ☑

Listen for correct responses to questions about setting, character, and theme.
If students have difficulty, review how to identify the setting, characters, and important plot events. Say: *One detail is that Adika wears his finest shirt to the* ***market****. Do you think this detail will be important in figuring out the message of the story?*

OBJECTIVE: Determine Importance ☑

Listen for details in student responses that support their purposes for reading.
If students have difficulty, reread the last thing Mama says on **Anthology** page 223. Ask: *What is this part about?* (Mama is concerned that she will not have enough pancakes.) *What do you want to know more about?* (Possible response: I want to know how they will feed everyone with only two coins.) *As you read, look for more details about the topic.*

Mama **quickened her pace**.

"We had to invite Mzee," Adika said, "he's our oldest friend."

"Hurry up, you're a few steps behind," Mama **replied**.

"Look, Mama, it's Sawandi and Naiman." Adika's friends **tapped long reeds** against the thighs of their cattle, moving them along. "I'll be just a few steps ahead."

"Wait, Adika!" Mama called.

Mama hadn't gone too far before he returned.

"They'd be happy to come," Adika **panted**.

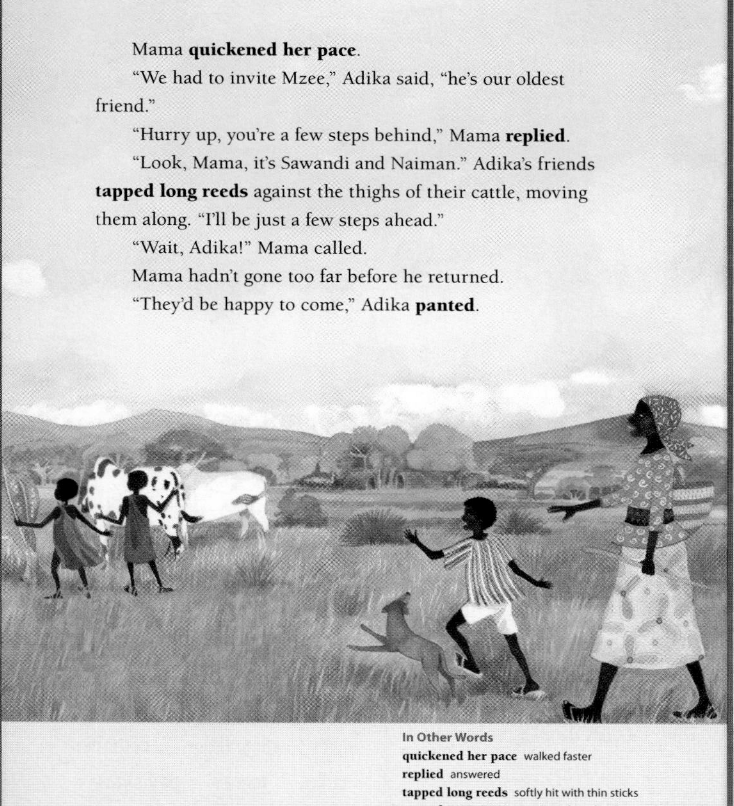

In Other Words
quickened her pace walked faster
replied answered
tapped long reeds softly hit with thin sticks
panted said while he was breathing hard

Mama Panya frowned, thinking about the coins in her wrap. **1**

"Ohhh! How many people will that be?"

"Let's see. Sawandi, Naiman, you and me," Adika counted. "And Mzee Odolo, that's only five."

"**Aiii!** How many pancakes do you think I can make today, son?"

"**I'm one step ahead of you**, Mama. You'll have a little bit and a little bit more. That's enough." **2**

In Other Words
Aiii! Oh no! (in Kiswahili)
I'm one step ahead of you I already thought of that

Before You Move On
1. **Make Inferences** How does Mama Panya feel about cooking for everyone? How can you tell?
2. **Point of View** Is the narrator a character in the story? How do you know?

Anthology
pages 222–223

Writing

4 Write About Characters

REVIEW Introduce: *Now you will write a paragraph that will describe a character from "Mama Panya's Pancakes" to a partner.* Model how to describe a minor character:

Think Aloud	Write
First, I describe a character's traits.	Mzee Odolo is friendly and thankful.
Then I give details that support my description.	Mzee Odolo accepts Adika's invitation and says "Thank you." He smiles and waves to Adika.

*For **Writing Routine 2**, see page BP48.*

Have each student write a paragraph about a major character in the story. Then have the partners share paragraphs before adding them to their Weekly Writing folders.

See **Differentiate**

WRAP-UP Have students relate story events so far to their own experience of inviting people to share a family meal.

Answers Before You Move On

1. **Make Inferences** I read that Mama Panya frowns when she thinks of the coins. I know it costs **money** to feed a lot of people. And so I think she's afraid she won't have enough food for everyone Adika has invited.
2. **Point of View** The narrator is not a story character and does not talk to the characters. The narrator uses the words *he, she,* and *they* and knows what the characters think and do.

Differentiate

EL English Learners

ISSUE Students lack the language proficiency to describe a character.

STRATEGY Provide a word bank that describes the story characters. Have students use it to complete a language frame: [character] is _____ and _____.

SN Special Needs

ISSUE Students have difficulty identifying the character's traits.

STRATEGY Have students review the sentences telling what the character says and does. Then have students read their sentences and choose a word that best describes the character.

Read and Comprehend

Realistic Fiction

OBJECTIVES

Thematic Connection: Community

- ☑ **Determine Theme**
- ☑ **Determine Importance**

PROGRAM RESOURCES

PRINT & TECHNOLOGY

Unit Concept Map: Practice Master PM4.1

TECHNOLOGY ONLY

Read with Me: Selection Recordings: MP3 or CD1 Tracks 20–21

My Vocabulary Notebook

Comprehension Coach

MATERIALS

timer

Power Writing

Have students write as much as they can as well as they can in one minute about the word *accomplish*.

*For **Writing Routine 1**, see page BP47.*

COMMON CORE STANDARDS

Reading	
Determine the Central Message	CC.3.Rlit.2
Describe Characters and Explain Characters' Actions	CC.3.Rlit.3
Distinguish Points of View	CC.3.Rlit.6
Read and Comprehend Literature	CC.3.Rlit.10
Read Orally with Accuracy and Appropriate Rate on Successive Readings	CC.3.Rfou.4.b
Writing	
Use Dialogue	CC.3.W.3.b
Write Over Shorter Time for Specific Tasks	CC.3.W.10
Speaking and listening	
Discuss Text, Building on Others' Ideas and Expressing Ideas Clearly	CC.3.SL.1
Language and Vocabulary	
Acquire and Use General Academic and Domain-Specific Words	CC.3.L.6

WARM-UP

Display the Key Words for the week. Set a timer for two minutes and have students use Key Words to write sentences about "Mama Panya's Pancakes."

Vocabulary Practice

1 Share Word Knowledge ☑

REVIEW Have students use the Three-Quarter Books from Day 3. Review the organizers.

Group each student with a partner who studied a different Key Word. Have partners follow **Vocabulary Routine 3**.

- Have partners take turns reading their organizers.
- Encourage partners to talk about how the pictures show the meanings of the Key Words.
- Have partners create sentences using both Key Words.
- Have each student add the sentences to **My Vocabulary Notebook**.

*For **Vocabulary Routine 3**, see page BP36.*

Key Words

accomplish · advertisement
buyer · cooperation · determine
market · money · paraphrase
pay · plenty · purpose
reward · seller · theme

Academic Talk

2 Summarize Reading

REVIEW Remind students: *When you summarize a story, it is important to describe the title, setting, characters, and events. These details may give clues about the **theme**, or main message, of the story.*

Explain that students will use Key Words as they summarize what they have read of "Mama Panya's Pancakes."

Write these Key Words: *accomplish, market, money, plenty, purpose*. Organize a **Fishbowl** to help students summarize.

- Have students on the inside summarize pages 218–220.
- Have students on the outside listen for Key Words and the most important details about plot, characters, and setting.
- Have groups change positions. The new inside group summarizes pages 221–223, building on the ideas presented by the first group.

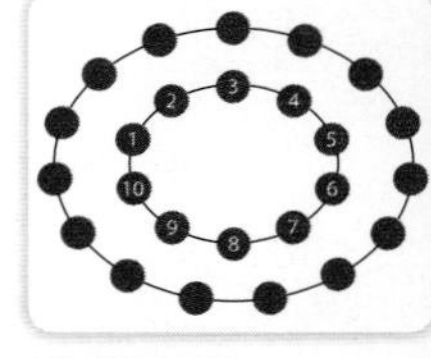

Fishbowl

*For **Fishbowl**, see page BP45.*

1 ▸ **Predict**
What will happen when Adika sees more friends at the **market**?

At the market, there were many **buyers** and **sellers**. Adika saw his friend Gamila at her **plantain** stand. "Mama, pancakes are her favorite."

"Now, now—don't you . . ." and before she could finish he ran to greet her.

Mama tried to catch up, arriving just in time to hear, "You will come, won't you?"

"Of course," Gamila replied.

EL Mama **shot a stare at Adika** and quickly grabbed his hand, **whisking** him away.

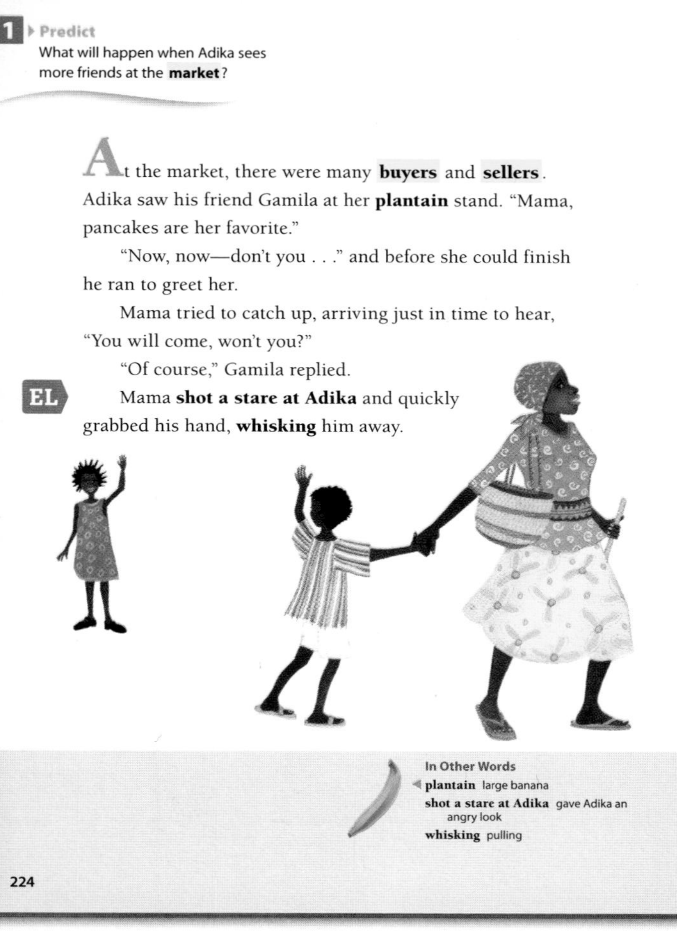

In Other Words
plantain large banana
shot a stare at Adika gave Adika an angry look
whisking pulling

224

"Mama, we'll be able to **stretch the flour**."

"**Ai Yi!** How much do you think I can stretch flour, son?"

Adika waved his hand. "Oh, a little bit and a little bit more."

At the **flour stand** Mama said, "Adika, you sit here."

After greeting Bibi and Bwana Zawenna, Mama asked, "What can you give me for my **money**?" She offered a coin to Bibi Zawenna, who **scooped some flour** onto a piece of paper. **2** AL

In Other Words
stretch the flour make many pancakes from a little flour
Ai Yi! Oh no! (in Kiswahili)
flour stand place to buy flour
scooped some flour took some flour out of a box and poured it

225

STUDENT TECHNOLOGY
Student eEdition
Read with Me
My Vocabulary Notebook
Comprehension Coach
NGReach.com

Anthology
pages 224–225

Reading

❸ Read and Build Comprehension

1 Predict Read aloud the predict question. Have students base their predictions on the pattern of Adika's behavior earlier in the story.

2 Analyze Characters *How would you describe Adika's personality?* (Possible responses: friendly, outgoing, cheerful, generous.) *What evidence from the text supports your answer?* (Possible responses: He talks to everyone. He invites everyone over for pancakes.)

Differentiate

EL English Learners

ISSUE Students have difficulty forming and expressing their predictions.

STRATEGY Name a story event, such as "Adika invites everyone he meets." Have students point to visuals that show Adika inviting his neighbors. Then provide sentence frames: I read that Adika _____. I predict that _____.

AL Above Level

ISSUE Students can analyze character's traits, but have difficulty supporting their conclusions.

STRATEGY Remind students to justify their descriptions by telling what the character does or says, what other characters say in response, or what the student knows from life experience about how the character acts.

Fluency

Practice Intonation, Accuracy, Rate As students read, monitor their intonation, accuracy, and rate.

Adika **popped up**. "Mama's making pancakes today. Can you come?"

"Oh, how wonderful! I think we can give a little more for that coin." Bwana Zawenna put more flour on the paper, then tied it up with string. "We'll see you later." **1**

Mama **tucked** the package into her bag. "**Ai-Yi-Yi!** You and I will be lucky to share half a pancake."

"But Mama, we have a little bit and a little bit more."

In Other Words
popped up jumped up to talk
tucked put
Ai-Yi-Yi! On no! (in Kiswahili)

226

Anthology page 226

Mini Lesson

Determine Viewpoint

Remind students that they have discussed story characters' ideas, thoughts, feelings, and responses. Explain: *A character's thoughts, ideas, and feelings make up the characters' viewpoint. They explain how the character looks at a situation or topic.*

Display **Student eEdition** page 226 and read what Adika says and does. Model identifying Adika's viewpoint: *I read that Adika "pops up" and tells a new person about the pancakes Adika is excited to greet and invite more friends. From Adika's viewpoint, the more people that come, the better.* Explain that the phrases in the text help readers understand Adika's viewpoint.

Then ask: *What does Mama think or feel about Adika inviting so many people?* (She is worried there won't be enough food to feed everyone.) *What words and phrases show that Mama is worried?* (Ai-Yi-Yi!; lucky to share half) Have students look for additional examples of words or phrases that show Mama's viewpoint on page 227. ("No, Adika!"; Mama just sighed.)

To check understanding, have students discuss the differences between Adika and Mama Panya's viewpoints. Then have students discuss their personal viewpoints about the situation. Ask: *How is your viewpoint different from or the same as the characters' viewpoint?*

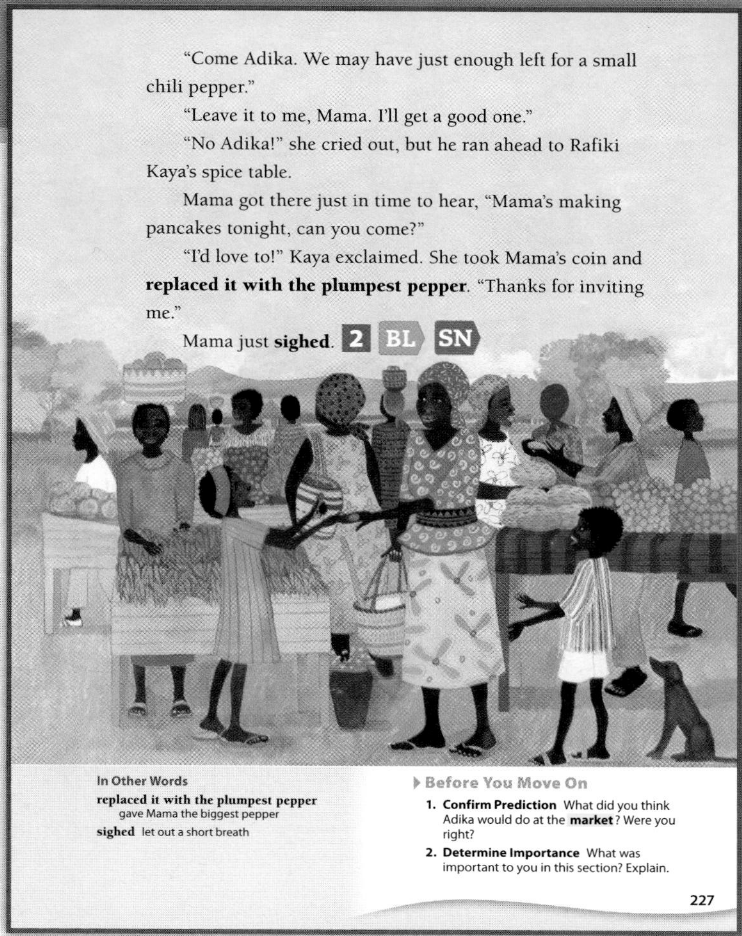

"Come Adika. We may have just enough left for a small chili pepper."
"Leave it to me, Mama. I'll get a good one."
"No Adika!" she cried out, but he ran ahead to Rafiki Kaya's spice table.
Mama got there just in time to hear, "Mama's making pancakes tonight, can you come?"
"I'd love to!" Kaya exclaimed. She took Mama's coin and replaced it with the plumpest pepper. "Thanks for inviting me."
Mama just sighed. 2 BL SN
In Other Words
replaced it with the plumpest pepper gave Mama the biggest pepper
sighed let out a short breath
Before You Move On
1. Confirm Prediction What did you think Adika would do at the market? Were you right?
2. Determine Importance What was important to you in this section? Explain.
227

Anthology page 227

Read and Build Comprehension

1. **Analyze Characters' Motives** *Why does Bwana Zawenna give Mama more flour for her coin?* (Bwana Zawenna wants to make sure there is **plenty** of flour for the extra pancakes.)
2. **Determine Theme** ☑ *What other clues about characters do you think will be important when figuring out the story's **theme**?* (Possible response: Adika welcomes everyone he sees. Bwana Zawenna and Rafiki Kaya give extra supplies to Mama. The **theme** might be about being generous.)

Differentiate

SN Special Needs

ISSUE Students lack focus necessary to analyze the characters' motives.

STRATEGY Tell students to focus on what a specific character says and does. Then ask: *If you saw someone do/say the same thing, what would that tell you about the person? Why would you do/say something like that?*

BL Below Level

ISSUE Students have difficulty distinguishing theme from plot.

STRATEGY Explain: *The plot of a story is events that only happen in this story. The **theme** of a story may be true for many situations and stories.* Display "Guardian Angel" on **Anthology** page 29. Provide the theme: *Showing kindness helps others.* Have students identify events that support the theme.

Answers Before You Move On

1. **Confirm Prediction** Possible response: My prediction was correct; Adika did invite more friends over for pancakes.
2. **Determine Importance** ☑ Possible response: I want to know how Mama Panya is going to have enough food to feed all those people. When I read that she gets extra flour, I learn that she has more than she thought she would have, but she still doesn't have enough.

1 ▸ Predict
SN Will Mama Panya have enough food to feed all the people?

They **headed** home.

"How many people did we invite for pancakes tonight?"

Adika, skipping two steps ahead, sang his reply, "All of our friends, Mama."

Mama piled small twigs and sticks into the firepit.

Adika ran to **fetch a pail** of water.

Mama crushed the chili pepper in a pot, while Adika added some water. She stirred in all the flour. Mama poured a **dollop** into the oiled pan on the fire. 2

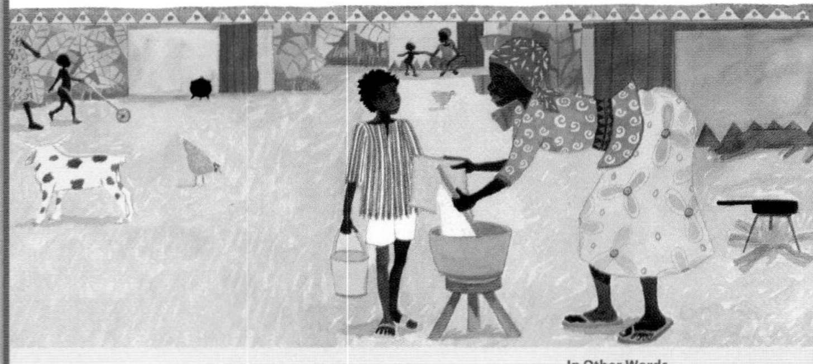

In Other Words
headed went
fetch a pail get a bucket
dollop small amount

228

Sawandi and Naiman were the first to arrive. They carried two **gourds** filled with milk and a small bucket of butter. "Mama Panya, we have extra from our cattle."

Mzee Odolo came soon after. "**Old-man river has given us three fish today.**"

Gamila arrived with a bunch of bananas. "They go very well with pancakes."

Bibi and Bwana Zawenna brought a package of flour and handed it to Adika. "**Store this away** for later." AL

◂ gourd

In Other Words
gourds containers
Old-man river has given us three fish today. I caught three fish in the river today.
Store this away Keep this

229

Anthology
pages 228–229

Read and Build Comprehension

1 **Predict** Read aloud the predict question. Have students base their predictions on what they have read and the illustrations they see.

2 **Analyze Narrator's Point of View** Remind students that when a third-person narrator tells a story, the narrator uses the words *he, she,* and *they* to describe the action. Ask: *Which sentences show that this story is told by a third-person narrator?* (Possible responses: They headed home. She stirred in all the flour.)

Differentiate

SN Special Needs

ISSUE Students lack the conceptual structure to make predictions.

STRATEGY Display a web with three circles labeled as follows: I Read, I Know, I Predict. Guide students to fill in the web with the information from the story to help them make a prediction.

AL Above Level

ISSUE Students read too quickly and fail to stop and confirm predictions.

STRATEGY Prompt students to stop after reading a set number of pages to check their predictions. If their predictions are confirmed, encourage them to make a new prediction. If it is not confirmed, have them either revise their predictions or continue reading.

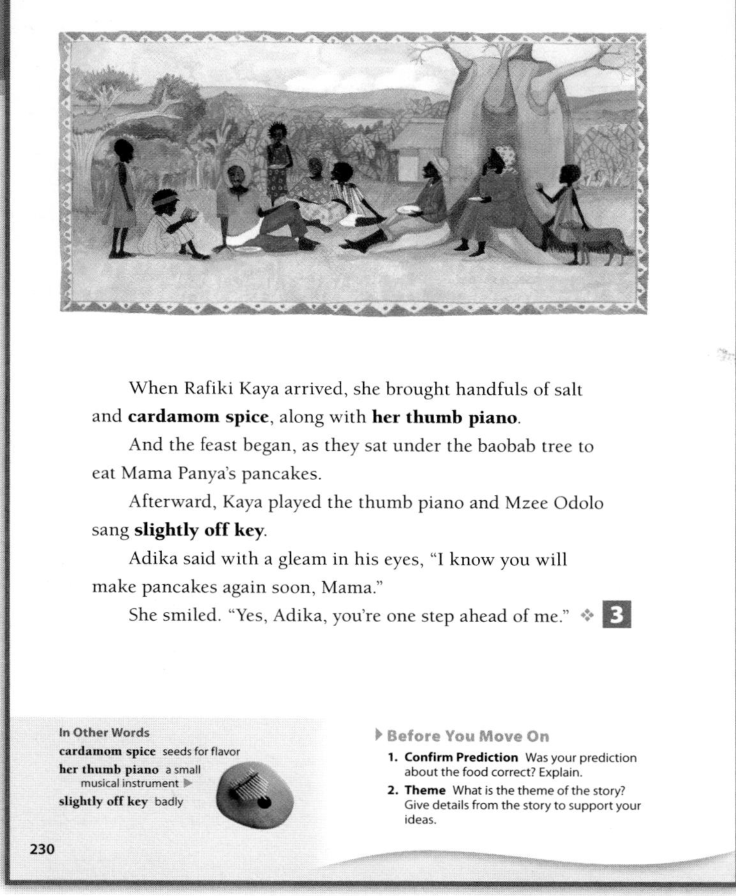

When Rafiki Kaya arrived, she brought handfuls of salt and **cardamom spice**, along with **her thumb piano**.

And the feast began, as they sat under the baobab tree to eat Mama Panya's pancakes.

Afterward, Kaya played the thumb piano and Mzee Odolo sang **slightly off key**.

Adika said with a gleam in his eyes, "I know you will make pancakes again soon, Mama."

She smiled. "Yes, Adika, you're one step ahead of me." ❖ **3**

In Other Words
cardamom spice seeds for flavor
her thumb piano a small musical instrument ▶
slightly off key badly

Before You Move On

1. **Confirm Prediction** Was your prediction about the food correct? Explain.
2. **Theme** What is the theme of the story? Give details from the story to support your ideas.

230

Anthology page 230

3 **Determine Importance** ☑ Ask: *What is important to you in this part? Explain what you learned.* (Possible response: This part is about the gathering for pancakes. I want to know more about feeding everyone. When I read "And the feast began," I know there was **plenty** of food for everyone.) *How did **determining** importance help you understand the story better?*

Check & Reteach

OBJECTIVE: Determine Theme ☑

Check for accurate responses to the comprehension questions about theme.

If students have difficulty, remind them that they can find clues about the theme based on important ideas in the title, setting, characters, and plot. If they still have difficulty, ask: *What message does the story teach about **cooperation**?*

OBJECTIVE: Determine Importance ☑

As students respond to questions about determining importance, make sure that they use the strategy correctly.

If students have difficulty, display **Student eEdition** page 230 and ask:

- *What is this part about?* (Adika is excited about having pancakes again.)
- *What do you want to know more about?* (Possible response: How does Mama feel about having pancakes again?)
- *What do you learn from reading Mama's response?* (She's not worried anymore.)

Answers Before You Move On

1. **Confirm Prediction** Possible response: My prediction was partially right. There was **plenty** of food for everyone. However, it wasn't because of Mama making smaller pancakes.
2. **Theme** ☑ Possible response: When everyone gives a little, everyone gets a lot. Mama makes pancakes. Sawandi and Naiman bring milk and butter. Mzee Odolo brings fish. Bibi and Bwana Zawenna bring extra flour. Rafiki Kaya brings salt and spices. All together, they had a feast.

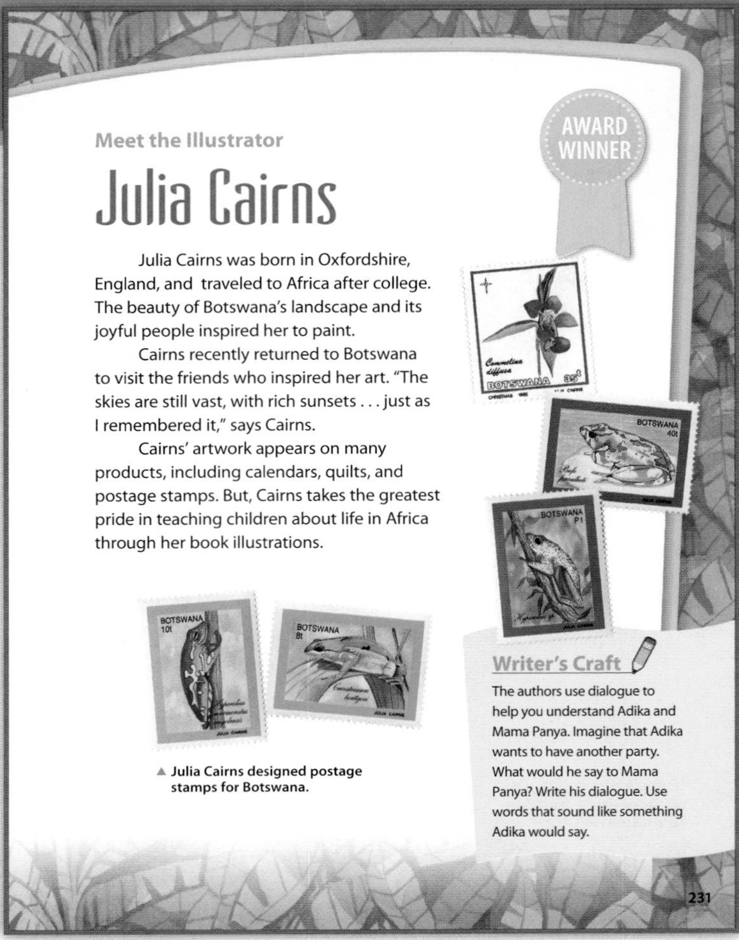

Meet the Illustrator
Julia Cairns
AWARD WINNER
Julia Cairns was born in Oxfordshire, England, and traveled to Africa after college. The beauty of Botswana's landscape and its joyful people inspired her to paint.
Cairns recently returned to Botswana to visit the friends who inspired her art. "The skies are still vast, with rich sunsets . . . just as I remembered it," says Cairns.
Cairns' artwork appears on many products, including calendars, quilts, and postage stamps. But, Cairns takes the greatest pride in teaching children about life in Africa through her book illustrations.
▲ Julia Cairns designed postage stamps for Botswana.
Writer's Craft
The authors use dialogue to help you understand Adika and Mama Panya. Imagine that Adika wants to have another party. What would he say to Mama Panya? Write his dialogue. Use words that sound like something Adika would say.
231

Anthology page 231

Best Practices

Encourage Elaboration As students answer questions, use general prompts:

- *What do you mean by that?*
- *Can you give some details to explain what you mean?*
- *Can you make a connection to what someone else said?*

4 Meet the Illustrator **Anthology** page 231

Have partners read the biography together. Ask: *How do the story illustrations help you learn about life in Africa?* (The pictures show how the people and the land of a Kenyan village look.)

After students read the biography, build comprehension:

- **Synthesize** *How do the illustrator's experiences in Africa help her illustrate the story better?* (Possible response: I read that the beauty of Botswana inspired Cairns to paint. I also read that the joyful people of Botswana inspired her as well. I connect the ideas and conclude that her positive experiences in Africa are shown in the illustrations of this story.)
- **Paraphrase Text** *Reread the last sentence of the biography. Use your own words to describe what pleases Cairns most about her work.* (Possible response: Cairns is proud to use her art to teach children about Africa.)
- **Make Inferences** *Why do you think Julia Cairns likes to teach children about life in Africa? Support your answers with information from the text and your own knowledge.* (Possible response: I read that she was inspired by the beauty of Africa and its people. I know I like to share things that inspire or excite me. And so, she must like to share her knowledge of Africa with children, who probably know little about it.)
- **Ask Questions** *After reading about her life, what questions could you ask Julia Cairns about how she illustrated the story?* (Possible responses: How long did the illustrations take? What materials did you use?)

Writing

5 Writer's Craft **Anthology** page 231

REVIEW Read aloud the instructions for the Writer's Craft feature on page 231 Remind students: *Dialogue is the words characters say. You can use dialogue to help readers understand what characters are like.* Have students identify dialogue from the story. Point out how it is set apart with quotation marks.

Explain: *Like the author of "Mama Panya's Pancakes," you can use dialogue to help your readers understand characters. Start by thinking about what your character could say to show what he or she is like.*

Model writing a brief dialogue that brings a character to life.

Think Aloud	Write
Eva is a confident and energetic fourth grader.	"That necklace is made for me!" Eva shouted. "I'll win the magazine-selling contest. Then I'll have a lot of money and can buy plenty of jewelry!"

*For **Writing Routine 2**, see page BP48.*

Have partners review words and phrases that Adika says in the story. Then have them work independently to write Adika's dialogue to Mama Panya about having another party. Remind them to use punctuation correctly. Have students add their brief dialogue to their Weekly Writing folders.

See **Differentiate**

WRAP-UP Remind students that Mama in "Mama Panya's Pancakes" is surprised to find that everyone has plenty to eat. Ask: *In your reading today, were you surprised by anything about **cooperation**? How did the author help you understand how working together can help **accomplish** something?* Have students add ideas to their unit concept maps.

Daily Language Arts

Daily Spelling and Word Work ☑
Practice page T207n

Daily Grammar ☑
Display **Anthology** page 229 and read aloud the last sentence of the first paragraph: *Mama Panya, we have extra from our cattle.* Then use page T207p to practice present-tense verbs and subject-verb agreement.

Daily Writing Skills ☑
Ask: *What do you think is the **purpose** of the biography on **Anthology** page 231?* (to inform) Use page T207r to have students practice writing for different purposes.

Differentiate

SN Special Needs

ISSUE Students have difficulty translating imagined dialogue into written form.

STRATEGY Have students make audio recordings of their dialogue. As they listen to their recordings, have them stop to write the words of the dialogue. Then have students go back and add appropriate punctuation and transitional language, as needed.

BL Below Level

ISSUE Dialogue is flat or still and does not reflect the character's personality.

STRATEGY Guide students to find examples of statements, questions, and exclamations that Adika makes in the story. Then have students review the sentences they wrote and think of ways to make the dialogue more lively and realistic. Have them add the examples to their dialogue so it sounds more like the character.

Review and Apply

OBJECTIVES

Thematic Connection: Community

☑ Determine Theme

☑ Read with Fluency

PROGRAM RESOURCES

PRINT & TECHNOLOGY

Unit Concept Map: Practice Master PM4.1

Test-Taking Strategy Practice: Practice Master PM4.5

Theme Chart: Practice Master PM4.6

Fluency Practice: Practice Master PM4.7

TECHNOLOGY ONLY

Online Vocabulary Games

Comprehension Coach

Read with Me: Fluency Models: MP3 or CD 1 Track 3

MATERIALS

timer

Power Writing

Have students write as much as they can as well as they can in one minute about the word *cooperation*.

*For **Writing Routine 1**, see page BP47.*

COMMON CORE STANDARDS

Reading	
Determine the Central Message	CC.3.Rlit.2
Explain Characters' Actions	CC.3.Rlit.3
Refer to Parts of Stories	CC.3.Rlit.5
Read and Comprehend Literature	CC.3.Rlit.10
Read Orally with Accuracy and Appropriate Rate on Successive Readings	CC.3.Rfou.4.b
Writing	
Write Over Shorter Time for Specific Purposes	CC.3.W.10
Speaking and Listening	
Discuss Topics, Expressing Ideas Clearly	CC.3.SL.1
Draw on Information to Explore Ideas	CC.3.SL.1.a
Language and Vocabulary	
Determine Meaning of Words and Phrases	CC.3.L.4
Acquire and Use General Academic and Domain-Specific Words	CC.3.L.6

WARM-UP

Remind students that "Mama Panya's Pancakes" is realistic fiction. Ask: *How is the setting like a place in real life?* (Possible response: The setting is similar to a real African village.) Then have partners discuss what other elements in the story are like real life, and what parts of the story are not.

Vocabulary Review

1 Apply Word Knowledge ☑

Write: ***determine***, ***paraphrase***, ***theme***. Point out the other Key Words on **Student eEdition** page 232. Then have students apply their knowledge of the Key Words to play a game called Picture It. Explain:

- *Each group will choose one Key Word and quietly discuss how to draw a picture that represents what the word means.*
- *When I call on a group, one group member will have 30 seconds to draw the picture. The other groups will discuss the picture quietly and write the group answer.*
- *Each team that guesses correctly gets a point.*
- *Another group takes a turn.*
- *After each team has drawn three pictures, show me your team's answers. The team with the most correct answers wins.*

Have students play the game.

*For **More Vocabulary Routines**, see pages BP41–BP43.*

Key Words

accomplish · advertisement · buyer
cooperation · determine · market
money · paraphrase · pay
plenty · purpose · reward
seller · theme

For additional practice, have students play the **Online Vocabulary Games** in pairs or individually.

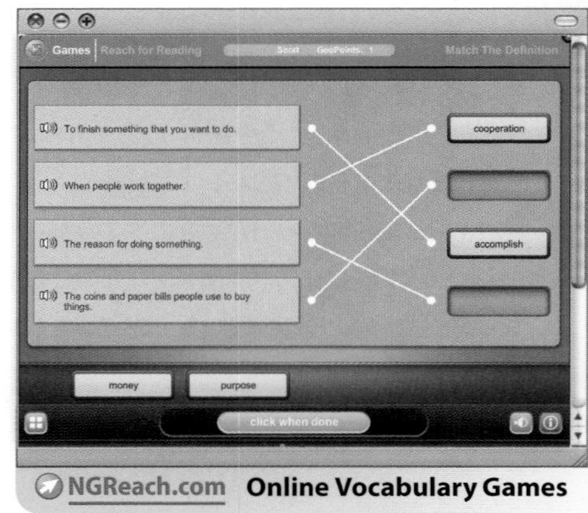

NGReach.com **Online Vocabulary Games**

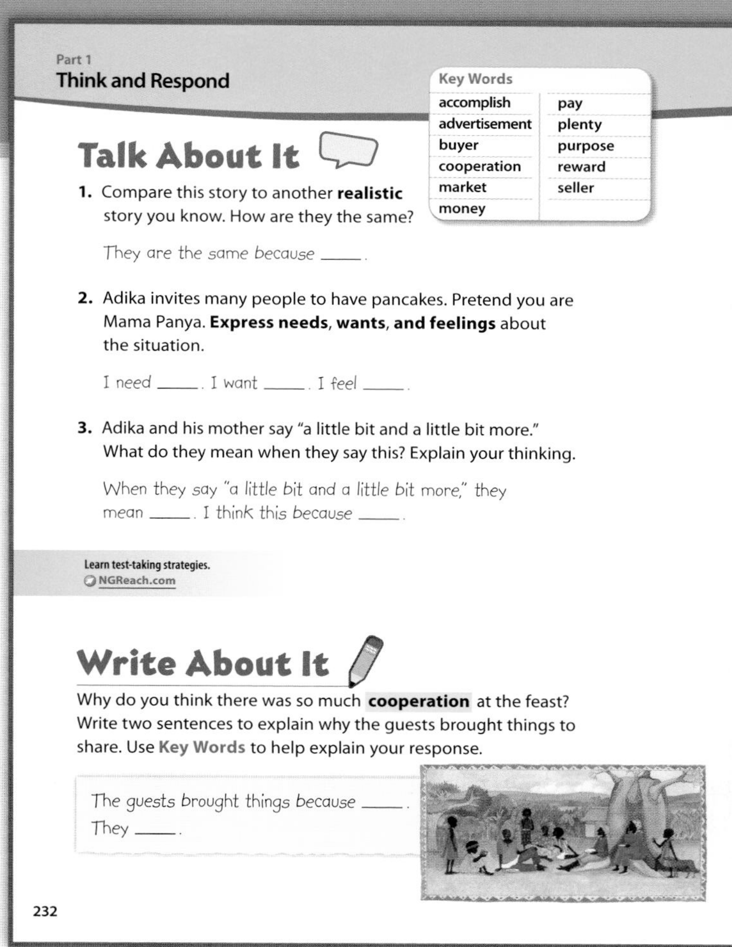
Part 1
Think and Respond

Key Words	
accomplish	pay
advertisement	plenty
buyer	purpose
cooperation	reward
market	seller
money	

Talk About It

1. Compare this story to another **realistic** story you know. How are they the same?

   They are the same because ____.

2. Adika invites many people to have pancakes. Pretend you are Mama Panya. **Express needs, wants, and feelings** about the situation.

   I need ____. I want ____. I feel ____.

3. Adika and his mother say "a little bit and a little bit more." What do they mean when they say this? Explain your thinking.

   When they say "a little bit and a little bit more," they mean ____. I think this because ____.

Learn test-taking strategies.
NGReach.com

Write About It

Why do you think there was so much **cooperation** at the feast? Write two sentences to explain why the guests brought things to share. Use **Key Words** to help explain your response.

The guests brought things because ____.
They ____.

232

Anthology page 232

Academic Talk

2 Talk About It **Anthology** page 232

Have partners use the Key Words as they discuss the **Talk About It** questions on **Student eEdition** page 232. Remind students to use clear language when they express needs, wants, and feelings. They should draw on information they know in order to explore ideas.

Then use the test-taking strategy lesson from **NGReach.com** and **Practice Master PM4.5** to ask more questions about the selection.

Writing

3 Write About It **Anthology** page 232

Read aloud the directions on page 232 and remind students that they can use the sentence frames to begin their writing.

Model using Key Words as you write sentences:

- *The guests brought things because they knew Mama Panya didn't have lots of* ***money*** *to* ***pay*** *for a big feast.*
- *They used* ***cooperation*** *to make sure everyone brought just a little and everyone would have* ***plenty*** *to eat.*

Have students add their sentences to their Weekly Writing folders.

Daily Language Arts

Daily Spelling and Word Work ☑

Test page T207m

Daily Grammar ☑

Write *She pays for the flour* and explain that *pays* is a verb that agrees with the subject *she*. Then use page T207p to review subject-verb agreement.

Daily Writing Skills ☑

Explain that the purpose of *Mama Panya's Pancakes* is to entertain and the purpose of *Meet the Illustrator Julia Cairns* is to inform. Then use page T207r to review purpose.

Answers Talk About It

1. **Realistic Fiction** They are the same because the events could happen in the real world.
2. **Express Needs, Wants, Feelings** Possible response: I need more food from the **market**. I want everyone to have **plenty** to eat. I feel nervous that I won't have enough food.
3. **Clarify Meaning** Possible response: They mean they only have a little bit of **money** to **pay** for basics, but somehow, what they have will be enough. I think this because they managed to have a big feast with only a little **money** because of everyone's **cooperation**.

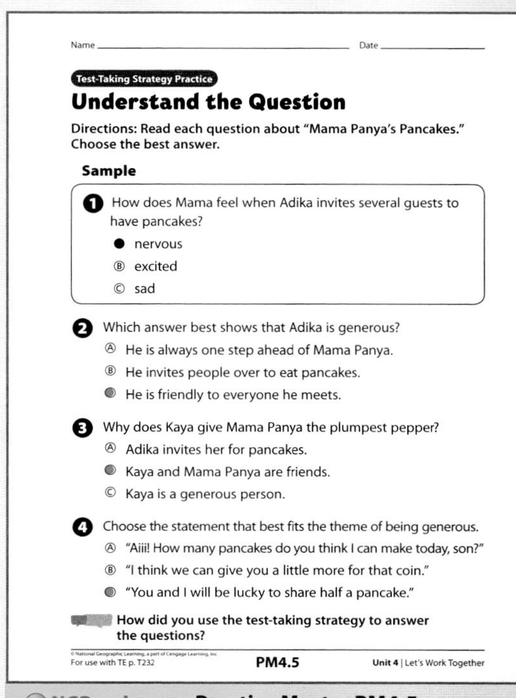
Name ____ Date ____

Test-Taking Strategy Practice

Understand the Question

Directions: Read each question about "Mama Panya's Pancakes." Choose the best answer.

Sample

1. How does Mama feel when Adika invites several guests to have pancakes?
   - ● nervous
   - Ⓑ excited
   - Ⓒ sad

2. Which answer best shows that Adika is generous?
   - Ⓐ He is always one step ahead of Mama Panya.
   - Ⓑ He invites people over to eat pancakes.
   - ● He is friendly to everyone he meets.

3. Why does Kaya give Mama Panya the plumpest pepper?
   - Ⓐ Adika invites her for pancakes.
   - ● Kaya and Mama Panya are friends.
   - Ⓒ Kaya is a generous person.

4. Choose the statement that best fits the theme of being generous.
   - Ⓐ "Aiii! How many pancakes do you think I can make today, son?"
   - Ⓑ "I think we can give you a little more for that coin."
   - ● "You and I will be lucky to share half a pancake."

How did you use the test-taking strategy to answer the questions?

For use with TE p. T232 — PM4.5 — Unit 4 | Let's Work Together

NGReach.com **Practice Master PM4.5**

Differentiate

SN Special Needs

ISSUE Students have difficulty identifying details to add to their theme charts.

STRATEGY Have partners point to details in the story text and read them aloud. Then have them work together to categorize details into the chart according to where they found the clues.

BL Below Level

ISSUE Students have difficulty placing information in the correct location on the theme chart.

STRATEGY Have students draw a simple picture or write a phrase at the top of each clue section to help remind them what goes in each part. For example, a speech balloon or the phrase "what people say and do" could go at the top of the "Clues from the Characters" section of the theme chart.

AL Above Level

ISSUE Students find too many details regarding characters and events to fit into the theme chart.

STRATEGY Have students review the clues they have listed. Then ask students to delete unimportant details and combine clues that could go together.

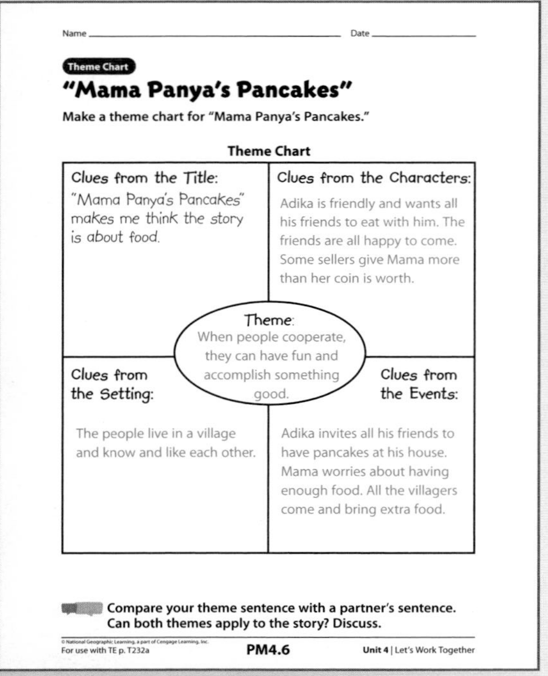
Name ________ Date ________

Theme Chart

"Mama Panya's Pancakes"

Make a theme chart for "Mama Panya's Pancakes."

Theme Chart

Clues from the Title: "Mama Panya's Pancakes" makes me think the story is about food.

Clues from the Characters: Adika is friendly and wants all his friends to eat with him. The friends are all happy to come. Some sellers give Mama more than her coin is worth.

Theme: When people cooperate, they can have fun and accomplish something good.

Clues from the Setting: The people live in a village and know and like each other.

Clues from the Events: Adika invites all his friends to have pancakes at his house. Mama worries about having enough food. All the villagers come and bring extra food.

Compare your theme sentence with a partner's sentence. Can both themes apply to the story? Discuss.

For use with TE p. T232a PM4.6 Unit 4 | Let's Work Together

NGReach.com **Practice Master PM4.6**

Comprehension

4 Theme ☑ Anthology page 233

REVIEW Display **Student eEdition** page 233. Read aloud the instructions and review theme: *The **theme** is the story's main message.*

Point out the sample theme chart and remind students: *The title, setting, events, and the characters' words and actions can give clues to the **theme**.* Read aloud the entry about the title in the theme chart. Then have students look for other clues from the characters to identify the theme of "Mama Panya's Pancakes." Demonstrate how to add them to the chart.

Have partners work together to complete **Practice Master PM4.6**. Circulate and use the questions below to help students find details in the story. Guide them to record the clues and then identify the theme in the chart.

See **Differentiate**

Clues	Guiding Question
Clues from the Title	• *Who is in this story?* • *What is the story about?*
Clues from the Characters	• *How does Adika act towards others?* • *How do his friends respond to him?* • *What do the **sellers** do to help?*
Clues from the Setting	• *Where do the characters live?* • *Do they know each other well?*
Clues from the Events	• *What do Adika and his Mama do?* • *What do the villagers bring?* • *In the end, what happens to the pancakes?*

Check & Reteach

OBJECTIVE: Determine Theme ☑

Ask students to identify the clues that helped them identify the story's theme.
If students have difficulty, review the story elements and discuss how they relate to the unit theme of working together. Ask: *How do the characters show **cooperation**? What happens when the characters cooperate? What main message is the author trying to tell in the story?*

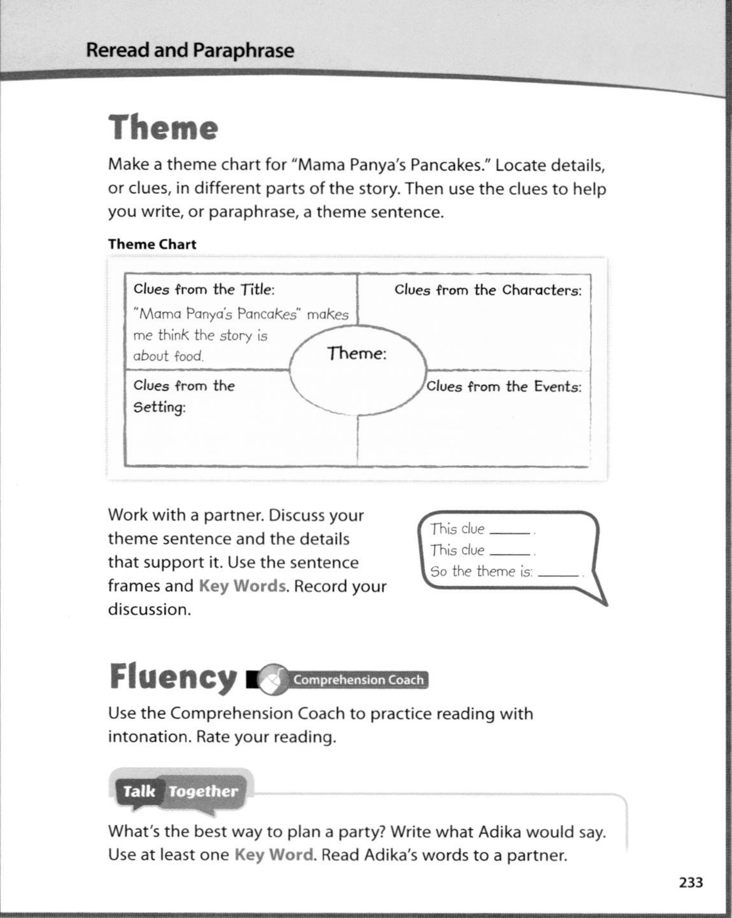

Reread and Paraphrase

Theme

Make a theme chart for "Mama Panya's Pancakes." Locate details, or clues, in different parts of the story. Then use the clues to help you write, or paraphrase, a theme sentence.

Theme Chart

Work with a partner. Discuss your theme sentence and the details that support it. Use the sentence frames and **Key Words**. Record your discussion.

This clue ____.
This clue ____.
So the theme is: ____.

Fluency Comprehension Coach

Use the Comprehension Coach to practice reading with intonation. Rate your reading.

Talk Together

What's the best way to plan a party? Write what Adika would say. Use at least one **Key Word**. Read Adika's words to a partner.

233

Anthology page 233

5 Fluency **Anthology** page 233

Have students read aloud the passage on **Practice Master PM4.7** or use the **Comprehension Coach** to practice fluency.

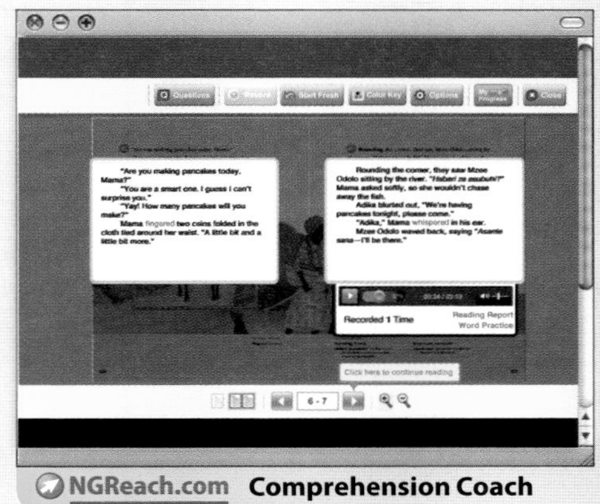

NGReach.com **Comprehension Coach**

Check & Reteach

OBJECTIVE: Read with Fluency

Monitor students' oral reading.

If students need additional fluency practice, have them read along with the **Fluency Models**.

6 Talk Together **Anthology** page 233

Have partners discuss what Adika would say about planning a party. Point out the Key Words on **Anthology** page 232 and remind students to refer to them.

WRAP-UP Ask students to share examples of cooperation they have read about this week and then add ideas to their unit concept maps.

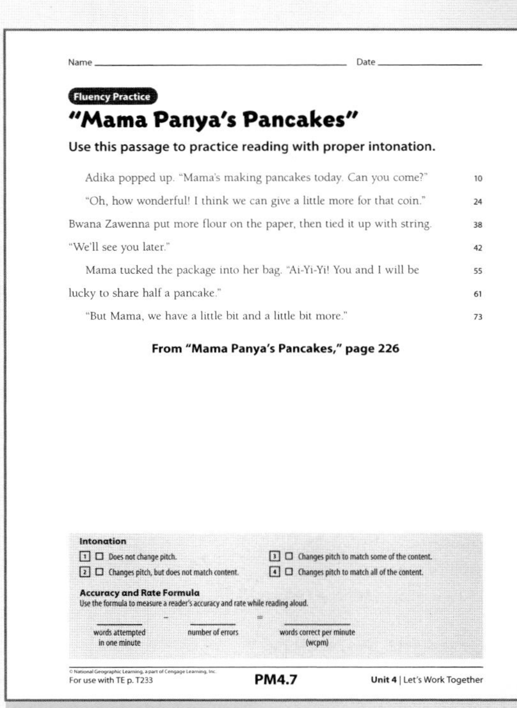

Name ____________ Date ____________

Fluency Practice

"Mama Panya's Pancakes"

Use this passage to practice reading with proper intonation.

Adika popped up. "Mama's making pancakes today. Can you come?" 10
"Oh, how wonderful! I think we can give a little more for that coin." 24
Bwana Zawenna put more flour on the paper, then tied it up with string. 38
"We'll see you later." 42
Mama tucked the package into her bag. "Ai-Yi-Yi! You and I will be 55
lucky to share half a pancake." 61
"But Mama, we have a little bit and a little bit more." 73

From "Mama Panya's Pancakes," page 226

Intonation

1 ☐ Does not change pitch.
2 ☐ Changes pitch, but does not match content.
3 ☐ Changes pitch to match some of the content.
4 ☐ Changes pitch to match all of the content.

Accuracy and Rate Formula

Use the formula to measure a reader's accuracy and rate while reading aloud.

______ words attempted in one minute − ______ number of errors = ______ words correct per minute (wcpm)

For use with TE p. T233 **PM4.7** **Unit 4** | Let's Work Together

NGReach.com **Practice Master PM4.7**

OBJECTIVES

Thematic Connection: Community

☑ **Write an Opinion Paragraph: Fluency**

PROGRAM RESOURCES

PRINT & TECHNOLOGY

Writing Rubric: Assessment Master A4.39

TECHNOLOGY ONLY

Sample Opinion Paragraph: eVisual 4.5

Writing Trait: Fluency: eVisual 4.6

Magazine Maker

SUGGESTED PACING

DAY 1	Study a Model
DAY 2	Prewrite
DAY 3	Draft
DAY 4	Revise/Edit and Proofread
DAY 5	Publish and Present

COMMON CORE STANDARDS

Writing	
Write Opinions on Topics	CC.3.W.1
Provide Reasons	CC.3.W.1.b
Plan, Revise, and Edit Writing	CC.3.W.5
Write Over Extended Time Frames	CC.3.W.10
Language and Vocabulary	
Demonstrate Command of Grammar	CC.3.L.1
Form and Use Verbs	CC.3.L.1.d
Use Knowledge of Conventions	CC.3.L.3

Write an Opinion Paragraph

Display and read aloud the prompt.

> Write an opinion paragraph about whether you think it is easier to work with others or to work on your own. Be sure to explain why. The paragraph is to be published in a student newsletter. Your goal is to make the readers agree with you.

Study a Model

Read an Opinion Paragraph

Explain: *Let's read one student's opinion paragraph.* Display and read aloud **eVisual 4.5**.

Sample Opinion Paragraph

Let's Work Together!

In my opinion, it's easier to work with others than to work on your own. First, you get more done if you work with others. For example, one of my brother's chores is taking care of the yard. He finishes faster if we work as a team to mow, weed, trim, and rake. Second, if you work with others, they can give you advice on how to do something. Last week, the chain fell off my bicycle. I asked my friend, Ryan, for help. He told me how to fix it and worked with me to get it done. Finally, working with others can be a lot of fun. I often help my dad clean out the garage, and we make the work feel playful. So go ahead—try working with others, and see how great it is!

NGReach.com **Opinion Paragraph: eVisual 4.5**

INTERACTIVE WHITEBOARD TIP: Underline the opinion and the evidence that supports the opinion.

Teach the Trait: Fluency

Introduce the concept: *When you write with fluency, your sentences flow together smoothly. To achieve this, vary sentence lengths and types of sentences. In addition, be sure to include words that link ideas, such as the transition words* first, then, *and* finally.

Display and read aloud **eVisual 4.6**.

Writing Trait: Fluency

Writing that is fluent
- has sentences that vary in length and type
- includes transition words to link ideas together

NGReach.com **Writing Trait: Fluency: eVisual 4.6**

INTERACTIVE WHITEBOARD TIP: Check each point as you explain it.

Display and read aloud: *My brother mows the lawn. I trim the bushes. We take a break.* Ask: *What do these sentences have in common?* (They are short.) *How could we improve them?* (Vary the length by combining them.)

Prewrite

Choose a Topic

Reread the first sentence of the prompt. Ask: *What is your role?* (writer for a newsletter) Continue with the remainder of the prompt in order to determine the Role, Audience, and Form for the RAFT.

Role: Writer for a newsletter
Audience: Other students
Form: Opinion paragraph

Have students work in pairs. One partner brainstorms reasons for working alone, while the other partner brainstorms reasons for working together. Then have them discuss the reasons and add them to two separate lists. Have each student choose one of the positions and individually complete the RAFT.

Get Organized

Review the sample: *In "Let's Work Together!" the writer states an opinion in the first sentence. This is the main idea. The writer then uses evidence to support the opinion. These are the details.* Display a main idea and details diagram and say: *A main idea and details diagram helps you see if you have enough evidence to support your opinion.* Model using the events from "Let's Work Together!" to complete the diagram.

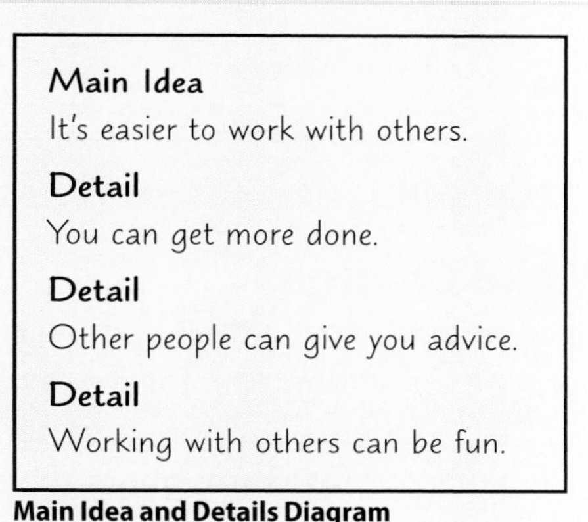

Main Idea
It's easier to work with others.
Detail
You can get more done.
Detail
Other people can give you advice.
Detail
Working with others can be fun.

Main Idea and Details Diagram

Have students use a main idea diagram to plan their opinion paragraphs. Tell them that all the details, or evidence, need to support the main idea, or opinion.

Draft

Write Ideas

Allow students adequate class time to plan, organize, and write their drafts. When they have finished writing their opinion paragraphs, instruct students to experiment with page layouts for their paragraph using **Magazine Maker**. Remind students to focus on fluency as they write their opinion paragraphs.

See **Differentiate**

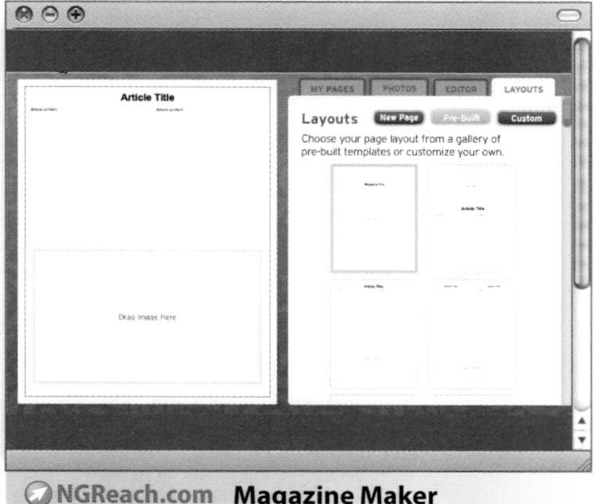

NGReach.com **Magazine Maker**

Differentiate

EL English Learner

ISSUE Students have difficulty generating sentences for their opinion paragraphs.

STRATEGY Provide students with the following sentence frames:

- I think it's better to work with other people because ______. Another person can help ______ and ______.
- I think it's easier to work alone because ______. Someone working alone can ______.

Daily Language Arts

Daily Spelling and Word Work
Practice Pages T207m–T207n

Daily Grammar
Point out examples of subject-verb agreement in the student sample on page T233d. Then use pages T207o–T207p to have students practice using present-tense action verbs and subject-verb agreement.

Daily Writing Skills
Ask: *What purpose have you established for writing? What are other possible author's purposes?* Use pages T207q–T207r to have students practice establishing and following a purpose for writing.

Best Practices

Encourage Collaboration When students work with their peers during the revision process, they are able to practice the type of thoughtful reflection that helps them learn to assess their own work carefully.

Differentiate

Below Level

ISSUE Students have difficulty writing persuasive texts.

STRATEGY Have students read their opinion paragraphs to a partner. For each sentence, have partners ask: *Does this sentence make me want to work alone/together?* Have partners discuss how they might strengthen the sentences to better persuade someone that this way of working is better.

Revise

Read, Retell, Respond

Have students read their drafts to partners. Have listeners retell the opinion paragraphs in their own words and offer ideas to improve fluency. Use language frames to guide the discussion.

Language Frames

Retell	Make Suggestions
• Your opinion is ______. • You believe this because ______.	• Several of your sentences ______. Can you change them to add variety? • The sentence about ______ doesn't really fit your purpose for writing. You could delete it. • These sentences don't flow together well. Can you add a transition word?

Make Changes

Have students revise their opinion paragraphs. Remind them that writers have a purpose for writing: to inform or explain, to entertain, to persuade, or to express. In this case, students' purpose is to persuade. Tell students that they must establish and follow this purpose throughout the entire paragraph.

Tell students that the title should make readers want to read the paragraph. Once students have a strong title, have them experiment with different type fonts and colors in **Magazine Maker** to make their titles stand out.

See **Differentiate**

Student Sample: Revise

Sample Analysis

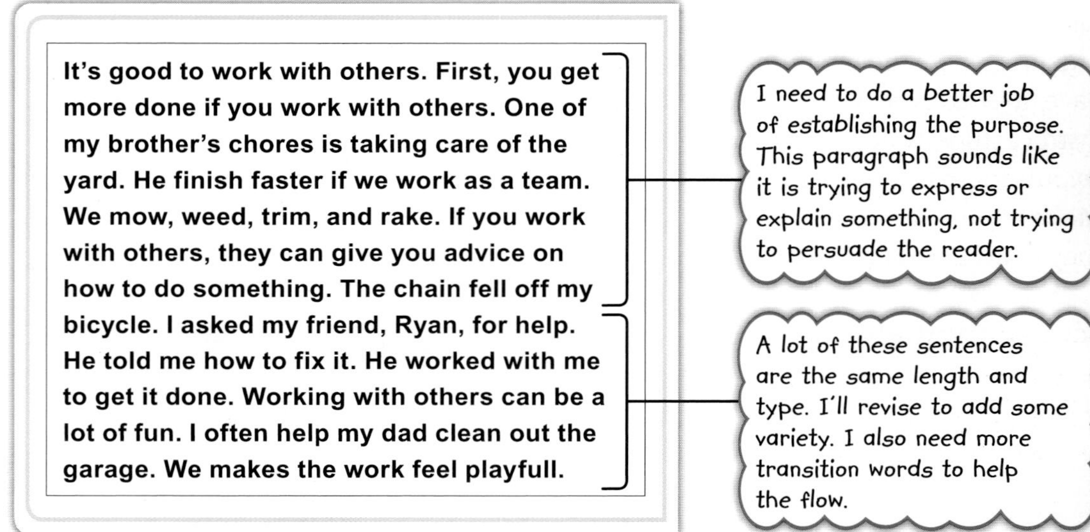

It's good to work with others. First, you get more done if you work with others. One of my brother's chores is taking care of the yard. He finish faster if we work as a team. We mow, weed, trim, and rake. If you work with others, they can give you advice on how to do something. The chain fell off my bicycle. I asked my friend, Ryan, for help. He told me how to fix it. He worked with me to get it done. Working with others can be a lot of fun. I often help my dad clean out the garage. We makes the work feel playfull.
I need to do a better job of establishing the purpose. This paragraph sounds like it is trying to express or explain something, not trying to persuade the reader.
A lot of these sentences are the same length and type. I'll revise to add some variety. I also need more transition words to help the flow.

Edit and Proofread

Check the Opinion Paragraph

Have students check their grammar and spelling, focusing on the Week 1 spelling words and using proper subject-verb agreement.

Student Sample: Edit and Proofread

In my opinion, it's easier to work with others than to work on your own. First, you get more done if you work with others. For example, one of my brother's chores is taking care of the lawn. He finish faster if we work together to mow, weed, trim, and rake. Second, if you work with others, they can give you advice on how to do something. Last week, the chain fell off my bicycle. I asked my friend, Ryan, for help. He told me how to fix it and worked with me to get it done. Finally, working with others can be a lot of fun. I often help my dad clean out the garage, and we makes the work feel playfull. So go ahead—try working with others, and see how great it is!

Sample Analysis

Some of the subjects don't agree with the verbs. I need to go through the paragraph and fix the subject-verb agreement.

I misspelled *playful*. I'll correct that.

Best Practices

Review Each Pass Use **eVisual 4.6** to review students' opinion paragraphs after each step in the writing process.

Publish and Present

Make a Final Copy

Students may want to use only one photo. Show how to delete a photo box in **Magazine Maker**: *Click on the box and press the Remove key.*

Share with Others

Form two groups: students who think it's easier to work with others, and those who think it's easier to work alone. Have students take turns reading aloud their opinion paragraphs. Remind students to speak clearly and at an understandable pace. Have the class vote on which group is more persuasive.

Have students make copies of their work and add it to the Weekly Writing folders. Use the **Writing Rubric** to assess each student's paragraph.

Student Sample: Publish

Let's Work Together!

In my opinion, it's easier to work with others than to work on your own. First, you get more done if you work with others. For example, one of my brother's chores is taking care of the yard. He finishes faster if we work as a team to mow, weed, trim, and rake. Second, if you work with others, they can give you advice on how to do something. Last week, the chain fell off my bicycle. I asked my friend, Ryan, for help. He told me how to fix it and worked with me to get it done. Finally, working with others can be a lot of fun. I often help my dad clean out the garage, and we make the work feel playful. So go ahead--try working with others, and see how great it is!

© Bruce Dale/NGS

Writing Rubric

A4.39

NGReach.com **Assessment Master A4.39**

Week 1 Assessment & Reteaching

☑ = TESTED

Assess

OBJECTIVES	ASSESSMENTS

Reading

- ☑ Determine Theme
- ☑ Determine Importance

Reading Comprehension Test

Directions: Read the story. Then answer the questions about the story.

The Cleaning Party

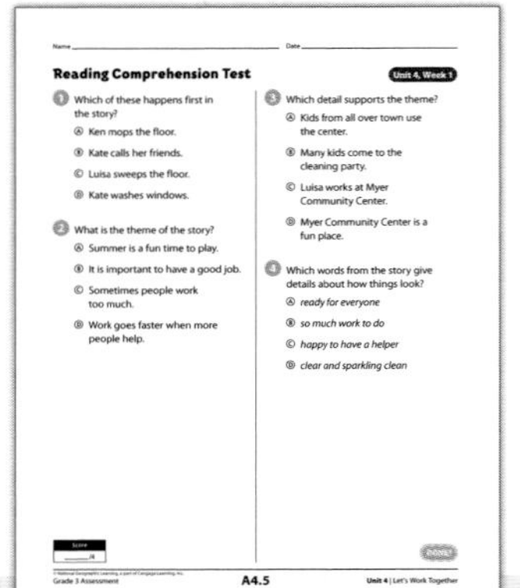

Reading Comprehension Test

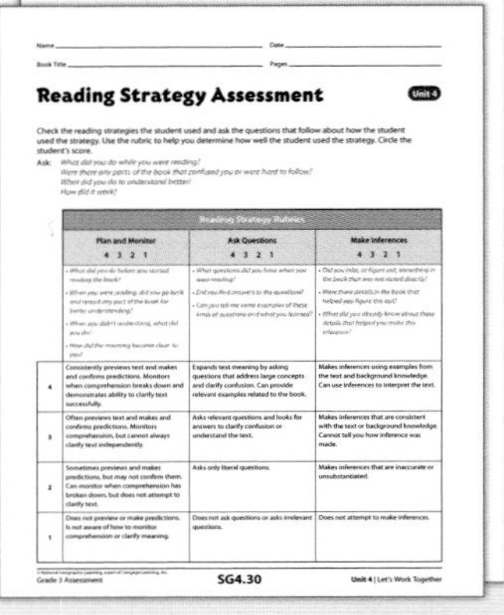

Reading Strategy Assessment

Reading Comprehension Test
A4.4–A4.5

Reading Strategy Assessment
SG4.30–SG4.31

Fluency

- ☑ Intonation
- ☑ Accuracy and Rate

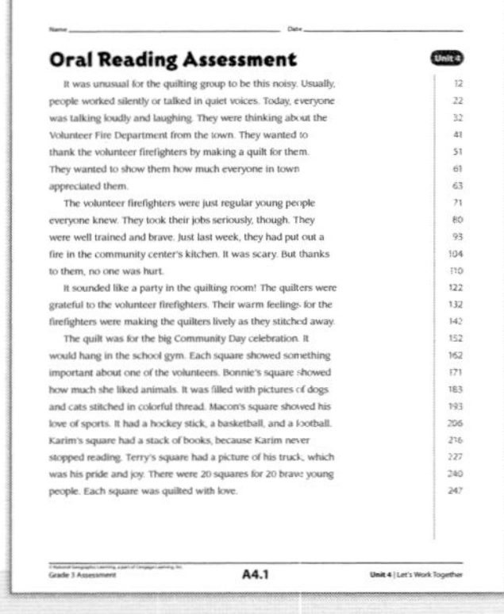

Oral Reading Assessment

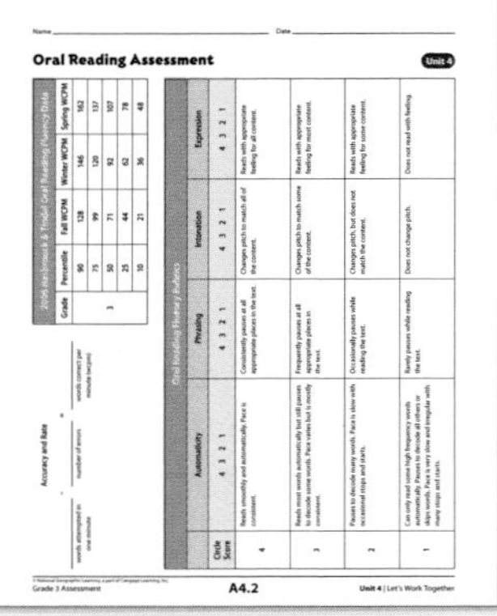

Oral Reading Assessment

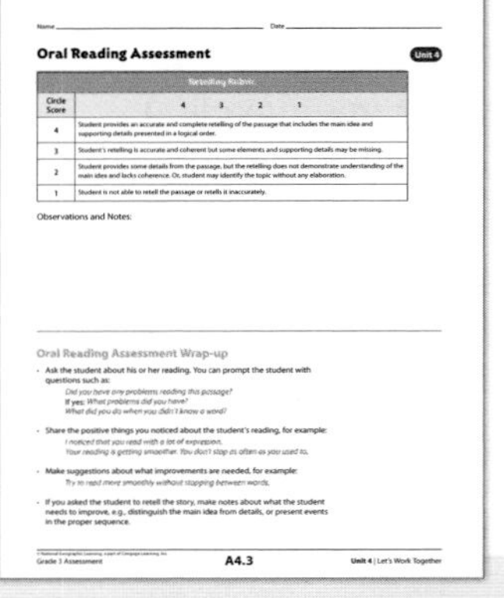

Oral Reading Assessment

Oral Reading Assessment
A4.1–A4.3

Use these passages throughout Unit 4. Work with Below Level students this week.

Vocabulary and Spelling

- ☑ Use Domain-Specific Words
- ☑ Use Academic Words
- ☑ Spell Words with *a: ai, ay*
- ☑ Use Commonly Misspelled Words Correctly

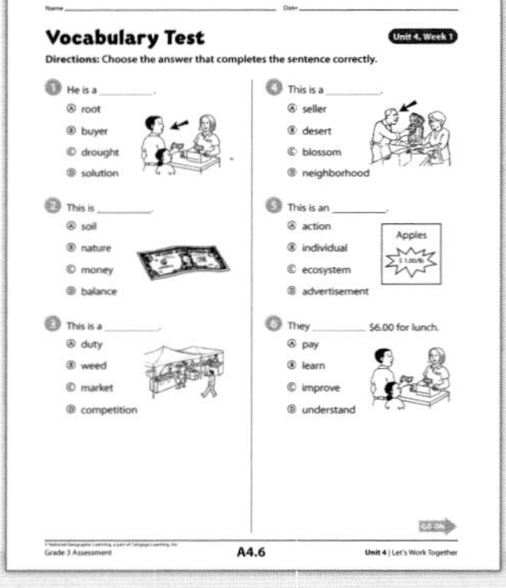

Vocabulary Test

Directions: Choose the answer that completes the sentence correctly.

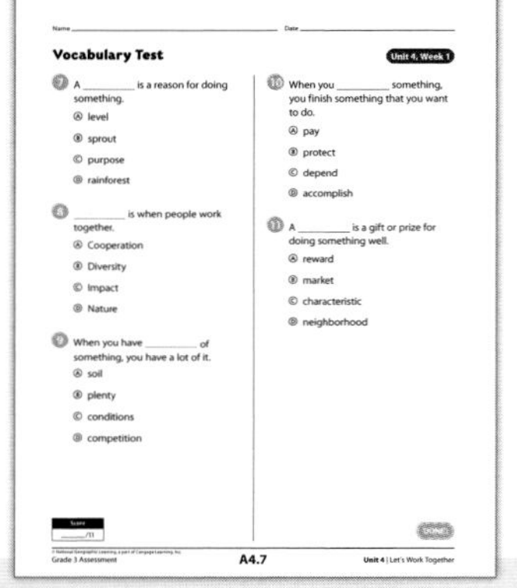

Vocabulary Test

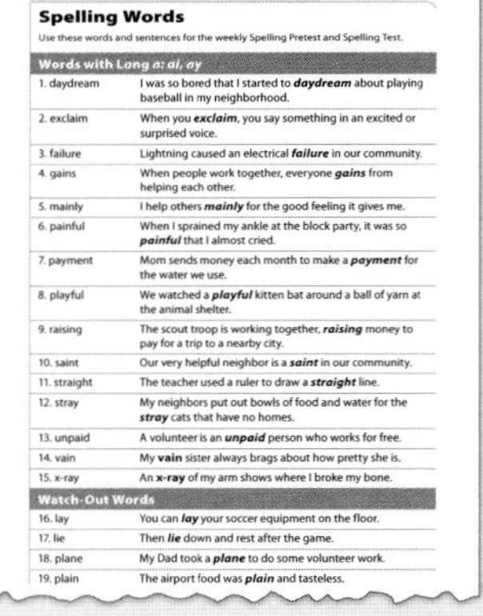

Spelling Words

Use these words and sentences for the weekly Spelling Pretest and Spelling Test.

Words with Long *a: ai, ay*	
1. daydream	I was so bored that I started to *daydream* about playing baseball in my neighborhood.
2. exclaim	When you *exclaim*, you say something in an excited or surprised voice.
3. failure	Lightning caused an electrical *failure* in our community.
4. gains	When people work together, everyone *gains* from helping each other.
5. mainly	I help others *mainly* for the good feeling it gives me.
6. painful	When I sprained my ankle at the block party, it was so *painful* that I almost cried.
7. payment	Mom sends money each month to make a *payment* for the water we use.
8. playful	We watched a *playful* kitten bat around a ball of yarn at the animal shelter.
9. raising	The scout troop is working together, *raising* money to pay for a trip to a nearby city.
10. saint	Our very helpful neighbor is a *saint* in our community.
11. straight	The teacher used a ruler to draw a *straight* line.
12. stray	My neighbors put out bowls of food and water for the *stray* cats that have no homes.
13. unpaid	A volunteer is an *unpaid* person who works for free.
14. vain	My *vain* sister always brags about how pretty she is.
15. x-ray	An *x-ray* of my arm shows where I broke my bone.
Watch-Out Words	
16. lay	You can *lay* your soccer equipment on the floor.
17. lie	Then *lie* down and rest after the game.
18. plane	My Dad took a *plane* to do some volunteer work.
19. plain	The airport food was *plain* and tasteless.

Vocabulary Test
A4.6–A4.7

Spelling Pretest/ Spelling Test
T207m

Grammar and Writing

- ☑ Use Present-Tense Verbs
- ☑ Use Action Verbs
- ☑ Use Subject-Verb Agreement: *he, she, it*
- ☑ Establish and Follow a Purpose

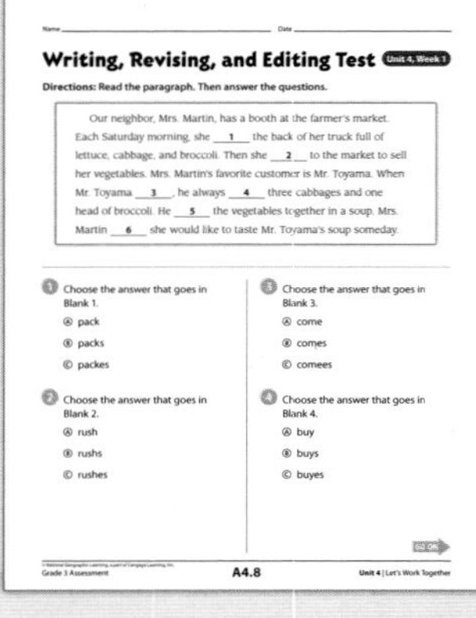

Writing, Revising, and Editing Test

Directions: Read the paragraph. Then answer the questions.

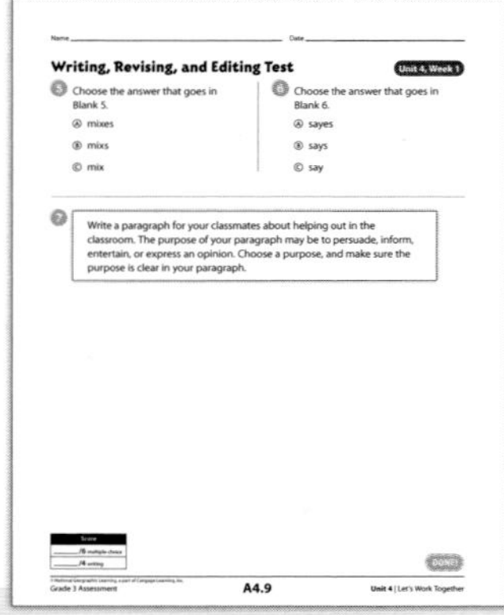

Writing, Revising, and Editing Test

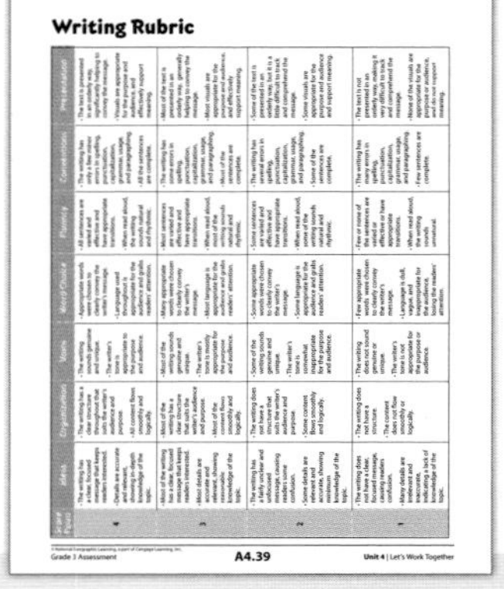

Writing Rubric

Writing, Revising, and Editing Test
A4.8–A4.9

Writing Rubric
A4.39

NGReach.com

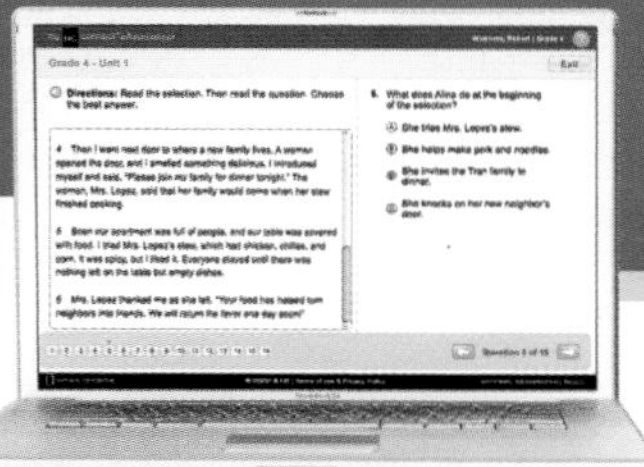

ExamView®

REPORTS

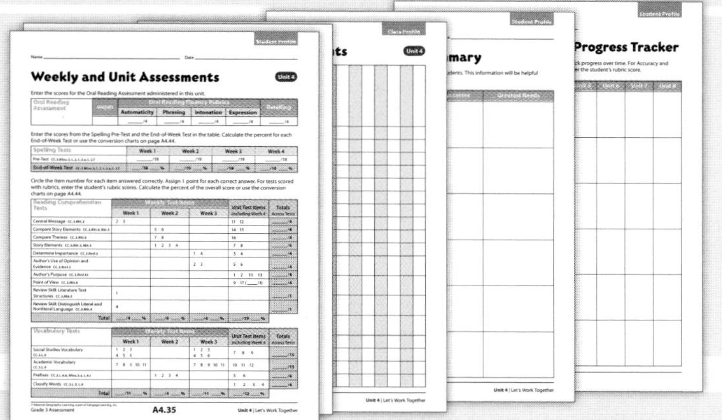

PRINT & ONLINE

Report Forms

Student Profile: Weekly and Unit Assessments	A4.35–A4.36
Class Profile: Weekly and Unit Assessments	A4.37
Student Profile: Strengths and Needs Summary	A4.38
Student Profile: Oral Reading Assessment Progress Tracker	A1.3

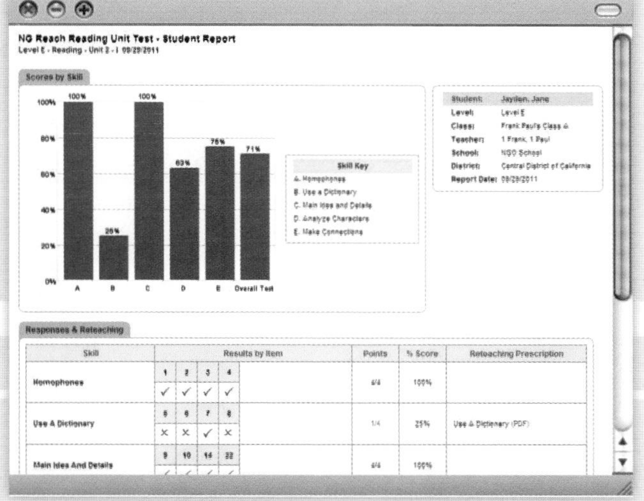

eAssessment™

ONLINE ONLY

Automated Reports

Student Profile: Weekly and Unit Tests

Class Profile: Weekly and Unit Tests

Standards Summary Report

Reteach and Practice

RESOURCES AND ROUTINES

Reading

RETEACH

Theme: Reteaching Master RT4.1

Determine Importance: Reteaching Master RT4.2

ADDITIONAL PRACTICE

Comprehension Coach NGReach.com

Fluency

RETEACH

Fluency Routines, page BP33

ADDITIONAL PRACTICE

Comprehension Coach NGReach.com

Vocabulary and Spelling

RETEACH

Vocabulary Routine 6, page BP40

Spelling and Word Work Routine, page BP52

ADDITIONAL PRACTICE

Vocabulary Games NGReach.com

Daily Spelling Practice, pages T207m–T207n

Grammar and Writing

RETEACH

Verbs: Anthology Handbook, pages 592, 594

Writing: Reteaching Writing Routine, page BP51

Writing Trait: Fluency: Reteaching Master RT4.3

ADDITIONAL PRACTICE

More Grammar Practice PM4.8

Daily Writing Skills Practice, pages T207q–T207r

Week 2 Planner

Online Lesson Planner
NGReach.com

☑ = TESTED

	Day 1	Day 2
WHOLE GROUP TIME	**Listen and Comprehend**	**Read and Comprehend**
Anthology — **Speaking and Listening** 5–10 minutes	**Academic Talk** CC.3.SL.4 Discuss the Big Question T233s	**Academic Talk** CC.3.SL.1 Preview and Predict T234c
Language and Vocabulary 15–25 minutes	**Daily Spelling and Word Work** CC.3.Rfou.3; CC.3.L.2; CC.3.L.2.e; CC.3.L.2.f ☑ Pretest: Words with Long *e: ee, ea; Long o: oa,ow;* and Commonly Misspelled Words T233m **Daily Grammar** CC.3.L.1; CC.3.L.1.e; CC.3.L.1.f; CC.3.L.2 ☑ More Subject-Verb Agreement T233o **Vocabulary Strategy** CC.3.Rfou.3.a; CC.3.L.4.b; CC.3.L.4.c ☑ Prefixes T233s	**Daily Spelling and Word Work** CC.3.Rfou.3; CC.Rfou.3.c; CC.3.L.2 ☑ Practice T233m **Daily Grammar** CC.3.L.1; CC.3.L.1.e; CC.3.L.1.f; CC.3.L.2 ☑ Plural Present-Tense Verbs T233o **Vocabulary Strategy** CC.3.Rfou.3.a; CC.3.L.1.i; CC.3.L.4.b; CC.3.L.4.c ☑ More Prefixes T234c
Reading 20–40 minutes	**Reading** CC.3.Rlit.3; CC.3.Rlit.5 Read Aloud: Realistic Fiction T234a **Comprehension** CC.3.Rlit.3; CC.3.Rlit.5 ☑ Describe Story Elements T234a **Fluency** CC.3.Rfou.4; CC.3.Rfou.4.b ☑ Model Expression T234a	**Reading** CC.3.Rlit.10 Read Realistic Fiction T235–T237 **Comprehension** CC.3.Rlit.2, 3, 6 ☑ Describe Story Elements T235, T236 ☑ Determine Importance T235, T236 Theme T236 **Fluency** CC.3.Rfou.4; CC.3.Rfou.4.b ☑ Practice Expression, Accuracy, and Rate T235
Writing 15–45 minutes	**Power Writing** T233s CC.3.W.10 **Daily Writing Skills** CC.3.W.3.a ☑ Introduce Characters T233q **Writing** CC.3.Rlit.3; CC.3.W.10 Write About Story Elements T234b **Writing Project: Realistic Fiction** CC.3.W.3.a; CC.3.W.5 ☑ Study a Model T239i	**Power Writing** T234c CC.3.W.10 **Daily Writing Skills** CC.3.W.3.a ☑ Introduce Characters T233q **Writing** CC.3.W.10 Write About a Character's Actions T237 **Writing Project: Realistic Fiction** CC.3.W.3.a; CC.3.W.5; CC.3.W.10 ☑ Prewrite T239j
SMALL GROUP READING TIME	**Read Social Studies Articles**	**Read Fiction Books**
Fiction & Nonfiction 20 minutes	**Vocabulary** CC.3.L.6 Social Studies Vocabulary SG10–SG11 **Reading** CC.3.Rinf.2; CC.3.Rinf.10 Identify Supporting Details SG10 Build Comprehension SG11	**Vocabulary** CC.3.L.6 Learn Story Words SG12–SG13 **Reading** CC.3.Rfou.4.a; CC.3.Rlit.3, 5, 10 Introduce SG12–SG13 Read SG14–SG15 ☑ Describe Story Elements SG14–SG15 Determine Importance SG14–SG15

LEARNING STATION TIME/DAILY PHONICS INTERVENTION

20 minutes

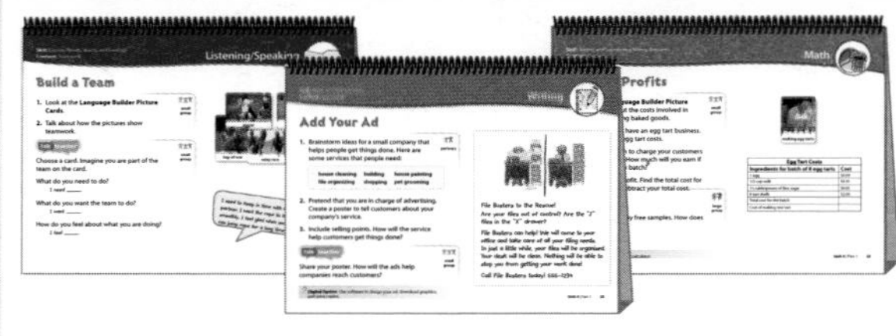

Speaking and Listening T233i CC.3.SL.1; CC.3.SL.4
Language and Vocabulary T233i CC.3.L.6
Writing T233i CC.3.W.2.a; CC.3.W.10
Cross-Curricular T233j CC.3.SL.2
Reading and Intervention T233j CC.3.Rlit.9; CC.3.Rlit.10; CC.3.Rinf.10; CC.3.Rfou.3
Daily Phonics Intervention T233k–T233l CC.3.Rfou.3; CC.3.Rfou.3.c; CC.3.L.2.e; CC.3.L.2.f

BIG Question What's the best way to get things done?

Day 3

Read and Comprehend

Academic Talk CC.3.SL.1.b
Talk Together T238

Daily Spelling and Word Work CC.3.L.2.e; CC.3.L.2.f
☑ Practice T233n

Daily Grammar CC.3.L.1; CC.3.L.1.e; CC.3.L.1.f; CC.3.L.2
☑ Present-Tense Action Verbs; Subject-Verb Agreement T233p, T238a

Vocabulary Review CC.3.L.6
Review Social Studies and Academic Vocabulary T237a

Reading CC.3.Rlit.10
Reread Realistic Fiction T237a

Comprehension CC.3.Rlit.1; CC.3.Rlit.3
Compare Characters T237a

Fluency CC.3.Rfou.4; CC.3.Rfou.4.b
☑ Practice Expression T238

Power Writing T237a CC.3.W.10

Daily Writing Skills CC.3.W.3.a
☑ Introduce Characters T233r

Writing CC.3.L.1; CC.3.L.1.e, f; CC.3.L.2, 3
Write to Reinforce Grammar T239

Writing Project: Realistic Fiction CC.3.W.3.a; CC.3.W.5; CC.3.W.10
☑ Draft T239j

Read Fiction Books

Vocabulary CC.3.L.6
Expand Vocabulary Through Wide Reading SG12–SG15

Reading CC.3.Rfou.4.a; CC.3.Rlit.3, 5, 10
Read and Integrate Ideas SG14–SG15
☑ Describe Story Elements SG14–SG15
Determine Importance SG14–SG15

Day 4

Read and Comprehend

Academic Talk CC.3.Rlit.3; CC.3.SL.1; CC.3.SL.1.a
Discuss Story Elements T239d

Daily Spelling and Word Work CC.3.L.2; CC.3.L.2.f; CC.3.L.4.d
☑ Practice T233n

Daily Grammar CC.3.W.5; CC.3.L.1; CC.3.L.1.e; CC.3.L.1.f; CC.3.L.2
☑ Grammar and Writing T233p

Vocabulary Practice CC.3.Rfou.3.a; CC.3.L.4.b; CC.3.L.4.c
☑ Prefixes T239c

Reading CC.3.Rlit.10
Read Short Stories T239a–T239b

Comprehension CC.3.Rlit.3; CC.3.Rlit.5; CC.3.Rlit.9
☑ Compare Story Elements T239a–T239b

Fluency CC.3.Rfou.4; CC.3.Rfou.4.b
☑ Model and Practice Expression T239b

Power Writing T239c CC.3.W.10

Daily Writing Skills CC.3.W.3.a
☑ Introduce Characters T233r

Writing CC.3.W.10
Write to Compare Story Elements T239d

Writing Project: Realistic Fiction CC.3.W.3.a; CC.3.W.5; CC.3.W.10; CC.3.L.1; CC.3.L.1.d; CC.3.L.3
☑ Revise/Edit and Proofread T239k–T239l

Read Fiction Books

Vocabulary CC.3.L.6
Expand Vocabulary Through Wide Reading SG12–SG15

Reading CC.3.Rfou.4.a; CC.3.Rlit.3, 5, 10
Introduce SG14–SG15
Read and Integrate Ideas SG14–SG15
☑ Describe Story Elements SG14–SG15
Determine Importance SG14–SG15

Day 5

Review and Apply

Academic Talk CC.3.SL.1; CC.3.SL.1.b
Relate Readings to the Big Question T239h

Daily Grammar CC.3.L.1; CC.3.L.1.e; CC.3.L.1.f; CC.3.L.2
☑ Review T233p

Vocabulary Practice CC.3.Rfou.3.a; CC.3.L.4.b; CC.3.L.4.c
☑ Prefixes T239e

Reading CC.3.Rlit.10
Reread Short Stories T239f–T239g

Comprehension CC.3.Rlit.9
Determine Themes T239f
Compare Themes T239g

Power Writing T239e CC.3.W.10

Daily Writing Skills CC.3.W.3.a
☑ Introduce Characters T233r

Writing CC.3.W.10
Write to Compare Themes T239g

Writing Project: Realistic Fiction CC.3.SL.5
☑ Publish and Present T239l

Read Fiction Books

Vocabulary CC.3.L.6
Expand Vocabulary Through Wide Reading SG12–SG15

Reading CC.3.Rlit.10; CC.3.Rfou.4.a; CC.3.SL.1.a
Connect Across Texts SG15

Writing CC.3.W.10
Choose a Writing Option SG14–SG15

ASSESSMENT & RETEACHING

Assessment and Reteaching T239m–T239n

☑ Reading Comprehension Test A4.10–A4.13 CC.3.Rlit.3; CC.3.Rlit.5

☑ Reading Strategy Assessment SG4.30–SG4.31 CC.3.Rfou.4.a

☑ Oral Reading Assessment A4.1–A4.3 CC.3.Rfou.4

☑ Vocabulary Test A4.14 CC.3.Rfou.3.a; CC.3.L.4.b; CC.3.L.4.c

☑ Spelling Test: Words with Long *e: ee, ea;* Long *o: oa,ow;* and Commonly Misspelled Words T233m CC.3.Rfou.3; CC.3.Rfou.3.c; CC.3.L.2; CC.3.L.2.e; CC.3.L.2.f

☑ Writing, Revising, and Editing Test A4.15–A4.16 CC.3.W.5; CC.3.L.1.e; CC.3.L.1.f

Reteaching Masters RT4.4–RT4.6

Week 2 Learning Stations

Speaking and Listening

Option 1: Build a Team

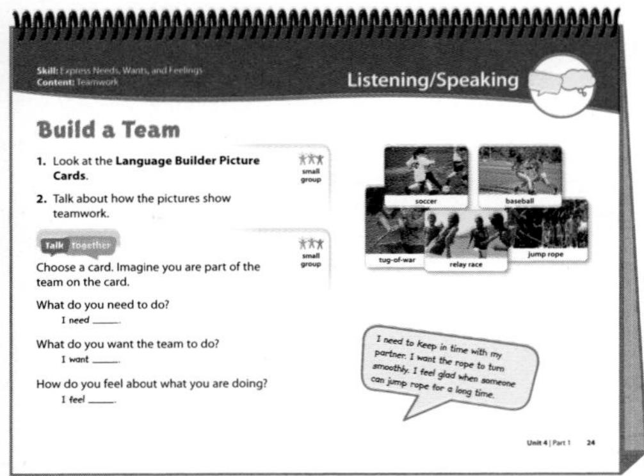

PROGRAM RESOURCES

Language and Literacy Teamwork Activities: Card 24

Digital Library: Language Builder Picture Cards D38–D42

Teacher's Guide on NGReach.com

Discuss Topics, Expressing Ideas Clearly	CC.3.SL.1
Recount an Experience	CC.3.SL.4

Option 2: Tell a True Story

I remember when I helped my friends run a bake sale at school. Our goal was to raise money for our soccer team. First we decided . . .

Have groups of three or four students each recount a time when they worked with others to achieve a goal.

- Students should describe the experience and provide as many details as possible.
- When one student is finished, another group member should tell his or her cooperation story.

Recount an Experience	CC.3.SL.4

Language and Vocabulary

Key Words

accomplish · advertisement · buyer · cooperation
determine · market · money · paraphrase · pay
plenty · purpose · reward · seller · theme

Option 1: Vocabulary Games

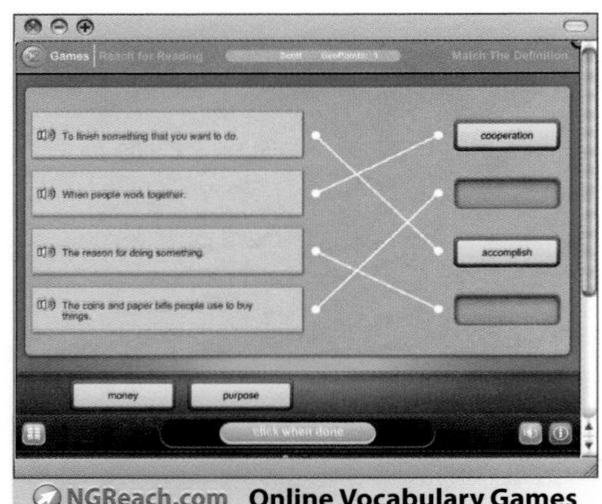

NGReach.com **Online Vocabulary Games**

Acquire and Use Academic and Domain-Specific Words	CC.3.L.6

Option 2: My Vocabulary Notebook

NGReach.com **My Vocabulary Notebook**

Have students expand their word knowledge.

- Under Add More Information > Use This Word > Write a Sentence, have students write sentences using each of the Key Words.
- Under Add More Information > Add What I Know > Related Wordshave students list words that are related to the vocabulary word.

Acquire and Use Conversational, Academic, and Domain-Specific Words	CC.3.L.6

Writing

Option 1: Add Your Ad

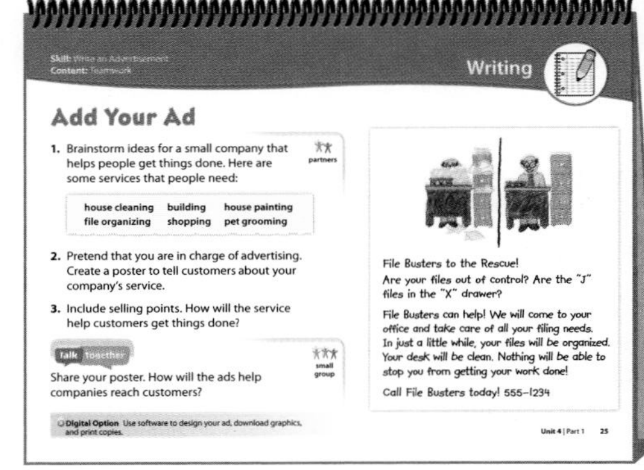

PROGRAM RESOURCES & MATERIALS

Language and Literacy Teamwork Activities: Card 25

Teacher's Guide on NGReach.com

poster board • art supplies

Include Illustrations	CC.3.W.2.a
Write Over Shorter Time for Specific Audiences	CC.3.W.10

Option 2: Write A Letter

Dear Grace Lin,
Thank you for writing the story "Ba's Business."

Have students work individually to write a letter to Grace Lin, the author of "Ba's Business."

- Have students write a friendly letter to Lin, telling her what they liked about the story and its illustrations.
- Students can share their letters with the class.

Write Over Shorter Time for Specific Purposes	CC.3.W.10

= one student = two students = three or more students

Cross-Curricular

Option 1: Egg Tart Profits

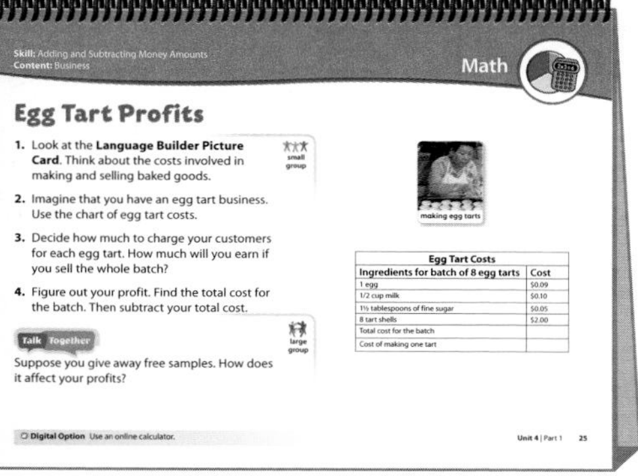
Skill: Adding and Subtracting Money Amounts
Content: Business

Math

Egg Tart Profits

1. Look at the **Language Builder Picture Card**. Think about the costs involved in making and selling baked goods.
2. Imagine that you have an egg tart business. Use the chart of egg tart costs.
3. Decide how much to charge your customers for each egg tart. How much will you earn if you sell the whole batch?
4. Figure out your profit. Find the total cost for the batch. Then subtract your total cost.

small group

making egg tarts

Egg Tart Costs	
Ingredients for batch of 8 egg tarts	**Cost**
1 egg	$0.09
1/2 cup milk	$0.10
1½ tablespoons of fine sugar	$0.05
8 tart shells	$2.00
Total cost for the batch	
Cost of making one tart	

Talk Together

large group

Suppose you give away free samples. How does it affect your profits?

Digital Option Use an online calculator.

Unit 4 | Part 1 25

PROGRAM RESOURCES

Cross-Curricular Teamwork Activities: Card 25

Digital Library: Language Builder Picture Card D25

Teacher's Guide on NGReach.com

Option 2: Working Together

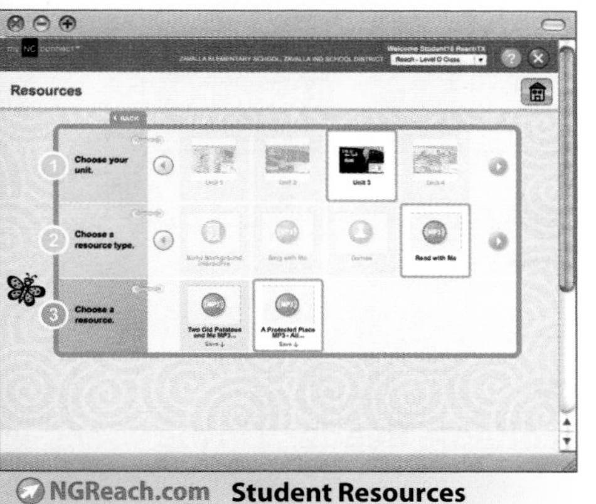

NGReach.com **Student Resources**

Have small groups watch a video about the ways people are working together in China to stop the spread of deserts. Go to: Resources > Unit 4 > Learning Stations > Week 2 > Deserts.

Ask groups to discuss why working together is necessary for a challenge as large as this one.

Determine the Main Ideas and Supporting Details of Information Presented Visually and Orally in Diverse Media	CC.3.SL.2

Reading

Option 1: Author Study

Grace Lin

Character Comparison Chart

	Character	Character
Detail		
Detail		

MATERIALS

books by Grace Lin such as Dim Sum for Everyone *and* The Ugly Vegetables

As students read multiple books by Grace Lin over the week, have them develop a character comparison chart. Then have partners use their charts to discuss the characters of the stories.

Students may wish to select from additional recommended books. See **Independent Reading** on page SG68.

Compare and Contrast Stories	CC.3.Rlit.9
Read and Comprehend Literature	CC.3.Rlit.10

Option 2: Read a Blog Post

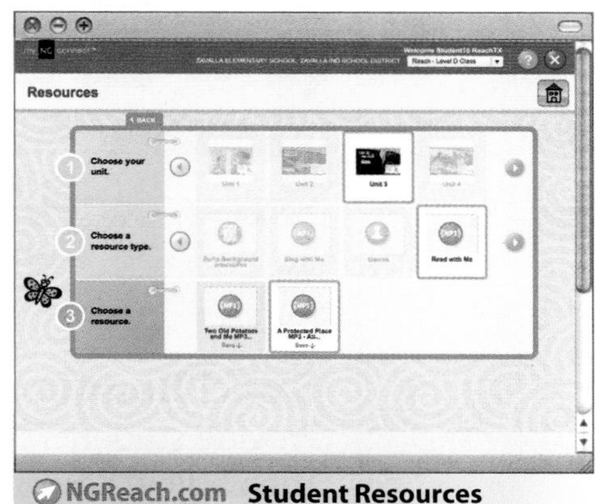

NGReach.com **Student Resources**

Have students read a blog entry describing a school garden in Kenya.

- To view the blog, have students go to Resources > Unit 4 > Learning Stations > Week 2 > Gardening Project.
- Have students read the blog entry, study the accompanying photographs, and write one or two sentences describing how the students in the blog are working together.

Read and Comprehend Informational Text	CC.3.Rinf.10

Intervention

Option 1: Phonics Games

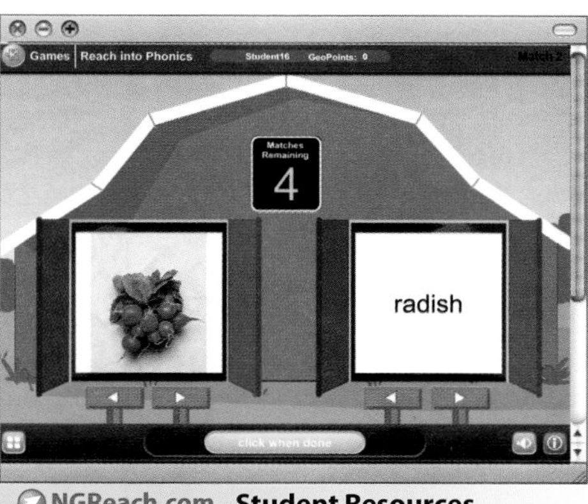

NGReach.com **Student Resources**

Apply Phonics and Word Analysis Skills	CC.3.Rfou.3

For Reteaching Masters, see pages RT4.4–RT4.6.

Additional Resources

ESL Kit

ESL Teacher's Edition pages T234a–T240h

Week 2 Daily Phonics Intervention

OBJECTIVES

Thematic Connection: Jobs and Money

Build Oral Vocabulary; Develop Phonological Awareness

Build Reading Fluency and Concepts of Print (title; paragraphs)

Use Word Patterns to Decode Long Vowel Words

Recognize High Frequency Words and Compound Words

Teach Day 1

PROGRAM RESOURCES

Word Builder: Transparency 43

Reach into Phonics

Lesson 50, page T84

Word Patterns

Follow Lesson 50 to teach word patterns and how to use word patterns to decode short and long vowel sounds. Guide students through **Transparency 43**.

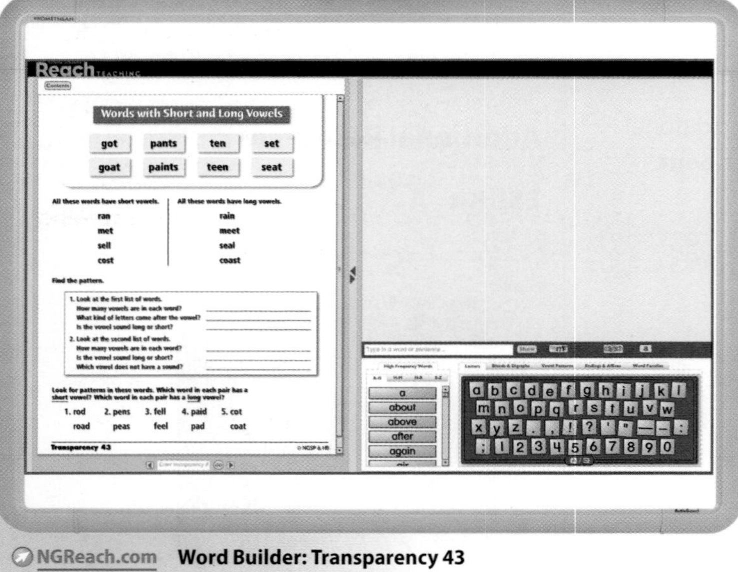

NGReach.com **Word Builder: Transparency 43**

Practice Day 2

PROGRAM RESOURCES

Word Builder: Transparency 44

Decodable Reader: *On the River*

Reach into Phonics

Lesson 51, pages T85

Lesson 52, pages T86–T88

Multisyllabic Words

Follow Lesson 51 to teach how to decode multisyllabic, compound words. Guide students through **Transparency 44**. Use **Reading Routine 3** to guide students as they read Decodable text.

*For **Reading Routine 3**, see Reach into Phonics page ix.*

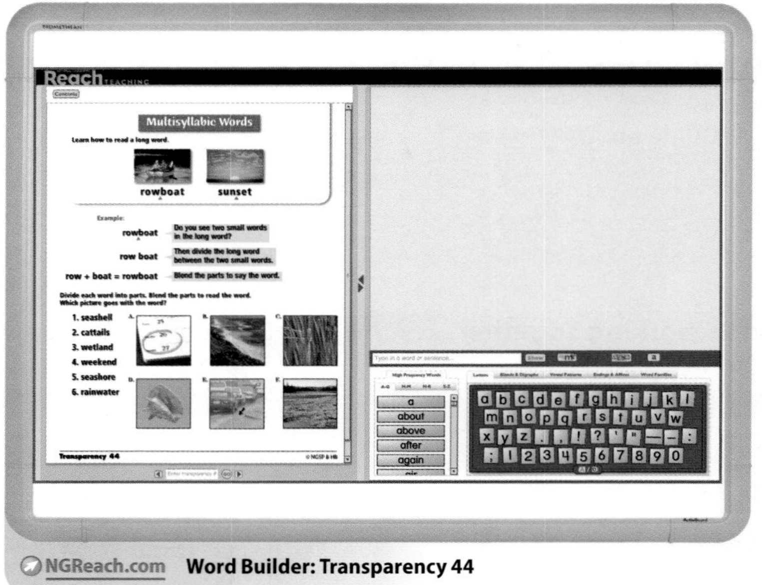

NGReach.com **Word Builder: Transparency 44**

Build Reading Fluency

Provide students with the **Decodable Reader**, *On the River*. Then follow Lesson 52.

= one student = two students = three or more students

Multisyllabic Words and Word Patterns

COMMON CORE STANDARDS

Apply Word Analysis Skills	CC.3.Rfou.3
Decode Multisyllabic Words	CC.3.Rfou.3.c
Use Conventional Spelling	CC.3.L.2.e
Use Spelling Patterns and Generalizations	CC.3.L.2.f

Words and Pictures Day 3  Option 1

MATERIALS

index cards, 16 per pair

Prepare

- Ask partners to write each word below on separate cards.

ran	bed	check	cot
train	bead	cheek	coat

- Have partners draw an illustration for each word on separate cards.
- Have partners combine the 16 cards and place them face down in four rows of four cards each.

Play a Game

Have Partner 1 turn over two cards and read the word or identify the picture. If the word and picture match, Partner 1 uses the word in a sentence and keeps the cards. If no match is made, Partner 1 returns the cards, and Partner 2 plays. Play continues until all matches are made.

Bingo! Day 3 Option 2

MATERIALS

32 squares of colored paper, each about two inches square

Prepare

- Students play in groups of three with one student as the host. The other students each make a bingo card by folding a sheet of paper in half twice horizontally and twice vertically to create 16 squares. The host cuts his or her card into individual squares.
- The host reads aloud the words below. As the host reads and writes each word on a square of paper, the players print the word in any empty square on the bingo card.

river	water	always	place	rainbow	claim
seaweed	airmail	daydream	snowman	sailboat	
something	maid	stem	steam	clam	

Play a Game

- Tell the host to read each word in a different order than before.
- The first player to find the word on his or her card identifies the word by spelling it. The host listens for accuracy. Then the other player does the same. Each player who identifies the word correctly places a colored square over the word. If the word is not identified correctly, the player leaves the space uncovered.
- Players call out "Bingo!" when they have four colored squares in a row.

Compound Word Day 4 

MATERIALS

index cards, five per pair of students • timer

Prepare

- Have students write each phonogram on a separate card: *air, sea, water, sun, snow.*
- Then have them place the cards face down in a pile.

Play a Game

- One partner picks and displays a card.
- Players have two minutes to write as many compound words as they can that contain the word shown. Remind students the word can come at the beginning or end of the compound word.
- After time is up, Player 1 reads his or her list of compound words. Player 2 listens for any repeats or nonsense words. Players receive one point for each compound word that contains the word shown.
- Have partners take turns choosing cards, reading lists, and listening. Partners continue to brainstorm compound words.

Review Day 5 

PROGRAM RESOURCES

Word Builder: Transparency 45

Reach into Phonics **Lesson 53, page T89**

Review

Follow Lesson 53 to review words with long *a, e, o,* and to review how to use word patterns to decode words. Guide students through **Transparency 45**.

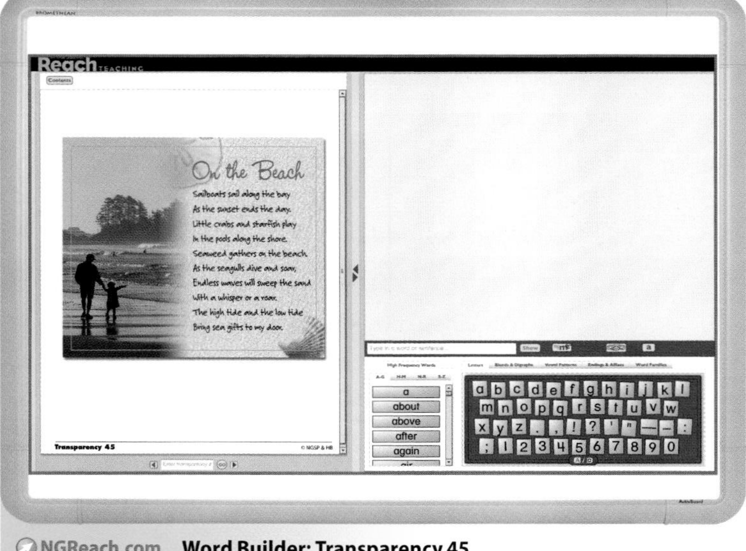

NGReach.com **Word Builder: Transparency 45**

Daily Spelling & Word Work

OBJECTIVES

Thematic Connection: Jobs and Money

- ☑ **Spell Words with Long *e: ee, ea;* Long *o: oa, ow***
- ☑ **Use Commonly Misspelled Words Correctly**

SUGGESTED PACING

DAY 1	Spelling Pretest
DAY 2–4	Daily Practice Options
DAY 5	Spelling Test

Spelling Pretest Day 1 

Spelling Test Day 5

Spelling Words

Use these words and sentences for the weekly Spelling Pretest and Spelling Test.

Words with Long *e: ee, ea;* Long *o: oa, ow*	
1. appeal	The toy's bright colors will ***appeal*** to young children.
2. asleep	My mom bought a fluffy pillow to help her fall ***asleep*** at night.
3. beast	A grizzly bear is a ***beast*** that no human wants to meet on a hike.
4. borrow	We need to ***borrow*** money from a bank in order to buy the house.
5. cheap	That toy is ***cheap***, so we should have enough money to buy it.
6. follower	If you are a ***follower***, you let someone else lead you.
7. healing	The ointment we bought is ***healing*** my cut.
8. lowered	The shop owner ***lowered*** the blinds on the window to show that the store was closed.
9. meek	***Meek*** people are afraid to stand up for themselves.
10. overthrow	The people want to ***overthrow*** their cruel king.
11. repeat	If you ***repeat*** something, you do it again.
12. roam	Let's just ***roam*** around the store until we find something we want to buy.
13. teenager	A ***teenager*** is older than 12 and younger than 20.
14. tomorrow	Today I will look for a job, and ***tomorrow*** I hope I will have one.
15. unload	Please help me ***unload*** shopping bags from the car.
Watch-Out Words	
16. raise	We watch the shop owner ***raise*** the blinds on her window to show that her shop is open.
17. rays	The sun's powerful ***rays*** shone through the window.
18. son	Both her daughter and ***son*** help her in the store.
19. sun	It is early in the morning, and the ***sun*** has just come up.

Words with Long *e* or *o* Day 2 — **Option 1**

Teach

Display *cheap, asleep,* and *roam* and read them aloud. Circle the *ea* in *cheap*, the *ee* in *asleep*, and the *oa* in *roam*.

Explain: *When two vowels appear together in a word, the first vowel is usually long, which means it says its own name. The second vowel is usually silent.*

Read the words aloud again, elongating the long-vowel sounds. Then display *borrow*, circle the *ow*, and read the word aloud. Explain: *In some words, the letter* w *can act as a vowel. In* borrow, *the* w *is acting as a vowel, so the* o *at the end of* borrow *is long.*

Prepare

Have students fold a sheet of paper vertically into four columns. Tell them to write a heading at the top of each column, as follows: Long e: ee as in tree; Long e: ea as in eat; Long o: oa as in oats; Long o: ow as in low.

Word Sort

- Have partners quietly partner-read a spelling word, listening for the target long *e* or long *o* sound or sounds.
- Tell them to print each word under the correct heading and to pronounce the word again as they write it. Tell them to underline the two vowels in the pattern.

Apply Phonics and Word Analysis Skills	CC.3.Rfou.3
Decode Multisyllabic Words	CC.3.Rfou.3.c

Classify Day 2 — **Option 2**

MATERIALS

index cards, 15 per pair of students • sheets of green and yellow construction paper, one of each per pair of students

Prepare

Have partners collaborate to write each of the first 15 spelling words on a separate index card. Then have students shuffle all the cards and place them face down.

Play a Game

- Give each pair of students a sheet of green and a sheet of yellow construction paper. Have them say the color names aloud, listening for the long-vowel sounds.
- Have students work together to see how quickly they can turn over the cards, pronounce and spell each word, and place it on the color whose name has the same long-vowel sound.
- When all cards are placed, have students choose three or more cards from each sheet. Then have them collaborate to write a silly sentence using the words on the related sheet of construction paper.

Apply Phonics and Word Analysis Skills	CC.3.Rfou.3
Demonstrate Command of Spelling	CC.3.L.2

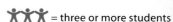

= one student = two students = three or more students

Words with Long *e: ee, ea;* Long *o: oa, ow*

Sound Signals Day 3  Option 1

MATERIALS
index cards, 17 per group • highlighters, one per student

Prepare
- Have groups of three students collaborate to write each of the first 15 spelling words, as well as *rays* and *raise*, on a separate card. Have them highlight the two letters in each word that work together to make the long vowel sound.
- Tell students to spread the cards face up.

Play a Game
- Player 1 makes a long *e*, a long *o*, or a long *a* sound. Player 2 chooses a spelling word that contains that sound.
- Player 2 reads the spelling word aloud to Player 3, who spells the word and uses it in a sentence. If Player 3 makes an error, the other students help correct it.
- Once a word is spelled correctly, players remove the card and switch roles. Play continues until all cards have been used.

Use Conventional Spelling	CC.3.L.2.e
Use Spelling Patterns and Generalizations	CC.3.L.2.f

Picture It Day 3  Option 2

MATERIALS
index cards, 19 per student

Prepare
- Have partners collaborate on drawing simple illustrations of as many spelling words as they can on index cards. Have them include all four Watch-Out Words. One sketch is drawn on each card.
- Tell students to write the word on the back of the card. Partners check each other's spelling.

Play a Game
- Have partners take turns displaying a drawing and asking the other to guess and spell the word.
- Play continues until each partner has spelled each word correctly.

Use Conventional Spelling	CC.3.L.2.e

Use a Dictionary Day 4 Option 1

MATERIALS
dictionaries, one per group

Prepare
Arrange students in groups of three and give each student six or seven spelling words to write, each on a separate slip of paper.

meek cheap raise

Play a Game
- Have players turn the slips of paper face down and mix them up.
- Player 1 chooses a word, reads it aloud, spells it, then puts it back down, face up.
- The other two players collaborate to look up the word in a dictionary and read the meaning aloud.
- Now Player 2 chooses a word, reads it, and spells it for the other two players to look up.
- Players take turns repeating the steps above until all 19 spelling words are face up on the table.

Use Glossaries and Dictionaries	CC.3.L.4.d

Word Combos Day 4  Option 2

MATERIALS
timer, one per group

Prepare
- Arrange students in groups of four, and arrange each group in two teams.
- Have each team secretly choose two spelling words, one with *ee* or *ea* and one with *oa* or *ow*.

Play a Game
- Team 1 calls out its two spelling words and starts the timer.
- Team 2 has one minute to compose and write a sentence that makes sense and contains the two target words. Have them underline the two words.
- If Team 2 writes a complete sentence before the buzzer rings and spells the words correctly, they score a point.
- Have teams take turns as Team 1 and Team 2 until each spelling word has been used at least once.

Meredith lowered the blinds so she could fall asleep.

Demonstrate Command of Spelling	CC.3.L.2
Use Spelling Patterns and Generalizations	CC.3.L.2.f

Week 2 Daily Grammar

OBJECTIVES

Thematic Connection: Jobs and Money

☑ **Grammar: Use Subject-Verb Agreement**

☑ **Grammar: Use Present-Tense Action Verbs**

COMMON CORE STANDARDS

Edit Writing	CC.3.W.5
Demonstrate Command of Grammar	CC.3.L.1
Form and Use Verb Tenses	CC.3.L.1.e

Day 1

PROGRAM RESOURCES

More Subject-Verb Agreement: eVisual 4.10

Game: Practice Master 4.9

Teach the Rules

Use the suggestion on page T234b to begin discussion of subject-verb agreement for action verbs that end with *-y*. Then use **eVisual 4.10** to show the spelling rules for action verbs that end in *-y*.

More Subject-Verb Agreement

For the **subject he**, **she**, or **it**:

• Change **y** to **i** and add **-es** for action verbs that end in a consonant and **-y**.	**hurry** → hurr**ies** **He** hurr**ies** to help her.
• Just add **-s** for verbs that end in a vowel and **-y**.	**buy** → buy**s** **She** buy**s** a gerbil. **It** scurr**ies** and play**s**.

NGReach.com **Subject-Verb Agreement: eVisual 4.10**

Play a Game

Distribute **Practice Master PM4.9** and have groups of three play the game.

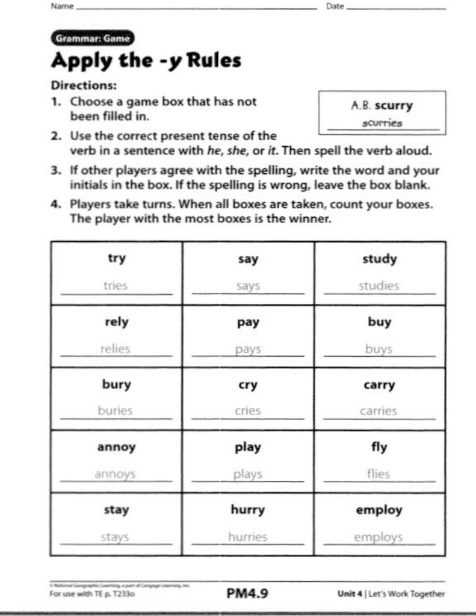

Name ______________ Date ______

Grammar: Game

Apply the -*y* Rules

Directions:

1. Choose a game box that has not been filled in.
2. Use the correct present tense of the verb in a sentence with *he, she,* or *it*. Then spell the verb aloud.
3. If other players agree with the spelling, write the word and your initials in the box. If the spelling is wrong, leave the box blank.
4. Players take turns. When all boxes are taken, count your boxes. The player with the most boxes is the winner.

A.B. **scurry** scurries

try tries	**say** says	**study** studies
rely relies	**pay** pays	**buy** buys
bury buries	**cry** cries	**carry** carries
annoy annoys	**play** plays	**fly** flies
stay stays	**hurry** hurries	**employ** employs

© National Geographic Learning, a part of Cengage Learning, Inc.
For use with TE p. T233o PM4.9 Unit 4 | Let's Work Together

NGReach.com **Practice Master PM4.9**

Differentiate

BL Below Level

ISSUE Students understand and retain the spelling rules more clearly with visual applications.

STRATEGY Make separate slips of paper for *stud | y | i | es*. Help students form the word *study* with *stud* and *y*. Have them remove the *y*, replace it with *i*, and add *-es*. Use the same steps with *say* and *-s* to show a word that does not change spelling.

Day 2

PROGRAM RESOURCES

Plural Present-Tense Verbs: eVisual 4.15

Game: Practice Master 4.10

MATERIALS

coins or game markers, one per group • index cards, seven per group

Teach the Rules

Use the suggestion on page T236 to begin discussion of present-tense action verbs that do *not* add *-s* or *-es* for subject-verb agreement. Then use **eVisual 4.15** to teach subject-verb agreement with *I, you, we,* and *they*.

Plural Present-Tense Verbs

For the **subject I**, **you, we,** or **they**, do not add **-s** or **-es** to present-tense action **verbs**.

I bake oat muffins.

You sell them.

We invite friends.

They buy our muffins.

NGReach.com **Plural Present-Tense Verbs: eVisual 4.15**

Play a Game

Distribute **Practice Master PM4.10** and have groups of three play the game.

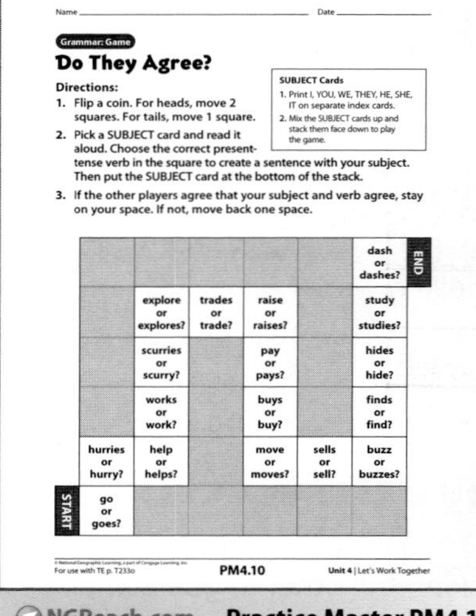

Name ______________ Date ______

Grammar: Game

Do They Agree?

Directions:

1. Flip a coin. For heads, move 2 squares. For tails, move 1 square.
2. Pick a SUBJECT card and read it aloud. Choose the correct present-tense verb in the square to create a sentence with your subject. Then put the SUBJECT card at the bottom of the stack.
3. If the other players agree that your subject and verb agree, stay on your space. If not, move back one space.

SUBJECT Cards

1. Print I, YOU, WE, THEY, HE, SHE, IT on separate index cards.
2. Mix the SUBJECT cards up and stack them face down to play the game.

						dash or dashes?	END
		explore or explores?	trades or trade?	raise or raises?		study or studies?	
		scurries or scurry?		pay or pays?		hides or hide?	
		works or work?		buys or buy?		finds or find?	
	hurries or hurry?	help or helps?		move or moves?	sells or sell?	buzz or buzzes?	
START	go or goes?						

© National Geographic Learning, a part of Cengage Learning, Inc.
For use with TE p. T233o PM4.10 Unit 4 | Let's Work Together

NGReach.com **Practice Master PM4.10**

Differentiate

SN Special Needs

ISSUE Students have difficulty following the game rules.

STRATEGY Have students place each subject card next to the square on the board as they play. Then have them use each verb in their sentence and listen to see which sentence sounds correct.

= one student = two students = three or more students

Subject-Verb Agreement
Present-Tense Action Verbs

Ensure Subject-Verb Agreement CC.3.L.1.f
Demonstrate Command of Spelling CC.3.L.2

Day 3

Teach the Rules

Use **Anthology** page 239 to review subject-verb agreement with present-tense action verbs. Then copy and display the chart below to reinforce the concept.

Present-Tense Action Verbs	Subject-Verb Agreement
When the subject is one person or thing, the verb is singular, too. Add an -s to the action verb.	Ba sells. He grins. His business grows.
Exception: When the subject is the pronoun *I* or *you*, meaning one person, do not add -s to the action verb.	I work hard. You help me with my work.
When the subject is more than one person or thing, the verb is plural, too. Do not add an -s to the verb.	Adika and Mama buy flour. Adika says to Bibi and Kaya, "You visit us." They eat together.

Generate Sentences

Have students write sentences to demonstrate subject-verb agreement and use present-tense action verbs. Explain:

- *Think of a business in your community. Write a sentence about it. Use a singular pronoun as your subject. Put a present-tense action verb in the second position.*
- *Think of the workers in the business. What do they do? Write a sentence about their work. Use a plural pronoun as your subject. Put a present-tense action verb in the second position.*

Have students share their best sentences.

*For **Writing Routine 3**, see page BP49.*

Differentiate

BL Below Level

ISSUE Students have difficulty with subject-verb agreement.

STRATEGY Work with students to create sentence frames to support their sentence writing, such as: It _____ s. They _____ . I _____ .

Day 4

PROGRAM RESOURCES

Grammar and Writing: Practice Master PM4.16

Grammar and Writing

Distribute **Practice Master PM4.16** Have students use editing and proofreading marks to correct errors with present-tense verbs and subject-verb agreement.

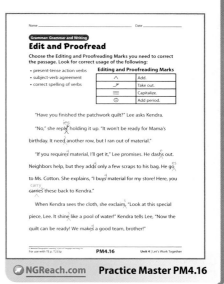

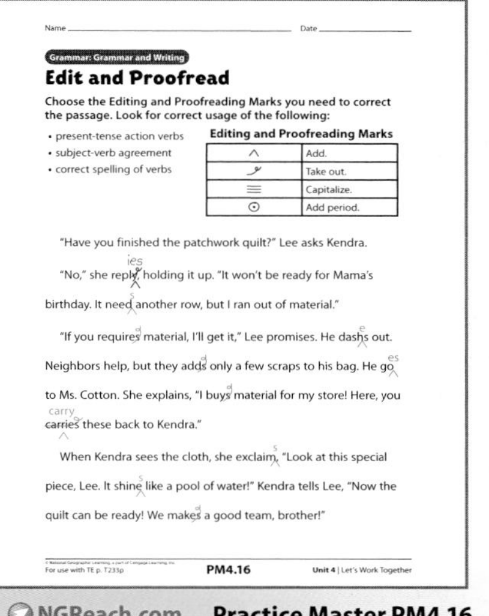

Name ______ Date ______

Grammar: Grammar and Writing

Edit and Proofread

Choose the Editing and Proofreading Marks you need to correct the passage. Look for correct usage of the following:

- present-tense action verbs
- subject-verb agreement
- correct spelling of verbs

Editing and Proofreading Marks

Mark	Meaning
^	Add.
℘	Take out.
≡	Capitalize.
⊙	Add period.

"Have you finished the patchwork quilt?" Lee asks Kendra.

"No," she reply, holding it up. "It won't be ready for Mama's birthday. It need another row, but I ran out of material."

"If you requires material, I'll get it," Lee promises. He dashs out. Neighbors help, but they adds only a few scraps to his bag. He go to Ms. Cotton. She explains, "I buys material for my store! Here, you carries these back to Kendra."

When Kendra sees the cloth, she exclaim, "Look at this special piece, Lee. It shine like a pool of water!" Kendra tells Lee, "Now the quilt can be ready! We makes a good team, brother!"

For use with TE p. T233p PM4.16 Unit 4 | Let's Work Together

NGReach.com **Practice Master PM4.16**

Day 5

PROGRAM RESOURCES

Writing, Revising, and Editing Test: Assessment Masters A4.15–A4.16

Review and Assess

Display the chart, and have partners write each verb with one of the subjects in each column. For example: it walks, I walk, they walk. Tell students to use each subject pronoun at least once.

Have partners tell each other how they made verbs agree with subjects and which verbs had spelling changes.

Verbs	Subject-Verb Agreement		
	he, she, it	I, you	we, you they
walk carry mix whisper			

☑ Administer the **Writing, Revising, and Editing Test**.

Week 2 Daily Writing Skills

OBJECTIVE

Thematic Connection: Jobs and Money

☑ **Introduce Characters**

COMMON CORE STANDARDS

Introduce Characters CC.3.W.3.a

Introduce Characters Day 1 

PROGRAM RESOURCES

Introduce Characters: eVisual 4.11
Character Chart: eVisual 4.12

Teach the Skill

Display **eVisual 4.11**.

Introduce Characters

Sammy walked into the gym carrying two folding chairs. He was helping his teacher set up the gym. He had to be careful, though. His class was just about to start their fourth-grade holiday concert and he didn't want his dressy clothes to get dirty.

Sammy looked down at his shirt. Oh no! There was a big black stain on his sleeve!

Suddenly, the doors opened. People started entering the gym. What was he going to do?

NGReach.com **Introduce Characters: eVisual 4.11**

INTERACTIVE WHITEBOARD TIP: Circle details that help introduce Sammy.

Have volunteers read the passage. Explain: *This passage introduces Sammy. A good character introduction includes clues about the character's gender, age, appearance, and traits or characteristics. Good writers often include these elements at the beginning of a story.* Display and explain **eVisual 4.12**.

Character Chart

Element	Details in the Text
gender	"Sammy," "He," "His"; the character is male
age	The story mentions his fourth-grade holiday concert, so he is about 9 years old.
appearance	He is wearing his nice clothes.
traits	He sets up the chairs, so he is helpful.

NGReach.com **Character Chart: eVisual 4.12**

INTERACTIVE WHITEBOARD TIP: Underline more details about Sammy's traits.

Interview a Character Day 2 Option 1

MATERIALS

timer

Introduce

Arrange students in pairs. Explain that writers usually know their characters well before they start writing a story. It's almost as if they interviewed the character first.

Practice

- Have partners use role-play to invent story characters. Give pairs of students five minutes to interview a partner. Have students ask questions like those below.
- Explain that the interviewee will role-play a character for a story. The character should be an animal or an imaginary character, such as a clever fox, an industrious pig, or a character from a fairy tale.
- Have each interviewer take notes about the interviewee's answers. Have students save their interview notes for use on Day 3.

- What is your name?
- What gender are you?
- How old are you?
- What do you look like?
- What are some good traits that you have?
- What are some traits that you aren't proud of?
- What are some of your hobbies?

Make a Character Profile Day 2  Option 2

MATERIALS

construction paper, one sheet per student • colored pencils

Practice

Have students create a character profile about a character they have read about. It may be a person such as Adika, a pig from "When the Pigs Took Over," or an animal from another story they have read. Tell students to include the following information and save their profile for use on Day 3.

- Character's Name
- Character's Age and Gender
- A Drawing of the Character
- Five Character Traits

= one student = two students

= three or more students

SUGGESTED PACING

DAY 1 Teach the Skill
DAY 2–4 Daily Practice Options
DAY 5 Review and Assess

Introduce Characters Day 3  Option 1

Introduce

Have students work with the same partner they had on Day 2 and revisit their interview notes. Tell partners to decide which of the two interviewed characters to include in a silly story in which the character is looking for a job.

Practice

Have partners work together to brainstorm a funny short story. Remind them that the character is looking for a job. Have them write just the beginning of the story—one that introduces the character and establishes the silly situation.

Encourage students to include clues to at least three of the following: gender, age, appearance, good traits, bad traits, and hobbies.

Reveal Character Traits Day 3  Option 2

Introduce

Tell students they will use the character profile they created on Day 2 to write a story opening that introduces their character. Have students imagine that their character is in a completely new story in which he or she is looking for a job.

Practice

Tell students that their paragraph should include the character's gender, age, appearance, and traits. When they are finished, have students exchange paragraphs with a partner. Have them mark the following:

- underline details that describe the character's gender
- double-underline details that describe the character's age
- circle details that describe the character's appearance
- draw boxes around the details that describe the character's traits

Revise Your Opening Day 4 

Practice

Have each student select a narrative piece from his or her Weekly Writing folder. Tell students to rewrite or revise the beginning of the narrative by creating a story opening that tells about the main character and pulls the reader into the narrative.

Copy and display the following list to remind students of details they can use to introduce their characters.

- Include your character's gender.
- Give details about your character's age.
- Give details about your character's appearance.
- Include details about your character's traits.

As students write, provide suggestions. For example, remind them that they don't have to tell the character's age. They can imply age through the character's situation, setting, or actions.

Review and Assess Day 5 

PROGRAM RESOURCES

Writing, Revising, and Editing Test: Assessment Masters A4.15–A4.16

Review the Skill

Copy and display the following sentences. Have partners decide which clue(s) the author presents in each sentence.

- Annie put on her green coat and walked out the door. gender, appearance
- Juan closed his eyes, took a deep breath, and began playing his violin in front of the audience. gender, traits
- Anish stamped his foot and said, "I'm 12 years old! I'm too old to play with those toys!" gender, age, traits

Have partners collaborate to write a sentence of their own that includes at least two clues about a character. Then tell them to read their sentence to another pair of students and have the other pair decide which clues have been provided and what words and phrases provide the clues.

☑ Administer the **Writing, Revising, and Editing Test**.

Day 1 Listen and Comprehend

Realistic Fiction

OBJECTIVES

Thematic Connection: Jobs and Money

☑ **Use Prefixes to Determine Word Meanings**

☑ **Describe Story Elements**

PROGRAM RESOURCES

TECHNOLOGY ONLY

Read Aloud: eVisual 4.9

MATERIALS

timer • dictionaries • index cards

Power Writing

Have students write as much as they can as well as they can in one minute about the word *buyer*.

*For **Writing Routine 1**, see page BP47.*

COMMON CORE STANDARDS

Reading	
Describe Characters and Explain Characters' Actions	CC.3.Rlit.3
Describe How Successive Parts Build	CC.3.Rlit.5
Identify Meaning of Prefixes and Suffixes	CC.3.Rfou.3.a
Read with Fluency to Support Comprehension	CC.3.Rfou.4
Read Orally with Accuracy and Appropriate Rate on Successive Readings	CC.3.Rfou.4.b
Writing	
Write Over Shorter Time for Specific Purposes	CC.3.W.10
Speaking and Listening	
Recount an Experience	CC.3.SL.4
Language and Vocabulary	
Use Affixes as Clues	CC.3.L.4.b
Use Root Words as Clues	CC.3.L.4.c

WARM-UP

Have students review the readings from Week 1, including "Mama Panya's Pancakes" and the **Small Group Reading** books. Have partners think of examples from last week's readings where characters worked together.

Academic Talk

1 Discuss the Big Question

Remind students that they know how to tell about their own experiences by telling events in order and including facts and details.

Model recounting an experience in answer to the Big Question: What's the best way to get things done? *I remember when I needed to paint my kitchen. I did not have a ladder, and I knew that painting would take a long time. A friend brought over her ladder and helped me. Working together was fun, and we quickly finished the job.* ***Cooperation*** *is the best way to get things done.*

Use a **Roundtable** to have students discuss the Big Question, recounting their experiences of working with someone else to get a job done. Remind students to speak clearly and at an understandable pace.

- Seat students around tables in groups of four.
- Have students take turns answering the Big Question by recounting experiences to the group.

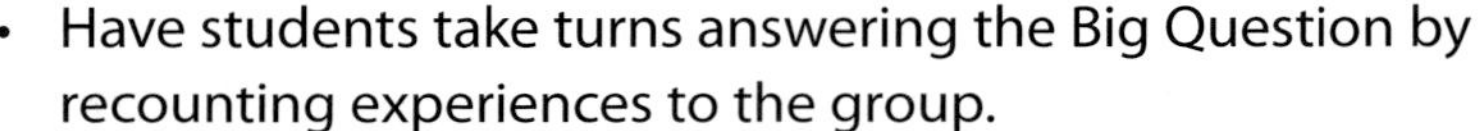

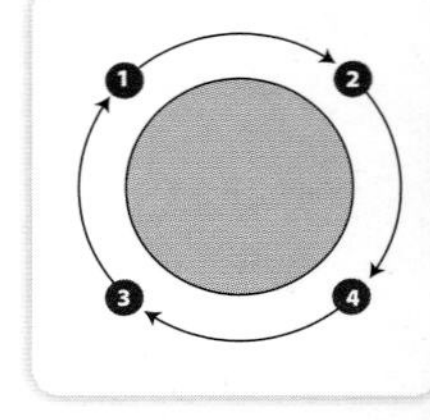

Roundtable

*For **Roundtable**, see page BP46.*

Vocabulary Strategy

2 Prefixes ☑ **Anthology** page 234

Project **Student eEdition** page 234 and read aloud the first two sentences. Elaborate: *Another word part is the base word. When you know the meaning of the base word in a longer word, the prefix helps you define the complete word. In the word* preview *the base word is* view. *What does* view *mean?* (to look at) *This helps you understand that the longer word* preview *has to do with looking at something.*

Write the word *unfold*. Ask: *Which part of the word is the prefix?* (un-) *Which part of the word is the base word?* (-fold) *What does* fold *mean?* (to bend one part over another part) *This helps you understand that the longer word* unfold *has to do with bending something.* Have students follow the same process to determine the meaning of *pregame*.

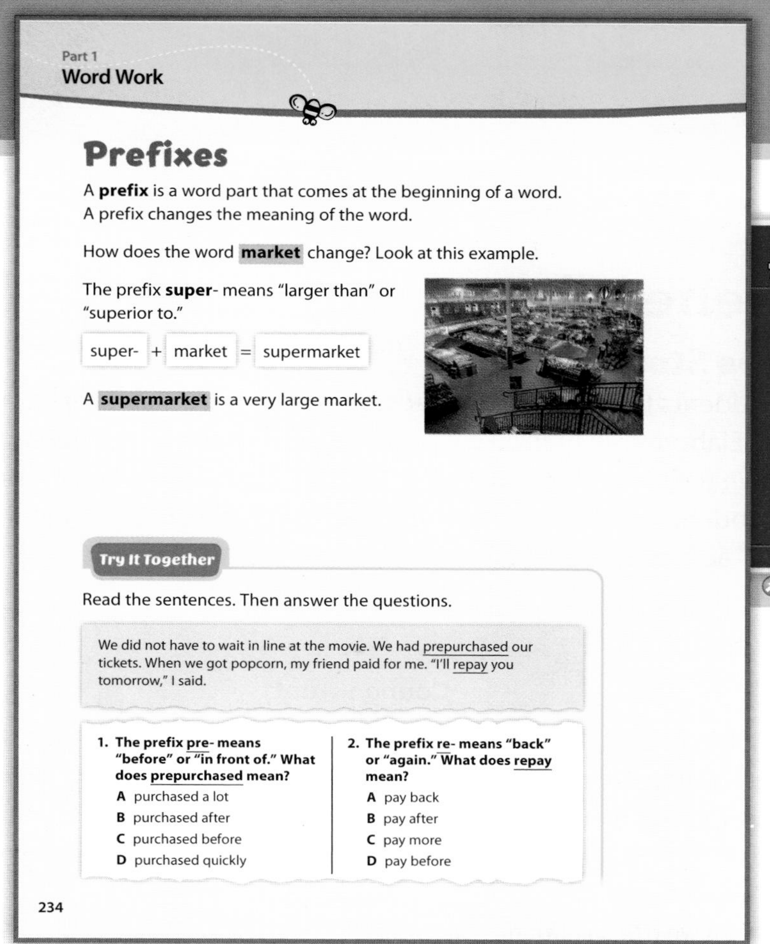
Part 1
Word Work

Prefixes

A **prefix** is a word part that comes at the beginning of a word. A prefix changes the meaning of the word.

How does the word **market** change? Look at this example.

The prefix **super**- means "larger than" or "superior to."

super- + market = supermarket

A **supermarket** is a very large market.

Try It Together

Read the sentences. Then answer the questions.

We did not have to wait in line at the movie. We had prepurchased our tickets. When we got popcorn, my friend paid for me. "I'll repay you tomorrow," I said.

1. The prefix pre- means "before" or "in front of." What does prepurchased mean?
A purchased a lot
B purchased after
C purchased before
D purchased quickly

2. The prefix re- means "back" or "again." What does repay mean?
A pay back
B pay after
C pay more
D pay before

234

Anthology page 234

STUDENT TECHNOLOGY

Student eEdition

Resources

NGReach.com

Read each step of the explanation of *supermarket* aloud as you model how to figure out the word's meaning: *I see a place where people buy things. I know that a* ***market*** *is a place where people buy things. I know that* super *means "larger than." When the prefix* super- *is added to the base word* ***-market****, it forms* supermarket. *I can figure out that a supermarket is a very large* ***market****.*

3 Try It Together **Anthology** page 234

Read the directions aloud. Then read aloud the example sentences as students follow along. Have partners work together to answer the questions. (question 1: C; question 2: A)

See **Differentiate**

Check & Reteach

OBJECTIVE: Use Prefixes to Determine Word Meanings ☑

As students answer the questions, determine whether they are able to use the meanings of prefixes and base words to define the longer words.

If students have difficulty, ask them to write each word and draw a vertical line after the prefix *pre-* or *re-*. Ask: *What words are left over?* (purchased; ***pay***) Model how to put these words together with the prefix meanings, "before" and "back," to define the complete words.

Weekly Writing

Gather students' writing throughout the week:

- ✓ Daily Writing Skills Practice (T233q–T233r)
- ✓ Power Writing (T233s, T234c, T237a, T239c, T239e)
- ✓ Writing (T234b, T237, T239, T239d, T239g)
- ✓ Writing Project (T239i–T239l)

Differentiate

EL English Learners

ISSUE Students have difficulty identifying the base words and understanding their meanings.

STRATEGY Have students cover the prefixes *pre-* or *re-* in each word and identify the remaining letters as the base word. Allow them to use dictionaries to define each base word in order to answer each question.

AL Above Level

ISSUE Students are ready to define more words with prefixes.

STRATEGY Provide students with additional words with the prefixes, such as *rejoin, preview,* and *supercenter.* Have them identify the prefixes and define each word. Then have students explain how they determined the words' meanings.

Fluency

Model Expression As you read the **Read Aloud**, model how to use expression to read realistic fiction. Explain: *When you read with expression, you change your voice to match what is happening in the story and how the characters feel.*

Comprehension

4 Describe Story Elements 

Remind students that they know that stories always contain characters, settings, and plots. Elaborate: *In many stories, the actions of characters cause certain events to happen in the plot. These actions tell you what the character is like.* Display **eVisual 4.9**. Ask students to listen for clues about the setting of the story and how the characters' actions cause events to happen.

Read Aloud

Realistic Fiction

Coupon Hunt

Zach is eating breakfast at the kitchen table with his dad and his little sister, Molly. He glances at a newspaper and spies an **advertisement** for a new cereal.

"Dad, can we try this kind of cereal?" Zach asks.

Dad thinks about it. "I'm sorry, but that cereal is more expensive than the one we usually get," he said.

"What if we had a coupon?" Zach asks.

"What's a coupon?" asks Molly.

Zach shows Molly the coupon section of the newspaper. "If Dad uses these when he shops, he can save **money**. For example, if he uses this coupon, he will **pay** 50 cents less than the regular price on this type of peanut butter. Coupons will help Dad save **money**."

Dad smiles and says, "If you can find a coupon for the cereal, I will use it."

Zach and Molly are excited as they work together to find coupons. "I'll search on the computer," Zach tells Molly. "You check Dad's newspapers. **Cooperation** makes the job easier."

At the end of the week, Zach and Molly match coupons to Dad's shopping list. Zach says, "Dad can save $14.00 with all these coupons. We even found a coupon for the cereal I wanted!"

Dad is impressed. "You're pretty good at this," he tells them.

"If you want, we can do this every week," Zach says.

Dad laughs and says, "And we can discuss the shopping list over bowls of your new favorite cereal."

NGReach.com **Read Aloud: eVisual 4.9**

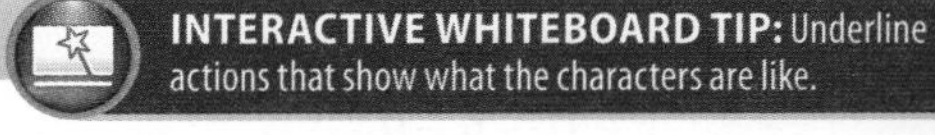

INTERACTIVE WHITEBOARD TIP: Underline actions that show what the characters are like.

Have partners identify the three characters in the story (Dad, Molly, Zach) and the setting (their house). Ask: *What does Dad do that causes another event?* (Dad refuses to buy the cereal Zach wants.) *What event does that cause to happen?* (Zach suggests using coupons to save money.) *What does Zach's action tell you about him?* (Zach knows a lot about how to save money.) Have students discuss how other characters' actions cause events in the plot to happen.

See **Differentiate**

Check & Reteach

OBJECTIVE: Describe Story Elements ☑

As students discuss the story, check if they can describe the story elements and explain how characters' actions relate to the plot. If students have difficulty, ask: *What does Zach do that causes another event?* (Zach explains to his sister how coupons work.) *What event does that cause to happen?* (Zach and Molly look for coupons together.) *What does Zach's action tell you about him?* (Zach is patient and good at explaining things to his sister.)

Writing

5 Write About Story Elements

Tell students they will write descriptions of story elements. Model writing a description about one story element in "Coupon Hunt":

Think Aloud	Write
The characters in "Coupon Hunt" are Zach, Dad, and Molly. I will describe each of them.	Dad is careful with money. Zach understands how to save money, too. He suggests a way to save enough money to buy the cereal he wants. Molly is helpful. She helps Zach find coupons to save money.

*For **Writing Routine 2**, see page BP48.*

Organize the class into small groups. Assign character, setting, or plot to each group. Have each group work together to write a description of their assigned story element. Have groups share their descriptions with the class. Have students copy and add their groups' descriptions to their Weekly Writing folders.

WRAP-UP Have partners describe the main characters and setting in "Mama Panya's Pancakes" and explain how the characters' actions cause events in the plot.

Daily Language Arts

Daily Spelling and Word Work ☑
Pretest page T233m

Daily Grammar ☑
Write the following sentence: *He spies an advertisement*. Point out that *he* is the subject of the verb *spies*. Then use page T233o to teach subject-verb agreement with verbs that end in *-y*.

Daily Writing Skills ☑
Ask: *Who are the three characters in the* ***Read Aloud****?* (Zach, Molly, Dad) Then use page T233q to teach how to introduce characters.

Differentiate

BL Below Level

ISSUE Students have difficulty describing how the characters' actions affect the plot.

STRATEGY Have students use cause-and-effect chains to track how actions lead to events.

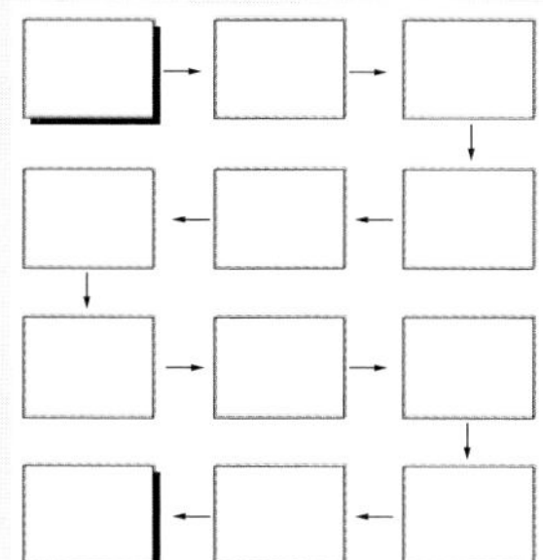

SN Special Needs

ISSUE Students have trouble remembering which character performs which action.

STRATEGY Have students write each character's name on a card. As you reread "Coupon Hunt," pause and have students hold up cards to answer questions, such as: *Who said this, Molly, Zach, or Dad?* or *Who is looking through newspapers?*

Day 2 Read and Comprehend
Realistic Fiction

OBJECTIVES

Thematic Connection: Jobs and Money

- ☑ Use Prefixes to Determine Word Meanings
- ☑ Determine Importance
- ☑ Describe Story Elements

MATERIALS

timer

Power Writing

Have students write as much as they can as well as they can for one minute about the word *seller.*

*For **Writing Routine 1**, see page BP47.*

COMMON CORE STANDARDS

Reading	
Recount Stories and Determine the Central Message	CC.3.Rlit.2
Describe Characters and Explain Characters' Actions	CC.3.Rlit.3
Distinguish Points of View	CC.3.Rlit.6
Read and Comprehend Literature	CC.3.Rlit.10
Identify Meaning of Prefixes and Suffixes	CC.3.Rfou.3.a
Read with Fluency to Support Comprehension	CC.3.Rfou.4
Read Orally with Accuracy and Appropriate Rate on Successive Readings	CC.3.Rfou.4.b
Writing	
Write Over Shorter Time for Specific Tasks	CC.3.W.10
Speaking and Listening	
Discuss Texts, Expressing Ideas Clearly	CC.3.SL.1
Language and Vocabulary	
Produce Simple Sentences	CC.3.L.1.i
Use Affixes as Clues	CC.3.L.4.b
Use Root Words as Clues	CC.3.L.4.c

WARM-UP

Ask partners to think about places where people buy food. Have them list as many places as they can think of. Partners can then share their lists with the class.

Vocabulary Strategy

1 More Prefixes ☑

Review the prefixes discussed on Day 1: *pre-*, *re-*, and *super-*. Ask students to recall the meaning of each prefix. Then display the prefixes *un-*, *mis-*, and *dis-*. Explain: *These three prefixes have similar meanings:* un- *and* dis- *mean "not," or "the opposite of." For example,* unbelievable *means "not believable" and* disassemble *means the opposite of* assemble. Mis- *means "not correctly," so* misread *means "to read incorrectly."*

Display the words *unable*, *reread*, *disagree*, *misbehave*, *preview*, and *supersize*, and underline each prefix. Model using a prefix and a base word to determine word meanings: *The base word* able *means "can do something." I know that* un- *means "not."* Unable *must mean "cannot do something."*

Have partners use the prefixes and base words to determine meanings for the remaining words. Then have each student use a word with a prefix to make a statement about a selection read in this unit.

Check & Reteach

OBJECTIVE: Use Prefixes to Determine Word Meanings ☑

Listen as partners work together to determine whether they use meanings of base words and prefixes to define words with prefixes.

If students have difficulty using meanings of prefixes and base words to define words with prefixes, break down the thinking: *The base word of* reread *is* read. Read *means "to look at and understand text." I know that* re- *means "again."* Reread *must mean "to look at and understand text again."*

Academic Talk

2 Preview and Predict

Say: *Before you begin reading, study the title and illustrations to preview the text. Then predict what the text will be about.* Project **Student eEdition** pages 235–237. Have students silently read the title and study the illustrations. Then have partners discuss their predictions.

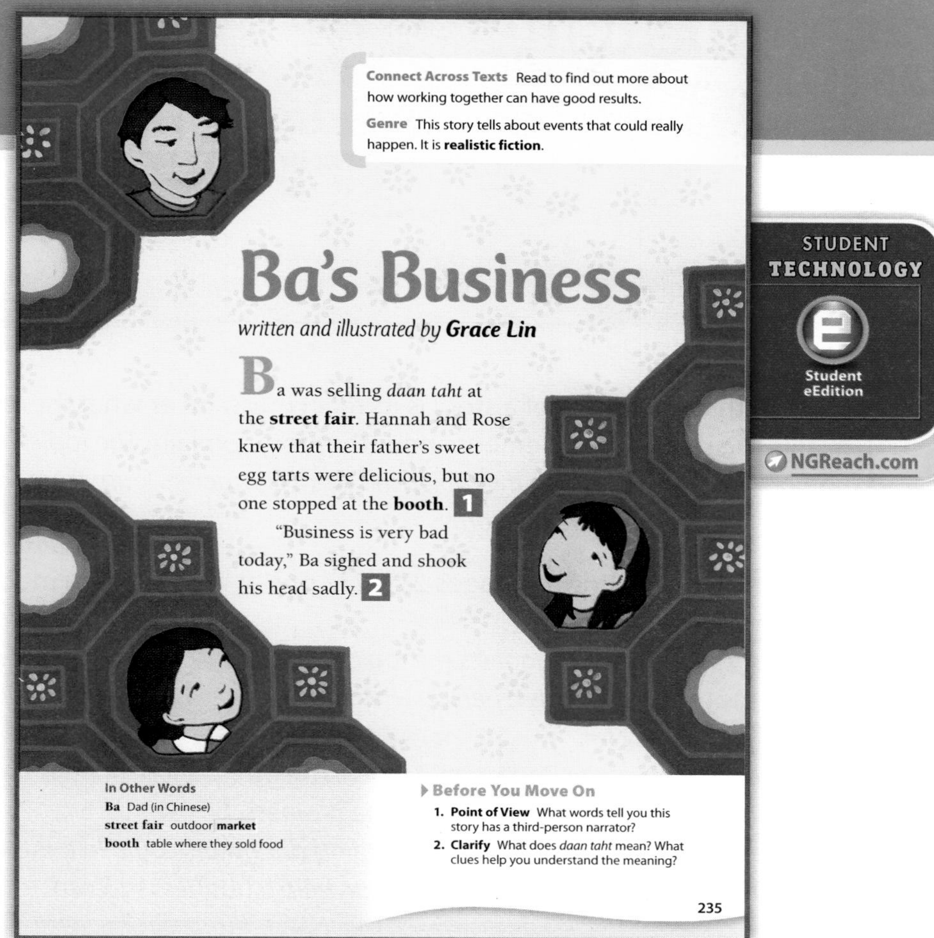

Anthology page 235

STUDENT TECHNOLOGY

Student eEdition

NGReach.com

Reading

3 Read Realistic Fiction

CONNECT ACROSS TEXTS Project **Student eEdition** page 235. Ask students to recall the results of the villagers working together in "Mama Panya's Pancakes." Then have a volunteer read aloud **Connect Across Texts**.

GENRE Read aloud the explanation of the genre. Point out the base word *real* in *realistic*. Explain that *–istic* means "in the style of." Clarify: *The story is not about real people and events, but the people seem real and the events could really happen.*

SOCIAL STUDIES BACKGROUND *Daan taht* is an English pastry popular in China. It has a sweet filling made with eggs. The filling is similar to *flan*.

Read and Build Comprehension

1 **Describe Story Elements** *What kind of person is Ba?* (Ba is a businessman who sells egg tarts.) *Describe where and when the story takes place.* (The story takes place in an outdoor market. It could be happening today.) *What do you know about the plot so far?* (Business is bad because no one is stopping at Ba's booth.)

2 **Determine Importance** *What is page 235 about?* (This part of the story is about how Ba's business is bad.) *What do you want to know after reading page 235?* (I want to know if Ba's business will get better.) *What will you read and learn in the rest of the story?* (I will read and learn about how working together can help a business.)

Fluency

Practice Expression, Accuracy, Rate As students read, monitor their expression, accuracy, and rate.

Answers Before You Move On

1. **Point of View** The words *his* and *their* tell me this story has a third-person narrator.
2. **Clarify** *Daan taht* is an egg tart. The second sentence in the story states that Ba's sweet egg tarts were delicious. This helps me know that *daan taht* is another name for sweet egg tarts.

Read and Comprehend

Realistic Fiction

Monday

Mini Lesson

Theme

Explain that the theme of a story is its main message or what the author wants the reader to remember about the story. Explain: *The topic, how important details relate to the topic, and what characters learn from the story are clues to the theme of a selection.*

Project **Student eEdition** pages 235–237 one at a time as you model the thinking:

- *A story's title usually suggests the topic of the story. The title "Ba's Business" tells me that the topic is a person who earns money by providing something that people pay for.*
- *The girls' actions are important details in the story. Those actions show how the family worked together to help the business.*
- *Ba learned that working together with his daughters could help his business.*
- *The theme is that working together can help a business succeed.*

Daily Language Arts

Daily Spelling and Word Work ☑
Practice Page T233m

Daily Grammar ☑
Display **Anthology** page 236, point to the sign, and say: *They take free samples.* Then use page T233o to teach more about subject-verb agreement.

Daily Writing Skills ☑
Point out that Hannah and Rose are helpful characters in "Ba's Business." Then use page T233q to practice creating characters.

Read and Build Comprehension

1 Describe Story Elements ☑ *What do Hannah and Rose do to help Ba's business?* (They make a sign and hand out free samples so people find out how good the tarts are and want to buy more.)

2 Determine Importance ☑ *What is page 236 about?* (This part of the story is about the girls' actions.) *What do you want to know after reading page 236?* (I want to know if the girls' actions help Ba's business.) *What do you read and learn on page 237?* (When I read that Ba sells all his tarts, I learn that working together can help a business succeed.)

Answers Before You Move On

1. **Determine Importance** ☑ Possible response: The most important part of the story to me is when Hannah and Rose help their father by making a sign and offering free samples. This is the most important part since it explains how Ba's business gets better because his daughters worked together to help their family.
2. **Theme** The theme is that when people work together, they can cause good results. At first, people are not buying any of Ba's egg tarts. The sisters work together to make a sign and give away free samples. These actions make a big difference and help their father's business succeed.

Check & Reteach

OBJECTIVE: Describe Story Elements ☑

Check for accurate responses to all the questions about story elements.
If students have difficulty describing story elements, explain: *What the characters do causes certain events to happen. By making a sign and handing out free samples, the girls cause people to buy all the daan taht.*

OBJECTIVE: Determine Importance ☑

Check for accurate responses to the questions about determining importance.
If students cannot determine importance, have them revisit each page of the story and prompt with these questions: *What is this page about? What do you want to know more about? What do you learn from reading this page or what will you learn from the next page?*

"Maybe we can make it better," Hannah whispered to Rose.

So Hannah made a large sign and Rose **offered free samples**.

People lined up to try the small pieces of *daan taht*.

"This is delicious!" everyone said. "I have to buy some for my family!" 1

FREE Samples daan taht

In Other Words
offered free samples gave people free pieces of *daan taht* to try

By the end of the day, Ba had sold **every last** *daan taht*.

"Business was very good today!" Hannah and Rose said to Ba.

Ba nodded and **grinned** at his daughters.

"With your help," he said, as he put an arm around each girl, "our business will be good every day." 2 BL SN

In Other Words
every last all of the
grinned smiled

Before You Move On

1. **Determine Importance** What part of the story is most important to you? Why?
2. **Theme** Write a sentence to tell the theme of the story. Give details to support your ideas.

Anthology
pages 236–237

Writing

4 Write About a Character's Actions

Tell students that they will write about a character in a story. Remind students that characters can cause events in a story. Elaborate: *Characters can also change during a story. If you think about what a character does or says at different times in the story, you can learn how the character changes.*

Model writing about how a character in "Mama Panya's Pancakes" changed: *In the beginning of the story, Mama Panya frowns because she is worried that she will not have enough food. At the end of the story, Mama Panya smiles at Adika because she knows she had worried for nothing.*

Have partners write about how a character changes in "Ba's Business." Have students add their responses to their Weekly Writing folders.

See **Differentiate**

WRAP-UP Have students recall characters' actions in stories they have read. Then have partners discuss how characters' actions cause events.

Best Practices

Model Academic Language As students talk, prompt their use of content and academic vocabulary words:

- *Can you say that in a different way?*
- *What Key Words relate to what you are saying?*

Differentiate

BL Below Level

ISSUE Students have difficulty explaining Ba's change.

STRATEGY Provide sentence frames:
At first, ______ feels ______. I know this because ______. Later, ______ feels ______. I know this because ______.

SN Special Needs

ISSUE Students have difficulty interpreting Ba's actions.

STRATEGY Mimic Ba's actions. Have students smile when they hear about actions that indicate "happy," and frown for those that indicate "not happy."

Day 3 Read and Comprehend

Realistic Fiction

OBJECTIVES

Thematic Connection: Jobs and Money

Compare Characters

☑ **Grammar: Use Present-Tense Action Verbs**

PROGRAM RESOURCES

PRINT & TECHNOLOGY

Comparison Chart: Practice Master PM4.11

Grammar Practice: Practice Master PM4.12

TECHNOLOGY ONLY

Grammar Passage: eVisual 4.16

MATERIALS

timer • index cards

Power Writing

Have students write as much as they can as well as they can in one minute about the word *reward*.

For ***Writing Routine 1,*** *see page BP47.*

COMMON CORE STANDARDS

Reading

Ask and Answer Questions About Text	CC.3.Rlit.1
Describe Characters and Explain Characters' Actions	CC.3.Rlit.3
Read and Comprehend Literature	CC.3.Rlit.10
Read with Fluency to Support Comprehension	CC.3.Rfou.4
Read Orally with Accuracy and Appropriate Rate on Successive Readings	CC.3.Rfou.4.b
Writing	
Write Over Shorter Time for Specific Tasks	CC.3.W.10
Speaking and Listening	
Follow Rules for Discussions	CC.3.SL.1.b
Language and Vocabulary	
Demonstrate Command of Grammar	CC.3.L.1
Form and Use Verb Tenses	CC.3.L.1.e
Ensure Subject-Verb Agreement	CC.3.L.1.f
Demonstrate Command of Spelling	CC.3.L.2
Use Knowledge of Language and Conventions	CC.3.L.3
Acquire and Use General Academic and Domain-Specific Words	CC.3.L.6

WARM-UP

Have partners review "Mama Panya's Pancakes" and "Ba's Business." Have Partner A choose one of the stories and retell it while pointing to the illustrations. Then Partner B retells the other selection using its illustrations.

Vocabulary Review

1 Review Social Studies and Academic Vocabulary

Project **Student eEdition** page 238 and point out the Key Words. Also display *theme, paraphrase,* and *determine*. Chorally read all the words as a class. Pause after each word and have a volunteer give the definition.

Have students write each word on a separate index card. Have each pair of students pick two cards and use the two words in a sentence that tells about the importance of working together.

Review and Integrate Ideas

2 Compare Characters **Anthology** page 238

Read aloud the introduction on **Student eEdition** page 238. As a class, summarize each story in a few sentences. Ask students to recall how Mama Panya and Ba changed as each story progressed.

Explain how the chart is organized and how to complete each row. Then have partners reread "Ba's Business" aloud and use **Practice Master PM4.11** to record how and why the characters in each story changed. Then read aloud the questions below the chart on page 238 and have partners use their charts to discuss answers to the questions.

Check & Reteach

OBJECTIVE: Compare Characters

As partners compare the characters, determine whether they can identify how and why the characters changed. If students have trouble, ask questions to guide discussion:

- *How does Mama Panya feel at the beginning of the story?* (worried) *How does she feel when people bring extra food?* (happy) *Why is she happy?* (because now there is enough food for everyone)
- *How does Ba feel at the beginning of the story? Why?* (worried; because he is not selling enough food) *How does Ba feel at the end of the story? Why?* (happy; because he sold all of his food)
- *What does Mama Panya learn from her guests?* (She learns not to worry because her friends will help when she is in need.) *What does Ba learn from his daughters?* (The girls have good ideas that can help him with his business.)

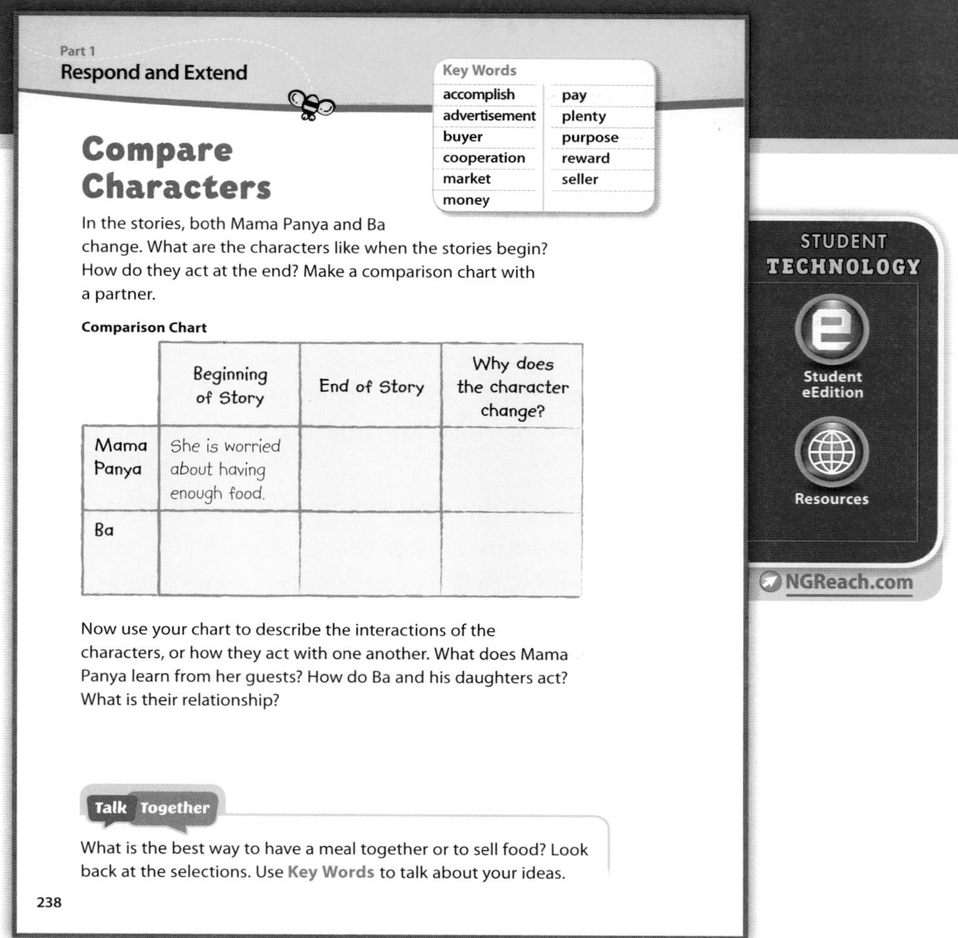

Part 1
Respond and Extend

Key Words

accomplish	pay
advertisement	plenty
buyer	purpose
cooperation	reward
market	seller
money	

Compare Characters

In the stories, both Mama Panya and Ba change. What are the characters like when the stories begin? How do they act at the end? Make a comparison chart with a partner.

Comparison Chart

	Beginning of Story	End of Story	Why does the character change?
Mama Panya	She is worried about having enough food.		
Ba			

Now use your chart to describe the interactions of the characters, or how they act with one another. What does Mama Panya learn from her guests? How do Ba and his daughters act? What is their relationship?

Talk Together

What is the best way to have a meal together or to sell food? Look back at the selections. Use **Key Words** to talk about your ideas.

238

Anthology page 238

Academic Talk

3 Talk Together **Anthology** page 238

Remind students that they have learned the rules for discussion (take turns speaking, acknowledge what others say, and state your own ideas). Read aloud the **Talk Together** question.

Use **Team Word Webbing** to have students discuss how people share meals and interact with others while buying food.

- Arrange students into teams of four.
- Have each team sit around a large piece of paper.
- Give each student on each team a different colored marker.
- Have teams write the topic in the center of the web: sharing food or buying food.
- Have students on each team add ideas to the nearest part of the web.
- Signal students to rotate the paper and have each student add to the ideas already on the nearest part of the web.
- Repeat the process until each team member has added to each part of the web.
- Have groups discuss the results of their word webs.

*For **Team Word Webbing**, see page BP46.*

A B C D

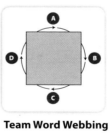

Team Word Webbing

Fluency

Practice Expression As partners reread the realistic fiction aloud, circulate and listen for correct expression.

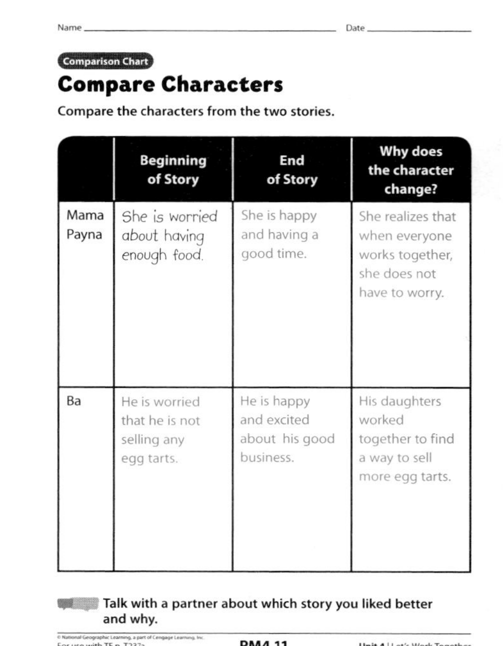

Name ______________________ Date __________

Comparison Chart

Compare Characters

Compare the characters from the two stories.

	Beginning of Story	End of Story	Why does the character change?
Mama Panya	She is worried about having enough food.	She is happy and having a good time.	She realizes that when everyone works together, she does not have to worry.
Ba	He is worried that he is not selling any egg tarts.	He is happy and excited about his good business.	His daughters worked together to find a way to sell more egg tarts.

Talk with a partner about which story you liked better and why.

For use with TE p. T237a PM4.11 Unit 4 | Let's Work Together

NGReach.com **Practice Master PM4.11**

Differentiate

EL English Learners

ISSUE In Chinese, Haitian, Creole, Hmong, and Vietnamese languages, verbs are not inflected for person and number.

STRATEGY To help speakers of these languages become familiar with present-tense verb inflections in English, provide students with present-tense action-verb conjugation charts showing, for example, *I eat, you eat, he eats, she eats*, and so on.

AL Above Level

ISSUE Students have mastered subject/present-tense action-verb agreement.

STRATEGY Have students explain why the action verbs in the first two sentences have *-s* at the ends. Then have them explain why the verb in the last sentence does not have *-s* at the end.

Name ______________ Date ______________

Grammar: Practice

Farmer's Market

Grammar Rules Present-Tense Action Verbs

A present-tense action verb must agree with its subject.

Use **-s** at the end of an action verb if the subject is ***he***, ***she***, or ***it***.	Carmella **loves** street fairs. She **takes** me along with her.
Do **not** add *-s* to the verb if the subject is ***I***, ***you***, ***we***, or ***they***.	Buyers **walk** slowly through the fairs. They **buy** a lot of things.

Fill in each blank with the present-tense verb form that agrees with the subject.

My parents take (take) us to the farmer's market. We enjoy (enjoy) all the sights, smells, and sounds. Farmers sell (sell) vegetables and fruit. One farmer sells (sell) flowers, too. My mother buys (buy) flowers every week. She loves (love) flowers. One man cooks (cook) delicious burritos. A woman paints (paint) faces. Two men carve (carve) wooden toys. They call (call) out to buyers. The farmer's market is so much fun! It makes (make) me smile.

Choose three verbs from the story and write new sentences. Read them to a partner.

For use with TE p. T238a PM4.12 Unit 4 | Let's Work Together

NGReach.com **Practice Master PM4.12**

Grammar Focus

4 Present-Tense Action Verbs ☑ Anthology page 239

Project **Student eEdition** page 239. Have a volunteer read aloud the introduction. Have a volunteer explain what they know about subject/action-verb agreement.

Read aloud and explain each rule and example shown in the chart. Clarify the relationship between the nouns *Adika, Mama,* and *The fire* and the words *he, she,* and *it* and explain how the words *we* and *they* and sometimes *you* take the place of plural nouns in sentences like this: *Dad and I wash the dishes together.* (*We wash the dishes together.*) *You and Mom read together.* (*You read together.*)

Then display **eVisual 4.16** and read aloud the passage.

Grammar Passage

Greta helps Dad prepare dinner. First, Dad puts the rolls in the oven. Then Greta and Dad mix the ingredients for pasta and bean salad. Greta walks to her friend's house. She asks her friend to join the family for dinner. Greta and her friend walk to Greta's house. The families eat dinner together. They enjoy the food and the company.

NGReach.com **Grammar Passage: eVisual 4.16**

INTERACTIVE WHITEBOARD TIP: Circle each subject. Underline each action verb.

Identify the first subject and action verb (Greta; helps) and ask: *Do the subject and verb agree?* (Yes.) *How do you know?* (The subject is Greta. I can use *she* in place of *Greta*. When the subject is *he* or *she*, the verb should end in *-s*.) Have students identify the remaining subjects and present-tense action verbs in the passage.

5 Read Present-Tense Action Verbs Anthology page 239

Read aloud the directions and the sentences about Mama Panya and Adika. Then have partners work together to follow the directions.

See **Differentiate**

6 Write Present-Tense Action Verbs Anthology page 239

Read aloud the directions and have students work independently. Provide support as necessary. Assign **Practice Master PM4.12**.

Check & Reteach

OBJECTIVE: Grammar: Use Present-Tense Action Verbs ☑

As students write, check to make sure their subjects and verbs agree.

If students have difficulty, ask: *What is the subject of your sentence?* If students use a proper noun, have them replace it with the appropriate pronoun. Then point to the corresponding rule in the chart. Ask: *What is the verb in your sentence? Should it end in an -s?* Then help students point to the rule in the chart to check the answer.

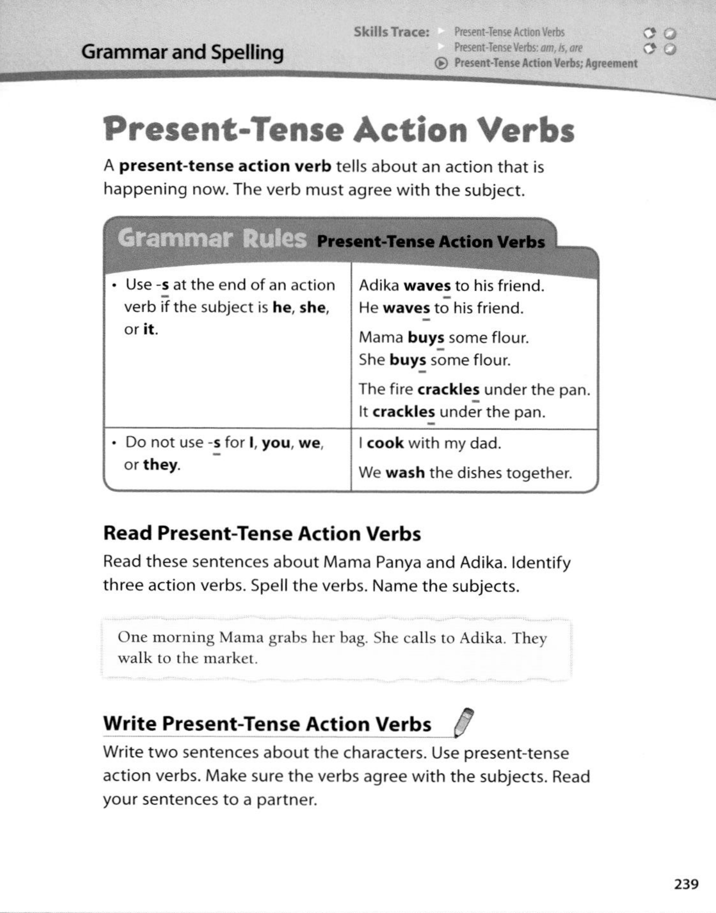

Grammar and Spelling

Skills Trace: Present-Tense Action Verbs; Present-Tense Verbs: *am, is, are*; **Present-Tense Action Verbs; Agreement**

Present-Tense Action Verbs

A **present-tense action verb** tells about an action that is happening now. The verb must agree with the subject.

Grammar Rules Present-Tense Action Verbs

• Use -**s** at the end of an action verb if the subject is **he**, **she**, or **it**.	Adika **waves** to his friend. He **waves** to his friend. Mama **buys** some flour. She **buys** some flour. The fire **crackles** under the pan. It **crackles** under the pan.
• Do not use -**s** for **I**, **you**, **we**, or **they**.	I **cook** with my dad. We **wash** the dishes together.

Read Present-Tense Action Verbs

Read these sentences about Mama Panya and Adika. Identify three action verbs. Spell the verbs. Name the subjects.

> One morning Mama grabs her bag. She calls to Adika. They walk to the market.

Write Present-Tense Action Verbs

Write two sentences about the characters. Use present-tense action verbs. Make sure the verbs agree with the subjects. Read your sentences to a partner.

239

Anthology page 239

Writing

7 Write to Reinforce Grammar

Have each student choose one of the readings from the week and write a paragraph describing part of its plot. Tell students that they should use present-tense action verbs that agree with subjects in their writing. Model writing a sentence: Adika runs ahead of Mama. Then circle *Adika,* underline *runs,* and explain how the subject and verb agree.

After students write their paragraphs, have them circle each subject and underline each present-tense action verb. Have partners use the Grammar Rules chart on page 239 to check each other's work for subject-verb agreement. Then have students add their paragraphs to their Weekly Writing folders.

WRAP-UP Have students think about what the characters in each story learned. Ask: *What might the characters do the next time they are at a* ***market****? How will their actions be different than before?* Ask students to share their ideas with a partner.

Daily Language Arts

Daily Spelling and Word Work

Practice Page T233n

Daily Grammar

Display the last sentence of the **Read Aloud** on page T238a: *They enjoy the food and the company.* Then use page T233p to teach more about present-tense action verbs.

Daily Writing Skills

Point out the characters in the **Grammar Passage** and then use page T233r to continue practicing how to introduce characters.

Day 4 Read and Comprehend

Short Stories

OBJECTIVES

Thematic Connection: Jobs and Money

- ☑ **Compare Story Elements**
- ☑ **Use Prefixes to Determine Word Meanings**

PROGRAM RESOURCES

PRINT & TECHNOLOGY

Mark-Up Reading: Practice Masters PM4.13–PM4.15

TECHNOLOGY ONLY

Mark-Up Model 4.1 or Model 4.1 PDF

Vocabulary Strategy Practice: eVisual 4.17

Name ______________ Date ______________

Mark-Up Reading

The Bird Bank by Grace Lin

During the winter, Hannah and Rose earned nickels from their father. Sometimes they would shovel snow or sweep the house. Ba would give them each a nickel and they put the nickels in their green bird bank.

Every time Hannah and Rose put their nickels in the bird bank it would sing "Tweet! Tweet!"

But in the spring, the bird bank stopped singing. It would not swallow Rose's nickel.

"Hannah!" Rose said. "Our bird bank is full!"

Shopping by Grace Lin

Hannah and Rose looked at all the stores. What should they buy?

"Look at the birds!" Rose said, pointing at a pet store window. "I like the yellow one."

"I like the blue one," Hannah said. "Let's go buy them!"

But Hannah and Rose did not have enough money for a yellow bird or a blue bird. On the shelf there was a birdhouse.

"We can buy the birdhouse," Rose said. "Should we buy that instead?"

Hannah nodded and they did.

© National Geographic Learning, a part of Cengage Learning, Inc.
For use with TE pp. T239a–T239h PM4.13 Unit 4 | Let's Work Together!

NGReach.com **Practice Masters PM4.13–PM4.15**

COMMON CORE STANDARDS

Reading	
Describe Characters	CC.3.Rlit.3
Refer to Parts of Stories	CC.3.Rlit.5
Describe How Successive Parts Build	CC.3.Rlit.5
Compare and Contrast Stories	CC.3.Rlit.9
Read and Comprehend Literature	CC.3.Rlit.10
Read with Fluency to Support Comprehension	CC.3.Rfou.4
Read Orally with Accuracy and Appropriate Rate on Successive Readings	CC.3.Rfou.4.b
Writing	
Write Over Shorter Time for Specific Purposes	CC.3.W.10
Speaking and Listening	
Discuss Texts, Expressing Ideas Clearly	CC.3.SL.1
Draw on Preparation to Explore Ideas	CC.3.SL.1.a
Language and Vocabulary	
Identify Meaning of Prefixes and Suffixes	CC.3.Rfou.3.a
Use Affixes as Clues	CC.3.L.4.b
Use Root Words as Clues	CC.3.L.4.c

WARM-UP

Give examples of small businesses that students could run, such as dog walking and leaf raking, and have them suggest others. Have them think of clever ways to let people know about the product or service of each business.

Comprehension

1 Compare Story Elements ☑

Remind students that they have already learned how to identify the story elements of character, setting, and plot.

SCREEN 1

1 Explain that students will compare elements in multiple stories. Display and read aloud **Mark-Up Model 4.1**. Have students follow along using **Practice Master PM4.13**. Invite volunteers to highlight text that identifies the characters and click the Characters button. Have students mark up **Practice Master PM4.13**.

2 Remind students that setting is time and place. Ask: *Which words in the story show time?* (*during the winter, in the spring*) *Which words tell where the story happens?* (*the house*) Have volunteers highlight these words and click the Settings button. Ask: *What is the first event in this story?* (Hannah and Rose earn money doing chores for their father.) Ask: *What are the events or plot in this story?* (The girls earn money doing chores, put money in a bird bank, and fill their bank.) Click on the arrow.

SCREEN 2

3 Read aloud the next story. Have students highlight the characters and click the Characters button. Ask: *Are these the same characters from "The Bird Bank"?* (Yes.) Remind students that stories can have multiple settings. Invite volunteers to highlight setting clues and click the Settings button. Ask: *Do the stories share a setting?* (No.) Have volunteers summarize the plot. (The sisters go shopping, enter a pet store to buy birds, and buy a birdhouse.) Click on the arrow to the next screen.

SCREEN 3

4 Have students review the characters, settings, and plot in "The Bird Bank" and erase the left side of the diagram to confirm answers. Have students add the information to **Practice Master PM4.15**. Ask: *Why aren't Hannah and Rose listed here?* (They appear in both stories.) Have students discuss the story elements in "Shopping," erase the diagram to confirm, and mark up **Practice Master PM4.15**.

Have students read **Practice Master PM4.14** and highlight characters and settings. Then have students complete the Venn diagram on **Practice Master PM4.15**. Remind them to also list the events. Have partners share their mark-ups.

SCREEN 1

NATIONAL GEOGRAPHIC Reach for Reading

The Bird Bank

by Grace Lin

1 During the winter, Hannah and Rose earned nickels from their father. Sometimes they would shovel snow or sweep the house. Ba would give them each a nickel and they put the nickels in their green bird bank.

Every time Hannah and Rose put their nickels in the bird bank it would sing "Tweet! Tweet!"

But in the spring, the bird bank stopped singing. It would not swallow Rose's nickel.

"Hannah!" Rose said. "Our bird bank is full!"

2 Highlight in yellow the characters.
Highlight in green the settings.

Characters Settings

NGReach.com **Mark-Up Model 4.1**

SCREEN 2

NATIONAL GEOGRAPHIC Reach for Reading

Shopping

by Grace Lin

3 Hannah and Rose looked at all the stores. What should they buy?

"Look at the birds!" Rose said, pointing at a pet store window. "I like the yellow one."

"I like the blue one," Hannah said. "Let's go buy them!"

But Hannah and Rose did not have enough money for a yellow bird or a blue bird. On the shelf there was a birdhouse.

"We can buy the birdhouse," Rose said. "Should we buy that instead?"

Hannah nodded and they did.

3 Highlight in yellow the characters.
Highlight in green the settings.

SCREEN 3

NATIONAL GEOGRAPHIC Reach for Reading

4 Erase to reveal which story elements are only in one story and which are in both stories.

"The Bird Bank"	Both	"Shopping"
Ba, their father	sisters Hannah and Rose	pet store and other stores
the house	in the spring	sisters go shopping
during the winter		enter store to buy birds
sisters earn money doing chores		buy a birdhouse
put money in bird bank		
fill bird bank		

Check & Reteach

OBJECTIVE: Compare Story Elements ☑

Review students' marked-up **Practice Masters PM4.13–PM4.15** to check if they can compare the characters, setting, and plot in the three stories.

If students have difficulty comparing story elements, ask questions such as these:

- *Which characters appear in only one story?* (Ba and Mrs. Alexis)
- *Which stories are set in the house?* ("The Bird Bank" and "Tweet! Tweet!")
- *In which stories do Hannah and Rose buy a birdhouse?* ("Shopping" and "Tweet! Tweet!")

Fluency ✓

Model and Practice Expression Explain: *When you read, change your voice to match the feelings expressed by the author.* Model reading the first two paragraphs from **Practice Master PM4.14** with expression. Point out sentences such as "What should they buy?" and "'Look at the birds!'" Have partners read the remainder of the selection aloud several times, improving their expression with each reading.

Daily Language Arts

Daily Spelling and Word Work ☑
Practice page T233n

Daily Grammar ☑
Point out the subject-verb agreement in the last line of dialogue on **Practice Master 4.13.** (*we buy*) Then use page T233p to correct errors with subject-verb agreement and present-tense verbs.

Daily Writing Skills ☑
Point out how the characters are introduced on **Practice Master PM4.13.** Then use page T233r to review how to introduce characters.

Power Writing

Have students write as much as they can as well as they can in one minute about a bird.

*For **Writing Routine 1**, see page BP47.*

Vocabulary Practice

2 Prefixes ☑

Remind students that they have learned how to use context clues to identify the meaning of words with prefixes. Display **eVisual 4.17**.

Vocabulary Strategy Practice

1. Hannah disliked the cold, but her sister Rose enjoyed winter weather.
2. Rose had mislaid the broom, so she had to hunt for it before she could sweep the house.
3. Hannah recounted the nickels in their bank several times, so the sisters knew what they could spend.
4. The birdhouse they bought looked unfinished, so they decided to paint it.
5. Hannah and Rose bought superfine sandpaper to smooth out the rough edges of the birdhouse.

NGReach.com **Vocabulary Strategy: eVisual 4.17**

INTERACTIVE WHITEBOARD TIP: Have students circle the context clues.

For each sentence, have one partner identify and list the word with a prefix and the meaning of the prefix. Have the other partner identify a context clue to the meaning of the word and then use the clue to write its meaning. Then have partners switch tasks. Model the strategy with *disliked*: *The word with a prefix in the first sentence is* disliked. *The prefix* dis- *means "not." The context clue* but her sister Rose enjoyed *shows that* disliked *means the opposite, or "did not enjoy."*

Check & Reteach

OBJECTIVE: Use Prefixes to Determine Word Meanings ☑

Review partners' lists to check if students can use context to identify the meaning of words with prefixes.

If students have difficulty using context, support the process by asking questions such as the following:

- *If Rose had to hunt for the broom, does* mislaid *mean that the broom was where she expected to find it or that it was lost?* (It was lost.)
- *What does* several times *show about the meaning of* recount? (*Recount* means "to add up more than once.")
- *If the birdhouse looked unfinished, does* unfinished *mean that it was decorated or that it needed to be painted?* (needed to be painted)
- *What does* smooth out the rough edges *show about the meaning of* superfine? (*Superfine* means "very smooth or fine.")

Academic Talk

3 Discuss Story Elements

Form small groups. Explain: *In your groups you will discuss one story element—characters, setting, or plot—in "Ba's Business" and* ***Practice Masters PM4.13–PM4.14****.* Have students discuss what new information they have learned about Hannah and Rose and their lives. Remind students to use discussion rules. Give groups time to hold their discussions.

Writing

4 Write to Compare Story Elements

Introduce the activity: *Now write a paragraph comparing the characters, setting, and plot in the stories in* ***Practice Masters PM4.13–PM4.14****.* Model the process by comparing the story elements of "Ba's Business" and the "The Bird Bank," the first story in **Practice Master PM4.13**. Remind students that they can use the diagram on **Practice Master PM4.15** to help them.

Think Aloud	Write
First, I'll compare the characters in both stories.	Hannah and Rose help their father in both "Ba's Business" and "The Bird Bank."
Then, I'll compare the settings.	"Ba's Business" takes place in one day. "The Bird Bank" takes place over several months.
Last, I'll compare how events in both stories are similar or different.	In "Ba's Business," Hannah and Rose help their father earn money. In "The Bird Bank," they earn money doing chores.

For ***Writing Routine 2****, see page BP48.*

Have students write their own comparisons. After students read aloud their comparisons, have them add their paragraphs to their Weekly Writing folders.

See **Differentiate**

WRAP-UP Form small groups. Ask: *What if Hannah and Rose had enough money to buy the birds they wanted? How would the events in "Shopping" and "Tweet!, Tweet!" have changed?* Have students brainstorm three events that could have happened. As students brainstorm, prompt them with questions: *Where would they have kept the birds? What might Ba have said?* Then have groups share their events with the class.

Differentiate

BL Below Level

Students have difficulty comparing story elements.

STRATEGY Have students review the stories to answer the following questions:

- *Who are the main people in each story? Which characters appear in both stories?*
- *When does the first story happen? When does the second story happen? Do the stories happen at the same time?*
- *Where does the first story happen? Where does the second story happen? Do the stories happen in the same place?*
- *What are the main things that happen in the first story? What are the main things that happen in the second story? Which events are the same? Which are different?*

AL Above Level

ISSUE Students satisfy the minimum requirements for the assignment.

STRATEGY Challenge students to extend their comparisons by showing the effects of different story events. Have students answer the following questions:

- *Do the events in one story create more suspense than the other story's events?*
- *Are one story's events funnier—or sadder—than the other story's events?*
- *Does one story's ending seem more surprising than the other story's ending?*

Review and Compare

Short Stories and Realistic Fiction

OBJECTIVES

Thematic Connection: Jobs and Money

☑ Use Prefixes to Determine Word Meanings

☑ Compare Themes

PROGRAM RESOURCES

PRINT & TECHNOLOGY

Mark-Up Reading: Practice Masters PM4.13–PM4.15

TECHNOLOGY ONLY

Vocabulary Strategy Practice: eVisual 4.18

Comparison Chart: eVisual 4.19

Power Writing

Have students write as much as they can as well as they can in one minute about the word *share*.

*For **Writing Routine 1,** see page BP47.*

COMMON CORE STANDARDS

Reading	
Compare and Contrast Stories	CC.3.Rlit.9
Read and Comprehend Literature	CC.3.Rlit.10
Writing	
Write Over Shorter Time for Specific Purposes	CC.3.W.10
Speaking and Listening	
Discuss Texts, Building on Others' Ideas	CC.3.SL.1
Discuss Texts, Expressing Ideas Clearly	CC.3.SL.1
Follow Rules for Discussions	CC.3.SL.1.b
Language and Vocabulary	
Identify Meanings of Prefixes and Suffixes	CC.3.Rfou.3.a
Use Affixes as Clues	CC.3.L.4.b
Use Root Words as Clues	CC.3.L.4.c

WARM-UP

Form teams. Give each team one of the following prefixes: *super-*, *pre-*, *re-*, *un-*, *dis-*, and *mis-*. Give teams one minute to list as many words as they can with their prefixes. The team with the most words wins.

Vocabulary Practice

1 Prefixes ☑

Remind students that they have learned how to use context clues to identify the meanings of words with prefixes. Display **eVisual 4.18**.

Vocabulary Strategy Practice

"I misplaced the dog-walking fliers," Sean told his brother Jamie. "I need to find them so we can pass them out to our neighbors with dogs. I guess I'll turn on the printer and reprint them."

"You're so disorganized," Jamie said. "It's good that I'm neat. The fliers are on the kitchen table."

"Great," Sean said. "Thanks. You are unbelievable! You always know where everything is."

 **Vocabulary Strategy: eVisual 4.18**

 **INTERACTIVE WHITEBOARD TIP:** Have students circle the context clues.

Have partners determine the meanings of the words with prefixes. One partner identifies the word with a prefix in each sentence and gives the meaning of the prefix. The other partner identifies a context clue for the word and uses the clue to determine the word's meaning. Then partners switch tasks.

Check & Reteach

OBJECTIVE: Use Prefixes to Determine Word Meanings ☑

Monitor partners' exchanges to check if students can use context to determine the meanings of words with prefixes.

If students have difficulty, ask questions:

- *What does the context clue* turn on the printer *tell you about the meaning of* reprint? (It means Sean will "print again.")
- *If Jamie thinks it's good that he is neat, he is saying that Sean isn't. So, what does* disorganized *probably mean?* (the opposite of *neat*, or "messy")
- *If messy Sean thinks that Jamie is "unbelievable" because he never loses anything, what might* unbelievable *mean?* (amazing)

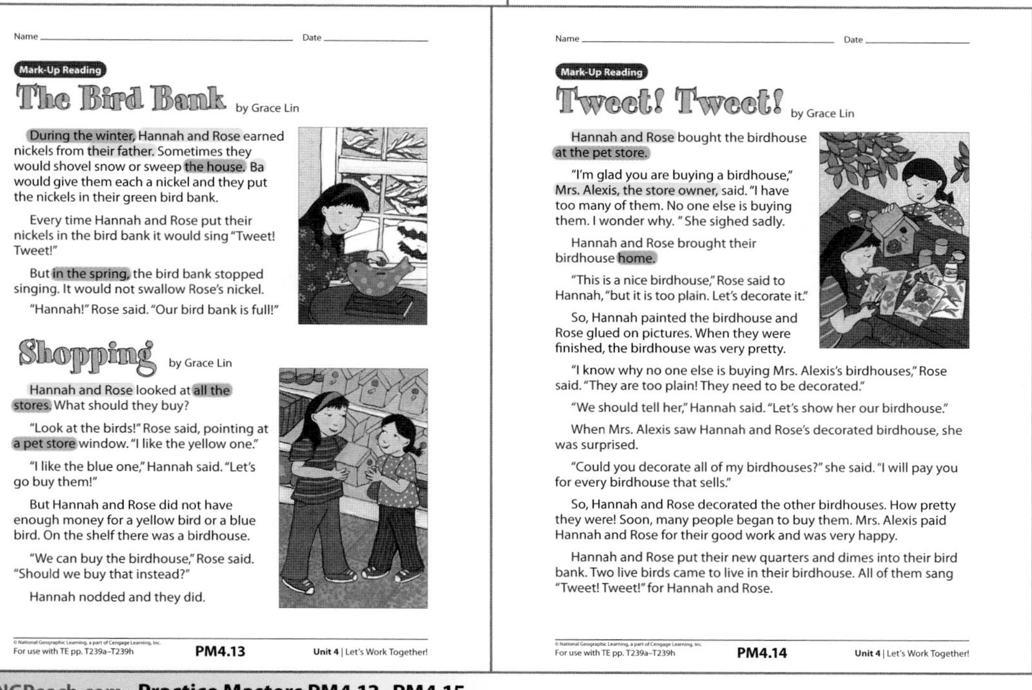
Name ______________________ Date ______________

Mark-Up Reading

The Bird Bank by Grace Lin

During the winter, Hannah and Rose earned nickels from their father. Sometimes they would shovel snow or sweep the house. Ba would give them each a nickel and they put the nickels in their green bird bank.

Every time Hannah and Rose put their nickels in the bird bank it would sing "Tweet! Tweet!"

But in the spring, the bird bank stopped singing. It would not swallow Rose's nickel.

"Hannah!" Rose said. "Our bird bank is full!"

Shopping by Grace Lin

Hannah and Rose looked at all the stores. What should they buy?

"Look at the birds!" Rose said, pointing at a pet store window. "I like the yellow one."

"I like the blue one," Hannah said. "Let's go buy them!"

But Hannah and Rose did not have enough money for a yellow bird or a blue bird. On the shelf there was a birdhouse.

"We can buy the birdhouse," Rose said. "Should we buy that instead?"

Hannah nodded and they did.

© National Geographic Learning, a part of Cengage Learning, Inc.
For use with TE pp. T239a–T239h PM4.13 Unit 4 | Let's Work Together!

Name ______________________ Date ______________

Mark-Up Reading

Tweet! Tweet! by Grace Lin

Hannah and Rose bought the birdhouse at the pet store.

"I'm glad you are buying a birdhouse," Mrs. Alexis, the store owner, said. "I have too many of them. No one else is buying them. I wonder why." She sighed sadly.

Hannah and Rose brought their birdhouse home.

"This is a nice birdhouse," Rose said to Hannah, "but it is too plain. Let's decorate it."

So, Hannah painted the birdhouse and Rose glued on pictures. When they were finished, the birdhouse was very pretty.

"I know why no one else is buying Mrs. Alexis's birdhouses," Rose said. "They are too plain! They need to be decorated."

"We should tell her," Hannah said. "Let's show her our birdhouse."

When Mrs. Alexis saw Hannah and Rose's decorated birdhouse, she was surprised.

"Could you decorate all of my birdhouses?" she said. "I will pay you for every birdhouse that sells."

So, Hannah and Rose decorated the other birdhouses. How pretty they were! Soon, many people began to buy them. Mrs. Alexis paid Hannah and Rose for their good work and was very happy.

Hannah and Rose put their new quarters and dimes into their bird bank. Two live birds came to live in their birdhouse. All of them sang "Tweet! Tweet!" for Hannah and Rose.

© National Geographic Learning, a part of Cengage Learning, Inc.
For use with TE pp. T239a–T239h PM4.14 Unit 4 | Let's Work Together!

NGReach.com **Practice Masters PM4.13–PM4.15**

Review and Integrate Ideas

2 Determine Themes

Remind students that the main message of a story is its theme. Explain: *To figure out the theme, look for clues from the characters, settings, and plot of the story.* Create a chart like the one below. Model for "The Bird Bank": *By working hard and saving their money, the sisters filled their bank. So, their hard work was rewarding.* Have students copy and complete the chart for the other two stories on **Practice Masters PM4.13–PM4.14**.

	Clues from Characters	Clues from Setting	Clues from Events	Theme
"The Bird Bank"	• are workers • are savers	can earn money at home	They earn and save money.	Hard work can be rewarding.
"Shopping"	want to buy birds spend what they can	see birds in the pet store	They don't have enough money for birds, so they buy a birdhouse.	Make the most of what you have.
"Tweet! Tweet!"	are creative share ideas are workers	store gives them a new way to earn money	Sisters decorate their birdhouse. Mrs. Alexis has them decorate more and pays for ones sold.	New ideas can help you and others.

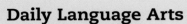

Daily Language Arts

Daily Spelling and Word Work
Test page T233m

Daily Grammar
Emphasize the subject-verb agreement in this sentence: Mrs. Alexis sells birdhouses. Then use page T233p to review and assess students' understanding of subject-verb agreement and present- tense verbs.

Daily Writing Skills
Point out how Mrs. Alexis is introduced on **Practice Master PM4.14**. Then use page T233r to review and assess students' understanding of how to introduce characters.

❸ Compare Themes

Explain to students that they will compare themes of "Ba's Business" and the stories on **Practice Masters PM4.13–PM4.14**. Display **eVisual 4.19**.

Comparison Chart

"Ba's Business"	"The Bird Bank"	"Shopping"	"Tweet! Tweet!"
Theme New ideas help others.	Theme Hard work can be rewarding.	Theme Make the most of what you have.	Theme New ideas can help you and others.

Comparison and Contrast

- In "Ba's Business," "The Bird Bank," and "Tweet! Tweet!" characters work hard.
- In "Ba's Business" and "Tweet! Tweet!" the characters share their ideas.
- Both "Ba's Business" and "Tweet! Tweet!" show that sharing ideas can help others and be rewarding.
- "Ba's Business," "The Bird Bank," and "Tweet! Tweet!" all show the rewards of working and helping.

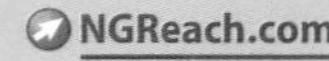
NGReach.com **Comparison Chart: eVisual 4.19**

INTERACTIVE WHITEBOARD TIP: Have students highlight similar themes.

Have students copy and complete both parts of the chart, using clues from their earlier entries. Then have partners compare themes. Ask:

- *Which themes seem most alike?* ("Ba's Business" and "Tweet! Tweet!")
- *Which themes seem most different?* ("The Bird Bank" and "Shopping")
- *Which themes relate to business?* ("Ba's Business" and "Tweet! Tweet!")

Check & Reteach

OBJECTIVE: Compare Themes

Monitor partners' discussions to check if students are able to compare themes.

If students have difficulty, model: *I look at themes in the chart and think about the events in each story. In "Ba's Business," Hannah and Rose come up with ideas to help their dad. In "Tweet! Tweet!" Hannah and Rose come up with ideas that make them happy, help Mrs. Alexis, and make them money. So both these themes are about how new ideas can help.*

Writing

❹ Write to Compare Themes

Introduce the activity: *Now you will write a paragraph comparing themes of two of the stories. Start by stating the themes. Then explain how they are alike and different by telling about the main events in each story and how these affect the characters.* Have students add their paragraphs to their Weekly Writing folders.

See **Differentiate**

Differentiate

EL English Learners

ISSUE Students lack the language skills necessary for comparing themes.

STRATEGY Provide language frames for comparing or contrasting the themes of two stories:

- The theme of [story title] is similar to the theme of [story title].
- The reason the themes are similar is that both stories ________.
- The theme of [story title] is different from the theme of [story title].
- The reason the themes are different is that ________.

SN Special Needs

ISSUE Students have difficulty organizing ideas for their paragraphs.

STRATEGY Give students a procedure for comparing themes:

Step 1 Write the themes of two of the stories.
Step 2 Explain how the themes are different.
Step 3 Explain how the themes are alike.

Academic Talk

5 Relate Readings to the Big Question

Have students recall the unit's Big Question: What's the best way to get things done? *Think about "Mama Panya's Pancakes," "Ba's Business,"* ***Practice Masters PM4.13–PM4.14,*** *and a* ***Small Group Reading*** *book you have read. What do these selections show about the importance of a group effort in accomplishing goals?*

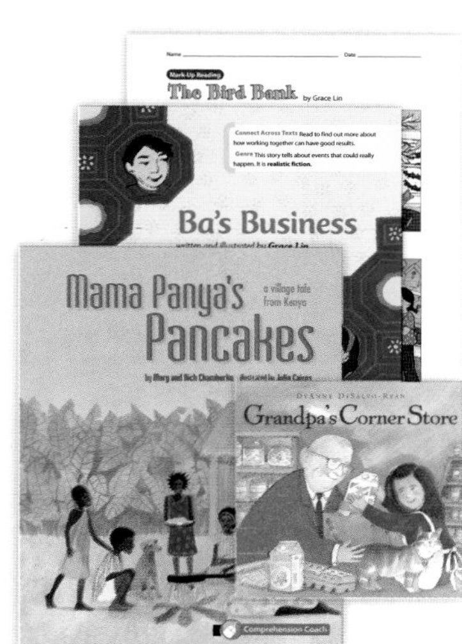

Model a response to the question for "Ba's Business": *Good ideas about how to get things done often come when people share ideas. Hannah and Rose know their father's egg tarts are delicious, but no one at the street fair is buying them until the sisters come up with their idea to give free samples.*

Use a **Think, Pair, Share** to have students continue discussion about how the readings relate to the Big Question. Remind students to follow the rules for discussion.

- Suggest a topic for students to think about, such as:
  - *Which kinds of projects can groups of people handle best?*
  - *Which attitudes help people to work together well?*
  - *How should people working together share their ideas about a project?*
  - *How can people share their different talents to get things done?*
- Have pairs discuss the topic.
- Have students individually share information with the class.

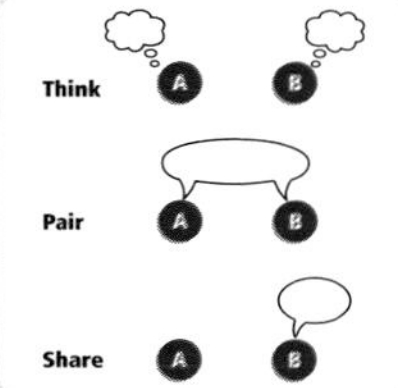

Think, Pair, Share

Best Practices

Link to Experience As students talk, connect selection topics to students' personal experiences: *Hannah and Rose help their father with his business. What are some ways you help your family?*

WRAP-UP Form small groups. Distribute markers and poster board. Have each group create a poster based on one of the stories they have read. It might be an invitation to Mama Panya's pancake dinner, an advertisement offering free samples of Ba's sweet egg tarts, or a flier showing Hannah's and Rose's decorated birdhouses for sale. When the groups have finished their posters, display them in the classroom.

OBJECTIVES

Thematic Connection: Jobs and Money
☑ **Write Realistic Fiction: Voice**

PROGRAM RESOURCES

PRINT & TECHNOLOGY
Writing Rubric: Assessment Master A4.39
TECHNOLOGY ONLY
Sample Realistic Fiction: eVisual 4.13
Writing Trait: Voice: eVisual 4.14
Magazine Maker

SUGGESTED PACING

DAY 1	Study a Model
DAY 2	Prewrite
DAY 3	Draft
DAY 4	Revise/Edit and Proofread
DAY 5	Publish and Present

Write Realistic Fiction

Display and read aloud the prompt.

> Write a short, realistic story about people working together. Write your story to entertain. You will read your story to the class and make an audio recording of it.

Study a Model

Read Realistic Fiction

Explain: *Let's read one student's story.* Display and read aloud **eVisual 4.13**.

Sample Realistic Fiction

Attack of the Swamp Beast!

I pull back my baseball cap and look through the camera. My friends are almost in place. Just a few more seconds and we will be ready to start filming the first scene of our third-grade movie, *Attack of the Swamp Beast!* I feel impatient.

"Are we almost ready?" I call out. "Maria, you need to move over."

Maria takes her place next to the birdbath. Her job is to walk her dog, Pip, past the bushes. Then José will jump out from behind a tree. He is playing the Swamp Beast. He has green streamers taped to his arms. They are supposed to be weeds.

"Maria, take your place," I say. I look through the camera. "Okay! Ready, set, and—"

Suddenly, a squirrel darts out of the bushes! Pip howls and pulls on the leash, yanking it out of Maria's hand. The terrified squirrel runs around the birdbath and under the picnic table. Pip runs after it, knocking over the birdbath and dumping water everywhere. Then Pip slams into the corner of the table. The table falls onto its side. Plates full of food crash onto the ground. Pip jumps from the noise, then turns around and runs inside the house.

Maria and I stare at the mess in shock. What happened?

José, the Swamp Beast, peeks his head out from around the tree. "Hey, Andrew," he asks, "did you say *action*?"

NGReach.com **Realistic Story: eVisual 4.13**

INTERACTIVE WHITEBOARD TIP: Underline the dialogue.

Review the Trait: Voice

Review the concept: *Every writer has a special way of saying things, known as voice. In a realistic story, use language that sounds natural. Write dialogue that sounds like something real people might say.*

COMMON CORE STANDARDS

Writing	
Introduce Narrator and/or Characters	CC.3.W.3.a
Plan, Revise, and Edit Writing	CC.3.W.5
Write Over Extended Time Frames	CC.3.W.10
Language and Vocabulary	
Create Audio Recordings	CC.3.SL.5
Demonstrate Command of Grammar	CC.3.L.1
Form and Use Verbs	CC.3.L.1.d
Use Knowledge of Conventions	CC.3.L.3

Display and read aloud **eVisual 4.14**.

Writing Trait: Voice

Realistic writing that has a strong voice

- sounds natural
- uses dialogue that sounds like real people talk

NGReach.com **Writing Trait: Voice: eVisual 4.14**

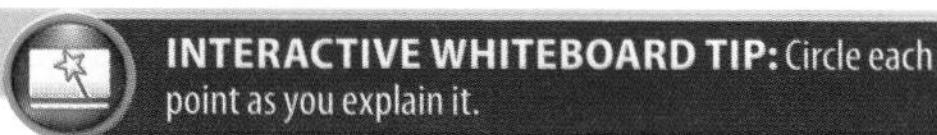

INTERACTIVE WHITEBOARD TIP: Circle each point as you explain it.

As a class, review examples of playful language and realistic dialogue in the sample.

Prewrite

Choose a Topic

Reread the first sentence of the prompt.
Ask: *What is your role?* (Storyteller) Continue with the remainder of the prompt in order to determine the Role, Audience, and Form for the RAFT.

Role: Storyteller
Audience: Other students
Form: Realistic story

Help students choose a topic for their realistic stories. Students can brainstorm topics with a partner or view **Magazine Maker** photos to get ideas. Have students complete a RAFT.

NGReach.com **Magazine Maker**

Get Organized

Review the sample: *"Attack of the Swamp Beast!" tells the story events in sequence. This helps the reader understand what is happening.* Display a story map and explain: *Using a story map, you can plan the beginning, middle, and end of the story.*

Model using events from the sample to complete a story map, then have students create story maps to plan their realistic fiction.

Andrew and his friends are ready to shoot a movie.
↓
Pip, the dog, chases a squirrel that jumps out of the bushes.
↓
Pip makes a mess and leaves everyone shocked.

Story Map

Draft

Write Ideas

Have students draft their stories. Remind them to focus on voice. Suggest they introduce characters in a way that gets readers' attention. Refer students to the sample and its use of first-person and dialogue.
See **Differentiate**

Differentiate

SN Special Needs

ISSUE Students struggle with drafting their stories to include story events, introduce characters, and add dialogue.

STRATEGY Have students break drafting into smaller steps: First, students turn their story maps into stories, telling events in order. Next, students focus on introducing the characters. Then, students add dialogue. Finally, students retell the story to a partner and note any details they should add.

Daily Language Arts

Daily Spelling and Word Work
Practice Pages T233m–T233n

Daily Grammar
Point out *I look* in paragraph four of "Attack of the Swamp Beast!" as an example of present-tense subject-verb agreement Then use pages T233o–T233p to have students practice subject-verb agreement with present-tense action verbs.

Daily Writing Skills
Have students note that the characters in "Attack of the Swamp Beast!" include a dog and squirrel as well as three children. Use pages T233q–T233r to have students practice introducing characters.

Revise

Read, Retell, Respond

Have students read their stories to partners. Have listeners restate their understanding of the story and offer suggestions. Use language frames to guide the discussion.

Language Frames

Retell	Make Suggestions
• This story is about ______. • In the beginning, ______. • In the middle, ______. • At the end, ______.	• The words you use in the part about ______ sound natural. • Can you change what ______ says to make it sound more like real speech?

Make Changes

Have students revise their realistic stories. Remind students to focus on voice and to make sure their writing sounds natural. As students revise their stories, have them provide clues about each character's gender, age, appearance, and traits.

Students can move or resize images in **Magazine Maker**. Model how to select an image from the library and drag it onto the page. Click the upper left corner of the image to move it around. To resize it, click and drag the lower right corner.

See **Differentiate**.

Student Sample: Revise

I look through the camera. My friends are almost in place. Just a few more seconds. Then we will be ready to start filming.

I ask if they are almost ready. I ask Maria to move over.

Maria takes her place next to the birdbath. Her job is to walk her dog, Pip. She will walk past the bushes. Then José will jump out . He will jump out from behind a tree. He is playing the Swamp Beest. He has green streamers taped to his arms. They are supposed to be weeds.

I tell Maria to take her place. I look back through the camera. I am ready to film.

Sample Analysis

I didn't do a good job of introducing the characters. I need to add information that will help the readers get to know my characters and understand what they are doing.

The voice doesn't sound natural. It sounds choppy. Plus I should probably change some of these sentences and make them dialogue.

Differentiate

BL Below Level

ISSUE Students have difficulty revising to introduce the characters in their realistic stories.

STRATEGY Use **eVisual 4.12** from page T233q to help students provide more clues about their characters. Have students use the chart to answer the following questions about each major character:

- What gender is your character?
- How old is your character?
- What does your character look like?
- What traits describe your character?

Have students use their answers to help provide more clues about each character.

Edit and Proofread

Check the Stories

Have students check their grammar and spelling, focusing on the Week 2 spelling words and on using proper subject-verb agreement.

Student Sample: Edit and Proofread

Suddenly, a squirrel dart out of the bushes! Pip howls and pulls on the leash, yanking it out of Maria's hand. The terrified squirrel runs around the birdbath and under the picnic table. Pip runs after it, knocking over the birdbath and dumping water everywhere. Then Pip slams into the corner of the table. The table falls onto its side. Plates full of food crash onto the ground. Pip jumps from the noise, then turns around and runs inside the house.

Maria and I stare at the mess in shock. What happened?

José, the Swamp Beest, peek his head out from around the tree. "Hey, Andrew," he asks, "did you say *action*?"

Sample Analysis

Some of my subjects and verbs don't agree. I'll need to fix that.

I misspelled *beast*. I'll go back and correct my mistake.

Best Practices

Focus on the Target Skill As you review students' stories, focus on their spelling and use of subject-verb agreement. Make sure they understand how to use these grammar skills correctly.

Publish and Present

Make a Final Copy

As students use **Magazine Maker** to style and resize text, remind them that their final layouts should not be distracting for the reader.

Share with Others

Invite volunteers to read their realistic stories to the class. Then help students record their readings. Tell students to speak clearly into the microphone at a normal volume and appropriate pace.

Have students make copies of their stories and add them to their Weekly Writing folders. Use the **Writing Rubric** to assess each student's story.

Student Sample: Publish

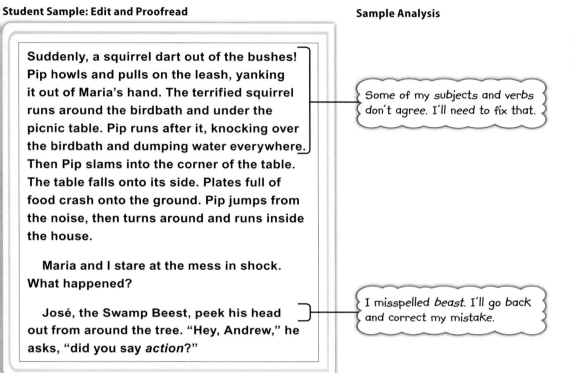

Attack of the *Swamp Beast*!

I pull back my baseball cap and look through the camera. My friends are almost in place. Just a few more seconds and we will be ready to start filming the first scene of our third-grade movie, *Attack of the Swamp Beast!*. I feel impatient.

"Are we almost ready?" I call out. "Maria, you need to move over."

Maria takes her place next to the birdbath. Her job is to walk her dog, Pip, past the bushes. Then José will jump out from behind a tree. He is playing the Swamp Beast. He has green streamers taped to his arms. They are supposed to be weeds.

"Maria, take your place," I say. I look back through the camera. "Okay! Ready, set, and—"

Suddenly, a squirrel darts out of the bushes! Pip howls and pulls on the leash, yanking it out of Maria's hand. The terrified squirrel runs around the birdbath and under the picnic table. Pip runs after it, knocking over the birdbath and dumping water everywhere. Then Pip slams into the corner of the table. The table falls onto its side. Plates full of food crash onto the ground. Pip jumps from the noise, then turns around and runs inside the house.

Maria and I stare at the mess in shock. What happened?

José, the Swamp Beast, peeks his head out from around the tree. "Hey, Andrew," he asks, "did you say *action*?"

© Bruce Dale/NGS

Writing Rubric

Score Point	Ideas	Organization	Voice	Word Choice	Fluency	Conventions	Presentation
4	• The writing has a clear, focused message that keeps readers interested. • Details are accurate and relevant, showing in-depth knowledge of the topic.	• The writing has a clear structure throughout that suits the writer's audience and purpose. • All content flows smoothly and logically.	• The writing sounds genuine and unique. • The writer's tone is appropriate to the purpose and audience.	• Appropriate words were chosen to clearly convey the writer's message. • Language used throughout is appropriate for the audience and grabs readers' attention.	• All sentences are varied and effective and have appropriate transitions. • When read aloud, the writing sounds natural and rhythmic.	• The writing has only a few minor errors in spelling, punctuation, capitalization, grammar, usage, and paragraphing. • All the sentences are complete.	• The text is presented in an orderly way, significantly helping to convey the message. • Visuals are appropriate for the purpose and audience, and effectively support meaning.
3	• Most of the writing has a clear, focused message that keeps readers interested. • Most details are accurate and relevant, showing reasonable knowledge of the topic.	• Most of the writing has a clear structure that suits the writer's audience and purpose. • Most of the content flows smoothly and logically.	• Most of the writing sounds genuine and unique. • The writer's tone is mostly appropriate for the purpose and audience.	• Many appropriate words were chosen to clearly convey the writer's message. • Most language is appropriate for the audience and grabs readers' attention.	• Most sentences are varied and effective and have appropriate transitions. • When read aloud, most of the writing sounds natural and rhythmic.	• The writing has some errors in spelling, punctuation, capitalization, grammar, usage, and paragraphing. • Most of the sentences are complete.	• Most of the text is presented in an orderly way, generally helping to convey the message. • Most visuals are appropriate for the purpose and audience, and effectively support meaning.
2	• The writing has a fairly unclear and unfocused message, causing readers some confusion. • Some details are relevant and accurate, showing minimum knowledge of the topic.	• The writing does not have a structure that suits the writer's audience and purpose. • Some content flows smoothly and logically.	• Some of the writing sounds genuine and unique. • The writer's tone is somewhat inappropriate for the purpose and audience.	• Some appropriate words were chosen to clearly convey the writer's message. • Some language is appropriate for the audience and grabs readers' attention.	• Some sentences are varied and effective and have appropriate transitions. • When read aloud, some of the writing sounds natural and rhythmic.	• The writing has several errors in spelling, punctuation, capitalization, grammar, usage, and paragraphing. • Some of the sentences are complete.	• Some of the text is presented in an orderly way, but it is a little difficult to track and comprehend the message. • Some visuals are appropriate for the purpose and audience and support meaning.
1	• The writing does not have a clear, focused message, causing readers confusion. • Many details are irrelevant and inaccurate, indicating a lack of knowledge of the topic.	• The writing does not have a structure. • The content does not flow smoothly or logically.	• The writing does not sound genuine or unique. • The writer's tone is not appropriate for the purpose or audience.	• Few appropriate words were chosen to clearly convey the writer's message. • Language is dull, vague, and inappropriate for the audience, losing the readers' attention.	• Few or none of the sentences are varied or effective or have appropriate transitions. • When read aloud, the writing sounds unnatural.	• The writing has many errors in spelling, punctuation, capitalization, grammar, usage, and paragraphing. • Few sentences are complete.	• The text is not presented in an orderly way, making it very difficult to track and comprehend the message. • None of the visuals are appropriate for the purpose or audience, and do not support meaning.

Grade 3 Assessment A4.39 Unit 4 | Let's Work Together

NGReach.com Assessment Master A4.39

☑ = TESTED

Assess

OBJECTIVES | **ASSESSMENTS**

Reading

- ☑ Describe Story Elements
- ☑ Compare Story Elements
- ☑ Compare Themes
- ☑ Determine Importance

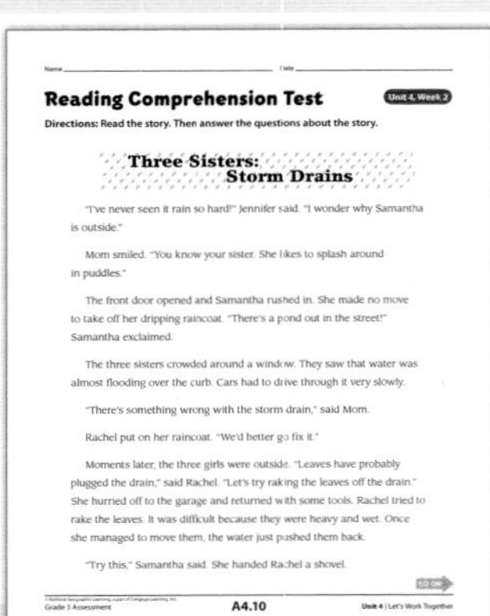
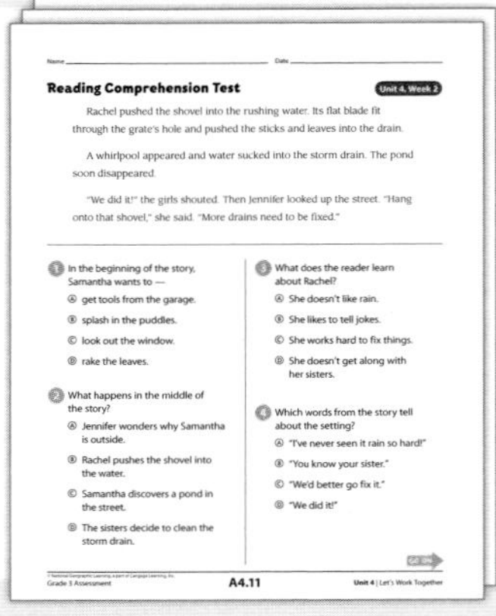
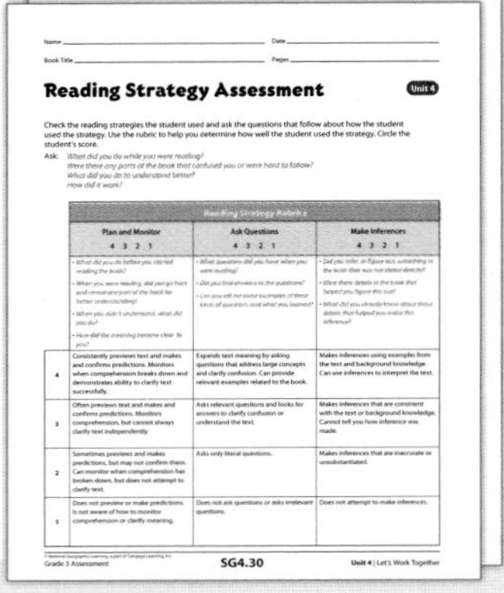

Reading Comprehension Test
A4.10–A4.13

Reading Strategy Assessment
SG4.30–SG4.31

Fluency

- ☑ Expression
- ☑ Accuracy and Rate

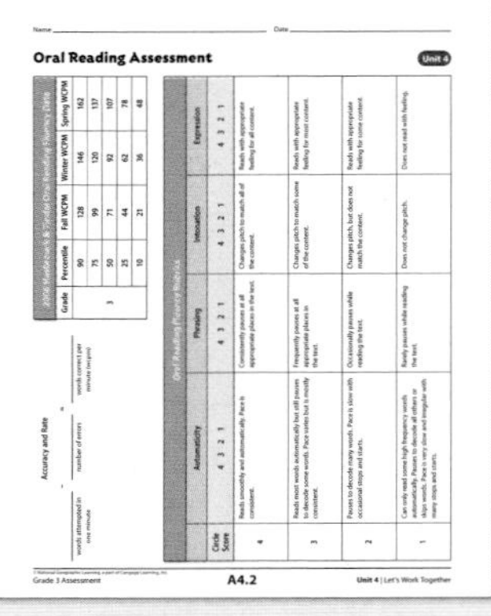
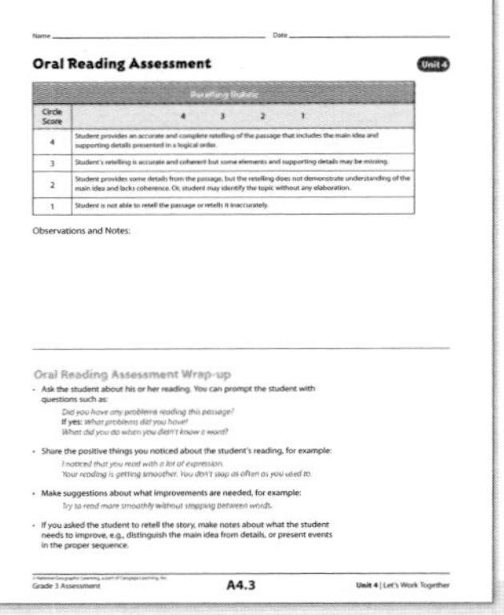

Oral Reading Assessment
A4.1–A4.3

Use these passages throughout Unit 4. Work with On Level students this week.

Vocabulary and Spelling

- ☑ Use Prefixes to Determine Word Meanings
- ☑ Spell Words with Long *e: ee, ea;* Long *o: oa, ow*
- ☑ Use Commonly Misspelled Words Correctly

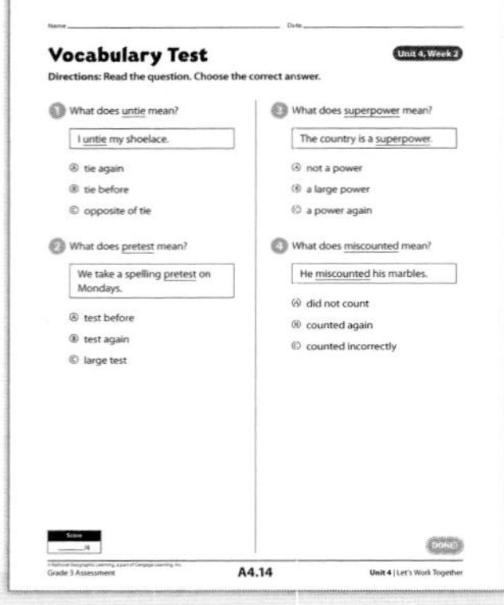
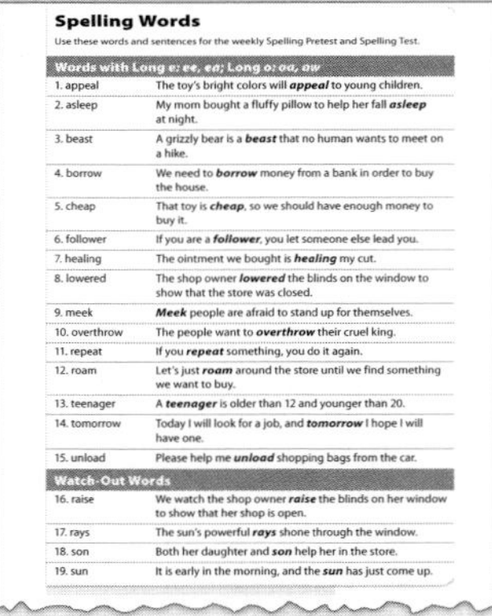

Vocabulary Test
A4.14

Spelling Pretest/ Spelling Test
T233m

Grammar and Writing

- ☑ Use Subject-Verb Agreement
- ☑ Use Present-Tense Action Verbs
- ☑ Introduce Characters

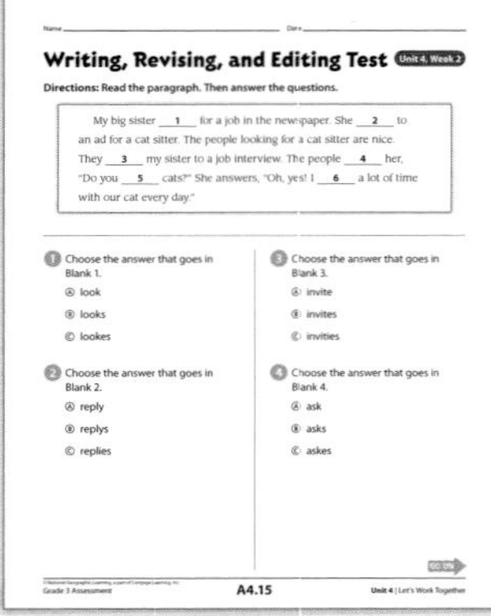
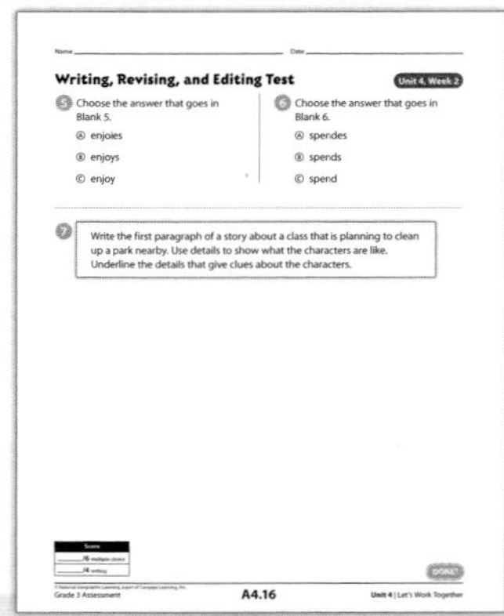
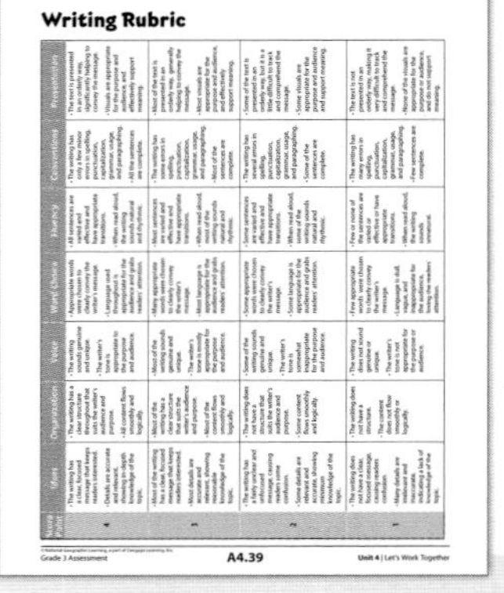

Writing, Revising, and Editing Test
A4.15–A4.16

Writing Rubric
A4.39

NGReach.com

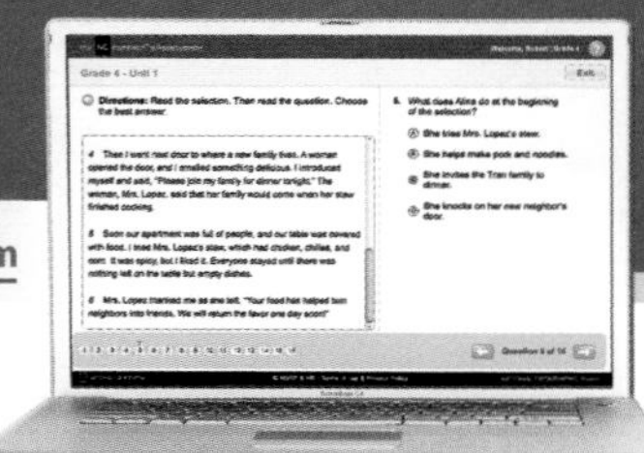

ExamView®

REPORTS

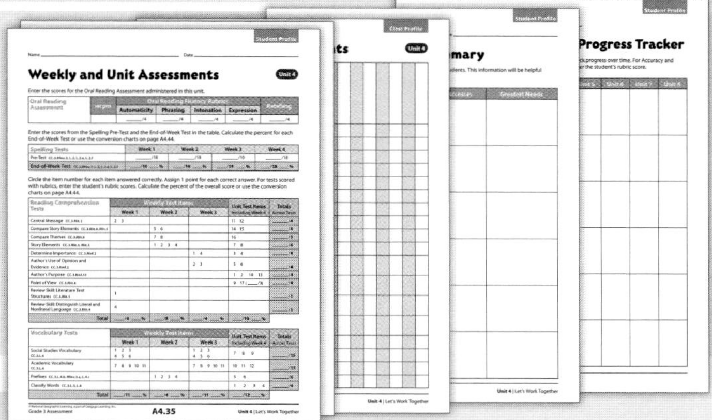

PRINT & ONLINE
Report Forms

Student Profile: Weekly and Unit Assessments	A4.35–A4.36
Class Profile: Weekly and Unit Assessments	A4.37
Student Profile: Strengths and Needs Summary	A4.38
Student Profile: Oral Reading Assessment Progress Tracker	A1.3

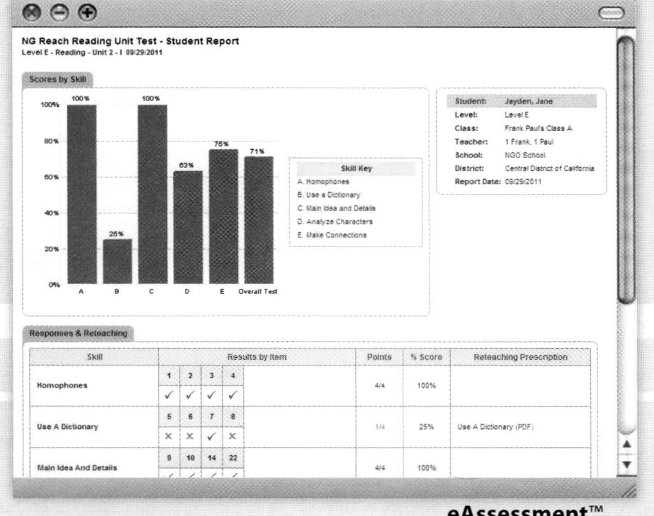

eAssessment™

ONLINE ONLY
Automated Reports

Student Profile: Weekly and Unit Tests

Class Profile: Weekly and Unit Tests

Standards Summary Report

Reteach and Practice

RESOURCES AND ROUTINES

Reading

RETEACH

Describe Story Elements: Reteaching Master RT4.4

Determine Importance: Reteaching Master RT4.5

ADDITIONAL PRACTICE

Comprehension Coach NGReach.com

Fluency

RETEACH

Fluency Routines, page BP33

ADDITIONAL PRACTICE

Comprehension Coach NGReach.com

Vocabulary and Spelling

RETEACH

Vocabulary Routine 6, page BP40

Spelling and Word Work Routine, page BP52

ADDITIONAL PRACTICE

Vocabulary Games NGReach.com

Daily Spelling Practice, pages T233m–T233n

Grammar and Writing

RETEACH

Verbs: Anthology Handbook, pages 592, 594

Writing: Reteaching Writing Routine, page BP51

Writing Trait: Voice: Reteaching Master RT4.6

ADDITIONAL PRACTICE

More Grammar Practice PM4.17

Daily Writing Skills Practice, pages T233q–T233r

Week 3 Planner

Online Lesson Planner
NGReach.com

☑ = TESTED

	Day 1	Day 2
WHOLE GROUP TIME	**Listen and Comprehend**	**Read and Comprehend**
Anthology — **Speaking and Listening** 5–10 minutes	**Academic Talk** CC.3.SL.1.d; CC.3.SL.3 Persuade T240	**Academic Talk** CC.3.SL.1; CC.3.SL.1.d Make an Argument T242a
Language and Vocabulary 15–25 minutes	**Daily Spelling and Word Work** CC.3.Rfou.3; CC.3.L.1.e; CC.3.L.2; CC.3.L.2.e; CC.3.L.2.f ☑ Verbs Ending in *ed* and Commonly Misspelled Words T239u **Daily Grammar** CC.3.L.1; CC.3.L.1.a; CC.3.L.1.d ☑ Helping Verbs T239w **Social Studies Vocabulary** CC.3.SL.1.d; CC.3.L.6 ☑ Learn Key Words T240 **agriculture crop farmer field harvest plow**	**Daily Spelling and Word Work** CC.3.L.1.e; CC.3.L.2.e; CC.3.L.2.f ☑ Practice T239u **Daily Grammar** CC.3.L.1; CC.3.L.1.a; CC.3.L.1.d ☑ More Helping Verbs T239w **Academic Vocabulary** CC.3.L.4; CC.3.L.6 ☑ Learn More Key Words T242a **alternative conservation evidence future method opinion summarize sustain**
Reading 20–40 minutes	**Reading** Read Aloud: Letter T241a **Comprehension** CC.3.Rinf.10 ☑ Identify Opinion and Evidence T241a **Fluency** CC.3.Rfou.4 ☑ Model Phrasing T241a	**Reading** CC.3.Rfou.4 Read a Persuasive Speech T244 **Comprehension** CC.3.Rinf.2 ☑ Determine Importance T244 **Fluency** CC.3.Rfou.4 ☑ Practice Phrasing T244
Writing 15–45 minutes	**Power Writing** T240 CC.3.W.10 **Daily Writing Skills** CC.3.W.6; CC.3.W.7 ☑ Evaluate Information T239y **Writing** CC.3.W.1.c; CC.3.W.10 Write and Support an Opinion T242 **Research Project: Conservation** CC.3.W.7; CC.3.W.8 ☑ Plan T259a	**Power Writing** T242a CC.3.W.10 **Daily Writing Skills** CC.3.W.6; CC.3.W.7 ☑ Evaluate Information T239y **Writing** CC.3.W.10 Write a Summary T244 **Research Project: Conservation** CC.3.W.7; CC.3.W.8 ☑ Research T259a
SMALL GROUP READING TIME	**Read Social Studies Articles**	**Read Nonfiction Books**
Fiction & Nonfiction  20 minutes	**Vocabulary** CC.3.L.6 Learn Social Studies Vocabulary SG16 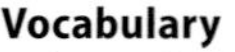 **Reading** CC.3.Rinf.6; CC.3.Rinf.10 Distinguish Points of View SG17 Build Comprehension SG17 	**Vocabulary** CC.3.L.6 Learn Story Words SG18–SG19 **Reading** CC.3.Rinf.10; CC.3.Rinf.2 Introduce SG18–SG19 Read and Integrate Ideas SG20–SG21 ☑ Opinion and Evidence SG20–SG21 ☑ Determine Importance SG20–SG21 

LEARNING STATION TIME/DAILY PHONICS INTERVENTION

 20 minutes

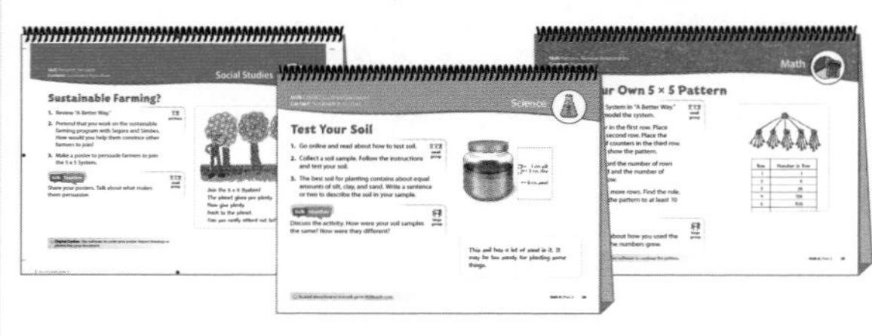

- **Speaking and Listening** T239q CC.3.SL.2; CC.3.SL.3
- **Language and Vocabulary** T239q CC.3.L.6
- **Writing** T239q CC.3.W.10; CC.3.L.6
- **Cross-Curricular** T239r CC.3.Rinf.10; CC.3.W.10
- **Reading and Intervention** T239r; SG68 CC.3.Rlit.10; CC.3.Rinf.10; CC.3.Rfou.3; CC.3.Rfou.4.b
- **Daily Phonics Intervention** T239s–T239t CC.3.Rfou.3; CC.3.Rfou.3.d; CC.3.L.2; CC.3.L.2.e, f

BIG Question What's the best way to get things done?

Day 3

Read and Comprehend

Academic Talk CC.3.Rinf.5
Preview and Predict T246

Daily Spelling and Word Work CC.3.L.1.e; CC.3.L.2.e
☑ Practice T239v

Daily Grammar CC.3.L.1; CC.3.L.1.a; CC.3.L.1.d
☑ Forms of *do* T239x

Vocabulary Practice CC.3.L.6
☑ Expand Word Knowledge T246

Reading
Read a Persuasive Article T247–T252

Comprehension
☑ Opinion and Evidence T248–249, T252 CC.3.Rinf.2, 5, 6
☑ Determine Importance T248–249, T252
Distinguish Viewpoint T250–251

Fluency CC.3.Rfou.4; CC.3.Rfou.4.b
☑ Practice Phrasing, Accuracy, and Rate T248–249

Power Writing T246 CC.3.W.10

Daily Writing Skills CC.3.W.6; CC.3.W.7
☑ Evaluate Information T239z

Writing CC.3.W.10
Write a Summary T253

Research Project: Conservation CC.3.W.7; CC.3.W.8
☑ Research T259a

Read Nonfiction Books

Vocabulary CC.3.L.6
Expand Vocabulary Through Wide Reading SG18–SG21

Reading CC.3.Rinf.10; CC.3.Rinf.2
Read and Integrate Ideas SG20–SG21
☑ Opinion and Evidence SG20–SG21
☑ Determine Importance SG20–SG21

Day 4

Read and Comprehend

Academic Talk CC.3.SL.1; CC.3.SL.1.d
Summarize Reading T254

Daily Spelling and Word Work CCC.3.L.2; CC.3.L.2.e CC.3.L.4.d
☑ Practice T239v

Daily Grammar CC.3.W.5; CC.3.L.1; CC.3.L.1.a; CC.3.L.1.d
☑ Grammar and Writing T239x

Vocabulary Practice CC.3.L.6
☑ Share Word Knowledge T254

Reading
Read a Persuasive Article T255–T256

Comprehension CC.3.Rinf.2
☑ Opinion and Evidence T255, T256
☑ Determine Importance T255, T256

Fluency CC.3.Rfou.4.b
☑ Practice Phrasing, Accuracy, and Rate T255

Power Writing T254 CC.3.W.10

Daily Writing Skills CC.3.W.6; CC.3.W.7
☑ Evaluate Information T239z

Writing CC.3.W.10
Write About Viewpoint T257

Research Project: Conservation CC.3.W.7; CC.3.W.8
☑ Organize T259b

Read Nonfiction Books

Vocabulary CC.3.L.6
Expand Vocabulary Through Wide Reading SG18–SG21

Reading CC.3.Rinf.10; CC.3.Rinf.2
Read and Integrate Ideas SG20–SG21
Opinion and Evidence SG20–SG21
☑ Determine Importance SG20–SG21

Day 5

Review and Apply

Academic Talk CC.3.SL.1; CC.3.SL.1.a; CC.3.SL.1.d
Talk About "A Better Way" T258

Daily Grammar CC.3.W.5; CC.3.L.1; CC.3.L.1.a; CC.3.L.1.d
☑ Review T239x

Vocabulary Review CC.3.L.6
☑ Apply Word Knowledge T257a

Reading
Reread a Persuasive Article T247–T256

Comprehension CC.3.SL.1; CC.3.SL.1.a, d
☑ Opinion and Evidence T259

Fluency CC.3.Rfou.4.b
☑ Check Phrasing, Accuracy, and Rate T259

Power Writing T257a CC.3.W.10

Daily Writing Skills CC.3.W.6; CC.3.W.7
☑ Evaluate Information T239z

Writing CC.3.W.1; CC.3.W.10
Write About "A Better Way" T258

Research Project: Conservation CC.3.SL.4.b
☑ Present T259b

Read Nonfiction Books

Vocabulary CC.3.L.6
Expand Vocabulary Through Wide Reading SG18–SG21

Reading CC.3.Rinf.2; CC.3.SL.1.a
Connect Across Texts SG21

Writing CC.3.W.10
Choose a Writing Option SG20–SG21

ASSESSMENT & RETEACHING

Assessment and Reteaching T259c–T259d

☑ Reading Comprehension Test A4.17–A4.18 CC.3.Rinf.2
☑ Reading Strategy Assessment SG4.30–SG4.31 CC.3.Rinf.2
☑ Oral Reading Assessment A4.1–A4.3 CC.3.Rfou.4
☑ Vocabulary Test A4.19–A4.20 CC.3.L.6

☑ Spelling Test: Verbs Ending in *ed* and Commonly Misspelled Words T239u CC.3.Rfou.3; CC.3.L.1.e; CC.3.L.2; CC.3.L.2.e; CC.3.L.2.f
☑ Writing, Revising, and Editing Test A4.21–A4.22 CC.3.W.5; CC.3.L.1.a; CC.3.L.1.d
Reteaching Masters RT4.7–RT4.8

Week 3 Learning Stations

Speaking and Listening

Option 1: Scenes of Cooperation (two students)

PROGRAM RESOURCES

Digital Library: Language Builder Picture Cards D38–D51

Students use picture cards to ask and answer questions about cooperation.

- Have one student select a picture card and briefly describe to a partner what the card shows.
- Have the other student ask questions about the first student's description. The first student should answer the questions with as much detail as possible.
- Students should then switch roles.

Ask and Answer Questions	CC.3.SL.3

Option 2: Spatulatta (two students)

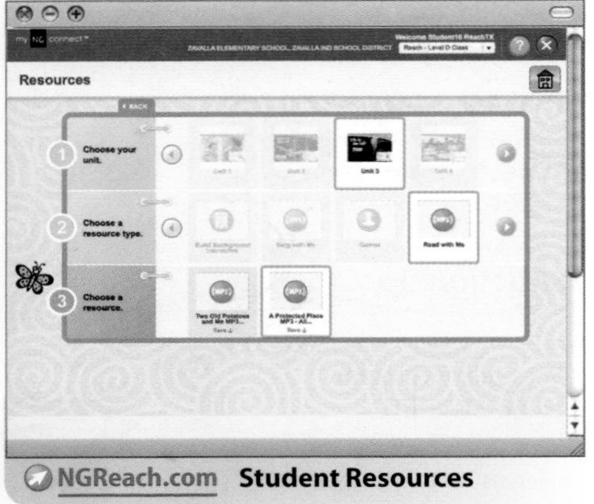

NGReach.com **Student Resources**

Students read and discuss an article about an online service created by grade-school students.

- To read the article, have students go to Resources > Unit 4 > Learning Stations > Week 3 > Spatulatta.
- Have partners read the article and discuss the main idea and supporting details.

Determine the Main Ideas and Supporting Details of Information Presented Visually and Orally in Diverse Media	CC.3.SL.2

Language and Vocabulary

Key Words

agriculture · alternative · conservation · crop
evidence · farmer · field · future · harvest
method · opinion · plow · summarize · sustain

Option 1: Vocabulary Games (one student)

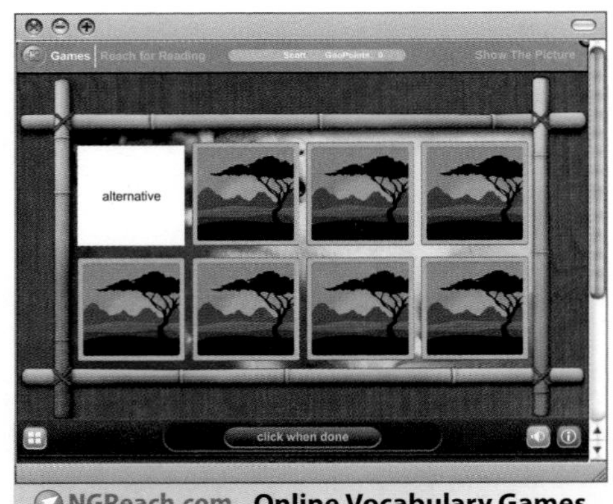

NGReach.com **Online Vocabulary Games**

Acquire and Use Conversational, Academic, and Domain-Specific Words	CC.3.L.6

Option 2: My Vocabulary Notebook (one student)

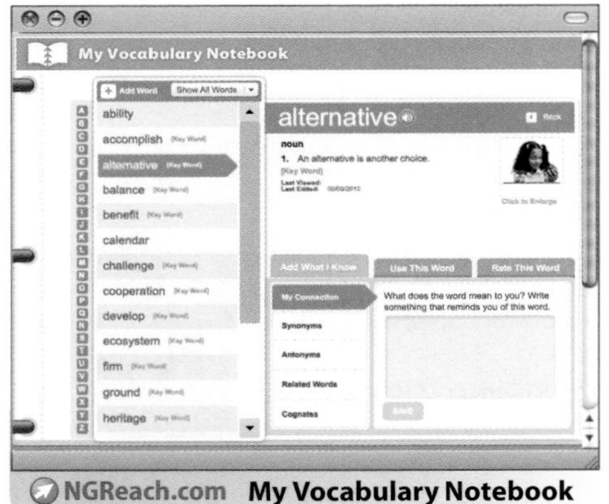

NGReach.com **My Vocabulary Notebook**

Have students expand their word knowledge.

- Under Add More Information > Add What I Know > My Connection have students write sentences that connect the Key Word to their own lives.
- Under Add More Information > Use This Word > Write a Sentence, have students use helping verbs to write sentences about the Key Word.

Acquire and Use Conversational, Academic, and Domain-Specific Words	CC.3.L.6

Writing

Option 1: Sustainable Farming? (one student)

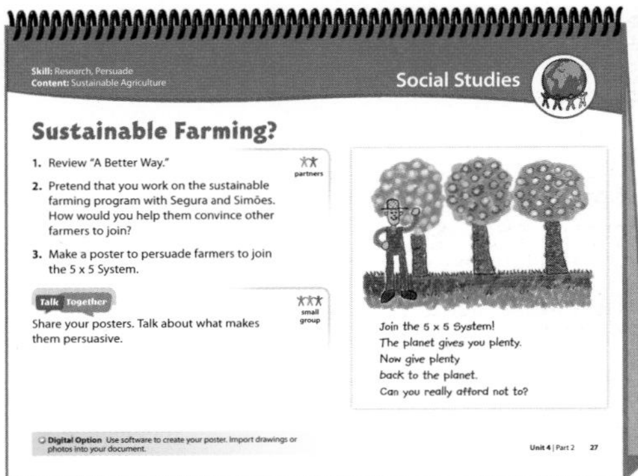
Social Studies

Sustainable Farming?

1. Review "A Better Way."
2. Pretend that you work on the sustainable farming program with Segura and Simões. How would you help them convince other farmers to join?
3. Make a poster to persuade farmers to join the 5 x 5 System.

Talk Together

Share your posters. Talk about what makes them persuasive.

Join the 5 x 5 System! The planet gives you plenty. Now give plenty back to the planet. Can you really afford not to?

PROGRAM RESOURCES & MATERIALS

Cross-Curricular Teamwork Activities: Card 27

Teacher's Guide on NGReach.com

Student Resources Directory

drawing paper • poster board • markers • crayons

Write Over Shorter Time for Specific Tasks	CC.3.W.10

Option 2: Write a Paragraph (one student)

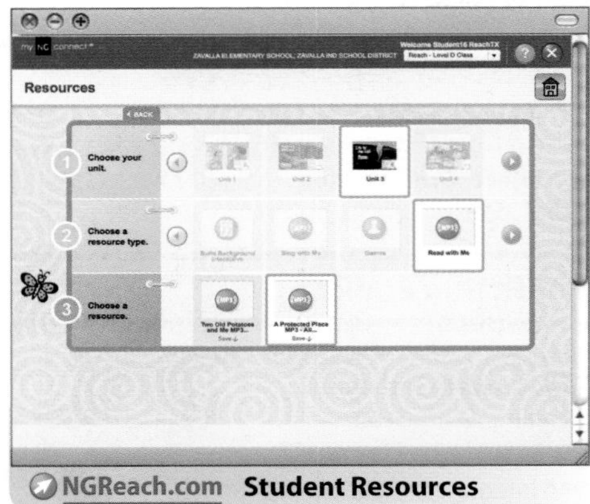

NGReach.com **Student Resources**

Students view an online photo of the Pantanal and write short paragraphs describing it.

- Go to Resources > Unit 4 > Learning Stations > Week 3 > Pantanal Photo.
- Have students focus on what they think is happening in the photograph.
- Encourage students to use Key Words in their paragraphs.

Write Over Shorter Time for Specific Tasks	CC.3.W.10
Acquire and Use Domain-Specific Words	CC.3.L.6

(one student icon) = one student (two students icon) = two students (three students icon) = three or more students

Cross-Curricular

Option 1: Test Your Soil

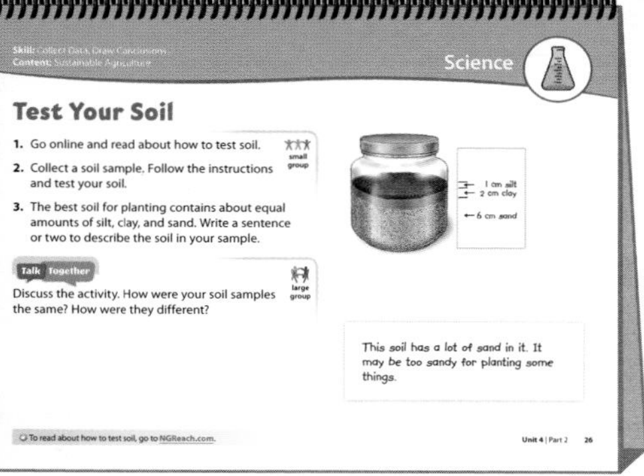
Science

Test Your Soil

1. Go online and read about how to test soil.
2. Collect a soil sample. Follow the instructions and test your soil.
3. The best soil for planting contains about equal amounts of silt, clay, and sand. Write a sentence or two to describe the soil in your sample.

Talk Together

Discuss the activity. How were your soil samples the same? How were they different?

This soil has a lot of sand in it. It may be too sandy for planting some things.

PROGRAM RESOURCES & MATERIALS

Cross-Curricular Teamwork Activities: Card 26

Teacher's Guide on NGReach.com

Student Resources Directory

plastic cup • towel • 1-quart or 1-liter jar • dishwashing detergent • soil • water • measuring spoons • index cards • ruler

Write Over Shorter Time for Specific Purposes CC.3.W.10

Option 2: Make Your Own 5 x 5 Pattern

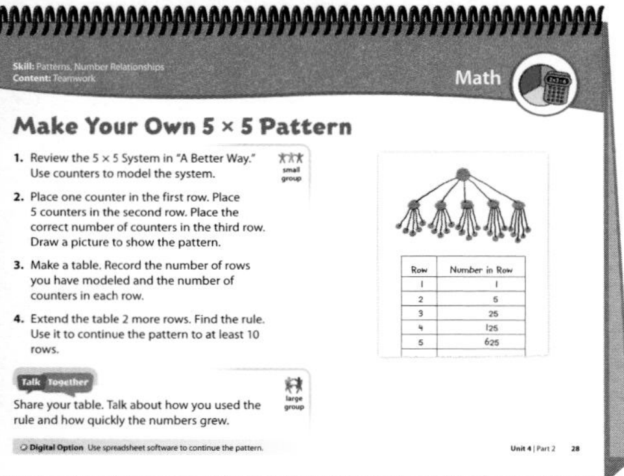
Math

Make Your Own 5 × 5 Pattern

1. Review the 5 × 5 System in "A Better Way." Use counters to model the system.
2. Place one counter in the first row. Place 5 counters in the second row. Place the correct number of counters in the third row. Draw a picture to show the pattern.
3. Make a table. Record the number of rows you have modeled and the number of counters in each row.
4. Extend the table 2 more rows. Find the rule. Use it to continue the pattern to at least 10 rows.

Row	Number in Row
1	1
2	5
3	25
4	125
5	625

Talk Together

Share your table. Talk about how you used the rule and how quickly the numbers grew.

PROGRAM RESOURCES & MATERIALS

Cross-Curricular Teamwork Activities: Card 28

Teacher's Guide on NGReach.com

Student Resources Directory

counters • drawing paper • markers • crayons

Read and Comprehend Informational Texts CC.3.Rinf.10

Reading

Option 1: Comprehension Coach

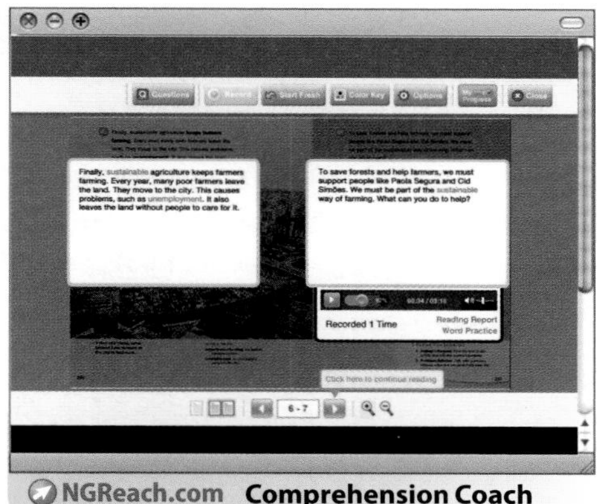

NGReach.com **Comprehension Coach**

Read and Comprehend Literature CC.3.Rlit.10
Read Orally with Accuracy and Appropriate Rate on Successive Readings CC.3.Rfou.4.b

Option 2: Read More About Brazil

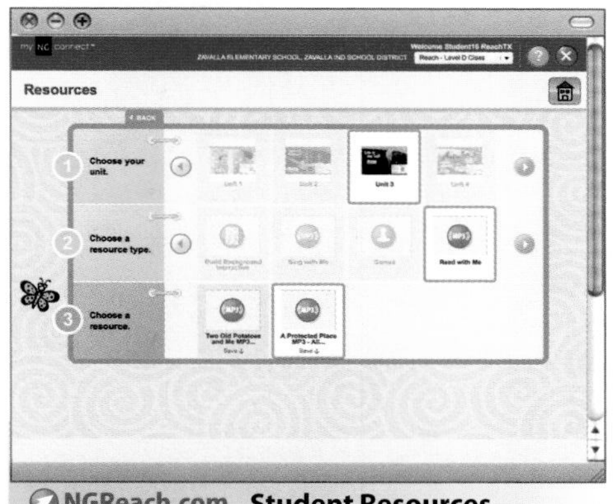

NGReach.com **Student Resources**

Have students read an online article about the land and people of Brazil.

- To read the article, have students go to Resources > Unit 4 > Learning Stations > Week 3 > Brazil.
- Have students create fact-sheets listing three or four important facts about Brazil.

Read and Comprehend Informational Text CC.3.Rinf.10

Intervention

Phonics Games

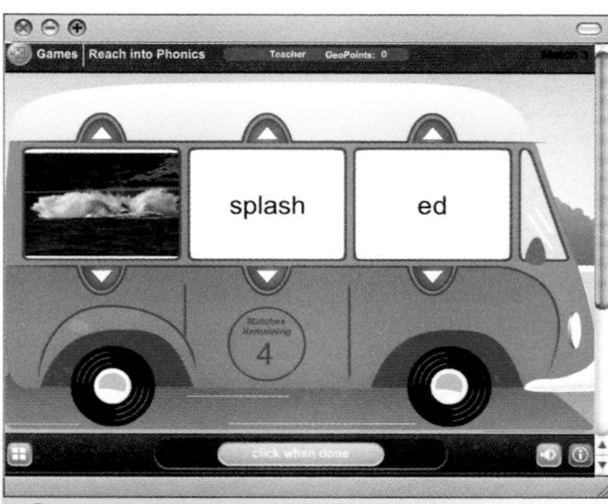

NGReach.com **Online Phonics Games**

Apply Phonics and Word Analysis Skills CC.3.Rfou.3

For Reteaching Masters, see pages RT4.7–RT4.8.

Additional Resources

ESL Kit

ESL Teacher's Edition pages T240–T259

Week 3 Daily Phonics Intervention

OBJECTIVES

Thematic Connection: Goods and Services

Recognize High Frequency Words

Develop Phonological Awareness: Count Syllables Contrast/Isolate Sounds

Associate Sounds and Spellings /d/-*ed*; /t/-*ed*; /ed/-*ed*

Identify Verb Endings (-*ed*); Blend Sounds to Decode Words with Endings

Teach Day 1

PROGRAM RESOURCES

High Frequency Words: Teaching Master 15

Word Builder: Transparencies 46, 47, 48, 49

Decodable Passage: *They Hiked at a Lake* Practice Book, page 114

Reach into Phonics

Lesson 54, page T90

Lesson 56, pages T92–T93

Lesson 57, pages T94–T95

High Frequency Words

Follow Lesson 54 to present High Frequency Words:

saw was where their said

Verbs Ending in *-ed*

Follow Lessons 56 and 57 to teach sounds for the *-ed* ending. Guide students through **Transparencies 46–49**. Use **Reading Routine 3** to guide students as they read Decodable text.

*For **Reading Routine 3**, see Reach into Phonics page ix.*

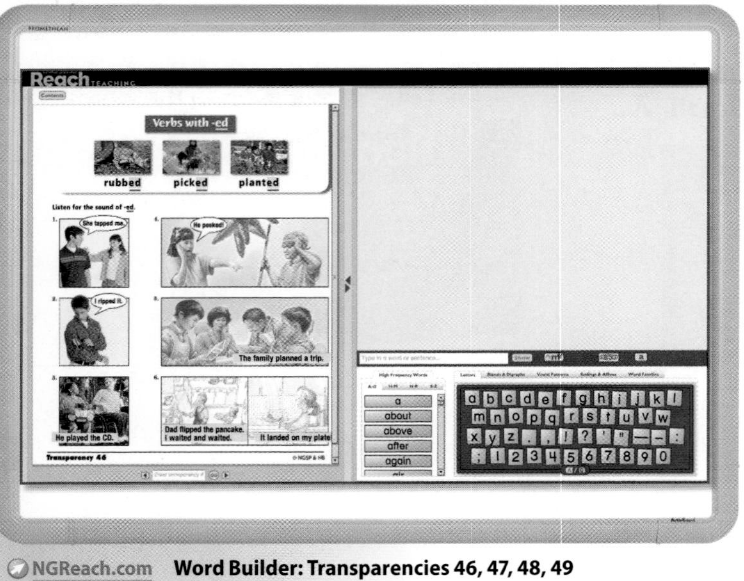

NGReach.com **Word Builder: Transparencies 46, 47, 48, 49**

Teach Day 2

PROGRAM RESOURCES

High Frequency Words: Teaching Master 16

Decodable Reader: *About Duke* Practice Book, page 159

Reach into Phonics

Lesson 55, page T91

Lesson 58, pages T96–T98

High Frequency Words

Follow Lesson 55 to present High Frequency Words:

began about thought dance again

Build Reading Fluency

Provide students with the **Decodable Reader**, *About Duke*. Then follow Lesson 58.

= one student = two students = three or more students

COMMON CORE STANDARDS

Demonstrate Command of Spelling	CC.3.L.2
Use Conventional Spelling	CC.3.L.2.e
Use Spelling Patterns and Generalizations	CC.3.L.2.f
Apply Phonics Skills	CC.3.Rfou.3
Read Irregularly Spelled Words	CC.3.Rfou.3.d

Oh, No! Day 3  Option 1

MATERIALS

index cards, 16 per pair of students • timer

Prepare

- Arrange two pairs of students in a group of four.
- Have each pair collaborate to write each word from the word bank below on a separate card and then write "Oh, No!" on the two remaining cards.

stubbed	packed	chanted	baked	paved
stained	mopped	nodded	hiked	healed
were	thought	again	said	

Play a Game

- Have groups shuffle all the cards, including the "Oh, No!" cards, and place them face down in a pile.
- Set a timer for ten minutes. Players take turns selecting a card and reading it aloud to the player on his or her right. Players should pay close attention to the end sound. Remind students the *-ed* ending can make the /d/, /t/, and /ed/ sounds.
- If the player reads the word correctly, he or she keeps the card. If not, it goes back in the pile.
- If a student draws an "Oh, No!" card, all his or her cards go back in the pile.
- When time is called, the player with the most cards wins.

Name the Final Sound Day 3  Option 2

MATERIALS

index cards, 12 per pair of students

Prepare

Have partners write each word from the word bank below on a separate card and place the cards face down in a pile.

grabbed	sealed	framed	planned	biked	packed
creaked	shopped	patted	mended	graded	smiled

Play a Game

- One partner picks and displays a card. The viewer identifies the final sound, names the root word, and reads the past-tense verb.
- The partner decides if the viewer has identified the final sound and read the past-tense verb correctly. If so, the viewer keeps the card. If not, the card goes back in the pile.
- Play ends after students have displayed all the cards and pronounced the words correctly. The partner with the most cards wins.

Tic Tac Toe Day 4 

MATERIALS

masking tape • large index cards, nine per pair of students • five red markers • five blue markers

Prepare

- Have partners work together to write each High Frequency Word from the word bank below on separate cards.
- Have partners use tape to make a Tic Tac Toe grid on the classroom floor. Tell students to tape a word card in each box of the grid.

saw	was	where	their	again
began	about	thought	dance	

Play a Game

- Players choose colors and collect markers for that color.
- Have Player 1 toss a marker onto the grid. Player 1 reads the word. If the player reads the word correctly, then the marker stays. If the player does not read the word correctly, he or she picks up the marker. Have Player 2 repeat the process.
- The first player to get three markers in a row reads all the words. If all the words are read correctly, that player wins.

Hop and Read Day 5 

MATERIALS

masking tape • large index cards, 11 per pair of students • markers

Prepare

- Have partners work together to write each High Frequency Word from the word bank below on separate cards.
- Have partners use tape to make a hopscotch grid on the classroom floor. Have students tape a word card in each box of the grid.

about	always	new	there	together	were
again	animals	really	thought	was	

Play a Game

- Have Player 1 toss a marker inside the first box and then hop through the boxes reading each word, skipping the box the marker is on.
- If Player 1 reads all the words correctly, he or she picks up the marker. If not, Player 1 waits for the next turn. Player 2 repeats the process.
- The first player to complete the hopscotch grid wins.

Week 3 Daily Spelling & Word Work

OBJECTIVES

Thematic Connection: Goods a

- ☑ **Spell Verbs Ending in *-ed***
- ☑ **Use Commonly Misspelled Word**

SUGGESTED PACING

DAY 1	Spelling Pretest
DAY 2–4	Daily Practice Options
DAY 5	Spelling Test

Spelling Pretest — Day 1

Spelling Test — Day 5

Spelling Words

Use these words and sentences for the weekly Spelling Pretest and Spelling Test.

Verbs Ending in *-ed*	
1. arranged	The store worker ***arranged*** canned goods in neat rows on the shelf.
2. blessed	Our family is ***blessed*** with many things, such as food, clothing, and a house.
3. calmed	The nice cashier ***calmed*** down the angry customer.
4. comforted	The vet ***comforted*** the scared puppy by holding him.
5. commanded	His boss ***commanded*** him to finish his work right away.
6. completed	The doctor ***completed*** his rounds, visiting every single one of his patients.
7. eased	Doctor Wu carefully ***eased*** the cast off my arm.
8. emptied	Workers ***emptied*** garbage from the office building.
9. included	The shoe store ***included*** socks with every box of new shoes.
10. joined	The workers ***joined*** together two boards with a hammer and nails.
11. opposed	Shoppers ***opposed*** the rise in the milk prices because they did not want to pay more money.
12. planted	The farmer ***planted*** corn in his empty field.
13. pitied	The vet ***pitied*** the injured dog, so she gave it some strong medicine.
14. provided	His extra job ***provided*** enough money to pay for his art classes.
15. worried	The nurse ***worried*** about having enough bandages for the patients.
Watch-Out Words	
16. some	We bought ***some*** vegetables for our soup.
17. sum	The ***sum*** of two cans plus two cans is four cans.
18. we'd	The tomatoes are ripe, so ***we'd*** better pick them now.
19. weed	That ***weed*** should not be growing next to the tomato plants.

…bs Ending in *-ed* — Day 2 — Option 1

…ch

…y the words *join, provide,* and *worry.* Say: *These verbs tell about …s that are happening now. We add* -ed *to many verbs to tell about …s that happened in the past.* Demonstrate adding *-ed* to join to …ake *joined.*

Point to *provide* and explain: *When a verb already has an* e *at the end, like* provide, *you drop the* e *and add* -ed *to form the past tense:* provided.

Point to *empty* and explain: *When a verb ends in a consonant and* y, *like* empty, *you change the* y *to* i *and add* -ed *to form the past tense:* emptied.

Prepare

Have students fold a paper vertically to create three columns. Then have them write a heading for each column: Drop e̲ and add -e̲d̲; Add -e̲d̲; Change y̲ to i̲ and add -e̲d̲.

Word Sort

- Have students first quietly read aloud a spelling word, listening for the *ed* at the end that signals a past action.
- Have them print each verb under the right heading and then underline the letters that form the pattern.

Form and Use Verb Tenses	CC.3.L.1.e
Use Spelling Patterns and Generalizations	CC.3.L.2.f

Oh, No! — Day 2 — Option 2

MATERIALS

index cards, 21 per group • timers, one per group

Prepare

Arrange students in small groups. Have students collaborate to write each of the 19 spelling words on a separate card. Tell them to write "Oh, No!" on two cards.

Play a Game

pitied

Oh, No!

- Have students shuffle the cards and place them face down in a pile. One student sets the timer for ten minutes, and play begins.
- Have players take turns selecting a card and reading it aloud to the player on his or her right.
- That player spells the word. If it is correct, the speller keeps the card. If not, it goes back in the pile.
- If a student draws an "Oh, No!" card, all his or her cards go in the pile.
- When time is called, the player with the most cards wins.

Form and Use Verb Tenses	CC.3.L.1.e
Use Conventional Spelling	CC.3.L.2.e

= one student = two students 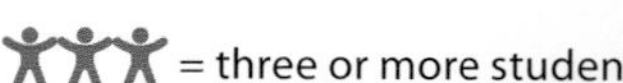 = three or more students

Verbs Ending in *-ed*

Fill in the Blank — Day 3  Option 1

MATERIALS

sentence strips, 19 per pair of students • vinyl sleeves, one per pair • erasable markers • erasers

Prepare

- Arrange students in pairs and have each partner write a sentence for each of nine or ten spelling words, leaving a blank for the word itself. Partners should choose different spelling words and write their sentences on separate sentence strips.
- Have students put one sentence at a time in the sleeve.

Play a Game

- Have partners take turns selecting a sentence strip, writing the missing word, and checking that the word makes sense and is spelled correctly.
- If the word makes sense and is spelled correctly, the student gets a point. If not, the strip goes back to the sleeve.
- Have students play until all the sentences have been correctly completed with words correctly spelled. The partner with more points wins.

Use Conventional Spelling — CC.3.L.2.e

Game Show! — Day 3  Option 2

Prepare

include

- Have small groups of students collaborate to write each of the first 15 spelling words on a slip of paper. On the backs, students write the present tense of the verbs.
- Have students place all the slips in the middle of the table with the present-tense verbs showing (leaving the spelling words hidden).

Play a Game

- Choose the first Game Show Host. The other students become Contestants. The Host calls out a present-tense verb from a slip.
- Contestants who can spell the past tense of the verb put their thumbs in the air. The Host calls on the Contestant who put a thumb up first.
- That Contestant says the past-tense form of the verb aloud and spells it. The Host checks the spelling on the back of the slip. If correct, the Contestant keeps the slip. If not, it goes back on the table.
- The student sitting to the right of the Host becomes the new Host.
- Play continues until all verbs are in the hands of students.

Form and Use Verb Tenses — CC.3.L.1.e

Mystery Words — Day 4  Option 1

Prepare

- Arrange students in groups of four. Divide groups into Pair 1 and Pair 2. Assign a "mystery word" to each Pair in the group.
- Have partners quietly collaborate to create four clues about the word and arrange their order so each one narrows down the possible answers, with the last clue being the most obvious.
- Explain that one clue should be about syllables or the word's meaning. Tell partners to consult a dictionary to check syllabication and word meaning as necessary.

> Mystery Word: completed
> Clue 1: The word has nine letters. (c o m p l e t e d)
> Clue 2: The word has three syllables.
> Clue 3: The word is spelled by dropping an *e* and adding *-ed*
> Clue 4: The word will work in this sentence:
> Julie ____ her work on time. (completed)

Play a Game

- Have Pair 1 present its clues, one clue at a time, to Pair 2.
- After hearing each clue, players in Pair 2 write down all of the words that match the clues to that point. Tell players to cross off words that do not match each new clue.
- When Pair 2 has the answer, the partners call it out and spell it.
- As soon as the correct word has been called, Pair 2 presents its clues. Continue until all "mystery words" have been identified.

Use Conventional Spelling — CC.3.L.2.e
Use Glossaries and Dictionaries — CC.3.L.4.d

Comic Strips — Day 4  Option 2

Make a Drawing

- Have partners collaborate to create comic strips using as many spelling words as possible, including at least three Watch-Out Words.
- Have students underline the Watch-Out Words in their strips and draw wavy lines under the regular spelling words.

Demonstrate Command of Spelling — CC.3.L.2

Week 3 Daily Grammar

OBJECTIVES

Thematic Connection: Goods and Services

- **Grammar: Use Helping Verbs**
- **Grammar: Use Forms of *Do***

COMMON CORE STANDARDS

Edit Writing	CC.3.W.5
Demonstrate Command of Grammar	CC.3.L.1
Explain the Function of Verbs	CC.3.L.1.a

Day 1

PROGRAM RESOURCES

Helping Verbs: eVisual 4.21

Game: Practice Master PM4.19

MATERIALS

index cards, ten per pair of students

Teach the Rules

Use the suggestion on page T242 to introduce helping verbs. Explain: *Some verbs are made up of a helping verb and a main verb.* Use **eVisual 4.21** to teach *can* and *could.*

Helping Verbs

A **helping verb** works with an action verb. The action verb is the **main verb**.

• The helping verb **can** tells that someone is able to do something.	She **can buy** shoes. He **can sell** them.
• The helping verb **could** tells that someone has a choice or something is possible.	She **could buy** tennis shoes or sandals. He **could sell** two pairs of shoes.

NGReach.com **Helping Verbs: eVisual 4.21**

Play a Game

Distribute **Practice Master PM4.19** and index cards. Have students play the game.

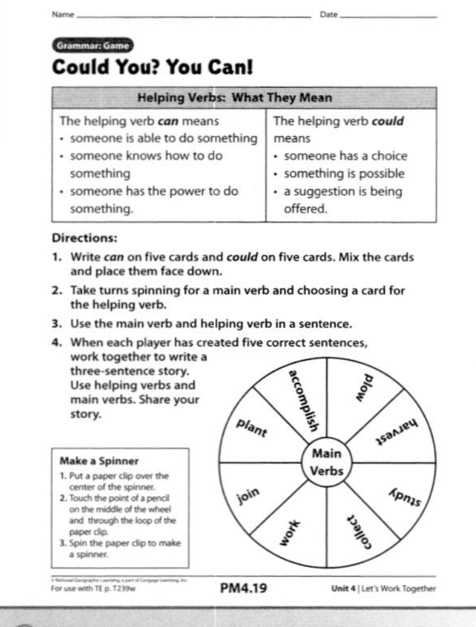
Name ______ Date ______

Grammar: Game

Could You? You Can!

Helping Verbs: What They Mean	
The helping verb *can* means • someone is able to do something • someone knows how to do something • someone has the power to do something.	The helping verb *could* means • someone has a choice • something is possible • a suggestion is being offered.

Directions:

1. Write *can* on five cards and *could* on five cards. Mix the cards and place them face down.
2. Take turns spinning for a main verb and choosing a card for the helping verb.
3. Use the main verb and helping verb in a sentence.
4. When each player has created five correct sentences, work together to write a three-sentence story. Use helping verbs and main verbs. Share your story.

Make a Spinner

1. Put a paper clip over the center of the spinner.
2. Touch the point of a pencil on the middle of the wheel and through the loop of the paper clip.
3. Spin the paper clip to make a spinner.

PM4.19 Unit 4 | Let's Work Together

NGReach.com **Practice Master PM4.19**

Differentiate

AL Above Level

ISSUE Students need a challenge to make the game fun.

STRATEGY After students form each sentence, have them tell which meaning of *can* or *could* best fits the meaning of the sentence.

Day 2

PROGRAM RESOURCES

More Helping Verbs: eVisual 4.23

Teach the Rules

Use the suggestion on page T244 to introduce another helping verb. Review: *A helping verb is used to help the main verb express an action.* Use **eVisual 4.23** to teach two more helping verbs.

More Helping Verbs

A **helping verb** works with an action verb. The action verb is the **main verb**.

• Use **must** to tell that somebody has to do something.	You **must buy** those shoes. He **must charge** the right price.
• Use **should** to give an opinion or advice.	You **should try** the shoes on first, though.

NGReach.com **More Helping Verbs: eVisual 4.23**

Generate Sentences

Prompt students to write sentences with helping verbs:

- *Write about something you have to do at home. Use* must *in the second position. Use an action verb in the third position.*
- *Write about something you should do at school. Use* should *in the second position. Use an action verb in the third position.*
- *Write a sentence telling someone to do something. Use* must *in the fourth position and an action verb in the fifth position.*
- *Write a sentence giving someone advice on how to do something. Use* should *in the fourth position and an action verb in the fifth position.*

*For **Writing Routine 3**, see page BP49.*

Differentiate

AL Above Level

ISSUE Students are able to complete their writing quickly.

STRATEGY Challenge students to link their four sentences by writing about farmers in the rainforest.

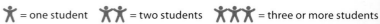

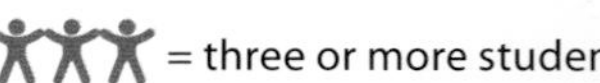

Form and Use Verbs (irregular)

CC.3.L.1.d

Day 3

PROGRAM RESOURCES

Forms of *do*: eVisual 4.24

MATERIALS

timer

Teach the Rules

Use the suggestion on page T253 to introduce the helping verb *do*. Then use **eVisual 4.24** to teach the forms of *do*.

Forms of *do*

The helping verb **do** adds emphasis to a **verb**.

• Use the form **do** with *I, you, we,* and *they.*	We **need** to share with those in need. We **do need** to share with those in need.
• Use the form **does** with *he, she,* and *it.*	She **agrees** to help. She **does agree** to help.

NGReach.com **Forms of *do*: eVisual 4.24**

Play a Game

Arrange students in pairs and allow ten minutes for them to find and rewrite sentences in the **Anthology** using *do*. Explain the rules of the game:

- *Use pages 245–253. Find sentences that you can add emphasis to by adding the helping verb* do.
- *For example, on page 249, I see the sentence "Some people blame humans." I can add do to the main verb* blame *to make a stronger statement: "Some people* do *blame humans."*

Afterward, have partners share their sentences with another pair and decide which pair has more sentences written correctly.

Have students vote on the most effective sentences with *do*. Have them copy the sentences, underlining *do*, to display.

Differentiate

SN Special Needs

ISSUE Students are overwhelmed by the number of pages to scan.

STRATEGY Have students look for sentences on **Anthology** pages 250–253 only. Focus on present-tense verbs such as *agree, believe,* and *think* on page 250. Remove the time limit and competitive element of the activity.

Day 4

PROGRAM RESOURCES

Grammar and Writing: Practice Master PM4.20

Grammar and Writing

Distribute **Practice Master PM4.20**. Have students use editing and proofreading marks to correct errors with helping verbs.

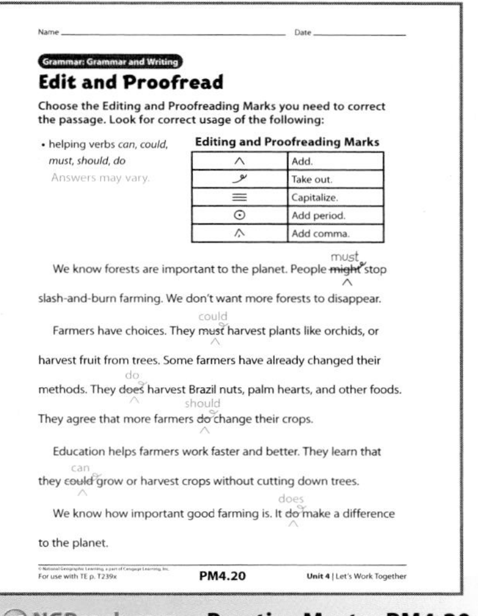
Name ______ Date ______

Grammar: Grammar and Writing

Edit and Proofread

Choose the Editing and Proofreading Marks you need to correct the passage. Look for correct usage of the following:

- helping verbs *can, could, must, should, do*

Answers may vary.

Editing and Proofreading Marks

^	Add.
⸗	Take out.
≡	Capitalize.
⊙	Add period.
^	Add comma.

We know forests are important to the planet. People ~~might~~ must stop slash-and-burn farming. We don't want more forests to disappear.

Farmers have choices. They ~~must~~ could harvest plants like orchids, or harvest fruit from trees. Some farmers have already changed their methods. They ~~does~~ do harvest Brazil nuts, palm hearts, and other foods. They agree that more farmers ~~do~~ should change their crops.

Education helps farmers work faster and better. They learn that they ~~could~~ can grow or harvest crops without cutting down trees.

We know how important good farming is. It ~~do~~ does make a difference to the planet.

© National Geographic Learning, a part of Cengage Learning, Inc.
For use with TE p. T239x PM4.20 Unit 4 | Let's Work Together

NGReach.com **Practice Master PM4.20**

Day 5

PROGRAM RESOURCES

Writing, Revising, and Editing Test: Assessment Masters A4.21–A4.22

Review and Assess

Copy and display the chart. Arrange students in small groups and have each group copy the chart. Tell them to complete columns two through five with the meaning or meanings of each helping verb and then use the helping verb in one example sentence.

can	could	must	should	do
"be able to" We can find a better way.				

☑ Administer the **Writing, Revising, and Editing Test.**

Daily Writing Skills

OBJECTIVES

Thematic Connection: Goods and Services

☑ **Evaluate Information**

COMMON CORE STANDARDS

Use Technology	CC.3.W.6
Conduct Research	CC.3.W.7

Introduce Evaluating Sources — Day 1 (three or more students)

PROGRAM RESOURCES

Web Site URLs: eVisual 4.22

MATERIALS

computers with Internet access • magazines • reference books • novels • encyclopedias

Teach the Skill

Introduce: *When you research, it's important to use reliable sources.*

Explain the qualities of a reliable source:

- The author is an expert; that is, someone who has special knowledge of, or experience in, the subject. Sometimes the author represents, or is part of, a well-respected group.
- The purpose is to give facts or information, not to persuade or entertain.
- It was published recently. Look for the date that the book or magazine was published or when the Web site was last updated.
- Another reliable source contains the same information.

Model evaluating materials using each criterion above. Then display **eVisual 4.22**. Explain the URL endings. Tell students to consider the expert or organization responsible as they decide if the site is reliable.

Explain that they should evaluate Web sites on all four criteria. Visit some of the Web sites below and discuss why they are more reliable than sources such as blogs or advertisements.

Explain that unreliable Web sites may contain incorrect facts and that incorrect facts can lead to misinformed opinions.

Web Site URLs

URL Ending	Example
.gov (government organization)	nps.gov nasa.gov
.edu (school, college, or university)	si.edu eo.ucar.edu/kids/
.com, .org, and .net (private organization, person, or business)	secretyellowstone.com tarpits.org nationalgeographic.com

NGReach.com
Web Site URLs: eVisual 4.22

INTERACTIVE WHITEBOARD TIP: Circle the URL endings in the examples.

Identify Research Sources — Day 2 (two students) — Option 1

Introduce

Explain to students that they will decide which selections in Units 3 and 4 are good sources of information to use in writing a research report.

Review the criteria for evaluating sources of information from Day 1 and relate it to "A Protected Place" on **Anthology** pages 180–193: *I believe that this nonfiction article is a reliable source. Its purpose is to inform. I think I can find the same information in other reliable sources.*

Practice

Tell partners to decide together if "Mama Panya's Pancakes" on **Anthology** pages 216–229 is a reliable source for research. Have students talk about the purpose of the selection as they decide.

Have partners choose two more selections from **Anthology** Units 3 and 4 and evaluate the reliability of each. Then have each student write a sentence or two to explain which selections are good sources for research and why.

Identify Research Sources — Day 2 (two students) — Option 2

PROGRAM RESOURCES

Small Group Reading Books for Units 3 and 4

Practice

Arrange students in pairs and have each pair select five different Unit 3 or 4 **Small Group Reading Books**.

Have partners look for information about the author and find the publication date of each book. Tell them to think about the purpose the author had in mind in writing the book.

Tell partners to collaborate to write a sentence or two about each book, explaining why they could or could not use the book as part of their research for a research report.

= one student = two students = three or more students

Evaluate Information

UGGESTED PACING

AY 1	Teach the Skill
AY 2–4	Daily Practice Options
AY 5	Review and Assess

Verify Information Day 3   Option 1

ATERIALS

ealth and science books • encyclopedias • computers with Internet access, ne per group

ntroduce

ell students that they will evaluate information by comparing nformation from more than one source. Copy and display the ollowing sentences.

> Broccoli has twice as much vitamin C as oranges.
> Carrots come in orange, white, yellow, and purple.
> The part of the potato that people eat is called the tuber.

ractice

rrange students in small groups. Have each group select one of the isplayed facts. Then have each group find one or two reliable sources hat confirm the information. Allow students to use both online and rint resources.

lave each group write sentences telling which sources they used and vhy they consider the source or sources reliable.

Verify Information Day 3  Option 2

ATERIALS

cience books and magazines • computers with Internet access, one per group

ntroduce

oint out the time line of the history of wolves in Yellowstone on **nthology** page 110. Remind students that one way to validate a ource and its information is to compare what it says to information ound in other sources.

ractice

rrange students in groups of three. Have each group member select different fact from the time line and search for other reliable sources ontaining the same information. Allow students to use both online and rint resources.

lave each student write a sentence or two telling which source they ised and why that source is reliable.

)nce each group has verified the information from the time line, have hem share their sources with another group and explain why they think heir sources are reliable.

Find Reliable Sources Day 4

MATERIALS

books about rainforests • encyclopedias • computers with Internet access, one per pair of students

Introduce

Tell students that they will locate and evaluate sources of information about rainforests. Review the four criteria for a reliable source. Provide sources such as the **Anthology**, other print materials, and digital media.

Practice

Copy and display the following chart. Have partners create and complete similar charts for two sources they find.

Source	Reliable/Unreliable	Why

Then have them compare their findings with those of another pair of students.

Review and Assess Day 5 

PROGRAM RESOURCES

Writing, Revising, and Editing Test: Assessment Masters A4.21–A4.22

Review the Skill

Copy and display the following chart.

Source	Why Source is Reliable or Unreliable
Web site written by experts	
Persuasive essay	
Web advertisement	
Personal Web site	

Have small groups complete the chart by explaining why each source is either reliable or unreliable.

☑ Administer the **Writing, Revising, and Editing Test**.

Day 1 Listen and Comprehend

Letter

OBJECTIVES

Thematic Connection: Goods and Services

☑ **Use Domain-Specific Words**

☑ **Identify Opinions and Evidence to Comprehend Text**

PROGRAM RESOURCES

PRINT & TECHNOLOGY

Family Newsletter 4

Opinion Chart: Practice Master PM4.18

TECHNOLOGY ONLY

Sing with Me MP3

Digital Library: Key Word Images

My Vocabulary Notebook

Read Aloud: eVisual 4.20

MATERIALS

timer

Power Writing

Have students write as much as they can as well as they can in one minute about the word *vegetable*.

*For **Writing Routine 1**, see page BP47.*

COMMON CORE STANDARDS

Reading	
Read and Comprehend Informational Text	CC.3.Rinf.10
Read with Fluency to Support Comprehension	CC.3.Rfou.4
Writing	
Link Opinions and Reasons	CC.3.W.1.c
Write Over Shorter Time for Specific Purposes	CC.3.W.10
Speaking/Listening	
Explain Ideas and Understanding	CC.3.SL.1.d
Elaborate	CC.3.SL.3
Language and Vocabulary	
Acquire and Use General Academic and Domain-Specific Words	CC.3.L.6

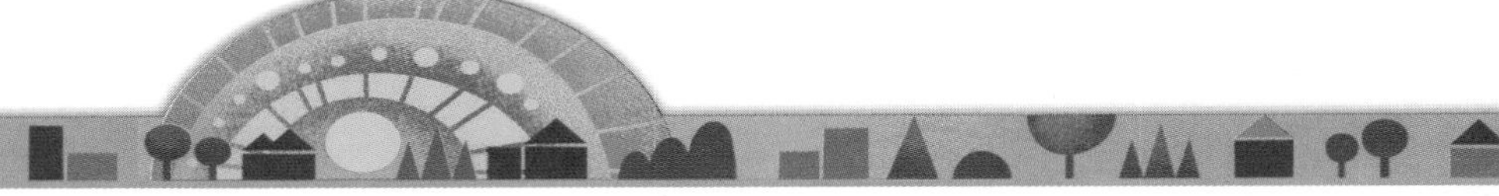

WARM-UP

Introduce: *Today we will listen to a chant about planting a garden.* Have partners share three reasons why planting a garden is a good idea.

Academic Talk

1 Persuade **Anthology** page 240

Read aloud the instructions and play the **Sing with Me Language Song**: "A Healthy Idea." Explain: *When you persuade, you try to get someone to do or to believe something.* Discuss how Clara persuades her friends to plant a garden.

Use the following steps to model persuading someone to eat more fruit:

- *First, state your idea: Everyone should eat at least three pieces of fruit every day.*
- *Next, elaborate by giving facts or examples to explain your ideas and understanding: We could eat sweet berries for dessert, instead of cookies.*

Have partners give persuasive statements about why people should recycle, using facts and examples to elaborate on their ideas and to explain their understanding.

Social Studies Vocabulary

2 Key Words ☑ **Anthology** page 241

Key Words

agriculture · crop · farmer
field · harvest · plow

Explain and model using **Vocabulary Routine 1** and the photos and captions to teach the Key Words.

- ***Pronounce the word** and point to the image:* **agriculture**.
- ***Rate the word.** Hold up your fingers to show how well you know the word. (1=very well; 2=a little; 3=not at all) Tell what you know about this word.*
- ***Define the word:*** ***Agriculture*** *is farming.*
- ***Elaborate:*** *Relate words to knowledge and experience:* ***Agriculture*** *grows food.*

*For **Vocabulary Routine 1**, see page BP34.*

*For more images of the Key Words, use the **Digital Library**.*

Have partners repeat the routine for each Key Word. Have each student add the words to **My Vocabulary Notebook**.

See **Differentiate**

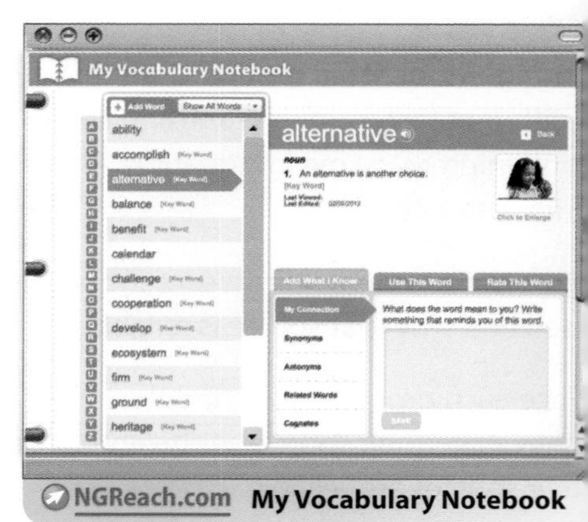

NGReach.com **My Vocabulary Notebook**

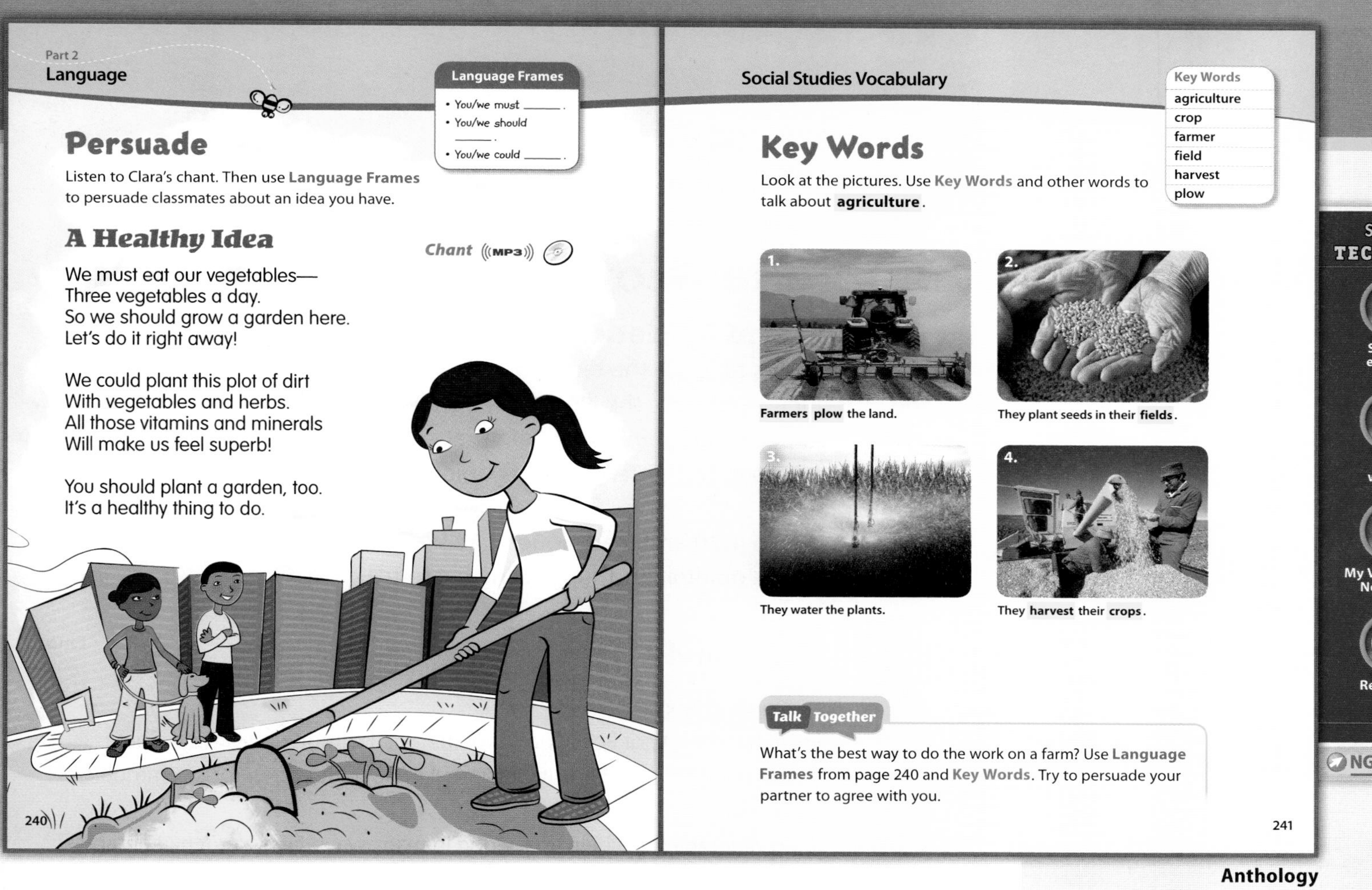

Part 2
Language
Language Frames
• You/we must ______.
• You/we should ______.
• You/we could ______.
Persuade
Listen to Clara's chant. Then use Language Frames to persuade classmates about an idea you have.
A Healthy Idea
Chant (MP3)
We must eat our vegetables—
Three vegetables a day.
So we should grow a garden here.
Let's do it right away!
We could plant this plot of dirt
With vegetables and herbs.
All those vitamins and minerals
Will make us feel superb!
You should plant a garden, too.
It's a healthy thing to do.
240
Social Studies Vocabulary
Key Words
agriculture
crop
farmer
field
harvest
plow
Key Words
Look at the pictures. Use Key Words and other words to talk about agriculture.
1. Farmers plow the land.
2. They plant seeds in their fields.
3. They water the plants.
4. They harvest their crops.
Talk Together
What's the best way to do the work on a farm? Use Language Frames from page 240 and Key Words. Try to persuade your partner to agree with you.
241
STUDENT TECHNOLOGY
Student eEdition
Sing with Me
My Vocabulary Notebook
Resources
NGReach.com

Anthology
pages 240–241

❸ Talk Together **Anthology** page 241

Read aloud the directions for **Talk Together**. Explain that the photographs on page 241 are examples of work that farmers do. Say: *Use the photographs and text on page 241 to discuss the best way to do work on a farm.* Provide an example: ***Farmers** must use big tractors to **plow** the land.*

Have students try to persuade their partners to agree with their ideas about farming. Remind them to state their ideas and support them with facts and examples.

Check & Reteach

OBJECTIVE: Use Domain-Specific Words ☑

As students make persuasive statements, listen for correct usage of the Key Words.

If students use words incorrectly, provide sentence frames for them to complete orally:

- ***Farmers** ______ the land to create rows for seeds.* (**plow**)
- ***Farmers** plant seeds in their ______.* (**fields**)
- ***Farmers harvest** their ______.* (**crops**)

Weekly Writing

Gather students' writing throughout the week:

✓ Daily Writing Skills Practice (T239y–T239z)
✓ Power Writing (T240, T242a, T246, T254, T257a)
✓ Writing (T242, T244–T245, T253, 257, T258)
✓ Research Project (T259a–T259b)

Differentiate

EL English Learners

ISSUE Students do not understand definitions.

STRATEGY Provide translations of the Key Words. Access **Family Newsletter 4** for translations in seven languages. Use a cognate for Spanish speakers:

agriculture/agricultura

BL Below Level

ISSUE Students have difficulty defining Key Words.

STRATEGY Pair students with more proficient partners and have them consult the **Picture Dictionary** to find a definition, photo, and example. Then have partners work together to paraphrase the definition using their own words.

Word Maps

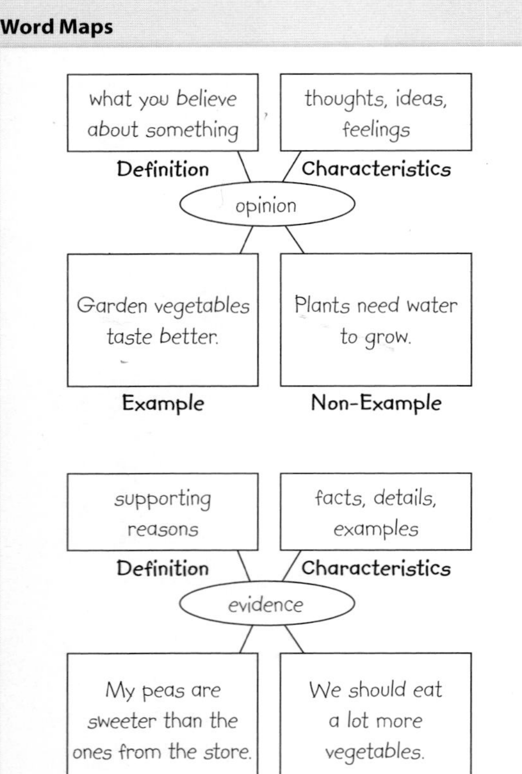

Fluency

Model Phrasing Explain the concept: *When you read with proper phrasing, you group the words together into meaningful parts. Punctuation like commas and periods can help you determine where to pause in your phrasing.* Model phrasing with sentences from the **Read Aloud**. Have students practice phrasing by reading aloud the speech balloons from **Anthology** page 242.

Comprehension

4 Opinion and Evidence  Anthology page 242

Use Word Maps to teach the terms ***opinion*** and ***evidence***. Then read aloud the introduction and use the illustrations and speech balloons to point out how evidence supports an opinion. Explain that signal words such as *first, finally, because, therefore*, and *since*, often link opinions and evidence.

Display **eVisual 4.20** and read aloud Clara's letter to the editor. Ask students to listen for Clara's opinion and supporting evidence.

Read Aloud

Letter

Dear Newspaper Editor:

I believe that the city of Rosewood should have a community garden. There is an empty field next to my school. It would make the perfect spot for a community vegetable garden.

Growing vegetables will help Rosewood in many ways. First, garden vegetables taste fresher than the ones we buy at the market. Secondly, since we will grow the vegetables ourselves, they will cost less. Finally, gardening is wonderful exercise.

Planting vegetables will give us fresh-tasting food, save money, and help people exercise. Therefore, Rosewood residents should start planting now!

Sincerely,
Clara Thorpe

NGReach.com **Read Aloud: eVisual 4.20**

INTERACTIVE WHITEBOARD TIP: Draw a box around an opinion. Underline evidence that supports it.

5 Map and Talk Anthology page 242

Have students read how to make an opinion chart. Ask: *What signal words tell you when Clara states her* ***opinion****?* (believe; should) *What* ***evidence*** *does Clara give to support her* ***opinion****?* (Vegetables will be fresher.) Have students vote for the most persuasive evidence in Clara's letter.

6 Talk Together Anthology page 242

Have students use **Practice Master PM4.18** to make an opinion chart about their partner's opinion.

Check & Reteach

OBJECTIVE: Identify Opinions and Evidence to Comprehend Text

As partners discuss their opinions, listen to make sure that students can consistently identify opinions and supporting evidence.

If students have difficulty, say: *Clara says, "I believe." The word* believe *is a signal word that shows that she is stating her* ***opinion****. What is Clara's* ***opinion****? What reasons does Clara give to show that it is a good idea? This is* ***evidence*** *that supports her* ***opinion****.*

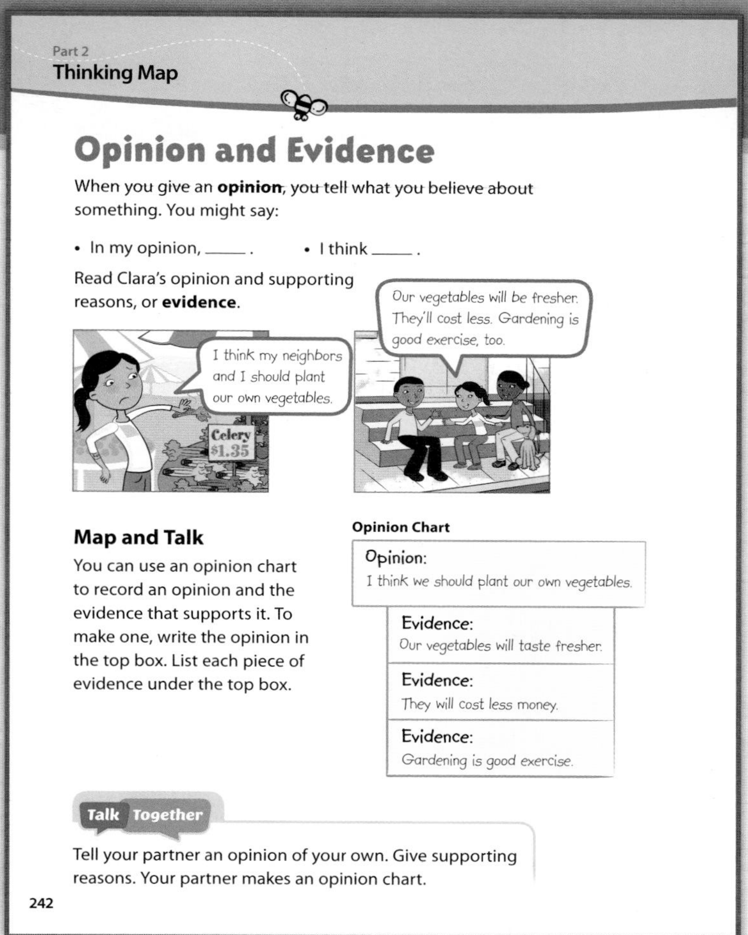

Part 2
Thinking Map

Opinion and Evidence

When you give an **opinion**, you tell what you believe about something. You might say:

- In my opinion, ____.
- I think ____.

Read Clara's opinion and supporting reasons, or **evidence**.

Map and Talk

You can use an opinion chart to record an opinion and the evidence that supports it. To make one, write the opinion in the top box. List each piece of evidence under the top box.

Opinion Chart

Opinion: I think we should plant our own vegetables.
Evidence: Our vegetables will taste fresher.
Evidence: They will cost less money.
Evidence: Gardening is good exercise.

Talk Together

Tell your partner an opinion of your own. Give supporting reasons. Your partner makes an opinion chart.

242

Anthology page 242

Writing

7 Write and Support an Opinion

Introduce: *Now you will write sentences about the* ***opinions*** *you discussed with your partner.* Model the process using the opinion chart on **Anthology** page 242.

Think Aloud	Write
First, I will write my ***opinion***.	I think we should plant our own vegetables.
Then I will support my ***opinion*** *with* ***evidence***.	I think we should plant our own vegetables because they will taste fresher and cost less.

For ***Writing Routine 2****, see page BP48.*

Have students use their opinion charts from **Talk Together** to help them write sentences that state and support their opinions. Remind them to link their opinions and reasons. Then have them add the sentences to their Weekly Writing folders.

WRAP-UP Ask students to use Key Words to persuade a partner that farmers are important people.

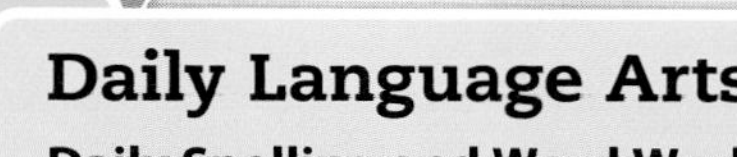

Daily Language Arts

Daily Spelling and Word Work
Pretest page T239u

Daily Grammar
Point out the verb phrase *could plant* in the second stanza of the chant on **Anthology** page 240. Then use page T239w to introduce helping verbs.

Daily Writing Skills
Point out that students should use reliable sources when they write reports. Then use page T239y to teach how to evaluate sources.

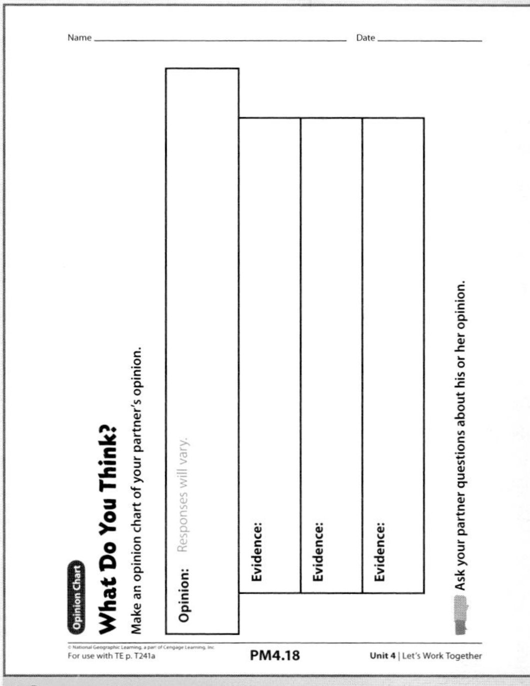

Name ____ Date ____

Opinion Chart

What Do You Think?

Make an opinion chart of your partner's opinion.

Opinion: Responses will vary.

Evidence:

Evidence:

Evidence:

Ask your partner questions about his or her opinion.

For use with TE p. T241a

PM4.18

Unit 4 | Let's Work Together

NGReach.com **Practice Master PM4.18**

Day 2 Read and Comprehend

Persuasive Speech

OBJECTIVES

Thematic Connection: Goods and Services

☑ Use Academic Words

☑ Determine Importance

PROGRAM RESOURCES

PRINT & TECHNOLOGY

Weekly Writing Folders

TECHNOLOGY ONLY

Digital Library: Key Word Images

My Vocabulary Notebook

Family Newsletter 4

MATERIALS

timer

Power Writing

Have students write as much as they can as well as they can in one minute about the word *agriculture*.

*For **Writing Routine 1**, see page BP47.*

COMMON CORE STANDARDS

Reading	
Determine the Main Idea of Text and Recount Key Details	CC.3.Rinf.2
Read with Fluency to Support Comprehension	CC.3.Rfou.4
Writing	
Write Over Shorter Time for Specific Tasks	CC.3.W.10
Speaking and Listening	
Discuss Topics, Expressing Ideas Clearly	CC.3.SL.1
Explain Ideas and Understanding	CC.3.SL.1.d
Language and Vocabulary	
Determine Meaning of Words and Phrases	CC.3.L.4
Acquire and Use General Academic Words	CC.3.L.6

WARM-UP

Ask students to imagine they are planting their own gardens. Have them work with a partner and explain what plants they would grow and why.

Academic Talk

1 Make an Argument

Explain: *When you make an argument, you state your **opinion** and then give reasons and **evidence** to support it.*

Model making an argument: *I think we should collect rainwater to water our gardens. If we use rainwater, we won't have to take as much water from lakes and rivers. Rainwater also has nutrients that are healthier for plants.*

Discuss your argument, asking students to point out your opinion and reasons. Explain how you expressed your ideas and explained your understanding clearly.

Ask: *Is it better to eat homegrown food or store-bought food?* Divide the class into two groups and have them discuss the topic. Use a **Fishbowl**:

- Group 1 sits in the center and makes an argument for or against eating homegrown food. Students should explain their opinions and reasons.
- Group 2 listens to identify Group 1's opinions and reasons.
- The groups reverse positions. Group 2 gives and supports opinions while Group 1 listens.

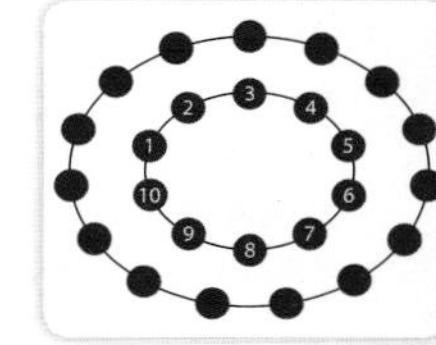

Fishbowl

*For **Fishbowl**, see page BP45.*

Academic Vocabulary

2 More Key Words ☑ Anthology page 243

Say: *Let's learn some more words to help us talk about making a better world.* Explain and model using **Vocabulary Routine 1** and the images in the **Student eEdition** to teach the Key Words.

Key Words

alternative · conservation
future · method · sustain

- ***Pronounce the word*** *and point to the image:* **alternative**.
- ***Rate the word.*** *Hold up your fingers to show how well you know the word. (1 = very well; 2 = a little; 3 = not at all) Tell what you know about this word.*
- ***Define the word:*** *An **alternative** is another choice.*
- ***Elaborate.*** *Relate the words to your experience: Biking is an **alternative** to driving.*

*For **Vocabulary Routine 1**, see page BP34.*

*For more images of the Key Words, use the **Digital Library**.*

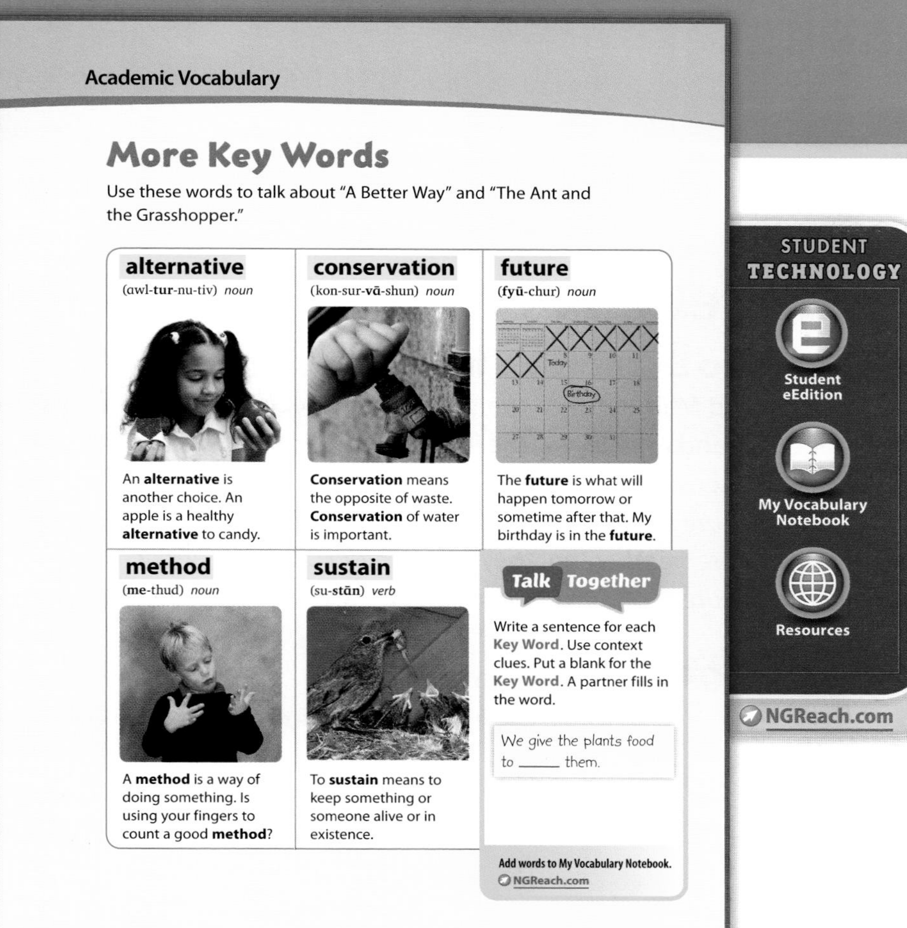
Academic Vocabulary

More Key Words

Use these words to talk about "A Better Way" and "The Ant and the Grasshopper."

alternative
(awl-**tur**-nu-tiv) *noun*

An **alternative** is another choice. An apple is a healthy **alternative** to candy.

conservation
(kon-sur-**vā**-shun) *noun*

Conservation means the opposite of waste. **Conservation** of water is important.

future
(**fyū**-chur) *noun*

The **future** is what will happen tomorrow or sometime after that. My birthday is in the **future**.

method
(**me**-thud) *noun*

A **method** is a way of doing something. Is using your fingers to count a good **method**?

sustain
(su-**stān**) *verb*

To **sustain** means to keep something or someone alive or in existence.

Talk Together

Write a sentence for each Key Word. Use context clues. Put a blank for the Key Word. A partner fills in the word.

We give the plants food to ______ them.

Add words to My Vocabulary Notebook.
NGReach.com

STUDENT TECHNOLOGY

Student eEdition

My Vocabulary Notebook

Resources

NGReach.com

Anthology page 243

Have partners use page 243 to take turns repeating the routine for each word. Have students add the words to **My Vocabulary Notebook**.

See **Differentiate**

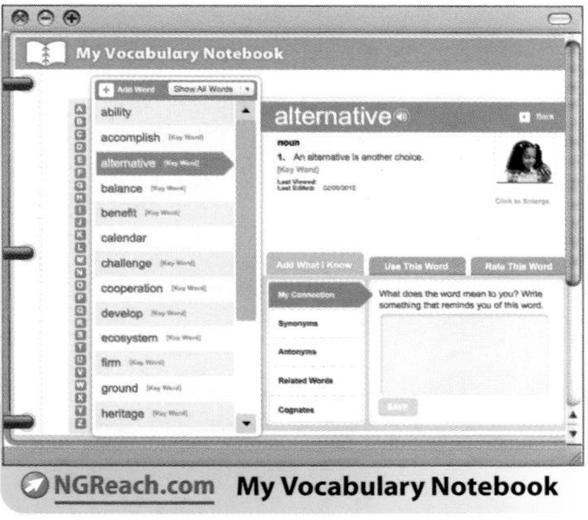

NGReach.com **My Vocabulary Notebook**

3 Talk Together **Anthology** page 243

Read aloud the instructions. Have students write a cloze sentence for each Key Word. Then have partners exchange papers and choose the correct Key Words to complete each other's sentences.

Check & Reteach

OBJECTIVE: Use Academic Words ☑

As partners share and discuss sentences, listen for correct usage of the Key Words.

If students use the words incorrectly, ask questions about the words:

Which word means "the opposite of waste"? (***conservation***)

Which word tells about something that will happen tomorrow or later? (***future***)

Which word means "a way of doing something"? (***method***)

Best Practices

Model Academic Language If Academic Talk discussions reflect too much informal talk, model an academic conversation with or between two students. Then have students echo the model to role-play an academic discussion.

Differentiate

EL English Learners

ISSUE Students do not understand definitions.

STRATEGY Provide translations of the Key Words. Access **Family Newsletter 4**. Use cognates for Spanish speakers:

alternative/alternativa	*conservation/conservación*
future/futuro	*method/método*

BL Below Level

ISSUE Students have trouble elaborating on words.

STRATEGY Have students review the images and examples of each Key Word on **Anthology** page T243. Ask: *What does this remind you of?*

Word Map

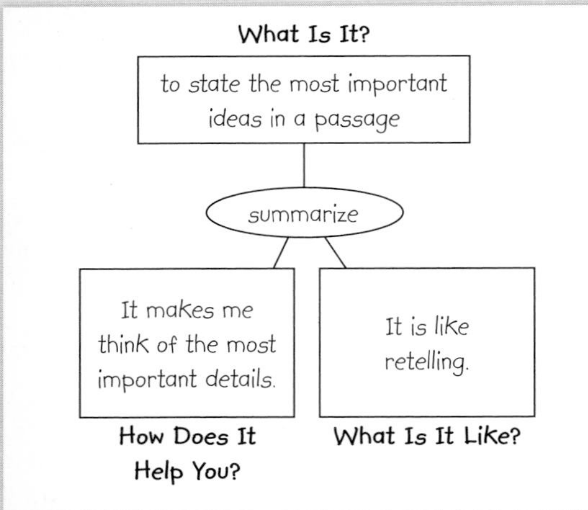
What Is It?
to state the most important ideas in a passage
summarize
It makes me think of the most important details.
It is like retelling.
How Does It Help You?
What Is It Like?

Daily Language Arts

Daily Spelling and Word Work ☑
Practice page T239u

Daily Grammar ☑
On **Anthology** page 245, point out the helping verb *should* in the second sentence of the persuasive speech. Then use page T239w to teach more helping verbs.

Daily Writing Skills ☑
Remind students that it is important to use reliable sources when they write. Then use page T239y to practice identifying good sources.

Fluency

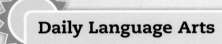

Practice Phrasing As partners read aloud "Window Dressing," circulate and listen for correct phrasing.

Comprehension

4 Learn to Determine Importance ☑ **Anthology** pages 244–245

Use a Word Map to teach the term ***summarize***. Then project **Student eEdition** page 244 and read aloud the instructions. Point to details in the illustration as you model determining importance and relating ideas. Say:

- *This picture is about a woman and a girl who are planting herbs.*
- *I should remember that they are planting basil and peppermint.*
- *This picture shows that the girl and the woman plant basil and peppermint.*

5 Talk Together **Anthology** page 245

Read aloud the instructions on page 245. Have students chorally read the first two paragraphs of "Window Dressing." Read aloud the sample summary. Ask: *How can summarizing help you identify what Clara wants the reader to do?* (Possible response: When I **summarize**, I identify the main idea and important details.)

Have partners read the rest of the speech and pause to summarize parts of the text. Circulate and monitor their conversations.

Check & Reteach

OBJECTIVE: Determine Importance ☑

Ask students to summarize the last paragraph of Clara's speech.

If students have difficulty summarizing, remind them to include only the most important ideas. Reread the third paragraph and say: *I read a detail about spaghetti. If I left that detail out, the summary of my speech would still make sense.* Ask students what detail in the paragraph is important to include. (Fresh herbs are good for cooking.)

Writing

6 Write a Summary

Introduce: *We are going to write a summary that tells the most important ideas of Clara's speech.* Model the process using the second paragraph of Clara's speech.

Think Aloud	Write
First, I will think about the topic of this paragraph.	planting an herb garden
Next, I will think about the most important details I remember.	You need soil, seedlings, sunlight, and water.
Finally, I will ***summarize*** *the most important details of this part of the text and write it as a complete sentence.*	You need soil, seedlings, sunlight, and a little water to plant and **sustain** an herb garden.

*For **Writing Routine 2**, see page BP48.*

Learn to Determine Importance

Look at the picture. What does it show? Determine which parts are important. Then think of a sentence or two to briefly tell, or **summarize**, what the picture shows.

Basil

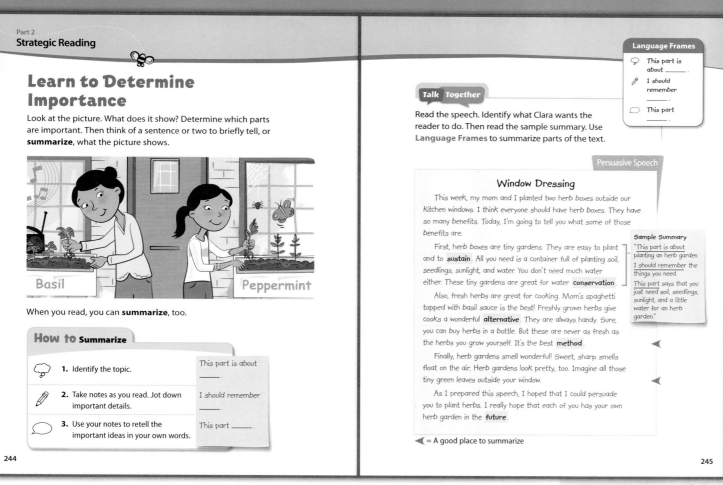

Peppermint

When you read, you can **summarize**, too.

How to Summarize

1. Identify the topic.	This part is about ___.
2. Take notes as you read. Jot down important details.	I should remember ___.
3. Use your notes to retell the important ideas in your own words.	This part ___.

Language Frames

- This part is about ___.
- I should remember ___.
- This part ___.

Talk Together

Read the speech. Identify what Clara wants the reader to do. Then read the sample summary. Use **Language Frames** to summarize parts of the text.

Persuasive Speech

Window Dressing

This week, my mom and I planted two herb boxes outside our kitchen windows. I think everyone should have herb boxes. They have so many benefits. Today, I'm going to tell you what some of those benefits are.

First, herb boxes are tiny gardens. They are easy to plant and to **sustain**. All you need is a container full of planting soil, seedlings, sunlight, and water. You don't need much water either. These tiny gardens are great for water **conservation**.

Also, fresh herbs are great for cooking. Mom's spaghetti topped with basil sauce is the best! Freshly grown herbs give cooks a wonderful **alternative**. They are always handy. Sure, you can buy herbs in a bottle. But these are never as fresh as the herbs you grow yourself. It's the best **method**.

Finally, herb gardens smell wonderful! Sweet, sharp smells float on the air. Herb gardens look pretty, too. Imagine all those tiny green leaves outside your window.

As I prepared this speech, I hoped that I could persuade you to plant herbs. I really hope that each of you has your own herb garden in the **future**.

Sample Summary
"This part is about planting an herb garden. I should remember the things you need. This part says that you just need soil, seedlings, sunlight, and a little water for an herb garden."

◄ = A good place to summarize

Anthology
pages 244–245

Have students write their own summaries of the entire speech, recounting the main idea and key details. Remind students to relate their ideas clearly. Then have them exchange summaries with a partner and determine if they included all of the most important details.

Have students add their summaries to their Weekly Writing folders.

See **Differentiate**

WRAP-UP Have partners debate whether their community should build a new playground or create a new flower garden. Partners should take different sides. Each partner has two minutes to convince the other. Have the class award points to the more persuasive argument.

Differentiate

AL Above Level

ISSUE Students' summaries include too many unimportant details.

STRATEGY Challenge students to write the shortest summary that still includes the most important details and information. Have students present their completed summaries to the group to critique for completeness. The shortest complete summary wins.

Read and Comprehend

Persuasive Article

OBJECTIVES

Thematic Connection: Goods and Services

- ☑ **Identify Opinions and Evidence to Comprehend Text**
- ☑ **Determine Importance**

PROGRAM RESOURCES

TECHNOLOGY ONLY

My Vocabulary Notebook

Read with Me: Selection Recordings: MP3 or CD 1 Tracks 10–11

Comprehension Coach

MATERIALS

timer

Power Writing

Have students write as much as they can as well as they can in one minute about the word *sustain*.

*For **Writing Routine 1**, see page BP47.*

COMMON CORE STANDARDS

Reading	
Recount Key Details	CC.3.Rinf.2
Use Text Features	CC.3.Rinf.5
Distinguish Points of View	CC.3.Rinf.6
Read with Fluency to Support Comprehension	CC.3.Rfou.4
Read Orally with Accuracy and Appropriate Rate on Successive Readings	CC.3.Rfou.4.b
Writing	
Write Over Shorter Time for Specific Audiences	CC.3.W.10
Language and Vocabulary	
Acquire and Use General Academic and Domain-Specific Words	CC.3.L.6

WARM-UP

Display the photo on **Student eEdition** page 247. Ask: *What do you see in this **field**? What do you think it was like before people changed the environment?*

Vocabulary Practice

1 Expand Word Knowledge ☑

Students will practice Key Words by creating Word Maps. Use **Vocabulary Routine 2** to model how to make a Word Map for the word ***sustain***.

- Write the word.
- Add a picture.
- Add a definition.
- Add an example.
- Add a non-example.

*For **Vocabulary Routine 2**, see page BP35.*

Key Words

agriculture · alternative · conservation
crop · evidence · farmer · field
future · harvest · method · opinion
plow · summarize · sustain

Assign a Key Word to each set of partners. After they complete their Word Maps, have them add the examples to **My Vocabulary Notebook**.

Academic Talk

2 Preview and Predict

REVIEW Remind students: *One way to preview a nonfiction text is to look at the text features that help organize and give information.* Point out the section heading on **Anthology** page 248 and read it aloud. Say: *The section heading helps me predict that this section will be about how trees are lost or destroyed. I think that the text will explain why this happens.*

Display these Key Words: *agriculture, crop, farmers, method*. Have students use a **Think, Pair, Share** to discuss their predictions about "A Better Way."

- Have students independently preview and make predictions about the article using the section heads on **Anthology** pages 248–257.
- Have students form pairs and discuss their predictions.
- Have students individually share their predictions with the class. Encourage students to use Key Words as they discuss the selection.

Think A B
Pair A B
Share A B

Think, Pair, Share

*For **Think, Pair, Share**, see page BP46.*

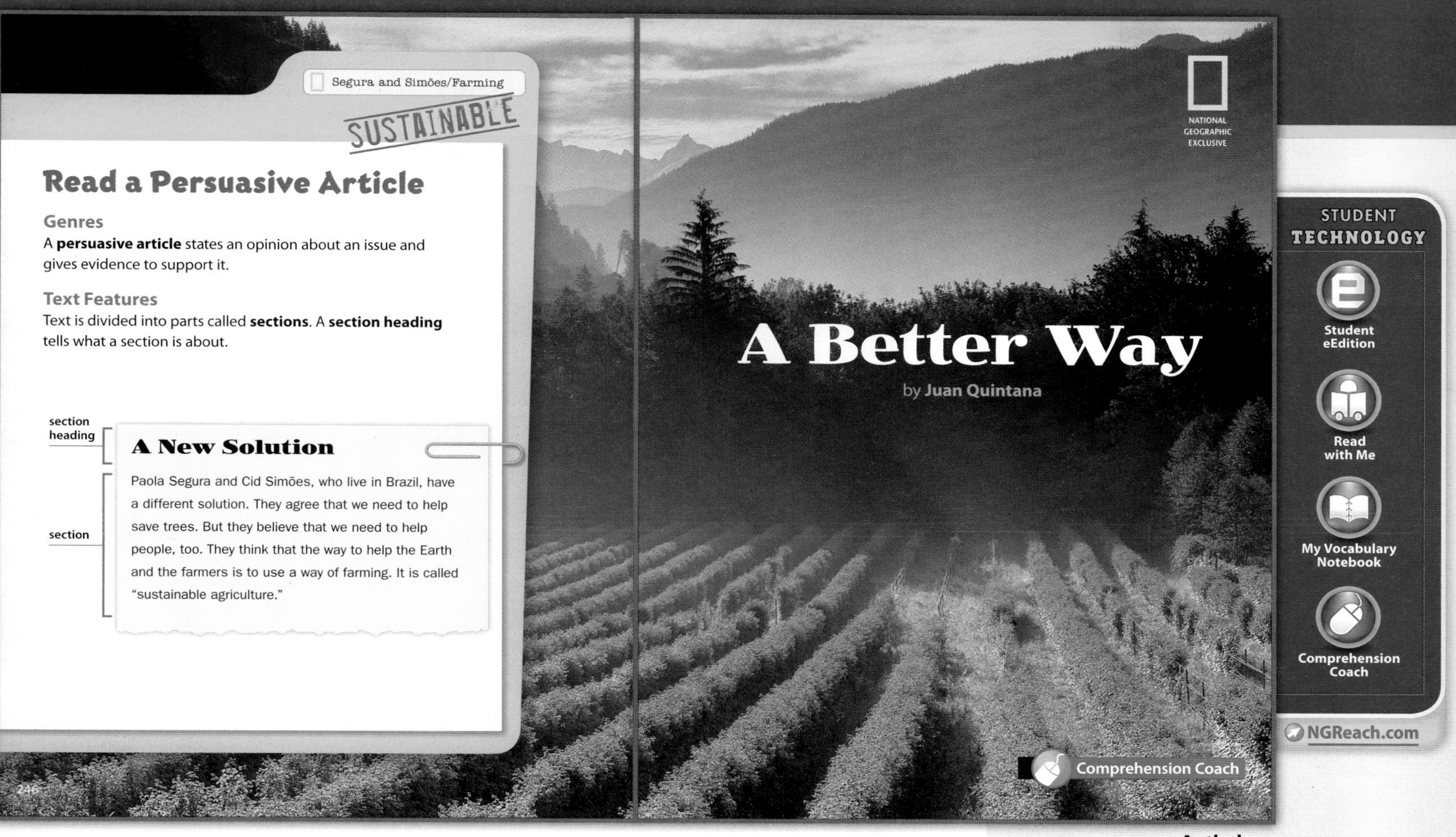

Segura and Simões/Farming
SUSTAINABLE
Read a Persuasive Article
Genres
A persuasive article states an opinion about an issue and gives evidence to support it.
Text Features
Text is divided into parts called sections. A section heading tells what a section is about.
section heading
section
A New Solution
Paola Segura and Cid Simões, who live in Brazil, have a different solution. They agree that we need to help save trees. But they believe that we need to help people, too. They think that the way to help the Earth and the farmers is to use a way of farming. It is called "sustainable agriculture."
NATIONAL GEOGRAPHIC EXCLUSIVE
A Better Way
by Juan Quintana
Comprehension Coach
STUDENT TECHNOLOGY
Student eEdition
Read with Me
My Vocabulary Notebook
Comprehension Coach
NGReach.com

Anthology
pages 246–247

Reading

3 Read a Persuasive Article **Anthology** pages 246–247

GENRE Have a volunteer read aloud the definition of a persuasive article. Elaborate: *A persuasive article wants the reader to believe or to do something.*

TEXT FEATURES Ask a volunteer to read aloud the definition of section headings. Elaborate: *A section heading can give clues about what you will read.*

SCIENCE BACKGROUND Share information to build background:

- *When forests are destroyed, animals lose their homes. Some become endangered.*
- *When too many trees are removed from a forest, there is nothing left to hold the soil in place. The soil washes away and causes pollution in streams and rivers.*

Have students read pages 246–253. See **Differentiate**

Differentiate

BL Below Level

TEXT-TALK READ ALOUD Use **Vocabulary Routine 5**. As you read, pause to provide a short explanation of each Key Word.

OL On Level

READ TOGETHER Have partners read the selection together. Use the questions to build comprehension.

AL Above Level

READ INDEPENDENTLY As students read silently, have them identify opinions and use the questions to build comprehension.

Best Practices

Encourage Participation If a student does not have the background experience to fully participate in a discussion, encourage him or her to ask questions as part of the background discussion.

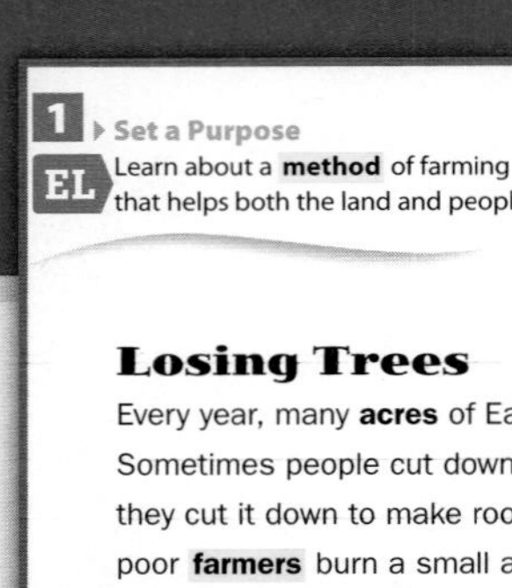

1 ▸ Set a Purpose
EL Learn about a **method** of farming that helps both the land and people.

Losing Trees

Every year, many **acres** of Earth's precious forests are cut down. Sometimes people cut down the forest for wood. Other times, they cut it down to make room for **cattle** or large farms. Often, poor **farmers** burn a small area of forest to **clear it of** trees. In the cleared area, they plant **crops** to feed their families. This is called **slash**-and-burn **agriculture**.

Slash-and-Burn Agriculture

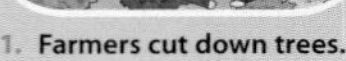

1. Farmers cut down trees.

2. Farmers burn the dry trees to clear the land.

3. Farmers plant crops. When the land wears out, they clear new land.

In Other Words
acres large areas
cattle cows
clear it of get rid of the
slash cut

248

For all of these reasons, forests have been disappearing. Some people blame humans. They think farming is the problem. To them, the solution is clear. People should stay out of the forest. **Farming must be limited!**

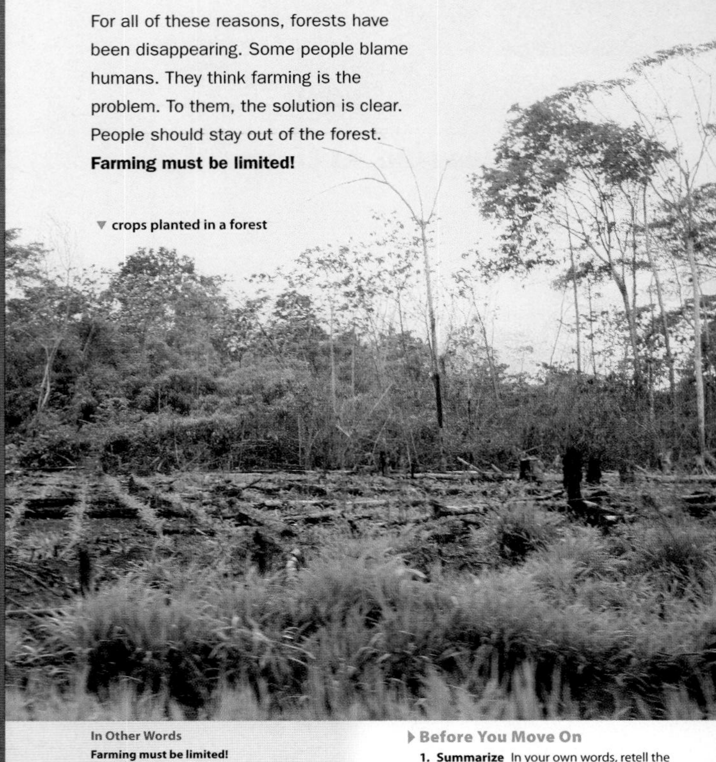

▾ crops planted in a forest

In Other Words
Farming must be limited! People must not farm very much!

▸ **Before You Move On**
1. **Summarize** In your own words, retell the important ideas in this section.
2. **Steps in a Process** What is the second step in slash-and-burn **agriculture**? Point to where you found the information.

249

Anthology
pages 248–249

Fluency

Practice Phrasing, Accuracy, Rate As students read, monitor their phrasing, accuracy, and rate.

Answers Before You Move On

1. **Summarize** ☑ Possible response: This part is about losing trees. I should remember why people cut down trees. This part says people slash-and-burn the forest for wood and to make room for cattle, large farms, and small farms.
2. **Steps in a Process** The second step in slash-and-burn **agriculture** is when people burn the dry trees to clear the land. Picture 2 on page 248 shows this step of the process.

Read and Build Comprehension

1 **Set a Purpose** Have a student read aloud the purpose statement. Discuss what students expect to find out about farming.

2 **Identify Opinion and Evidence** ☑ *What is one of Segura and Simões's* ***opinions*** *on page 250?* (Possible response: We need to save trees, but we need to help people, too.) *What* ***evidence*** *supports this* ***opinion****?* (Sustainable **agriculture** will give **farmers** an income without destroying more trees.)

3 **Determine Importance** ☑ *What is the most important idea on pages 250–251?* (Possible response: Segura and Simões believe that sustainable **agriculture** will help both **farmers** and trees.)

Differentiate

EL English Learners

ISSUE Students do not understand what it means to set a purpose for reading.

STRATEGY Together, have students look at the text features, photographs, and illustrations. Ask:

- *Do you think we will read facts about farming or a funny story about farming?*
- *Will you read to be entertained or to learn about a new* ***method*** *of farming?*

BL Below Level

ISSUE Students have difficulty identifying an opinion.

STRATEGY Remind students that one way to express an opinion is by using words like *think* or *believe*. Have students locate examples of the signal words on page 250. Then have them identify Simões and Segura's opinions about farming.

A New Solution

Paola Segura and Cid Simões, who live in Brazil, have a different solution. They agree that we need to help save trees. But they believe that we need to help people, too. They think that the way to help the Earth and the farmers is to use a way of farming. It is called "sustainable agriculture."

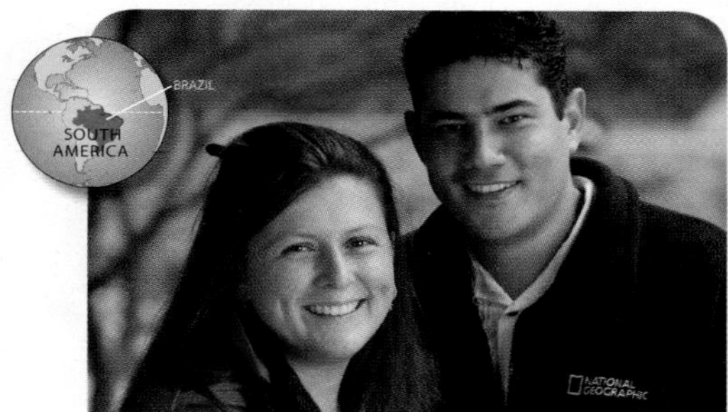

▲ Segura and Simões were named "Emerging Explorers" by the National Geographic Society. The Society wanted to thank them for their work.

Segura and Simões met in Costa Rica at Earth University. There they studied sustainable agriculture. They believe that farmers can earn money from a small piece of land. They can live there and **raise** their families. They can have healthy land and a community that **lasts.** 2 BL

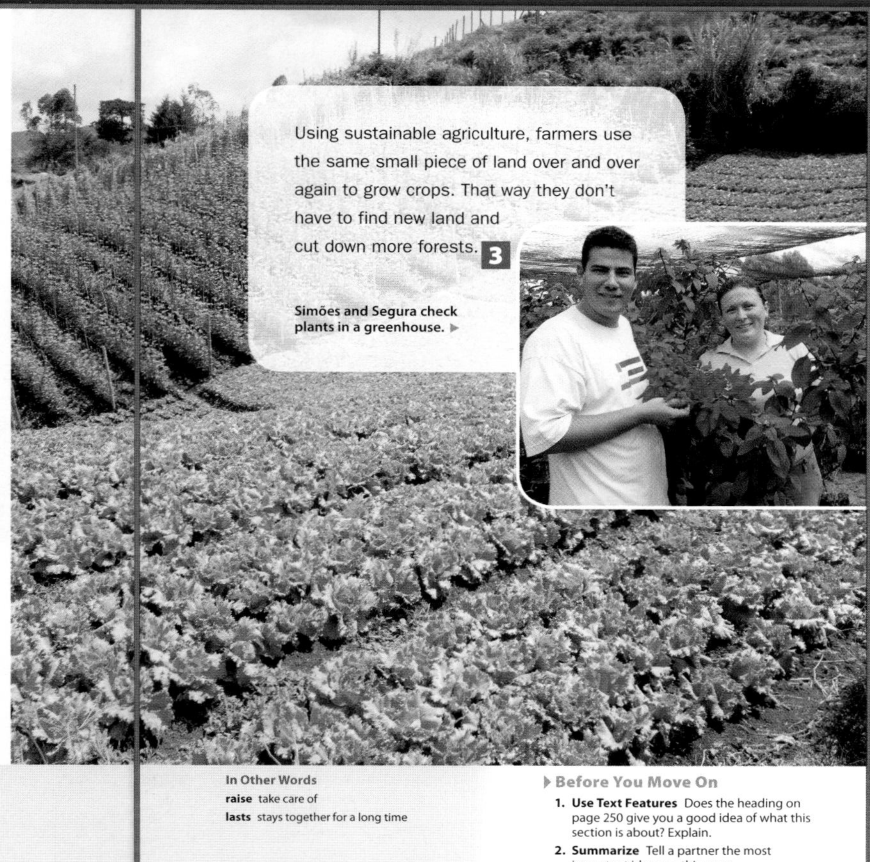

Using sustainable agriculture, farmers use the same small piece of land over and over again to grow crops. That way they don't have to find new land and cut down more forests. 3

Simões and Segura check plants in a greenhouse. ▶

In Other Words
raise take care of
lasts stays together for a long time

▶ Before You Move On

1. **Use Text Features** Does the heading on page 250 give you a good idea of what this section is about? Explain.
2. **Summarize** Tell a partner the most important ideas on this page.

Anthology
pages 250–251

Mini Lesson

Distinguish Viewpoint

Project **Student eEdition** pages 248 and 249. Review: *Remember that a viewpoint is someone's personal* ***opinion*** *or belief about something. Most authors have* ***opinions*** *about the topic they are writing about. You can look for clues about the author's viewpoint in the text.*

Point out the phrase *precious forests* on page 248 and explain: *The word* precious *tells us that the author thinks trees are important.* Point out the phrase *blame humans* on page 249 and explain: *These words are negative. They show that the author feels humans are the reason for the disappearing forests.*

Have partners identify other persuasive or negative words and phrases on page 249 that express a viewpoint. (People should stay out of the forest; Farming must be limited)

Then have partners compare their own viewpoints about farming to the author's. Encourage students to find evidence from the text or their own prior knowledge to support their opinions during the discussion. Then have pairs share the arguments with the class.

Answers Before You Move On

1. **Use Text Features** Possible response: Yes, the heading is *A New Solution*, and the text tells about a solution to the problem of disappearing forests.
2. **Summarize** ☑ Possible response: This section is about sustainable farming. I should remember that **farmers** can earn money by using the same land over and over. This part says sustainable farming is good for people and trees. We can save trees and help people farm in the same place and earn money.

Day 3

Helping Farmers

Today, Segura and Simões teach farmers about crops that grow well in the forest. Fruit trees and flowers can provide a good **income**. Fruit trees don't have to be replanted every year. Their deep roots help keep water and healthy nutrients in the soil. Some flowers, such as orchids, grow on less land than other crops. Farmers can sell their flowers to markets around the world. 1 2

People like to buy beautiful flowers. These are orchids.

Inside the fruit of a cocoa tree are seeds. The seeds can be sold to make chocolate.

In Other Words
income way to make money

252

Branching Out

To make a difference, many farmers need to grow crops this way. Segura and Simões use a special plan to teach more farmers. It is called the 5 x 5 System. First, they teach one family how to grow crops that don't ruin the land. Then that family teaches five new families what they learned. Each new family teaches five more families. Think of all the land that could be saved in the **future**!

5 x 5 System

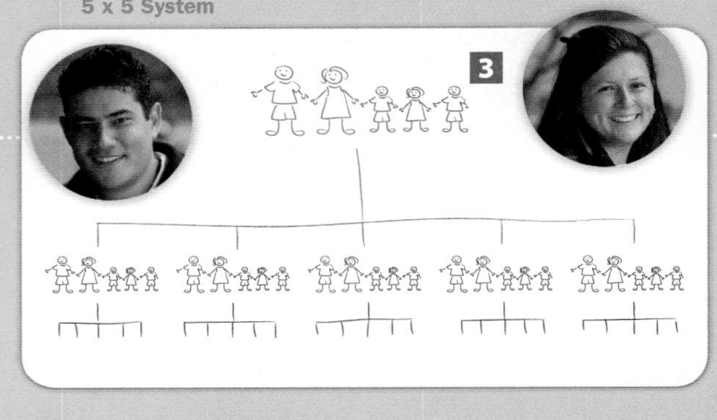

Before You Move On
1. **Details** What are two types of sustainable crops for a forest?
2. **Summarize** Explain briefly in your own words how the 5 x 5 System works.

253

Anthology
pages 252–253

Read and Build Comprehension

1 **Identify Opinion and Evidence** ☑ *How do Segura and Simões believe farmers can earn money without cutting down trees?* (They think **farmers** should plant fruit trees and flowers.) *Find* ***evidence*** *that supports this* ***opinion***.

2 **Determine Importance** ☑ *In your own words, retell the important ideas on page 252.* (Possible response: This part is about what Segura and Simões teach about forest **crops**. I should remember what they say about different kinds of plants. This part says fruit trees and flowers are good **crops** for forest land.)

3 **Analyze Text Features** *What does the diagram on page 253 help you understand?* (how the 5 X 5 system works)

Check & Reteach

OBJECTIVE: Identify Opinions and Evidence to Comprehend Text ☑

Check for accurate responses to comprehension questions about opinions and evidence.
If students have difficulty, have them look for signal words such as *believe*, *think*, and *need* to identify an opinion. Then have them point out evidence in the text that supports the opinion.

OBJECTIVE: Determine Importance ☑

Check for accurate responses to questions about determining importance.
If students have difficulty summarizing, ask: *What is this section about? What important details do you need to remember? What does this part tell about?*

Answers Before You Move On

1. **Details** Two types of sustainable forest **crops** are fruit and flowers, such as orchids.
2. **Summarize** ☑ Possible response: This part is about a farming **method**. I should remember how those **farmers** learn the process. This part says each new family teaches the **method** to five more families, and those five families teach five more, and so on.

Writing

4 Write a Summary

Explain: *Now you will write a paragraph that summarizes one section of the persuasive article. Your audience will be a friend or classmate, so you can use less formal language in your summary.*

Model writing a summary for pages 248–249.

Think Aloud	Write
First, I think about what this part of the article is about.	losing trees
Next, I think about what I need to remember about this part of the article.	why people cut down trees and why some people think this is a problem
Finally, I write a summary that retells the important ideas in this section.	Some **farmers** destroy the forest for wood, to make room for their cattle, and to plant **crops**. Some people believe that we should keep out of the forest and stop **farmers** from taking them over.

*For **Writing Routine 2**, see page BP48.*

Have each student write a summary about another section of the article on pages 250–253. Remind students that they should consider their audience and choose the appropriate language as they write.

Have partners exchange papers to make sure that the summaries are complete. Then have students add their summaries to their Weekly Writing folders.

See **Differentiate**

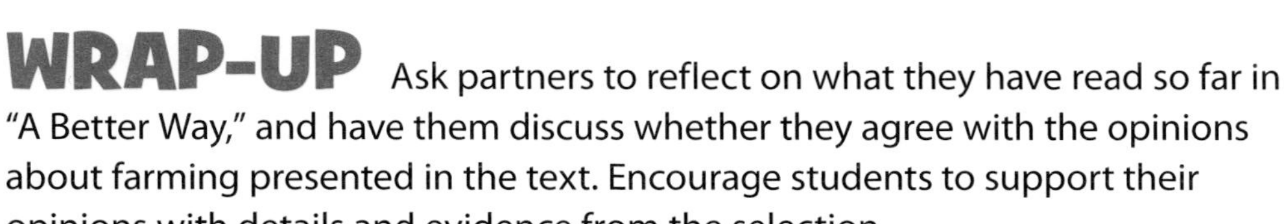

WRAP-UP Ask partners to reflect on what they have read so far in "A Better Way," and have them discuss whether they agree with the opinions about farming presented in the text. Encourage students to support their opinions with details and evidence from the selection.

Daily Language Arts

Spelling and Word Work ☑
Practice page T239v

Daily Grammar ☑
Display the photograph on **Anthology** page 249 and say: *We do need to protect forests.* Then use T239x to teach forms of *do*.

Daily Writing Skills ☑
Tell students that one way of checking if a source is good is by comparing the facts in it to facts in another source. Then use page T239z to practice validating facts in sources.

Differentiate

SN Special Needs

ISSUE Students have difficulty organizing their thoughts in writing.

STRATEGY Have students use the organization of the selection to help them organize their written summary. Point to the first paragraph on page 250. Have students retell the most important details from that paragraph. Explain that their summary should begin with those details. Have students write what they retell. Continue with the other paragraphs.

EL English Learners

ISSUE Students lack the language skills to write a summary.

STRATEGY Provide sentence frames to organize students' summaries:

- Sustainable farming is good for people and trees because _____.
- Segura and Simões teach farmers to _____ because _____.

Day 4 Read and Comprehend

Persuasive Article

OBJECTIVES

Thematic Connection: Goods and Services

☑ **Identify Opinions and Evidence to Comprehend Text**

☑ **Determine Importance**

PROGRAM RESOURCES

PRINT & TECHNOLOGY

Family Newsletter 4

TECHNOLOGY ONLY

Read with Me: Selection Recordings: MP3 or CD 1 Track 12

My Vocabulary Notebook

Comprehension Coach

MATERIALS

timer • Word Maps from Day 3

Power Writing

Have students write as much as they can as well as they can in one minute about the word *conservation*.

*For **Writing Routine 1**, see page BP47.*

COMMON CORE STANDARDS

Reading	
Recount Key Details	CC.3.Rinf.2
Distinguish Points of View	CC.3.Rinf.6
Read Orally with Accuracy and Appropriate Rate on Successive Readings	CC.3.Rfou.4.b
Writing	
Write Over Shorter Time for Specific Audiences	CC.3.W.10
Speaking and Listening	
Discuss Texts, Expressing Ideas Clearly	CC.3.SL.1
Explain Ideas and Understanding Clearly	CC.3.SL.1.d
Language and Vocabulary	
Acquire and Use General Academic and Domain-Specific Words	CC.3.L.6

WARM-UP

Have partners share their family activity drawings from **Family Newsletter 4** and talk about how people cooperate during family activities. Partners can then share their ideas with the class.

Vocabulary Practice

1 Share Word Knowledge ☑

Key Words

agriculture · alternative · conservation
crop · evidence · farmer · field
future · harvest · method · opinion
plow · summarize · sustain

REVIEW Have students use the Word Maps they made on Day 3. Review what the Word Maps show.

Pair each student with a partner who studied a different Key Word. Have partners follow **Vocabulary Routine 3**.

- Have partners take turns reading their Word Maps.
- Encourage partners to talk about how the pictures show the meanings of the Key Words.
- Have partners create sentences using both Key Words.
- Have each student add the sentences to **My Vocabulary Notebook**.

*For **Vocabulary Routine 3**, see page BP36.*

Academic Talk

2 Summarize Reading

REVIEW Remind students: *When you **summarize** an article, you briefly tell the most important ideas and recount the key details. Remember to express your ideas clearly as you discuss the text.* Explain that students will use Key Words as they summarize what they have read so far in "A Better Way."

Write these Key Words: *agriculture, alternative, crop, farmer, field, method*. Use a **Fishbowl** to help students summarize.

- Have half of the students sit in a close circle facing inward; have the other half sit in a larger circle around them.
- Have students on the inside summarize pages 248–250 using Key Words in their summary. Have students on the outside listen for the most important details and Key Words.
- Have students reverse positions. This time have students on the inside summarize pages 251–253.

Fishbowl

*For **Fishbowl**, see page BP45.*

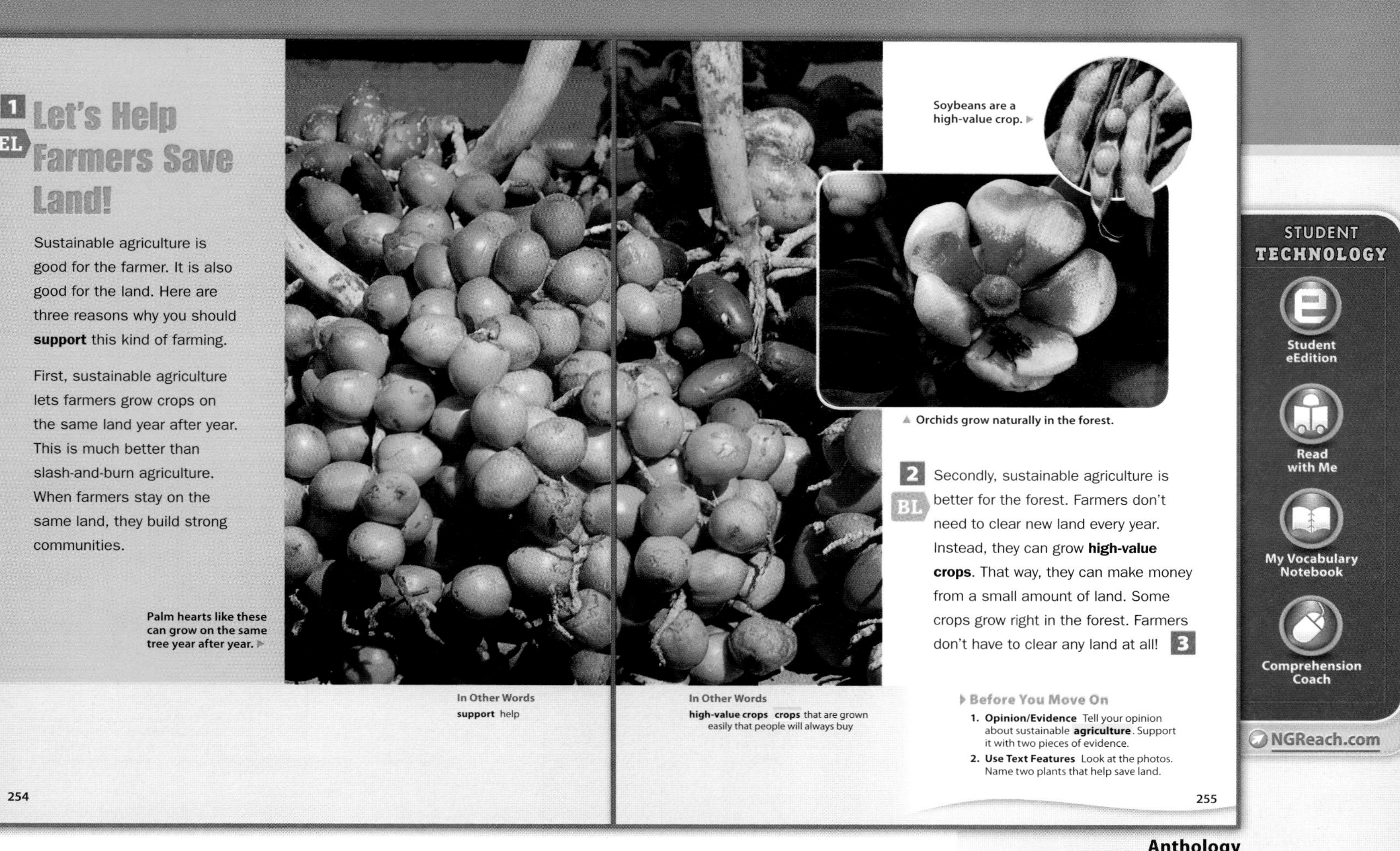

1 EL Let's Help Farmers Save Land!
Sustainable agriculture is good for the farmer. It is also good for the land. Here are three reasons why you should **support** this kind of farming.
First, sustainable agriculture lets farmers grow crops on the same land year after year. This is much better than slash-and-burn agriculture. When farmers stay on the same land, they build strong communities.
Palm hearts like these can grow on the same tree year after year.
Soybeans are a high-value crop.
Orchids grow naturally in the forest.
2 BL Secondly, sustainable agriculture is better for the forest. Farmers don't need to clear new land every year. Instead, they can grow **high-value crops**. That way, they can make money from a small amount of land. Some crops grow right in the forest. Farmers don't have to clear any land at all! 3
In Other Words
support help
In Other Words
high-value crops crops that are grown easily that people will always buy
Before You Move On
1. Opinion/Evidence Tell your opinion about sustainable agriculture. Support it with two pieces of evidence.
2. Use Text Features Look at the photos. Name two plants that help save land.
254
255
STUDENT TECHNOLOGY
Student eEdition
Read with Me
My Vocabulary Notebook
Comprehension Coach
NGReach.com

Anthology
pages 254–255

Reading

3 Read and Build Comprehension

1 **Use Text Features** *What information does the section head on page 254 give?* (This section is about ways to help **farmers** save land.)

2 **Identify Opinions and Evidence** ☑ *What* ***evidence*** *from the text supports the* ***opinion*** *that sustainable* ***agriculture*** *is better for the forest?* ("When **farmers** stay on the same land, they build strong communities."; "**Farmers** don't need to clear new land every year.")

3 **Determine Importance** ☑ *What is important to remember on pages 254–255?* (Possible response: This part is about sustainable **agriculture**. I should remember that it builds farming communities. It also helps save forest land. This part explains how sustainable agriculture helps **farmers** and forests.)

Differentiate

EL English Learners

ISSUE Students have difficulty analyzing section heads.

STRATEGY Provide frames: The section head says ______. This section is about ______.

BL Below Level

ISSUE Students have difficulty connecting evidence to opinions.

STRATEGY Have students use a graphic organizer to record opinions and list reasons or evidence for the opinions to help visualize the connections.

Fluency

Practice Phrasing, Accuracy, and Rate
As students read, monitor their phrasing, accuracy, and rate.

Best Practices

Encourage Elaboration As students respond to questions, use general prompts:

- *What do you mean by that?*
- *Can you give some details to explain what you mean?*
- *Can you make a connection to what someone else said?*

Answers Before You Move On

1. **Opinion/Evidence** ☑ Possible response: I believe that sustainable **agriculture** is good because **farmers** can grow **crops** on the same land for years. They don't need to clear land every year. That means that the **method sustains** both the **farmers** and the land.
2. **Use Text Features** According to the photos, palm hearts, soybeans, and orchids help save land.

Day 4

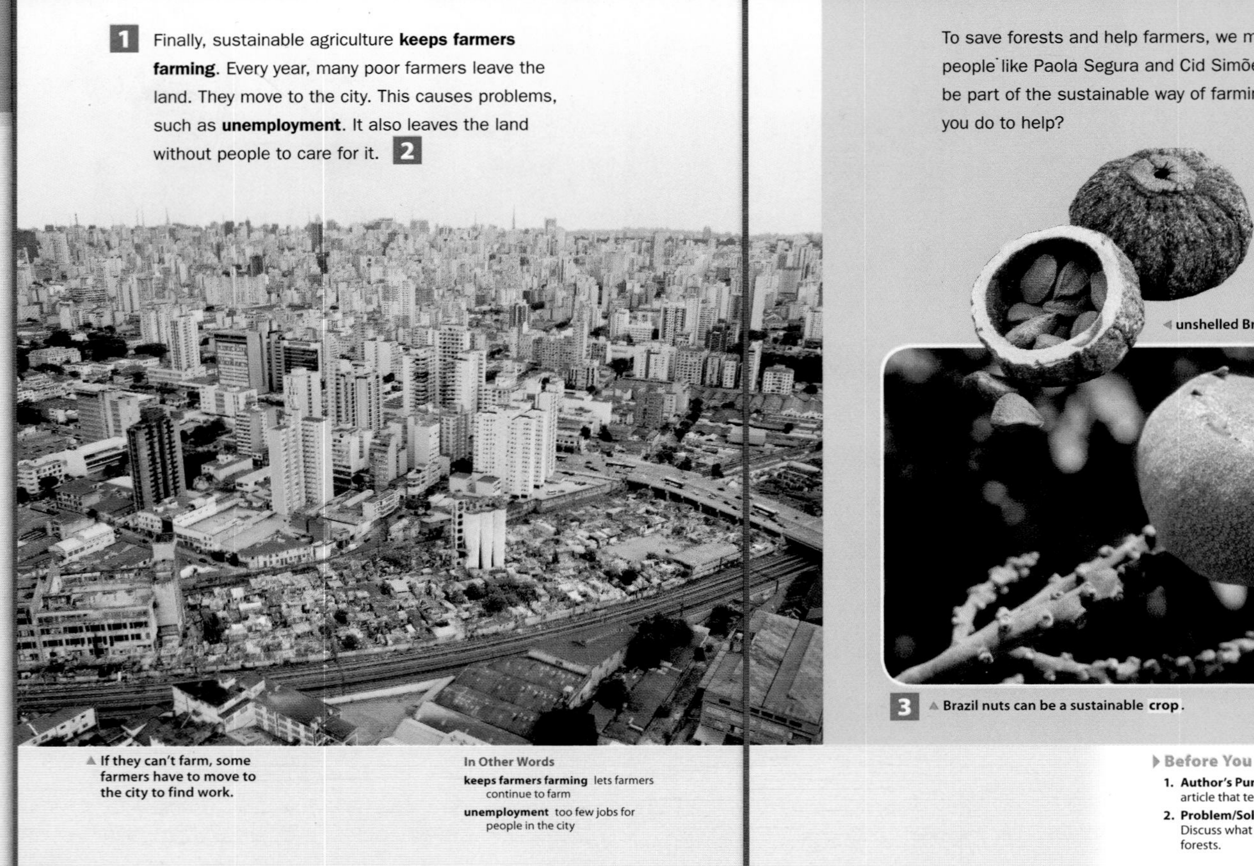
1 Finally, sustainable agriculture **keeps farmers farming**. Every year, many poor farmers leave the land. They move to the city. This causes problems, such as **unemployment**. It also leaves the land without people to care for it. 2
If they can't farm, some farmers have to move to the city to find work.
In Other Words
keeps farmers farming lets farmers continue to farm
unemployment too few jobs for people in the city
256
To save forests and help farmers, we must support people like Paola Segura and Cid Simões. We must be part of the sustainable way of farming. What can you do to help?
unshelled Brazil nuts
3 Brazil nuts can be a sustainable crop.
Before You Move On
1. Author's Purpose Find the text in the article that tells the author's purpose.
2. Problem/Solution Talk with a partner. Discuss what you can do to help save the forests.
257

Anthology
pages 256–257

Read and Build Comprehension

1 **Identify Opinions and Evidence** *What is the author's* ***opinion*** *on page 256?* (Sustainable **agriculture** helps **farmers** keep farming instead of looking for other jobs.) *Look for* ***evidence*** *that supports this* ***opinion****.*

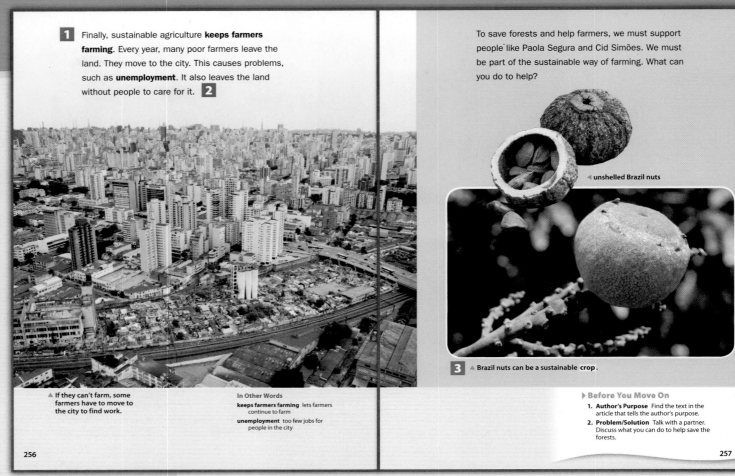

2 **Determine Importance** *Summarize page 256.* (This part is about keeping **farmers** farming. I should remember what helps **farmers**. This part says that sustainable **agriculture** keeps **farmers** from moving to the city, facing unemployment, and leaving the land with no one to care for it.)

3 **Use Text Features** *What information do the photo captions and labels give on page 257?* (Brazil nuts can be a sustainable **crop**.)

Check & Reteach

OBJECTIVE: Identify Opinions and Evidence to Comprehend Text

Check for accurate responses to questions about identifying opinions and evidence.
If students have difficulty, point out different statements in the article. Ask: *Can this information be proved or is it just something that someone believes?* Have students identify evidence from the text that supports any opinions they identify.

OBJECTIVE: Determine Importance

Check for accurate responses to questions about determining importance.
If students have difficulty, have them ask questions such as: *What is this section about? What does the author want me to remember about this part?*

Answers Before You Move On

1. **Author's Purpose** Possible response: The author's purpose is to persuade people to support sustainable farming. The author uses **evidence** like the fact that if **farmers** plant trees, they don't have to replant each year and clear more land.
2. **Problem/Solution** Possible response: I can help save the forests by buying and eating food grown by sustainable farming methods.

Writing

5 Write About Viewpoint

Review author's viewpoint: *Many authors have **opinions** or beliefs about the topic they are writing about. They can use positive and negative words to help readers recognize their viewpoints.*

Remind students that the author uses the positive word *precious* to express the opinion that trees are important and the negative word *blame* to tell how people feel about farming in the forests. Point out that authors also use words like *must* and *should* to express their viewpoint of what they think readers should do.

Introduce: *You will write a paragraph that identifies the author's viewpoint and the evidence he includes to support that viewpoint. Then you'll add your own opinion about whether you agree or disagree.* Explain that you will be their audience, so they should use appropriate, formal language to express their ideas.

Model writing about the author's viewpoint.

Think Aloud	Write
*First, I will write the author's viewpoint about a topic. I'll include **evidence** that supports his **opinion**.*	The author believes sustainable farming has many benefits for **farmers**. He thinks it is good because farming the same land year after year helps **farmers** stay in one place and build strong communities.
*Next, I will write my own **opinion** to tell whether I agree or disagree with the author.*	I agree with the author. I believe sustainable farming is good for **farmers** because they can stay in one place and not leave the land with no one to care for it.

*For **Writing Routine 2**, see page BP48.*

Have each student write a paragraph that tells the author's viewpoint and evidence from the article that supports it. Students should also include their own viewpoints and explain whether they agree or disagree with the author. Have students add their paragraphs to their Weekly Writing folders.

See **Differentiate**

WRAP-UP Have students reflect on what they learned from reading "A Better Way" and their **Small Group Reading** books. Ask: *How did this week's readings change the way you think about **agriculture**? What will you do differently in your own life based on what you learned?*

Daily Language Arts

Daily Spelling and Word Work ☑
Practice page T239v

Daily Grammar ☑
Point out the word *must* in the first sentence on **Anthology** page 257 and explain that it is a helping verb. Then use page T239x to have students practice using helping verbs.

Daily Writing Skills ☑
Remind students that they should always use reliable sources when researching a topic. Then use page T239z to practice finding reliable sources.

Differentiate

SN Special Needs

ISSUE Students need help organizing ideas.

STRATEGY Have students create a T chart with the author's opinion on the left and supporting evidence for each opinion on the right. They can follow the same process to organize their own opinions. Guide students in using their notes to create a paragraph.

BL Below Level

ISSUE Students have difficulty writing about author's viewpoint.

STRATEGY Provide sentence frames to help students begin their writing:

- The author believes ______.
- He thinks this because ______.
- I (agree/disagree) with his viewpoint because ______.

Day 5 Review and Apply

OBJECTIVES

Thematic Connection: Goods and Services

☑ Identify Opinions and Evidence to Comprehend Text

☑ Read with Fluency

PROGRAM RESOURCES

PRINT & TECHNOLOGY

Bingo Card from NGReach.com

Unit Concept Map: Practice Master PM4.1

Test-Taking Strategy Practice: Practice Master PM4.21

Opinion Chart: Practice Master PM4.22

Fluency Practice: Practice Master PM4.23

TECHNOLOGY ONLY

Online Vocabulary Games

Comprehension Coach

Read with Me: Fluency Models: MP3 or CD 1 Track 14

MATERIALS

timer • Bingo cards • markers for Bingo • index cards

Power Writing

Have students write as much as they can as well as they can in one minute about the word *harvest*.

*For **Writing Routine 1**, see page BP47.*

COMMON CORE STANDARDS

Reading	
Read Orally with Accuracy and Appropriate Rate on Successive Readings	CC.3.Rfou.4.b
Writing	
Write Opinions on Texts	CC.3.W.1
Write Over Shorter Time for Specific Tasks	CC.3.W.10
Speaking and Listening	
Discuss Texts, Expressing Ideas Clearly	CC.3.SL.1
Draw on Preparation to Explore Ideas	CC.3.SL.1.a
Explain Ideas and Understanding	CC.3.SL.1.d
Language and Vocabulary	
Acquire and Use General Academic and Domain-Specific Words	CC.3.L.6

WARM-UP

Have students think about what they read in "A Better Way." Ask: *Do you think **farmers** will change their **methods** of farming? Why or why not?* Ask students to share their opinions and support their opinions with evidence from the text.

Vocabulary Review

1 Apply Word Knowledge ☑

Write: ***opinion***, ***evidence***, ***summarize***. Call students' attention to the other Key Words on **Student eEdition** page 258. Then have students apply their knowledge of the Key Words to play Vocabulary Bingo.

Key Words

agriculture · alternative · conservation
crop · evidence · farmer · field
future · harvest · method · opinion
plow · summarize · sustain

Download a copy of a blank Bingo card from **NGReach.com** and make enough copies for each student. Then explain the rules and goals of the game:

- *I will give each student a blank Bingo card and a set of markers.*
- *You will write the Key Words in random order on the cards. Fill in every space of the card. You may need to write some words more than once.*
- *I will say definitions for the Key Words, one at a time.*
- *If you hear the definition of a word on your card, put a marker on the card for each time the Key Word appears.*
- *When you have a complete row of five markers in a straight row, column, or diagonal line, call out "Bingo!"*
- *We will review your answers together to make sure that you covered the Key Words that match the definitions I gave.*
- *The first person to call "Bingo!" with all the correct answers wins the game.*

Have students play the game.

*For **More Vocabulary Routines**, see pages BP41–BP43.*

For additional practice, have students play the **Online Vocabulary Games** in pairs or individually.

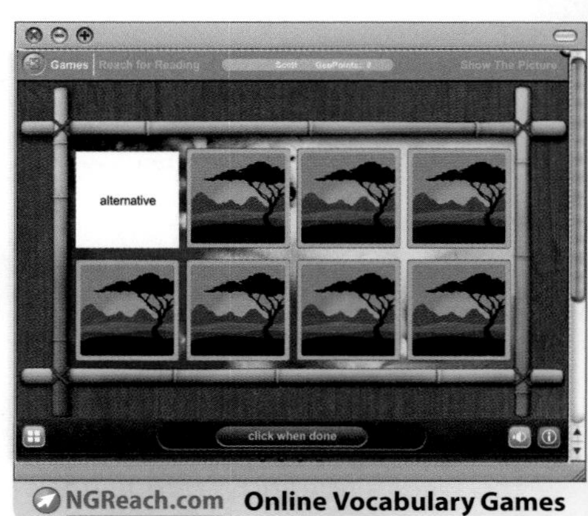

NGReach.com **Online Vocabulary Games**

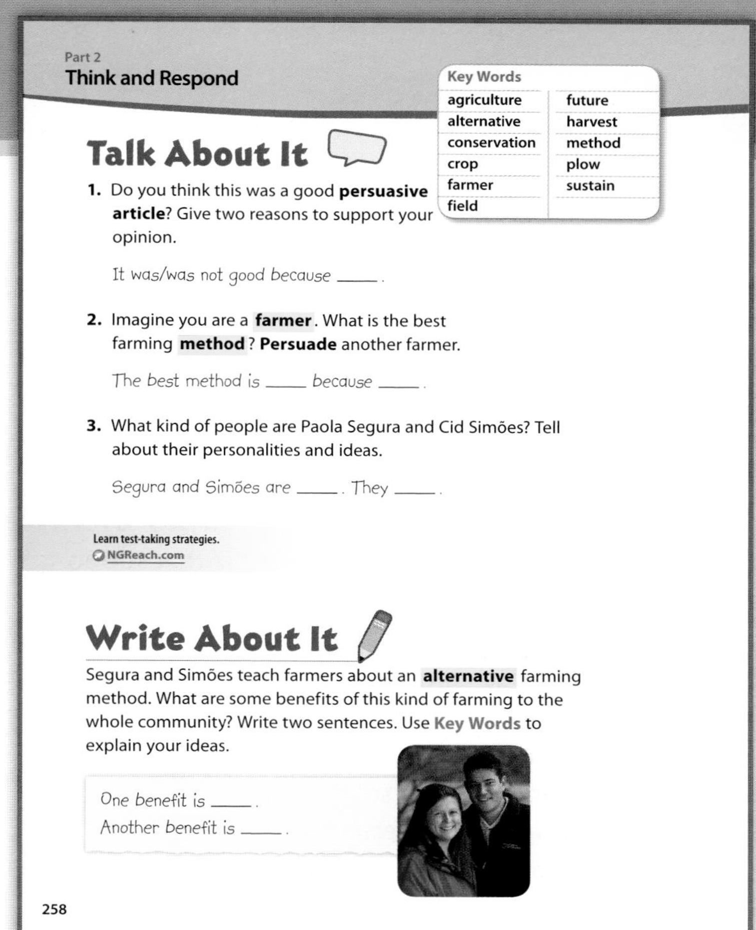
Part 2
Think and Respond

Key Words

agriculture	future
alternative	harvest
conservation	method
crop	plow
farmer	sustain
field	

Talk About It

1. Do you think this was a good **persuasive article**? Give two reasons to support your opinion.

   It was/was not good because ___.

2. Imagine you are a **farmer**. What is the best farming **method**? **Persuade** another farmer.

   The best method is ___ because ___.

3. What kind of people are Paola Segura and Cid Simões? Tell about their personalities and ideas.

   Segura and Simões are ___. They ___.

Learn test-taking strategies.
NGReach.com

Write About It

Segura and Simões teach farmers about an **alternative** farming method. What are some benefits of this kind of farming to the whole community? Write two sentences. Use **Key Words** to explain your ideas.

One benefit is ___.
Another benefit is ___.

258

Anthology page 258

Daily Language Arts

Daily Spelling and Word Work
Test page T239u

Daily Grammar
Write the sentence *We must visit Brazil.* Underline the helping verb *must.* Then use page T239x to review and assess students' understanding of helping verbs.

Daily Writing Skills
Remind students that they need to use reliable sources when they are writing reports. Then use page T239z to review students' understanding of evaluating sources.

Academic Talk

2 Talk About It Anthology page 258

Have partners use Key Words as they answer the **Talk About It** questions. Prompt students to use evidence from the text to make clear arguments and to explain their ideas and understanding of the text. If students have difficulty expressing their opinions, encourage them to preview the questions and provide time for them to prepare their responses before joining the group discussion.

Then use the test-taking strategy lesson from **NGReach.com** and **Practice Master PM4.21** to ask more questions about the selection.

Writing

3 Write About It Anthology page 258

Read aloud the directions on page 258. Point out the sentence frames and explain: *You can use these sentence frames to explain your ideas about the benefits of alternative farming.*

Model using Key Words as you write about the benefits of alternative farming:

One benefit is that **farmers** do not need to cut down more trees in the forest. Another benefit is that **farmers** do not have to move to the cities.

Have students add their sentences to their Weekly Writing folders.

Answers Talk About It

1. **Persuasive Article** Possible response: It was good because the author provided evidence to support his **opinion** that sustainable **agriculture** is best.
2. **Persuade** Possible response: The best farming **method** is sustainable **agriculture** because it is good for both **farmers** and the land.
3. **Analyze** Possible response: Segura and Simões are caring people. They work to help the environment and **farmers**.

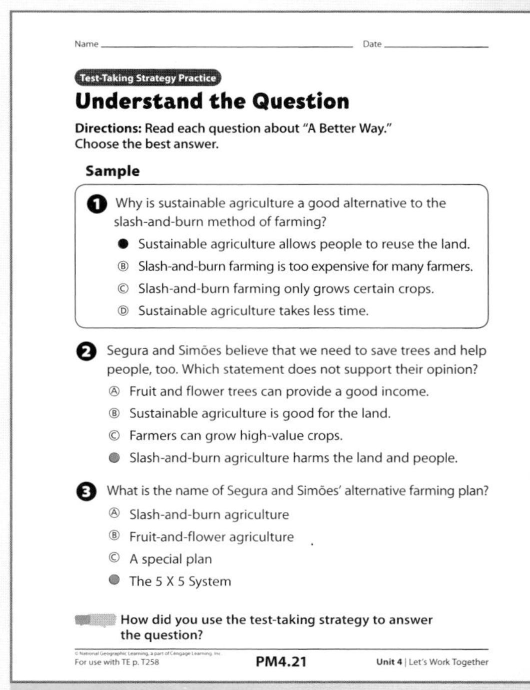
Name ___ Date ___

Test-Taking Strategy Practice

Understand the Question

Directions: Read each question about "A Better Way." Choose the best answer.

Sample

1. Why is sustainable agriculture a good alternative to the slash-and-burn method of farming?
   - ● Sustainable agriculture allows people to reuse the land.
   - Ⓑ Slash-and-burn farming is too expensive for many farmers.
   - Ⓒ Slash-and-burn farming only grows certain crops.
   - Ⓓ Sustainable agriculture takes less time.

2. Segura and Simões believe that we need to save trees and help people, too. Which statement does not support their opinion?
   - Ⓐ Fruit and flower trees can provide a good income.
   - Ⓑ Sustainable agriculture is good for the land.
   - Ⓒ Farmers can grow high-value crops.
   - ● Slash-and-burn agriculture harms the land and people.

3. What is the name of Segura and Simões' alternative farming plan?
   - Ⓐ Slash-and-burn agriculture
   - Ⓑ Fruit-and-flower agriculture
   - Ⓒ A special plan
   - ● The 5 X 5 System

How did you use the test-taking strategy to answer the question?

For use with TE p. T258 PM4.21 Unit 4 | Let's Work Together

NGReach.com **Practice Master PM4.21**

Differentiate

SN Special Needs

ISSUE Students struggle with identifying an opinion in the text.

STRATEGY Help students identify the author's opinions by having them review the text and point out signal words such as *think, believe, should*, and *must*. Have students read the text around the signal words to identify the author's opinion.

EL English Learners

ISSUE Students lack sufficient vocabulary to explain the text.

STRATEGY Encourage students to use visuals and gestures if they have difficulty completing the sentence frames with words.

BL Below Level

ISSUE Students have difficulty identifying evidence that supports the author's opinion.

STRATEGY Remind students that evidence can be reasons or facts that explain why the author has an opinion. Have students point to an opinion in the text. Read the surrounding text aloud. Ask: *Which words tell why the author has his opinion?* Have students record the evidence in their charts.

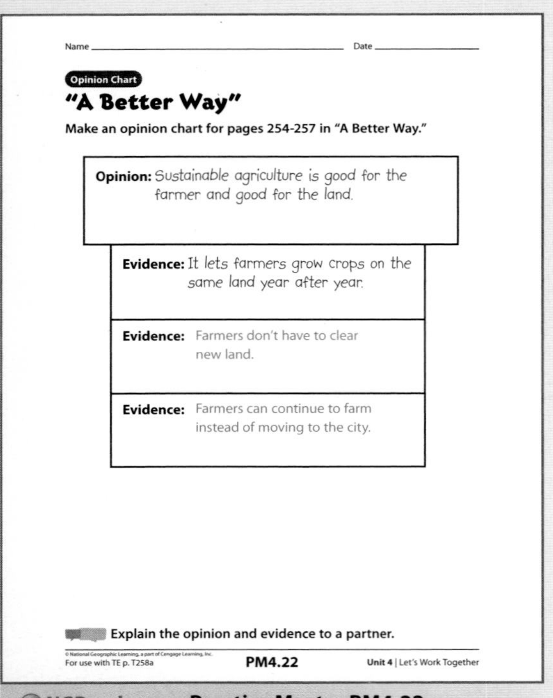
Name ____ Date ____

Opinion Chart

"A Better Way"

Make an opinion chart for pages 254-257 in "A Better Way."

Opinion: Sustainable agriculture is good for the farmer and good for the land.

Evidence: It lets farmers grow crops on the same land year after year.

Evidence: Farmers don't have to clear new land.

Evidence: Farmers can continue to farm instead of moving to the city.

Explain the opinion and evidence to a partner.

For use with TE p. T258a PM4.22 Unit 4 | Let's Work Together

NGReach.com **Practice Master PM4.22**

Comprehension

4 Opinion and Evidence ☑ Anthology page 259

REVIEW Display **Student eEdition** page 259 and read aloud the instructions. Remind students: *An **opinion** is what a person believes about something. Authors use **evidence**, such as reasons and facts, to support their **opinions**.* Read aloud the opinion in the opinion chart. Then work with students to review the text and enter another piece of evidence from pages 254–257 that supports the author's opinion.

Have partners work together to complete **Practice Master PM4.22**. Circulate and use the questions below to guide students in completing the opinion chart.

- *How will sustainable **agriculture** help the trees and forests?*
- *Why is it important for **farmers** to make money farming?*
- *How can sustainable **agriculture** affect where **farmers** live?*
- *How will sustainable **agriculture** help the land?*

After students complete their charts, explain that they will take turns explaining pages 254–257 to a partner. Remind students to use their opinion charts to guide their explanations.

See **Differentiate**

Check & Reteach

OBJECTIVE: Identify Opinions and Evidence to Comprehend Text ☑

As partners discuss the article, check to make sure that students can identify the author's opinion on pages 254–257 and identify evidence to support the opinion.

If students have difficulty, ask

- *Does the author think sustainable **agriculture** is good or bad for **farmers**?* (good) *This is what the author thinks. It is his **opinion**.*
- *Why does the author think sustainable **agriculture** is a good **method** for **farmers** to use?* (They can keep farming instead of moving to cities and looking for work.) *This is **evidence** that supports the author's **opinion** that sustainable **agriculture** is good for farmers.*

5 Fluency ☑ Anthology page 259

Have students read aloud the passage on **Practice Master PM4.23** or use the **Comprehension Coach** to practice fluency.

Check & Reteach

OBJECTIVE: Read with Fluency ☑

Monitor students' oral reading.

If students need additional fluency practice, have them read along with the **Fluency Models**.

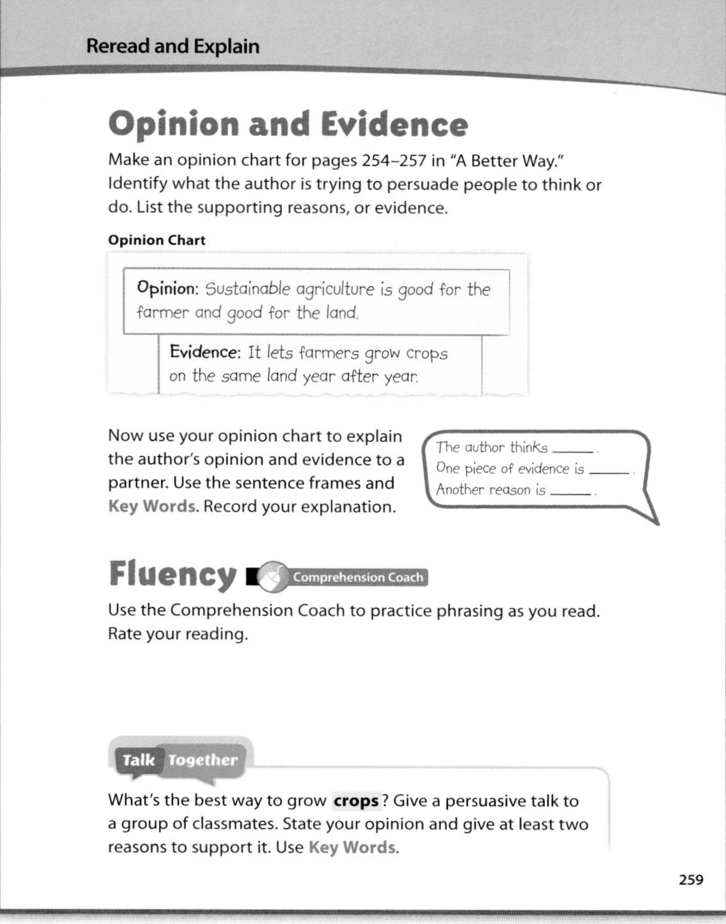

Reread and Explain

Opinion and Evidence

Make an opinion chart for pages 254–257 in "A Better Way." Identify what the author is trying to persuade people to think or do. List the supporting reasons, or evidence.

Opinion Chart

Opinion: Sustainable agriculture is good for the farmer and good for the land.

Evidence: It lets farmers grow crops on the same land year after year.

Now use your opinion chart to explain the author's opinion and evidence to a partner. Use the sentence frames and Key Words. Record your explanation.

The author thinks ____.
One piece of evidence is ____.
Another reason is ____.

Fluency Comprehension Coach

Use the Comprehension Coach to practice phrasing as you read. Rate your reading.

Talk Together

What's the best way to grow **crops**? Give a persuasive talk to a group of classmates. State your opinion and give at least two reasons to support it. Use Key Words.

259

Anthology page 259

Best Practices

Encourage Respect Provide sentence frames that embed respect for diverse opinions:

- *I've heard that too, but now I think that **farmers** should grow high-value **crops**.*
- *That's a good argument, but maybe it's better for **farmers** to grow orchids instead.*

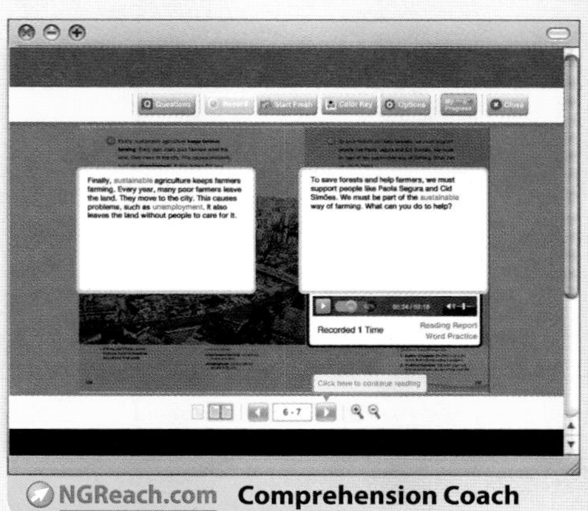

NGReach.com **Comprehension Coach**

6 Talk Together **Anthology** page 259

Read aloud the instructions and have partners discuss their ideas first. When students are ready, have partners draw on their preparation to present their persuasive talks to another pair of students. Post the Key Words so that students can refer to them during their talks. Have students add the most persuasive ideas to their unit concept maps.

WRAP-UP Have partners role-play an encounter between a farmer who uses the 5x5 system and a farmer who doesn't. Give the 5x5 farmer one minute to convince the other farmer to adopt the 5x5 farming system. Then have the other farmer speak for one minute.

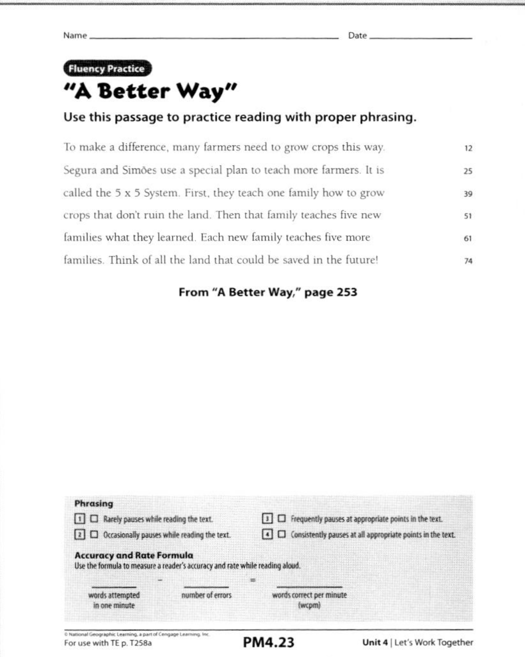

Name ______________________ Date ______________

Fluency Practice

"A Better Way"

Use this passage to practice reading with proper phrasing.

To make a difference, many farmers need to grow crops this way. 12
Segura and Simões use a special plan to teach more farmers. It is 25
called the 5 x 5 System. First, they teach one family how to grow 39
crops that don't ruin the land. Then that family teaches five new 51
families what they learned. Each new family teaches five more 61
families. Think of all the land that could be saved in the future! 74

From "A Better Way," page 253

Phrasing

1 ☐ Rarely pauses while reading the text.
2 ☐ Occasionally pauses while reading the text.
3 ☐ Frequently pauses at appropriate points in the text.
4 ☐ Consistently pauses at all appropriate points in the text.

Accuracy and Rate Formula

Use the formula to measure a reader's accuracy and rate while reading aloud.

______ (words attempted in one minute) – ______ (number of errors) = ______ (words correct per minute (wcpm))

For use with TE p. T258a PM4.23 Unit 4 | Let's Work Together

NGReach.com **Fluency PM4.23**

Week 3 Research Project

OBJECTIVES

Thematic Connection: Goods and Services

☑ **Research Conservation**

☑ **Evaluate Information**

☑ **Report on a Topic**

PROGRAM RESOURCES

PRINT & TECHNOLOGY

Research Rubric: Assessment Master A4.40

TECHNOLOGY ONLY

Project Checklist: eVisual 4.25

MATERIALS

index cards • print and online almanacs, encyclopedias, atlases, magazines, newspapers, and other reference books about conservation

SUGGESTED PACING

DAY 1	Plan
DAY 2	Research
DAY 3	Research
DAY 4	Organize
DAY 5	Present

Research Conservation

Display and read the prompt aloud.

> Paola Segura and Cid Simões have chosen you to write about conservation. You'll describe a place where an area or animals living there were saved. Gather information from several print and digital resources. Then present the paper to your classmates as an oral report.

Plan

Choose a Topic

Guide discussion to unpack the prompt and determine the Role, Audience, and Form for the RAFT:

Role: Researcher
Audience: Paola Segura, Cid Simões, and the class
Form: Paper also presented as oral report

REVIEW Explain that students must first choose a place where people saved the area or the animals living in the area. Then they must narrow their topic even further.

Model this process: *I remember reading about people in Florida trying to protect the environment. But I need to be more specific. I know that scientists are trying to protect the coral reefs in the Florida Keys, so I'll write about that.*

Have students choose an animal or place to research and complete the RAFT.

Develop Research Questions

REVIEW Remind students: *Before you gather information for your research report, write questions to guide your research.* Ask students to write and number at least three questions on separate index cards.

1. Why do the coral reefs in the Florida Keys need to be protected?

Research

Gather Information

Ask students to look for information from print and digital sources. For example:

- Print sources: nonfiction books, encyclopedias, newspapers, and magazines
- Digital sources: online encyclopedias, trusted websites, and documentaries

Review how to evaluate information (see page T239y). Remind students to look critically at the information to make sure it relates to their topic. Have students note down information that answers each question, using their numbered index cards.

See **Differentiate**

COMMON CORE STANDARDS

Writing	
Conduct Research	CC.3.W.7
Gather Information	CC.3.W.8
Speaking and Listening	
Report on a Topic	CC.3.SL.4

Organize

Arrange Information

Have students review their notes to make sure all information relates to the topic. Then, have them organize the cards in logical order by grouping related information together. Finally, have students plan an attention-getting introduction and a conclusion that summarizes the topic. Display and read aloud **eVisual 4.25**.

Project Checklist

- Use information from both print and digital resources.
- Make sure the information relates to the topic.
- Be sure to answer all of your research questions.
- Include an introduction and conclusion.

NGReach.com **Project Checklist: eVisual 4.25**

INTERACTIVE WHITEBOARD TIP: Underline important words as you read each point.

Draft Ideas

Have students create a written draft of their reports. Suggest they begin with a brief introduction that explains why their area or the animals living in it need to be saved. Then have students discuss steps people took to make that happen. Remind students to include facts and descriptive details in their reports. Have students finish their reports with a conclusion that briefly summarizes it.

When students finish their drafts, have them plan how to present the information as an oral report. They should not just read their reports. Point out that they might find their note cards helpful as prompts during the oral presentation. Suggest that they display related visuals as they present important facts.

Present

Practice Speaking Skills

Explain: *When giving an oral report, be sure to speak clearly and slowly. To engage the interest of your audience, make eye contact and speak at a volume that everyone can hear.* Have students work with partners to rehearse their oral reports.

Share with Others

Have students take turns presenting their oral reports. Allow time for the class to ask each presenter questions. Explain that this will be the opportunity to tell more of the descriptive details from the written report. Also have students provide a copy of their written reports for interested students to read.

Use the **Research Rubric** to evaluate students' oral reports.

Daily Language Arts

Daily Spelling and Word Work ☑
Practice Pages T239u–T239v

Daily Grammar ☑
Use pages T239w–T239x to have students practice using helping verbs.

Daily Writing Skills ☑
Use pages T239y–T239z to have students practice evaluating information.

Differentiate

BL Below Level

ISSUE Students have difficulty finding print and digital sources.

STRATEGY Have students reference pages 567–571 of the **Student eEdition** for information on print and digital sources. Model how to access these sources for students.

SN Special Needs

ISSUE Students have trouble working with digital sources.

STRATEGY Work with students by finding information in digital sources together. If using the Internet, ask students to provide a topic or key word and type it into the search box. Print out relevant information for students to use in their reports.

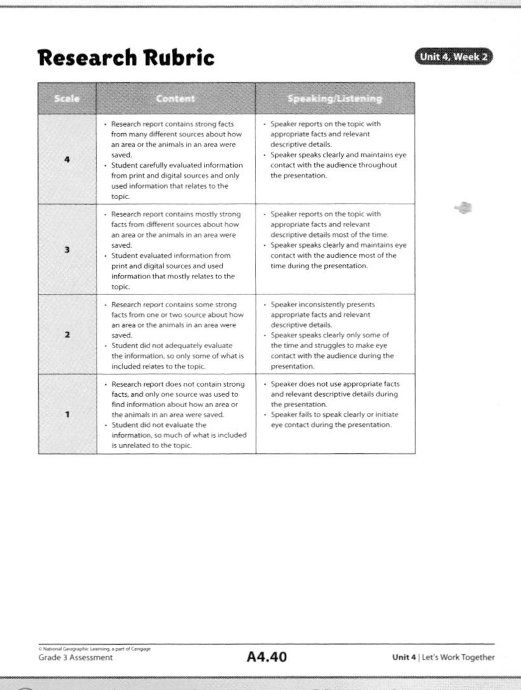

Research Rubric Unit 4, Week 2

Scale	Content	Speaking/Listening
4	• Research report contains strong facts from many different sources about how an area or the animals in an area were saved. • Student carefully evaluated information from print and digital sources and only used information that relates to the topic.	• Speaker reports on the topic with appropriate facts and relevant descriptive details. • Speaker speaks clearly and maintains eye contact with the audience throughout the presentation.
3	• Research report contains mostly strong facts from different sources about how an area or the animals in an area were saved. • Student evaluated information from print and digital sources and used information that mostly relates to the topic.	• Speaker reports on the topic with appropriate facts and relevant descriptive details most of the time. • Speaker speaks clearly and maintains eye contact with the audience most of the time during the presentation.
2	• Research report contains some strong facts from one or two source about how an area or the animals in an area were saved. • Student did not adequately evaluate the information, so only some of what is included relates to the topic.	• Speaker inconsistently presents appropriate facts and relevant descriptive details. • Speaker speaks clearly only some of the time and struggles to make eye contact with the audience during the presentation.
1	• Research report does not contain strong facts, and only one source was used to find information about how an area or the animals in an area were saved. • Student did not evaluate the information, so much of what is included is unrelated to the topic.	• Speaker does not use appropriate facts and relevant descriptive details during the presentation. • Speaker fails to speak clearly or initiate eye contact during the presentation.

Grade 3 Assessment A4.40 **Unit 4** | Let's Work Together

NGReach.com **Assessment Master A4.40**

☑ = TESTED

Assess

OBJECTIVES	ASSESSMENTS			
Reading ☑ Identify Opinions and Evidence to Comprehend Text ☑ Determine Importance	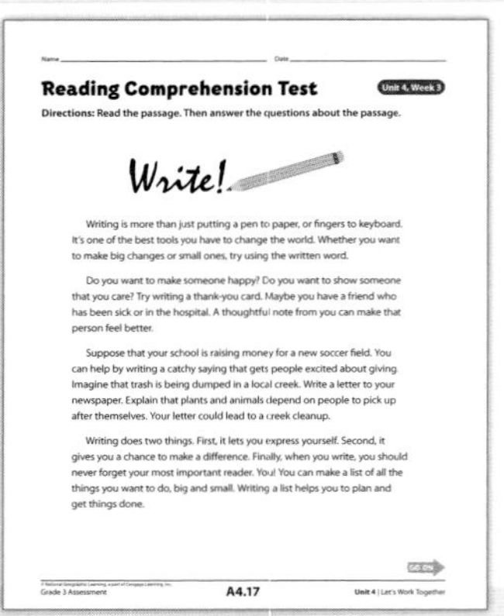	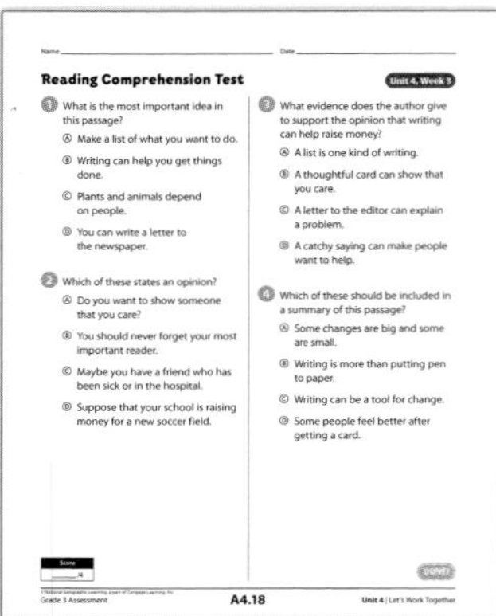	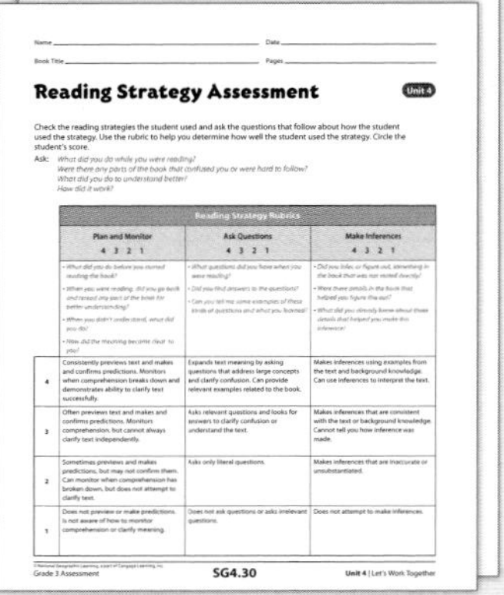	**Reading Comprehension Test** A4.17–A4.18 **Reading Strategy Assessment** SG4.30–SG4.31
Fluency ☑ Phrasing ☑ Accuracy and Rate	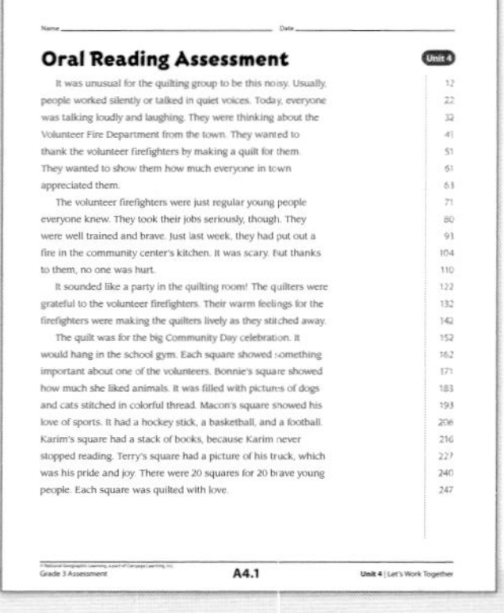	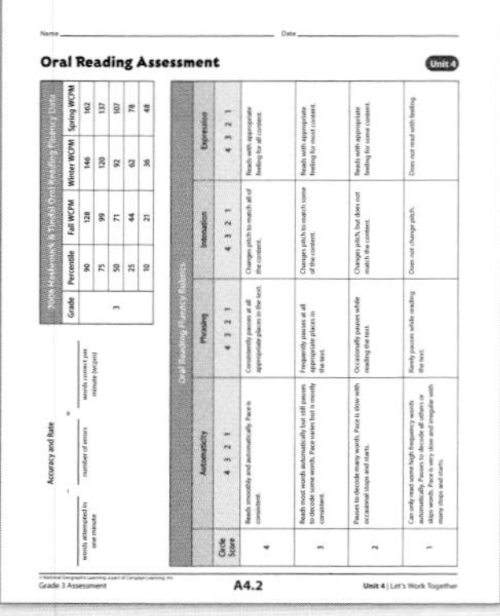	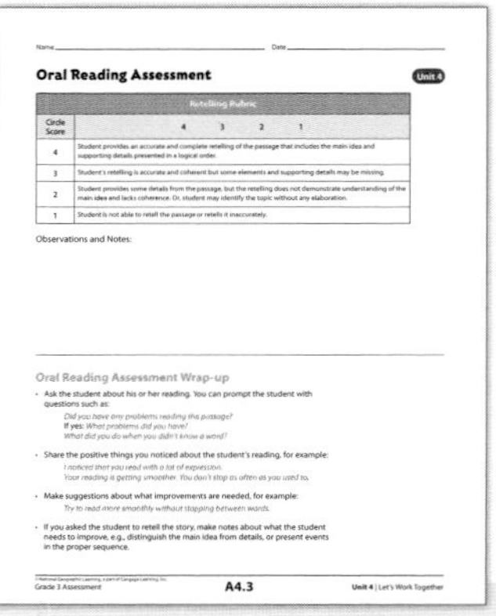	**Oral Reading Assessment** A4.1–A4.3 *Use these passages throughout Unit 4. Work with Above Level students this week.*
Vocabulary and Spelling ☑ Use Domain-Specific Words ☑ Use Academic Words ☑ Spell Words Ending in *-ed* ☑ Use Commonly Misspelled Words Correctly	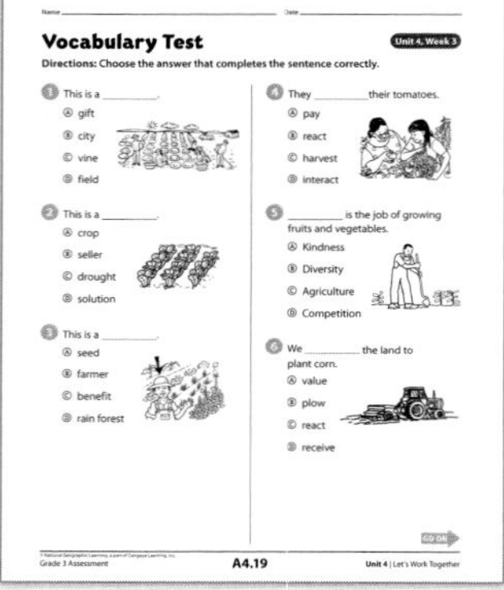	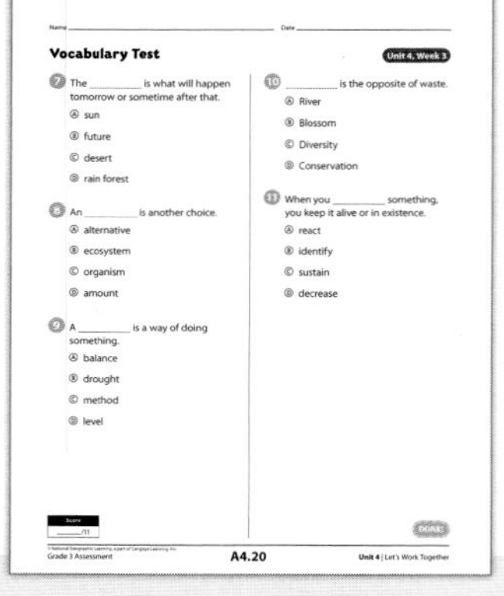	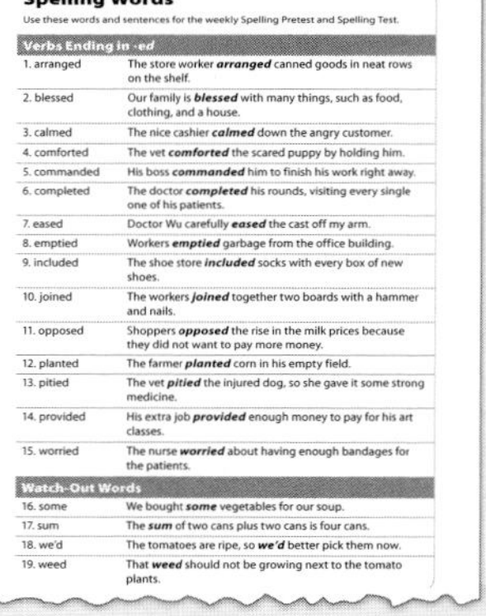	**Vocabulary Test** A4.19–A4.20 **Spelling Pretest/ Spelling Test** T239u
Grammar and Writing ☑ Use Helping Verbs ☑ Use Forms of *Do* ☑ Evaluate Information	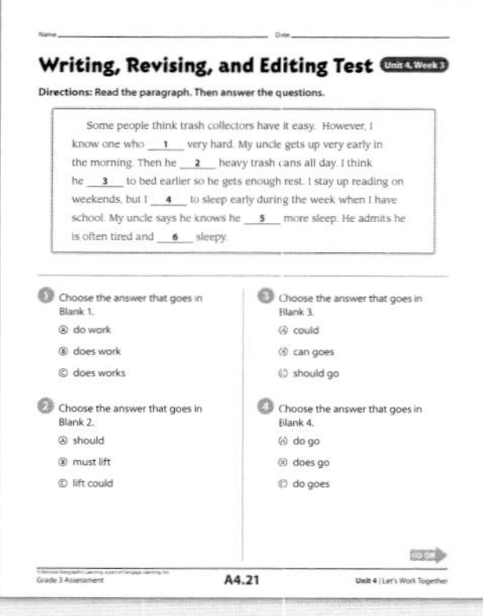	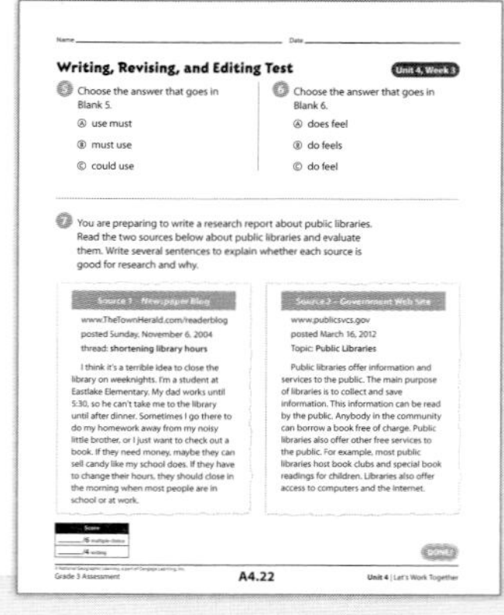	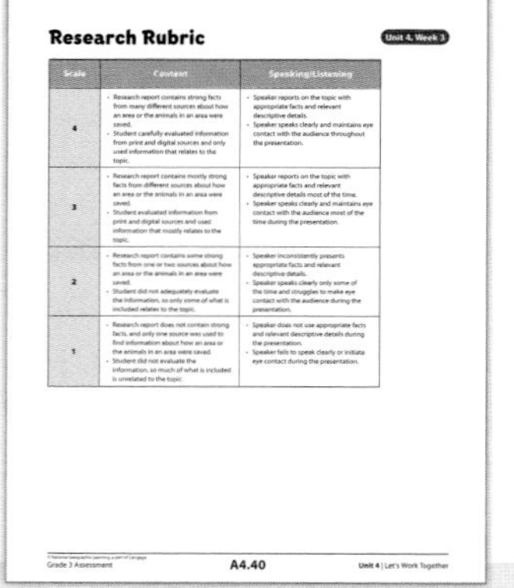	**Writing, Revising, and Editing Test** A4.21–A4.22 **Research Project Rubric** A4.40

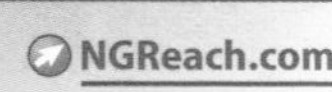
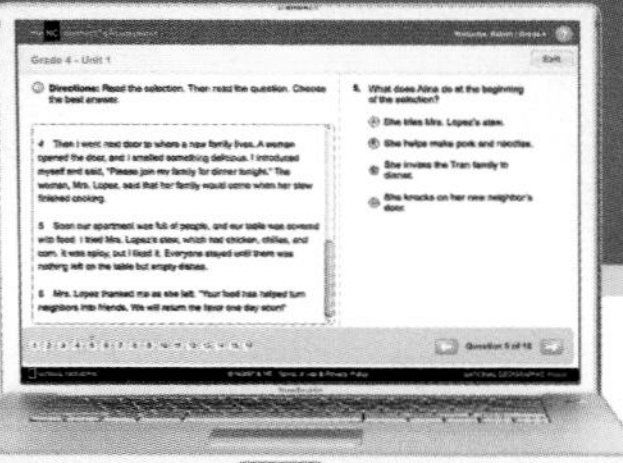

ExamView®

REPORTS

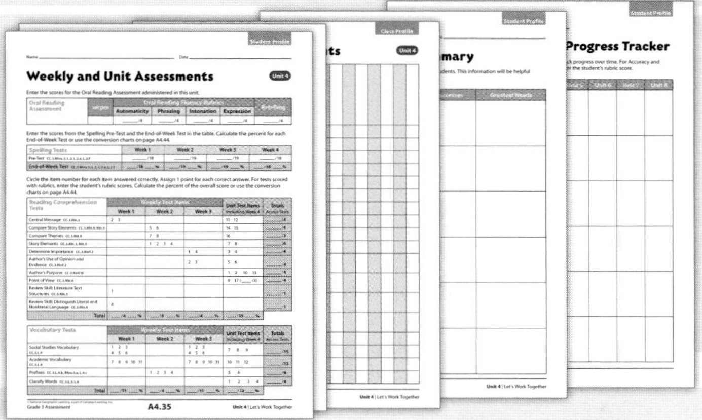

PRINT & ONLINE

Report Forms

Student Profile: Weekly and Unit Assessments	A4.35–A4.36
Class Profile: Weekly and Unit Assessments	A4.37
Student Profile: Strengths and Needs Summary	A4.38
Student Profile: Oral Reading Assessment Progress Tracker	A1.3

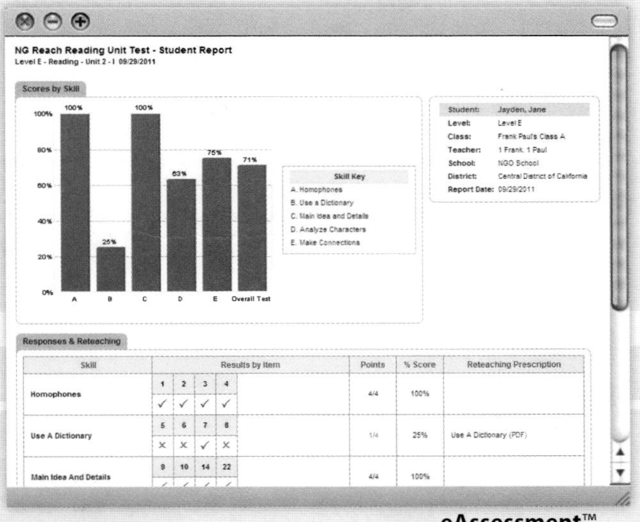

eAssessment™

ONLINE ONLY

Automated Reports

Student Profile: Weekly and Unit Tests

Class Profile: Weekly and Unit Tests

Standards Summary Report

Reteach and Practice

RESOURCES AND ROUTINES

Reading

RETEACH

Opinion and Evidence: Reteaching Master RT4.7

Determine Importance: Reteaching Master RT4.8

ADDITIONAL PRACTICE

Comprehension Coach NGReach.com

Fluency

RETEACH

Fluency Routines, page BP33

ADDITIONAL PRACTICE

Comprehension Coach NGReach.com

Vocabulary and Spelling

RETEACH

Vocabulary Routine 6, page BP40

Spelling and Word Work Routine, page BP52

ADDITIONAL PRACTICE

Vocabulary Games NGReach.com

Daily Spelling Practice, pages T239u–T239v

Grammar and Writing

RETEACH

Verbs: Anthology Handbook, page 593

Writing: Reteaching Writing Routine, page BP51

ADDITIONAL PRACTICE

More Grammar Practice PM4.24

Daily Writing Skills Practice, pages T239y–T239z

Week 4 Planner

☑ = TESTED

	Day 1	Day 2
WHOLE GROUP TIME	**Listen and Comprehend**	**Read and Comprehend**
Anthology — **Speaking and Listening**  5–10 minutes	**Academic Talk** CC.3.SL.1 Discuss the Big Question T259q	**Academic Talk** CC.3.SL.1 Preview and Predict T260c
Language and Vocabulary  15–25 minutes	**Daily Spelling and Word Work** CC.3.Rfou.3; CC.3.L.1.e; CC.3.L.2; CC.3.L.2.e; CC.3.L.2.f ☑ Pretest: Verbs Ending in *-ing* and Commonly Misspelled Words T259k **Daily Grammar** CC.3.L.1; CC.3.L.1.a; CC.3.L.1.d ☑ Forms of *be* T259m **Vocabulary Strategy** CC.3.L.5; CC.3.L.6 ☑ Classify Words T259q	**Daily Spelling and Word Work** CC.3.L.1.e; CC.3.L.2; CC.3.L.2.f ☑ Practice T259k **Daily Grammar** CC.3.L.1; CC.3.L.1.a; CC.3.L.1.d ☑ Forms of *have* T259m **Vocabulary Strategy** CC.3.L.5; CC.3.L.6 ☑ Classify More Words T260c
Reading 20–40 minutes	**Reading** CC.3.Rlit.10; CC.3.Rinf.10 Read Aloud: Persuasive Text; Note; Story T260a **Comprehension** CC.3.Rlit.10; CC.3.Rinf.10 ☑ Determine Author's Purpose T260a **Fluency** CC.3.Rfou.4 ☑ Model Phrasing T260a	**Reading** CC.3.Rlit.10; Read a Fable T261, T262–263 **Comprehension** CC.3.Rlit.2; CC.3.Rlit.3 ☑ Identify Author's Purpose T261, T262–263 ☑ Determine Importance T261, T262–263 **Fluency** CC.3.Rfou.4 ☑ Practice Phrasing, Accuracy, and Rate T261
Writing 15–45 minutes	**Power Writing** T259q CC.3.W.10 **Daily Writing Skills** CC.3.W.1; CC.3.W.1.a; CC.3.W.1.b; CC.3.W.1.c ☑ Link Opinions and Reasons T259o **Writing** CC.3.W.10 Write for a Purpose T260b **Writing Project: Persuasive Essay** CC.3.W.1; CC.3.W.1.a; CC.3.W.1.b; CC.3.W.1.c; CC.3.W.5; CC.3.W.10 ☑ Study a Model T268	**Power Writing** T260c CC.3.W.10 **Daily Writing Skills** CC.3.W.1; CC.3.W.1.a; CC.3.W.1.b; CC.3.W.1.c ☑ Link Opinions and Reasons T259o **Writing** CC.3.Rlit.2; CC.3.W.10 Explain the Moral T264–265 **Writing Project: Persuasive Essay** CC.3.W.1; CC.3.W.1.a; CC.3.W.1.b; CC.3.W.1.c; CC.3.W.5; CC.3.W.10 ☑ Prewrite T268–T269
SMALL GROUP READING TIME	**Read Social Studies Articles**	**Read Nonfiction Books**
Fiction & Nonfiction 20 minutes	**Vocabulary** CC.3.L.6 Learn Social Studies Vocabulary SG22–SG23 **Reading** CC.3.Rinf.3, 8, 10 Explain Text Structure SG22 Build Comprehension SG23 	**Vocabulary** CC.3.L.6 Learn Story Words SG24–SG25 **Reading** CC.3.Rinf.10 Introduce SG24–SG25 Read SG26–SG27 Determine Importance SG26–SG27 ☑ Determine Author's Purpose SG26–SG27 

LEARNING STATION TIME/DAILY PHONICS INTERVENTION

20 minutes

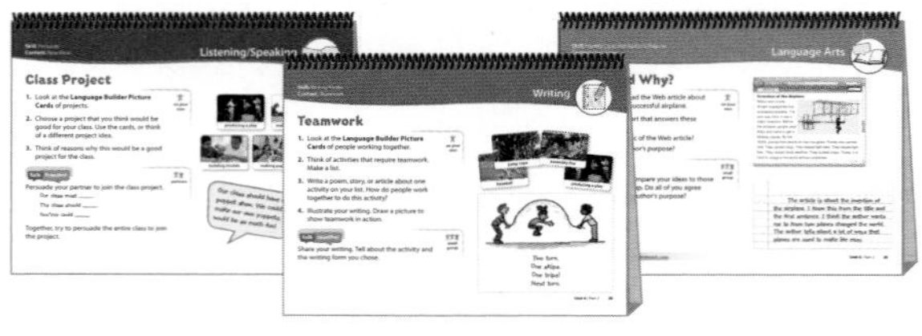

- **Speaking and Listening** T259g CC.3.SL.1; CC.3.SL.2
- **Language and Vocabulary** T259g CC.3.L.6
- **Writing** T259g CC.3.W.1; CC.3.W.1.a; CC.3.W.2.a; CC.3.W.4
- **Cross-Curricular** T259h CC.3.Rinf.10; CC.3.W.2
- **Reading and Intervention** T259h CC.3.Rinf.10; CC.3.Rfou.3; CC.3.Rfou.4.b
- **Daily Phonics Intervention** T259i–T259j CC.3.Rfou.3; CC.3.Rfou.3.d; CC.3.L.2.e; CC.3.L.2.f

BIG Question What's the best way to get things done?

Day 3

Read and Comprehend

Academic Talk CC.3.SL.1; CC.3.SL.1.a; CC.3.SL.1.d
Talk Together T266

Daily Spelling and Word Work CC.3.L.1.e; CC.3.L.2.e
☑ Practice T259l

Daily Grammar CC.3.W.5; CC.3.L.1; CC.3.L.1.a; CC.3.L.1.d; CC.3.L.1.f
☑ Subject-Verb Agreement T259n, T266a

Vocabulary Review CC.3.L.6
Review Social Studies and Academic Vocabulary T265a

Reading CC.3.Rlit.10
Reread a Fable T265a–T266

Comprehension CC.3.Rlit.10
☑ Compare Purposes T265a

Fluency CC.3.Rfou.4
☑ Practice Phrasing T266

Power Writing T265a CC.3.W.10

Daily Writing Skills CC.3.W.1; CC.3.W.1.a; CC.3.W.1.b; CC.3.W.1.c
☑ Link Opinions and Reasons T259p

Writing CC.3.L.1; CC.3.L.1.d, f; CC.3.L.3
Write to Reinforce Grammar T267

Writing Project: Persuasive Essay CC.3.W.1; CC.3.W.1.a; CC.3.W.1.b; CC.3.W.1.c; CC.3.W.5; CC.3.W.10
☑ Draft T269

Read Nonfiction Books

Vocabulary CC.3.L.6
Expand Vocabulary Through Wide Reading SG24–SG27

Reading
Read and Integrate Ideas SG26–SG27 CC.3.Rinf.10
Determine Importance SG26–SG27
☑ Determine Author's Purpose SG26–SG27

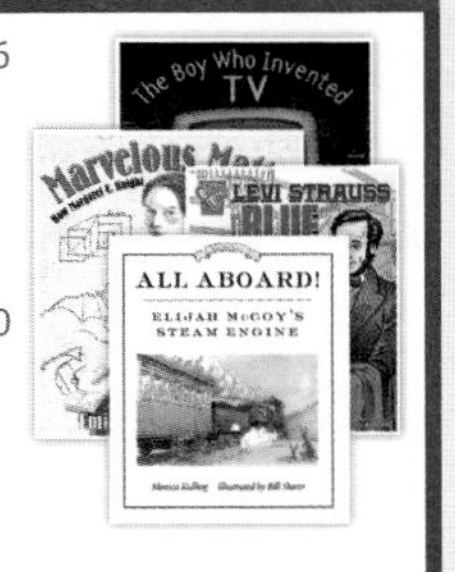

Day 4

Read and Comprehend

Academic Talk CC.3.Rlit.2; CC.3.SL.4
Retell a Story T267d

Daily Spelling and Word Work CC.3.L.2; CC.3.L.2.e; CC.3.L.2.g
☑ Practice T259l

Daily Grammar CC.3.W.5; CC.3.L.1; CC.3.L.1.a; CC.3.L.1.d; CC.3.L.1.f
☑ Grammar and Writing T259n

Vocabulary Practice CC.3.L.5; CC.3.L.6
☑ Classify Words T267c

Reading CC.3.Rlit.10
☑ Read Fables T267a–T267b

Comprehension CC.3.Rlit.6
☑ Distinguish Viewpoint T267a

Fluency CC.3.Rfou.4
☑ Model and Practice Phrasing T267b

Power Writing T267c CC.3.W.10

Daily Writing Skills CC.3.W.1; CC.3.W.1.a; CC.3.W.1.b; CC.3.W.1.c
☑ Link Opinions and Reasons T259p

Writing CC.3.W.10
Write About Viewpoint T267d

Writing Project: Persuasive Essay CC.3.W.1; CC.3.W.1.a; CC.3.W.1.b; CC.3.W.1.c; CC.3.W.5; CC.3.W.10; CC.3.L.1; CC.3.L.1.d; CC.3.L.3
☑ Revise/Edit and Proofread T270

Read Nonfiction Books

Vocabulary CC.3.L.6
Expand Vocabulary Through Wide Reading SG24–SG27

Reading CC.3.Rinf.10
Introduce SG26–SG27
Read and Integrate Ideas SG26–SG27
Determine Importance SG26–SG27
☑ Determine Author's Purpose SG26–SG27

Day 5

Review and Apply

Academic Talk CC.3.SL.1; CC.3.SL.1.b
Relate Readings to the Big Question T267h

Daily Grammar CC.3.W.5; CC.3.L.1; CC.3.L.1.a; CC.3.L.1.d; CC.3.L.1.f
☑ Review T259n

Vocabulary Practice CC.3.L.5; CC.3.L.6
☑ Classify Words T267e

Reading CC.3.Rlit.10
Reread Fables T267f–T267g

Comprehension CC.3.Rlit.6; CC.3.Rlit.9
☑ Distinguish Viewpoint T267f
Compare Viewpoints T267g

Power Writing T267e CC.3.W.10

Daily Writing Skills CC.3.W.1; CC.3.W.1.a; CC.3.W.1.b; CC.3.W.1.c
☑ Link Opinions and Reasons T259p

Writing CC.3.W.10
Write About the Moral T267g

Writing Project: Persuasive Essay
☑ Publish T271

Read Nonfiction Books

Vocabulary CC.3.L.6
Expand Vocabulary Through Wide Reading SG24–SG27

Reading CC.3.Rinf.10; CC.3.SL.1.a
Connect Across Texts SG27

Writing CC.3.W.10
Choose a Writing Option SG26–SG27

ASSESSMENT & RETEACHING

Assessment and Reteaching T271a–T271b

☑ Reading Comprehension Unit Test A4.23–A4.28 CC.3.Rlit.2
☑ Reading Strategy Assessment SG4.30–SG4.31 CC.3.Rlit.3
☑ Oral Reading Assessment A4.1–A4.3 CC.3.Rfou.4
☑ Vocabulary Unit Test A4.29–A4.30 CC.3.L.5; CC.3.L.6
☑ Spelling Test: Verbs Ending in *-ing* and Commonly Misspelled Words T259k CC.3.Rfou.3; CC.3.L.1.e; CC.3.L.2; CC.3.L.2.e; CC.3.L.2.f; CC.3.L.2.g
☑ Writing, Revising, and Editing Unit Test A4.31–A4.34 CC.3.L.1.d; CC.3.L.1.f
Reteaching Masters RT4.9–RT4.12

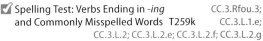

Week 4 Learning Stations

Speaking and Listening

Option 1: Class Project

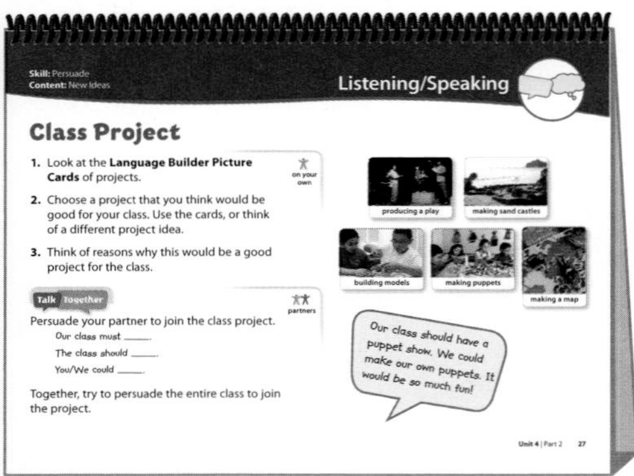

PROGRAM RESOURCES & MATERIALS

Language and Literacy Teamwork Activities: Card 27

Digital Library Images: Language Builder Picture Cards D47–D51

Teacher's Guide on NGReach.com

Discuss Topics, Expressing Ideas Clearly CC.3.SL.1

Option 2: Discuss a Video

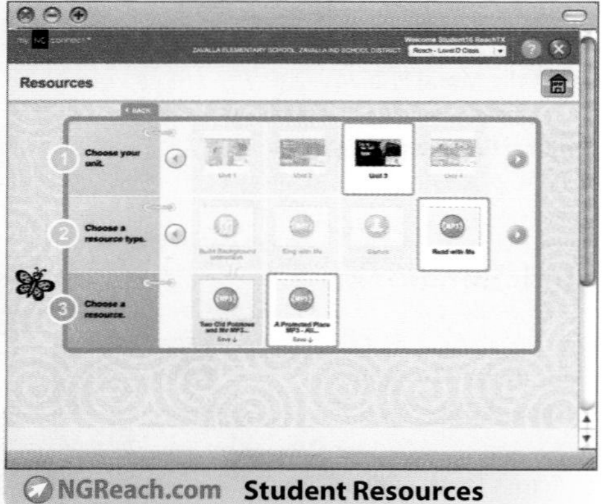

NGReach.com **Student Resources**

Have students view and discuss a video about the relationship between ants and acacia trees.

- Have students go to Resources > Unit 4 > Learning Stations > Week 4 > Acacia Ants.
- Have small groups talk about how the ants and the tree help each other.

Determine the Main Ideas and Supporting Details of Information Presented Visually and Orally in Diverse Media CC.3.SL.2

Language and Vocabulary

Key Words

accomplish · alternative · conservation · crop
evidence · farmer · field · future · harvest
method · opinion · plow · summarize · sustain

Option 1: Vocabulary Games

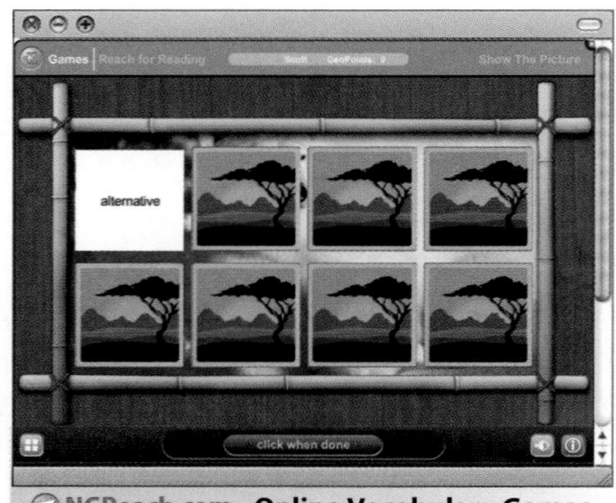

NGReach.com **Online Vocabulary Games**

Acquire and Use Conversational, Academic and Domain-Specific Words CC.3.L.6

Option 2: My Vocabulary Notebook

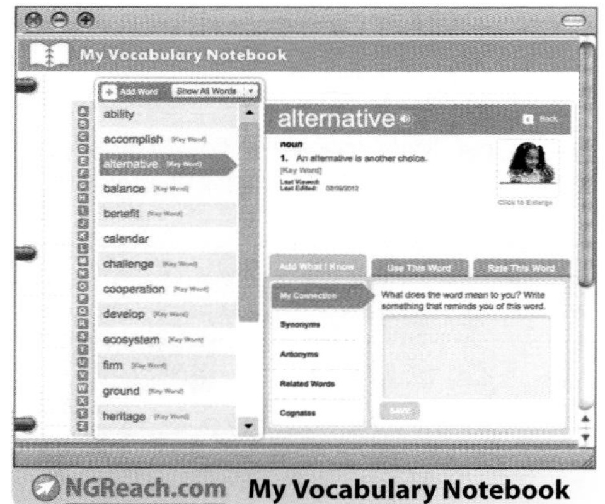

NGReach.com **My Vocabulary Notebook**

Have students expand their word knowledge.

- Under Add More Information > Add What I Know > My Connection, have students write what the word means to them, or something that reminds them of the word.

Acquire and Use Conversational, Academic, and Domain-Specific Words CC.3.L.6

Writing

Option 1: Teamwork

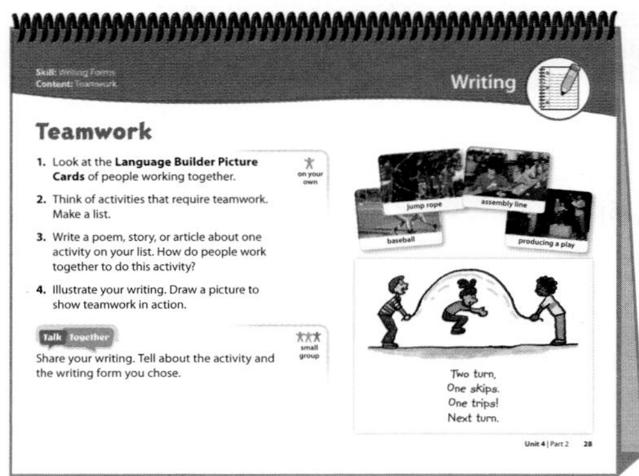

PROGRAM RESOURCES & MATERIALS

Language and Literacy Teamwork Activities: Card 28

Digital Library Images: Language Builder Picture Cards D39–D47

Teacher's Guide on NGReach.com

crayons and markers

Include Illustrations CC.3.W.2.a
Use Appropriate Development and Organization CC.3.W.4

Option 2: Write an Opinion

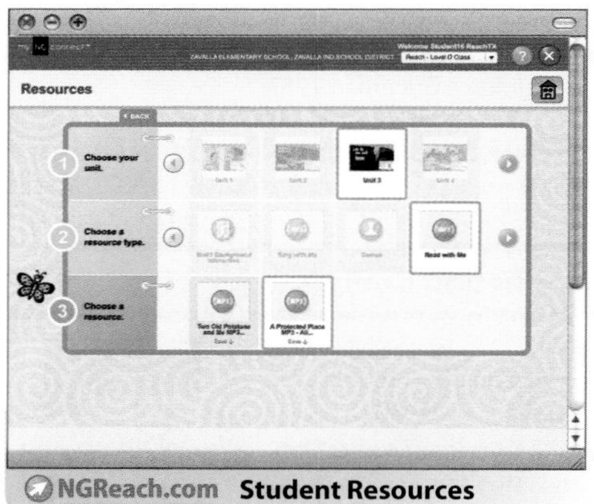

NGReach.com **Student Resources**

Have students write an opinion paragraph about saving native plants.

- Go to Resources > Unit 4 > Learning Stations > Week 4 > Invasive Plants.
- Have students read the article and decide whether they agree with the author.
- Then have students write a paragraph that includes reasons for their opinion.

Write Opinions on Topics CC.3.W.1
Provide Reasons CC.3.W.1.b

= one student  = two students 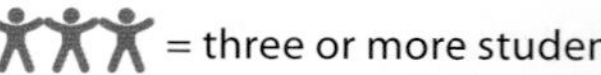 = three or more students

Cross-Curricular

Option 1: What and Why?

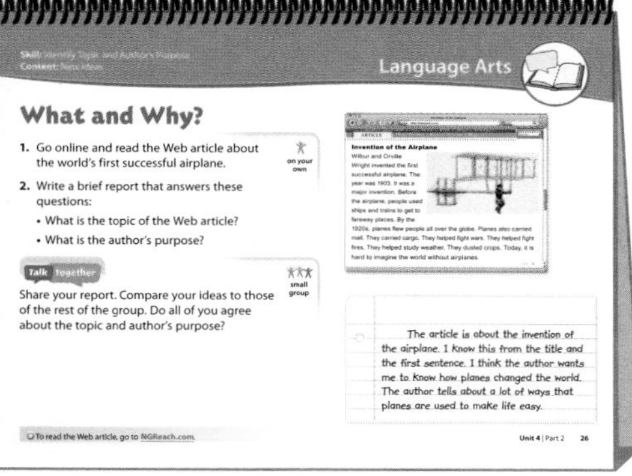

PROGRAM RESOURCES & MATERIALS

Language and Literacy Teamwork Activities: Card 26

Student Resources Directory

Teacher's Guide on NGReach.com

Write Informative/Explanatory Text to Convey Information	CC.3.W.2

Option 2: Write a Response

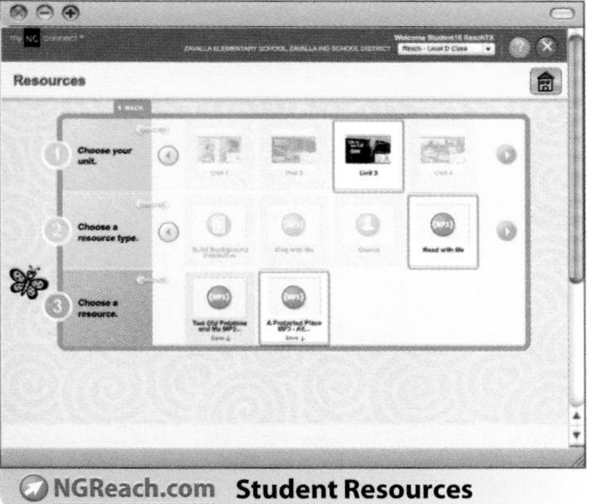

NGReach.com **Student Resources**

Have students read about ants.

- To read the article, have students go to Resources > Unit 4 > Learning Stations > Week 4 > Trapjaw Ants.
- Have students read the article and create a factsheet based on the information contained in the article.
- Students should list three to five ant facts in their factsheets.

Read and Comprehend Informational Text	CC.3.Rinf.10

Reading

Option 1: Read a Fable Aloud

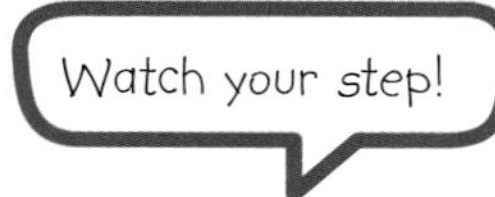

Have students read aloud "The Ant and the Grasshopper" on pages 261–265 of the **Anthology**.

- Have partners look at the dialogue and discuss how it should be read, including what their voice should sound like and what facial gestures and body language they should use.
- Have partners take turns reading aloud the parts of the ant, the grasshopper, and the narrator.

Read Orally with Expression on Successive Readings	CC.3.Rfou.4.b

Option 2: Read a Blog

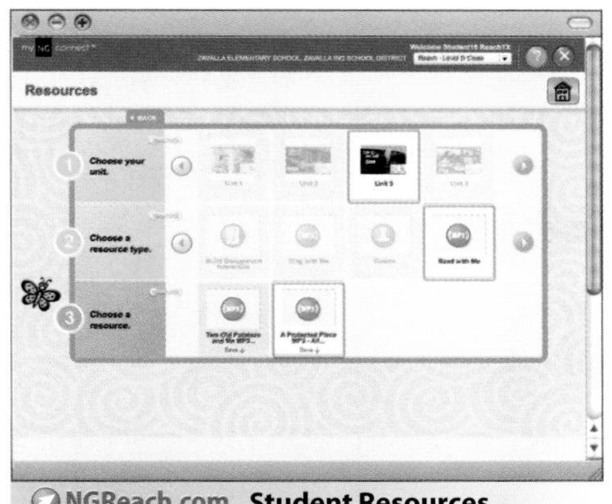

NGReach.com **Student Resources**

Students read a blog entry about a student exploring the Amazon rainforest.

- To read the blog entry, have students go to Resources > Unit 4 > Learning Stations > Week 4 > Rainforest Blog.
- Have students read the blog entry and write a sentence about what they learned.

Read and Comprehend Informational Text	CC.3.Rinf.10

Intervention

Phonics Games

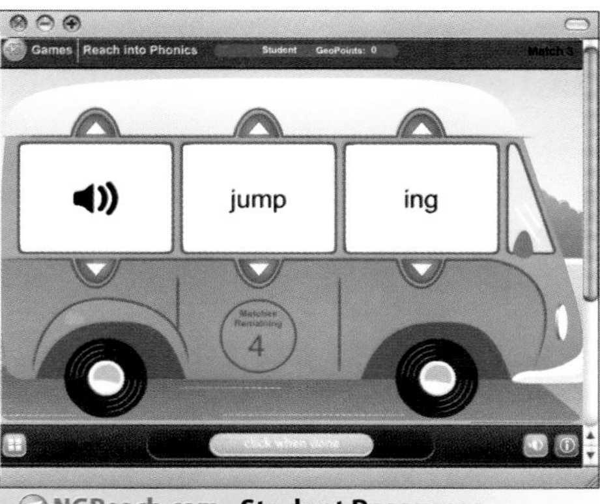

NGReach.com **Student Resources**

Apply Phonics and Word Analysis Skills	CC.3.Rfou.3

For Reteaching Masters, see pages RT4.9–RT4.12.

Additional Resources

ESL Kit

ESL Teacher's Edition pages T260a–T273

Week 4 Daily Phonics Intervention

OBJECTIVES

Thematic Connection: Innovations

Recognize High Frequency Words

Develop Phonological Awareness: Count Syllables and Contrast Final Sounds

Identify Verb Endings (*-ing*); Decode Words with Endings

Build Reading Fluency; Concepts of Print (dialogue)

Teach Day 1

PROGRAM RESOURCES

High Frequency Words: Teaching Master 17

Word Builder: Transparencies 51, 52

Reach into Phonics

Lesson 60, page T100

Lesson 62, pages T102–T103

High Frequency Words

Follow Lesson 60 to present High Frequency Words:

celebrate	most	young	children	started

Verbs Ending in *-ing*

Follow Lesson 62 to teach words with *-ing* ending. Guide students through **Transparencies 51** and **52**.

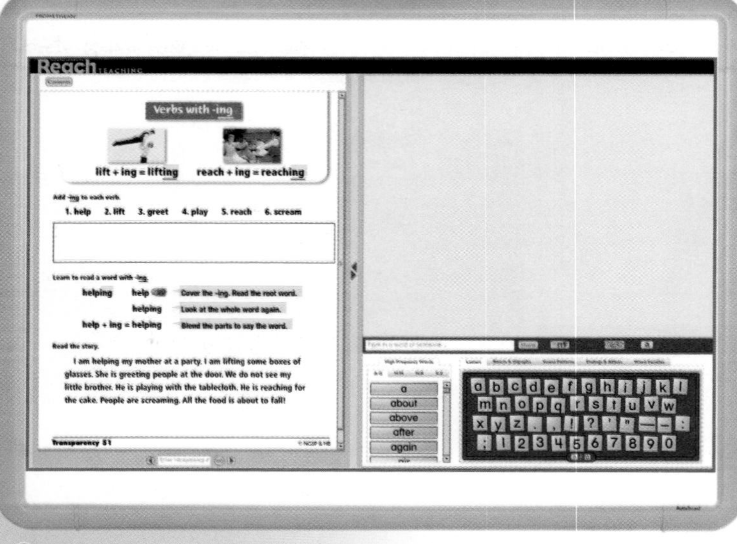

NGReach.com **Word Builder: Transparencies 51, 52**

Practice Day 2

PROGRAM RESOURCES

More High Frequency Words: Teaching Master 18

Decodable Reader: *Celebrate the Past*, Practice Book, page 163

Reach into Phonics

Lesson 61, page T101

Lesson 63, pages T104–T106

High Frequency Words

Follow Lesson 61 to present High Frequency Words:

beginning	change	another	only	following

Build Reading Fluency

Provide students with the **Decodable Reader**, *Celebrate the Past*. Then follow Lesson 63. Use **Reading Routine 3** to guide students as they read Decodable texts.

*For **Reading Routine 3**, see Reach into Phonics page ix.*

= one student = two students = three or more students

COMMON CORE STANDARDS

Apply Word Analysis Skills	CC.3.Rfou.3		
Read Grade-Appropriate Irregularly-Spelled Words	CC.3.Rfou.3.d	Use Spelling Patterns and Generalizations	CC.3.L.2.f
Use Conventional Spelling	CC.3.L.2.e		

Pick It Up! Day 3  Option 1

MATERIALS

index cards, 14 per group

Prepare

- Arrange students in groups of three to six. Have students print the vowels *a, e, i* and the consonants *c, k, l, n, m, p, p, s, t, w,* separately on index cards. Have students print the ending *-ing* on the final index card.
- Students line up the vowel cards together and then arrange the consonant and *-ing* cards together on a desk.

Play a Game

- A "Caller" calls out a word from the following word bank below.

sipping	**planting**	**wiping**	**tapping**	**clapping**	**skating**
slipping	**melting**	**swiping**	**taping**	**packing**	**sailing**

- A "Word Builder" picks up the letters needed to build the word. The Word Builder places the cards down in order and reads the word.
- Group members listen and watch as the Word Builder builds the word. If a student notices an error, he or she takes the Word Builder's place.
- Students take turns as the Caller and Word Builder.

Mystery Word Day 3  Option 2

Prepare

- Display the words in the word bank below. Assign a "mystery word" from the word bank to each pair of students.
- Have partners work together to create five clues to help other students identify the word.

reading	**another**	**changing**	**young**	**taking**	**helping**

> Mystery Word: helping
> Clue 1: The mystery word has 2 syllables.
> Clue 2: The mystery word has 7 letters.
> Clue 3: The mystery word does not drop a letter to add -ing.
> Clue 4: The first syllable of the mystery word has a short vowel.
> Clue 5: The mystery word will complete this sentence: I like ________ my parents around the house. (helping)

Play a Game

- Have each pair of students present the clues to the other pairs of players, one clue at a time.
- After hearing each clue, other pairs collaborate to write down all the mystery words that match the clues to that point. After the next clue, players cross off words that do not match the new clue.
- When a pair has the answer, the partners call it out.

Crack the Code! Day 4 

MATERIALS

computer

Prepare

- Have partners use a computer to type the alphabet on one line. Tell them to paste that line onto the next line, and then change the second line to a symbol font.
- Next, have partners type all the words from the word bank below in random order and then change their typing of the words into the same symbol font.
- Tell partners to type a blank line next to each word.

celebrate	**children**	**beginning**	**grading**	**drifting**	**dripping**

Play a Game

- Have pairs use the symbol alphabet to decode the letters used in each word and then write the word.
- Remind students that they might be able to figure out the word after decoding only a few of its letters.

Review and Assess Day 5 

PROGRAM RESOURCES

Word Builder: Transparency 53

Reach into Phonics

Lesson 64, page T107

Progress Check 4, pages T290-T291

Review and Assess

Follow Lesson 64 to review verbs ending in *-ing*. Guide students through **Transparency 53**. Administer Progress Check 4 on pages T290-T291 to measure learning.

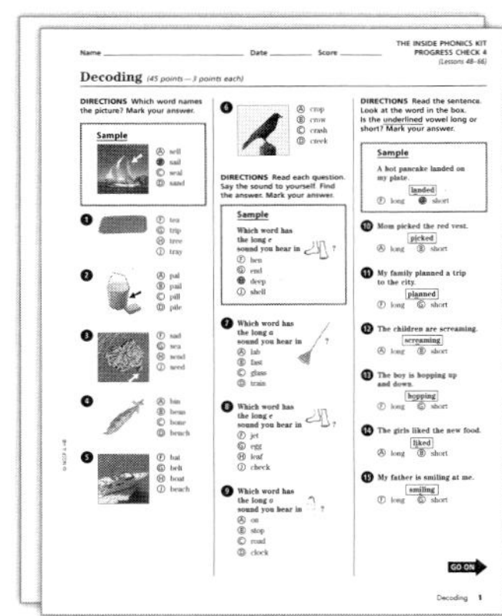
Decoding

Week 4 Daily Spelling & Word Work

OBJECTIVES

Thematic Connection: Innovation

☑ **Spell Verbs Ending in *-ing***

☑ **Use Commonly Misspelled Words Correctly**

SUGGESTED PACING

DAY 1	Spelling Pretest
DAY 2–4	Daily Practice Options
DAY 5	Spelling Test

Spelling Pretest — Day 1

Spelling Test — Day 5

Spelling Words

Use these words and sentences for the weekly Spelling Pretest and Spelling Test.

Verbs Ending in *-ing*	
1. announcing	Use a microphone when you are ***announcing*** the winner of the science fair.
2. attending	I am ***attending*** the meeting about new inventions, but I have to leave early.
3. beautifying	Our club is ***beautifying*** the main street with flowers.
4. collecting	We're ***collecting*** soil samples by digging them up and putting each one in a plastic bag.
5. considering	Students are ***considering*** which recent invention has changed their lives the most.
6. doubling	I am ***doubling*** the recipe because twice as many people are coming for dinner.
7. educating	Good teachers are always ***educating*** their students about the real world.
8. erasing	The teacher is ***erasing*** the chalkboard.
9. forgiving	Dad is ***forgiving*** when people say they are sorry.
10. gathering	Nathan is ***gathering*** facts on the Internet about new kinds of footwear.
11. hiring	Few companies are ***hiring*** people for jobs here.
12. mistreating	Is he ***mistreating*** his dog with that shock collar?
13. notifying	The principal will be ***notifying*** our parents in a weekly newsletter about innovations at school.
14. realizing	Mindi is ***realizing*** that too much TV and computer time is bad for her.
15. spreading	Dad is ***spreading*** peanut butter on each slice of bread with a fancy new knife.
Watch-Out Words	
16. bring	Please ***bring*** my lunch to me in the workroom.
17. take	I can't use this toolbox, so will you please ***take*** it?
18. where	***Where*** did you put that box of nails?
19. were	We ***were*** working on a secret new mousetrap.

Verbs Ending in *-ing* — Day 2 — Option 1

Teach

Write *collect, realize,* and *notify* on the board and read each aloud. Say: *These verbs tell about actions that are happening now: I* collect old buttons. *If I want to show that the action continues over time, I use a helping verb* (am, is, *or* are) *and add* -ing *to the verb: I* am collecting *old buttons all day today.*

Point to *realize* and explain: *When a verb ends with* e*, drop the* e *before you add* -ing. Demonstrate erasing the *e* and adding *-ing* to make *realizing*.

Point to *notify* and explain: *When a verb ends in a consonant and* y*, just add* -ing. Demonstrate that you do *not* change the word *notify* to make *notifying*. (Students may recall that you do change the *y* to *i* before adding *-ed: notified.*)

Prepare

Have each student fold a piece of paper to create two columns. Tell them to head one column, "Just add *-ing*," and to head the other column, "Drop the e, and add *-ing*."

Word Sort

- Have students quietly read aloud each of the first 15 spelling words, listening for the *-ing* at the end of the word that signals an action continuing over time.
- Tell them to print each verb under the right heading, pronouncing the word again as they write it. Have them underline the letters that form the pattern.

Form and Use Verb Tenses	CC.3.L.1.e
Use Spelling Patterns and Generalizations	CC.3.L.2.f

Comic Strips — Day 2 — Option 2

Make a Drawing

- Have partners collaborate to create a comic strip using as many spelling words as possible. Tell them to include at least three of the Watch-Out Words.
- Have students underline the Watch-Out Words in their strips and draw a wavy line under the regular spelling words. Partners who include the most spelling words are the day's spelling champs.

Demonstrate Command of Spelling	CC.3.L.2

= one student = two students = three or more students

Trace Words — Day 3  Option 1

MATERIALS

index cards, 19 per pair of students • timer • tracing paper

Prepare

- Have student pairs collaborate to write each spelling word on a separate index card.
- Have partners use tracing paper to trace around each word to make a bubble in the shape of the word.
- Have students set the index cards aside and place the word bubble outlines in front of them.

Play a Game

- Have one partner choose a bubble and write the correct spelling word inside the bubble, based on the shape of the bubble.
- Have the other partner check to make sure that the correct spelling word is written in the bubble.
- If the word is incorrect, the first partner tries once more. If the student spells it correctly the first or second time, he or she keeps the word.
- Students take turns until ten minutes are up.

Use Conventional Spelling — CC.3.L.2.e

Game Show! — Day 3  Option 2

Prepare

- Have small groups write each of the first 15 spelling words on slips of paper. On the back, students write the present tense of the verb.
- Have students place all the slips in the middle of the table with the present-tense verbs showing (leaving the spelling words hidden).

Play a Game

- Choose the first Host. The other students are Contestants. The Host calls out a present-tense verb from a slip.
- Contestants who can spell the *-ing* form of the verb put their thumbs in the air. The Host calls on the Contestant who put a thumb up first.
- That Contestant says the *-ing* form of the verb aloud and spells it. The Host checks the spelling. If correct, the Contestant keeps the slip. If not, it goes back on the table.
- The student sitting to the right of the Host becomes the new Host.
- Play continues until all verbs are in the hands of students.

Form and Use Verb Tenses — CC.3.L.1.e
Use Conventional Spelling — CC.3.L.2.e

Beat the Clock — Day 4  Option 1

MATERIALS

index cards, 19 per group • markers, three different colors per group

Prepare

- Arrange students in teams of three. Tell students that they will try to "Beat the Clock" by being the first team to finish the game.
- Have each team member choose six to seven spelling words, so that all 19 words are chosen.
- Have each student choose a color and write each of his or her words on separate cards with a marker of that color.
- Tell students to place their cards face down.

Play a Game

- Choose one player to go first. Have that player pick a card and read aloud the word on that card for the other team members to chorally spell. If the word is spelled correctly, he or she places the card on the floor to begin a list. If spelled incorrectly, the reader then spells the word correctly and places the card on the floor.
- The player to the left of the first player picks up the top card from his or her pile and reads it for the others to chorally spell and add to the list on the floor. Play continues alphabetically.
- The team that builds a list in the shortest time wins.

Use Conventional Spelling — CC.3.L.2.e

Word Families — Day 4  Option 2

MATERIALS

dictionaries, one per pair of students

Use Graphic Organizers

- Have partners draw a large house outline on a sheet of paper. Tell them to choose a spelling word and write its present-tense form in the house to begin a word family.
- Have students add prefixes and suffixes to the present-tense word. Tell them to use a dictionary to see if the word they formed is a real word, and to be sure to include the *-ing* form of the verb.
- Tell partners to see how many word families they can create, using one house per spelling word.

educating
uneducated
educate
educated
educator

Demonstrate Command of Spelling — CC.3.L.2
Consult References — CC.3.L.2.g

Week 4 Daily Grammar

OBJECTIVES

Thematic Connection: Innovations

☑ **Grammar: Use Forms of *be***

☑ **Grammar: Use Forms of *have***

COMMON CORE STANDARDS

Edit Writing	CC.3.W.5
Demonstrate Command of Grammar	CC.3.L.1
Explain the Function of Verbs	CC.3.L.1.a

Day 1

PROGRAM RESOURCES

Forms of *be*: eVisual 4.28

Game: Practice Master PM4.25

MATERIALS

timer • glue

Teach the Rules

Use the suggestion on page T260b to introduce the linking verb *be*. Explain: *The verb* to be *is not an action verb. To be links the subject of a sentence to a word in the predicate that tells something about the subject.* Use **eVisual 4.28** to teach about forms of *be*.

Forms of *be*

- The verb **to be** is a **linking verb**. It links the **subject** of a sentence to a **noun** that tells what the subject is. Or it links the **subject** to a word that **describes** the subject.
- The verb **to be** has special forms: **I am you are she/he/it is we are they are**

I am a **student**.

You are a **friend**.

He is a **farmer**.

We are **busy**.

They are **helpers**.

The **fields** are **golden**.

The **corn** is **ripe**.

NGReach.com **Forms of *be*: eVisual 4.28**

Play a Game

Distribute **Practice Master PM4.25** and have groups of three students each play the game.

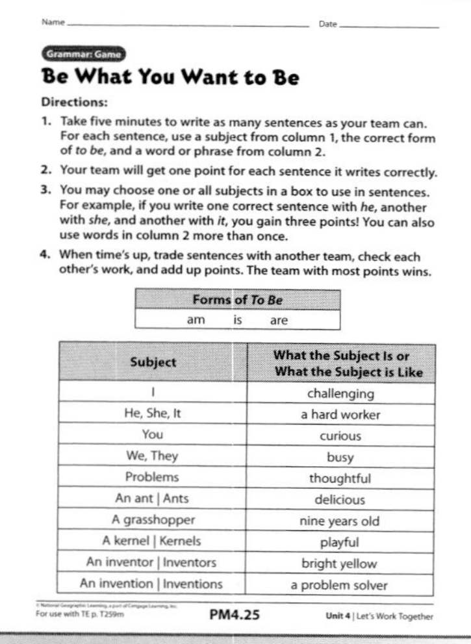

Name ________________ Date ________

Grammar: Game

Be What You Want to Be

Directions:

1. Take five minutes to write as many sentences as your team can. For each sentence, use a subject from column 1, the correct form of *to be*, and a word or phrase from column 2.
2. Your team will get one point for each sentence it writes correctly.
3. You may choose one or all subjects in a box to use in sentences. For example, if you write one correct sentence with *he*, another with *she*, and another with *it*, you gain three points! You can also use words in column 2 more than once.
4. When time's up, trade sentences with another team, check each other's work, and add up points. The team with most points wins.

Forms of *To Be*
am is are

Subject	What the Subject Is or What the Subject is Like
I	challenging
He, She, It	a hard worker
You	curious
We, They	busy
Problems	thoughtful
An ant | Ants	delicious
A grasshopper	nine years old
A kernel | Kernels	playful
An inventor | Inventors	bright yellow
An invention | Inventions	a problem solver

For use with TE p. T259m PM4.25 Unit 4 | Let's Work Together

NGReach.com **Practice Master PM4.25**

Differentiate

SN Special Needs

ISSUE Students may have difficulty building sentences.

STRATEGY Have students write forms of *to be* on strips of paper and glue them between the two columns.

Day 2

PROGRAM RESOURCES

Forms of *have*: eVisual 4.32

Game: Practice Master PM4.26

MATERIALS

game markers, one per student • coins, one per pair of students

Teach the Rules

Use the suggestion on page T262–263 to introduce the verb *have*. Explain: *The verb* to have *can be a helping verb, or it can be the main verb.* Then use **eVisual 4.32** to teach.

Forms of *have*

- The verb **to have** can be a **main verb** telling what the **subject** has.

I **have** a problem.

You **have** a solution.

Ria **has** the supplies.

- The verb **to have** can also be the **helping verb** before the **main verb**.
- The verb to have has special forms: **I have, you have, he/she/it has, we have, they have.**

Ravi and I **have** **planned** a new game.

Milo **has** **helped** us.

We **have** **delighted** many friends.

NGReach.com **Forms of *have*: eVisual 4.32**

Play a Game

Distribute **Practice Master PM4.26** and have partners play the game.

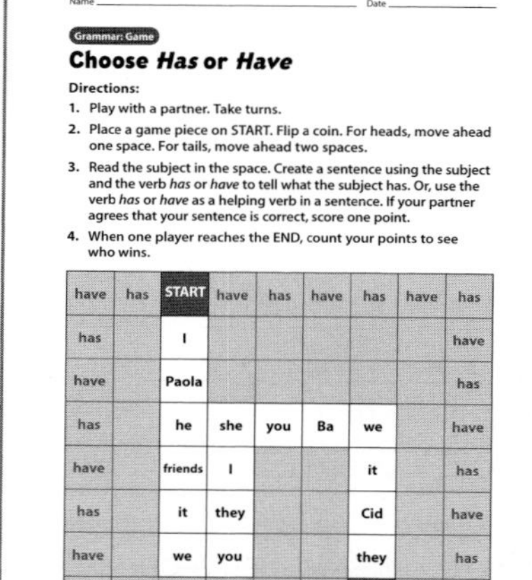

Name ________________ Date ________

Grammar: Game

Choose *Has* or *Have*

Directions:

1. Play with a partner. Take turns.
2. Place a game piece on START. Flip a coin. For heads, move ahead one space. For tails, move ahead two spaces.
3. Read the subject in the space. Create a sentence using the subject and the verb *has* or *have* to tell what the subject has. Or, use the verb *has* or *have* as a helping verb in a sentence. If your partner agrees that your sentence is correct, score one point.
4. When one player reaches the END, count your points to see who wins.

have	has	START	have	has	have	has	have	has
has		I						have
have		Paola						has
has		he	she	you	Ba	we		have
have		friends	I			it		has
has		it	they			Cid		have
have		we	you			they		has
has	have	has	have	has	have	END	has	have

For use with TE p. T259m PM4.26 Unit 4 | Let's Work Together

NGReach.com **Practice Master PM4.26**

Differentiate

EL English Learners

ISSUE In Korean, the verb *be* can be used in place of *have*. For example, "I am idea" instead of "I have an idea."

STRATEGY Emphasize that *has* or *have* tells what a subject owns or possesses and that English uses *am, is,* or *are* to link the subject to a noun or adjective that tells more about the subject.

= one student 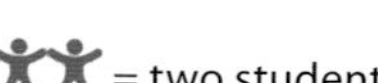 = two students  = three or more students

Forms of *be* and *have*

Form and Use Verbs — CC.3.L.1.d
Ensure Subject-Verb Agreement — CC.3.L.1.f

Day 3

MATERIALS

index cards, 16 per group

Review the Rules

Use **Anthology** page T267 to review subject-verb agreement with *to be* and *to have*. Extend the lesson with this hint: *Subject-verb agreement can be hard with irregular verb forms. Remember that most singular verbs end in -s.* Point out that the pronouns *I* and *you* follow special rules.

Copy and display the chart below to present irregular forms in an order that emphasizes where forms are the same and different.

Subject	be	have
he, she, it	is	has
Adika, Hannah	is	has
I	am	have
you (singular + plural)	are	have
we	are	have
they	are	have
Paola and Cid	are	have

Play a Game

Have partners collaborate to write each subject from the chart on a separate card, then write each of these verbs on a separate card: *am, is, are, has,* and *have*. Explain:

- *Spread the verb cards face up. Mix the subject cards and stack them face down.*
- *Take turns drawing a card from the subject stack. Choose a correct verb form and make up a sentence.*
- *If your partner agrees that your subject and verb agree, keep the subject card. Put the verb back. If the sentence is incorrect, replace both cards. Put the subject card at the bottom of the stack.*

Differentiate

BL Below Level

ISSUE Students continue to have difficulty with subject-verb agreement

STRATEGY Have students create a reference sheet with drawings to show subject-verb agreement. Examples: For *I* (self-portrait) *am, have*; for *it* (ant) *is, has*; for *we* (self-portrait and friend) *are, have*.

Day 4

PROGRAM RESOURCES

Grammar and Writing:
Practice Master PM4.31

Grammar and Writing

Distribute **Practice Master PM4.31**. Have students use editing and proofreading marks to correct errors with the verbs *be* and *have*.

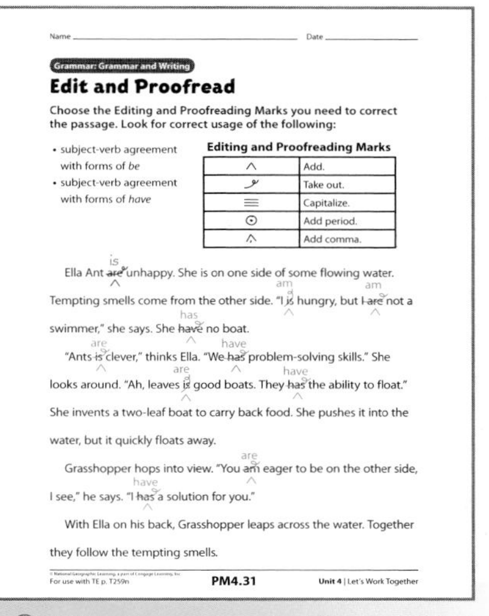

Name ________________ Date ________

Grammar: Grammar and Writing

Edit and Proofread

Choose the Editing and Proofreading Marks you need to correct the passage. Look for correct usage of the following:

- subject-verb agreement with forms of *be*
- subject-verb agreement with forms of *have*

Editing and Proofreading Marks

Mark	Meaning
∧	Add.
℘	Take out.
≡	Capitalize.
⊙	Add period.
∧	Add comma.

Ella Ant ~~are~~ is unhappy. She is on one side of some flowing water. Tempting smells come from the other side. "I ~~is~~ am hungry, but I ~~are~~ am not a swimmer," she says. She ~~have~~ has no boat.

"Ants ~~is~~ are clever," thinks Ella. "We ~~has~~ have problem-solving skills." She looks around. "Ah, leaves ~~is~~ are good boats. They ~~has~~ have the ability to float." She invents a two-leaf boat to carry back food. She pushes it into the water, but it quickly floats away.

Grasshopper hops into view. "You ~~am~~ are eager to be on the other side, I see," he says. "I ~~has~~ have a solution for you."

With Ella on his back, Grasshopper leaps across the water. Together they follow the tempting smells.

For use with TE p. T259n — PM4.31 — Unit 4 | Let's Work Together

NGReach.com **Practice Master PM4.31**

Day 5

PROGRAM RESOURCES

Writing, Revising, and Editing Unit Test: Assessment Masters A4.33–A4.36

Review and Assess

Copy and display the chart. Have small groups write singular and plural subject pronouns and the correct form of *to be* and *to have*.

Then have them write three sentences to illustrate correct use of the verb *to be*, one sentence using *have* as a main verb, and one sentence using *has* as a helping verb.

Subject	To Be	To Have	Sentences
I	am	have	I have an innovation!
He	is	has	He has studied it.

☑ Administer the **Writing, Revising, and Editing Unit Test.**

Week 4 Daily Writing Skills

OBJECTIVES

Thematic Connection: Innovation

☑ **Link Opinions and Reasons**

COMMON CORE STANDARDS

Write Opinions on Topics	CC.3.W.1
Introduce the Topic, State an Opinion, and Create a Structure	CC.3.W.1.a
Provide Reasons	CC.3.W.1.b
Link Opinions and Reasons	CC.3.W.1.c

Introduce the Skill — Day 1 

PROGRAM RESOURCES

Persuasive Passage: eVisual 4.29
Linking Words and Phrases: eVisual 4.30

Teach the Skill

Display **eVisual 4.29** and have volunteers collaboratively read it aloud.

Persuasive Passage

Every summer, people use sprinklers to water their lawns. However, in my opinion, a soaker hose is a far better choice. There are many reasons why it is better. First, a soaker hose puts water directly on the grass, so you don't waste water like you do with a sprinkler. Secondly, because you use less water, you save money. And lastly, a soaker hose doesn't get the plants' leaves wet. Wet leaves can cause plant diseases. In conclusion, the soaker hose is a great innovation that not only saves water for the future, but also saves money.

NGReach.com **Persuasive Passage: eVisual 4.29**

INTERACTIVE WHITEBOARD TIP: Underline the linking words and phrases.

Explain: *A persuasive essay tells what you think about something and why. When you write a persuasive essay, you need to state your opinion clearly and back up your opinion with reasons. Reasons can be facts, examples, or any information that supports your opinion by explaining why.*

Display **eVisual 4.30**. Reread the passage. In the chart, circle the words and phrases the writer included to link reasons to the opinion (first, so, secondly, because, lastly). Point out how the linking words and phrases, along with *in conclusion*, help to provide an easy-to-read structure.

Linking Words and Phrases

To Show Cause and Effect	• because • so • since • therefore
To Introduce Examples	• for example • such as
To Show Sequence	• first • next • secondly • lastly

NGReach.com **Linking Words and Phrases: eVisual 4.30**

INTERACTIVE WHITEBOARD TIP: Circle words the writer used in the passage.

Link Opinions and Reasons — Day 2 — Option 1

PROGRAM RESOURCES

Linking Words and Phrases: eVisual 4.30

Introduce

Copy and display the model opinion chart below. Tell students that they will create similar opinion charts showing their opinion of the selection "A Better Way," on **Anthology** pages 246–257. Display **eVisual 4.30** for student reference.

Opinion: People should use soaker hoses instead of sprinklers.
Reason: Soaker hoses don't waste water.
Reason: Because soaker hoses use less water, they save money.

Practice

Have partners briefly review "A Better Way" and agree on an opinion of it that both can support. Provide an example: *"A Better Way" gives good advice*, or *"A Better Way" is unrealistic.* Then have them follow the model above to create an opinion chart about the article. Tell them to write at least two reasons that support their opinion.

Then, have partners exchange their charts with another pair of students. Tell each pair to use carets (^) to insert linking words and phrases into the other pair's chart. Tell them they may use words and phrases from **eVisual 4.30** or others.

Link Opinions and Reasons — Day 2  — Option 2

PROGRAM RESOURCES

Small Group Reading Books for Unit 4
Linking Words and Phrases: eVisual 4.30

Introduce

Copy and display the model opinion chart above. Tell students that they will create an opinion chart for a review they could write of one of the **Small Group Reading** books they have read in Unit 4. Display **eVisual 4.30** for student reference.

Practice

Have each student choose a **Small Group Reading** book and create an opinion chart supported by three reasons Then, have students exchange their charts with a partner. Have each student use carets (^) to insert linking words and phrases into his or her partner's chart.

= one student = two students = three or more students

Link Opinions and Reasons

SUGGESTED PACING

DAY 1	Teach the Skill
DAY 2–4	Daily Practice Options
DAY 5	Review and Assess

Write An Opinion Day 3  Option 1

PROGRAM RESOURCES

Linking Words and Phrases: eVisual 4.30

Introduce

Provide pairs of students with the following opinion: *When it comes to agriculture, innovation is a good thing.* Explain that partners will work together to write a paragraph that states this opinion and provides reasons to support it.

Copy and display the following steps for students to follow:

1. Begin your paragraph with the opinion. It will be your topic sentence.
2. Support the opinion with two or three reasons.
3. Use linking words or phrases to link your reasons to the opinion.

Display **eVisual 4.30** for student reference.

Practice

Have partners co-write their paragraph. Remind them to use linking words or phrases to link reasons to the opinion.

When partners have finished writing, have them exchange papers with another pair of students and underline the linking words and phrases.

Write An Opinion Day 3  Option 2

Introduce

Have partners choose an innovation they know about that has helped people or the planet. Provide examples, such as growing plants in the shade of rainforest trees, wind farms that produce power, medicines such as vaccines, and helmets and kneepads for sports.

Practice

Have partners co-write a short paragraph stating their opinion and supporting it with reasons. If needed, remind them to use linking words and phrases to link supporting details to their opinion.

When partners have finished writing, have them exchange papers with another pair of students and underline the linking words and phrases.

Write a Report Day 4

PROGRAM RESOURCES

Linking Words and Phrases: eVisual 4.30

Introduce

Have each student select an opinion piece from his or her Weekly Writing folder. Tell students that they will revise their pieces to include words and phrases that link their supporting sentences to their statements of opinion. Display **eVisual 4.30** for reference.

Practice

Have students revise their opinion pieces and underline their linking words and phrases.

If time allows, have students take out another opinion piece from their Weekly Writing folder and use different linking words and phrases to revise it.

Review and Assess Day 5 

PROGRAM RESOURCES

Writing, Revising, and Editing Unit Test: Assessment Masters A4.31–A4.34

Review the Skill

Remind students of the opinion charts they created on Day 2. Have small groups choose a general topic (such as school lunches, recess time, or acquiring a class pet) that they can narrow down and on which they can agree on an opinion.

Have groups collaborate to create an opinion chart that begins with a clear statement of an opinion. After completing their opinion chart, have each group use carets (^) to insert words and phrases that could be used to link reasons to their stated opinion.

☑ Administer the **Writing, Revising and Editing Unit Test.**

Listen and Comprehend

Persuasive Text, Note, and Story

OBJECTIVES

Thematic Connection: Innovation

☑ **Classify Words to Understand Word Relationships**

☑ **Determine Author's Purpose to Comprehend Literature**

PROGRAM RESOURCES

TECHNOLOGY ONLY

Author's Purpose Chart: eVisual 4.26

Read Aloud: eVisual 4.27

MATERIALS

timer • picture dictionaries

Power Writing

Have students write as much as they can as well as they can in one minute about farmers.

*For **Writing Routine 1**, see page BP47.*

COMMON CORE STANDARDS

Reading	
Read and Comprehend Literature	CC.3.Rlit.10
Read and Comprehend Informational Texts	CC.3.Rinf.10
Read with Fluency to Support Comprehension	CC.3.Rfou.4
Writing	
Write Over Shorter Time for Specific Tasks	CC.3.W.10
Speaking and Listening	
Discuss Topics, Building on Others' Ideas and Expressing Ideas Clearly	CC.3.SL.1
Language and Vocabulary	
Understand Word Relationships	CC.3.L.5
Acquire and Use General Academic Words	CC.3.L.6

WARM-UP

Have small groups review the readings from Week 3, including "A Better Way" and the **Small Group Reading** books. Have each group write three questions about each selection. Have the class answer all the questions.

Academic Talk

1 Discuss the Big Question

Remind students that they have learned how to state their opinions and give reasons to support them. Have students recall how they can build on other people's ideas and state their ideas clearly to strengthen their arguments.

Use "A Better Way" to demonstrate how to make an argument in answer to the Big Question: What is the best way to get things done?: *The best way to get things done is to listen to new ideas. I think more **farmers** should study the research about the benefits of sustainable **agriculture**. If they study the research, they will learn that using approaches like the 5x5 System can help save trees and keep soil and water healthy.*

Have a volunteers who agree with you build on your argument by giving their own reasons for why they agree. Use a **Think, Pair, Share** to have students discuss arguments based on the readings for Week 3 in answer to the Big Question.

- Have each partner think independently about an argument based on a reading and the Big Question.
- Have partners share their arguments and help each other add support for their opinions.
- Have volunteers share arguments with the class.

*For **Think, Pair, Share,** see page BP47.*

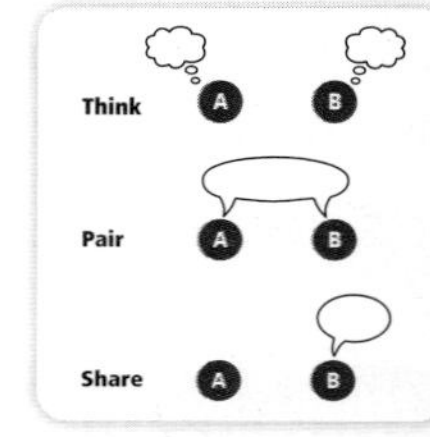

Think, Pair, Share

Vocabulary Strategy

2 Classify Words ☑ Anthology page 260

Project **Student eEdition** page 260 and read aloud the first two sentences. Display these words: *pan, fry, boil, chef* and ask: *What topic do all these words tell about?* (cooking) *What other words belong with this topic?* (Answers will vary.)

Read aloud the introduction to the word web. Have students look at the topic and the other words in the web. Model using the strategy: *I see that the topic is* farm *and all the words around it are related to that topic: a farm involves people* (farmer)*, places* (field)*, products* (crop)*, steps in a process* (plow, harvest)*, and important concepts* (agriculture).

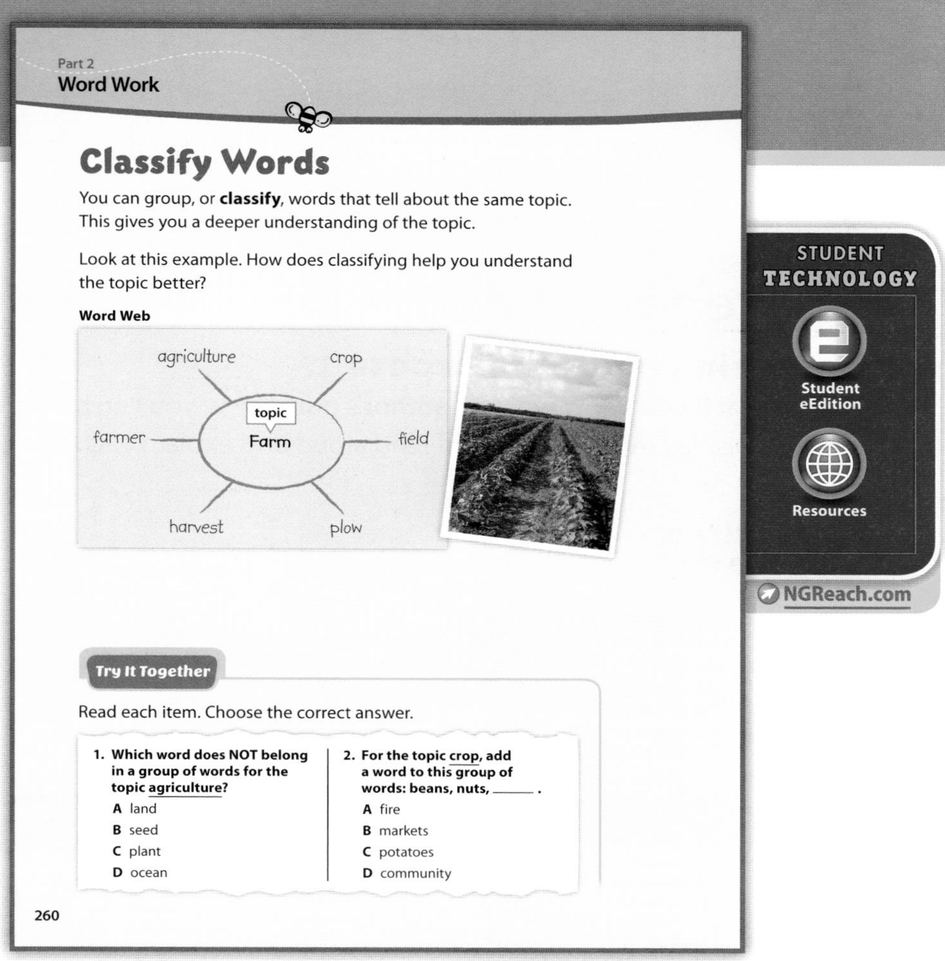

Part 2
Word Work

Classify Words

You can group, or **classify**, words that tell about the same topic. This gives you a deeper understanding of the topic.

Look at this example. How does classifying help you understand the topic better?

Word Web

Try It Together

Read each item. Choose the correct answer.

1. **Which word does NOT belong in a group of words for the topic agriculture?**
   A land
   B seed
   C plant
   D ocean

2. **For the topic crop, add a word to this group of words: beans, nuts, ______ .**
   A fire
   B markets
   C potatoes
   D community

260

STUDENT TECHNOLOGY
Student eEdition
Resources
NGReach.com

Anthology page 260

3 Try It Together **Anthology** page 260

Read the directions aloud and have partners work together to answer the questions. (question 1: D; question 2: C)

See **Differentiate**

Check & Reteach

OBJECTIVE: Classify Words to Understand Word Relationships ☑

As students answer the questions, determine whether they are able to correctly classify words for a particular topic.

If students have difficulty classifying words, draw a word web for the first question. Then model the thinking: *The topic is* **agriculture**, *the science of farming.* **Farmers** *need land, so* land *belongs in the web because it relates to the topic of farming.* **Farmers** *also need seeds to grow plants. So* seeds *and* plants *relate to the topic. Farming happens on land, not in the ocean, so the word* ocean *does not relate to the topic.*

Weekly Writing

Gather students' writing throughout the week:

- ✓ Daily Writing Skills Practice (T259o–T259p)
- ✓ Power Writing (T259q, T260c, T265a, T267c, T267e)
- ✓ Writing (T260b, T264–265, T267, T267d, T267g)
- ✓ Writing Project (T268-T271)

Differentiate

EL English Learners

ISSUE Students lack sufficient vocabulary to answer the questions.

STRATEGY Encourage students to consult picture dictionaries to understand the meanings of the answer choices.

BL Below Level

ISSUE Students have difficulty understanding the concept of classifying words.

STRATEGY Provide question frames to guide students' thinking about each of the choices.

For question 1: Is ______ used in **agriculture**?

For question 2: Is ______ a **crop**?

Fluency

Model Phrasing As you read the **Read Aloud**, model how to read text that has many facts and details. Explain: *When you read with appropriate phrasing, you group words together to support the meaning of the text.*

Comprehension

4 Determine Author's Purpose ☑

Explain that if you know what an author's purpose is, you can better understand the text. Display **eVisual 4.26** and read aloud and explain each row.

Purpose Chart

The author wants the reader to...	The author's purpose is...
learn something	to inform, describe, or explain
enjoy a story	to entertain
believe or do something	to persuade
know how he or she feels	to express deep feelings

NGReach.com **Purpose Chart: eVisual 4.26**

INTERACTIVE WHITEBOARD TIP: Add notes to clarify.

Display **eVisual 4.27** and read aloud the first text.

Read Aloud

The Most Amazing Insect
by Cheryl Stafford

If you knew more about ants, you would think they are truly amazing! Each can lift 20 times its own body weight. The queen of an ant colony can lay millions of eggs.

Hi, Carly!

The article you showed me about how ants work together was so inspiring! Oh! How I wish people could be more like ants!

Marco

My Mother's Aunts
by Rebecca Toale

When I was a little girl, my mother took me to visit her aunts. I asked how we could find such tiny ants in such a big house. Mom looked confused and then laughed, "Silly girl, my aunts are people, not bugs!"

NGReach.com **Read Aloud: eVisual 4.27**

INTERACTIVE WHITEBOARD TIP: Underline words that are clues to each author's purpose.

Explain that an author might have more than one purpose for writing. Model: *The first author says that ants are truly amazing. This shows that the author wants me to know how she feels. The author gives facts to convince me. This shows that she is trying to persuade me to believe what she believes. So, this author has two purposes: to express deep feelings and to persuade.*

Best Practices

Encourage Respect Have students repeat what the person before them said before they express their own ideas. For example: *You said that the author's purpose in the third paragraph is to inform, but I think that the author's purpose is to entertain.*

Read aloud the note to Carly. Have partners work together to identify the author's purpose and words that indicate that purpose. Have partners read the third paragraph and identify the author's purpose(s) and discuss words or sentences that helped them identify the purpose(s).

See **Differentiate**

Check & Reteach

OBJECTIVE: Determine Author's Purpose to Comprehend Literature

As partners discuss the **Read Aloud**, check if they can identify each author's purpose. If students have difficulty, display **eVisual 4.26** and review the four purposes. Then model the process with "My Mother's Aunts."

Writing

5 Write for a Purpose

Tell students that they will write for a specific purpose. Model writing with the purpose to persuade.

Think Aloud	Write
My purpose for writing is to persuade people to use less paper and plastic. First, I will write the main idea that I want the readers to believe.	Our planet is drowning in a sea of trash! If we want Earth to be healthy, we should all use less paper and plastic!
Next, I will write facts that will convince the readers that I am right.	American families throw away approximately 7.6 billion tons of waste each year.

*For **Writing Routine 2**, see page BP48.*

Form four groups and assign each one a different purpose for writing. Allow time for each group to choose a topic to write about that is related to the unit topic: Let's Work Together. Then have students in each group take turns writing sentences for a paragraph about the topic, building on each other's ideas. Have students copy their teams' paragraphs and add them to their Weekly Writing folders.

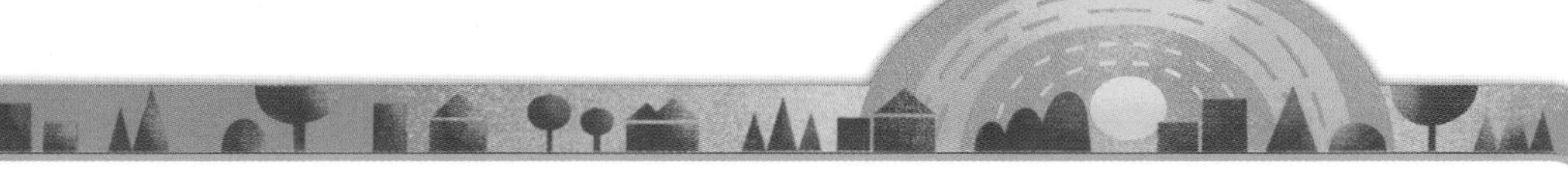

WRAP-UP Have partners discuss the types of texts they most enjoy reading: text that entertains, informs, persuades, or expresses deep feelings. Have students explain their preferences.

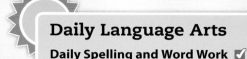

Daily Language Arts

Daily Spelling and Word Work
Spelling Pretest page T259k

Daily Grammar
Point out the verb *are* in the first sentence of the **Read Aloud**, and explain that it is a form of the verb *be*. Then use page T259m to teach forms of *be*.

Daily Writing Skills
Display the **Read Aloud** and point out that the purpose of "The Most Amazing Insect" is to convince readers that ants are the most amazing insect in the world. Then use page T259o to introduce persuasive writing.

Differentiate

SN Special Needs

ISSUE Students have difficulty focusing on an author's purpose instead of the facts in the text.

STRATEGY Ask forced-choice questions, such as: *Is the author in a serious mood or remembering a funny experience? Is the author trying to convince you that aunts are people or trying to make you laugh?*

AL Above Level

ISSUE Students can easily determine an author's purpose.

STRATEGY Have students explain why they think each author wanted to write for the specific purpose. Ask: *What is the author more interested in: facts or fun? What kind of reader does the author think will want to read the text?*

OBJECTIVES

Thematic Connection: Innovation

- ☑ Classify Words to Understand Word Relationships
- ☑ Determine Importance
- ☑ Determine Author's Purpose to Comprehend Literature

MATERIALS

timer

Power Writing

Have students write as much as they can as well as they can for one minute about the word *field*.

*For **Writing Routine 1**, see page BP47.*

COMMON CORE STANDARDS

Reading	
Recount Fables	CC.3.Rlit.2
Describe Characters and Explain Characters' Actions	CC.3.Rlit.3
Read and Comprehend Literature	CC.3.Rlit.10
Read with Fluency to Support Comprehension	CC.3.Rfou.4
Writing	
Write Over Shorter Time for Specific Audiences	CC.3.W.10
Speaking and Listening	
Discuss Texts, Building on Others' Ideas and Expressing Ideas Clearly	CC.3.SL.1
Language and Vocabulary	
Understand Word Relationships	CC.3.L.5
Acquire and Use General Academic Words	CC.3.L.6

WARM-UP

Set a timer and, within the time limit, have partners brainstorm ways people at school work together.

Vocabulary Strategy

1 Classify More Words ☑

Remind students that they can classify words to better understand a topic. Display these words from "The Ant and the Grasshopper": *dance, fiddle, hungry, play,* and *merry* and model how to classify them for the topic *fun*: *The words* dance *and* fiddle *make me think of music. I think music is fun. The word* play *is also related to fun. I don't think being hungry is fun, so it does not belong in this category. Does the word* merry *fit the category of* fun? (Yes. Being merry is having fun.)

Display two topics: *food* and *time* and two sets of words: *gather, long, future hungry; kernel, winter, corn, year.* Form small groups and assign one set of words to each. Have each group sort the words according to the assigned topic and add other appropriate words. Then have groups explain their thinking to the class.

Check & Reteach

OBJECTIVE: Classify Words to Understand Word Relationships ☑

Listen as groups work together. Check to see if groups classify the words appropriately. If students have difficulty, reteach the process with the category *working together* and these words: *cooperate, help, problem, warning.*

Academic Talk

2 Preview and Predict

Say: *Before you begin reading a story, study the title and the illustrations to preview and predict what the text will be about.* Project **Student eEdition** page 261. Have students silently read the title and study the illustration. Model thinking about illustrations: *This art is very different from the photographs that illustrate "A Better Way." The art looks like the art I have seen in cartoons. This tells me that this selection will not be a nonfiction text.*

Have partners study the illustrations throughout the selection to identify the author's purpose and make predictions about what the story will be like. Remind students to build on each other's ideas and express their own ideas clearly.

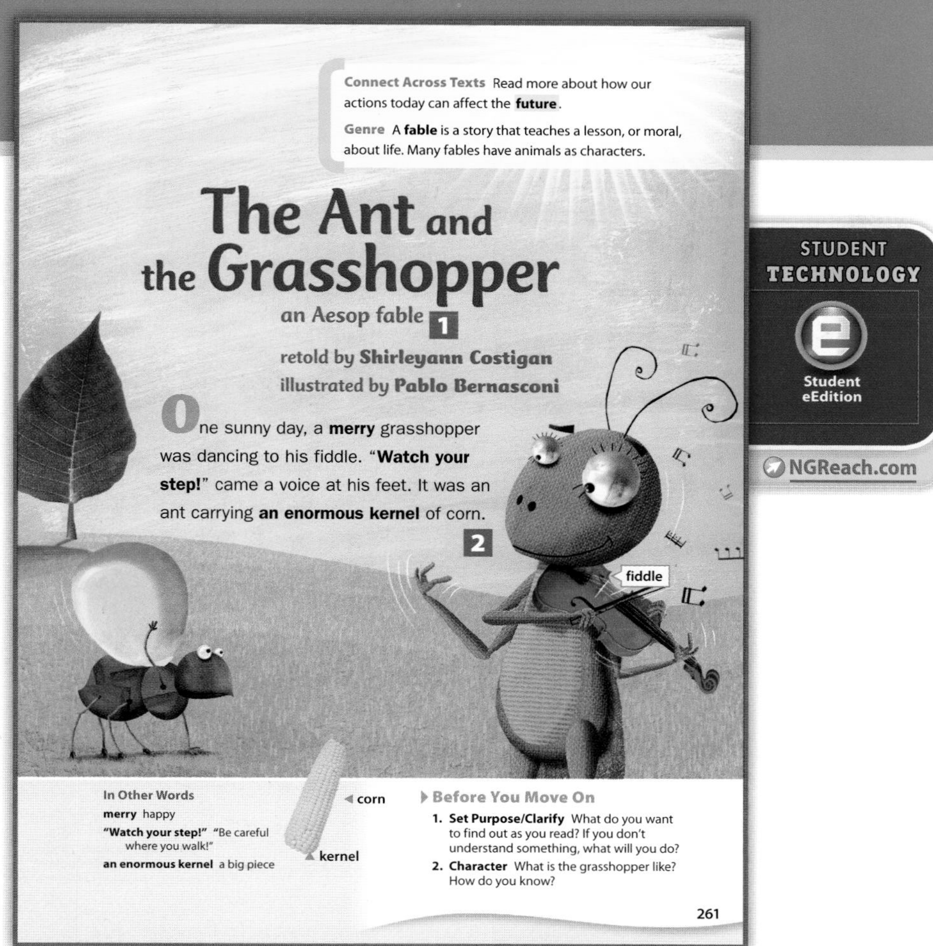

Connect Across Texts Read more about how our actions today can affect the **future**.

Genre A **fable** is a story that teaches a lesson, or moral, about life. Many fables have animals as characters.

The Ant and the Grasshopper

an Aesop fable 1

retold by **Shirleyann Costigan**
illustrated by **Pablo Bernasconi**

One sunny day, a **merry** grasshopper was dancing to his fiddle. "**Watch your step!**" came a voice at his feet. It was an ant carrying **an enormous kernel** of corn. 2

In Other Words
merry happy
"Watch your step!" "Be careful where you walk!"
an enormous kernel a big piece

Before You Move On

1. **Set Purpose/Clarify** What do you want to find out as you read? If you don't understand something, what will you do?
2. **Character** What is the grasshopper like? How do you know?

261

STUDENT TECHNOLOGY
Student eEdition
NGReach.com

Anthology page 261

Reading

3 Read a Fable

CONNECT ACROSS TEXTS Project **Student eEdition** page 261. Ask students to recall how the sustainable **agriculture methods** in "A Better Way" help save forests for the **future**. Then have a volunteer read aloud **Connect Across Texts**.

GENRE Read aloud the explanation of the genre. Clarify: *The animals in fables often talk and act like people. Fables are often very short and many times the author clearly states at the end of the story the lesson the story is designed to teach.*

SOCIAL STUDIES BACKGROUND Tell students that many people believe that popular fables were written long ago by a Greek man named Aesop. Elaborate: *One legend says that Aesop was a slave. According to the legend, Aesop's master set him free because he was so clever.*

Read and Build Comprehension

1 **Identify Author's Purpose** ☑ *The subtitle of this story is* an Aesop fable. *The subtitle is a clue to the author's purpose. What do you think is the author's purpose?* (The author wants to teach a lesson.)

2 **Determine Importance** ☑ *What is this part of the story about?* (This part is about the grasshopper meeting the ant.) *What should you remember after reading this part of the story?* (The grasshopper is dancing to his fiddle and the ant is carrying a large kernel of corn.) *What are the most important details?* (The grasshopper was having fun while the ant was working hard.)

Fluency

Practice Phrasing, Accuracy, Rate As students read, monitor their phrasing, accuracy, and rate.

Answers Before You Move On

1. **Set Purpose/Clarify** Possible answers: I want to know why the ant is carrying a big kernel of corn. If I don't understand something, I can look at the illustrations, reread the text, or read on to try to find the answer.
2. **Character** Possible answer: The grasshopper likes to have fun and is carefree. I know this because he is playing a fiddle and smiling.

"Come dance with me!" **urged** the grasshopper.

"No time, no time," the ant answered without stopping. "I must gather food for winter. Why aren't you gathering food? It's a bad idea to wait until it snows."

"**Nonsense**," said the grasshopper. "Winter is a long time away."

"**Suit yourself**," said the ant, and she **staggered forward** under her heavy load.

In Other Words
urged said
Nonsense That's silly
Suit yourself Do what you want
staggered forward walked with difficulty

Before You Move On
1. **Summarize** Reread this page. Tell the ideas in your own words.
2. **Character** How do you think the ant and the grasshopper would describe each other? Do you think they'll get along? Explain.

262 263

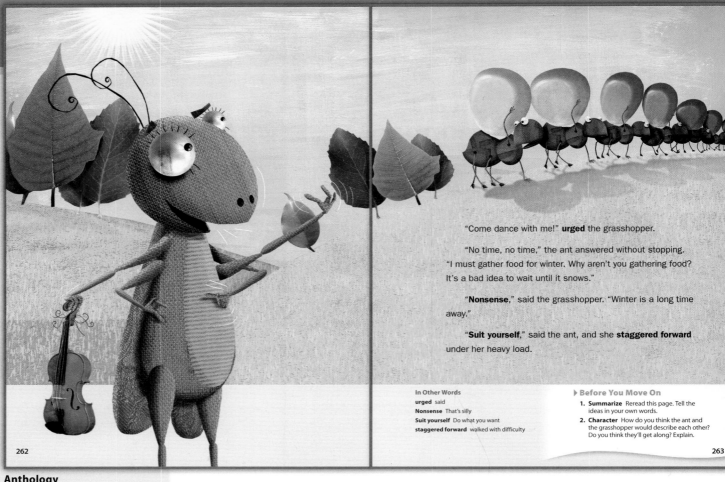

Anthology
pages 262–263

Da[illegible]

Dai[illegible]
Pra[illegible]

Daily [illegible]
Display **Anthology** page 261, point to the grasshopper and say: *The grasshopper has a fiddle.* Then use page T259m to teach forms of *have.*

Daily Writing Skills
Remind students that opinions in a persuasive essay need to be backed up with facts and examples. Then use page T259o to practice persuasive writing.

Read and Build Comprehension

1. **Determine Importance** *What is this part of the story about? ?* (This part of the story is about what the grasshopper learned from his experience.) *Why should you remember the end of the story?* (The grasshopper learned a lesson about listening when someone tells him to save for the future.) *Retell the end of the story.* (The ant shares food with the hungry grasshopper and the grasshopper remembers the ant's lesson.)
2. **Identify Author's Purpose** *Why do you think the author wrote this story?* (Possible answers: to entertain readers with a story; to teach readers what happens when they don't plan for the future; to persuade readers to save for the future)

Check & Reteach

OBJECTIVE: Determine Author's Purpose to Comprehend Literature

Check students' responses to both of the comprehension questions about author's purpose.
If students have difficulty, ask: *What does the author want readers to think or do?*

OBJECTIVE: Determine Importance

Check students' responses to both of the comprehension questions about determining importance.
If students have difficulty, use the How To on page 244 to model with details on page 263.

Answers Before You Move On

1. **Summarize** Possible response: This part is about the grasshopper urging the ant to come and dance. I should remember that the ant said he had no time and warned the grasshopper that he should be working. This part states the lesson that the grasshopper learned: to save for the future.
2. **Character** Answers will vary. Students should use supporting details from the story in their explanations.

Soon winter came, and snow covered the land. Not a kernel of food could be found. "Oh!" **lamented** the grasshopper. "I'm so hungry I **must surely** die!"

"Hey, Grasshopper!" cried a voice at his feet. It was the same ant. She was carrying another kernel of corn.

"I warned you this day would come," said the ant.

In Other Words
lamented cried
must surely am sure I will

264

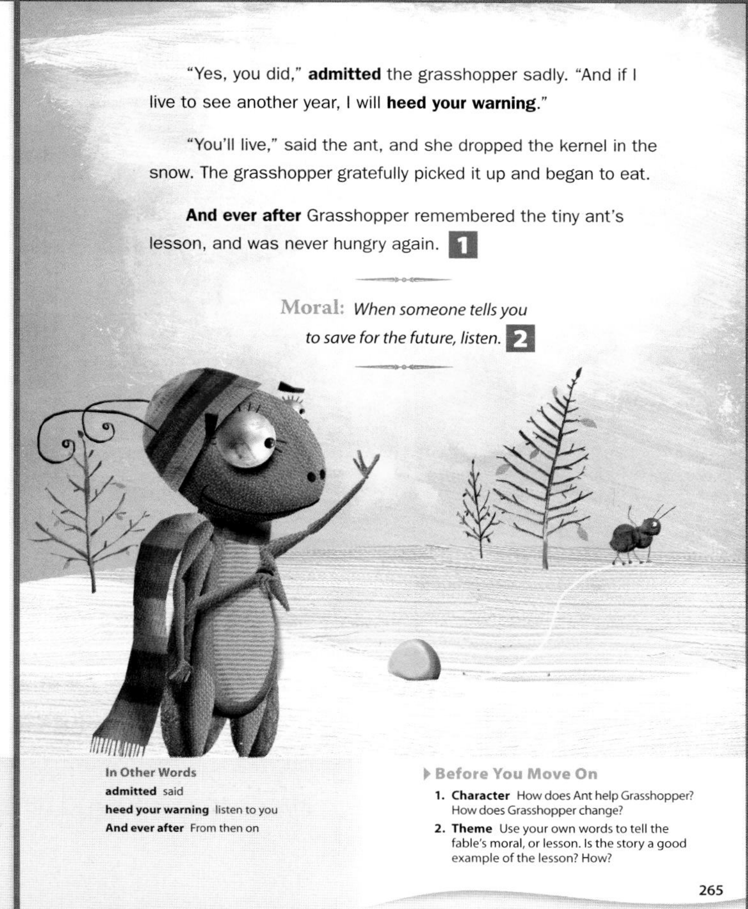

"Yes, you did," **admitted** the grasshopper sadly. "And if I live to see another year, I will **heed your warning**."

"You'll live," said the ant, and she dropped the kernel in the snow. The grasshopper gratefully picked it up and began to eat.

And ever after Grasshopper remembered the tiny ant's lesson, and was never hungry again. **1**

Moral: *When someone tells you to save for the future, listen.* **2**

In Other Words
admitted said
heed your warning listen to you
And ever after From then on

Before You Move On

1. **Character** How does Ant help Grasshopper? How does Grasshopper change?
2. **Theme** Use your own words to tell the fable's moral, or lesson. Is the story a good example of the lesson? How?

265

Anthology
pages 264–265

Writing

4 Explain the Moral

Tell students to imagine that they want to explain the moral or lesson of "The Ant and the Grasshopper" to a younger sibling or friend. Clarify: *First state the moral of the fable, or what the reader should learn. Then use details from the story to tell how the characters learned that lesson.*

Have individuals write their explanations. Then have students add their explanations to their Weekly Writing folders.

See **Differentiate**

WRAP-UP Help partners discuss how an author with a different purpose might write about ants and grasshoppers. Say: *For example, what if the author's purpose was to inform the reader about ants and grasshoppers?* Have partners share their ideas with the class.

Answers Before You Move On

1. **Charact**[illegible]

[illegible] wer: It is a good [illegible] future. The story is a good example because it shows what can happen if you don't plan and save for the future.

Differentiate

EL English Learners

ISSUE Students lack the language proficiency to express ideas.

STRATEGY Provide language frames: *The moral of the fable is ____. I know the grasshopper learned this because ____. The ant ____.*

BL Below Level

ISSUE Students have difficulty supporting with evidence from the text.

STRATEGY Remind students to mention the grasshopper's problem, how the ant helped, and what the grasshopper learned.

Day 3 Review and Compare
Persuasive Article and Fable

OBJECTIVES

Thematic Connection: Innovations

☑ Determine Author's Purpose to Comprehend Literature

☑ Grammar: Use Forms of *be* and *have*

PROGRAM RESOURCES

PRINT & TECHNOLOGY

Comparison Chart: Practice Master PM4.27

Grammar Practice: Practice Master PM4.28

TECHNOLOGY ONLY

Grammar Passage: eVisual 4.33

MATERIALS

timer • index cards

Power Writing

Have students write as much as they can as well as they can in one minute about the word *harvest*.

*For **Writing Routine 1,** see page BP47.*

COMMON CORE STANDARDS

Reading	
Read and Comprehend Literature	CC.3.Rlit.10
Read with Fluency to Support Comprehension	CC.3.Rfou.4
Writing	
Write Over Shorter Time for Specific Tasks	CC.3.W.10
Speaking and Listening	
Discuss Texts, Expressing Ideas Clearly	CC.3.SL.1
Draw on Preparation to Explore Ideas	CC.3.SL.1.a
Explain Ideas and Understanding	CC.3.SL.1.d
Language and Vocabulary	
Demonstrate Command of Grammar	CC.3.L.1
Form and Use Verbs	CC.3.L.1.d
Ensure Subject-Verb Agreement	CC.3.L.1.f
Use Knowledge of Language and Conventions	CC.3.L.3
Acquire and Use Academic and Domain Specific Words	CC.3.L.6

WARM-UP

Have partners review "A Better Way" and "The Ant and the Grasshopper" and discuss the different ways the authors taught lessons about the same topic.

Vocabulary Review

1 Review Science and Academic Vocabulary

Project **Student eEdition** page 266 and point out the Key Words. Also display *opinion, evidence*, and *summarize*. Chorally read all the words as a class. Pause after each word and have a volunteer give the definition.

Have each group write each word on a separate index card and place the cards face down in a pile. Have students in each group take turns drawing cards and saying the definitions of the words on the cards. Then have each student make a word web that classifies the word on the card with at least two other words.

farmer

Review and Integrate Ideas

2 Compare Purposes ☑ **Anthology** page 266

Display **Student eEdition** page 266. Read aloud the first paragraph and the bulleted list. Remind students that a comparison chart shows how two things are similar and different. Then read the second paragraph aloud.

Point out the headings in the chart and read the sample text in each. Then model how to fill in each column of the chart. Remind students that an author may have more than one purpose for writing a text. Have partners read "The Ant and the Grasshopper" aloud. Then assign **Practice Master PM4.27**.

Read aloud the questions below the chart on page 266 and have partners discuss their answers.

Check & Reteach

OBJECTIVE: Determine Author's Purpose to Comprehend Literature ☑

Check students' work on the chart. Can they determine the authors' purposes?

If students have difficulty, remind them that specific parts of the text provide clues to the authors' purposes. Model the thinking: *On page 251, the author states facts about sustainable **agriculture**. That shows that the author wants to teach the reader about the topic. So his purpose is to inform or explain.*

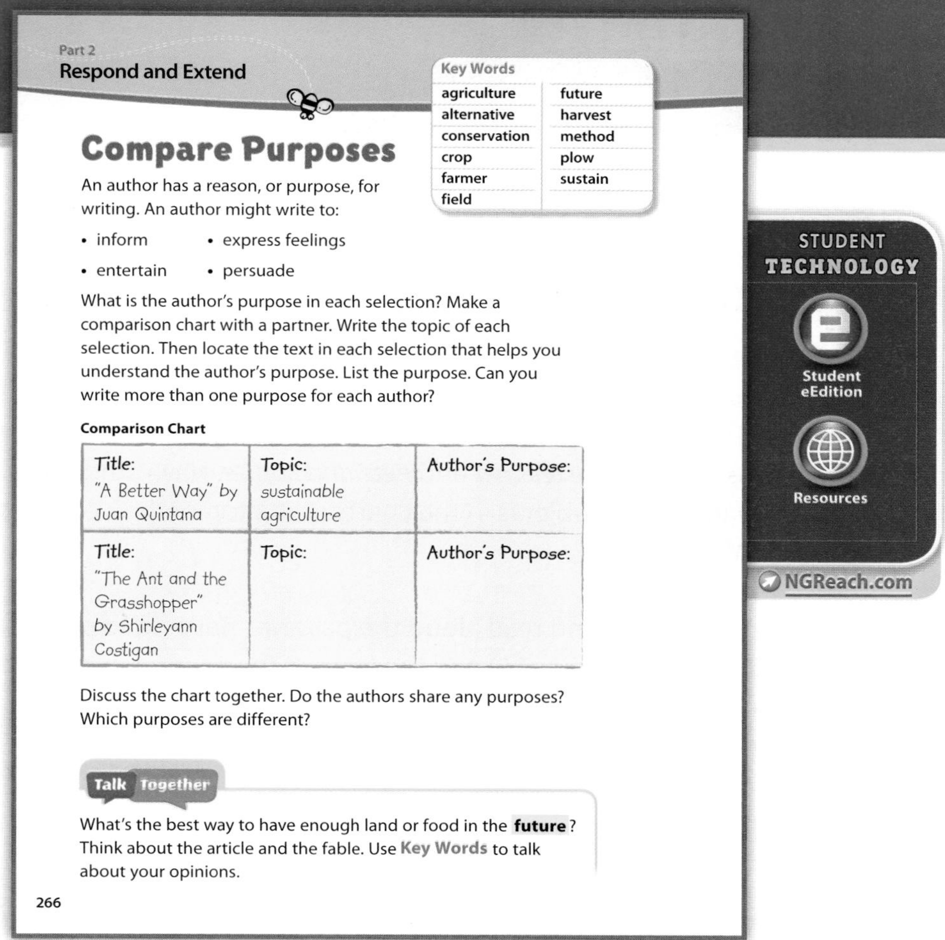

Part 2
Respond and Extend

Compare Purposes

Key Words	
agriculture	future
alternative	harvest
conservation	method
crop	plow
farmer	sustain
field	

An author has a reason, or purpose, for writing. An author might write to:

- inform
- express feelings
- entertain
- persuade

What is the author's purpose in each selection? Make a comparison chart with a partner. Write the topic of each selection. Then locate the text in each selection that helps you understand the author's purpose. List the purpose. Can you write more than one purpose for each author?

Comparison Chart

Title:	Topic:	Author's Purpose:
Title: "A Better Way" by Juan Quintana	Topic: sustainable agriculture	Author's Purpose:
Title: "The Ant and the Grasshopper" by Shirleyann Costigan	Topic:	Author's Purpose:

Discuss the chart together. Do the authors share any purposes? Which purposes are different?

Talk Together

What's the best way to have enough land or food in the **future**? Think about the article and the fable. Use **Key Words** to talk about your opinions.

266

STUDENT TECHNOLOGY

Student eEdition

Resources

NGReach.com

Anthology page 266

Academic Talk

3 Talk Together **Anthology** page 266

Review the methods for preparing for the future in "A Better Way" and "The Ant and the Grasshopper." Use a **Jigsaw** to have students discuss ways to prepare for the future . Remind students to use information from the selections to express their ideas and understanding of the topic clearly.

- Group students into two expert groups. Members of one group become experts about "A Better Way" and members of the other group become experts about "The Ant and the Grasshopper."
- Have each expert group study their selection and discuss how the text shows ways to prepare for the future.
- Regroup students so that each new group has at least one member from each expert group.
- Have the experts report on their ideas and understandings of the topic to help other students learn more about the topic.

Expert Group 1 A B C D — A's
Expert Group 2 A B C D — B's
Expert Group 3 A B C D — C's
Expert Group 4 A B C D — D's

Jigsaw

*For **Jigsaw**, see page BP46.*

Fluency

Practice Phrasing As partners reread the fable aloud, circulate and listen for correct phrasing.

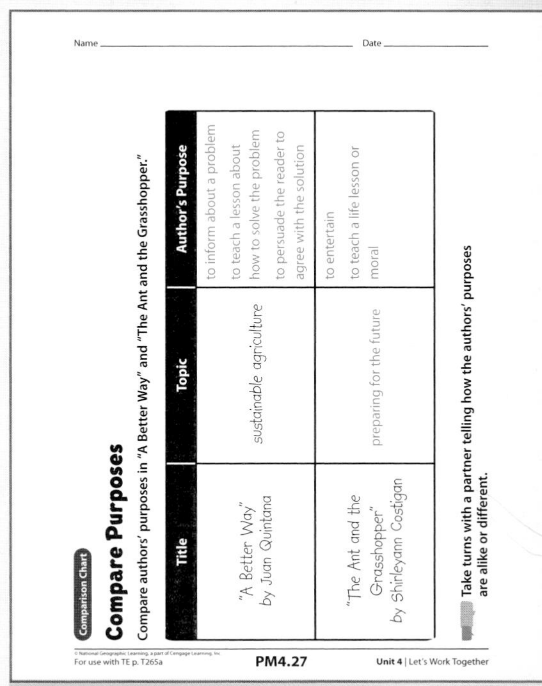

Name ____________ Date ____________

Comparison Chart

Compare Purposes

Compare authors' purposes in "A Better Way" and "The Ant and the Grasshopper."

Title	Topic	Author's Purpose
"A Better Way" by Juan Quintana	sustainable agriculture	to inform about a problem to teach a lesson about how to solve the problem to persuade the reader to agree with the solution
"The Ant and the Grasshopper" by Shirleyann Costigan	preparing for the future	to entertain to teach a life lesson or moral

Take turns with a partner telling how the authors' purposes are alike or different.

© National Geographic Learning, a part of Cengage Learning, Inc.
For use with TE p. T265a PM4.27 Unit 4 | Let's Work Together

NGReach.com **Practice Master PM4.27**

Differentiate

BL Below Level

ISSUE Students have difficulty identifying matching subjects for the verbs *be* and *have*.

STRATEGY Tell students to find the form of *be* or *have* first and then underline the verb and the words that follow it. Then have students find the subject by answering the following question:

Who or what ______?

AL Above Level

ISSUE Students readily understand forms of *be* and *have* and subject-verb agreement.

STRATEGY Encourage students to search through a variety of texts and compete to see who can find the most sentences that match each row of the chart, using both the pronoun from the first column and an appropriate verb from the second or third column.

Name ______________________ Date ____________

Grammar: Practice

What Is in the Garden?

Grammar Rules Subject-Verb Agreement: *be* and *have*

The verbs *be* and *have* are irregular. The subject and verb must agree. Use these correct forms:

I am	We are	I have	We have
You are	You are	You have	You have
He, she, it is	They are	He, she, it has	They have

Write the correct form of be or have to complete each sentence. Choose the correct form for the subject.

Jenna and Jake __have__ a large garden. Jake's favorite vegetable __is__ corn. He __has__ several rows of corn in the garden. The corn __is__ almost ready to harvest. Both Jenna and Jake __are__ excited to roast ears of corn. They also grow tomatoes. Tomatoes __are__ their mother's favorite vegetable. Jenna planted sunflowers, too. They __have__ delicious seeds and pretty blooms.

I __am__ planning to help them pick some corn. I __have__ a basket I will take with me.

Imagine a garden. Tell your partner about it, using forms of *be* and *have*.

For use with TE p. T266a PM4.28 Unit 4 | Let's Work Together

NGReach.com **Practice Master PM4.28**

Grammar Focus

4 Forms of *be, have* Anthology page 267

Project **Student eEdition** page 267. Have volunteers read aloud the introduction. Then teach each concept in the chart. Provide detailed explanations for subjects with nouns, such as *The teacher* and *Pete and Sun Ye*. Have students add notes about the additional subjects in the charts at the top of their copies of **Practice Master PM4.28.**

Display **eVisual 4.33** and read aloud the passage, pausing to point out the subject of the first sentence (I) and the form of the verb *be* that agrees (*am*) and explain: *The Grammar Rules chart shows that* am *is the form of* be *that agrees with the subject* I.

Grammar Passage

I am at the farmer's market today with my family. We are here to buy vegetables. My uncle has a stall here. My cousin is at the stall to help my uncle. They have a lot of fresh fruits to sell.

My mother has many recipes for what we buy at the market. Her dishes are the best. She has an excellent recipe for strawberry jam. It is delicious!

NGReach.com **Grammar Passage: eVisual 4.33**

INTERACTIVE WHITEBOARD TIP: Underline each subject. Circle each *be* or *have* verb.

Have partners identify the subject of each remaining sentence and the verb form that agrees with it.

5 Read Forms of *be/have* Anthology page 267

Read aloud the directions and the sentences based on "A Better Way."

See **Differentiate**

6 Write Forms of *be/have* Anthology page 267

Read aloud the directions and have students work independently. Provide support as necessary. Assign **Practice Master PM4.28**.

Check & Reteach

OBJECTIVE: Grammar: Use Forms of *be* and *have*

As students write their sentences, check for subject-verb agreement with forms of *be* and *have*.

If students have trouble, model using the Grammar Rules chart and the additional information students added to **Practice Master PM4.28**: *I want to write about Paola and Cid. Since I could use* they *to talk about two people, I look at the row for* they *to find a form of* be *or* have. *I find that* have *agrees with the subject* Paola and Cid. *So I write* Paola and Cid have good ideas about farming.

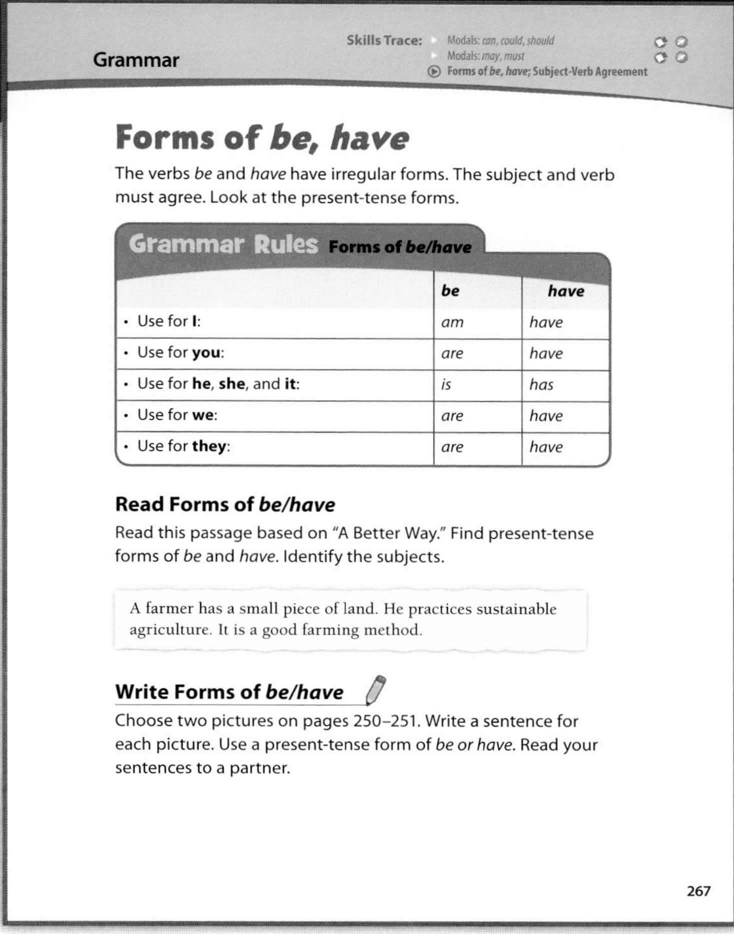

Grammar

Skills Trace: Modals: can, could, should
Modals: may, must
Forms of be, have; Subject-Verb Agreement

Forms of *be, have*

The verbs *be* and *have* have irregular forms. The subject and verb must agree. Look at the present-tense forms.

Grammar Rules **Forms of *be/have***

	be	*have*
• Use for **I**:	*am*	*have*
• Use for **you**:	*are*	*have*
• Use for **he**, **she**, and **it**:	*is*	*has*
• Use for **we**:	*are*	*have*
• Use for **they**:	*are*	*have*

Read Forms of *be/have*

Read this passage based on "A Better Way." Find present-tense forms of *be* and *have*. Identify the subjects.

A farmer has a small piece of land. He practices sustainable agriculture. It is a good farming method.

Write Forms of *be/have*

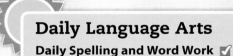

Choose two pictures on pages 250–251. Write a sentence for each picture. Use a present-tense form of *be or have*. Read your sentences to a partner.

267

Anthology page 267

Writing

7 Write to Reinforce Grammar

Have students write paragraphs about preparing for the future, using forms of *be* and *have* and subjects that agree with them. Remind students to use as many of the Key Words on page 266 as they can.

Model writing a paragraph: *I have a lot of good ideas about how to prepare for the* ***future****. My family is happy to start reducing the amount of stuff we throw away. We are also ready to recycle or reuse many containers. Our neighbors are eager to help. They have a compost pile where we can all recycle scraps from our garden* ***crops****.*

After students write their paragraphs, have them underline the subjects, circle the forms of *have* and *be*, and use the Grammar Rules chart to check for subject-verb agreement. Then have students add their paragraphs to their Weekly Writing folders.

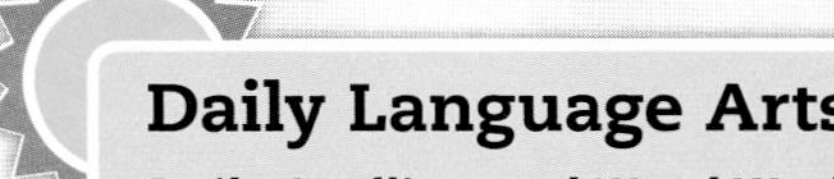

Daily Language Arts

Daily Spelling and Word Work
Practice Page T259l

Daily Grammar
Point out the sentence *It is delicious!* in the last sentence of the **Grammar Passage**. Then use page T259n to review forms of *be* and *have*.

Daily Writing Skills
Remind students that they should always use facts, examples, or experiences, to support their opinions. Then use page T259p to practice linking opinions and reasons.

WRAP-UP Have each student choose one lesson similar to the moral stated at the end of "The Ant and the Grasshopper" and tell a partner why everyone should learn the lesson.

OBJECTIVES

Thematic Connection: Innovation

- ☑ **Classify Words to Understand Word Relationships**
- ☑ **Distinguish Viewpoint**

PROGRAM RESOURCES

PRINT & TECHNOLOGY

Mark-Up Reading: Practice Masters PM4.29–PM4.30

TECHNOLOGY ONLY

Mark-Up Model 4.2 or Model 4.2 PDF

Vocabulary Strategy Practice: eVisual 4.34

MATERIALS

highlighters of three different colors

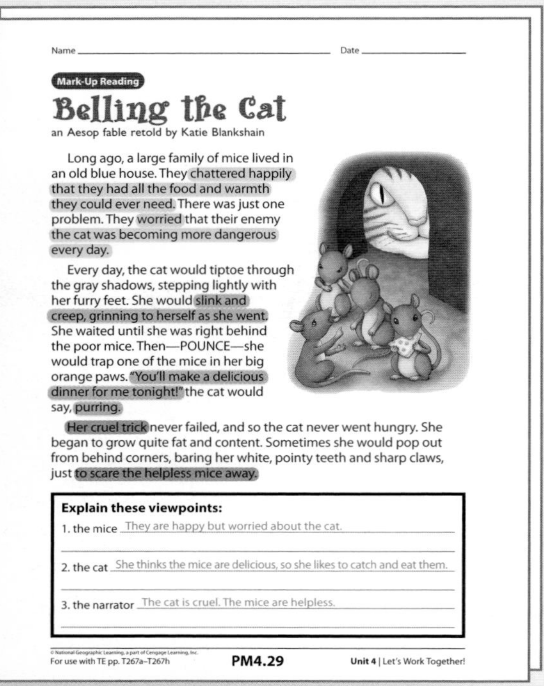

Name ____________ Date ____________

Mark-Up Reading

Belling the Cat

an Aesop fable retold by Katie Blankshain

Long ago, a large family of mice lived in an old blue house. They chattered happily that they had all the food and warmth they could ever need. There was just one problem. They worried that their enemy the cat was becoming more dangerous every day.

Every day, the cat would tiptoe through the gray shadows, stepping lightly with her furry feet. She would slink and creep, grinning to herself as she went. She waited until she was right behind the poor mice. Then—POUNCE—she would trap one of the mice in her big orange paws. "You'll make a delicious dinner for me tonight!" the cat would say, purring.

Her cruel trick never failed, and so the cat never went hungry. She began to grow quite fat and content. Sometimes she would pop out from behind corners, baring her white, pointy teeth and sharp claws, just to scare the helpless mice away.

Explain these viewpoints:

1. the mice They are happy but worried about the cat.
2. the cat She thinks the mice are delicious, so she likes to catch and eat them.
3. the narrator The cat is cruel. The mice are helpless.

© National Geographic Learning, a part of Cengage Learning, Inc.
For use with TE pp. T267a–T267h PM4.29 Unit 4 | Let's Work Together!

NGReach.com **Practice Masters PM4.29–PM4.30**

WARM-UP

Create two teams and give each a fable: 1. A huge wind uproots a strong, unbending tree, but a weak reed bends and springs back. 2. A fox that can't reach grapes calls them sour. The first team to come up with the moral of its fable wins.

Comprehension

1 Distinguish Viewpoints ☑

Remind students they have learned to identify characters' viewpoints. Explain that they will now distinguish viewpoints of characters and the narrator in a fable.

SCREEN 1

1 Display **Mark-Up Model 4.2**. Read aloud the definition of viewpoint and then the text. Have students follow along using **Practice Master PM4.29**. Model: *Characters' words and actions can reveal what the characters think and feel. The phrase "chattered happily," tells me that the mice feel happy.* Ask: *What is the mice's viewpoint about the cat?* (They worry the cat is getting more dangerous.)

Ask volunteers to highlight words and phrases that show clues to the mice's viewpoint and click the Viewpoint button to confirm. Have a volunteer explain the mice's viewpoint and erase the Explanation box. Have students mark up **Practice Master PM4.29** and write their explanations. Click the arrow to the next screen.

SCREEN 2

2 Read aloud the next part of the fable. Have volunteers highlight words and phrases that show clues to the cat's viewpoint and click the Viewpoint button. Ask: *Why does the cat hunt the mice?* (She enjoys it; she thinks they taste good.) *What actions reveal this viewpoint?* (The cat grins as she hunts and purrs when she traps a mouse.) *Which words reveal this viewpoint?* ("You'll make a delicious dinner for me tonight!")

3 Have a volunteer explain the cat's viewpoint and erase the Explanation box. Have students mark up **Practice Master PM4.29** and write explanations. Click the arrow.

SCREEN 3

4 Read aloud the next part of the fable. Explain that the narrator also has a viewpoint about the characters and events. Have volunteers highlight text that shows clues to the narrator's viewpoint and click the Viewpoint button. Have students mark up **Practice Master PM4.29** and write their explanations of the narrator's viewpoint.

Explain that characters' viewpoints can change in a story. Have students mark up **Practice Master PM4.30** by highlighting text clues that show the different viewpoints and then explaining these viewpoints. Have partners share and compare their mark-ups of **Practice Masters PM4.29–PM4.30**.

COMMON CORE STANDARDS

Reading	
Recount Fables	CC.3.Rlit.2
Distinguish Points of View	CC.3.Rlit.6
Read and Comprehend Literature	CC.3.Rlit.10
Read with Fluency to Support Comprehension	CC.3.Rfou.4
Writing	
Write Over Shorter Time for Specific Tasks	CC.3.W.10
Speaking and Listening	
Tell a Story	CC.3.SL.4
Language and Vocabulary	
Understand Word Relationships	CC.3.L.5
Acquire and Use General Academic Words	CC.3.L.6

SCREEN 1

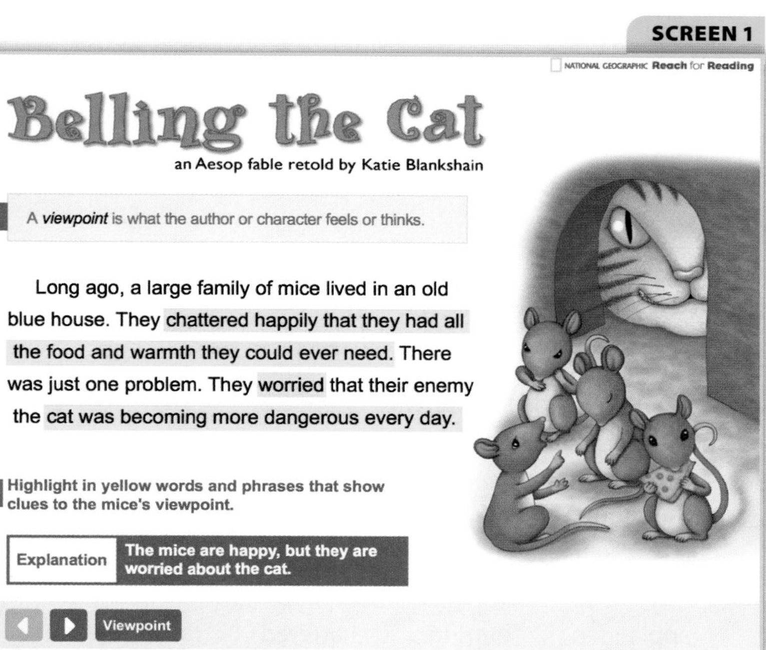

NGReach.com **Mark-Up Model 4.2**

SCREEN 2

NATIONAL GEOGRAPHIC Reach for Reading

Belling the Cat

(continued)

3 Every day, the cat would tiptoe through the gray shadows, stepping lightly with her furry feet. She would slink and creep, grinning to herself as she went. She waited until she was right behind the poor mice. Then—POUNCE—she would trap one of the mice in her big orange paws. "You'll make a delicious dinner for me tonight!" the cat would say, purring.

3 Highlight in green words and phrases that show clues to the cat's viewpoint.

4 Explanation | **She thinks the mice are delicious, so she likes to catch and eat them.**

Viewpoint

SCREEN 3

NATIONAL GEOGRAPHIC Reach for Reading

Belling the Cat

(continued)

5 Her cruel trick never failed, and so the cat never went hungry. She began to grow quite fat and content. Sometimes she would pop out from behind corners, baring her white, pointy teeth and sharp claws, just to scare the helpless mice away.

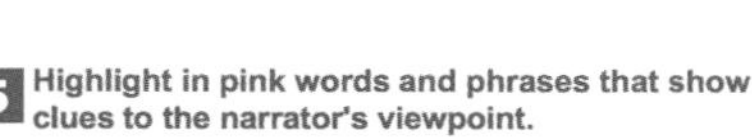

5 Highlight in pink words and phrases that show clues to the narrator's viewpoint.

Explanation | **The cat is cruel. The mice are helpless.**

Viewpoint

Fluency ✓

Model and Practice Phrasing Explain: *Fluent readers recognize groups of words that go together. They should be read together, without long pauses between words.* Model phrasing by reading the first two paragraphs from **Practice Master PM4.29**. Point out phrases such as *a large family of mice* and *slink and creep*. Have students mark up copies of the selection, putting brackets around phrases as they identify them, and then practice using the brackets to phrase as they read aloud.

Check & Reteach

OBJECTIVE: Distinguish Viewpoint ✓

Review students' marked-up **Practice Masters PM4.29–PM4.30** to check if they can distinguish the viewpoints of the characters and the narrator.

If students have difficulty, have them identify a character's viewpoint from these quotes:

- *"She would slink and creep, grinning to herself as she went."* (The cat enjoys hunting the mice.)
- *"She will never sneak up on us again!"* (The mice believe their plan will work.)

Daily Language Arts

Daily Spelling and Word Work
Practice page T259l

Daily Grammar
Write: *The cat has an easy life. The mice have tough lives.* Have students find the form of *have* in each sentence. Then use page T259n to practice correcting errors with forms of *be* and *have*.

Daily Writing Skills
Point out the opinion and reason in the first paragraph on **Practice Master 4.30**. ("We have lived in fear of the cat for too long. She must be stopped.") Ask: *How could I link these two sentences?* (with the word *so*) Then use page T259p to review how to link opinions and reasons.

Power Writing

Have students write as much as they can as well as they can in one minute about the word *plan*.

*For **Writing Routine 1**, see page BP47.*

Vocabulary Practice

2 Classify Words

Remind students that they have learned how to classify words in categories. Display **eVisual 4.34**.

Vocabulary Strategy Practice

Category: responses to a problem
Words: plan meeting idea outwit
Category: movement (ways of moving)
Words: slink creep tiptoe pounce
Category: location (words that tell where)
Words: in on behind under forward
Category: sounds
Words: say applauded purring chattered ring
Category: emotions
Words: happily fear grinning content joyfully

Word Bank

happily	tiptoe	ring	purring	in	meeting	slink	outwit
say	under	creep	behind	grinning	pounce	plan	forward
joyfully	idea	fear	on	content	chattered	applauded	

NGReach.com **Vocabulary Strategy: eVisual 4.34**

INTERACTIVE WHITEBOARD TIP: Have students write other related words for each topic.

Model classifying words: *First I look at the category, "responses to a problem." Then I look in the Word Bank for words that are related to this topic. Having an idea or a solution are two kinds of responses to a problem. Making a plan and having a meeting are other ways to respond to a problem. So I can classify all four words in the "responses to a problem" category.* Have partners write the categories and then list words from the Word Bank that fit each category. Have them discuss how the words are related to the topic.

Check & Reteach

OBJECTIVE: Classify Words to Understand Word Relationships

Review partners' lists to check if students can group words in categories.

If students have difficulty seeing how words are related, support the process by naming the categories first and then having students find the words on **Practice Masters PM4.29–PM4.30**. For example, ask:

- *Which words in the story tell how the cat and mice move around?* (creep, slink, tiptoe, pounce)
- *Which category names how these words are related?* (They are all words about movement.)

Academic Talk

3 Retell a Story

Explain: *When you retell a story, use words such as* first, next, *and* finally *to signal the beginning, middle, and end. Speak clearly and at a pace the audience can understand.* Model retelling "The Ant and the Grasshopper." Then form small groups. Explain: *In your groups you will take turns retelling the fable in **Practice Masters PM4.29–PM4.30**. Be sure to include the moral.* Give students time to do their retellings.

Writing

4 Write About Viewpoint

Introduce the activity: *Now write a paragraph describing the viewpoint of one of the characters or of the narrator in **Practice Masters PM4.29–PM4.30**. Include examples to support the viewpoint.* Model the process using the viewpoint of a character from "The Ant and the Grasshopper."

Think Aloud	Write
First, I'll describe the ant's viewpoint.	The ant believes that people need to save for the future.
Then I'll describe what the ant says.	When the grasshopper plays all summer, the ant tells him he is foolish.
Last, I'll describe what the ant does.	The ant works hard all summer to gather food. When winter comes, she is ready. Her actions support her viewpoint.

*For **Writing Routine 2**, see page BP48.*

Have students write their own descriptions. After students have read their descriptions aloud, have them add their paragraphs to their Weekly Writing folders.

See **Differentiate**

WRAP-UP Explain: *Imagine that the moral of "Belling the Cat" was "What seems impossible can really happen."* Form small groups. Give each group a few minutes to think of an alternative ending to the fable in which the mice find a way to put the bell on the cat. Then have each group describe its alternative ending to the class.

Differentiate

BL Below Level

ISSUE Students have difficulty describing a character's viewpoint.

STRATEGY Tell students to focus on what the character says and does. Ask:

- *The young mouse says, "...we should attach a small bell to the cat using this collar." What do those words tell us about what the young mouse thinks or feels?*
- *The cat's actions tell us things, too. Sometimes the cat pops out just to scare the mice. She isn't even hungry! What does that action tell us about what the cat thinks and feels?*

AL Above Level

ISSUE Students satisfy the minimum requirements for the assignment.

STRATEGY Challenge students to develop the viewpoint of a different character more fully by answering the following questions:

- *How does this character's viewpoint differ from that of the other characters in the fable?*
- *How does this character's viewpoint differ from that of the narrator?*
- *How is this character's viewpoint related to the moral of the fable?*

OBJECTIVES

Thematic Connection: Innovation

- ☑ Classify Words to Understand Word Relationships
- ☑ Distinguish Viewpoint

PROGRAM RESOURCES

PRINT & TECHNOLOGY

Mark-Up Reading: Practice Masters PM4.29–PM4.30

TECHNOLOGY ONLY

Vocabulary Strategy Practice: eVisual 4.35

Comparison Chart: eVisual 4.36

Power Writing

Have students write as much as they can as well as they can in one minute about the word *future*.

*For **Writing Routine 1**, see page BP47.*

COMMON CORE STANDARDS

Reading	
Distinguish Points of View	CC.3.Rlit.6
Compare and Contrast Stories	CC.3.Rlit.9
Read and Comprehend Literature	CC.3.Rlit.10
Writing	
Write Over Shorter Time for Specific Tasks	CC.3.W.10
Speaking and Listening	
Discuss Texts, Building on Others' Ideas	CC.3.SL.1
Discuss Texts, Expressing Ideas Clearly	CC.3.SL.1
Follow Rules for Discussions	CC.3.SL.1.b
Language and Vocabulary	
Understand Word Relationships	CC.3.L.5
Acquire and Use General Academic Words	CC.3.L.6

WARM-UP

Give teams five words, one them unrelated: *sea, hill, ocean, river, lake*. Teams race to be the first to identify category and unrelated word.

Vocabulary Practice

1 Classify Words ☑

Remind students that they have learned how to classify related words by topic. Display **eVisual 4.35**.

Vocabulary Strategy Practice

Category: ways to describe a problem
Words: trouble worry difficulty danger
Category: time
Words: tomorrow yesterday soon next
Category: people with ideas
Words: creator designer author inventor
Category: story elements
Words: plot character setting theme
Category: persuasion
Words: convince agree opinion evidence

Word Bank

tomorrow	designer	character	opinion	next	convince	plot
inventor	soon	trouble	theme	danger	agree	worry
yesterday	difficulty	author	setting	evidence	creator	

NGReach.com **Vocabulary Strategy: eVisual 4.35**

INTERACTIVE WHITEBOARD TIP: Have students write other related words for each category.

Students will classify words by category. Have partners identify and list related words for each category. Then have them brainstorm and add additional words for each category. Have partners share their results with other pairs.

Check & Reteach

OBJECTIVE: Classify Words to Understand Word Relationships ☑

If students have difficulty, pick a category and have them determine which words in the Word Bank belong in it.

Review partners' lists to check if students can sort words by category.

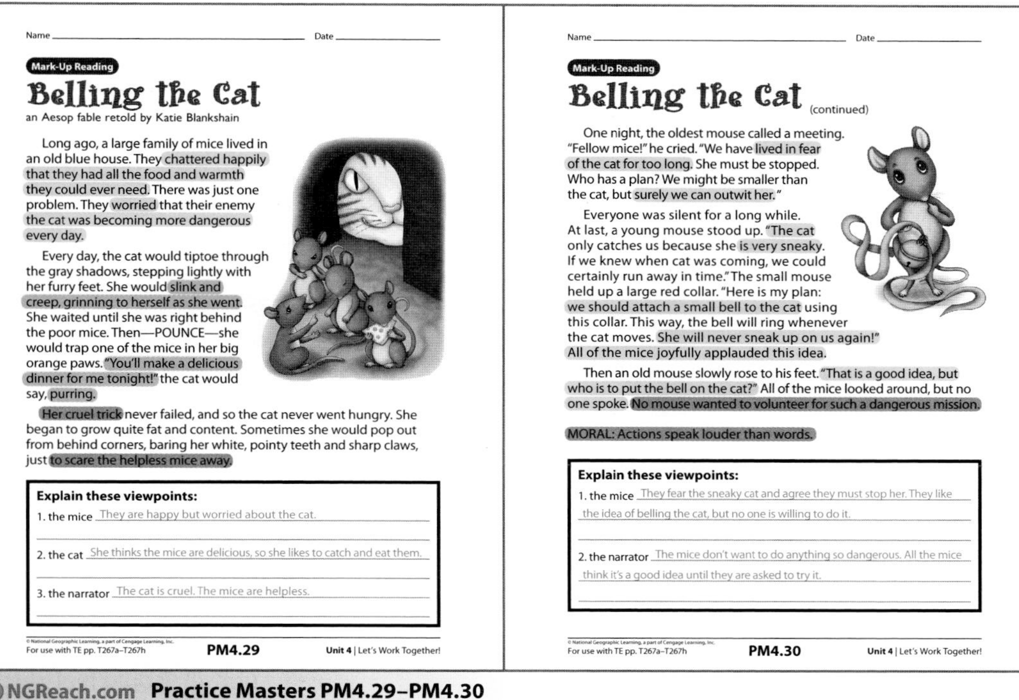

Name ______ Date ______

Mark-Up Reading

Belling the Cat

an Aesop fable retold by Katie Blankshain

Long ago, a large family of mice lived in an old blue house. They chattered happily that they had all the food and warmth they could ever need. There was just one problem. They worried that their enemy the cat was becoming more dangerous every day.

Every day, the cat would tiptoe through the gray shadows, stepping lightly with her furry feet. She would slink and creep, grinning to herself as she went. She waited until she was right behind the poor mice. Then—POUNCE—she would trap one of the mice in her big orange paws. "You'll make a delicious dinner for me tonight!" the cat would say, purring.

Her cruel trick never failed, and so the cat never went hungry. She began to grow quite fat and content. Sometimes she would pop out from behind corners, baring her white, pointy teeth and sharp claws, just to scare the helpless mice away.

Explain these viewpoints:

1. the mice They are happy but worried about the cat.
2. the cat She thinks the mice are delicious, so she likes to catch and eat them.
3. the narrator The cat is cruel. The mice are helpless.

For use with TE pp. T267a–T267h **PM4.29** **Unit 4** | Let's Work Together!

Name ______ Date ______

Mark-Up Reading

Belling the Cat (continued)

One night, the oldest mouse called a meeting. "Fellow mice!" he cried. "We have lived in fear of the cat for too long. She must be stopped. Who has a plan? We might be smaller than the cat, but surely we can outwit her."

Everyone was silent for a long while. At last, a young mouse stood up. "The cat only catches us because she is very sneaky. If we knew when cat was coming, we could certainly run away in time." The small mouse held up a large red collar. "Here is my plan: we should attach a small bell to the cat using this collar. This way, the bell will ring whenever the cat moves. She will never sneak up on us again!" All of the mice joyfully applauded this idea.

Then an old mouse slowly rose to his feet. "That is a good idea, but who is to put the bell on the cat?" All of the mice looked around, but no one spoke. No mouse wanted to volunteer for such a dangerous mission.

MORAL: Actions speak louder than words.

Explain these viewpoints:

1. the mice They fear the sneaky cat and agree they must stop her. They like the idea of belling the cat, but no one is willing to do it.
2. the narrator The mice don't want to do anything so dangerous. All the mice think it's a good idea until they are asked to try it.

For use with TE pp. T267a–T267h **PM4.30** **Unit 4** | Let's Work Together!

NGReach.com **Practice Masters PM4.29–PM4.30**

Review and Integrate Ideas

❷ Distinguish Viewpoint ☑

Ask students to look back at the viewpoints they recorded for the mice, the cat, and the narrator in "Belling the Cat" on **Practice Masters PM4.29–PM4.30**. Help them distinguish between viewpoints by evaluating their own responses to them. Ask questions to elicit students' sympathy, agreement, or other responses to a character's viewpoint. Have them add any background knowledge that helps them distinguish between viewpoints:

- *Do you agree with the mice that the cat is a problem? Why?* (Possible responses: Yes, the cat wants to eat the mice; yes, all cats are a problem for mice.)
- *How dangerous do you think the cat really is for the mice? Why? What does she think, do, or have that makes her dangerous or not dangerous?* (Possible responses: She is very dangerous because she wants to eat them for dinner. She has pointy teeth and sharp claws. She can pounce. She sneaks up.)

Check & Reteach

OBJECTIVE: Distinguish Viewpoint ☑

Evaluate students' ability to understand the actions, dialogue, and other story information that underlie each viewpoint. If students have difficulty distinguishing viewpoints, ask:

- *What is the cat's viewpoint?* (She likes catching and scaring the mice.)
- *Do you think the cat should feel that way? Why, or why not?* (Possible responses: Cats have to eat, too; it is normal for cats to eat mice. It's not nice to scare the mice for no reason.)

Review and Compare

Fables

Daily Language Arts

Daily Spelling and Word Work
Test page T259k

Daily Grammar
Write: The grasshopper has a lot of fun. Ask: *What subject word could replace the word* grasshopper *in this sentence?* (*he*) Then use page T259n to review and assess students' understanding of forms of *be* and *have*.

Daily Writing Skills
Say: *Cats are great because they hunt mice.* Ask: *What word did I use to link my opinion and reason?* (*because*) Then use page T259p to review and assess how to link opinions and reasons.

Differentiate

EL English Learners

ISSUE Students lack the language to express their opinions and reasons.

STRATEGY Provide sentence frames:

- I agree with the moral because ______.
- I disagree with the moral because ______.
- Another reason is that ______.

AL Above Level

ISSUE Students think no further than the boundaries of the assignment.

STRATEGY Have students brainstorm two or more new morals, or new ways of stating the moral, of each fable. Some possible examples include:

"Belling the Cat"

- Don't suggest an idea unless you're willing to carry it out yourself.
- A plan that doesn't work is no plan all.

"The Ant and the Grasshopper"

- Don't put off for tomorrow what you should do today.
- Balance work and play.

3 Compare Viewpoints

Explain to students that they will compare the characters' and narrators' viewpoints in "The Ant and the Grasshopper" and "Belling the Cat" on **Practice Masters PM4.29–PM4.30** with their own viewpoints. Display **eVisual 4.36**.

Comparison Chart

Character	Character's Viewpoint	My Viewpoint
the grasshopper	thinks he doesn't need to plan ahead	Possible response: should plan ahead but have fun, too
the ant	thinks it's important to plan ahead	Possible response: should plan ahead but have fun, too
the narrator of "The Ant and the Grasshopper"	thinks you should listen to good advice	Possible response: Listen to advice but think for yourself.
the mice	scared of the cat	Possible response: should feel scared
the cat	likes to catch, eat, and scare mice	Possible response: shouldn't scare mice for no reason
the narrator of "Belling the Cat"	the cat is cruel	Possible response: It's cruel when she scares mice for no reason.

NGReach.com **Comparison Chart: eVisual 4.36**

INTERACTIVE WHITEBOARD TIP: Have students add their own viewpoints.

Have students copy the chart and use it to compare the characters' and narrators' viewpoints with their own viewpoints. Model comparing the grasshopper's viewpoint with a personal viewpoint: *The grasshopper thinks it is silly to plan ahead for winter. I think you should plan ahead so that you don't freeze or go hungry, but also make time for fun.*

Writing

4 Write About the Moral

Introduce the activity: *Now you will write a paragraph in which you agree or disagree with the moral in "The Ant and the Grasshopper" or "Belling the Cat" in* ***Practice Masters PM4.29–PM4.30****. Be sure to give reasons for your opinions.* Allow time for students to review the two fables, determine their opinions, and write their paragraphs. Have volunteers share their paragraphs. Have students add their paragraphs to their Weekly Writing folders.

See **Differentiate**

Academic Talk

5 Relate Readings to the Big Question

Have students recall the unit's Big Question: What's the best way to get things done? *Think about "A Better Way," "The Ant and the Grasshopper,"* ***Practice Masters PM4 .29–PM4.30****, and a* ***Small Group Reading*** *book you have read. Why is it important to think about the rewards and difficulties of taking any kind of action?*

Model a response to the question for "Belling the Cat" in **Practice Masters PM4.29–PM4.30**: *The young mouse's plan to put a bell on the cat sounds really great at first. But the older mouse points out the problem—none of the mice want to be the one to put the bell on the cat.*

Use a **Three-Step Interview** to have students continue discussion about how the readings relate to the Big Question. Remind students to follow the rules for discussion.

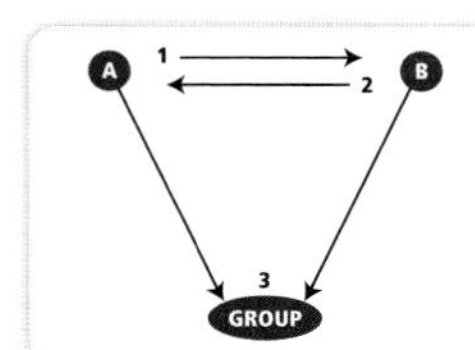

Three-Step Interview

- Have students form pairs.
- Student A interviews Student B about a topic related to the readings. Possible questions:
  - *How does careful planning help get things done right?*
  - *Why might the first solution to a problem not be the best solution?*
  - *How might some solutions be too hard to do?*
  - *How might some solutions cause more harm than good?*
- Partners reverse roles.
- Student A shares information from Student B with the class; then Student B shares information from Student A.

WRAP-UP Form small groups. Explain that each group will write a fable about a greedy animal that takes over its environment. For example, students may write about a hawk that eats all the mice in a field or gophers that dig so many holes the plants won't grow. Elaborate: *The moral of your fable should be "Greed today can become loss tomorrow."* Have groups read or act out their fables for the class.

Best Practices

Encourage Elaboration As students talk, use general prompts:

- *What do you mean by that?*
- *Can you give some details to explain what you mean?*
- *Can you make a connection to what someone else said?*

Week 4 Writing Project

OBJECTIVES

Thematic Connection: Innovation

☑ **Write a Persuasive Essay: Ideas**

PROGRAM RESOURCES

PRINT & TECHNOLOGY

Writing Rubric: Assessment Master A4.39

TECHNOLOGY ONLY

Writing Trait: Ideas: eVisual 4.31

SUGGESTED PACING

DAY 1	Study a Model
DAY 2	Prewrite/Gather Information
DAY 3	Get Organized/Draft
DAY 4	Revise/Edit and Proofread
DAY 5	Publish and Present

Study a Model

Read the Persuasive Essay **Anthology** page 268

Read aloud the prompt and the model on **Student eEdition** page 268. Then have volunteers read aloud the notes next to the student sample. Have them identify the features of the model persuasive essay (writer's opinion, evidence that supports the opinion and develops the writer's ideas, and an ending that restates the opinion).

Teach the Trait: Ideas

Reinforce for students that a persuasive essay contains a writer's opinion and evidence to support the writer's opinion.

Display and read aloud **eVisual 4.31**. Point out the important ideas in the model persuasive essay. (Opinion: You should make a neighborhood garden; Evidence: It's a chance for neighbors to get to know each other; It's something to do; It's something everyone can enjoy.) Finally, tell students that a persuasive essay has an ending that restates the writer's opinion and makes the essay feel complete.

Writing Trait: Ideas

Persuasive writing that has well-developed ideas
- clearly presents the writer's opinion about a topic
- includes evidence that supports the writer's opinion

NGReach.com **Writing Trait: Ideas: eVisual 4.31**

INTERACTIVE WHITEBOARD TIP: Underline Key Words: *opinion, evidence.*

Prewrite

Choose a Topic **Anthology** page 269

Have students reread the prompt. Help them unpack the prompt with a RAFT. Ask questions such as *What is the writing form?*

Role: Yourself
Audience: Other students
Form: Persuasive essay

Have students read step 1 on **Anthology** page 269. Then have partners use the language frames to talk about their ideas. If possible, have students brainstorm different things that could be done better at school or in their neighborhood. Then have students complete a RAFT.

Gather Information **Anthology** page 269

Have a volunteer read step 2. Then have students review their opinions and brainstorm evidence that supports their opinions. Encourage students to gather details or examples that help support their opinions. Remind them that the evidence should guide them to develop ideas that are worthwhile and interesting.

COMMON CORE STANDARDS

Writing	
Write Opinions on Topics	CC.3.W.1
Introduce the Topic, State an Opinion, and Create a Structure	CC.3.W.1.a
Provide Reasons	CC.3.W.1.b
Link Opinions and Reasons	CC.3.W.1.c
Plan, Revise, and Edit Writing	CC.3.W.5
Write Over Extended Time Frames	CC.3.W.10
Language and Vocabulary	
Demonstrate Command of Grammar	CC.3.L.1
Form and Use Verbs	CC.3.L.1.d
Use Knowledge of Conventions	CC.3.L.1.3

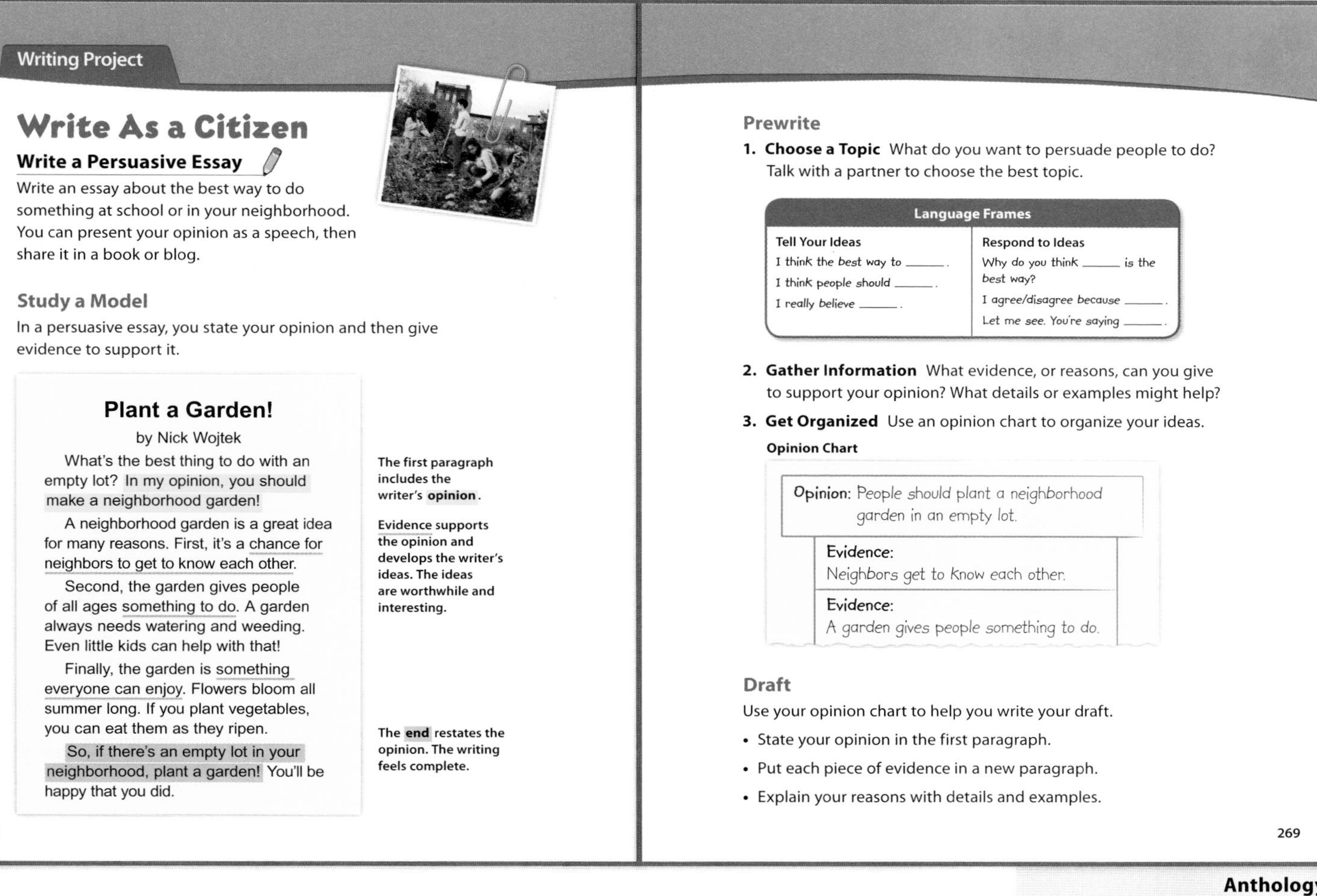

Writing Project

Write As a Citizen

Write a Persuasive Essay

Write an essay about the best way to do something at school or in your neighborhood. You can present your opinion as a speech, then share it in a book or blog.

Study a Model

In a persuasive essay, you state your opinion and then give evidence to support it.

Plant a Garden!

by Nick Wojtek

What's the best thing to do with an empty lot? In my opinion, you should make a neighborhood garden!

A neighborhood garden is a great idea for many reasons. First, it's a chance for neighbors to get to know each other.

Second, the garden gives people of all ages something to do. A garden always needs watering and weeding. Even little kids can help with that!

Finally, the garden is something everyone can enjoy. Flowers bloom all summer long. If you plant vegetables, you can eat them as they ripen.

So, if there's an empty lot in your neighborhood, plant a garden! You'll be happy that you did.

The first paragraph includes the writer's **opinion**.

Evidence supports the opinion and develops the writer's ideas. The ideas are worthwhile and interesting.

The **end** restates the opinion. The writing feels complete.

268

Prewrite

1. **Choose a Topic** What do you want to persuade people to do? Talk with a partner to choose the best topic.

Language Frames

Tell Your Ideas	Respond to Ideas
I think the best way to _____.	Why do you think _____ is the best way?
I think people should _____.	I agree/disagree because _____.
I really believe _____.	Let me see. You're saying _____.

2. **Gather Information** What evidence, or reasons, can you give to support your opinion? What details or examples might help?
3. **Get Organized** Use an opinion chart to organize your ideas.

Opinion Chart

Opinion: People should plant a neighborhood garden in an empty lot.

Evidence: Neighbors get to know each other.

Evidence: A garden gives people something to do.

Draft

Use your opinion chart to help you write your draft.

- State your opinion in the first paragraph.
- Put each piece of evidence in a new paragraph.
- Explain your reasons with details and examples.

269

Anthology
pages 268–269

Get Organized **Anthology** page 269

Have a volunteer read step 3. Draw students' attention to the graphic organizer. Explain: *Use a chart to organize your opinions and the evidence that supports them. First, write your opinion in the top box. Then, list your evidence in the boxes below.*

Have students use opinion charts to organize their ideas. Point out that for each item of evidence they provide, they should be able to give an example or more details.

Draft

Write Ideas **Anthology** page 269

Invite a volunteer to read the instructions aloud. Ask students to review the main features of a persuasive essay (writer's opinion, evidence that supports the opinion and develops the writer's ideas, and an end that restates the opinion).

Then have students use the opinion charts to write their persuasive essays. Review with students how to organize their ideas: *Start by stating your opinion in the first paragraph. Then begin a new paragraph and give the evidence that supports your opinion. Your last paragraph should restate the opinion and make your writing feel complete.*

See **Differentiate**

Differentiate

BL Below Level

ISSUE Students struggle to restate their opinions in a different way for their conclusions.

STRATEGY Help students use a dictionary or a thesaurus to look up important words in their opinions and find other words that could be used in restating the opinions.

Daily Language Arts

Daily Spelling and Word Work
Practice Pages T259k–T259l

Daily Grammar
On **Anthology** page 268, point to the linking verb *is* in the second paragraph of the student model. Then use pages T259m–T259n to have students practice working with the verbs *be* and *have*.

Daily Writing Skills
Have students note the transition word *so* in the last paragraph of the student model on **Anthology** page 268. Use pages T259o–T259p to have students practice linking opinions to reasons.

Differentiate

AL Above Level

ISSUE Students have written too many reasons in support of their opinions.

STRATEGY Have students organize their evidence by *more important, important,* and *less important.* Tell students to include only evidence that is *more important* and *important* in their persuasive essays.

Revise

Read, Retell, Respond **Anthology** page 270

Read aloud step 1 on page 270. Have partners take turns reading their persuasive essays to each other and then retelling what they have heard. Then have them hold peer conferences to aid in revising. Model how to offer feedback: *You stated your opinion in the first paragraph. However, you did not include enough evidence to support your opinion. Can you give a detail or example to help support your opinion?*

Make Changes **Anthology** page 270

Read aloud the instructions and the sample changes in step 2 on page 270. Check understanding:

- In the first revision, why did the writer edit the second sentence? (The second sentence states the writer's opinion.)
- In the second revision, why did the writer change the second sentence? (The second sentence adds an important detail and example.)

Have students use revising marks to edit their own drafts. Remind students to make sure that they state their opinions in the first paragraph. They should also include evidence that supports their opinions.

See **Differentiate**

Edit and Proofread

Check the Persuasive Essay **Anthology** page 271

Have students work with a partner to edit and proofread their essays. Have them check the forms of the verbs *be* and *have*. In addition, make sure that they are using proper subject-verb agreement in their sentences. Then have students edit and proofread their drafts, focusing on the Week 4 spelling words.

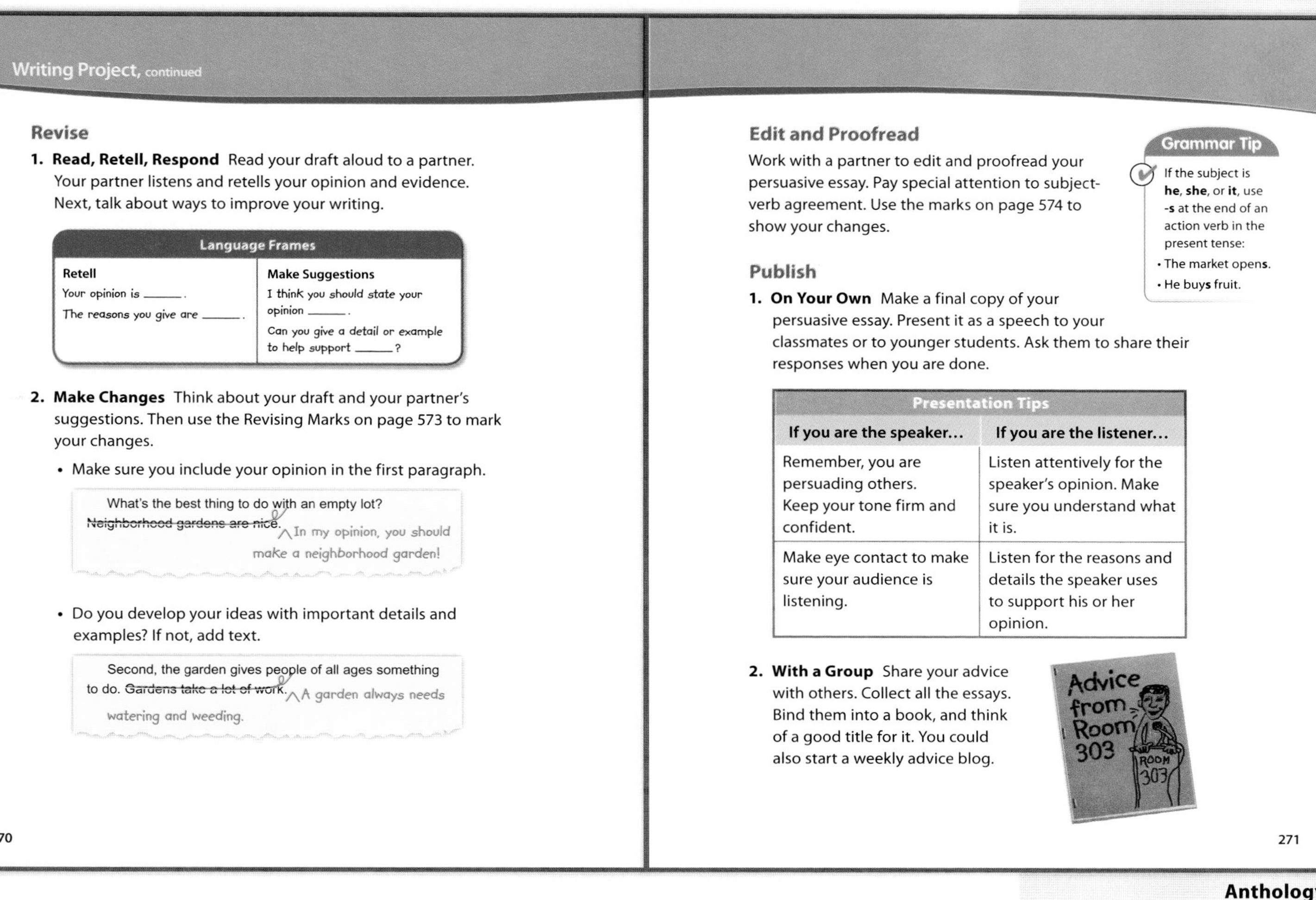

Writing Project, continued

Revise

1. **Read, Retell, Respond** Read your draft aloud to a partner. Your partner listens and retells your opinion and evidence. Next, talk about ways to improve your writing.

Language Frames	
Retell Your opinion is ____. The reasons you give are ____.	**Make Suggestions** I think you should state your opinion ____. Can you give a detail or example to help support ____?

2. **Make Changes** Think about your draft and your partner's suggestions. Then use the Revising Marks on page 573 to mark your changes.
   - Make sure you include your opinion in the first paragraph.

     What's the best thing to do with an empty lot? ~~Neighborhood gardens are nice.~~ In my opinion, you should make a neighborhood garden!

   - Do you develop your ideas with important details and examples? If not, add text.

     Second, the garden gives people of all ages something to do. ~~Gardens take a lot of work.~~ A garden always needs watering and weeding.

270

Edit and Proofread

Work with a partner to edit and proofread your persuasive essay. Pay special attention to subject-verb agreement. Use the marks on page 574 to show your changes.

Grammar Tip

If the subject is **he**, **she**, or **it**, use **-s** at the end of an action verb in the present tense:
- The market open**s**.
- He buy**s** fruit.

Publish

1. **On Your Own** Make a final copy of your persuasive essay. Present it as a speech to your classmates or to younger students. Ask them to share their responses when you are done.

Presentation Tips	
If you are the speaker...	**If you are the listener...**
Remember, you are persuading others. Keep your tone firm and confident.	Listen attentively for the speaker's opinion. Make sure you understand what it is.
Make eye contact to make sure your audience is listening.	Listen for the reasons and details the speaker uses to support his or her opinion.

2. **With a Group** Share your advice with others. Collect all the essays. Bind them into a book, and think of a good title for it. You could also start a weekly advice blog.

271

Anthology
pages 270–271

Publish

On Your Own **Anthology** page 271

Have students write final drafts of their persuasive essays and present them as speeches to their fellow classmates or younger students.

Review Presentation Tips before students read their persuasive essays aloud. Explain that the purpose of a persuasive essay is to convince readers to think, feel, or act in a certain way. Therefore, students should use a tone that is firm and confident. Model reading a persuasive essay using Presentation Tips. Ask students to listen and think about what they hear.

With a Group **Anthology** page 271

Combine all of the persuasive essays into a book. Work with students to think of a good title for their book. Then post the book online. Use the **Writing Rubric** to assess each student's essay.

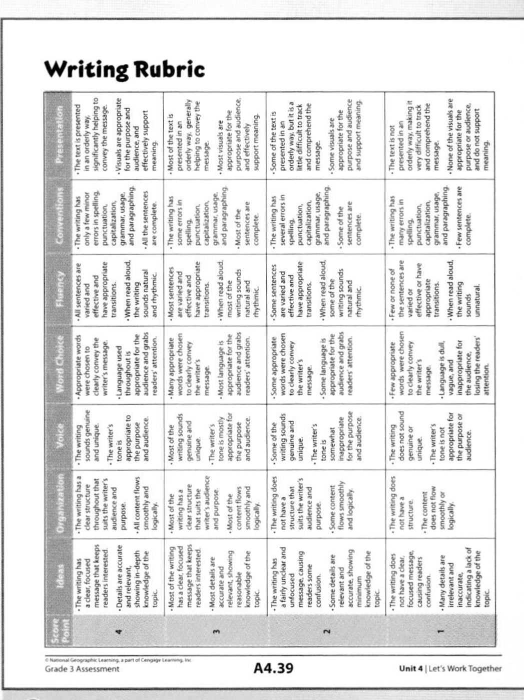

Writing Rubric

Grade 3 Assessment A4.39 Unit 4 | Let's Work Together

NGReach.com **Assessment Master A4.39**

Week 4 Assessment & Reteaching

☑ = TESTED

Assess

OBJECTIVES | **ASSESSMENTS**

Reading

- ☑ Determine Theme
- ☑ Describe and Compare Story Elements
- ☑ Compare Themes
- ☑ Identify Opinions and Evidence
- ☑ Determine Author's Purpose
- ☑ Distinguish Viewpoint
- ☑ Determine Importance

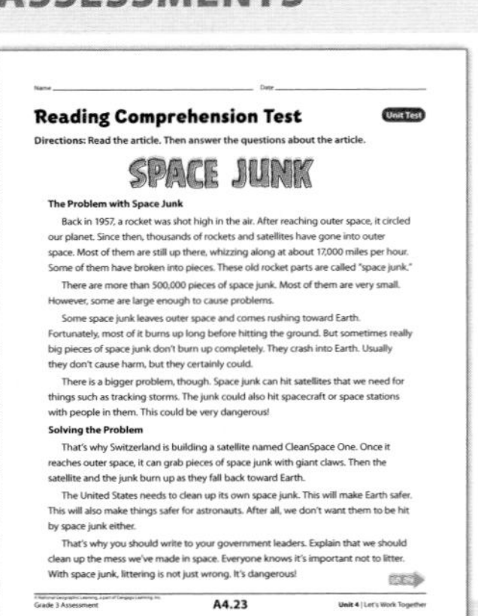
Reading Comprehension Test — SPACE JUNK — A4.23

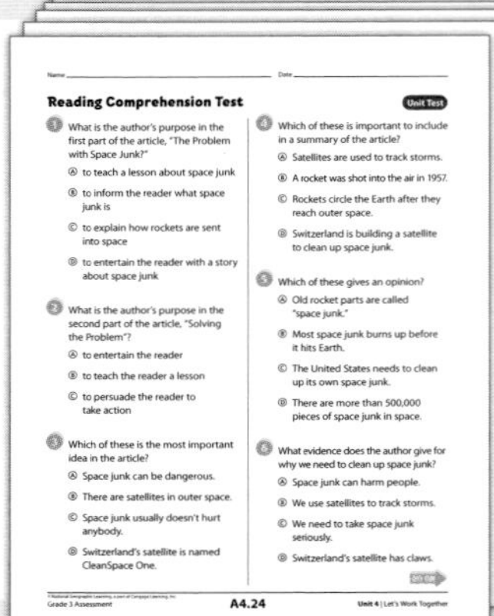
Reading Comprehension Test — A4.24

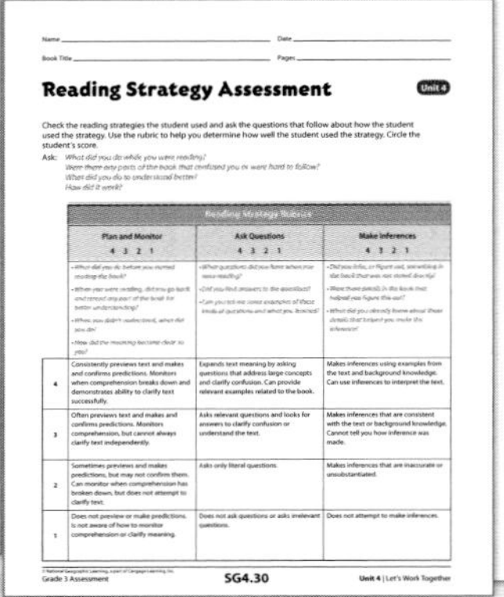
Reading Strategy Assessment — SG4.30

Reading Comprehension Unit Test
A4.23–A4.28

Reading Strategy Assessment
SG4.30–SG4.31

Fluency

- ☑ Phrasing
- ☑ Accuracy and Rate

Oral Reading Assessment — A4.1

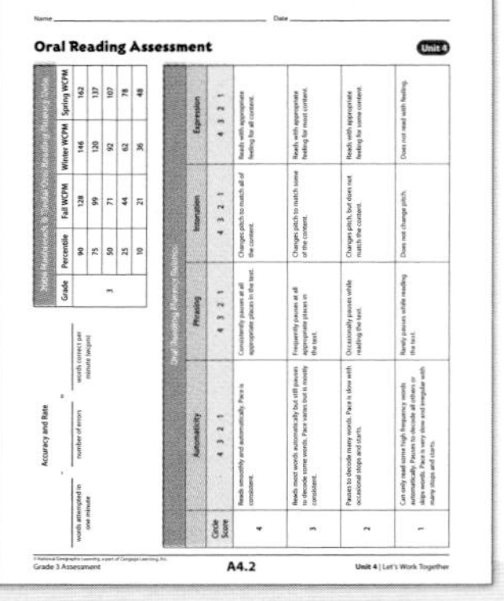
Oral Reading Assessment — A4.2

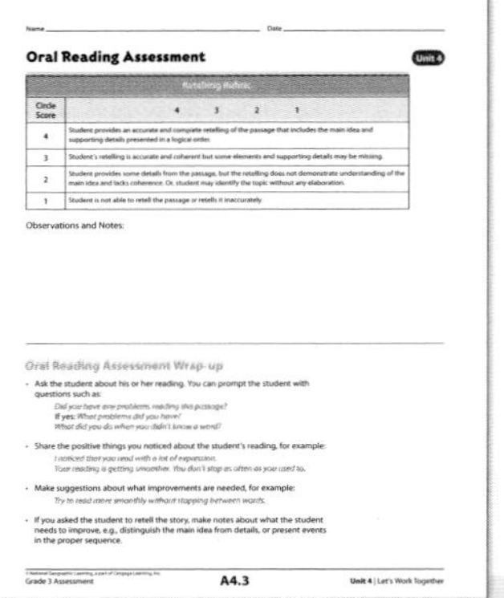
Oral Reading Assessment — A4.3

Oral Reading Assessment
A4.1–A4.3

Use these passages throughout Unit 4. Work with Below Level students this week.

Vocabulary and Spelling

- ☑ Use Domain-Specific Words
- ☑ Use Academic Words
- ☑ Use Prefixes to Determine Word Meanings
- ☑ Classify Words
- ☑ Spell Verbs Ending in *–ing*
- ☑ Use Commonly Misspelled Words Correctly

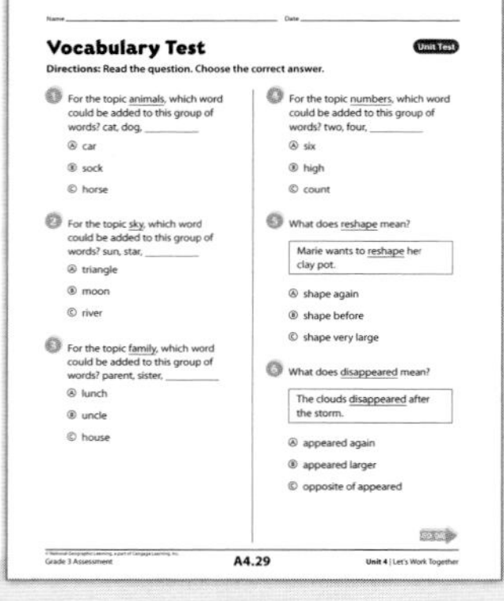
Vocabulary Test — A4.29

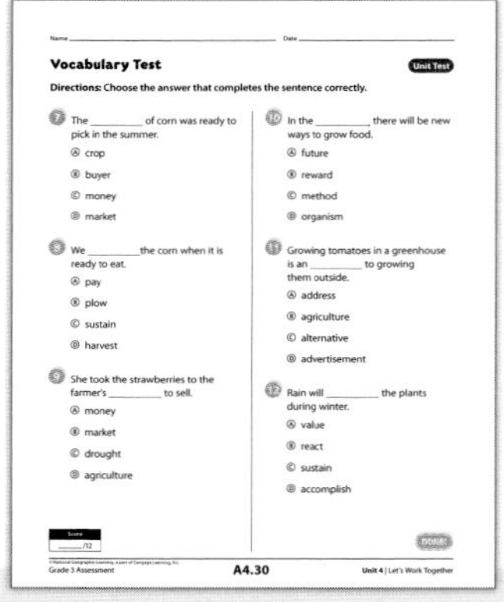
Vocabulary Test — A4.30

Spelling Words

Vocabulary Unit Test
A4.29–A4.30

Spelling Pretest/ Spelling Test
T259k

Grammar and Writing

- ☑ Use Present-Tense Verbs
- ☑ Use Action Verbs
- ☑ Use Subject-Verb Agreement: *he, she, it*
- ☑ Use Present-Tense Action Verbs
- ☑ Use Helping Verbs
- ☑ Use Forms of *Do*
- ☑ Link Opinions and Reasons

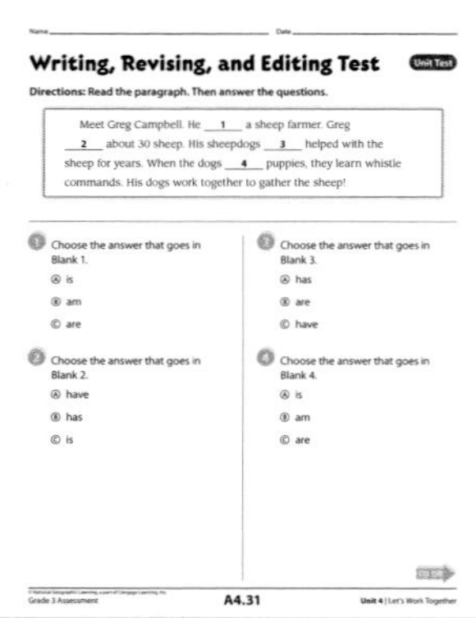
Writing, Revising, and Editing Test — A4.31

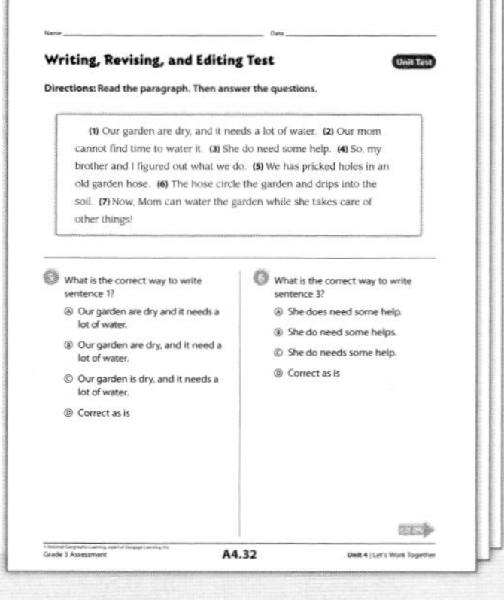
Writing, Revising, and Editing Test — A4.32

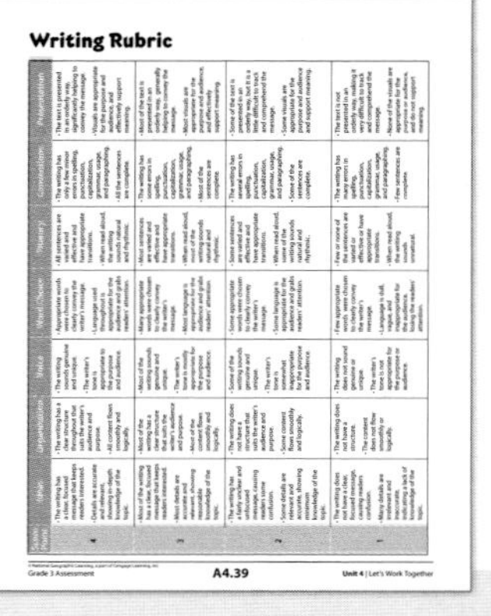
Writing Rubric — A4.39

Writing, Revising, and Editing Unit Test
A4.31–A4.34

Writing Rubric
A4.39

NGReach.com

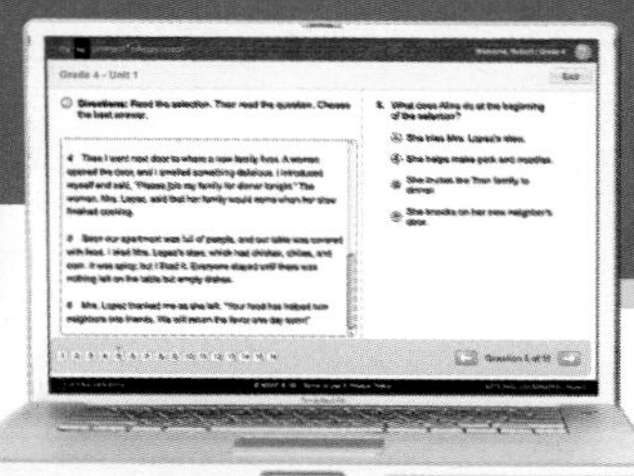

ExamView®

Reteach and Practice

REPORTS

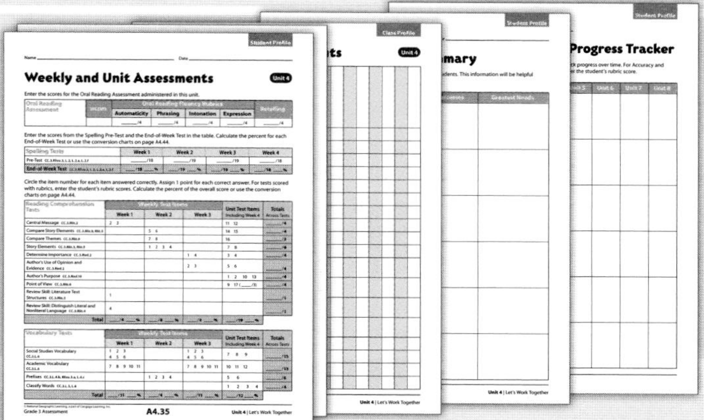

PRINT & ONLINE

Report Forms

Student Profile: Weekly and Unit Assessments	A4.35–A4.36
Class Profile: Weekly and Unit Assessments	A4.37
Student Profile: Strengths and Needs Summary	A4.38
Student Profile: Oral Reading Assessment Progress Tracker	A1.3

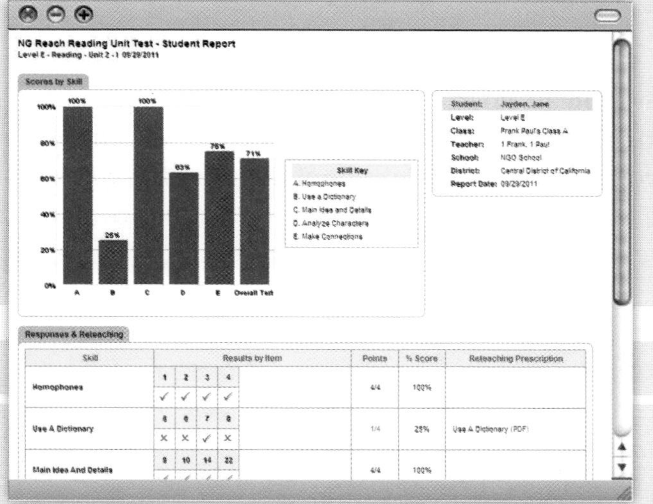

eAssessment™

ONLINE ONLY

Automated Reports

Student Profile: Weekly and Unit Tests

Class Profile: Weekly and Unit Tests

Standards Summary Report

RESOURCES AND ROUTINES

Reading

RETEACH

Determine Author's Purpose: Reteaching Master RT4.9

Distinguish Viewpoint: Reteaching Master RT4.10

Determine Importance: Reteaching Master RT4.11

ADDITIONAL PRACTICE

Comprehension Coach NGReach.com

Fluency

RETEACH

Fluency Routines, page BP33

ADDITIONAL PRACTICE

Comprehension Coach NGReach.com

Vocabulary and Spelling

RETEACH

Vocabulary Routine 6, page BP40

Spelling and Word Work Routine, page BP52

ADDITIONAL PRACTICE

Vocabulary Games NGReach.com

Daily Spelling Practice, pages T259k–T259l

Grammar and Writing

RETEACH

Verbs: Anthology Handbook, pages 592–593

Writing: Reteaching Writing Routine, page BP51

Writing Trait: Ideas: Reteaching Master RT4.12

ADDITIONAL PRACTICE

More Grammar Practice PM4.32

Daily Writing Skills Practice, pages T259o–T259p

See Weeks 1–3 for additional reteaching resources.

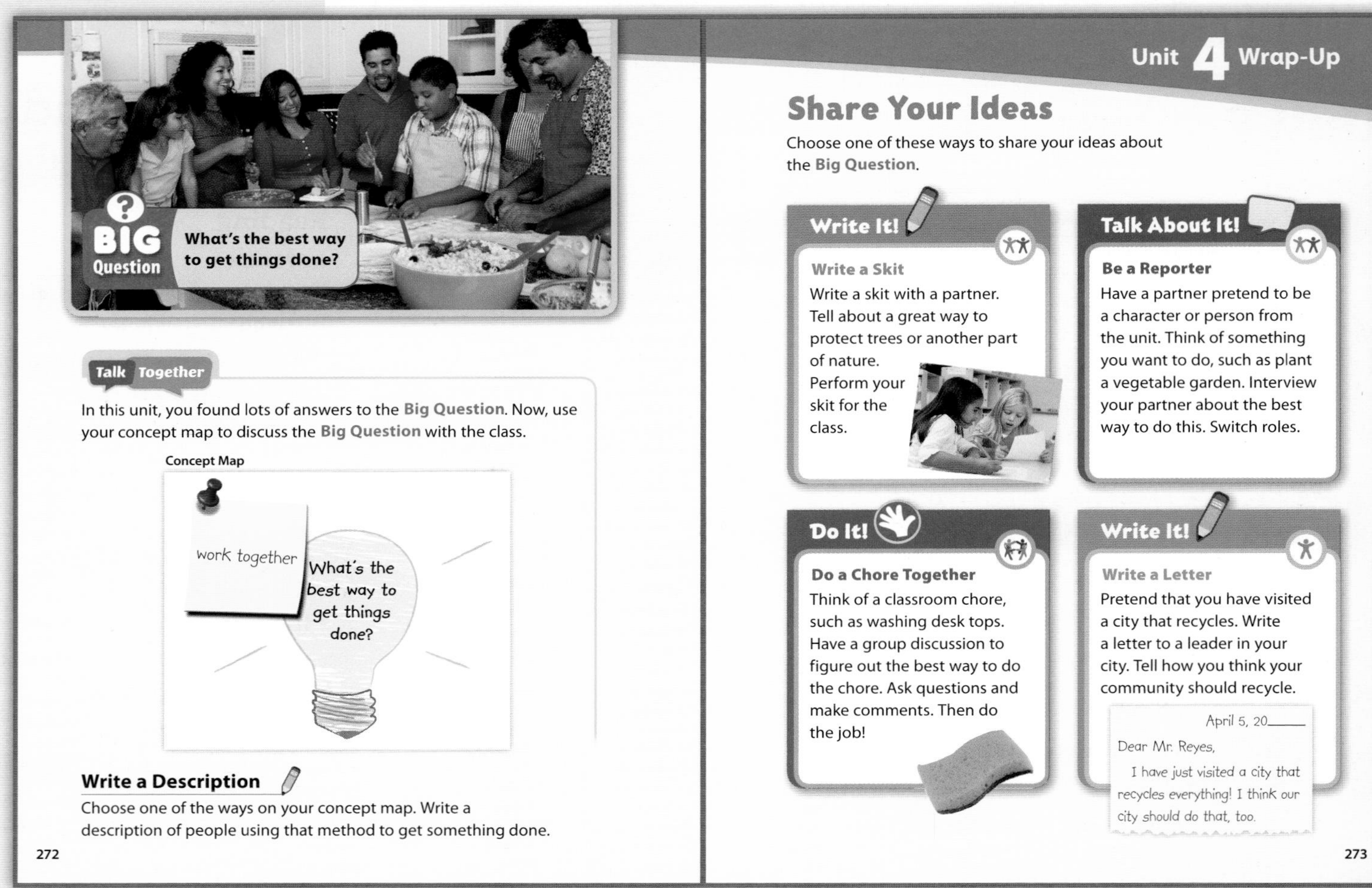

What's the best way to get things done?

BIG Question

Talk Together

In this unit, you found lots of answers to the Big Question. Now, use your concept map to discuss the Big Question with the class.

Concept Map

work together

What's the best way to get things done?

Write a Description

Choose one of the ways on your concept map. Write a description of people using that method to get something done.

272

Unit 4 Wrap-Up

Share Your Ideas

Choose one of these ways to share your ideas about the Big Question.

Write It!

Write a Skit

Write a skit with a partner. Tell about a great way to protect trees or another part of nature. Perform your skit for the class.

Talk About It!

Be a Reporter

Have a partner pretend to be a character or person from the unit. Think of something you want to do, such as plant a vegetable garden. Interview your partner about the best way to do this. Switch roles.

Do It!

Do a Chore Together

Think of a classroom chore, such as washing desk tops. Have a group discussion to figure out the best way to do the chore. Ask questions and make comments. Then do the job!

Write It!

Write a Letter

Pretend that you have visited a city that recycles. Write a letter to a leader in your city. Tell how you think your community should recycle.

April 5, 20____

Dear Mr. Reyes,

I have just visited a city that recycles everything! I think our city should do that, too.

273

Anthology
pages 272–273

OBJECTIVES

Thematic Connection: Working Together

PROGRAM RESOURCES

PRINT & TECHNOLOGY

Unit Concept Map: Practice Master PM4.1

Academic Talk

1 Talk Together **Anthology** page 272

Display the Big Question. Read aloud the first paragraph on page 272. Have students revisit **Practice Master PM4.1** to remind them of their answers to the Big Question. Encourage them to think about their class discussions, the selections in the unit, and the books they read during **Small Group Reading**. Have students tell about an experience related to getting something done, in order to support their opinions. Model the processs: *I think that working together is the best way to get things done. Once, the people in my neighborhood wanted to have a Fourth of July parade. One family brought frozen treats for the kids, another family made lemonade for everyone. Another neighbor asked the local fire station to lead the parade. Because everyone worked together, our parade was a big success.*

Writing

2 Write a Description **Anthology** page 272

Read aloud the instructions. Ask volunteers to say which thing from their concept map they would like to describe. Have students review "A Better Way" as a guide for describing how people can get things done.

COMMON CORE STANDARDS

Writing

Connect Opinions and Reasons	CC.3.W.1
Write Over Shorter Time for Specific Tasks and Purposes	CC.3.W.10

Speaking and Listening

Draw on Preparation to Explore Ideas	CC.3.SL.1.a

Unit Projects

3 Share Your Ideas **Anthology** page 273

Read aloud the project options. Have students who have chosen projects that require partners or small groups gather in designated areas. Have the other students work independently at their desks.

Write It!

Plan

Have partners brainstorm settings for their skit. Suggest places like a farm or forest, or even a talk-show interview about sustainable agriculture. Once they have chosen their setting, students should think about who their characters are and what they will say. Explain that they will use commas and quotation marks when writing their skit dialogues.

Write a Skit

Allow students ample time to write their skits and then practice them.

Have students perform their skits for the class.

Use Dialogue	CC.3.W.3.b
Use Commas and Quotation Marks in Dialogue	CC.3.L.2.c
Recognize Conventions of Spoken and Written English	CC.3.L.3.b

Talk About It!

Plan

Have partners brainstorm people in the unit and each choose one that they would like to pretend to be. Then have them think of something that person would like to do that is related to sustainable agriculture, such as planting a tree or teaching others how to plant a garden. Have them think of questions they will ask each other about the best way to accomplish this goal. Provide example questions, such as: *Why do you think this is the best way? Have you ever tried doing it this way? What problems might come up? What will you do then?*

Be a Reporter

Have students take turns interviewing each other.

Ask and Answer Questions and Elaborate	CC.3.SL.3

Do It!

Plan

Have students brainstorm all the things that have to be done around the class on a regular basis, such as putting away art supplies, straightening up books, watering plants, etc. Have students choose one chore, break it down into parts, and figure out how many people are needed to do each part and what materials they might need. Then have them assign each task to one or more students.

Do a Chore Together

Have students do the chore as planned. After they complete the chore, have students tell how the process went and suggest any changes that would make the chore go more smoothly next time.

Discuss Topics, Building on Others' Ideas	CC.3.SL.1
Ask Questions to Check Understanding and Link to Others' Remarks	CC.3.SL.1.c

Write It!

Plan

Discuss with students what kinds of items it is possible to recycle and why it is important to recycle. Have them make a list. Then explain that they will write a letter to the leaders of the community explaining what the community should recycle, stating their opinion about why it is important, and presenting all the reasons why it is important.

Write a Letter

Have students write their letters. Allow students to read them to the class. If practical, send the letters either through the postal service or as letters to the editor of the local newspaper.

Write Opinions on Topics	CC.3.W.1
Provide Reasons	CC.3.W.1.b
Write Over Shorter Time for Specific Audiences	CC.3.W.10

= one student 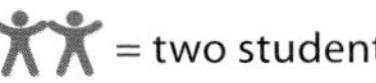 = two students 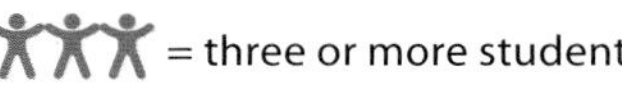 = three or more students

Unit 4 Reflection

Successful Teaching Moments	Adjustments for Next Year

Additional Notes or Resources

Contents at a Glance

Level D | Unit 4

Dear Family Member,

"What's the best way to get things done?" That is the big question we are exploring in this unit. To answer it, we are reading, writing, and talking about how working together can make things better. Be a part of our exploration! With your student, read the New Words on the next page. Then follow these directions.

Directions:

1. Talk together about activities your family does at home. Which ones are good to do together? Share why you think so. Try to use some of the New Words in your discussion.
2. In the space below, work together to draw a picture of your favorite family activity. Use the New Words when you can to add labels to the drawing.
3. Remind your student to bring the completed drawing to class.

What We're Reading

"Mama Panya's Pancakes"
by Mary and Rich Chamberlin
This story tells how a boy organizes a feast by getting everyone to contribute to it.

"Ba's Business"
by Grace Lin
This story tells how two sisters help their father with his business.

"A Better Way"
by Juan Quintana
In this persuasive article, the author describes the work of two Explorers who teach farmers.

"The Ant and the Grasshopper"
retold by Shirleyann Costigan
In this fable, Grasshopper learns why it's important to plan for the future.

And more!

COPY READY

COPY READY

New Words

Weeks 1 and 2

accomplish	market	purpose
advertisement	money	reward
buyer	pay	seller
cooperation	plenty	

Weeks 3 and 4

agriculture	farmer	method
alternative	field	plow
conservation	future	sustain
crop	harvest	

Learn and play with words. NGReach.com

BOLETÍN DE NOTICIAS

Nivel D | Unidad 4

Estimado miembro de la familia,

"¿Cuál es la mejor manera de hacer las cosas?" Esa es la gran pregunta que estamos explorando en esta unidad. Para responderla, estamos leyendo, escribiendo y hablando acerca de cómo trabajar unidos para hacer las cosas mejor. ¡Sea parte de nuestra exploración! Con su estudiante, lea las Nuevas Palabras en la siguiente página. Luego siga estas instrucciones.

Instrucciones:

1. Juntos, hablen acerca de las actividades que su familia hace en casa. ¿Cuáles actividades son apropiadas para hacerlas juntos? Compartan porqué lo creen así. Intenten usar algunas de las Nuevas Palabras en su conversación.
2. Juntos, dibujen su actividad familiar favorita usando el espacio que aparece abajo. Usen las Nuevas Palabras cada vez que puedan para agregar etiquetas al dibujo.
3. Recuerde a su estudiante traer el dibujo completo a clase.

Qué estamos leyendo

"Mama Panya's Pancakes"
por Mary y Rich Chamberlin
Esta historia nos cuenta la manera en que un niño organiza un festín, logrando que cada persona contribuya.

"Ba's Business"
por Grace Lin
Esta historia nos cuenta cómo dos hermanas ayudan a su padre en su negocio.

"A Better Way"
por Juan Quintana
En este convincente artículo, el autor describe el trabajo de dos exploradores que enseñan a los granjeros.

"The Ant and the Grasshopper"
re-narrada por Shirleyann Costigan
En esta fábula, el saltamontes aprende porqué es importante planear hacia el futuro.

¡Y más!

COPY READY

Nuevas Palabras

Semanas 1 y 2

accomplish
lograr

advertisement
publicidad

buyer
comprador

cooperation
cooperación

market
mercado

money
dinero

pay
pagar

plenty
suficiente

purpose
propósito

reward
recompensa

seller
vendedor

Semanas 3 y 4

agriculture
agricultura

alternative
alternativa

conservation
conservación

crop
cosecha

farmer
granjero

field
campo

future
futuro

harvest
cosecha

method
método

plow
arado

sustain
preservar

Aprenda y juegue con palabras. NGReach.com

Name ____________________ Date ____________

Unit Concept Map

Let's Work Together

Make a concept map with the answers to the Big Question: What's the best way to get things done?

COPY READY

Name ______________________ Date ____________

Theme Chart

Story Clues

Make a theme chart about your partner's story.

Title: ______________________

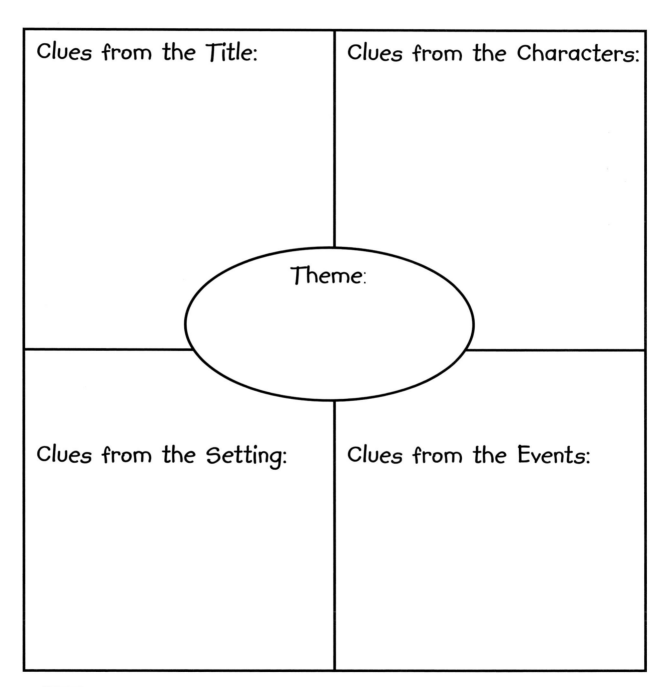

Clues from the Title:	Clues from the Characters:
Clues from the Setting:	Clues from the Events:

Theme:

Discuss the clues in the theme chart with a partner.

Name ______________________ Date ______________

Grammar: Game

Everyone Is Present

Directions:

1. **Make two pronoun cards for each pronoun: *he, she,* and *it*.**
2. **Shuffle the six cards and stack them face down.**
3. **Take turns drawing a card and tossing a marker onto a square.**
4. **Form a sentence using the word from the card and the verb your marker lands on. Write a sentence using the pronoun and the verb. For example: "It stretches."**
5. **Award yourself one point for using the correct present tense of the verb and one point for spelling it correctly.**
6. **Put the pronoun card at the bottom of the stack.**
7. **After eight turns each, the player with more points wins.**

hum	fetch	gather
leave	wave	tap
miss	rush	cheer
skip	chase	stretch
pour	visit	mix

COPY READY

COPY READY

Name ______________________ Date ____________

Grammar: Grammar and Writing

Edit and Proofread

Choose the Editing and Proofreading Marks you need to correct the passage. Look for correct usage of the following:

- present-tense action verbs
- subject-verb agreement with *he*, *she*, and *it*

Editing and Proofreading Marks

Mark	Meaning
∧	Add.
℘	Take out.
≡	Capitalize.
⊙	Add period.
∧,	Add comma.

Mimi finish∧e s cutting the strawberries. She places them into a bowl. She smile as she leaves the kitchen. Everything is ready, and neighbors will arrive soon.

Suddenly, Mimi hear a crash and rushs into the kitchen. It was the cat! She see the bowl of strawberries on the floor.

When Jeff gets home, Mimi discuss the problem with him. They have no dessert! Then Mimi's phone buzz. It's their neighbor, Mrs. Wong. She want to know what to bring. "Bring strawberries!" say Mimi.

Mimi smiles again. "That fix our dessert problem," she says.

Name ________________________________ Date ________________

Test-Taking Strategy Practice

Understand the Question

Directions: Read each question about "Mama Panya's Pancakes." Choose the best answer.

Sample

1 How does Mama feel when Adika invites several guests to have pancakes?

- ● nervous
- Ⓑ excited
- Ⓒ sad

2 Which answer best shows that Adika is generous?

- Ⓐ He is always one step ahead of Mama Panya.
- Ⓑ He invites people over to eat pancakes.
- Ⓒ He is friendly to everyone he meets.

3 Why does Kaya give Mama Panya the plumpest pepper?

- Ⓐ Adika invites her for pancakes.
- Ⓑ Kaya and Mama Panya are friends.
- Ⓒ Kaya is a generous person.

4 Choose the statement that best fits the theme of being generous.

- Ⓐ "Aiii! How many pancakes do you think I can make today, son?"
- Ⓑ "I think we can give you a little more for that coin."
- Ⓒ "You and I will be lucky to share half a pancake."

How did you use the test-taking strategy to answer the questions?

COPY READY

COPY READY

Name ______________________ Date ____________

Theme Chart

"Mama Panya's Pancakes"

Make a theme chart for "Mama Panya's Pancakes."

Theme Chart

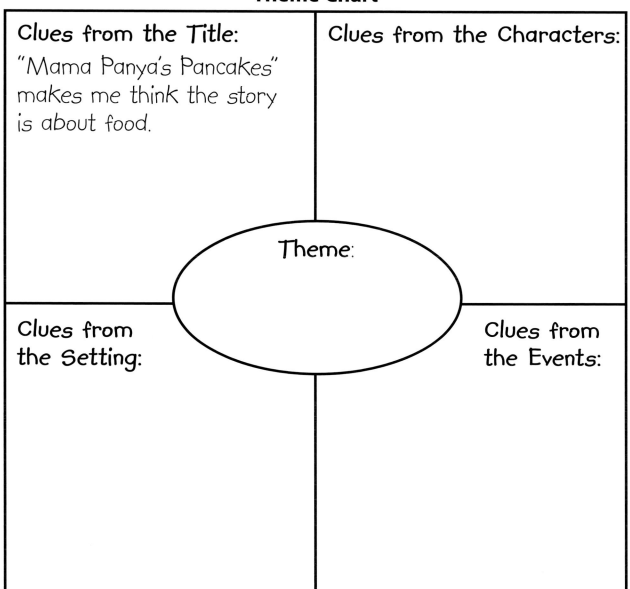

Clues from the Title: "Mama Panya's Pancakes" makes me think the story is about food.	Clues from the Characters:
Clues from the Setting:	Clues from the Events:

Theme:

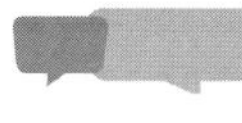

Compare your theme sentence with a partner's sentence. Can both themes apply to the story? Discuss.

Name ____________________ Date ____________

Fluency Practice

"Mama Panya's Pancakes"

Use this passage to practice reading with proper intonation.

Adika popped up. "Mama's making pancakes today. Can you come?" 10
"Oh, how wonderful! I think we can give a little more for that coin." 24
Bwana Zawenna put more flour on the paper, then tied it up with string. 38
"We'll see you later." 42
Mama tucked the package into her bag. "Ai-Yi-Yi! You and I will be 55
lucky to share half a pancake." 61
"But Mama, we have a little bit and a little bit more." 73

From "Mama Panya's Pancakes," page 226

Intonation

- 1 ☐ Does not change pitch.
- 2 ☐ Changes pitch, but does not match content.
- 3 ☐ Changes pitch to match some of the content.
- 4 ☐ Changes pitch to match all of the content.

Accuracy and Rate Formula

Use the formula to measure a reader's accuracy and rate while reading aloud.

________	–	________	=	________
words attempted in one minute		number of errors		words correct per minute (wcpm)

COPY READY

COPY READY

Name ______________________________ Date ______________

Grammar: Reteach

A Fair Trade

Grammar Rules Subject-Verb Agreement with Present Tense

A **present-tense action verb** tells about an action that happens now or all the time.

To show present tense for the subject **he**, **she**, or **it**, add -s or -*es* to most action verbs.

The baker **reads** the recipe.

"It **lists** cinnamon!" he **yells** to an assistant.

She **adds** cinnamon to the bowl.

He **mixes** the bread dough.

It bakes in the oven.

Circle the present-tense verb that completes each sentence.

1. A girl sits near the bakery. She (sniff/sniffs) the cinnamon scent.
2. The baker stomps up to her. He (glares/glare) at the young girl.
3. Then he (demand/demands), "You pay for enjoying the scent!"
4. The girl says, "It smells wonderful!" She (find/finds) her only coin.
5. She (tosses/toss) the coin, and it (sparkles/sparkle) in the light.
6. He (catches/catch) the coin and (twirl/twirls) it happily.
7. Then he (flip/flips) it high in the air, and the girl grabs the coin.
8. The baker says, "It belongs to me!" and he (step/steps) closer.
9. "I smelled the cinnamon. You felt the coin." The girl (grin/grins).
10. The baker frowns. Suddenly, he (flashes/flash) a smile. "It *is* a fair trade."

Tell a partner about an event or a trade that is fair. Include present-tense action verbs, and use *he*, *she*, and *it*.

Name ______________________ Date ______________

Grammar: Game

Apply the -*y* Rules

Directions:

1. **Choose a game box that has not been filled in.**
2. **Use the correct present tense of the verb in a sentence with *he*, *she*, or *it*. Then spell the verb aloud.**
3. **If other players agree with the spelling, write the word and your initials in the box. If the spelling is wrong, leave the box blank.**
4. **Players take turns. When all boxes are taken, count your boxes. The player with the most boxes is the winner.**

A.B. **scurry**
scurries

try __________	**say** __________	**study** __________
rely __________	**pay** __________	**buy** __________
bury __________	**cry** __________	**carry** __________
annoy __________	**play** __________	**fly** __________
stay __________	**hurry** __________	**employ** __________

COPY READY

COPY READY

Name ______________________________ Date ________________

Grammar: Game

Do They Agree?

SUBJECT Cards

1. Print I, YOU, WE, THEY, HE, SHE, IT on separate index cards.
2. Mix the SUBJECT cards up and stack them face down to play the game.

Directions:

1. **Flip a coin. For heads, move 2 squares. For tails, move 1 square.**
2. **Pick a SUBJECT card and read it aloud. Choose the correct present-tense verb in the square to create a sentence with your subject. Then put the SUBJECT card at the bottom of the stack.**
3. **If the other players agree that your subject and verb agree, stay on your space. If not, move back one space.**

						dash or dashes?	END
		explore or explores?	trades or trade?	raise or raises?		study or studies?	
		scurries or scurry?		pay or pays?		hides or hide?	
		works or work?		buys or buy?		finds or find?	
	hurries or hurry?	help or helps?		move or moves?	sells or sell?	buzz or buzzes?	
START	go or goes?						

Name ______________________ Date ______________

Comparison Chart

Compare Characters

Compare the characters from the two stories.

	Beginning of Story	End of Story	Why does the character change?
Mama Payna	She is worried about having enough food.		
Ba			

Talk with a partner about which story you liked better and why.

COPY READY

Name ____________________________ Date ______________

Grammar: Practice

Farmer's Market

Grammar Rules Present-Tense Action Verbs

A present-tense action verb must agree with its subject.

Use **-*s*** at the end of an action verb if the subject is ***he***, ***she***, or ***it***.	Carmella **loves** street fairs. She **takes** me along with her.
Do **not** add -*s* to the verb if the subject is ***I***, ***you***, ***we***, or ***they***.	Buyers **walk** slowly through the fairs. They **buy** a lot of things.

Fill in each blank with the present-tense verb form that agrees with the subject.

My parents ________ (take) us to the farmer's market. We ________ (enjoy) all the sights, smells, and sounds. Farmers ________ (sell) vegetables and fruit. One farmer ________ (sell) flowers, too. My mother ________ (buy) flowers every week. She ________ (love) flowers. One man ________ (cook) delicious burritos. A woman ________ (paint) faces. Two men ________ (carve) wooden toys. They ________ (call) out to buyers. The farmer's market is so much fun! It ________ (make) me smile.

Choose three verbs from the story and write new sentences. Read them to a partner.

Name ______________________ Date ______________

Mark-Up Reading

The Bird Bank

by Grace Lin

During the winter, Hannah and Rose earned nickels from their father. Sometimes they would shovel snow or sweep the house. Ba would give them each a nickel and they put the nickels in their green bird bank.

Every time Hannah and Rose put their nickels in the bird bank it would sing "Tweet! Tweet!"

But in the spring, the bird bank stopped singing. It would not swallow Rose's nickel.

"Hannah!" Rose said. "Our bird bank is full!"

Shopping

by Grace Lin

Hannah and Rose looked at all the stores. What should they buy?

"Look at the birds!" Rose said, pointing at a pet store window. "I like the yellow one."

"I like the blue one," Hannah said. "Let's go buy them!"

But Hannah and Rose did not have enough money for a yellow bird or a blue bird. On the shelf there was a birdhouse.

"We can buy the birdhouse," Rose said. "Should we buy that instead?"

Hannah nodded and they did.

Name ______________________ Date ______________

Mark-Up Reading

Tweet! Tweet!

by Grace Lin

Hannah and Rose bought the birdhouse at the pet store.

"I'm glad you are buying a birdhouse," Mrs. Alexis, the store owner, said. "I have too many of them. No one else is buying them. I wonder why. " She sighed sadly.

Hannah and Rose brought their birdhouse home.

"This is a nice birdhouse," Rose said to Hannah, "but it is too plain. Let's decorate it."

So, Hannah painted the birdhouse and Rose glued on pictures. When they were finished, the birdhouse was very pretty.

"I know why no one else is buying Mrs. Alexis's birdhouses," Rose said. "They are too plain! They need to be decorated."

"We should tell her," Hannah said. "Let's show her our birdhouse."

When Mrs. Alexis saw Hannah and Rose's decorated birdhouse, she was surprised.

"Could you decorate all of my birdhouses?" she said. "I will pay you for every birdhouse that sells."

So, Hannah and Rose decorated the other birdhouses. How pretty they were! Soon, many people began to buy them. Mrs. Alexis paid Hannah and Rose for their good work and was very happy.

Hannah and Rose put their new quarters and dimes into their bird bank. Two live birds came to live in their birdhouse. All of them sang "Tweet! Tweet!" for Hannah and Rose.

Name ______________________ Date ______________

Mark-Up Reading

Compare Story Elements

For each story, list the characters, settings, and story events found only in that story. Then list elements found in multiple stories.

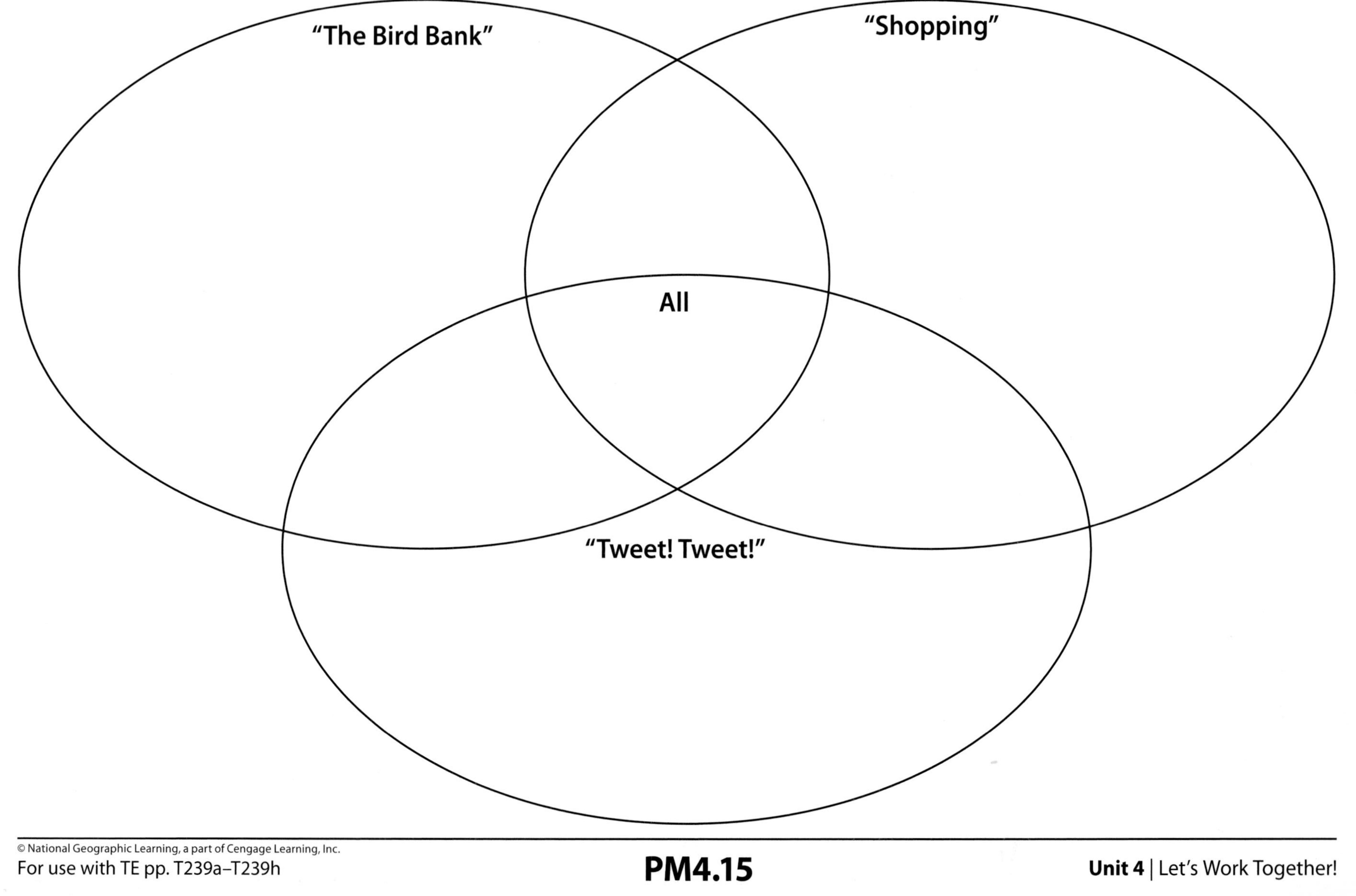

COPY READY

Name ________________________________ Date ______________

Grammar: Grammar and Writing

Edit and Proofread

Choose the Editing and Proofreading Marks you need to correct the passage. Look for correct usage of the following:

- present-tense action verbs
- subject-verb agreement
- correct spelling of verbs

Editing and Proofreading Marks

∧	Add.
	Take out.
≡	Capitalize.
⊙	Add period.

"Have you finished the patchwork quilt?" Lee asks Kendra.

"No," she reply, holding it up. "It won't be ready for Mama's birthday. It need another row, but I ran out of material."

"If you requires material, I'll get it," Lee promises. He dashs out. Neighbors help, but they adds only a few scraps to his bag. He go to Ms. Cotton. She explains, "I buys material for my store! Here, you carries these back to Kendra."

When Kendra sees the cloth, she exclaim, "Look at this special piece, Lee. It shine like a pool of water!" Kendra tells Lee, "Now the quilt can be ready! We makes a good team, brother!"

Name ________________________________ Date ________________

Grammar: Reteach

Pet Show

Grammar Rules Subject-Verb Agreement

Present-Tense Action Verbs

Singular subject: Use -***s*** or -***es*** if the subject is ***he***, ***she***, or ***it***.	**He** pat**s** his big dog. **It** swish**es** its long, fluffy tail. **She** hurr**ies** to the pet show.
Plural subject: Do not use *-s* or *-es* at the end of an action verb if the subject is ***we***, ***you***, or ***they.***	**We** help the judges. **You** watch the time for us. **They** walk around each pet.
Exceptions: For singular subjects ***I*** and ***you***, do not use *-s* or *-es*.	**I** take a video of the contest. **You** bring the prize ribbons.

Read each sentence. Write the correct form of the verb on the line.

1. Owners hold leashes and cages. They ________ (smile) eagerly.
2. Judges have a hard job. "We ________ (promise) to be fair to all pets."
3. A judge holds a gerbil. "He ________ (race) in his wheel," says the boy.
4. "I ________ (sing) great!" A judge laughs because the speaker is a parrot.
5. She ________ (study) the parrot. It ________ (reach) for a treat after singing.
6. Another judge says, "You ________ (lead) your dogs to the ring."

COPY READY

COPY READY

Name ______________________ Date ______________

Opinion Chart

What Do You Think?

Make an opinion chart of your partner's opinion.

Opinion:

Evidence:

Evidence:

Evidence:

Ask your partner questions about his or her opinion.

Name ______________________ Date ______________

Grammar: Game

Could You? You Can!

Helping Verbs: What They Mean	
The helping verb ***can*** means • someone is able to do something • someone knows how to do something • someone has the power to do something.	The helping verb ***could*** means • someone has a choice • something is possible • a suggestion is being offered.

Directions:

1. **Write *can* on five cards and *could* on five cards. Mix the cards and place them face down.**
2. **Take turns spinning for a main verb and choosing a card for the helping verb.**
3. **Use the main verb and helping verb in a sentence.**
4. **When each player has created five correct sentences, work together to write a three-sentence story. Use helping verbs and main verbs. Share your story.**

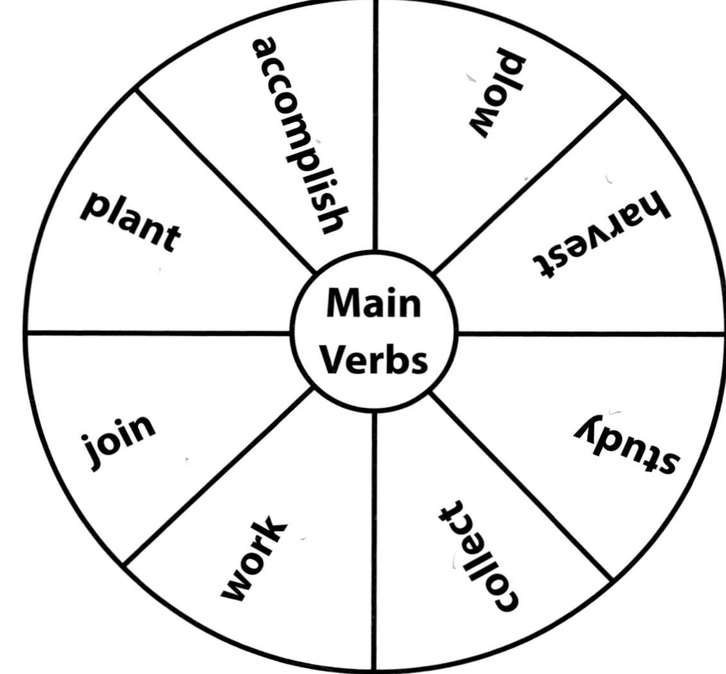

Make a Spinner

1. Put a paper clip over the center of the spinner.
2. Touch the point of a pencil on the middle of the wheel and through the loop of the paper clip.
3. Spin the paper clip to make a spinner.

COPY READY

Name ______________________ Date ____________

Grammar: Grammar and Writing

Edit and Proofread

Choose the Editing and Proofreading Marks you need to correct the passage. Look for correct usage of the following:

- helping verbs *can, could, must, should, do*

Editing and Proofreading Marks

Mark	Meaning
∧	Add.
↗	Take out.
≡	Capitalize.
⊙	Add period.
∧,	Add comma.

We know forests are important to the planet. People ~~might~~ must stop slash-and-burn farming. We don't want more forests to disappear.

Farmers have choices. They must harvest plants like orchids, or harvest fruit from trees. Some farmers have already changed their methods. They does harvest Brazil nuts, palm hearts, and other foods. They agree that more farmers do change their crops.

Education helps farmers work faster and better. They learn that they could grow or harvest crops without cutting down trees.

We know how important good farming is. It do make a difference to the planet.

Name ______________________ Date ____________

Test-Taking Strategy Practice

Understand the Question

Directions: Read each question about "A Better Way." Choose the best answer.

Sample

1 Why is sustainable agriculture a good alternative to the slash-and-burn method of farming?

● Sustainable agriculture allows people to reuse the land.

Ⓑ Slash-and-burn farming is too expensive for many farmers.

Ⓒ Slash-and-burn farming only grows certain crops.

Ⓓ Sustainable agriculture takes less time.

2 Segura and Simões believe that we need to save trees and help people, too. Which statement does not support their opinion?

Ⓐ Fruit and flower trees can provide a good income.

Ⓑ Sustainable agriculture is good for the land.

Ⓒ Farmers can grow high-value crops.

Ⓓ Slash-and-burn agriculture harms the land and people.

3 What is the name of Segura and Simões' alternative farming plan?

Ⓐ Slash-and-burn agriculture

Ⓑ Fruit-and-flower agriculture

Ⓒ A special plan

Ⓓ The 5 X 5 System

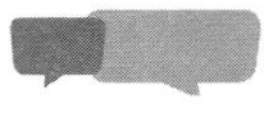

How did you use the test-taking strategy to answer the question?

COPY READY

Name ______________________ Date ____________

Opinion Chart

"A Better Way"

Make an opinion chart for pages 254-257 in "A Better Way."

Opinion: Sustainable agriculture is good for the farmer and good for the land.
Evidence: It lets farmers grow crops on the same land year after year.
Evidence:
Evidence:

Explain the opinion and evidence to a partner.

COPY READY

Name ____________________ Date ____________

Fluency Practice

"A Better Way"

Use this passage to practice reading with proper phrasing.

To make a difference, many farmers need to grow crops this way. 12
Segura and Simões use a special plan to teach more farmers. It is 25
called the 5 x 5 System. First, they teach one family how to grow 39
crops that don't ruin the land. Then that family teaches five new 51
families what they learned. Each new family teaches five more 61
families. Think of all the land that could be saved in the future! 74

From "A Better Way," page 253

Phrasing

1 ☐ Rarely pauses while reading the text.

2 ☐ Occasionally pauses while reading the text.

3 ☐ Frequently pauses at appropriate points in the text.

4 ☐ Consistently pauses at all appropriate points in the text.

Accuracy and Rate Formula

Use the formula to measure a reader's accuracy and rate while reading aloud.

______ − ______ = ______

words attempted in one minute − number of errors = words correct per minute (wcpm)

COPY READY

COPY READY

Name ______________________ Date ____________

Grammar: Reteach

Traveling Straight Up

Grammar Rules Helping Verbs

A **helping verb** works with the main verb to tell something about the action. • Use ***can*** to tell that someone is able to do something. • Use ***could*** to tell that someone has a choice or something is possible. • Use ***must*** to tell that somebody has to do something. • Use ***should*** to give an opinion or advice about doing something. • Use ***do*** to add emphasis to a verb.	People **can** see skyscrapers in big cities. You **could** visit New York City to see some. People **must** use elevators in skyscrapers. You **should** visit. I **do** ride in a glass elevator! It **does** go fast!

Read each sentence. Write the correct form of the verb on the line.

1. This is advice:

They __________ go to the Empire State Building.

2. They are able:

They __________ reach the 102nd floor of the building.

3. You have to do this:

You __________ see the view across the city from there!

4. This is a choice.

You __________ stop at the 86th floor.

 **Tell a partner if he or she should ride elevators to reach the 102nd floor. Use three helping verbs.**

Name ________________________ Date ____________

Grammar: Game

Be What You Want to Be

Directions:

1. **Take five minutes to write as many sentences as your team can. For each sentence, use a subject from column 1, the correct form of *to be*, and a word or phrase from column 2.**
2. **Your team will get one point for each sentence it writes correctly.**
3. **You may choose one or all subjects in a box to use in sentences. For example, if you write one correct sentence with *he*, another with *she*, and another with *it*, you gain three points! You can also use words in column 2 more than once.**
4. **When time's up, trade sentences with another team, check each other's work, and add up points. The team with most points wins.**

Forms of *To Be*
am is are

Subject	What the Subject Is or What the Subject is Like
I	challenging
He, She, It	a hard worker
You	curious
We, They	busy
Problems	thoughtful
An ant | Ants	delicious
A grasshopper	nine years old
A kernel | Kernels	playful
An inventor | Inventors	bright yellow
An invention | Inventions	a problem solver

COPY READY

COPY READY

Name ____________________ Date ____________

Grammar: Game

Choose *Has* or *Have*

Directions:

1. Play with a partner. Take turns.
2. Place a game piece on START. Flip a coin. For heads, move ahead one space. For tails, move ahead two spaces.
3. Read the subject in the space. Create a sentence using the subject and the verb *has* or *have* to tell what the subject has. Or, use the verb *has* or *have* as a helping verb in a sentence. If your partner agrees that your sentence is correct, score one point.
4. When one player reaches the END, count your points to see who wins.

have	has	START	have	has	have	has	have	has
has		I						have
have		Paola						has
has		he	she	you	Ba	we		have
have		friends	I			it		has
has		it	they			Cid		have
have		we	you			they		has
has	have	has	have	has	have	END	has	have

Name ______________________ Date ______________

Comparison Chart

Compare Purposes

Compare authors' purposes in "A Better Way" and "The Ant and the Grasshopper."

Title	Topic	Author's Purpose
"A Better Way" by Juan Quintana	sustainable agriculture	
"The Ant and the Grasshopper" by Shirleyann Costigan		

Take turns with a partner telling how the authors' purposes are alike or different.

COPY READY

COPY READY

Name ______________________________ Date ______________

Grammar: Practice

What Is in the Garden?

Grammar Rules Subject-Verb Agreement: *be* and *have*

The verbs *be* and *have* are irregular. The subject and verb must agree. Use these correct forms:

I am	We are	I have	We have
You are	You are	You have	You have
He, she, it is	They are	He, she, it has	They have

Write the correct form of be or have to complete each sentence. Choose the correct form for the subject.

Jenna and Jake ___have___ a large garden. Jake's favorite vegetable __________ corn. He __________ several rows of corn in the garden. The corn __________ almost ready to harvest. Both Jenna and Jake __________ excited to roast ears of corn. They also grow tomatoes. Tomatoes __________ their mother's favorite vegetable. Jenna planted sunflowers, too. They __________ delicious seeds and pretty blooms.

I __________ planning to help them pick some corn. I __________ a basket I will take with me.

Imagine a garden. Tell your partner about it, using forms of *be* and *have*.

Name ______________________ Date ______________

Mark-Up Reading

Belling the Cat

an Aesop fable retold by Katie Blankshain

Long ago, a large family of mice lived in an old blue house. They chattered happily that they had all the food and warmth they could ever need. There was just one problem. They worried that their enemy the cat was becoming more dangerous every day.

Every day, the cat would tiptoe through the gray shadows, stepping lightly with her furry feet. She would slink and creep, grinning to herself as she went. She waited until she was right behind the poor mice. Then—POUNCE—she would trap one of the mice in her big orange paws. "You'll make a delicious dinner for me tonight!" the cat would say, purring.

Her cruel trick never failed, and so the cat never went hungry. She began to grow quite fat and content. Sometimes she would pop out from behind corners, baring her white, pointy teeth and sharp claws, just to scare the helpless mice away.

Explain these viewpoints:

1. the mice ______________________

2. the cat ______________________

3. the narrator ______________________

COPY READY

COPY READY

Name ______________________ Date ______________

Mark-Up Reading

Belling the Cat (continued)

One night, the oldest mouse called a meeting. "Fellow mice!" he cried. "We have lived in fear of the cat for too long. She must be stopped. Who has a plan? We might be smaller than the cat, but surely we can outwit her."

Everyone was silent for a long while. At last, a young mouse stood up. "The cat only catches us because she is very sneaky. If we knew when cat was coming, we could certainly run away in time." The small mouse held up a large red collar. "Here is my plan: we should attach a small bell to the cat using this collar. This way, the bell will ring whenever the cat moves. She will never sneak up on us again!" All of the mice joyfully applauded this idea.

Then an old mouse slowly rose to his feet. "That is a good idea, but who is to put the bell on the cat?" All of the mice looked around, but no one spoke. No mouse wanted to volunteer for such a dangerous mission.

MORAL: Actions speak louder than words.

Explain these viewpoints:

1. the mice ______________________

2. the narrator ______________________

Name ______________________ Date ____________

Grammar: Grammar and Writing

Edit and Proofread

Choose the Editing and Proofreading Marks you need to correct the passage. Look for correct usage of the following:

- subject-verb agreement with forms of *be*
- subject-verb agreement with forms of *have*

Editing and Proofreading Marks

Mark	Meaning
∧	Add.
ᒧ	Take out.
≡	Capitalize.
⊙	Add period.
∧,	Add comma.

Ella Ant ~~are~~ is unhappy. She is on one side of some flowing water. Tempting smells come from the other side. "I is hungry, but I are not a swimmer," she says. She have no boat.

"Ants is clever," thinks Ella. "We has problem-solving skills." She looks around. "Ah, leaves is good boats. They has the ability to float." She invents a two-leaf boat to carry back food. She pushes it into the water, but it quickly floats away.

Grasshopper hops into view. "You am eager to be on the other side, I see," he says. "I has a solution for you."

With Ella on his back, Grasshopper leaps across the water. Together they follow the tempting smells.

Name ______________________ Date ______________

Grammar: Reteach

The Science Museum

Grammar Rules Forms of *Be* and *Have*

• The linking verb ***to be*** tells what a subject is or is like.	I **am**	we **are**
	you **are**	you **are**
• The verb ***to be*** has irregular forms.	she, he, it **is**	they **are**
• The verb ***to have*** can tell what the subject of a sentence has.	I **have**	we **have**
	you **have**	you **have**
• The verb ***to have*** has irregular forms.	she, he, it **has**	they **have**

Read each sentence. Write the correct verb from the box. Then read your sentences again to make sure the subjects and verbs agree.

am	is	are	has	have

1. This science museum __________ many exciting inventions.
2. The can opener __________ one of the most practical ones.
3. Science certainly __________ come a long way!
4. Inventions __________ changed our lives.
5. Our lives __________ easier because of them.
6. Inventions __________ created by clever people.
7. I __________ hoping someday to invent something.
8. Jenna says she __________ going to invent something, too.

Tell a partner what inventions you think are interesting. Use at least one *be* verb and one *have* verb.

COPY READY

Answer Keys

Also available in Resource Directory NGReach.com

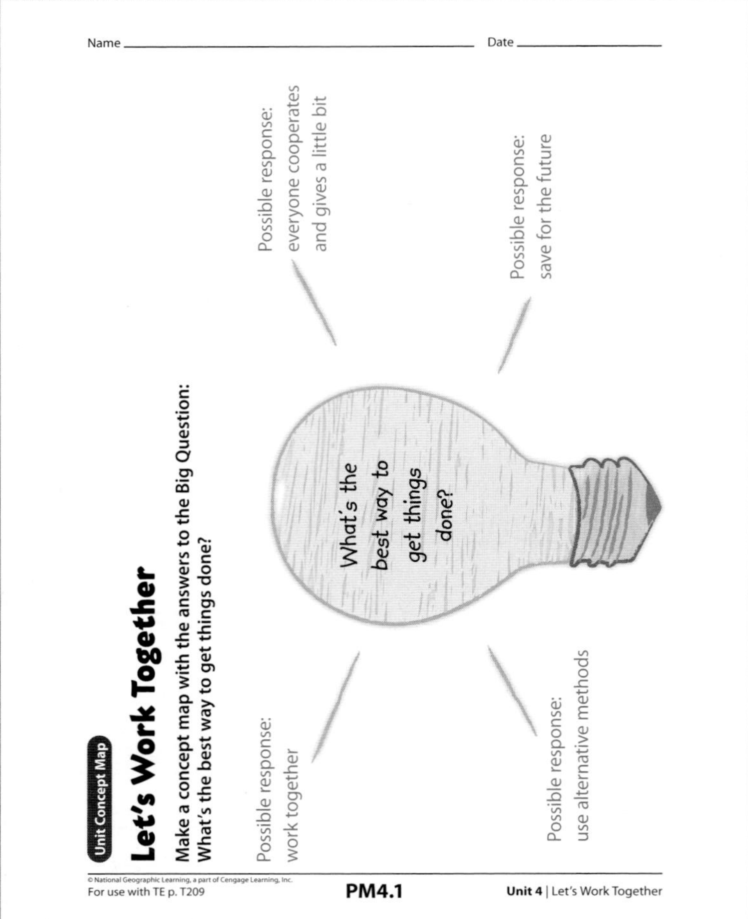
Name ______ Date ______

Unit Concept Map

Let's Work Together

Make a concept map with the answers to the Big Question:
What's the best way to get things done?

© National Geographic Learning, a part of Cengage Learning, Inc.
For use with TE p. T209 PM4.1 Unit 4 | Let's Work Together

Page PM4.1

Name ______ Date ______

Theme Chart

Story Clues

Make a theme chart about your partner's story.

Title: Possible response: The Birthday Party

Clues from the Title:	Clues from the Characters:
Possible response: This story will describe a birthday party.	Possible response: The birthday girl was happy all her friends were at the party. The friends smiled when they arrived.
Theme: Possible response: Birthday parties are a lot of fun for everyone.	
Clues from the Setting:	**Clues from the Events:**
Possible response: The room was decorated with streamers, balloons, and a "Happy Birthday!" sign.	Possible response: Everyone played lots of games. The birthday girl opened gifts, and then she gave presents to all her friends to thank them for coming to the party.

Discuss the clues in the theme chart with a partner.

© National Geographic Learning, a part of Cengage Learning, Inc.
For use with TE p. T212 PM4.2 Unit 4 | Let's Work Together

Page PM4.2

Name ______ Date ______

Grammar: Game

Everyone Is Present

Directions:

1. Make two pronoun cards for each pronoun: *he, she,* and *it*.
2. Shuffle the six cards and stack them face down.
3. Take turns drawing a card and tossing a marker onto a square.
4. Form a sentence using the word from the card and the verb your marker lands on. Write a sentence using the pronoun and the verb. For example: "It stretches."
5. Award yourself one point for using the correct present tense of the verb and one point for spelling it correctly.
6. Put the pronoun card at the bottom of the stack.
7. After eight turns each, the player with more points wins.

hums	fetches	gathers
leaves	waves	taps
misses	rushes	cheers
skips	chases	stretches
pours	visits	mixes

© National Geographic Learning, a part of Cengage Learning, Inc.
For use with TE p. T207p PM4.3 Unit 4 | Let's Work Together

Page PM4.3

Name ______ Date ______

Grammar: Grammar and Writing

Edit and Proofread

Choose the Editing and Proofreading Marks you need to correct the passage. Look for correct usage of the following:

- present-tense action verbs
- subject-verb agreement with *he, she,* and *it*

Editing and Proofreading Marks

Mark	Meaning
^	Add.
(take out mark)	Take out.
≡	Capitalize.
⊙	Add period.
^,	Add comma.

Mimi finish(^e)s cutting the strawberries. She places them into a bowl. She smile(^s) as she leaves the kitchen. Everything is ready, and neighbors will arrive soon.

Suddenly, Mimi hear(^s) a crash and rush(^es)s into the kitchen. It was the cat! She see(^s) the bowl of strawberries on the floor.

When Jeff gets home, Mimi discuss(^es) the problem with him. They have no dessert! Then Mimi's phone buzz(^es). It's their neighbor, Mrs. Wong. She want(^s) to know what to bring. "Bring strawberries!" say(^s) Mimi.

Mimi smiles again. "That fix(^es) our dessert problem," she says.

© National Geographic Learning, a part of Cengage Learning, Inc.
For use with TE p. T207p PM4.4 Unit 4 | Let's Work Together

Page PM4.4

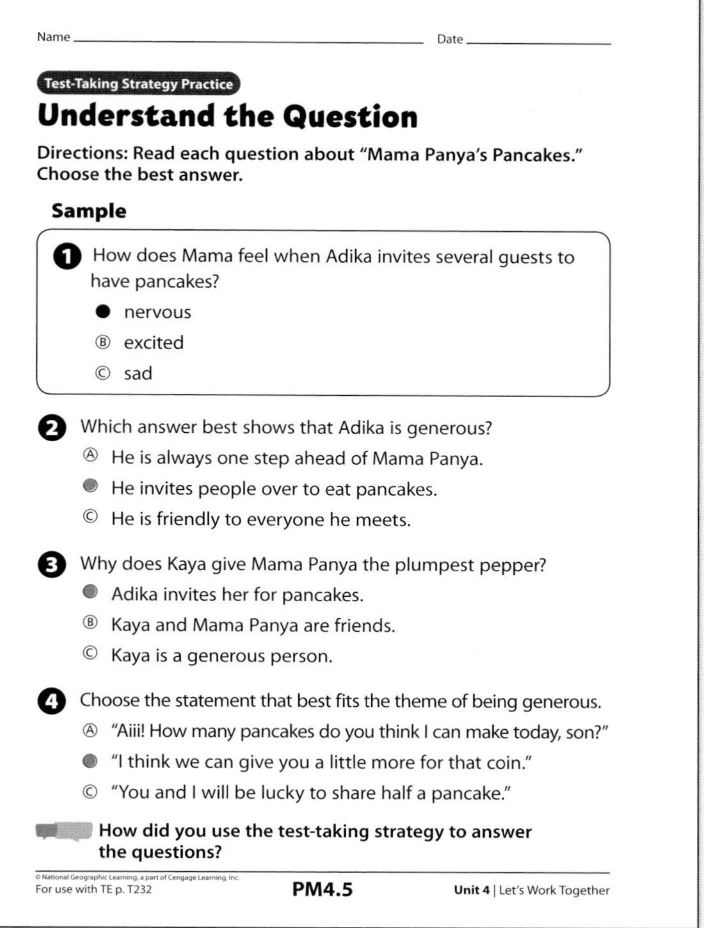

Name ______________________ Date ____________

Test-Taking Strategy Practice

Understand the Question

Directions: Read each question about "Mama Panya's Pancakes." Choose the best answer.

Sample

1. How does Mama feel when Adika invites several guests to have pancakes?
   - ● nervous
   - Ⓑ excited
   - Ⓒ sad

2. Which answer best shows that Adika is generous?
   - Ⓐ He is always one step ahead of Mama Panya.
   - ● He invites people over to eat pancakes.
   - Ⓒ He is friendly to everyone he meets.

3. Why does Kaya give Mama Panya the plumpest pepper?
   - ● Adika invites her for pancakes.
   - Ⓑ Kaya and Mama Panya are friends.
   - Ⓒ Kaya is a generous person.

4. Choose the statement that best fits the theme of being generous.
   - Ⓐ "Aiii! How many pancakes do you think I can make today, son?"
   - ● "I think we can give you a little more for that coin."
   - Ⓒ "You and I will be lucky to share half a pancake."

How did you use the test-taking strategy to answer the questions?

Page PM4.5

Name ______________________ Date ____________

Theme Chart

"Mama Panya's Pancakes"

Make a theme chart for "Mama Panya's Pancakes."

Theme Chart

Clues from the Title:	Clues from the Characters:
"Mama Panya's Pancakes" makes me think the story is about food.	Adika is friendly and wants all his friends to eat with him. The friends are all happy to come. Some sellers give Mama more than her coin is worth.

Theme: When people cooperate, they can have fun and accomplish something good.

Clues from the Setting:	Clues from the Events:
The people live in a village and know and like each other.	Adika invites all his friends to have pancakes at his house. Mama worries about having enough food. All the villagers come and bring extra food.

Compare your theme sentence with a partner's sentence. Can both themes apply to the story? Discuss.

Page PM4.6

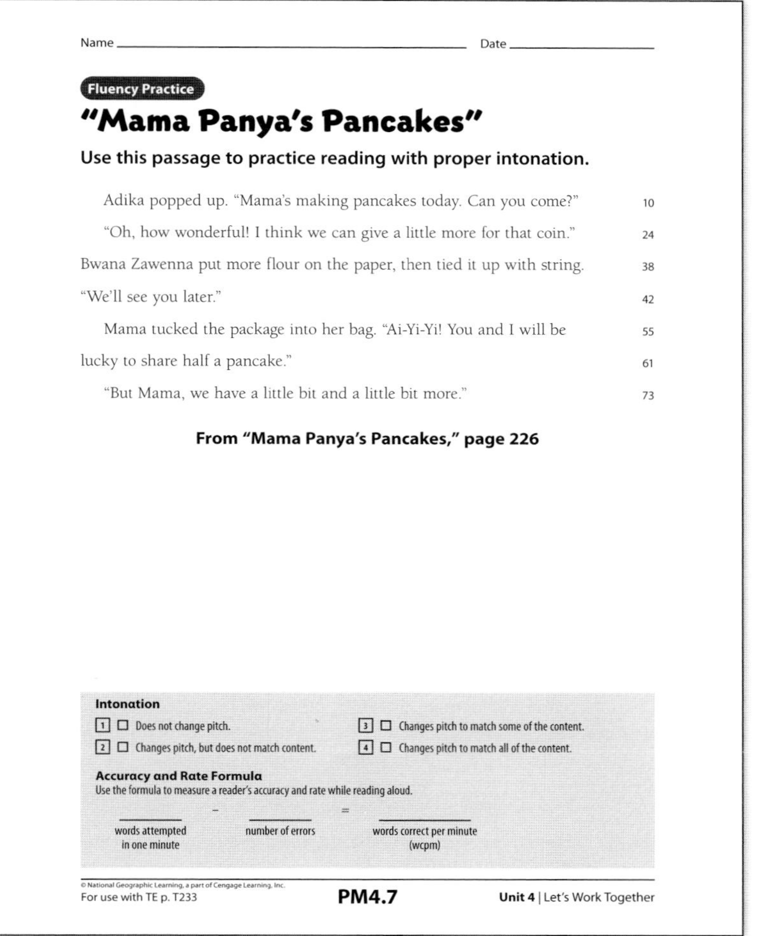

Name ______________________ Date ____________

Fluency Practice

"Mama Panya's Pancakes"

Use this passage to practice reading with proper intonation.

Adika popped up. "Mama's making pancakes today. Can you come?" 10

"Oh, how wonderful! I think we can give a little more for that coin." 24

Bwana Zawenna put more flour on the paper, then tied it up with string. 38

"We'll see you later." 42

Mama tucked the package into her bag. "Ai-Yi-Yi! You and I will be 55

lucky to share half a pancake." 61

"But Mama, we have a little bit and a little bit more." 73

From "Mama Panya's Pancakes," page 226

Intonation

1 ☐ Does not change pitch.
2 ☐ Changes pitch, but does not match content.
3 ☐ Changes pitch to match some of the content.
4 ☐ Changes pitch to match all of the content.

Accuracy and Rate Formula

Use the formula to measure a reader's accuracy and rate while reading aloud.

______ − ______ = ______

words attempted in one minute − number of errors = words correct per minute (wcpm)

Page PM4.7

Name ______________________ Date ____________

Grammar: Reteach

A Fair Trade

Grammar Rules Subject-Verb Agreement with Present Tense

A **present-tense action verb** tells about an action that happens now or all the time.	The baker **reads** the recipe. "It **lists** cinnamon!" he **yells** to an assistant.
To show present tense for the subject **he**, **she**, or **it**, add *-s* or *-es* to most action verbs.	She **adds** cinnamon to the bowl. He **mixes** the bread dough. It bakes in the oven.

Circle the present-tense verb that completes each sentence.

1. A girl sits near the bakery. She (sniff/sniffs) the cinnamon scent.
2. The baker stomps up to her. He (glares/glare) at the young girl.
3. Then he (demand/demands), "You pay for enjoying the scent!"
4. The girl says, "It smells wonderful!" She (find/finds) her only coin.
5. She (tosses/toss) the coin, and it (sparkles/sparkle) in the light.
6. He (catches/catch) the coin and (twirl/twirls) it happily.
7. Then he (flip/flips) it high in the air, and the girl grabs the coin.
8. The baker says, "It belongs to me!" and he (step/steps) closer.
9. "I smelled the cinnamon. You felt the coin." The girl (grin/grins).
10. The baker frowns. Suddenly, he (flashes/flash) a smile. "It *is* a fair trade."

Tell a partner about an event or a trade that is fair. Include present-tense action verbs, and use *he*, *she*, and *it*.

Page PM4.8

Name ______________________ Date ____________

Grammar: Game

Apply the -*y* Rules

Directions:

A.B. **scurry**
scurries

1. Choose a game box that has not been filled in.
2. Use the correct present tense of the verb in a sentence with *he*, *she*, or *it*. Then spell the verb aloud.
3. If other players agree with the spelling, write the word and your initials in the box. If the spelling is wrong, leave the box blank.
4. Players take turns. When all boxes are taken, count your boxes. The player with the most boxes is the winner.

try	**say**	**study**
tries	says	studies
rely	**pay**	**buy**
relies	pays	buys
bury	**cry**	**carry**
buries	cries	carries
annoy	**play**	**fly**
annoys	plays	flies
stay	**hurry**	**employ**
stays	hurries	employs

Page PM4.9

Name ______________________ Date ____________

Grammar: Game

Do They Agree?

SUBJECT Cards

1. Print I, YOU, WE, THEY, HE, SHE, IT on separate index cards.
2. Mix the SUBJECT cards up and stack them face down to play the game.

Directions:

1. Flip a coin. For heads, move 2 squares. For tails, move 1 square.
2. Pick a SUBJECT card and read it aloud. Choose the correct present-tense verb in the square to create a sentence with your subject. Then put the SUBJECT card at the bottom of the stack.
3. If the other players agree that your subject and verb agree, stay on your space. If not, move back one space.

						dash or dashes?	**END**
		explore or explores?	**trades or trade?**	**raise or raises?**		**study or studies?**	
		scurries or scurry?		**pay or pays?**		**hides or hide?**	
		works or work?		**buys or buy?**		**finds or find?**	
	hurries or hurry?	**help or helps?**		**move or moves?**	**sells or sell?**	**buzz or buzzes?**	
START	**go or goes?**						

Page PM4.10

Name ______________________ Date ____________

Comparison Chart

Compare Characters

Compare the characters from the two stories.

	Beginning of Story	End of Story	Why does the character change?
Mama Payna	She is worried about having enough food.	She is happy and having a good time.	She realizes that when everyone works together, she does not have to worry.
Ba	He is worried that he is not selling any egg tarts.	He is happy and excited about his good business.	His daughters worked together to find a way to sell more egg tarts.

Talk with a partner about which story you liked better and why.

Page PM4.11

Name ______________________ Date ____________

Grammar: Practice

Farmer's Market

Grammar Rules Present-Tense Action Verbs

A present-tense action verb must agree with its subject.

Use **-s** at the end of an action verb if the subject is ***he***, ***she***, or ***it***.	Carmella **loves** street fairs. She **takes** me along with her.
Do **not** add -*s* to the verb if the subject is ***I***, ***you***, ***we***, or ***they***.	Buyers **walk** slowly through the fairs. They **buy** a lot of things.

Fill in each blank with the present-tense verb form that agrees with the subject.

My parents _take_ (take) us to the farmer's market. We _enjoy_ (enjoy) all the sights, smells, and sounds. Farmers _sell_ (sell) vegetables and fruit. One farmer _sells_ (sell) flowers, too. My mother _buys_ (buy) flowers every week. She _loves_ (love) flowers. One man _cooks_ (cook) delicious burritos. A woman _paints_ (paint) faces. Two men _carve_ (carve) wooden toys. They _call_ (call) out to buyers. The farmer's market is so much fun! It _makes_ (make) me smile.

Choose three verbs from the story and write new sentences. Read them to a partner.

Page PM4.12

Name _______________ Date _______________

Mark-Up Reading

The Bird Bank

by Grace Lin

During the winter, Hannah and Rose earned nickels from their father. Sometimes they would shovel snow or sweep the house. Ba would give them each a nickel and they put the nickels in their green bird bank.

Every time Hannah and Rose put their nickels in the bird bank it would sing "Tweet! Tweet!"

But in the spring, the bird bank stopped singing. It would not swallow Rose's nickel.

"Hannah!" Rose said. "Our bird bank is full!"

Shopping

by Grace Lin

Hannah and Rose looked at all the stores. What should they buy?

"Look at the birds!" Rose said, pointing at a pet store window. "I like the yellow one."

"I like the blue one," Hannah said. "Let's go buy them!"

But Hannah and Rose did not have enough money for a yellow bird or a blue bird. On the shelf there was a birdhouse.

"We can buy the birdhouse," Rose said. "Should we buy that instead?"

Hannah nodded and they did.

Mark-Up Reading

Tweet! Tweet!

by Grace Lin

Hannah and Rose bought the birdhouse at the pet store.

"I'm glad you are buying a birdhouse," Mrs. Alexis, the store owner, said. "I have too many of them. No one else is buying them. I wonder why." She sighed sadly.

Hannah and Rose brought their birdhouse home.

"This is a nice birdhouse," Rose said to Hannah, "but it is too plain. Let's decorate it."

So, Hannah painted the birdhouse and Rose glued on pictures. When they were finished, the birdhouse was very pretty.

"I know why no one else is buying Mrs. Alexis's birdhouses," Rose said. "They are too plain! They need to be decorated."

"We should tell her," Hannah said. "Let's show her our birdhouse."

When Mrs. Alexis saw Hannah and Rose's decorated birdhouse, she was surprised.

"Could you decorate all of my birdhouses?" she said. "I will pay you for every birdhouse that sells."

So, Hannah and Rose decorated the other birdhouses. How pretty they were! Soon, many people began to buy them. Mrs. Alexis paid Hannah and Rose for their good work and was very happy.

Hannah and Rose put their new quarters and dimes into their bird bank. Two live birds came to live in their birdhouse. All of them sang "Tweet! Tweet!" for Hannah and Rose.

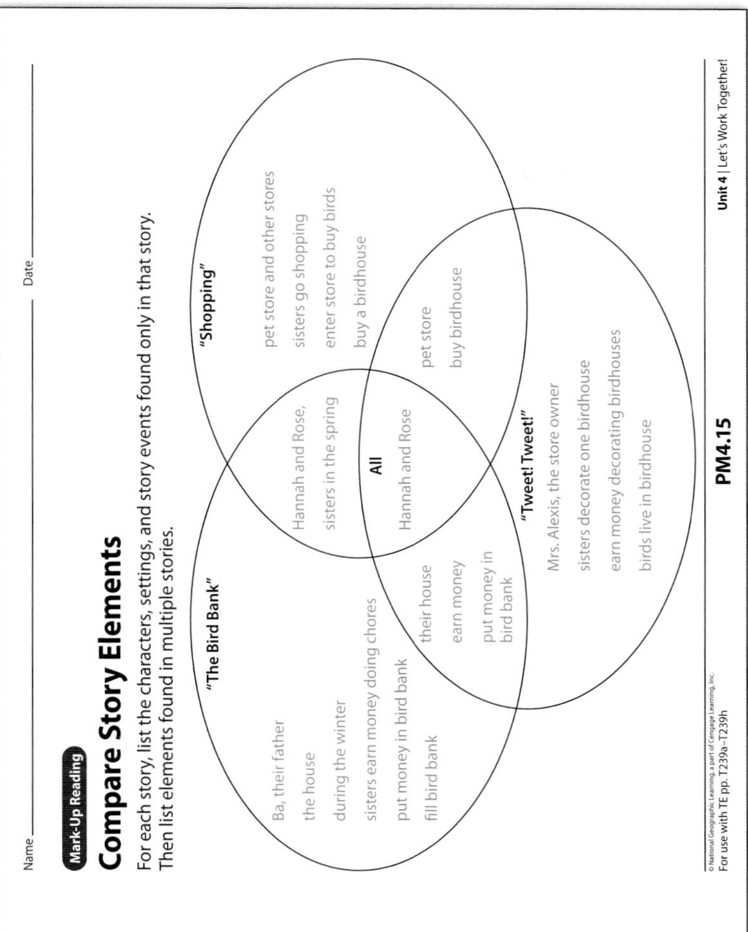
Name _______________ Date _______________

Mark-Up Reading

Compare Story Elements

For each story, list the characters, settings, and story events found only in that story. Then list elements found in multiple stories.

"The Bird Bank": Ba, their father; the house; during the winter; sisters earn money doing chores; put money in bird bank; fill bird bank

"Shopping": pet store and other stores; sisters go shopping; enter store to buy birds; buy a birdhouse

"Tweet! Tweet!": Mrs. Alexis, the store owner; sisters decorate one birdhouse; earn money decorating birdhouses; birds live in birdhouse

"The Bird Bank" and "Shopping": Hannah and Rose, sisters in the spring

"Shopping" and "Tweet! Tweet!": pet store; buy birdhouse

"The Bird Bank" and "Tweet! Tweet!": their house; earn money; put money in bird bank

All: Hannah and Rose

Name _______________ Date _______________

Grammar: Grammar and Writing

Edit and Proofread

Choose the Editing and Proofreading Marks you need to correct the passage. Look for correct usage of the following:

- present-tense action verbs
- subject-verb agreement
- correct spelling of verbs

Editing and Proofreading Marks

Mark	Meaning
∧	Add.
ᒧ	Take out.
≡	Capitalize.
⊙	Add period.

"Have you finished the patchwork quilt?" Lee asks Kendra.

"No," she repl~~y~~ies holding it up. "It won't be ready for Mama's birthday. It need[s] another row, but I ran out of material."

"If you require~~s~~ material, I'll get it," Lee promises. He dash[e]s out. Neighbors help, but they add~~s~~ only a few scraps to his bag. He go[es] to Ms. Cotton. She explains, "I buy~~s~~ material for my store! Here, you ~~carries~~ carry these back to Kendra."

When Kendra sees the cloth, she exclaim[s], "Look at this special piece, Lee. It shine[s] like a pool of water!" Kendra tells Lee, "Now the quilt can be ready! We make~~s~~ a good team, brother!"

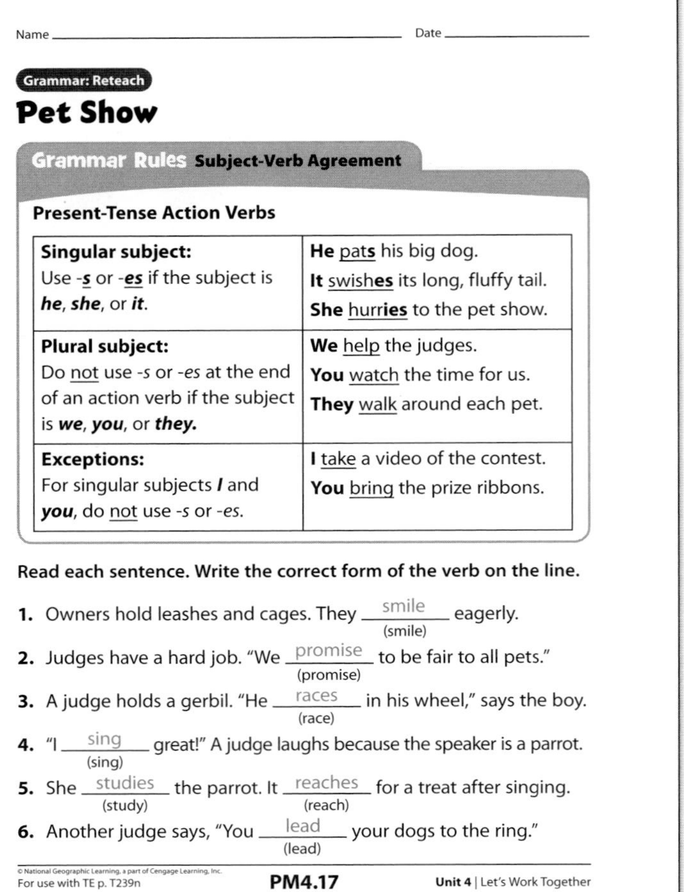

Name ________________ Date ________

Grammar: Reteach

Pet Show

Grammar Rules **Subject-Verb Agreement**

Present-Tense Action Verbs

Singular subject: Use -***s*** or -***es*** if the subject is ***he***, ***she***, or ***it***.	**He** pats his big dog. **It** swishes its long, fluffy tail. **She** hurries to the pet show.
Plural subject: Do not use -*s* or -*es* at the end of an action verb if the subject is ***we***, ***you***, or ***they***.	**We** help the judges. **You** watch the time for us. **They** walk around each pet.
Exceptions: For singular subjects ***I*** and ***you***, do not use -*s* or -*es*.	**I** take a video of the contest. **You** bring the prize ribbons.

Read each sentence. Write the correct form of the verb on the line.

1. Owners hold leashes and cages. They smile (smile) eagerly.
2. Judges have a hard job. "We promise (promise) to be fair to all pets."
3. A judge holds a gerbil. "He races (race) in his wheel," says the boy.
4. "I sing (sing) great!" A judge laughs because the speaker is a parrot.
5. She studies (study) the parrot. It reaches (reach) for a treat after singing.
6. Another judge says, "You lead (lead) your dogs to the ring."

© National Geographic Learning, a part of Cengage Learning, Inc.
For use with TE p. T239n PM4.17 Unit 4 | Let's Work Together

Page PM4.17

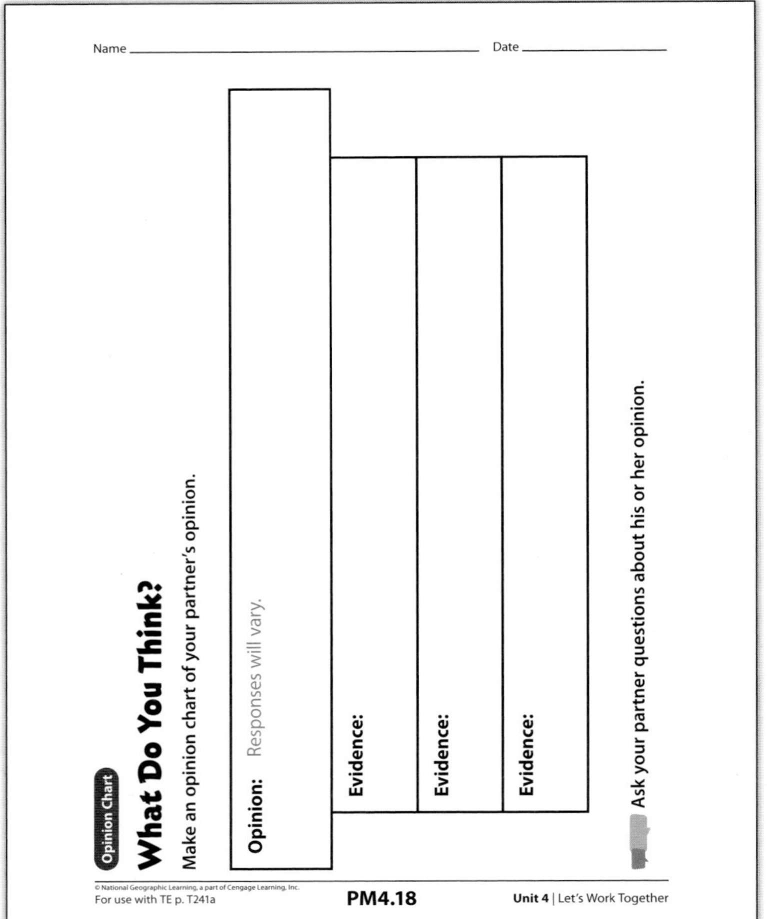

Name ________________ Date ________

Opinion Chart

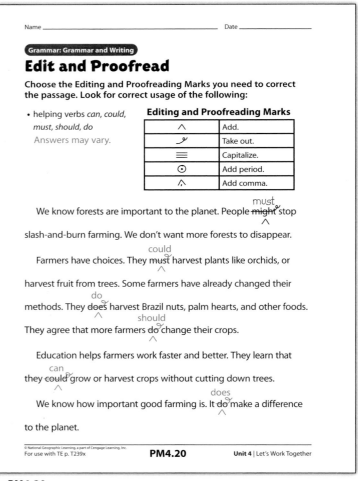

What Do You Think?

Make an opinion chart of your partner's opinion.

Opinion: Responses will vary.	
	Evidence:
	Evidence:
	Evidence:

Ask your partner questions about his or her opinion.

© National Geographic Learning, a part of Cengage Learning, Inc.
For use with TE p. T241a PM4.18 Unit 4 | Let's Work Together

Page PM4.18

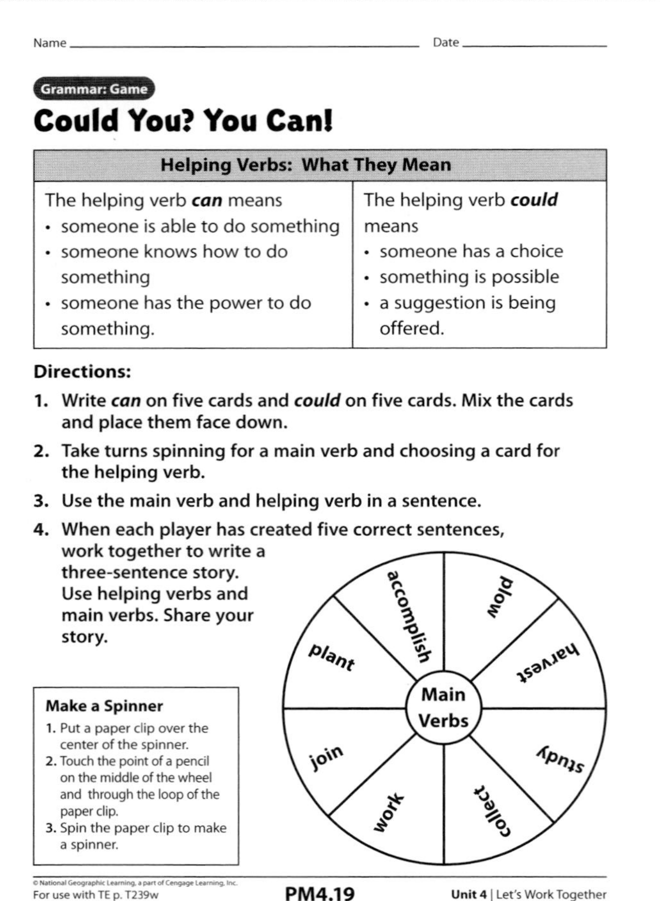

Name ________________ Date ________

Grammar: Game

Could You? You Can!

Helping Verbs: What They Mean	
The helping verb ***can*** means • someone is able to do something • someone knows how to do something • someone has the power to do something.	The helping verb ***could*** means • someone has a choice • something is possible • a suggestion is being offered.

Directions:

1. **Write *can* on five cards and *could* on five cards. Mix the cards and place them face down.**
2. **Take turns spinning for a main verb and choosing a card for the helping verb.**
3. **Use the main verb and helping verb in a sentence.**
4. **When each player has created five correct sentences, work together to write a three-sentence story. Use helping verbs and main verbs. Share your story.**

Make a Spinner
1. Put a paper clip over the center of the spinner.
2. Touch the point of a pencil on the middle of the wheel and through the loop of the paper clip.
3. Spin the paper clip to make a spinner.

© National Geographic Learning, a part of Cengage Learning, Inc.
For use with TE p. T239w PM4.19 Unit 4 | Let's Work Together

Page PM4.19

Name ________________ Date ________

Grammar: Grammar and Writing

Edit and Proofread

Choose the Editing and Proofreading Marks you need to correct the passage. Look for correct usage of the following:

- helping verbs *can, could, must, should, do*

Answers may vary.

Editing and Proofreading Marks

∧	Add.
~~ ~~	Take out.
≡	Capitalize.
⊙	Add period.
∧,	Add comma.

We know forests are important to the planet. People ~~might~~ must stop slash-and-burn farming. We don't want more forests to disappear.

Farmers have choices. They ~~must~~ could harvest plants like orchids, or harvest fruit from trees. Some farmers have already changed their methods. They ~~does~~ do harvest Brazil nuts, palm hearts, and other foods. They agree that more farmers ~~do~~ should change their crops.

Education helps farmers work faster and better. They learn that they ~~could~~ can grow or harvest crops without cutting down trees.

We know how important good farming is. It ~~do~~ does make a difference to the planet.

© National Geographic Learning, a part of Cengage Learning, Inc.
For use with TE p. T239x PM4.20 Unit 4 | Let's Work Together

Page PM4.20

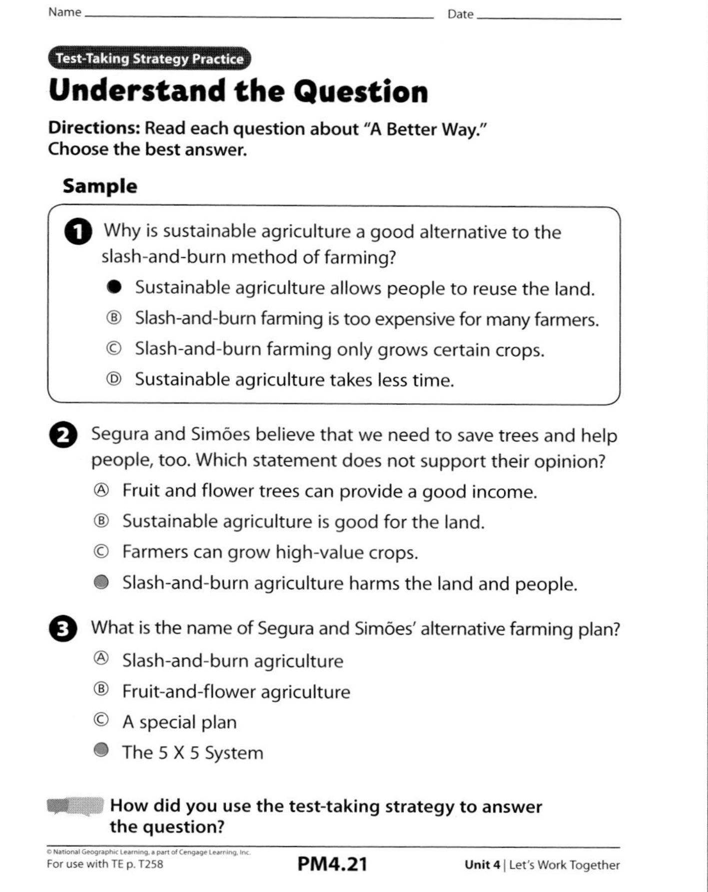

Name ______________________ Date ____________

Test-Taking Strategy Practice

Understand the Question

Directions: Read each question about "A Better Way." Choose the best answer.

Sample

1. Why is sustainable agriculture a good alternative to the slash-and-burn method of farming?
   - ● Sustainable agriculture allows people to reuse the land.
   - Ⓑ Slash-and-burn farming is too expensive for many farmers.
   - Ⓒ Slash-and-burn farming only grows certain crops.
   - Ⓓ Sustainable agriculture takes less time.

2. Segura and Simões believe that we need to save trees and help people, too. Which statement does not support their opinion?
   - Ⓐ Fruit and flower trees can provide a good income.
   - Ⓑ Sustainable agriculture is good for the land.
   - Ⓒ Farmers can grow high-value crops.
   - ● Slash-and-burn agriculture harms the land and people.

3. What is the name of Segura and Simões' alternative farming plan?
   - Ⓐ Slash-and-burn agriculture
   - Ⓑ Fruit-and-flower agriculture
   - Ⓒ A special plan
   - ● The 5 X 5 System

How did you use the test-taking strategy to answer the question?

Page PM4.21

Name ______________________ Date ____________

Opinion Chart

"A Better Way"

Make an opinion chart for pages 254-257 in "A Better Way."

Opinion: Sustainable agriculture is good for the farmer and good for the land.

Evidence: It lets farmers grow crops on the same land year after year.

Evidence: Farmers don't have to clear new land.

Evidence: Farmers can continue to farm instead of moving to the city.

Explain the opinion and evidence to a partner.

Page PM4.22

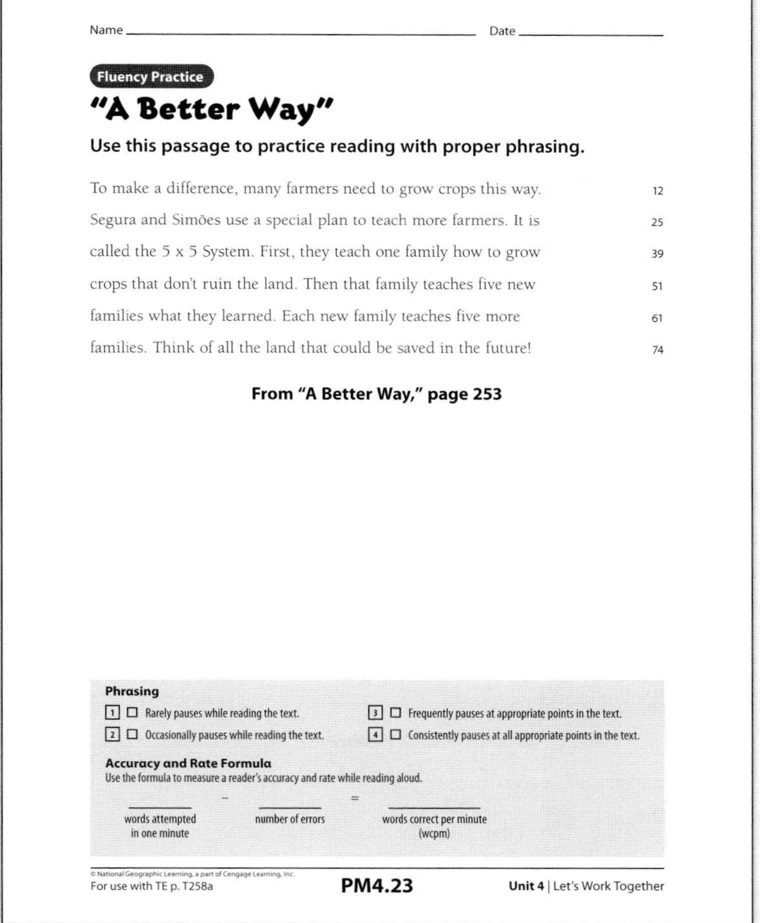

Name ______________________ Date ____________

Fluency Practice

"A Better Way"

Use this passage to practice reading with proper phrasing.

To make a difference, many farmers need to grow crops this way. 12
Segura and Simões use a special plan to teach more farmers. It is 25
called the 5 x 5 System. First, they teach one family how to grow 39
crops that don't ruin the land. Then that family teaches five new 51
families what they learned. Each new family teaches five more 61
families. Think of all the land that could be saved in the future! 74

From "A Better Way," page 253

Phrasing

1 ☐ Rarely pauses while reading the text.
2 ☐ Occasionally pauses while reading the text.
3 ☐ Frequently pauses at appropriate points in the text.
4 ☐ Consistently pauses at all appropriate points in the text.

Accuracy and Rate Formula

Use the formula to measure a reader's accuracy and rate while reading aloud.

______ words attempted in one minute − ______ number of errors = ______ words correct per minute (wcpm)

Page PM4.23

Name ______________________ Date ____________

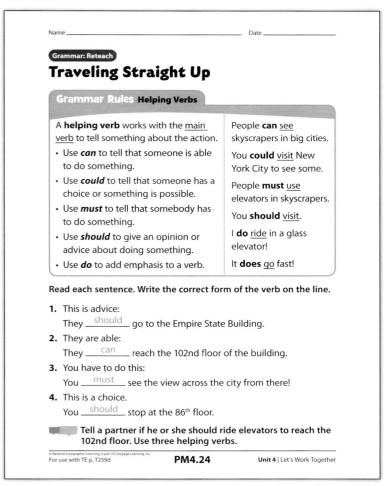

Grammar: Reteach

Traveling Straight Up

Grammar Rules Helping Verbs

A **helping verb** works with the main verb to tell something about the action. • Use ***can*** to tell that someone is able to do something. • Use ***could*** to tell that someone has a choice or something is possible. • Use ***must*** to tell that somebody has to do something. • Use ***should*** to give an opinion or advice about doing something. • Use ***do*** to add emphasis to a verb.	People **can** see skyscrapers in big cities. You **could** visit New York City to see some. People **must** use elevators in skyscrapers. You **should** visit. I **do** ride in a glass elevator! It **does** go fast!

Read each sentence. Write the correct form of the verb on the line.

1. This is advice:
   They should go to the Empire State Building.
2. They are able:
   They can reach the 102nd floor of the building.
3. You have to do this:
   You must see the view across the city from there!
4. This is a choice.
   You should stop at the 86th floor.

Tell a partner if he or she should ride elevators to reach the 102nd floor. Use three helping verbs.

Page PM4.24

Name ______________________ Date ____________

Grammar: Game

Be What You Want to Be

Directions:

1. Take five minutes to write as many sentences as your team can. For each sentence, use a subject from column 1, the correct form of *to be*, and a word or phrase from column 2.
2. Your team will get one point for each sentence it writes correctly.
3. You may choose one or all subjects in a box to use in sentences. For example, if you write one correct sentence with *he*, another with *she*, and another with *it*, you gain three points! You can also use words in column 2 more than once.
4. When time's up, trade sentences with another team, check each other's work, and add up points. The team with most points wins.

Forms of *To Be*		
am	is	are

Subject	What the Subject Is or What the Subject is Like
I	challenging
He, She, It	a hard worker
You	curious
We, They	busy
Problems	thoughtful
An ant | Ants	delicious
A grasshopper	nine years old
A kernel | Kernels	playful
An inventor | Inventors	bright yellow
An invention | Inventions	a problem solver

Page PM4.25

Name ______________________ Date ____________

Grammar: Game

Choose *Has* or *Have*

Directions:

1. Play with a partner. Take turns.
2. Place a game piece on START. Flip a coin. For heads, move ahead one space. For tails, move ahead two spaces.
3. Read the subject in the space. Create a sentence using the subject and the verb *has* or *have* to tell what the subject has. Or, use the verb *has* or *have* as a helping verb in a sentence. If your partner agrees that your sentence is correct, score one point.
4. When one player reaches the END, count your points to see who wins.

have	has	START	have	has	have	has	have	has
has		I						have
have		Paola						has
has		he	she	you	Ba	we		have
have		friends	I			it		has
has		it	they			Cid		have
have		we	you			they		has
has	have	has	have	has	have	END	has	have

Page PM4.26

Name ______________________ Date ____________

Comparison Chart

Compare Purposes

Compare authors' purposes in "A Better Way" and "The Ant and the Grasshopper."

Title	Topic	Author's Purpose
"A Better Way" by Juan Quintana	sustainable agriculture	to inform about a problem to teach a lesson about how to solve the problem to persuade the reader to agree with the solution
"The Ant and the Grasshopper" by Shirleyann Costigan	preparing for the future	to entertain to teach a life lesson or moral

Take turns with a partner telling how the authors' purposes are alike or different.

Page PM4.27

Name ______________________ Date ____________

Grammar: Practice

What Is in the Garden?

Grammar Rules Subject-Verb Agreement: *be* and *have*

The verbs *be* and *have* are irregular. The subject and verb must agree. Use these correct forms:

I am	We are	I have	We have
You are	You are	You have	You have
He, she, it is	They are	He, she, it has	They have

Write the correct form of be or have to complete each sentence. Choose the correct form for the subject.

Jenna and Jake __have__ a large garden. Jake's favorite vegetable __is__ corn. He __has__ several rows of corn in the garden. The corn __is__ almost ready to harvest. Both Jenna and Jake __are__ excited to roast ears of corn. They also grow tomatoes. Tomatoes __are__ their mother's favorite vegetable. Jenna planted sunflowers, too. They __have__ delicious seeds and pretty blooms.

I __am__ planning to help them pick some corn. I __have__ a basket I will take with me.

Imagine a garden. Tell your partner about it, using forms of *be* and *have*.

Page PM4.28

Name ________ Date ________

Mark-Up Reading

Belling the Cat

an Aesop fable retold by Katie Blankshain

Long ago, a large family of mice lived in an old blue house. They chattered happily that they had all the food and warmth they could ever need. There was just one problem. They worried that their enemy the cat was becoming more dangerous every day.

Every day, the cat would tiptoe through the gray shadows, stepping lightly with her furry feet. She would slink and creep, grinning to herself as she went. She waited until she was right behind the poor mice. Then—POUNCE—she would trap one of the mice in her big orange paws. "You'll make a delicious dinner for me tonight!" the cat would say, purring.

Her cruel trick never failed, and so the cat never went hungry. She began to grow quite fat and content. Sometimes she would pop out from behind corners, baring her white, pointy teeth and sharp claws, just to scare the helpless mice away.

Explain these viewpoints:

1. the mice They are happy but worried about the cat.
2. the cat She thinks the mice are delicious, so she likes to catch and eat them.
3. the narrator The cat is cruel. The mice are helpless.

Page PM4.29

Name ________ Date ________

Mark-Up Reading

Belling the Cat (continued)

One night, the oldest mouse called a meeting. "Fellow mice!" he cried. "We have lived in fear of the cat for too long. She must be stopped. Who has a plan? We might be smaller than the cat, but surely we can outwit her."

Everyone was silent for a long while. At last, a young mouse stood up. "The cat only catches us because she is very sneaky. If we knew when cat was coming, we could certainly run away in time." The small mouse held up a large red collar. "Here is my plan: we should attach a small bell to the cat using this collar. This way, the bell will ring whenever the cat moves. She will never sneak up on us again!" All of the mice joyfully applauded this idea.

Then an old mouse slowly rose to his feet. "That is a good idea, but who is to put the bell on the cat?" All of the mice looked around, but no one spoke. No mouse wanted to volunteer for such a dangerous mission.

MORAL: Actions speak louder than words.

Explain these viewpoints:

1. the mice They fear the sneaky cat and agree they must stop her. They like the idea of belling the cat, but no one is willing to do it.
2. the narrator The mice don't want to do anything so dangerous. All the mice think it's a good idea until they are asked to try it.

Page PM4.30

Name ________ Date ________

Grammar: Grammar and Writing

Edit and Proofread

Choose the Editing and Proofreading Marks you need to correct the passage. Look for correct usage of the following:

- subject-verb agreement with forms of *be*
- subject-verb agreement with forms of *have*

Editing and Proofreading Marks

Mark	Meaning
∧	Add.
℘	Take out.
≡	Capitalize.
⊙	Add period.
∧,	Add comma.

Ella Ant ~~are~~ is unhappy. She is on one side of some flowing water. Tempting smells come from the other side. "I ~~is~~ am hungry, but I ~~are~~ am not a swimmer," she says. She ~~have~~ has no boat.

"Ants ~~is~~ are clever," thinks Ella. "We ~~has~~ have problem-solving skills." She looks around. "Ah, leaves ~~is~~ are good boats. They ~~has~~ have the ability to float." She invents a two-leaf boat to carry back food. She pushes it into the water, but it quickly floats away.

Grasshopper hops into view. "You ~~am~~ are eager to be on the other side, I see," he says. "I ~~has~~ have a solution for you."

With Ella on his back, Grasshopper leaps across the water. Together they follow the tempting smells.

Page PM4.31

Name ________ Date ________

Grammar: Reteach

The Science Museum

Grammar Rules Forms of *Be* and *Have*

- The linking verb ***to be*** tells what a subject is or is like.
- The verb ***to be*** has irregular forms.

I **am**	we **are**
you **are**	you **are**
she, he, it **is**	they **are**

- The verb ***to have*** can tell what the subject of a sentence has.
- The verb ***to have*** has irregular forms.

I **have**	we **have**
you **have**	you **have**
she, he, it **has**	they **have**

Read each sentence. Write the correct verb from the box. Then read your sentences again to make sure the subjects and verbs agree.

am	is	are	has	have

1. This science museum has many exciting inventions.
2. The can opener is one of the most practical ones.
3. Science certainly has come a long way!
4. Inventions have changed our lives.
5. Our lives are easier because of them.
6. Inventions are created by clever people.
7. I am hoping someday to invent something.
8. Jenna says she is going to invent something, too.

Tell a partner what inventions you think are interesting. Use at least one *be* verb and one *have* verb.

Page PM4.32

Books at a Glance

LEXILE KEY

BL Below Level = 250L–400L
BL Below Level = 400L–550L
OL On Level = 550L–700L
AL Above Level = 700L–850L

Week	Days	Level* & Title	Author	Content Connection	Pages
Week 1 Community	DAY 1	Explorer Books, ***Our Human Footprint*** BL Pioneer Edition OL Pathfinder Edition	Barbara H. Seeber	Good Citizenship	SG4–SG5
	DAYS 2–5	BL ***The Runaway Rice Cake***	Ying Chang Compestine	Neighbors	SG6, SG8
		BL ***Under the Lemon Moon***	Edith Hope Fine	Neighbors	SG6, SG8
		OL ***Four Feet, Two Sandals***	Karen Lynn Williams	Strangers	SG7, SG9
		AL ***Sadako and the Thousand Paper Cranes***	Eleanor Coerr	Friends	SG7, SG9
Week 2 Jobs and Money	DAY 1	Explorer Books, ***Dogs at Work*** BL Pioneer Edition OL Pathfinder Edition	Terrell Smith	Community Service	SG10–SG11
	DAYS 2–5	BL ***Grandpa's Corner Store***	DyAnne DiSalvo-Ryan	Running a Business	SG12, SG14
		BL ***Uncle Willie and the Soup Kitchen***	DyAnne DiSalvo-Ryan	Community Service	SG12, SG14
		OL ***Pitching in for Eubie***	Jerdine Nolen	Fundraising	SG13, SG15
		AL ***My Rows and Piles of Coins***	Tololwa Mollel	Saving Money	SG13, SG15
Week 3 Goods and Services	DAY 1	Explorer Books, ***Working Hand in Hand*** BL Pioneer Edition OL Pathfinder Edition	Diane G. Silver	Sustainable Use of Animal Resources	SG16–SG17
	DAYS 2–5	BL ***Making Water Clean***	Rebecca Olien	Clean Water	SG18, SG20
		BL ***Farmers: Then and Now***	Lisa Zamosky	Agriculture	SG18, SG20
		OL ***A Weed is a Flower***	Aliki	Agriculture	SG19, SG21
		AL ***Ryan and Jimmy: And the Well in Africa That Brought Them Together***	Herb Shoveller	Clean Water	SG19, SG21
Week 4 Innovation	DAY 1	Explorer Books, ***First Flight*** BL Pioneer Edition OL Pathfinder Edition	Glen Phelan	Technology	SG22–SG23
	DAYS 2–5	BL ***All Aboard! Elijah McCoy's Steam Engine***	Monica Kulling	Technology	SG24, SG26
		BL ***Levi Strauss and Blue Jeans***	Nathan Olson	Fashion	SG24, SG26
		OL ***Marvelous Mattie: How Margaret E. Knight Became an Inventor***	Emily Arnold McCully	Industry	SG25, SG27
		AL ***The Boy Who Invented TV: The Story of Philo Farnsworth***	Kathleen Krull	Entertainment	

*See page R2 for Guided Reading (GR) and other leveling translation information.

Unit 4 Reading Routines

Fiction & Nonfiction

PROGRAM RESOURCES

PRINT ONLY

Fiction and Nonfiction Books

PRINT & TECHNOLOGY

Unit 3 Assessment Masters: SG3.29–SG3.32

Unit 4 Practice Masters: SG4.1–SG4.28

Unit 4 Assessment Masters: SG4.29–SG4.32

TECHNOLOGY ONLY

My Vocabulary Notebook

WEEK 1 Fiction

WEEK 2 Fiction

WEEK 3 Nonfiction

WEEK 4 Nonfiction

Introduce

Assign books. Use the summaries of the books in the Teaching Resources for an overview of content. Analyze the Unit 3 **Assessment Masters** and your conference notes to assign books according to students' interests and reading levels.

Introduce books. Activate prior knowledge and build background for the books, using the Teaching Resources. Remind students that all of the books connect to the Big Question: *What's the best way to get things done?*

Introduce vocabulary. Use **Vocabulary Routine 1** to teach the story words for each book.

1. **Display** the words for each book.
2. **Pronounce** each word.
3. Have students **rate** each word, holding up their fingers to show how well they know the word (1 = very well; 2 = a little; 3 = not at all). Ask: *What do you know about this word?*
4. Have students **define** each word, using the Story Words **Practice Masters**, for example: *To **decide** means to make a choice or a judgment.*
5. Relate each word to students' knowledge and experience. *The teacher will **decide** who wins the drawing contest.* Have students work in pairs to **elaborate**.
6. Have students **record** each word in **My Vocabulary Notebook**.

*For **Vocabulary Routine 1**, see page BP46.*

Read and Integrate Ideas

Have students read independently. Circulate to observe students as they read. Ask individuals to read sections aloud. Note any miscues as they read, and encourage students to self-correct. Model by asking questions like: *Did that make sense in the sentence? You said ____. Does that sound right?*

Monitor students' understanding. As students read, have them complete the Graphic Organizer **Practice Master** for their books. Prompt them to show you where in the books they gathered the information to complete their organizers.

Form homogeneous discussion groups. Group students who have read the same book. Distribute the Discussion Guide **Practice Master** for that book to each group member.

Monitor group discussions. Have students discuss the book they read, using the questions on the Discussion Guide. Use the build comprehension questions in the Teaching Resources to develop higher-order thinking skills. See the Discussion Guide Answer Keys on pages SG60–SG67.

Provide writing options. Have each student complete one of the writing options from the Teaching Resources. Encourage students to share their writing with their group.

BEFORE READING

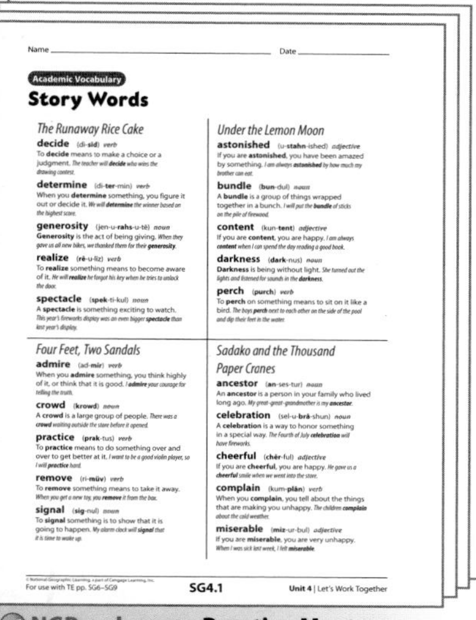
Academic Vocabulary

Story Words

The Runaway Rice Cake: decide, determine, generosity, realize, spectacle

Under the Lemon Moon: astonished, bundle, content, darkness, perch

Four Feet, Two Sandals: admire, crowd, practice, remove, signal

Sadako and the Thousand Paper Cranes: ancestor, celebration, cheerful, complain, miserable

SG4.1 Unit 4 | Let's Work Together

NGReach.com **Practice Masters**
SG4.1, SG4.8, SG4.15, SG4.22

AFTER READING

Speaking and Listening Observation Log

SG4.29

NGReach.com
Assessment Master SG4.29

DURING CONFERENCES

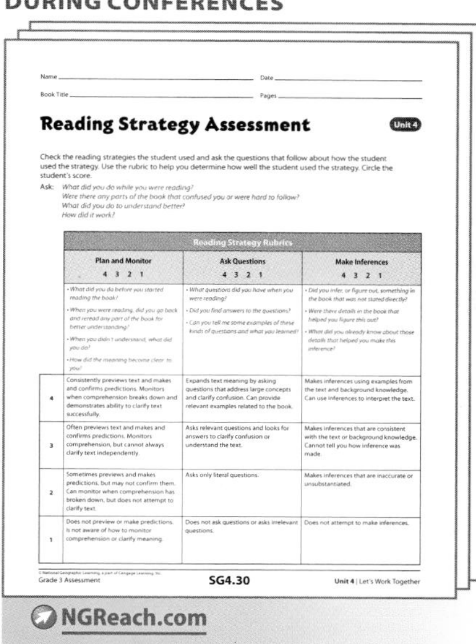
Reading Strategy Assessment

Reading Strategy Rubrics: Plan and Monitor, Ask Questions, Make Inferences

SG4.30

NGReach.com
Assessment Masters SG4.30–SG4.32

Connect Across Texts

Form heterogeneous groups. Group students who have read different books. Include at least one representative for each book read that week.

Introduce the activity. Distribute the Connect Across Texts **Practice Master** for the week. Explain to each group that they will share the books they read, talk about their themes, and discuss what the books say about working together.

Have students summarize. Ask students to summarize the books they just read, including new story words that helped them understand the themes and content. Have them refer to their graphic organizers as they share their books with the group.

Have students connect across texts. Have groups use the questions provided on the Connect Across Texts **Practice Masters** to guide discussions. See the Discussion Guide Answer Keys for possible responses.

Monitor groups. Use Unit 4 Speaking and Listening Observation Log **Assessment Master SG4.29** to assess students' participation in discussions.

Conduct Conferences

Assess reading. Have each student select and read aloud from a section of the book that connects to the Big Question. Listen for fluency. Ask: *Which strategies did you use to help you understand this section?* Use the reading strategy rubrics on **Assessment Masters SG4.30–SG4.31** to assess how well the student uses the reading strategies. Then have the student complete Reader Reflection **Assessment Master SG4.32**.

Assess writing. Have the student share a completed writing option. Say: *Tell me about what you wrote.* Monitor responses to gauge how well the writing relates to the book. Ask: *How did your writing help you understand the book?*

Plan intervention or acceleration. Ask the student to summarize what he or she has learned. Plan for further instruction:

- If the student needs additional support with identifying theme, determining importance, describing story elements, summarizing, or determining author's purpose, use the Assessment and Reteaching resources provided on pages RT4.1–RT4.14.
- If the student successfully applies the focus skills, use the Recommended Books on page SG68 to guide the student in choosing books for independent reading.

= one student = small group = four students

OBJECTIVES

Thematic Connection: Community

Read and Comprehend Informational Text

Use Visuals to Comprehend Text

Our Human Footprint by Barbara H. Seeber

Summary *Our Human Footprint* describes how human activities impact our planet Earth and how people can reduce their human footprint—the amount of things they buy, use, and throw away. In "Our Human Footprint," Barbara H. Seeber explains that people in the U.S. create tons of trash and use up lots of natural resources. People also put huge amounts of carbon dioxide into the air when they use energy. Seeber describes changes she can make in her daily habits to help keep Earth healthy. She also describes what others are doing worldwide to help Earth. One German artist creates art from trash, and college students use trash to make school supplies. "How Big Is Your Footprint?" describes ways to save water, replace plastic bags with reusable bags, and recycle.

Activate Prior Knowledge Display the front cover and ask: *How can people work together to take care of planet Earth?* (Possible responses: do not litter or pollute; recycle; use resources wisely)

Build Background Explain that every action has an effect on Earth. Actions with bad effects include creating trash, wasting resources, and putting lots of carbon dioxide into the air. Actions with good effects include conserving resources and reducing waste. Use the photos on pages 6–7 to discuss how these objects affect Earth. Have volunteers describe each photo and tell how they think it relates to Earth's resources.

PROGRAM RESOURCES

PRINT ONLY

***Our Human Footprint*, Pioneer Edition**

***Our Human Footprint*, Pathfinder Edition**

TECHNOLOGY ONLY

My Vocabulary Notebook

COMMON CORE STANDARDS

Reading	
Use Illustrations	CC.3.Rinf.7
Read and Comprehend Informational Text	CC.3.Rinf.10
Language	
cquire and Use Domain-Specific Words	CC.3.L.6

Mini Lesson

Use Visuals to Comprehend Text

Explain: *Often, nonfiction texts present information in a visual way to explain key points in the text and to add information. Such visual information may appear in photos and diagrams.* Point out that good readers know how to use visuals to understand a text.

Read aloud the following text from page 4 of the Pioneer Edition of *Our Human Footprint* as students listen.

> I had no idea how the things I do add up.
>
> This is called my human footprint. That's the stuff I buy, use, or throw away.

Text from Pioneer Edition

Then, think aloud to model how to use visual information: *The author says she had no idea how the things she buys, uses, or throws away add up. I will use the information in the diagram caption, labels, and photos on pages 4–5 to better understand how much stuff people use and throw away in a lifetime. The diagram caption says:*

- *An average person in the U.S. uses a lot in a lifetime.*

The diagram labels and photos add specific examples:

- *5,054 newspapers; the photo shows huge piles of newspaper*
- *13,056 pints of milk; the photo shows a huge line of milk crates*

By using the information in the diagram caption along with the examples in the labels and photos, I can understand and explain the vast amounts of stuff a person uses and throws away in a lifetime.

Have students use the visual information and the information from the text above to identify the total amount of other things people use and throw away. Then have students summarize what they learned from the text and photos of the diagram. (Possible response: An average person eats 14,518 candy bars. The photo shows five shopping carts full of candy wrappers. This is a huge amount of trash.)

BL BELOW LEVEL 430L

PIONEER EDITION

Lexile: 430L

Content Connection: Good Citizenship

Social Studies Vocabulary

Use Wordwise on page 9 to introduce new words:

carbon footprint energy landfill litter recycle

Have students add new words to **My Vocabulary Notebook**.

Build Comprehension

After reading, use the Concept Check on page 12. Remind students to use details and examples to support each answer.

1. **Main Idea** What three things make up a person's human footprint? (Creation of trash, use of natural resources, and release of CO_2 make up a human footprint.)
2. **Explain** What happens to trash after people throw it away? (Most of it is buried in landfills. Some trash is burned. Some ends up in the ocean.)
3. **Evaluate** What are the three best ways to shrink your human footprint? Tell why you think so. (Possible response: Buy things with less packaging. This makes less trash. Buy only what I need. This saves resources. Use low-watt light bulbs. This saves energy.)
4. **Details** What things do people make from recycled trash? (Some college students turn trash from schools into school supplies and toys. An artist turns trash into art. Also, people make glass into bracelets and candy wrappers into bags.)
5. **Use Visuals** How does the diagram on page 11 help you understand the number of plastic bags that people use every year? (It shows that there are so many bags that they could stretch back and forth between Earth and the moon 400 times.)

OL ON LEVEL 690L

PATHFINDER EDITION

Lexile: 690L

Content Connection: Good Citizenship

Social Studies Vocabulary

Use Wordwise on page 9 to introduce new words:

carbon footprint consume decompose landfill recycle release

Have students add new words to **My Vocabulary Notebook**.

Build Comprehension

After reading, use the Concept Check on page 12. Remind students to use details and examples to support each answer.

1. **Main Idea** Describe the three things that make up a human footprint. (Creation of trash, use of natural resources, and release of CO_2 make up a human footprint.)
2. **Explain** What happens to trash after it is thrown away? (Most trash is buried in landfills. Some trash is burned. Some trash ends up in the sea.)
3. **Evaluate** In your opinion, what are the three best ways to shrink your human footprint? Explain your choices. (Possible response: Use reusable bags. This makes less trash. Take short showers. This saves water. Ride a bike. This saves energy.)
4. **Details** What are some ways that people around the world reuse trash? (Possible response: College students turn trash into school supplies and toys. An artist turns trash into art. A factory in Australia recycles 75 percent of Australia's trash.)
5. **Use Visuals** How does the diagram on page 11 help you understand the quantity of plastic bags used in a year? (It shows that the number of bags could stretch back and forth between Earth and the moon 400 times.)

Check & Reteach

OBJECTIVE: Use Visuals to Comprehend Text

Have partners use "Trash Travels" on page 4 and the photo of the barge on page 5 to explain how much trash people create in the U.S. (Possible response: [Text] Each person throws out about five pounds a day. [Photo] There is so much trash in the U.S. that it is sent to other countries.) For students who cannot use visual information, reteach with the photo on page 8. Remind students that the text says that an artist turns trash into art and sets up his Trash People all over the world. Say: *The photo shows the artist's work. What does the photo tell you about the art and the artist's message?* Have students look at the photo. Make a class list of information students gather from the photo. (Possible response: It takes a lot of trash to make the art; the artist sets up his art in nature.) Have students use information from the photo and the text to explain the art. (Possible response: It shows how much trash people throw away and how trash can ruin nature.)

Week 1 Teaching Resources
Fiction

BL BELOW LEVEL AD300L

The Runaway Rice Cake
by Ying Chang Compestine

Content Connection:
Neighbors

Historical Fiction | Pages: 32 | Lexile: AD300L | GR: J

OBJECTIVES

Thematic Connection: Community

Read and Comprehend Literature

- ☑ **Theme**
- ☑ **Determine Importance**

PROGRAM RESOURCES

PRINT & TECHNOLOGY

Practice Master SG4.1, page SG28
Practice Master SG4.2, page SG29
Practice Master SG4.3, page SG30
Practice Master SG4.7, page SG34

TECHNOLOGY ONLY

Digital Library: Chinese Kitchen God

SUGGESTED PACING

DAY 2 Introduce and read pages 2–19
DAY 3 Read pages 20–32 and discuss
DAY 4 Reteach or conduct intervention
DAY 5 Connect across texts

Summary The Chang family is poor, but they make the traditional rice cake, *nián-gāo*, for a Chinese New Year treat. But their rice cake comes alive when the oven is opened, and it runs away. They chase it through the village until it comes to a hungry old woman. The Changs decide to give their only rice cake to the old woman. When others hear about how the Changs lost their holiday meal, they all bring food for them, and the whole village shares a magical, growing feast.

Activate Prior Knowledge Ask: *What are some traditional foods you and your family share on special holidays?*

Build Background Display the photo of the Chinese kitchen god from the **Digital Library**. Explain that many Chinese people hang a picture of the Chinese kitchen god, Tsao Chun, above their stoves. They believe that each year Tsao Chun tells the Jade Emperor in heaven about the family's good and bad deeds. This report affects the luck the family will have next year.

Story Words Use **Practice Master SG4.1** to extend vocabulary.

decide, page 3 | *determine*, page 32 | *generosity*, page 26
realize, page 20 | *spectacle*, page 30

BL BELOW LEVEL 520L

Under the Lemon Moon
by Edith Hope Fine

Content Connection:
Neighbors

Realistic Fiction | Pages: 32 | Lexile: 520L | GR: N

PROGRAM RESOURCES

PRINT & TECHNOLOGY

Practice Master SG4.1, page SG28
Practice Master SG4.2, page SG29
Practice Master SG4.4, page SG31
Practice Master SG4.7, page SG34

TECHNOLOGY ONLY

Digital Library: Outdoor Market

SUGGESTED PACING

DAY 2 Introduce and read pages 4–17
DAY 3 Read pages 18–29 and discuss
DAY 4 Reteach or conduct intervention
DAY 5 Connect across texts

Summary Rosalinda awakes to find a man stealing lemons from her tree. When the tree gets sick, Rosalinda seeks the help of Anciana, The Old One, who is known to help things grow. On the way to find Anciana, Rosalinda sees the thief selling her lemons in the market. Anciana tells Rosalinda that the man was wrong to steal, but perhaps he was in need. She shows Rosalinda how to heal her tree. The next day, Rosalinda shares her lemons with everyone, including the apologetic thief.

Activate Prior Knowledge Ask: *Have you ever made a bad situation better by being kind? What happened?*

Build Background Display the photo of an outdoor market from the **Digital Library**. Explain that an outdoor market is a place where people can go to socialize and where local farmers and artisans can sell their products. Markets provide people with easy access to healthy foods, and they help keep money in the local community.

Story Words Use **Practice Master SG4.1** to extend vocabulary.

astonished, page 24 | *bundle*, page 9 | *content*, page 32
darkness, page 5 | *perch*, page 27

OL ON LEVEL 620L

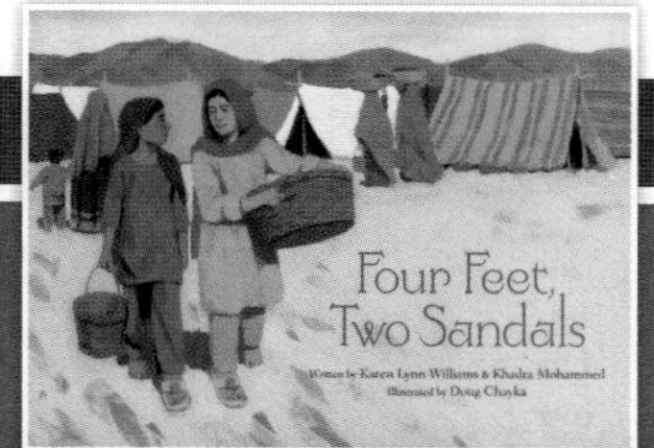

Four Feet, Two Sandals
by Karen Lynn Williams

Content Connection:
Strangers

Realistic Fiction | Pages: 32 | Lexile: 620L | GR: O

COMMON CORE STANDARDS

Reading

Determine the Central Message	CC.3.Rlit.2
Read and Comprehend Literature	CC.3.Rlit.10
Read with Purpose and Understanding	CC.3.Rfou.4.a

PROGRAM RESOURCES

PRINT & TECHNOLOGY

Practice Master SG4.1, page SG28
Practice Master SG4.2, page SG29
Practice Master SG4.5, page SG32
Practice Master SG4.7, page SG34

TECHNOLOGY ONLY

Digital Library: Map of the Middle East

SUGGESTED PACING

DAY 2 Introduce and read pages 4–17
DAY 3 Read pages 18–32
DAY 4 Reread and discuss
DAY 5 Connect across texts

Summary Two girls, Lina and Feroza, live in a refugee camp in Pakistan. Each finds one sandal of the same pair in a pile of used clothes. They share the sandals, taking turns each day or each wearing one, until Lina learns she and her mother will be moving to America. Feroza makes Lina take one sandal with her so she will always remember their friendship.

Activate Prior Knowledge Ask: *What are some things good friends do for each other?*

Build Background Display the map of the Middle East from the **Digital Library** and point to the border between Afghanistan and Pakistan and the city of Peshawar. Explain that the conflict between Afghanistan and Pakistan has been going on since Pakistan was named a country in 1947.

Story Words Use **Practice Master SG4.1** to extend vocabulary.

admire, page 26	*crowd*, page 6	*practice*, page 19
remove, page 13	*signal*, page 21	

AL ABOVE LEVEL

Sadako and the Thousand Paper Cranes
by Eleanor Coerr

Content Connection: **Friends**

Biographical Fiction | Pages: 76

Writing

Write Over Shorter Time for Specific Tasks	CC.3.W.10

Speaking and Listening

Draw on Preparation to Explore Ideas	CC.3.SL.1.a

Language and Vocabulary

Acquire and Use Academic Words	CC.3.L.6

PROGRAM RESOURCES

PRINT & TECHNOLOGY

Practice Master SG4.1, page SG28
Practice Master SG4.2, page SG29
Practice Master SG4.6, page SG33
Practice Master SG4.7, page SG34

SUGGESTED PACING

DAY 2 Introduce and read pages 4–23
DAY 3 Read pages 24–48
DAY 4 Read pages 49–76 and discuss
DAY 5 Connect across texts

Summary Sadako, a gifted runner, is diagnosed with leukemia, years after the U.S. dropped the atom bomb on Hiroshima. As she struggles with her illness, she folds paper cranes, hoping that after folding one thousand of them, the gods will grant her wish to be healthy. She dies before reaching her goal, but her classmates fold the rest in her honor and everyone remembers her as a symbol of peace.

Activate Prior Knowledge Ask: *If you could make one wish, what would it be?*

Build Background Explain that President Truman ordered the U.S. Air Force to drop an atom bomb on Hiroshima, Japan, on August 5, 1945, hoping the act would bring an end to World War II and save many lives. The bomb is estimated to have killed well over 100,000 people, both immediately and over the following years as a result of sickness caused by the bomb.

Story Words Use **Practice Master SG4.1** to extend vocabulary.

ancestor, page 7	*celebration*, page 50	*cheerful*, page 26
complain, page 55	*miserable*, page 28	

Week 1 Teaching Resources

Fiction

BL BELOW LEVEL AD300L

The Runaway Rice Cake
by Ying Chang Compestine

Build Comprehension

- **Make Inferences** *Why do you think the Changs gave the rice cake to the old woman, even though they were hungry?* (Possible response: The family was being generous because they thought she needed it more than they did.)
- **Explain** *How did the Changs' good deed make their New Year better?* (Possible response: Everyone brought them food because they heard that they had given away their only rice cake. If they kept the rice cake for themselves, they would not have ended up with a feast.)

Writing Options

- **Thank You Note** Have students write a thank you note from the Changs to the people of the village. Encourage them to tell what they are thankful for and how their neighbors made their New Year more special.
- **Friendly Letter** Have students write a letter from one of the Chang boys telling a friend about his New Year.
- **Journal Entry** Invite students to write about a special holiday meal they share with their family. Encourage them to tell the types of food they eat and any holiday traditions they have.

BL BELOW LEVEL 520L

Under the Lemon Moon
by Edith Hope Fine

Build Comprehension

- **Explain** *Why did Rosalinda tell the Night Man to plant the lemon seeds?* (Possible response: If he plants the seeds, he will have his own lemon trees to get lemons from, so he will not have to steal anymore.)
- **Character's Feelings** *How do Rosalinda's feelings for the Night Man change after talking with Anciana?* (Possible response: She realizes that he took the lemons to sell because he was very poor and needed them.)

Writing Options

- **Character Sketch** Have students write a character sketch telling how Rosalinda changes from the beginning to the end of the story.
- **Thank You Note** Have students write a note from the Night Man to Rosalinda thanking her for giving him the lemon and explaining what happened when he planted the seeds.
- **Journal Entry** Invite students to write about a time when someone helped them when they least expected it. Encourage them to tell how they felt before being helped and how they felt after being helped.

Check & Reteach

Ask students to describe the theme of each book.
If students have difficulty identifying the theme, refer them to their theme charts. Ask: *What clues can you get from the title, characters, setting, and events of the story?*

DURING READING

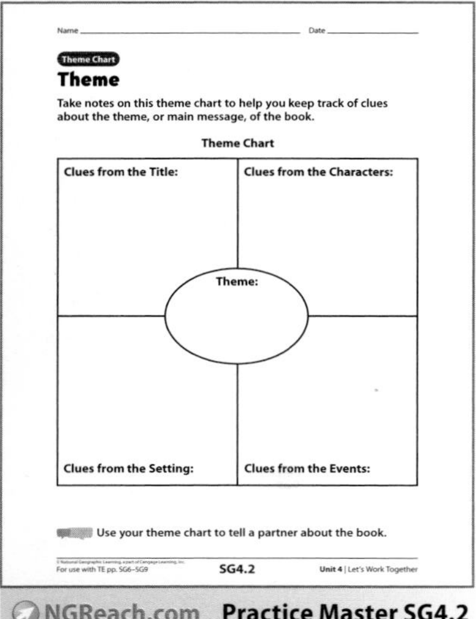

Name ______ Date ______

Theme Chart

Theme

Take notes on this theme chart to help you keep track of clues about the theme, or main message, of the book.

Theme Chart

Clues from the Title:	Clues from the Characters:
Theme:	
Clues from the Setting:	Clues from the Events:

Use your theme chart to tell a partner about the book.

For use with TE pp. SG6–SG9 SG4.2 Unit 4 | Let's Work Together

NGReach.com **Practice Master SG4.2**

AFTER READING

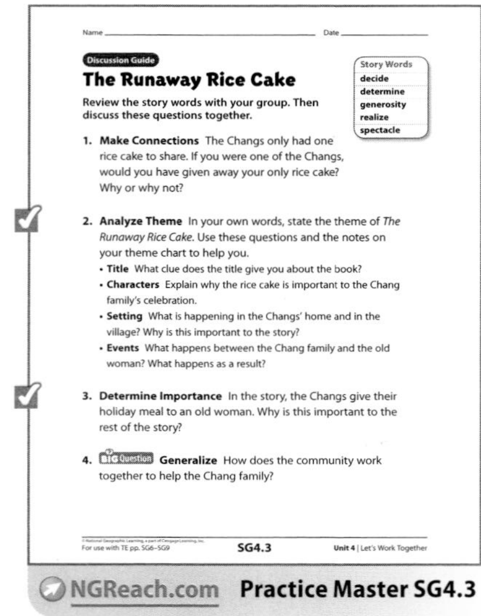

Name ______ Date ______

Discussion Guide

The Runaway Rice Cake

Review the story words with your group. Then discuss these questions together.

Story Words: decide, determine, generosity, realize, spectacle

1. **Make Connections** The Changs only had one rice cake to share. If you were one of the Changs, would you have given away your only rice cake? Why or why not?
2. **Analyze Theme** In your own words, state the theme of *The Runaway Rice Cake*. Use these questions and the notes on your theme chart to help you.
   - **Title** What clue does the title give you about the book?
   - **Characters** Explain why the rice cake is important to the Chang family's celebration.
   - **Setting** What is happening in the Changs' home and in the village? Why is this important to the story?
   - **Events** What happens between the Chang family and the old woman? What happens as a result?
3. **Determine Importance** In the story, the Changs give their holiday meal to an old woman. Why is this important to the rest of the story?
4. BIG Question **Generalize** How does the community work together to help the Chang family?

For use with TE pp. SG6–SG9 SG4.3 Unit 4 | Let's Work Together

NGReach.com **Practice Master SG4.3**

AFTER READING

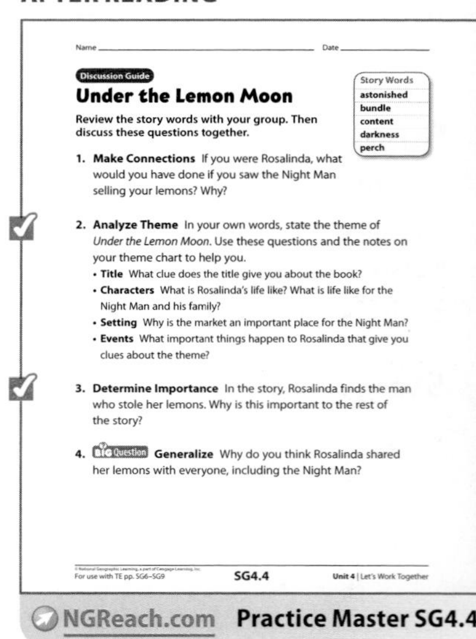

Name ______ Date ______

Discussion Guide

Under the Lemon Moon

Review the story words with your group. Then discuss these questions together.

Story Words: astonished, bundle, content, darkness, perch

1. **Make Connections** If you were Rosalinda, what would you have done if you saw the Night Man selling your lemons? Why?
2. **Analyze Theme** In your own words, state the theme of *Under the Lemon Moon*. Use these questions and the notes on your theme chart to help you.
   - **Title** What clue does the title give you about the book?
   - **Characters** What is Rosalinda's life like? What is life like for the Night Man and his family?
   - **Setting** Why is the market an important place for the Night Man?
   - **Events** What important things happen to Rosalinda that give you clues about the theme?
3. **Determine Importance** In the story, Rosalinda finds the man who stole her lemons. Why is this important to the rest of the story?
4. BIG Question **Generalize** Why do you think Rosalinda shared her lemons with everyone, including the Night Man?

For use with TE pp. SG6–SG9 SG4.4 Unit 4 | Let's Work Together

NGReach.com **Practice Master SG4.4**

OL ON LEVEL 620L

Four Feet, Two Sandals
by Karen Lynn Williams

Build Comprehension

- **Identify Problem and Solution** *What problem do the girls in the story have?* (Possible response: They only have one pair of sandals for the two of them.) *How do they solve this problem?* (Possible response: They share the sandals by taking turns or each wearing one.)
- **Character's Feelings** *Why does Feroza give one sandal to Lina at the end of the story?* (Possible response: She wants Lina to keep it so she will remember her.)

Writing Options

- **Sequel** Have students write a paragraph telling about what happens to Lina when she gets to America.
- **Book Review** Have students write a review of the book in which they tell about the story and what they did or did not like about it. Remind students to begin with a brief summary of the story's main points.
- **Journal Entry** Invite students to write about someone they consider to be a special friend and explain why this person is special to them.

AL ABOVE LEVEL

Sadako and the Thousand Paper Cranes
by Eleanor Coerr

Build Comprehension

- **Goal and Outcome** *Why did Sadako want to fold one thousand paper cranes?* (Possible response: She hoped that she would become well if she met her goal.) *How was her goal reached?* (Possible response: She died before she folded them, but her classmates folded the rest for her.)
- **Draw Conclusions** *How were the people in Japan affected by the atom bomb? Use examples from your book to support your answer.* (Student examples should reflect the idea that the atom bomb made many innocent people sick for many years after it was dropped.)

Writing Options

- **New Report** Have students write a news report in which they tell about Sadako's death, giving information about her life and about what her classmates did for her.
- **Blog Post** Have students write a blog post by one of Sadako's classmates, telling what the class is doing for Sadako and why. Encourage students to tell why others should join their cause.
- **Journal Entry** Invite students to write about a goal they have for the future and how they plan to reach it.

Connect Across Texts

AFTER READING Form heterogeneous groups, and have each member of the group summarize his or her book. Then have groups use **Practice Master SG4.7** to guide discussion.

AFTER READING

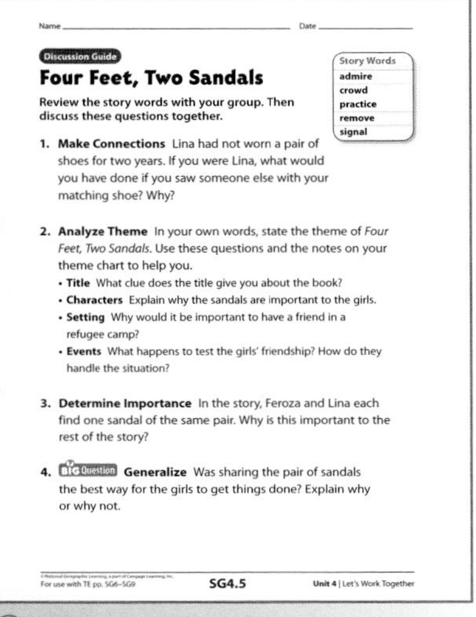

Name ______ Date ______

Discussion Guide

Four Feet, Two Sandals

Review the story words with your group. Then discuss these questions together.

Story Words
admire
crowd
practice
remove
signal

1. **Make Connections** Lina had not worn a pair of shoes for two years. If you were Lina, what would you have done if you saw someone else with your matching shoe? Why?
2. **Analyze Theme** In your own words, state the theme of *Four Feet, Two Sandals*. Use these questions and the notes on your theme chart to help you.
   - **Title** What clue does the title give you about the book?
   - **Characters** Explain why the sandals are important to the girls.
   - **Setting** Why would it be important to have a friend in a refugee camp?
   - **Events** What happens to test the girls' friendship? How do they handle the situation?
3. **Determine Importance** In the story, Feroza and Lina each find one sandal of the same pair. Why is this important to the rest of the story?
4. Big Question **Generalize** Was sharing the pair of sandals the best way for the girls to get things done? Explain why or why not.

For use with TE pp. SG6–SG9 SG4.5 **Unit 4** | Let's Work Together

NGReach.com **Practice Master SG4.5**

AFTER READING

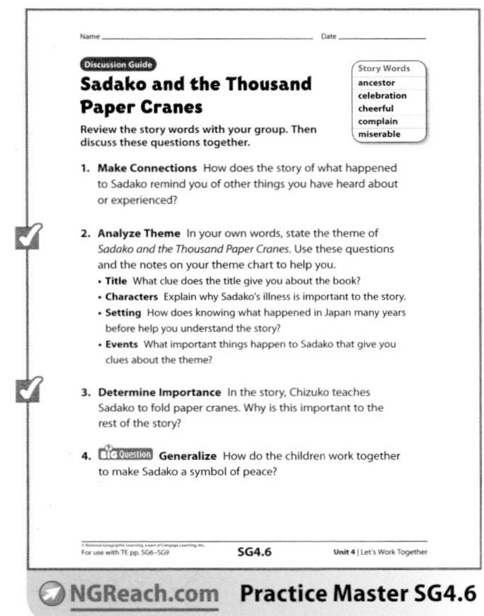

Name ______ Date ______

Discussion Guide

Sadako and the Thousand Paper Cranes

Review the story words with your group. Then discuss these questions together.

Story Words
ancestor
celebration
cheerful
complain
miserable

1. **Make Connections** How does the story of what happened to Sadako remind you of other things you have heard about or experienced?
2. **Analyze Theme** In your own words, state the theme of *Sadako and the Thousand Paper Cranes*. Use these questions and the notes on your theme chart to help you.
   - **Title** What clue does the title give you about the book?
   - **Characters** Explain why Sadako's illness is important to the story.
   - **Setting** How does knowing what happened in Japan many years before help you understand the story?
   - **Events** What important things happen to Sadako that give you clues about the theme?
3. **Determine Importance** In the story, Chizuko teaches Sadako to fold paper cranes. Why is this important to the rest of the story?
4. Big Question **Generalize** How do the children work together to make Sadako a symbol of peace?

For use with TE pp. SG6–SG9 SG4.6 **Unit 4** | Let's Work Together

NGReach.com **Practice Master SG4.6**

AFTER READING

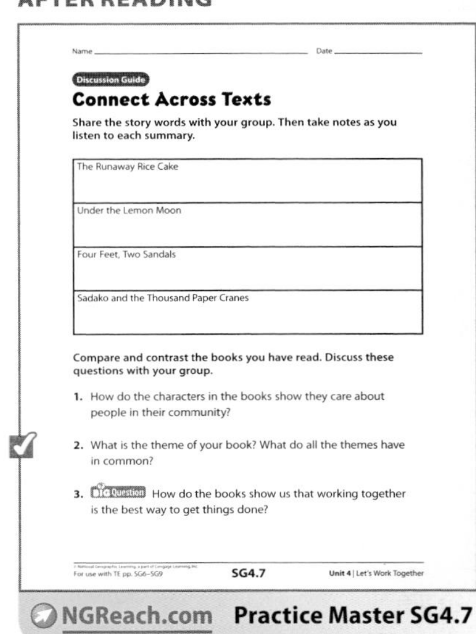

Name ______ Date ______

Discussion Guide

Connect Across Texts

Share the story words with your group. Then take notes as you listen to each summary.

The Runaway Rice Cake
Under the Lemon Moon
Four Feet, Two Sandals
Sadako and the Thousand Paper Cranes

Compare and contrast the books you have read. Discuss these questions with your group.

1. How do the characters in the books show they care about people in their community?
2. What is the theme of your book? What do all the themes have in common?
3. Big Question How do the books show us that working together is the best way to get things done?

For use with TE pp. SG6–SG9 SG4.7 **Unit 4** | Let's Work Together

NGReach.com **Practice Master SG4.7**

OBJECTIVES

Thematic Connection: Jobs and Money

Read and Comprehend Informational Text

Identify Supporting Details

Dogs at Work by Terrell Smith

Summary *Dogs at Work* explores the various types of work performed by service dogs and describes how seeing-eye dogs are trained. In "Working Like a Dog," author Terrell Smith explains that because dogs are smart, skilled, and love people, they can become great workers. Some dogs are trained to help disabled people accomplish daily tasks. Dogs are also used at airports to sniff out bombs and other dangerous items. They can do this because a dog's nose has 20 times more sniffing cells than a human's nose has. Search-and-rescue dogs also use their noses to find lost hikers and people buried under snow or rubble. "At Your Service" describes how seeing-eye dogs are trained. At eight weeks old, they begin learning good behavior. Then, at a year and a half, they learn voice commands. Next, they learn to guide people. Finally, they prove their skills by passing a test.

Activate Prior Knowledge Display the front cover and explain: *This dog has a job. It helps find missing people.* Then ask: *What jobs have you seen dogs do?* (Possible responses: guide people; sniff suitcases)

Build Background Explain that dogs are smart. They can be trained to help people and save lives. Point out that a dog's strong sense of smell is one reason that dogs are so good at certain kinds of jobs. Use the photos on pages 2–4 to discuss some of the work that dogs do. Have volunteers point to each photo and describe the job the dog is doing.

PROGRAM RESOURCES

PRINT ONLY

***Dogs at Work*, Pioneer Edition**

***Dogs at Work*, Pathfinder Edition**

TECHNOLOGY ONLY

My Vocabulary Notebook

COMMON CORE STANDARDS

Reading	
Explain How Key Details Support the Main Idea	CC.3.Rinf.2
Read and Comprehend Informational Text	CC.3.Rinf.10
Language	
Acquire and Use Domain-Specific Words	CC.3.L.6

Mini Lesson

Identify Supporting Details

Explain: *Authors provide details, such as facts and examples, to support main ideas, or show that they are true.* Point out that good readers can explain how key details support a main idea in a text.

Read aloud the following text from page 5 of the Pioneer Edition of *Dogs at Work* as students listen.

Dog Detectives

Some dogs use their noses to find people. Search-and-rescue (SAR) dogs search for missing people. They find lost hikers. Some SAR dogs save people after earthquakes. They find people under piles of rubble.

Text from Pioneer Edition

Then, think aloud to model how to identify key details and explain how they support the main idea of the text: *The main idea is stated in the first sentence of the paragraph:*

- *Some dogs use their noses to find people.*

The following sentences give details that support this main idea by explaining how dogs use their noses to find people. Two details are:

- *They search for missing people.*
- *They find lost hikers.*

Point out that these details are examples of the kinds of people dogs use their noses to find.

Have students identify more details about the people dogs find in the text above. Then have them explain how all the details support the main idea in the text. (Details: Dogs save people after earthquakes. They find people under piles of rubble. Possible response: The details support the main idea because they tell about the kinds of people dogs find and give specific examples.)

BL BELOW LEVEL 440L

PIONEER EDITION
Lexile: 440L | GR: P

Content Connection: Community Service

Social Studies Vocabulary

Use Wordwise on page 7 to introduce new words:

archaeologist *breed* *disability* *visually impaired*

Have students add new words to **My Vocabulary Notebook**.

Build Comprehension

After reading, use the Concept Check on page 12. Remind students to use details and examples to support each answer.

1. **Identify Supporting Details** How can dogs help people with disabilities? (Dogs help people do things that they cannot do on their own. For example, dogs open doors, turn on lights, and pick up things.)
2. **Explain** Why do dogs work at airports? (Because they have a better sense of smell than people have, dogs sniff bags to find dangerous things like bombs. They also sniff for food that is not allowed to come into the U.S.)
3. **Define** What is a search-and-rescue dog? (A search-and-rescue dog searches for missing people, such as hikers. The dog uses its sense of smell to find clues that the missing people have left behind.)
4. **Describe** How does one dog help an archaeologist discover the past? (The dog digs up bones of people who died long ago. Once, the dog helped him find a cemetery.)
5. **Evaluate** Why is a service dog's training so important? (People's safety depends on the dog. So, the dog has to know when to listen to people and when not to.)

OL ON LEVEL 730L

PATHFINDER EDITION
Lexile: 730L | GR: Q

Content Connection: Community Service

Social Studies Vocabulary

Use Wordwise on page 7 to introduce new words:

archaeologist *breed* *disability* *visually impaired*

Have students add new words to **My Vocabulary Notebook**.

Build Comprehension

After reading, use the Concept Check on page 12. Remind students to use details and examples to support each answer.

1. **Identify Supporting Details** How can dogs help people with disabilities? (Dogs help people do things that they cannot do on their own. For example, dogs open and close doors, turn lights on and off, pick up things, and pull wheelchairs.)
2. **Explain** Why are dogs good inspectors at airports? (Dogs have 20 times more sniffing cells than people. So, they can smell for things like bombs, drugs, money, and food, including fruit that might be carrying diseases.)
3. **Make Inferences** How is a search-and-rescue dog's job like a game? (A search-and-rescue dog loves to play. So, for the dog, looking for a missing person is like a game of hide-and-seek.)
4. **Compare** How are a dog archaeologist and a search-and-rescue dog alike? (Both look for people who are "hidden.")
5. **Evaluate** Why is a service dog's training so important? (People's safety depends on the dog. So, the dog has to know when to listen to people and when not to.)

Check & Reteach

OBJECTIVE: Identify Supporting Details

Have partners identify key details in the second paragraph on page 9 and explain how they support the main idea that training serves dogs well. (Details: dogs learn skills; they get confidence to do their job well. These details explain how training helps dogs.)

For students who cannot identify key details and explain how they support a main idea, reteach with the section "Step 4" on page 11. Say: *The main idea is that a service dog must pass tests. What details support, or explain, this idea?* Have students skim the text. Make a class list to record details. (Both versions: A dog leads trainer up stairs; crosses busy streets; Additional details in Pathfinder: A dog leads trainer along crowded sidewalks, through buildings and malls, onto escalators, and over curbs.) Guide students as they explain how the details support the main idea. (Possible response: The details give examples of the tests that service dogs must pass.)

Week 2 Teaching Resources
Fiction

BL BELOW LEVEL AD380L

Grandpa's Corner Store
by DyAnne DiSalvo-Ryan

Content Connection:
Running a Business

Realistic Fiction | Pages: 32 | Lexile: AD380L | GR: L

OBJECTIVES

Thematic Connection: Jobs and Money

- **Read and Comprehend Literature**
- **Determine Importance**
- ☑ **Describe Story Elements**

PROGRAM RESOURCES

PRINT & TECHNOLOGY

Practice Master SG4.8, page SG35
Practice Master SG4.9, page SG36
Practice Master SG4.10, page SG37
Practice Master SG4.14, page SG41

SUGGESTED PACING

DAY 2 Introduce and read pages 2–15
DAY 3 Read pages 16–32 and discuss
DAY 4 Reteach or conduct intervention
DAY 5 Connect across texts

Summary Lucy worries that Grandpa will have to close his corner store when a new supermarket opens nearby. As other stores begin closing, Grandpa plans to close his store, too. Lucy gets many neighbors together to spruce up the store and show Grandpa that the store is important to the community.

Activate Prior Knowledge Ask: *What are some important places in your community?* (Possible response: the grocery store; our school) *Why are these places important?* (Possible response: We get food there; we go there to learn.)

Build Background Explain that super stores are owned by large corporations that have stores just like it all over the country. Some people think that super stores will improve the community by providing jobs and bringing in more money. Others worry that they will force small, family-owned businesses to close and will take money out of the community by giving it to corporations who are not part of the community.

Story Words Use **Practice Master SG4.8** to extend vocabulary.

arrangement, page 11	*business*, page 14	*notice*, page 16
repair, page 17	*success*, page 32	

BL BELOW LEVEL 450L

Uncle Willie and the Soup Kitchen
by DyAnne DiSalvo-Ryan

Content Connection: **Community Service**

Realistic Fiction | Pages: 32 | Lexile: 450L | GR: M

PROGRAM RESOURCES

PRINT & TECHNOLOGY

Practice Master SG4.8, page SG35
Practice Master SG4.9, page SG36
Practice Master SG4.11, page SG38
Practice Master SG4.14, page SG41

TECHNOLOGY ONLY

Digital Library: Soup kitchen line

SUGGESTED PACING

DAY 2 Introduce and read pages 3–15
DAY 3 Read pages 16–32 and discuss
DAY 4 Reteach or conduct intervention
DAY 5 Connect across texts

Summary A boy visits a soup kitchen with Uncle Willie, who works there every day. The boy helps his uncle prepare for the day's lunch. Through his experience, the boy learns how many people work to make a soup kitchen work and about the hungry people a soup kitchen helps.

Activate Prior Knowledge Ask: *How do you know when you are hungry? What do you do?* (Possible response: I feel a pang in my stomach, so I get some food.) Explain that there are some Americans who feel hungry much of the time but have no food.

Build Background Display the photo of a line outside a soup kitchen from the **Digital Library**. Explain that the first soup kitchens started after the Civil War, but at the start of the Great Depression, and throughout the 1930s, they became common places where people in need could get a meal.

Story Words Use **Practice Master SG4.8** to extend vocabulary.

feast, page 14	*introduce*, page 18	*pretend*, page 4
separate, page 20	*toward*, page 5	

OL ON LEVEL AD540L

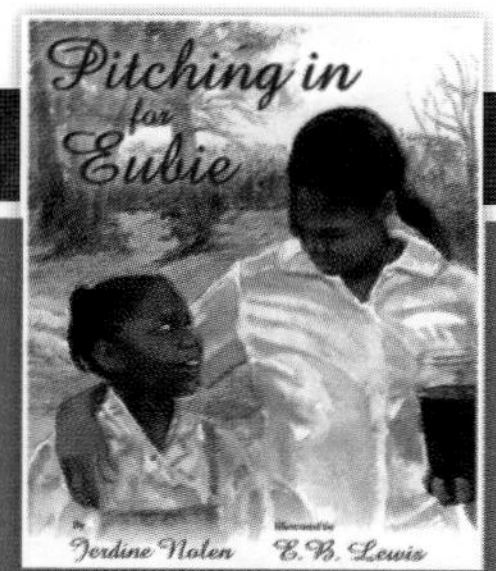

Pitching in for Eubie
by Jerdine Nolen

Content Connection:
Fundraising

Realistic Fiction | Pages: 32 | Lexile: AD540L | GR: N

COMMON CORE STANDARDS

Reading

Describe Characters and Explain Characters' Actions	CC.3.Rlit.3
Describe How Successive Parts Build	CC.3.Rlit.5
Read and Comprehend Literature	CC.3.Rlit.10
Read with Purpose and Understanding	CC.3.Rfou.4.a

PROGRAM RESOURCES

PRINT & TECHNOLOGY

Practice Master SG4.8, page SG35
Practice Master SG4.9, page SG36
Practice Master SG4.12, page SG39
Practice Master SG4.14, page SG41

SUGGESTED PACING

DAY 2 Introduce and read pages 4–15
DAY 3 Read pages 16–32
DAY 4 Reread and discuss
DAY 5 Connect across texts

Summary When Lily's sister gets a scholarship to college, she and her family have to figure out how to save the money to make up the rest of the fees. Lily wants to find a way to earn money to help. After a few failed attempts, she finally gets a job keeping an elderly woman company.

Activate Prior Knowledge Ask: *What are some ways you and your family help each other?*

Build Background Explain that there are many ways to make paying for college easier. Scholarships are money that is often awarded to students with very good grades and/or special talents, such as in sports or music. Some scholarships pay all the money needed for college. Others pay for some of it.

Story Words Use **Practice Master SG4.8** to extend vocabulary.

announce, page 32 | *contribute*, page 6 | *delivery*, page 5
dream, page 10 | *emergency*, page 5

AL ABOVE LEVEL AD700L

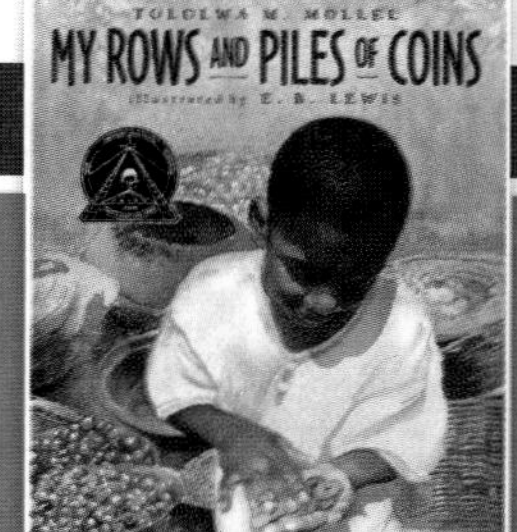

My Rows and Piles of Coins
by Tololwa Mollel

Content Connection:
Saving Money

Realistic Fiction | Pages: 32 | Lexile: AD700L | GR: Q

Writing

Write Over Shorter Time for Specific Tasks	CC.3.W.10

Speaking and Listening

Draw on Preparation to Explore Ideas	CC.3.SL.1.a

Language and Vocabulary

Acquire and Use Academic Words	CC.3.L.6

PROGRAM RESOURCES

PRINT & TECHNOLOGY

Practice Master SG4.8, page SG35
Practice Master SG4.9, page SG36
Practice Master SG4.13, page SG40
Practice Master SG4.14, page SG41

TECHNOLOGY ONLY

Digital Library: Map of Tanzania

SUGGESTED PACING

DAY 2 Introduce and read pages 4–13
DAY 3 Read pages 14–32
DAY 4 Reread and discuss
DAY 5 Connect across texts

Summary When Saruni's mother gives him a few coins to spend in the market, he decides to save up for a new bicycle to help his mother carry things to the market. After many weeks of saving coins and nights of counting and arranging the growing piles, Saruni discovers he does not have enough. So, his father sells his old bicycle to Saruni for the coins he has, gives the coins to Saruni's mother, who then gives them back to Saruni as a reward for being a good son.

Activate Prior Knowledge Ask: *Have you ever saved money to buy something? What was it? How did you earn the money?*

Build Background Display the map of Africa from the **Digital Library**. Point out Tanzania and explain that this country is part of East Africa. Open markets are common here. Local people buy and sell many things here, such as food, clothing, toys, and other items.

Story Words Use **Practice Master SG4.8** to extend vocabulary.

clutch, page 6 | *disappointed*, page 25 | *errand*, page 12
precious, page 22 | *various*, page 22

BL BELOW LEVEL AD380L

Grandpa's Corner Store
by DyAnne DiSalvo-Ryan

Build Comprehension

- **Identify Problem and Solution** *What problem does Lucy have?* (Possible response: She is worried that Grandpa is going to sell his store.) *How does she solve the problem?* (Possible response: She gets the neighbors together to show him how important his store is to them so he will not sell it.)
- **Draw Conclusions** *Why do you think so many people come to help out at the store?* (Possible response: They want to show that the store is important to them.)

Writing Options

- **Dialogue** Have students write a dialogue between Lucy and Grandpa in which they talk about closing the store.
- **Friendly Letter** Have students write a friendly letter to Grandpa from someone in the community, telling him why the corner store is important to the community.
- **Journal Entry** Invite students to write about a favorite place in their community and what makes it special.

BL BELOW LEVEL 450L

Uncle Willie and the Soup Kitchen
by DyAnne DiSalvo-Ryan

Build Comprehension

- **Explain** *How does the soup kitchen help people?* (Possible response: Many volunteers work there making food and serving it to people who are hungry and in need.)
- **Make Inferences** *How can you tell the soup kitchen is important to the community?* (Possible responses: Many local stores donate food to the soup kitchen. The soup kitchen helps many hungry people.)

Writing Options

- **Interview Questions** Have students write three questions they would like to ask Uncle Willie about the soup kitchen. Then have them share their questions with a partner.
- **Character Sketch** Have students write a character sketch in which they describe Uncle Willie. Encourage students to tell what he is like and to provide details from the text to support their opinions.
- **Journal Entry** Invite students to write about an idea for something their family or fellow classmates could do together to help a person or people in need.

Check & Reteach

Ask students to describe the story elements of each book.
If students have difficulty describing the story elements, refer them to their story maps. Ask: *Who are the characters? What is the setting? What happens at the beginning, middle, and end of the story?*

DURING READING

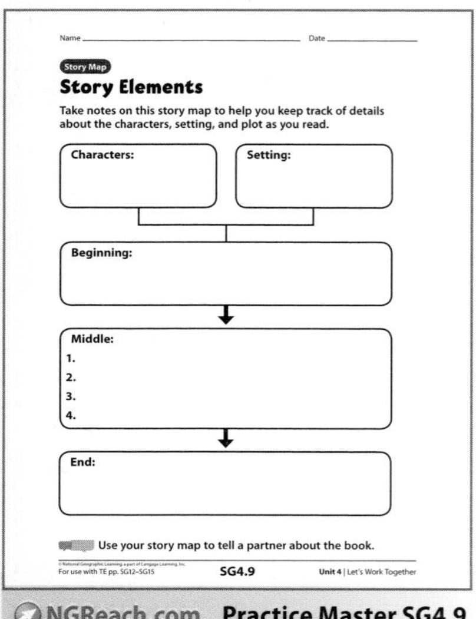
Name ________ Date ________

Story Map

Story Elements

Take notes on this story map to help you keep track of details about the characters, setting, and plot as you read.

Characters:
Setting:
Beginning:
Middle:
1.
2.
3.
4.
End:

Use your story map to tell a partner about the book.

SG4.9 Unit 4 | Let's Work Together

NGReach.com **Practice Master SG4.9**

AFTER READING

Name ________ Date ________

Discussion Guide

Grandpa's Corner Store

Story Words: arrangement, business, notice, repair, success

Review the story words with your group. Then discuss these questions together.

1. **Character Motivation** Why does Grandpa decide not to sell his store?
2. **Describe Story Elements** In your own words, tell about the parts of *Grandpa's Corner Store*. Use these questions and the notes on the story map to help you.
   - **Characters** Who are the main characters of the story?
   - **Setting** Where does the story take place?
   - **Beginning** What is happening in town at the beginning of the story?
   - **Middle** What happens in class to make Lucy want to help Grandpa?
   - **End** What decision does Grandpa make at the end of the story? Why does he make this decision?
3. **Determine Importance** In the story, a big supermarket is opening in the community. Why is this important to the rest of the story?
4. Big Question **Generalize** How does the community work together to stop Grandpa from selling the store?

SG4.10 Unit 4 | Let's Work Together

NGReach.com **Practice Master SG4.10**

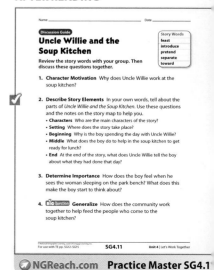

AFTER READING

Name ________ Date ________

Discussion Guide

Uncle Willie and the Soup Kitchen

Story Words: feast, introduce, pretend, separate, toward

Review the story words with your group. Then discuss these questions together.

1. **Character Motivation** Why does Uncle Willie work at the soup kitchen?
2. **Describe Story Elements** In your own words, tell about the parts of *Uncle Willie and the Soup Kitchen*. Use these questions and the notes on the story map to help you.
   - **Characters** Who are the main characters of the story?
   - **Setting** Where does the story take place?
   - **Beginning** Why is the boy spending the day with Uncle Willie?
   - **Middle** What does the boy do to help in the soup kitchen to get ready for lunch?
   - **End** At the end of the story, what does Uncle Willie tell the boy about what they had done that day?
3. **Determine Importance** How does the boy feel when he sees the woman sleeping on the park bench? What does this make the boy start to think about?
4. Big Question **Generalize** How does the community work together to help feed the people who come to the soup kitchen?

SG4.11 Unit 4 | Let's Work Together

NGReach.com **Practice Master SG4.11**

OL ON LEVEL AD540L

Pitching in for Eubie
by Jerdine Nolen

Build Comprehension

- **Goal and Outcome** *What is Lily's goal?* (Possible response: She wants to help earn money for her sister to go to school.) *How does she work toward this goal?* (Possible response: She tries to start a few businesses that do not work, but then she gets a job keeping an older woman company.)
- **Make Judgments** *Do you think Lily is a good sister? Explain.* (Possible response: Yes, she is a good sister because she wants to help earn money for Eubie to go to school.)

Writing Options

- **Character Sketch** Have students write a character sketch describing Lily. Encourage students to tell what she is like and to provide details from the text to support their opinions.
- **Sequel** Have students write a paragraph telling what happens to Lily's family after the story ends. Students may choose one member of the family to write about, such as Lily or Eubie, or they may choose to write about the whole family.
- **Journal Entry** Invite students to write about something they have done to help their family. Remind students to begin with a problem and tell what they did to help solve it.

AL ABOVE LEVEL AD700L

My Rows and Piles of Coins
by Tololwa Mollel

Build Comprehension

- **Character's Motivation** *Why does Saruni want to buy the bicycle?* (Possible responses: He wants to be able to race around and do errands and help his family on market days.)
- **Evaluate** *How does Saruni feel about his mother? How do you know?* (Possible response: He cares for her very much and wants to do all he can to help her. He wants a bicycle to help make her work easier.)

Writing Options

- **Thank You Note** Have students write a note from Saruni to his parents thanking them for the bicycle.
- **Book Review** Ask students to write a book review for *My Rows and Piles of Coins*. Remind students to tell what they did and did not like about the book, whether or not they would recommend it to others, and why they feel that way.
- **Journal Entry** Invite students to write about a time that they saved money for something they really wanted. Encourage students to tell what they did to earn the money they needed and whether or not they were successful.

Connect Across Texts

AFTER READING Form heterogeneous groups, and have each member of the group summarize his or her book. Then have groups use **Practice Master SG4.14** to guide discussion.

AFTER READING

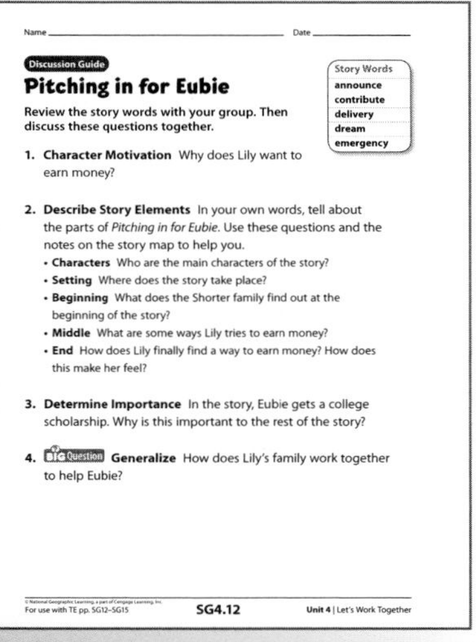

Name ____________ Date ____________

Discussion Guide

Pitching in for Eubie

Story Words: announce, contribute, delivery, dream, emergency

Review the story words with your group. Then discuss these questions together.

1. **Character Motivation** Why does Lily want to earn money?
2. **Describe Story Elements** In your own words, tell about the parts of *Pitching in for Eubie*. Use these questions and the notes on the story map to help you.
   - **Characters** Who are the main characters of the story?
   - **Setting** Where does the story take place?
   - **Beginning** What does the Shorter family find out at the beginning of the story?
   - **Middle** What are some ways Lily tries to earn money?
   - **End** How does Lily finally find a way to earn money? How does this make her feel?
3. **Determine Importance** In the story, Eubie gets a college scholarship. Why is this important to the rest of the story?
4. BIG Question **Generalize** How does Lily's family work together to help Eubie?

For use with TE pp. SG12–SG15 SG4.12 **Unit 4** | Let's Work Together

NGReach.com **Practice Master SG4.12**

AFTER READING

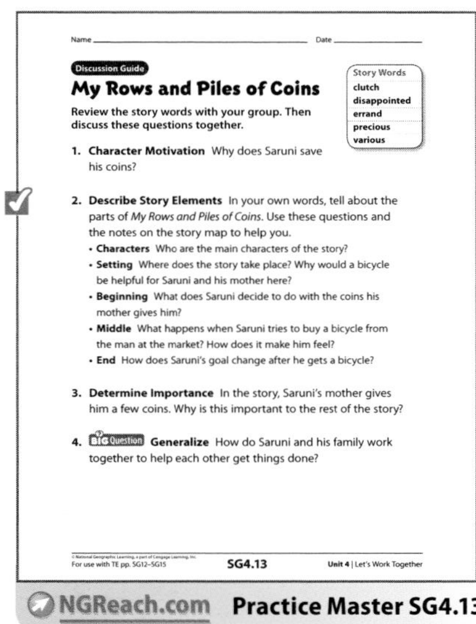

Name ____________ Date ____________

Discussion Guide

My Rows and Piles of Coins

Story Words: clutch, disappointed, errand, precious, various

Review the story words with your group. Then discuss these questions together.

1. **Character Motivation** Why does Saruni save his coins?
2. **Describe Story Elements** In your own words, tell about the parts of *My Rows and Piles of Coins*. Use these questions and the notes on the story map to help you.
   - **Characters** Who are the main characters of the story?
   - **Setting** Where does the story take place? Why would a bicycle be helpful for Saruni and his mother here?
   - **Beginning** What does Saruni decide to do with the coins his mother gives him?
   - **Middle** What happens when Saruni tries to buy a bicycle from the man at the market? How does it make him feel?
   - **End** How does Saruni's goal change after he gets a bicycle?
3. **Determine Importance** In the story, Saruni's mother gives him a few coins. Why is this important to the rest of the story?
4. BIG Question **Generalize** How do Saruni and his family work together to help each other get things done?

For use with TE pp. SG12–SG15 SG4.13 **Unit 4** | Let's Work Together

NGReach.com **Practice Master SG4.13**

AFTER READING

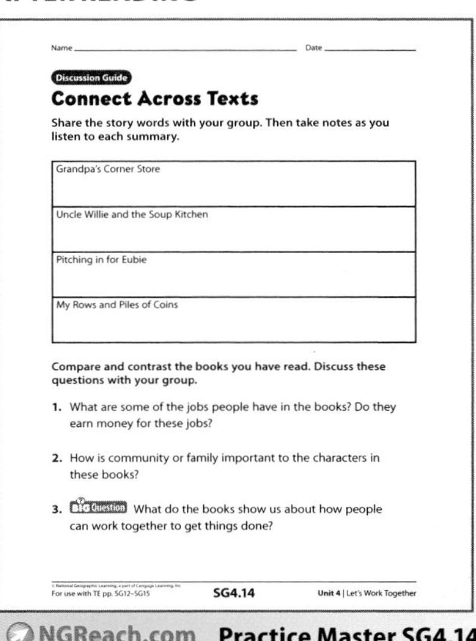

Name ____________ Date ____________

Discussion Guide

Connect Across Texts

Share the story words with your group. Then take notes as you listen to each summary.

Grandpa's Corner Store
Uncle Willie and the Soup Kitchen
Pitching in for Eubie
My Rows and Piles of Coins

Compare and contrast the books you have read. Discuss these questions with your group.

1. What are some of the jobs people have in the books? Do they earn money for these jobs?
2. How is community or family important to the characters in these books?
3. BIG Question What do the books show us about how people can work together to get things done?

For use with TE pp. SG12–SG15 SG4.14 **Unit 4** | Let's Work Together

NGReach.com **Practice Master SG4.14**

OBJECTIVES

Thematic Connection: Goods and Services

- **Read and Comprehend Informational Text**
- **Distinguish Points of View**

Working Hand in Hand by Diane G. Silver

Summary *Working Hand in Hand* describes two National Geographic Explorers dedicated to protecting endangered animals and helping people. In "Changing the Tide for Turtles," Diane G. Silver introduces marine biologist José Urteaga. He learned that because people had few ways to earn money, they were selling turtle eggs. As a result, Nicaragua's sea turtles were dying out. To help the turtles and the people, Urteaga protects the turtle eggs and shows people other ways to earn money. Today, the turtles are safer. "Team Turtle" presents information about Nicaragua's five species of endangered turtles. "Saving Elephants One Village at a Time" describes Hammer Simwinga. To save endangered elephants in Zambia, he taught villagers new ways to make money other than killing elephants for ivory tusks.

Activate Prior Knowledge Display the front cover and ask: *How can people work together to protect turtles and other animals?* (Possible responses: protect their environments; give money to organizations)

Build Background Explain that sea turtles have lived on Earth for more than 100 million years. Today, sea turtles in Nicaragua are in danger of dying out. A scientist named José Urteaga is working to save them. Use the photos on pages 8–9 to point out the five endangered species of turtles in Nicaragua. Have volunteers point to each picture and describe the turtles.

PROGRAM RESOURCES

PRINT ONLY

***Working Hand in Hand*, Pioneer Edition**
***Working Hand in Hand*, Pathfinder Edition**

TECHNOLOGY ONLY

My Vocabulary Notebook
Interactive Whiteboard Lesson—Turtle Travels

COMMON CORE STANDARDS

Reading	
Distinguish Points of View	CC.3.Rinf.6
Read and Comprehend Informational Text	CC.3.Rinf.10
Language	
Acquire and Use Domain-Specific Words	CC.3.L.6

Mini Lesson

Distinguish Points of View

Explain: *When authors write about a topic, they often have a particular viewpoint, or opinion, about that topic. Readers may feel the same way or have a different opinion.* Point out that good readers are able to distinguish between the author's viewpoint and their own opinions.

Read aloud the following text from page 4 of the Pioneer Edition of *Working Hand in Hand* as students listen.

> **Saving the Leatherbacks**
> Leatherbacks are Earth's biggest sea turtles. These gentle giants have lived on Earth for more than 100 million years.
> Urteaga knew that these amazing animals were dying out. He wanted to know why.

Text from Pioneer Edition

Then, think aloud to model how to determine the author's viewpoint about the topic: *In the first paragraph, the author describes leatherback sea turtles as "gentle giants." These are positive words that tell me the author has a good opinion about sea turtles.* Point out that adjectives, such as *gentle*, are clues that can help you figure out how the author feels about a topic. Then, model how to determine your own opinion about the topic and compare it to the author's viewpoint. *I like turtles, too. So, the author and I have the same viewpoint about turtles.*

Have students determine the author's viewpoint about the topic of the second paragraph above and compare it to their own opinion. Tell students to look for adjectives that give clues to the author's opinion of leatherbacks. (Possible response: The author says that leatherbacks are amazing animals. I think turtles are really amazing, too. So, the author and I have the same opinion of these turtles.)

BL BELOW LEVEL

PIONEER EDITION

Content Connection:
Sustainable Use of Animal Resources

Social Studies Vocabulary

Use Wordwise on page 6 to introduce new words:

achievement *earn* *poaching* *survive*

Have students add new words to **My Vocabulary Notebook**.

Build Comprehension

After reading, use the Concept Check on page 12. Remind students to use details and examples to support each answer.

1. **Explain** How is José Urteaga helping both turtles and people in Nicaragua? (He protects turtle eggs to keep sea turtles from dying out. He teaches people new ways to make money.)
2. **Distinguish Points of View** What does the author think of Urteaga's work? What do you think? (Possible response: The author thinks Urteaga's work is very important. I agree because it helps both turtles and people.)
3. **Evaluate** Which strategy on page 7 is best? Tell why you think so. (Possible response: I think the first strategy is best because it helps both the turtles and the people.)
4. **Details** What problems did Hammer Simwinga help solve in North Luangwa National Park? How did he help? (People poached elephants to make money. Hammer helped them find ways to earn money.)
5. **Compare and Contrast** How are José Urteaga and Hammer Simwinga alike? (Possible response: Both work to help people, animals, and the environment.) How are they different? (Possible response: Urteaga works in Nicaragua with sea turtles. Hammer works in Africa with elephants.)

OL ON LEVEL 790L

PATHFINDER EDITION

Lexile: 790L

Content Connection:
Sustainable Use of Animal Resources

Social Studies Vocabulary

Use Wordwise on page 6 to introduce new words:

business *earn* *economy* *income* *poacher*

Have students add new words to **My Vocabulary Notebook**.

Build Comprehension

After reading, use the Concept Check on page 12. Remind students to use details and examples to support each answer.

1. **Explain** What is José Urteaga doing to improve things for both turtles and people in Nicaragua? (He protects turtle eggs to keep sea turtles from dying out. He shows people new ways to earn money.)
2. **Distinguish Points of View** What opinion does the author have of José Urteaga's work? How do you feel about it? (Possible response: The author thinks Urteaga's work is important. I agree because it helps both turtles and people.)
3. **Evaluate** Which strategy on page 7 is best? Why so you think so? (Possible response: I think the first strategy is best. It helps both turtles and people.)
4. **Details** What problems did Hammer tackle in North Luangwa National Park? How did he solve them? (People poached elephants to make money. Hammer helped them find ways to earn money.)
5. **Compare and Contrast** How are José Urteaga and Hammer Simwinga similar? (Possible response: Both work to help people, animals, and the environment.) How are they different? (Possible response: Urteaga works in Nicaragua with sea turtles. Hammer works in Africa with elephants.)

Check & Reteach

OBJECTIVE: Distinguish Points of View

Have partners determine the author's viewpoint about Urteaga in the first paragraph on page 7. (The author says Urteaga is creative.) Then have students compare this to their own opinions. (Possible response: I agree because of the many ways he solves problems.)

For students who cannot distinguish an author's viewpoint from their own, reteach using the last paragraph of "Hope for the Future" on page 11. Say: *A viewpoint is someone's opinion about something. Authors often express their opinions when they write about a topic. What is the author's viewpoint about Hammer?* Help students skim the text. (Possible response: The author says the future will be better because of Hammer's work. The author thinks Hammer's work is important.) Ask: *Is your opinion the same or different?* Guide students as they explain their own opinions and compare them with the author's viewpoint. (Possible response: Hammer helps both animals and people. So, I think his work is important, too.)

BL BELOW LEVEL

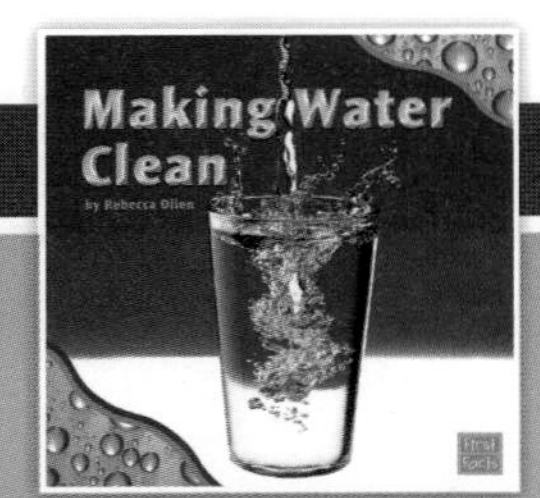

Making Water Clean
by Rebecca Olien

Content Connection:
Clean Water

Expository Nonfiction | Pages: 24

OBJECTIVES

Thematic Connection: Goods and Services

Read and Comprehend Text

- ☑ **Opinion and Evidence**
- ☑ **Determine Importance: Summarize**

PROGRAM RESOURCES

PRINT & TECHNOLOGY

Practice Master SG4.15, page SG42

Practice Master SG4.16, page SG43

Practice Master SG4.17, page SG44

Practice Master SG4.21, page SG48

SUGGESTED PACING

DAY 2 Introduce and read pages 4–13
DAY 3 Read pages 14–21 and discuss
DAY 4 Reteach or conduct intervention
DAY 5 Connect across texts

Summary We get our water by turning on a faucet, but the water that comes out has been cleaned to make it safe to drink. Water comes from many sources, and often these sources are polluted. Cities clean their water in treatment plants, where sediment is removed and chemicals are added to kill bacteria.

Activate Prior Knowledge Ask: *What are some places where we can find water?* (Possible responses: rivers; lakes; oceans)

Build Background Explain that safe drinking water is necessary for good health. When water used for drinking and cleaning is left untreated, many people can become sick. Each year, close to two million people die from diseases caused by unclean water.

Story Words Use **Practice Master SG4.15** to extend vocabulary.

connect, page 17	*material*, page 8	*remove*, page 9
simple, page 4	*source*, page 6	

BL BELOW LEVEL 530L

Farmers: Then and Now
by Lisa Zamosky

Content Connection:
Agriculture

Expository Nonfiction | Pages: 32 | Lexile: 530L | GR: N

PROGRAM RESOURCES

PRINT & TECHNOLOGY

Practice Master SG4.15, page SG42

Practice Master SG4.16, page SG43

Practice Master SG4.18, page SG45

Practice Master SG4.21, page SG48

SUGGESTED PACING

DAY 2 Introduce and read pages 4–13
DAY 3 Read pages 14–29 and discuss
DAY 4 Reteach or conduct intervention
DAY 5 Connect across texts

Summary Before farming, people moved from place to place to find food. Farming allowed people to stay in one place. At first, all farming was done by hand. As time passed, machines, such as the plow and then the tractor, were invented to make farming easier, and these machines allowed farmers to grow bigger crops. Farmers learned new ways to water their crops and protect them from pests. Now, crops can be shipped around the world.

Activate Prior Knowledge Ask: *What are some things we eat that are grown on farms?* (Possible response: vegetables; wheat; fruits; meat)

Build Background Explain that there are about two million farms in the U.S. today, and only about one percent of the population farms for a living. About forty percent of the land in the U.S. is used for farming, with the largest single crop being corn, followed by soybeans.

Story Words Use **Practice Master SG4.15** to extend vocabulary.

healthy, page 14	*improve*, page 25	*raise*, page 5
search, page 6	*trade*, page 21	

OL ON LEVEL AD640L

A Weed is a Flower
by Aliki

Content Connection: **Agriculture**

Picture Book Biography | Pages: 32 | Lexile: AD640L | GR: O

COMMON CORE STANDARDS

Reading

Read and Comprehend Informational Text	CC.3.Rinf.10

PROGRAM RESOURCES

PRINT & TECHNOLOGY

Practice Master SG4.15, page SG42
Practice Master SG4.16, page SG43
Practice Master SG4.19, page SG46
Practice Master SG4.21, page SG48

SUGGESTED PACING

DAY 2 Introduce and read pages 4–15
DAY 3 Read pages 16–32
DAY 4 Reread and discuss
DAY 5 Connect across texts

Summary George Washington Carver was born a slave. He was an inquisitive boy known for his interest in plants. Carver worked hard to find many uses for a single plant, including over 300 different uses for the peanut. He encouraged southern farmers to grow a bigger variety of crops because it would be better for the soil. He is remembered as a great scientist.

Activate Prior Knowledge Ask: *What is something you are really good at? Is this something you like to do?*

Build Background Explain that crop rotation is a method farmers use to keep soil healthy. Farmers take turns planting two different types of crops in the same soil from season to season. It helps to keep the soil healthy and control pests.

Story Words Use **Practice Master SG4.15** to extend vocabulary.

admit, page 14 *advice*, page 11 *entirely*, page 24
ordinary, page 5 *unusual*, page 9

AL ABOVE LEVEL 810L

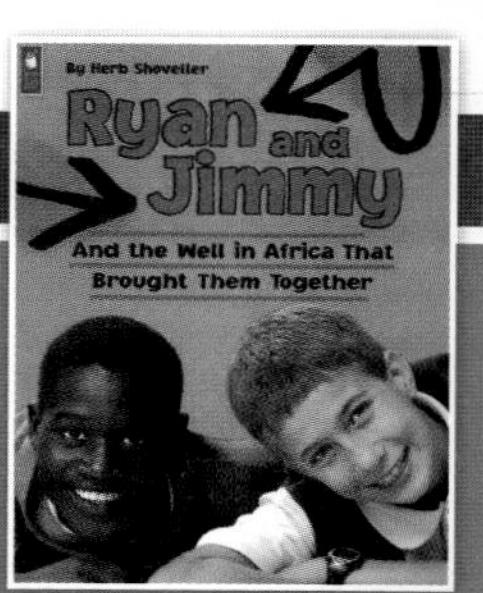

Ryan and Jimmy: And the Well in Africa That Brought Them Together
by Herb Shoveller

Content Connection: **Clean Water**

Photo Essay | Pages: 56 | Lexile: 810L | GR: S

Writing

Write Over Shorter Time for Specific Tasks	CC.3.W.10

Speaking and Listening

Draw on Preparation to Explore Ideas	CC.3.SL.1.a

Language and Vocabulary

Acquire and Use Academic Words	CC.3.L.6

PROGRAM RESOURCES

PRINT & TECHNOLOGY

Practice Master SG4.15, page SG42
Practice Master SG4.16, page SG43
Practice Master SG4.20, page SG47
Practice Master SG4.21, page SG48

SUGGESTED PACING

DAY 2 Introduce and read pages 4–15
DAY 3 Read pages 16–35
DAY 4 Read pages 36–54 and discuss
DAY 5 Connect across texts

Summary In 1998, six-year-old Ryan Hreljac began saving money to build a well in Africa. When the well was built, Ryan visited Uganda and met his pen pal, Akana Jimmy. Because of dangers that faced Jimmy in Uganda, the Hreljac family eventually brought Jimmy to Canada. Ryan and Jimmy continue to give speeches on behalf of the Ryan's Well Foundation, telling about the need for clean water around the world.

Activate Prior Knowledge Ask: *What is a goal you have worked hard to reach? What did you do to reach that goal?*

Build Background Explain that fighting, or civil war, began in the country of Uganda in the 1980s. Over the years, many villages have been victims of violent attacks, leaving hundreds of thousands of people homeless. Children were often kidnapped and made to fight in the war.

Story Words Use **Practice Master SG4.15** to extend vocabulary.

anxious, page 13 *distant*, page 4 *experience*, page 18
prepare, page 30 *skill*, page 18

Week 3 Teaching Resources
Nonfiction

BL BELOW LEVEL

Making Water Clean
by Rebecca Olien

Build Comprehension

- **Goal and Outcome** *Why does water need to be treated?* (Possible response: Water is polluted with dirt and bacteria that could make people sick.)
- **Explain** *How does water get from its source to our homes?* (Possible response: It comes from rivers and lakes, gets pumped through pipes to treatment plants, is filtered and disinfected, and then gets stored. Then it goes through pipes to our homes.)

Writing Options

- **News Report** Have students write a news report explaining how water gets cleaned and why this is important.
- **Interview Questions** Have students write three questions that they would like to ask someone who works in a water treatment plant.
- **Journal Entry** Invite students to write about how they use water each day. Encourage students to begin by first thinking about the different ways they use water throughout the day, from drinking to bathing to brushing their teeth.

BL BELOW LEVEL 530L

Farmers: Then and Now
by Lisa Zamosky

Build Comprehension

- **Draw Conclusions** *How did the invention of farm machinery change farming?* (Possible response: Machines made farming easier, so farmers could grow more crops.)
- **Make Comparisons** *What was life like for people before and after farming?* (Possible response: Before farming, it was hard to find food, and people had to move around to find it. After farming, people could stay in one place and grow more food than they needed.)

Writing Options

- **Email** Have students write an email to a friend telling him or her three things they learned from the book.
- **List** Have students make a list of three things farmers do and give a brief explanation for each item on the list. Then invite students to tell how that task was made easier by the invention of a new tool.
- **Journal Entry** Invite students to write about whether or not they would like to be a farmer and explain why or why not.

Check & Reteach

Ask students to give examples of opinions and supporting evidence from each book.
If students have difficulty finding opinions or evidence that supports the opinions, refer them to their opinion chart. Ask: *Do you see the words* think, believes, *or* should? *What does the person do to show this is how he or she really thinks or feels?*

DURING READING

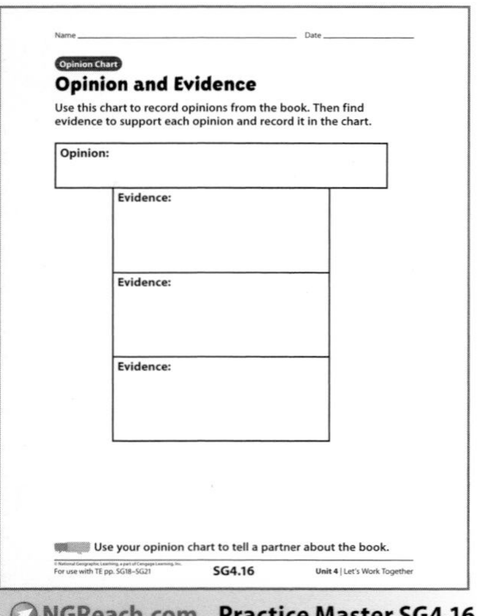

Name ________ Date ________

Opinion Chart

Opinion and Evidence

Use this chart to record opinions from the book. Then find evidence to support each opinion and record it in the chart.

Opinion:

Evidence:

Evidence:

Evidence:

Use your opinion chart to tell a partner about the book.

For use with TE pp. SG18–SG21 SG4.16 Unit 4 | Let's Work Together

NGReach.com **Practice Master SG4.16**

AFTER READING

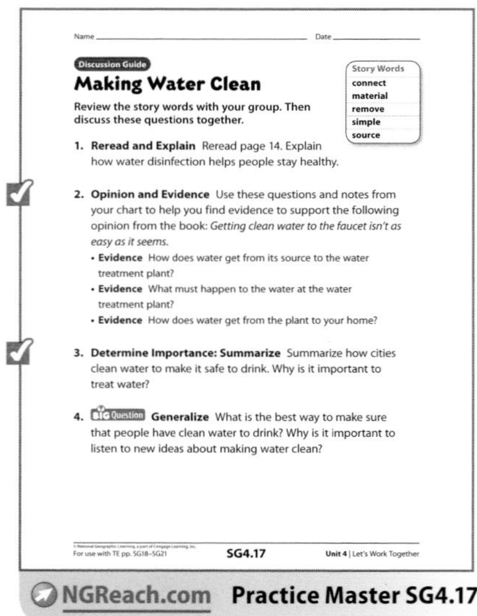

Name ________ Date ________

Discussion Guide

Making Water Clean

Review the story words with your group. Then discuss these questions together.

Story Words: connect, material, remove, simple, source

1. **Reread and Explain** Reread page 14. Explain how water disinfection helps people stay healthy.
2. **Opinion and Evidence** Use these questions and notes from your chart to help you find evidence to support the following opinion from the book: *Getting clean water to the faucet isn't as easy as it seems.*
   - **Evidence** How does water get from its source to the water treatment plant?
   - **Evidence** What must happen to the water at the water treatment plant?
   - **Evidence** How does water get from the plant to your home?
3. **Determine Importance: Summarize** Summarize how cities clean water to make it safe to drink. Why is it important to treat water?
4. Big Question **Generalize** What is the best way to make sure that people have clean water to drink? Why is it important to listen to new ideas about making water clean?

For use with TE pp. SG18–SG21 SG4.17 Unit 4 | Let's Work Together

NGReach.com **Practice Master SG4.17**

AFTER READING

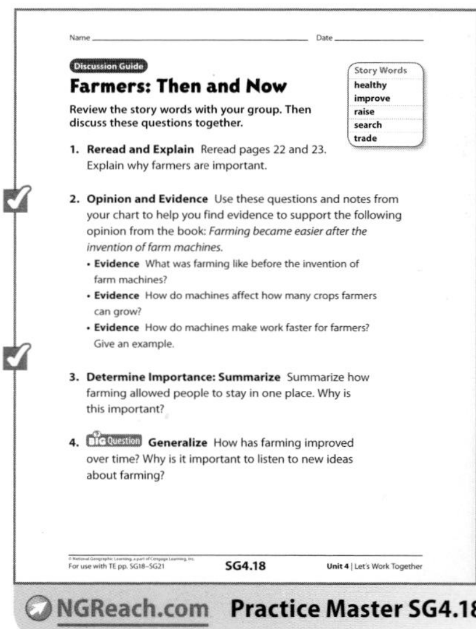

Name ________ Date ________

Discussion Guide

Farmers: Then and Now

Review the story words with your group. Then discuss these questions together.

Story Words: healthy, improve, raise, search, trade

1. **Reread and Explain** Reread pages 22 and 23. Explain why farmers are important.
2. **Opinion and Evidence** Use these questions and notes from your chart to help you find evidence to support the following opinion from the book: *Farming became easier after the invention of farm machines.*
   - **Evidence** What was farming like before the invention of farm machines?
   - **Evidence** How do machines affect how many crops farmers can grow?
   - **Evidence** How do machines make work faster for farmers? Give an example.
3. **Determine Importance: Summarize** Summarize how farming allowed people to stay in one place. Why is this important?
4. Big Question **Generalize** How has farming improved over time? Why is it important to listen to new ideas about farming?

For use with TE pp. SG18–SG21 SG4.18 Unit 4 | Let's Work Together

NGReach.com **Practice Master SG4.18**

OL ON LEVEL AD640L

A Weed is a Flower
by Aliki

Build Comprehension

- **Form Generalizations** *Why is George Washington Carver remembered as a great scientist?* (Possible response: He worked hard to find many uses for plants. His discoveries helped people all over the world.)
- **Identify Problem and Solution** *Why did Carver think it would be better for farmers to grow more than one thing?* (Possible response: Growing only one crop harms the soil. Changing the crops you plant keeps the soil healthy.)

Writing Options

- **Dialogue** Have students write a dialogue between George Washington Carver and a farmer in which he tries to convince the farmer to grow more than cotton. Encourage students to include both the farmer's concerns and Carver's ideas.
- **Character Sketch** Have students write a list of words that describe George Washington Carver. Then have them write a short character sketch of the man, using the words from their lists and facts from their books.
- **Journal Entry** Invite students to write about a time that someone gave them advice about something and tell how things turned out.

AL ABOVE LEVEL 810L

Ryan and Jimmy...
by Herb Shoveller

Build Comprehension

- **Analyze** *What does this book show you about what kids can do to make a difference? Explain.* (Possible response: It tells about a first grader who collects enough money to build a well in Africa and starts a foundation. This shows that kids can do great things.)
- **Explain** *Why was it important for the Hreljacs to get Jimmy out of Uganda?* (Possible response: His life was in danger because he had escaped the rebels more than once. If they caught him again, they would have killed him.)

Writing Options

- **Interview Questions** Have students write five questions that they would like to ask Ryan or Jimmy. Then have them share their questions with a partner.
- **Speech** Have students write a speech that Ryan or Jimmy might give, telling about their work.
- **Journal Entry** Invite students to write about a time they helped someone else. Encourage students to tell why they decided to help and how it turned out.

AFTER READING Form heterogeneous groups, and have each member of the group summarize his or her book. Then have groups use **Practice Master SG4.21** to guide discussion.

AFTER READING

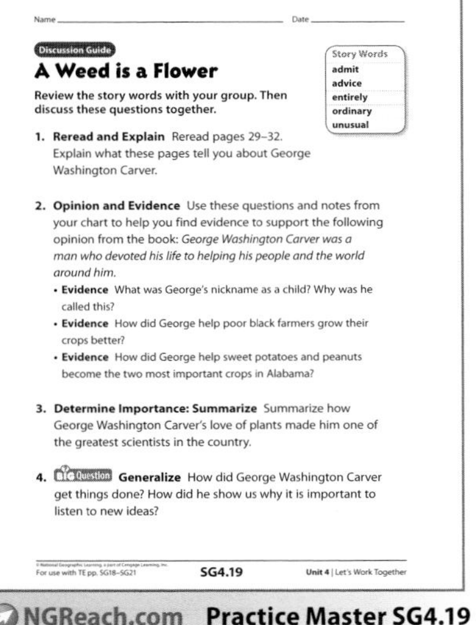

Name ______ Date ______

Discussion Guide

A Weed is a Flower

Review the story words with your group. Then discuss these questions together.

Story Words
admit
advice
entirely
ordinary
unusual

1. **Reread and Explain** Reread pages 29–32. Explain what these pages tell you about George Washington Carver.
2. **Opinion and Evidence** Use these questions and notes from your chart to help you find evidence to support the following opinion from the book: *George Washington Carver was a man who devoted his life to helping his people and the world around him.*
   - **Evidence** What was George's nickname as a child? Why was he called this?
   - **Evidence** How did George help poor black farmers grow their crops better?
   - **Evidence** How did George help sweet potatoes and peanuts become the two most important crops in Alabama?
3. **Determine Importance: Summarize** Summarize how George Washington Carver's love of plants made him one of the greatest scientists in the country.
4. Big Question **Generalize** How did George Washington Carver get things done? How did he show us why it is important to listen to new ideas?

For use with TE pp. SG18–SG21 SG4.19 Unit 4 | Let's Work Together

NGReach.com **Practice Master SG4.19**

AFTER READING

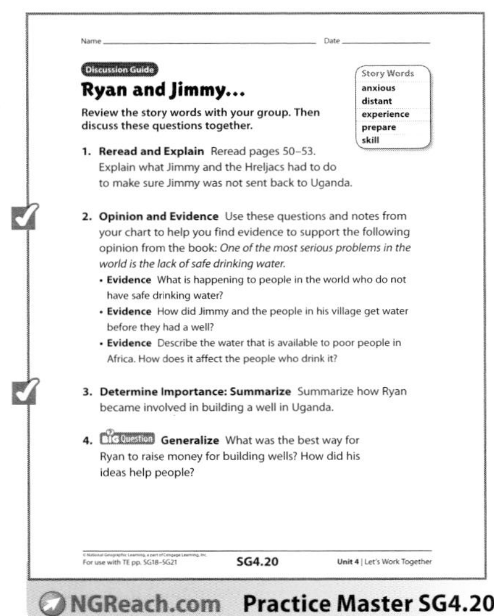

Name ______ Date ______

Discussion Guide

Ryan and Jimmy...

Review the story words with your group. Then discuss these questions together.

Story Words
anxious
distant
experience
prepare
skill

1. **Reread and Explain** Reread pages 50–53. Explain what Jimmy and the Hreljacs had to do to make sure Jimmy was not sent back to Uganda.
2. **Opinion and Evidence** Use these questions and notes from your chart to help you find evidence to support the following opinion from the book: *One of the most serious problems in the world is the lack of safe drinking water.*
   - **Evidence** What is happening to people in the world who do not have safe drinking water?
   - **Evidence** How did Jimmy and the people in his village get water before they had a well?
   - **Evidence** Describe the water that is available to poor people in Africa. How does it affect the people who drink it?
3. **Determine Importance: Summarize** Summarize how Ryan became involved in building a well in Uganda.
4. Big Question **Generalize** What was the best way for Ryan to raise money for building wells? How did his ideas help people?

For use with TE pp. SG18–SG21 SG4.20 Unit 4 | Let's Work Together

NGReach.com **Practice Master SG4.20**

AFTER READING

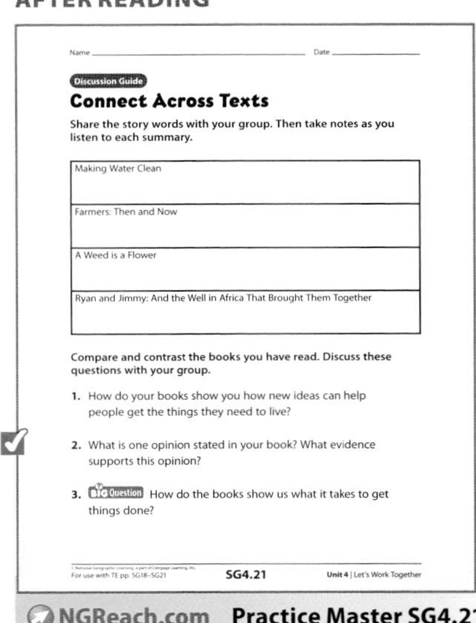

Name ______ Date ______

Discussion Guide

Connect Across Texts

Share the story words with your group. Then take notes as you listen to each summary.

Making Water Clean
Farmers: Then and Now
A Weed is a Flower
Ryan and Jimmy: And the Well in Africa That Brought Them Together

Compare and contrast the books you have read. Discuss these questions with your group.

1. How do your books show you how new ideas can help people get the things they need to live?
2. What is one opinion stated in your book? What evidence supports this opinion?
3. Big Question How do the books show us what it takes to get things done?

For use with TE pp. SG18–SG21 SG4.21 Unit 4 | Let's Work Together

NGReach.com **Practice Master SG4.21**

OBJECTIVES

Thematic Connection: Innovation

Read and Comprehend Informational Text

Explain Text Structure: Sequence

First Flight by Glen Phelan

Summary *First Flight* describes how Wilbur and Orville Wright invented the flying machine and explains how they made it fly. It also discusses the amazing achievements of aviator Amelia Earhart. In "First Flight," Glen Phelan explains that as children, the Wright brothers were interested in flying. As adults, their goal was to build a flying machine. After much study, they found that a flying machine needed wings, a power source, and controls. By 1902, they had perfected a glider. This enabled them to invent *Flyer 1*, the first airplane. In 1903, the brothers flew their machine at Kitty Hawk for 12 seconds. This launched the age of aviation. A diagram of *Flyer 1* shows key parts of the famous plane. "Amelia Earhart: Flying Into Fame" describes how Earhart became the first woman to cross the Atlantic in 1932. Then in 1934, she became the first person to fly across the Pacific. She disappeared in 1937, while on a flight around the world.

Activate Prior Knowledge Display the front cover and trace the airplane. Then ask: *How is this first flying machine like airplanes today?* (Possible responses: has wings, a pilot, and an engine; stays up in the air)

Build Background Explain that in 1903, Wilbur and Orville Wright made history. They built and flew the very first airplane. Use the diagram on pages 8–9 to describe the key parts of *Flyer 1*, the brother's amazing flying machine. Have volunteers explain what they think each part does.

PROGRAM RESOURCES

PRINT ONLY

***First Flight*, Pioneer Edition**

***First Flight*, Pathfinder Edition**

TECHNOLOGY ONLY

My Vocabulary Notebook

COMMON CORE STANDARDS

Reading	
Relate Ideas	CC.3.Rinf.3
Describe Text Structure	CC.3.Rinf.8
Read and Comprehend Informational Text	CC.3.Rinf.10
Language	
Acquire and Use Domain-Specific Words	CC.3.L.6

Mini Lesson

Explain Text Structure: Sequence

Explain: *Often, authors describe events in sequence, or in the order they happen. Authors may include dates and time order words, such as* next. Point out that good readers know how to explain the sequence connections in a text.

Read aloud the following text from page 6 of the Pioneer Edition of *First Flight* as students listen.

Kites and Gliders

Wilbur and Orville tested their idea on a kite.

Next, the Wrights built a glider. It took two years to get the design right.

The Right Wings

The Wright brothers tested their first glider in 1900.

Text from Pioneer Edition

Model identifying sequence connections: *The author tells events leading to the invention of the flying machine. The first event is:*

- *Wilbur and Orville tested their idea on a kite.*

I see the time order word next *and the phrase "took two years." These are clues that events are described in the order they happen:*

- *Next, the Wrights built a glider.*
- *It took two years to get the design right.*

The author is using sequence to make connections between events.

Have students identify another event in the text above. Then have them explain how the events are connected in a sequence. (Event: The brothers tested their first glider in 1900. Possible response: The author uses the date 1900 to tell what the Wrights did after getting the design right. The events occur in sequence. The author describes the events in the order they happen.)

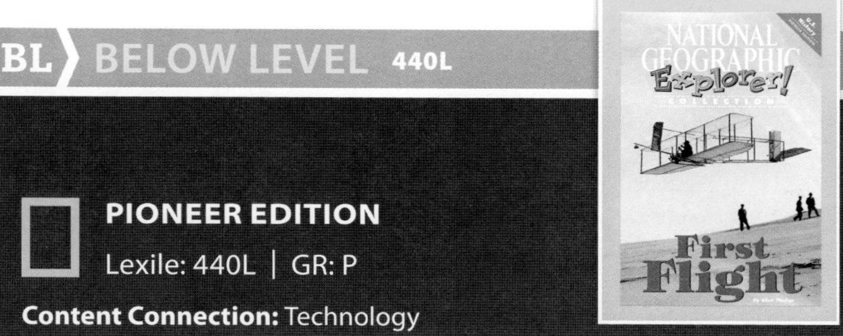

BL BELOW LEVEL 440L

PIONEER EDITION
Lexile: 440L | GR: P
Content Connection: Technology

Social Studies Vocabulary
Use Wordwise on page 7 to introduce new words:

glider *propeller* *warp*

Have students add new words to **My Vocabulary Notebook**.

Build Comprehension
After reading, use the Concept Check on page 12. Remind students to use details and examples to support each answer.

1. **Explain Text Structure: Sequence** What got the Wright brothers interested in flying? (In 1878 their father gave them a toy they called the Bat. They studied how it worked. When it broke, they looked at how it was put together. Next, they built a new one. They kept building better and better Bats. The author uses time order to connect the events.)
2. **Details** What was hardest about building a plane? (The hardest part was building controls to balance the plane.)
3. **Describe** How did buzzards help solve the problem? (The Wright brothers watched buzzards and saw that the birds twisted the tips of their wings for balance. So the brothers decided to try to twist, or warp, the wings of their plane to solve the balance problem.)
4. **Explain** What was *Flyer 1*? (It was the first flying machine the Wright brothers built. It became the first airplane in the world.)
5. **Evaluate** Who was Amelia Earhart? (a woman who lived in the early 1900s and who learned to fly) Why is she famous? (She was the first woman to fly across the Atlantic Ocean and the first person to fly across the Pacific. She set many flying records. She disappeared when trying to fly around the world.)

OL ON LEVEL 680L

PATHFINDER EDITION
Lexile: 680L | GR: Q
Content Connection: Technology

Social Studies Vocabulary
Use Wordwise on page 7 to introduce new words:

lift *rudder* *wing-warping*

Have students add new words to **My Vocabulary Notebook**.

Build Comprehension
After reading, use the Concept Check on page 12. Remind students to use details and examples to support each answer.

1. **Explain Text Structure: Sequence** How did the Wright brothers first become interested in flight? (In 1878 their father gave them a toy they called the Bat. They studied how it worked. Then when it broke, they looked at how it was put together. Next, they built a new one. They kept building better and better Bats. The author uses time order to connect the events.)
2. **Details** Why did the Wright brothers test their plane in Kitty Hawk? (There were strong, steady winds on the beach there.)
3. **Describe** What role did buzzards play in the Wright brothers' success? (The Wright brothers watched buzzards and saw that the birds twisted the tips of their wings for balance. So the brothers decided to try to twist, or warp, the wings of their plane to solve the balance problem.)
4. **Explain** Why is the Wright brothers' invention called the first airplane? (It was heavier than air and moved by its own power. It carried a passenger during a flight that a pilot controlled.)
5. **Make Inferences** How can Amelia Earhart be an inspiration to people today? (Possible response: She shows that people can follow their dreams and do things that others think are impossible. She also shows how to be brave.)

Check & Reteach
OBJECTIVE: Explain Text Structure: Sequence

Have partners explain how events in "Setting Records" on page 11 are connected in a sequence. (The author uses time order to make connections between events. Pioneer–dates: 1935, 1937. Pathfinder–dates: 1932, 1935; time order phrase: *Four years later*)
For students who cannot explain sequence connections, reteach with "Making History" (Pioneer) / "Powered Flight" (Pathfinder) on page 7. Say: *This section tells about testing* Flyer 1 *and finally flying the plane. How does the author present the events?* Have students skim the text for clue words. (Clues: Pioneer—*Then, a month passed, two days*; Pathfinder—*November 1903, December 15, two days*) Have groups discuss the connections and identify the order of events. (Order: propellers broke; tested and crashed; repaired plane; flew. The author uses sequence to connect events.)

Week 4 Teaching Resources
Nonfiction

BL BELOW LEVEL AD460L

All Aboard! Elijah McCoy's Steam Engine
by Monica Kulling

Content Connection: **Technology**

Picture Book Biography | Pages: 32 | Lexile: AD460L | GR: M

OBJECTIVES

Thematic Connection: Innovation

Read and Comprehend Text

Determine Importance

☑ **Determine Author's Purpose**

PROGRAM RESOURCES

PRINT & TECHNOLOGY

Practice Master SG4.22, page SG49

Practice Master SG4.23, page SG50

Practice Master SG4.24, page SG51

Practice Master SG4.28, page SG55

SUGGESTED PACING

DAY 2 Introduce and read pages 3–17
DAY 3 Read pages 18–32 and discuss
DAY 4 Reteach or conduct intervention
DAY 5 Connect across texts

Summary Elijah McCoy was the son of freed slaves. Even though he had studied to be an engineer, he worked shoveling coal in a steam locomotive. These trains stopped regularly so the engines could be oiled, a dangerous job. He invented an oil cup that was a safer and more efficient way to oil the engine and made train travel safer and faster.

Activate Prior Knowledge Ask: *When have you had an idea for how to do something better?*

Build Background Explain that the Industrial Revolution (1712–1942) was a period of innovation and invention. In 1712, Thomas Newcomen patented an early version of the steam engine. In 1769, James Watt's steam engine introduced the use of steam power. Then, in 1814, George Stephenson used the steam engine to power a train for the first time.

Story Words Use **Practice Master SG4.22** to extend vocabulary.

attach, page 26	*engineer*, page 6	*explode*, page 14
invent, page 25	*model*, page 26	

BL BELOW LEVEL GN600L

Levi Strauss and Blue Jeans
by Nathan Olson

Content Connection: **Fashion**

Graphic Novel Biography | Pages: 32 | Lexile: GN600L | GR: O

PROGRAM RESOURCES

PRINT & TECHNOLOGY

Practice Master SG4.22, page SG49

Practice Master SG4.23, page SG50

Practice Master SG4.25, page SG52

Practice Master SG4.28, page SG55

SUGGESTED PACING

DAY 2 Introduce and read pages 4–13
DAY 3 Read pages 14–29 and discuss
DAY 4 Reteach or conduct intervention
DAY 5 Connect across texts

Summary When the California Gold Rush began, Levi Strauss, a peddler in Kentucky, headed west to sell his goods. In California, he discovered there was a need for clothes that would last. Legend has it that he made pants from canvas and, eventually, denim. These first blue jeans were popular with gold miners—and later cowboys, railroad workers, and farmers—because they held up under rough conditions.

Activate Prior Knowledge Ask: *Do you like to wear blue jeans? What is it you like or do not like about them?*

Build Background Explain that in 1848, James Marshall found a few gold nuggets at Sutter's Mill near Sacramento, California. When news traveled east, the California Gold Rush began. Tens of thousands of people migrated to California in search of gold. Few people made it rich, but the California Gold Rush was an important step in the West becoming part of the United States.

Story Words Use **Practice Master SG4.22** to extend vocabulary.

comfortable, page 13	*rough*, page 15	*seeker*, page 5
typical, page 28	*voyage*, page 9	

OL ON LEVEL AD720L

Marvelous Mattie
by Emily Arnold McCully

Content Connection:
Industry

Picture Book Biography | Pages: 32 | Lexile: AD720L | GR: Q

COMMON CORE STANDARDS

Reading
Read and Comprehend Informational Text — CC.3.Rinf.10

Writing
Write Over Shorter Time for Specific Tasks — CC.3.W.10

Speaking and Listening
Draw on Preparation to Explore Ideas — CC.3.SL.1.a

Language and Vocabulary
Acquire and Use Academic Words — CC.3.L.6

PROGRAM RESOURCES

PRINT & TECHNOLOGY

Practice Master SG4.22, page SG49
Practice Master SG4.23, page SG50
Practice Master SG4.26, page SG53
Practice Master SG4.28, page SG55

SUGGESTED PACING

DAY 2 Introduce and read pages 4–15
DAY 3 Read pages 16–32
DAY 4 Reread and discuss
DAY 5 Connect across texts

Summary As a girl, Mattie Knight loved inventing things. At 12, she invented a metal guard that would keep shuttles from injuring mill workers. She was denied a patent because she was a little girl, but she kept inventing. Years later, she invented the machine that made paper bags with flat bottoms. Her idea was stolen, but she was able to prove in court that the invention was hers.

Activate Prior Knowledge Say: *Tell about a time you did something someone said you would not be able to do.*

Build Background Explain that a patent is an official document stating an inventor has rights as the only one to make, use, or sell an invention. The first patent was issued in 1790, after President George Washington signed a bill that started the American patent system.

Story Words Use **Practice Master SG4.22** to extend vocabulary.

entire, page 30 | *evidence*, page 30 | *mention*, page 21
sketch, page 7 | *sudden*, page 4

AL ABOVE LEVEL 860L

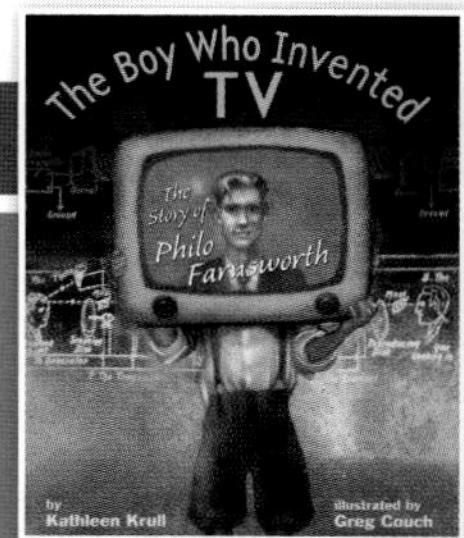

The Boy Who Invented TV
by Kathleen Krull

Content Connection:
Entertainment

Picture Book Biography | Pages: 40 | Lexile: 860L | GR: T

PROGRAM RESOURCES

PRINT & TECHNOLOGY

Practice Master SG4.22, page SG49
Practice Master SG4.23, page SG50
Practice Master SG4.27, page SG54
Practice Master SG4.28, page SG55

TECHNOLOGY ONLY

Digital Library: Early Television

SUGGESTED PACING

DAY 2 Introduce and read pages 3–15
DAY 3 Read pages 16–32
DAY 4 Reread and discuss
DAY 5 Connect across texts

Summary Philo Farnsworth was always interested in machines. When his family moved to Idaho, he saw power lines for the first time and learned about televisions, which people were trying to invent. He invented many gadgets to make chores easier. At 14, he got his idea for how a television could work, and at the age of 22, he finally had success.

Activate Prior Knowledge Ask: *Do you like to watch television? What shows do you like? What do you think it would be like to live without television?*

Build Background Display the photo of an early television set from the **Digital Library**. Explain that the first television show was the televised opening of the New York World's Fair on April 30, 1939, and Franklin D. Roosevelt was the first president to appear on television.

Story Words Use **Practice Master SG4.22** to extend vocabulary.

chore, page 3 | *complete*, page 19 | *effort*, page 3
interest, page 5 | *invisible*, page 8

Week 4 Teaching Resources
Nonfiction

BL BELOW LEVEL **AD460L**

All Aboard! Elijah McCoy's Steam Engine
by Monica Kulling

Build Comprehension
- **Identify Problem and Solution** *What problem did Elijah McCoy want to solve? What did he do?* (The train needed to be oiled often, and it was a dangerous job. He invented an oil cup so the train could be oiled as it kept moving.)
- **Draw Conclusions** *What kind of person was Elijah McCoy? How do you know?* (Possible response: He was smart and helpful. He cared about the safety of others. He had lots of ideas for inventions that would make trains operate more easily and more safely.)

Writing Options
- **Interview Questions** Have students write five questions that they would like to ask Elijah McCoy. Then have them share their questions with a partner.
- **Thank You Note** Have students write a thank you note from the grease monkey to McCoy, thanking him for his invention.
- **Journal Entry** Invite students to write about a time they had to do a chore or a job that they did not like. Encourage students to tell what they did to make it easier or more enjoyable.

BL BELOW LEVEL **GN600L**

Levi Strauss and Blue Jeans
by Nathan Olson

Build Comprehension
- **Goal and Outcome** *Why did Levi Strauss want to go to California?* (Possible responses: He thought he could sell his goods there. He thought he would follow those who were looking for gold.) *What happened when he got there?* (Possible response: He saw there was a great need for sturdy clothes. This led him to create blue jeans.)
- **Explain** *Why did Strauss add the orange pattern to the jeans' pockets?* (Possible response: So people could tell his blue jeans from the ones others were making.)

Writing Options
- **Advertisement** Have students imagine they work for Levi Strauss and he asks them to make an advertisement for his new blue jeans. Have them draw an ad and description for the new kind of pants, explaining why his are the best.
- **Friendly Letter** Have students write a letter in which Levi Strauss tells his brothers Louis and Jonas about his success in California.
- **Journal Entry** Invite students to write about their favorite article of clothing, explaining why it is their favorite.

Check & Reteach
Ask students to discuss the author's purpose for writing each book.
If students have difficulty discussing the author's purpose, refer them to their author's purpose charts. Ask: *What does the author want the reader to do? What is the author's purpose? What should the reader look for?*

DURING READING

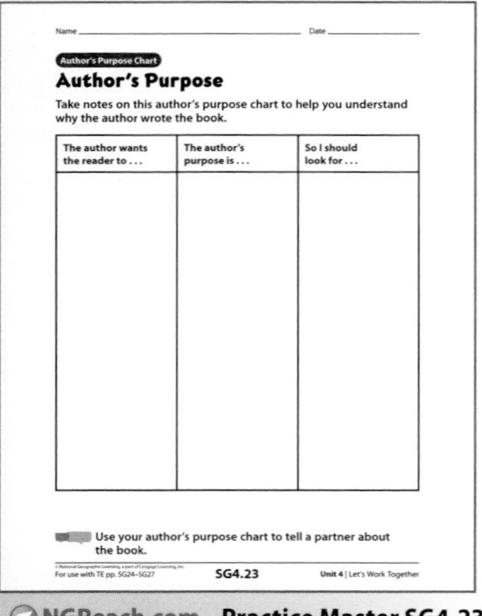
Name ______ Date ______

Author's Purpose Chart

Author's Purpose

Take notes on this author's purpose chart to help you understand why the author wrote the book.

The author wants the reader to . . .	The author's purpose is . . .	So I should look for . . .

Use your author's purpose chart to tell a partner about the book.

For use with TE pp. SG24–SG27 SG4.23 Unit 4 | Let's Work Together

NGReach.com Practice Master SG4.23

AFTER READING

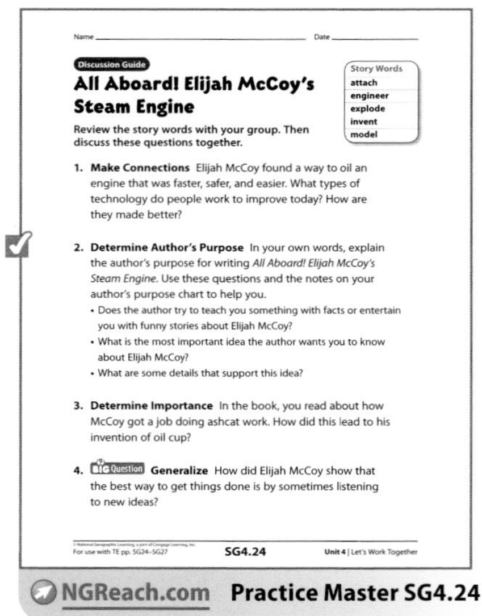
Name ______ Date ______

Discussion Guide

All Aboard! Elijah McCoy's Steam Engine

Story Words: attach, engineer, explode, invent, model

Review the story words with your group. Then discuss these questions together.

1. **Make Connections** Elijah McCoy found a way to oil an engine that was faster, safer, and easier. What types of technology do people work to improve today? How are they made better?
2. **Determine Author's Purpose** In your own words, explain the author's purpose for writing *All Aboard! Elijah McCoy's Steam Engine*. Use these questions and the notes on your author's purpose chart to help you.
   - Does the author try to teach you something with facts or entertain you with funny stories about Elijah McCoy?
   - What is the most important idea the author wants you to know about Elijah McCoy?
   - What are some details that support this idea?
3. **Determine Importance** In the book, you read about how McCoy got a job doing ashcat work. How did this lead to his invention of oil cup?
4. Big Question **Generalize** How did Elijah McCoy show that the best way to get things done is by sometimes listening to new ideas?

For use with TE pp. SG24–SG27 SG4.24 Unit 4 | Let's Work Together

NGReach.com Practice Master SG4.24

AFTER READING

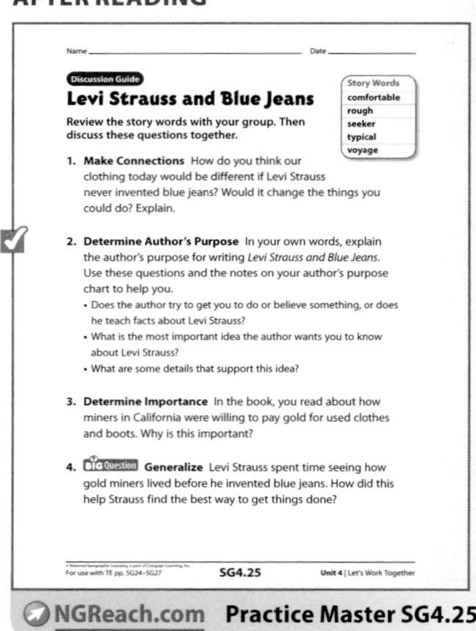
Name ______ Date ______

Discussion Guide

Levi Strauss and Blue Jeans

Story Words: comfortable, rough, seeker, typical, voyage

Review the story words with your group. Then discuss these questions together.

1. **Make Connections** How do you think our clothing today would be different if Levi Strauss never invented blue jeans? Would it change the things you could do? Explain.
2. **Determine Author's Purpose** In your own words, explain the author's purpose for writing *Levi Strauss and Blue Jeans*. Use these questions and the notes on your author's purpose chart to help you.
   - Does the author try to get you to do or believe something, or does he teach facts about Levi Strauss?
   - What is the most important idea the author wants you to know about Levi Strauss?
   - What are some details that support this idea?
3. **Determine Importance** In the book, you read about how miners in California were willing to pay gold for used clothes and boots. Why is this important?
4. Big Question **Generalize** Levi Strauss spent time seeing how gold miners lived before he invented blue jeans. How did this help Strauss find the best way to get things done?

For use with TE pp. SG24–SG27 SG4.25 Unit 4 | Let's Work Together

NGReach.com Practice Master SG4.25

OL ON LEVEL AD720L

Marvelous Mattie
by Emily Arnold McCully

Build Comprehension

- **Identify Problem and Solution** *Why did people need paper bags with flat bottoms?* (Possible response: The bags people had could not stand up on their own, and the bottoms kept splitting.)
- **Explain** *How did Mattie help to make work safer for mill workers?* (Possible response: She invented a metal guard that would keep a machine piece from flying out and hurting someone.)

Writing Options

- **News Brief** Have students write a news brief in which they explain what happened in court when Mattie tried to get her patent.
- **Diary Entry** Have students write a diary entry for Mattie, in which she tells about one of her inventions.
- **Journal Entry** Invite students to design an invention and write about how they think it could help people.

AL ABOVE LEVEL 860L

The Boy Who Invented TV
by Kathleen Krull

Build Comprehension

- **Make Judgments** *How would you describe Philo Farnsworth? Support your answer with an example from the book.* (Possible responses: He was creative and always wanted to learn. He did not like washing clothes, so he attached a motor to the washtub so that it would churn on its own, giving him more time to read.)
- **Form Opinions** *Do you think Farnsworth's invention of television was important? Explain.* (Possible response: Yes, it was important because most people watch television. It is a way for people to get the news and to watch the shows they like.)

Writing Options

- **Dialogue** Have students write a dialogue between Philo and Pem that they might have had after his Image Dissector exploded.
- **Book Review** Have students write a book review telling about the book, whether or not they liked it, and why.
- **Journal Entry** Invite students to write about whether or not they think Philo Farnsworth's invention was important and explain why or why not.

AFTER READING Form heterogeneous groups, and have each member of the group summarize his or her book. Then have groups use **Practice Master SG4.28** to guide discussion.

AFTER READING

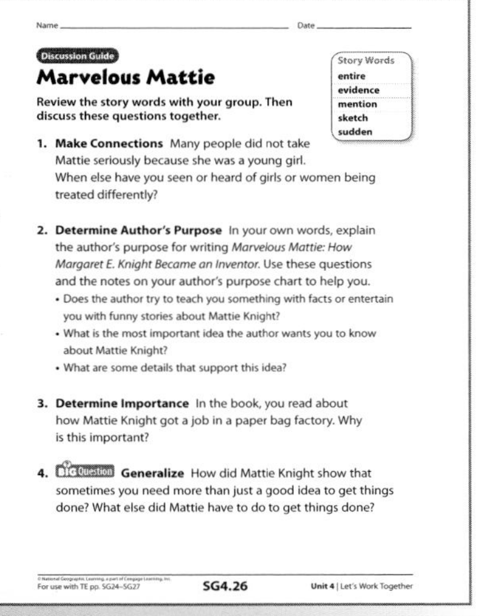

Name ______ Date ______

Discussion Guide

Marvelous Mattie

Review the story words with your group. Then discuss these questions together.

Story Words: entire, evidence, mention, sketch, sudden

1. **Make Connections** Many people did not take Mattie seriously because she was a young girl. When else have you seen or heard of girls or women being treated differently?
2. **Determine Author's Purpose** In your own words, explain the author's purpose for writing *Marvelous Mattie: How Margaret E. Knight Became an Inventor.* Use these questions and the notes on your author's purpose chart to help you.
   - Does the author try to teach you something with facts or entertain you with funny stories about Mattie Knight?
   - What is the most important idea the author wants you to know about Mattie Knight?
   - What are some details that support this idea?
3. **Determine Importance** In the book, you read about how Mattie Knight got a job in a paper bag factory. Why is this important?
4. Big Question **Generalize** How did Mattie Knight show that sometimes you need more than just a good idea to get things done? What else did Mattie have to do to get things done?

For use with TE pp. SG24–SG27 SG4.26 Unit 4 | Let's Work Together

NGReach.com **Practice Master SG4.26**

AFTER READING

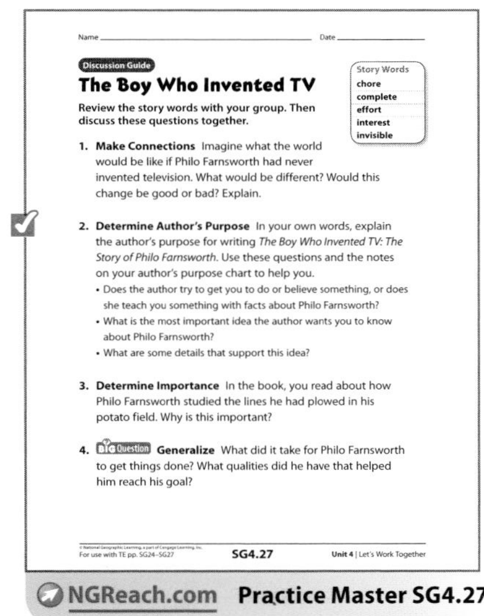

Name ______ Date ______

Discussion Guide

The Boy Who Invented TV

Review the story words with your group. Then discuss these questions together.

Story Words: chore, complete, effort, interest, invisible

1. **Make Connections** Imagine what the world would be like if Philo Farnsworth had never invented television. What would be different? Would this change be good or bad? Explain.
2. **Determine Author's Purpose** In your own words, explain the author's purpose for writing *The Boy Who Invented TV: The Story of Philo Farnsworth.* Use these questions and the notes on your author's purpose chart to help you.
   - Does the author try to get you to do or believe something, or does she teach you something with facts about Philo Farnsworth?
   - What is the most important idea the author wants you to know about Philo Farnsworth?
   - What are some details that support this idea?
3. **Determine Importance** In the book, you read about how Philo Farnsworth studied the lines he had plowed in his potato field. Why is this important?
4. Big Question **Generalize** What did it take for Philo Farnsworth to get things done? What qualities did he have that helped him reach his goal?

For use with TE pp. SG24–SG27 SG4.27 Unit 4 | Let's Work Together

NGReach.com **Practice Master SG4.27**

AFTER READING

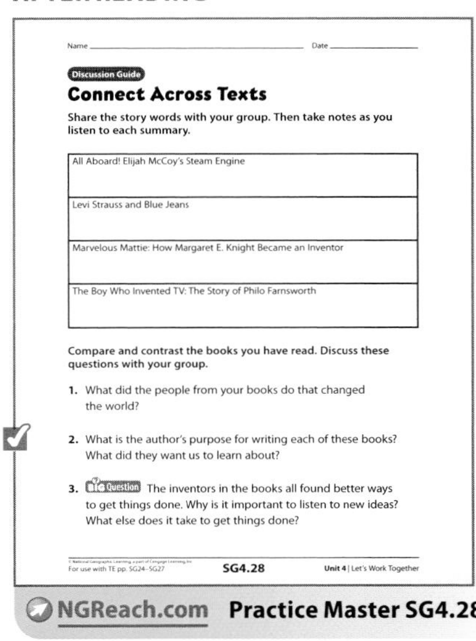

Name ______ Date ______

Discussion Guide

Connect Across Texts

Share the story words with your group. Then take notes as you listen to each summary.

All Aboard! Elijah McCoy's Steam Engine
Levi Strauss and Blue Jeans
Marvelous Mattie: How Margaret E. Knight Became an Inventor
The Boy Who Invented TV: The Story of Philo Farnsworth

Compare and contrast the books you have read. Discuss these questions with your group.

1. What did the people from your books do that changed the world?
2. What is the author's purpose for writing each of these books? What did they want us to learn about?
3. Big Question The inventors in the books all found better ways to get things done. Why is it important to listen to new ideas? What else does it take to get things done?

For use with TE pp. SG24–SG27 SG4.28 Unit 4 | Let's Work Together

NGReach.com **Practice Master SG4.28**

Name ______________________ Date ______________

Academic Vocabulary

Story Words

The Runaway Rice Cake

decide (di-**sīd**) ***verb***
To **decide** means to make a choice or a judgment. *The teacher will **decide** who wins the drawing contest.*

determine (di-**ter**-min) ***verb***
When you **determine** something, you figure it out or decide it. *We will **determine** the winner based on the highest score.*

generosity (jen-u-**rahs**-u-tē) ***noun***
Generosity is the act of being giving. *When they gave us all new bikes, we thanked them for their **generosity**.*

realize (**rē**-u-līz) ***verb***
To **realize** something means to become aware of it. *He will **realize** he forgot his key when he tries to unlock the door.*

spectacle (**spek**-ti-kul) ***noun***
A **spectacle** is something exciting to watch. *This year's fireworks display was an even bigger **spectacle** than last year's display.*

Under the Lemon Moon

astonished (u-**stahn**-ished) ***adjective***
If you are **astonished**, you have been amazed by something. *I am always **astonished** by how much my brother can eat.*

bundle (**bun**-dul) ***noun***
A **bundle** is a group of things wrapped together in a bunch. *I will put the **bundle** of sticks on the pile of firewood.*

content (kun-**tent**) ***adjective***
If you are **content**, you are happy. *I am always **content** when I can spend the day reading a good book.*

darkness (**dark**-nus) ***noun***
Darkness is being without light. *She turned out the lights and listened for sounds in the **darkness**.*

perch (**purch**) ***verb***
To **perch** on something means to sit on it like a bird. *The boys **perch** next to each other on the side of the pool and dip their feet in the water.*

Four Feet, Two Sandals

admire (ad-**mīr**) ***verb***
When you **admire** something, you think highly of it, or think that it is good. *I **admire** your courage for telling the truth.*

crowd (**krowd**) ***noun***
A **crowd** is a large group of people. *There was a **crowd** waiting outside the store before it opened.*

practice (**prak**-tus) ***verb***
To **practice** means to do something over and over to get better at it. *I want to be a good violin player, so I will **practice** hard.*

remove (ri-**müv**) ***verb***
To **remove** something means to take it away. *When you get a new toy, you **remove** it from the box.*

signal (**sig**-nul) ***noun***
To **signal** something is to show that it is going to happen. *My alarm clock will **signal** that it is time to wake up.*

Sadako and the Thousand Paper Cranes

ancestor (**an**-ses-tur) ***noun***
An **ancestor** is a person in your family who lived long ago. *My great-great-grandmother is my **ancestor**.*

celebration (sel-u-**brā**-shun) ***noun***
A **celebration** is a way to honor something in a special way. *The Fourth of July **celebration** will have fireworks.*

cheerful (**chēr**-ful) ***adjective***
If you are **cheerful**, you are happy. *He gave us a **cheerful** smile when we went into the store.*

complain (kum-**plān**) ***verb***
When you **complain**, you tell about the things that are making you unhappy. *The children **complain** about the cold weather.*

miserable (**miz**-ur-bul) ***adjective***
If you are **miserable**, you are very unhappy. *When I was sick last week, I felt **miserable**.*

COPY READY

COPY READY

Name ______________________ Date ____________

Theme Chart

Theme

Take notes on this theme chart to help you keep track of clues about the theme, or main message, of the book.

Theme Chart

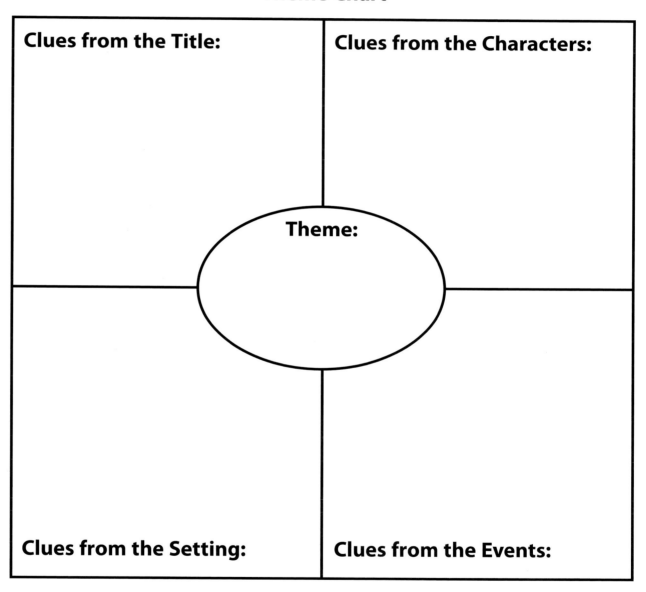

Clues from the Title:	**Clues from the Characters:**
Theme:	
Clues from the Setting:	**Clues from the Events:**

 Use your theme chart to tell a partner about the book.

Name ______________________ Date ______________

Discussion Guide

The Runaway Rice Cake

Story Words
decide
determine
generosity
realize
spectacle

Review the story words with your group. Then discuss these questions together.

1. **Make Connections** The Changs only had one rice cake to share. If you were one of the Changs, would you have given away your only rice cake? Why or why not?

2. **Analyze Theme** In your own words, state the theme of *The Runaway Rice Cake*. Use these questions and the notes on your theme chart to help you.
   - **Title** What clue does the title give you about the book?
   - **Characters** Explain why the rice cake is important to the Chang family's celebration.
   - **Setting** What is happening in the Changs' home and in the village? Why is this important to the story?
   - **Events** What happens between the Chang family and the old woman? What happens as a result?

3. **Determine Importance** In the story, the Changs give their holiday meal to an old woman. Why is this important to the rest of the story?

4. BIG Question **Generalize** How does the community work together to help the Chang family?

COPY READY

COPY READY

Name ______________________________ Date ________________

Discussion Guide

Under the Lemon Moon

Review the story words with your group. Then discuss these questions together.

1. **Make Connections** If you were Rosalinda, what would you have done if you saw the Night Man selling your lemons? Why?

2. **Analyze Theme** In your own words, state the theme of *Under the Lemon Moon*. Use these questions and the notes on your theme chart to help you.
   - **Title** What clue does the title give you about the book?
   - **Characters** What is Rosalinda's life like? What is life like for the Night Man and his family?
   - **Setting** Why is the market an important place for the Night Man?
   - **Events** What important things happen to Rosalinda that give you clues about the theme?

3. **Determine Importance** In the story, Rosalinda finds the man who stole her lemons. Why is this important to the rest of the story?

4. BIG Question **Generalize** Why do you think Rosalinda shared her lemons with everyone, including the Night Man?

Name ____________________ Date ____________

Discussion Guide

Four Feet, Two Sandals

Story Words
admire
crowd
practice
remove
signal

Review the story words with your group. Then discuss these questions together.

1. **Make Connections** Lina had not worn a pair of shoes for two years. If you were Lina, what would you have done if you saw someone else with your matching shoe? Why?

2. **Analyze Theme** In your own words, state the theme of *Four Feet, Two Sandals*. Use these questions and the notes on your theme chart to help you.
   - **Title** What clue does the title give you about the book?
   - **Characters** Explain why the sandals are important to the girls.
   - **Setting** Why would it be important to have a friend in a refugee camp?
   - **Events** What happens to test the girls' friendship? How do they handle the situation?

3. **Determine Importance** In the story, Feroza and Lina each find one sandal of the same pair. Why is this important to the rest of the story?

4. BIG Question **Generalize** Was sharing the pair of sandals the best way for the girls to get things done? Explain why or why not.

COPY READY

Name ______________________ Date ____________

Discussion Guide

Sadako and the Thousand Paper Cranes

Review the story words with your group. Then discuss these questions together.

Story Words
ancestor
celebration
cheerful
complain
miserable

COPY READY

1. **Make Connections** How does the story of what happened to Sadako remind you of other things you have heard about or experienced?

2. **Analyze Theme** In your own words, state the theme of *Sadako and the Thousand Paper Cranes*. Use these questions and the notes on your theme chart to help you.
   - **Title** What clue does the title give you about the book?
   - **Characters** Explain why Sadako's illness is important to the story.
   - **Setting** How does knowing what happened in Japan many years before help you understand the story?
   - **Events** What important things happen to Sadako that give you clues about the theme?

3. **Determine Importance** In the story, Chizuko teaches Sadako to fold paper cranes. Why is this important to the rest of the story?

4. BIG Question **Generalize** How do the children work together to make Sadako a symbol of peace?

Name ______________________________ Date ______________

Discussion Guide

Connect Across Texts

Share the story words with your group. Then take notes as you listen to each summary.

The Runaway Rice Cake
Under the Lemon Moon
Four Feet, Two Sandals
Sadako and the Thousand Paper Cranes

Compare and contrast the books you have read. Discuss these questions with your group.

1. How do the characters in the books show they care about people in their community?

2. What is the theme of your book? What do all the themes have in common?

3. BIG Question How do the books show us that working together is the best way to get things done?

COPY READY

Name ______________________________ Date ______________

Academic Vocabulary

Story Words

Grandpa's Corner Store

arrangement (u-**rānj**-munt) ***noun***
An **arrangement** is a plan for how something will be. *Living near my grandparents is a nice **arrangement** for my family.*

business (**biz**-nus) ***noun***
Business is the act of buying, selling, or making things. *Since **business** has been good this year, we have enough money to go on a family vacation.*

notice (**nō**-tis) ***verb***
To **notice** something means to be aware of it. *When I get to soccer practice, I **notice** that everyone is wearing uniforms.*

repair (ri-**pār**) ***verb***
To **repair** something means to fix it. *I took my broken watch to the shop so the watchmaker could **repair** it.*

success (suc-**ses**) ***noun***
If something is a **success**, it turned out well. *Our school bake sale was a huge **success**.*

Uncle Willie and the Soup Kitchen

feast (**fēst**) ***noun***
A **feast** is a big meal with large amounts of food, often for a special reason. *Every year, we have a **feast** at Thanksgiving.*

introduce (in-tru-**düs**) ***verb***
When you **introduce** someone, you let others meet that person for the first time. *Let me **introduce** you to my father.*

pretend (prē-**tend**) ***verb***
When you **pretend**, you act out something that is not real. *At the party, we all dress in animal costumes and **pretend** to be animals.*

separate (**sep**-ur-āt) ***verb***
To **separate** means to set apart. *Our teacher will **separate** us if we do not stop talking in class.*

toward (**tword**) ***adverb***
To move **toward** something is to go in the direction of it. *In a race, you run **toward** the finish line.*

Pitching in for Eubie

announce (u-**nowns**) ***verb***
When you **announce** something, you say it out loud for others to hear. *The judge will **announce** the winner.*

contribute (kun-**trib**-ūt) ***verb***
When you **contribute**, you give part of something. *If I earn part of the money for my new bike, my parents will **contribute** the rest.*

delivery (di-**li**-vu-rē) ***noun***
A **delivery** is something that is brought to a person or place. *We made a toy **delivery** to the children's hospital.*

dream (**drēm**) ***noun***
A **dream** is a hope you have for the future. *She has a **dream** of one day being a doctor.*

emergency (i-**mur**-jen-sē) ***noun***
An **emergency** is a time when help is needed right away. *When I broke my arm, it was an **emergency**.*

My Rows and Piles of Coins

clutch (**kluch**) ***verb***
To **clutch** something means to hold onto it tightly. *I felt her **clutch** my hand when she got the bad news.*

disappointed (dis-u-**poin**-ted) ***adjective***
You feel **disappointed** when something you hoped for doesn't happen. *I felt **disappointed** when I could not go to the party.*

errand (**er**-und) ***noun***
An **errand** is a short trip you take to get something done. *I was sent on an **errand** to buy milk.*

precious (**presh**-us) ***adjective***
Something that is **precious** is important to you. *My time is **precious**, so please do not be late.*

various (**vair**-ē-us) ***adjective***
Various means different kinds. *The store sells **various** flavors of ice cream.*

Name ______________________ Date ____________

Story Map

Story Elements

Take notes on this story map to help you keep track of details about the characters, setting, and plot as you read.

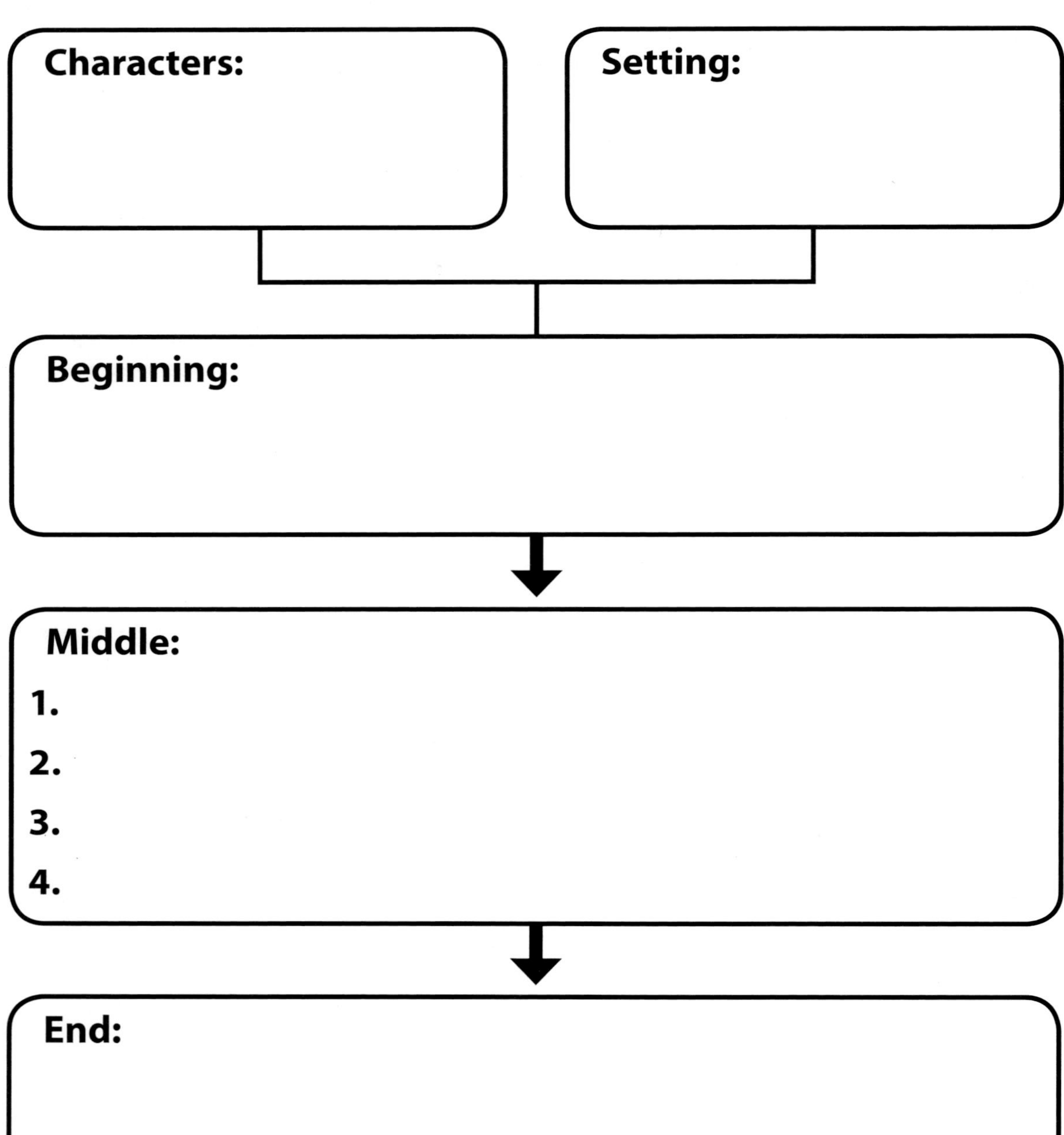

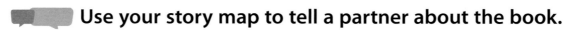

Use your story map to tell a partner about the book.

COPY READY

Name ______________________ Date ____________

Discussion Guide

Grandpa's Corner Store

Review the story words with your group. Then discuss these questions together.

Story Words
arrangement
business
notice
repair
success

1. **Character Motivation** Why does Grandpa decide not to sell his store?

2. **Describe Story Elements** In your own words, tell about the parts of *Grandpa's Corner Store*. Use these questions and the notes on the story map to help you.
   - **Characters** Who are the main characters of the story?
   - **Setting** Where does the story take place?
   - **Beginning** What is happening in town at the beginning of the story?
   - **Middle** What happens in class to make Lucy want to help Grandpa?
   - **End** What decision does Grandpa make at the end of the story? Why does he make this decision?

3. **Determine Importance** In the story, a big supermarket is opening in the community. Why is this important to the rest of the story?

4. BIG Question **Generalize** How does the community work together to stop Grandpa from selling the store?

COPY READY

Name ______________________ Date ______________

Discussion Guide

Uncle Willie and the Soup Kitchen

Story Words
feast
introduce
pretend
separate
toward

Review the story words with your group. Then discuss these questions together.

1. **Character Motivation** Why does Uncle Willie work at the soup kitchen?

2. **Describe Story Elements** In your own words, tell about the parts of *Uncle Willie and the Soup Kitchen*. Use these questions and the notes on the story map to help you.
   - **Characters** Who are the main characters of the story?
   - **Setting** Where does the story take place?
   - **Beginning** Why is the boy spending the day with Uncle Willie?
   - **Middle** What does the boy do to help in the soup kitchen to get ready for lunch?
   - **End** At the end of the story, what does Uncle Willie tell the boy about what they had done that day?

3. **Determine Importance** How does the boy feel when he sees the woman sleeping on the park bench? What does this make the boy start to think about?

4. BIG Question **Generalize** How does the community work together to help feed the people who come to the soup kitchen?

COPY READY

Name ______________________ Date ______________

Discussion Guide

Pitching in for Eubie

Story Words
announce
contribute
delivery
dream
emergency

Review the story words with your group. Then discuss these questions together.

1. **Character Motivation** Why does Lily want to earn money?

2. **Describe Story Elements** In your own words, tell about the parts of *Pitching in for Eubie*. Use these questions and the notes on the story map to help you.
   - **Characters** Who are the main characters of the story?
   - **Setting** Where does the story take place?
   - **Beginning** What does the Shorter family find out at the beginning of the story?
   - **Middle** What are some ways Lily tries to earn money?
   - **End** How does Lily finally find a way to earn money? How does this make her feel?

3. **Determine Importance** In the story, Eubie gets a college scholarship. Why is this important to the rest of the story?

4. BIG Question **Generalize** How does Lily's family work together to help Eubie?

COPY READY

Name ______________________ Date ____________

Discussion Guide

My Rows and Piles of Coins

Story Words
clutch
disappointed
errand
precious
various

Review the story words with your group. Then discuss these questions together.

1. **Character Motivation** Why does Saruni save his coins?

2. **Describe Story Elements** In your own words, tell about the parts of *My Rows and Piles of Coins*. Use these questions and the notes on the story map to help you.
   - **Characters** Who are the main characters of the story?
   - **Setting** Where does the story take place? Why would a bicycle be helpful for Saruni and his mother here?
   - **Beginning** What does Saruni decide to do with the coins his mother gives him?
   - **Middle** What happens when Saruni tries to buy a bicycle from the man at the market? How does it make him feel?
   - **End** How does Saruni's goal change after he gets a bicycle?

3. **Determine Importance** In the story, Saruni's mother gives him a few coins. Why is this important to the rest of the story?

4. BIG Question **Generalize** How do Saruni and his family work together to help each other get things done?

COPY READY

Name ______________________ Date ____________

Discussion Guide

Connect Across Texts

Share the story words with your group. Then take notes as you listen to each summary.

Grandpa's Corner Store
Uncle Willie and the Soup Kitchen
Pitching in for Eubie
My Rows and Piles of Coins

Compare and contrast the books you have read. Discuss these questions with your group.

1. What are some of the jobs people have in the books? Do they earn money for these jobs?

2. How is community or family important to the characters in these books?

3. BIG Question What do the books show us about how people can work together to get things done?

COPY READY

Name ______________________ Date ______________

Academic Vocabulary

Story Words

Making Water Clean

connect (ku-**nekt**) *verb*
When you **connect** things, you join them together. *Your fingers **connect** to your hands.*

material (ma-**tir**-ē-ul) *noun*
Material is a thing or a substance from which something can be made. *Wood is a **material** used to build a home.*

remove (ri-**müv**) *verb*
When you **remove** something, you take it away. *I help my mother in the garden when I **remove** the weeds.*

simple (**sim**-pul) *adjective*
Something that is **simple** is easy. *One plus one is a **simple** math problem.*

source (**sors**) *noun*
A **source** is where something came from. *The garbage can is the **source** of the smell.*

Farmers: Then and Now

healthy (**hel**-thē) *adjective*
If you are **healthy**, you are not sick. *If you exercise and eat the right foods, you will stay **healthy**.*

improve (im-**prüv**) *verb*
When you **improve** something, you make it better. *Studying more will **improve** your math grade.*

raise (**rāz**) *verb*
To **raise** something means to grow it. *They **raise** corn and soybeans on that farm.*

search (**surch**) *verb*
If you **search** for something, you look for it. *We helped Dad **search** for his lost keys.*

trade (**trād**) *verb*
When you **trade**, you give something in exchange for something else. *If you want, I'll **trade** you my tuna sandwich for your peanut butter and jelly sandwich.*

A Weed is a Flower

admit (ad-**mit**) *verb*
If you **admit** someone, you let them in. *The hospital will **admit** a patient after he or she has filled out paperwork.*

advice (ud-**vīs**) *noun*
Advice is something you give to help someone with a problem. *Saying you are sorry when you do something wrong is good **advice**.*

entirely (in-**tīr**-lē) *adverb*
When something is done **entirely**, it is done all the way. *You cannot have dessert until you have **entirely** finished your meal.*

ordinary (**or**-du-ner-ē) *adjective*
Something that is **ordinary** is nothing special. *Today started out as an **ordinary** day, but then something surprising happened.*

unusual (un-**yü**-zhu-wul) *adjective*
Something that is **unusual** is not common. *We have not had any snow this winter, which is **unusual**.*

Ryan and Jimmy. . .

anxious (**ank**-shus) *adjective*
When you are feeling **anxious**, you feel worried. *I feel **anxious** about my test tomorrow.*

distant (**dis**-tunt) *adjective*
If something is **distant**, it is far away. *Old age is part of a child's **distant** future.*

experience (ik-**spir**-ē-unts) *adjective*
If you have **experience** in something, that means you have done it before. *I asked my aunt to help me bake a pie for school because she has **experience** with baking.*

prepare (pri-**pār**) *verb*
When you **prepare** something, you get it ready. *The chef will **prepare** our dinner.*

skill (**skil**) *noun*
Skill is ability or talent. *It takes **skill** to play a sport well.*

COPY READY

COPY READY

Name ______________________ Date ____________

Opinion Chart

Opinion and Evidence

Use this chart to record opinions from the book. Then find evidence to support each opinion and record it in the chart.

Opinion:
Evidence:
Evidence:
Evidence:

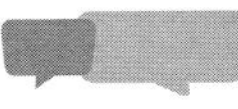

Use your opinion chart to tell a partner about the book.

Name ______________________ Date ______________

Discussion Guide

Making Water Clean

Story Words
connect
material
remove
simple
source

Review the story words with your group. Then discuss these questions together.

1. **Reread and Explain** Reread page 14. Explain how water disinfection helps people stay healthy.

2. **Opinion and Evidence** Use these questions and notes from your chart to help you find evidence to support the following opinion from the book: *Getting clean water to the faucet isn't as easy as it seems.*
   - **Evidence** How does water get from its source to the water treatment plant?
   - **Evidence** What must happen to the water at the water treatment plant?
   - **Evidence** How does water get from the plant to your home?

3. **Determine Importance: Summarize** Summarize how cities clean water to make it safe to drink. Why is it important to treat water?

4. BIG Question **Generalize** What is the best way to make sure that people have clean water to drink? Why is it important to listen to new ideas about making water clean?

COPY READY

Name ______________________ Date ______________

Discussion Guide

Farmers: Then and Now

Review the story words with your group. Then discuss these questions together.

1. **Reread and Explain** Reread pages 22 and 23. Explain why farmers are important.

2. **Opinion and Evidence** Use these questions and notes from your chart to help you find evidence to support the following opinion from the book: *Farming became easier after the invention of farm machines.*
   - **Evidence** What was farming like before the invention of farm machines?
   - **Evidence** How do machines affect how many crops farmers can grow?
   - **Evidence** How do machines make work faster for farmers? Give an example.

3. **Determine Importance: Summarize** Summarize how farming allowed people to stay in one place. Why is this important?

4. BIG Question **Generalize** How has farming improved over time? Why is it important to listen to new ideas about farming?

Name ______________________ Date ____________

Discussion Guide

A Weed is a Flower

Review the story words with your group. Then discuss these questions together.

Story Words
admit
advice
entirely
ordinary
unusual

1. **Reread and Explain** Reread pages 29–32. Explain what these pages tell you about George Washington Carver.

2. **Opinion and Evidence** Use these questions and notes from your chart to help you find evidence to support the following opinion from the book: *George Washington Carver was a man who devoted his life to helping his people and the world around him.*
   - **Evidence** What was George's nickname as a child? Why was he called this?
   - **Evidence** How did George help poor black farmers grow their crops better?
   - **Evidence** How did George help sweet potatoes and peanuts become the two most important crops in Alabama?

3. **Determine Importance: Summarize** Summarize how George Washington Carver's love of plants made him one of the greatest scientists in the country.

4. BIG Question **Generalize** How did George Washington Carver get things done? How did he show us why it is important to listen to new ideas?

COPY READY

Name ______________________ Date ______________

COPY READY

Discussion Guide

Ryan and Jimmy...

Story Words
anxious
distant
experience
prepare
skill

Review the story words with your group. Then discuss these questions together.

1. **Reread and Explain** Reread pages 50–53. Explain what Jimmy and the Hreljacs had to do to make sure Jimmy was not sent back to Uganda.

2. **Opinion and Evidence** Use these questions and notes from your chart to help you find evidence to support the following opinion from the book: *One of the most serious problems in the world is the lack of safe drinking water.*
   - **Evidence** What is happening to people in the world who do not have safe drinking water?
   - **Evidence** How did Jimmy and the people in his village get water before they had a well?
   - **Evidence** Describe the water that is available to poor people in Africa. How does it affect the people who drink it?

3. **Determine Importance: Summarize** Summarize how Ryan became involved in building a well in Uganda.

4. BIG Question **Generalize** What was the best way for Ryan to raise money for building wells? How did his ideas help people?

Name ______________________ Date ______________

Discussion Guide

Connect Across Texts

Share the story words with your group. Then take notes as you listen to each summary.

Making Water Clean
Farmers: Then and Now
A Weed is a Flower
Ryan and Jimmy: And the Well in Africa That Brought Them Together

Compare and contrast the books you have read. Discuss these questions with your group.

1. How do your books show you how new ideas can help people get the things they need to live?

2. What is one opinion stated in your book? What evidence supports this opinion?

3. BIG Question How do the books show us what it takes to get things done?

COPY READY

Name ______________________ Date ____________

Academic Vocabulary

Story Words

All Aboard! Elijah McCoy's Steam Engine

attach (u-**tach**) *verb*
When you **attach** something, you connect it to something else. *I can use a rope to **attach** the boat to the dock.*

engineer (en-ju-**nir**) *noun*
An **engineer** is a designer and builder of engines and machines. *The **engineer** is working on an invention that will allow cars to run on less gas.*

explode (**ik**-splōd) *verb*
To **explode** means to blow up. *If you put too much lighter fluid on the coals, the grill might **explode**.*

invent (in-**vent**) *verb*
To **invent** means to make something that has never been made before. *I wish someone would **invent** shoelaces that could tie themselves.*

model (**mah**-dul) *noun*
A **model** is something small that is built to look like something big. *My brother and I like to build **model** airplanes.*

Levi Strauss and Blue Jeans

comfortable (**kumpf**-tur-bul) *adjective*
If you are **comfortable**, you are relaxed. *You are a good host if you can make your guests feel **comfortable**.*

rough (**ruf**) *adjective*
Something that is **rough** is not smooth. *The **rough** rocks were worn smooth by the waves.*

seeker (**sē**-kur) *noun*
A **seeker** is someone who searches for something. *I try to learn something new every day because I am a **seeker** of knowledge.*

typical (**tip**-u-kul) *adjective*
When something is **typical**, that means it happens in an expected way. *A **typical** breakfast at my house includes cereal, milk, and orange juice.*

voyage (**voi**-ij) *noun*
A **voyage** is a long a trip. *My dream is to take a **voyage** around the world.*

Marvelous Mattie

entire (in-**tī**-ur) *adjective*
Entire means all of it. *This cake is so good I could eat the **entire** thing.*

evidence (**e**-vu-dents) *noun*
Evidence is clues that prove something. *Footsteps in the snow are **evidence** that someone was here.*

mention (**men**-shun) *verb*
When you **mention** something, you speak about it briefly. *Did I **mention** that I got an A on my spelling test?*

sketch (**skech**) *noun*
A **sketch** is a quick drawing. *I drew a **sketch** of my dog in my notebook.*

sudden (**su**-dun) *adjective*
Something that is **sudden** is not expected. *The sky was clear and then there was a **sudden** rainstorm.*

The Boy Who Invented TV

chore (**chor**) *noun*
A **chore** is a small job or task that is done on a regular basis. *My least favorite **chore** is washing the dishes.*

complete (kum-**plēt**) *adjective*
If something is **complete**, it is whole or finished. *We all must do our parts if we want the project to be a **complete** success.*

effort (**e**-furt) *noun*
If you make an **effort**, you try. *I put a lot of **effort** into my science project.*

interest (**in**-trest) *noun*
Interest is the attention you want to pay to something. *He does not have any **interest** in seeing that movie.*

invisible (in-**vi**-zu-bul) *adjective*
Something that is **invisible** cannot be seen. *The air we breathe is **invisible**.*

Name ______________________________ Date ______________

Author's Purpose Chart

Author's Purpose

Take notes on this author's purpose chart to help you understand why the author wrote the book.

The author wants the reader to . . .	The author's purpose is . . .	So I should look for . . .

COPY READY

Use your author's purpose chart to tell a partner about the book.

Name ______________________ Date ______________

Discussion Guide

All Aboard! Elijah McCoy's Steam Engine

Story Words
attach
engineer
explode
invent
model

Review the story words with your group. Then discuss these questions together.

1. **Make Connections** Elijah McCoy found a way to oil an engine that was faster, safer, and easier. What types of technology do people work to improve today? How are they made better?

2. **Determine Author's Purpose** In your own words, explain the author's purpose for writing *All Aboard! Elijah McCoy's Steam Engine*. Use these questions and the notes on your author's purpose chart to help you.
   - Does the author try to teach you something with facts or entertain you with funny stories about Elijah McCoy?
   - What is the most important idea the author wants you to know about Elijah McCoy?
   - What are some details that support this idea?

3. **Determine Importance** In the book, you read about how McCoy got a job doing ashcat work. How did this lead to his invention of oil cup?

4. BIG Question **Generalize** How did Elijah McCoy show that the best way to get things done is by sometimes listening to new ideas?

Name ______________________ Date ____________

Discussion Guide

Levi Strauss and Blue Jeans

Story Words
comfortable
rough
seeker
typical
voyage

Review the story words with your group. Then discuss these questions together.

1. **Make Connections** How do you think our clothing today would be different if Levi Strauss never invented blue jeans? Would it change the things you could do? Explain.

2. **Determine Author's Purpose** In your own words, explain the author's purpose for writing *Levi Strauss and Blue Jeans*. Use these questions and the notes on your author's purpose chart to help you.
   - Does the author try to get you to do or believe something, or does he teach facts about Levi Strauss?
   - What is the most important idea the author wants you to know about Levi Strauss?
   - What are some details that support this idea?

3. **Determine Importance** In the book, you read about how miners in California were willing to pay gold for used clothes and boots. Why is this important?

4. BIG Question **Generalize** Levi Strauss spent time seeing how gold miners lived before he invented blue jeans. How did this help Strauss find the best way to get things done?

COPY READY

Name ______________________ Date ______________

Discussion Guide

Marvelous Mattie

Story Words
entire
evidence
mention
sketch
sudden

Review the story words with your group. Then discuss these questions together.

1. **Make Connections** Many people did not take Mattie seriously because she was a young girl. When else have you seen or heard of girls or women being treated differently?

2. **Determine Author's Purpose** In your own words, explain the author's purpose for writing *Marvelous Mattie: How Margaret E. Knight Became an Inventor.* Use these questions and the notes on your author's purpose chart to help you.
   - Does the author try to teach you something with facts or entertain you with funny stories about Mattie Knight?
   - What is the most important idea the author wants you to know about Mattie Knight?
   - What are some details that support this idea?

3. **Determine Importance** In the book, you read about how Mattie Knight got a job in a paper bag factory. Why is this important?

4. BIG Question **Generalize** How did Mattie Knight show that sometimes you need more than just a good idea to get things done? What else did Mattie have to do to get things done?

COPY READY

Name ____________________ Date ____________

Discussion Guide

The Boy Who Invented TV

Review the story words with your group. Then discuss these questions together.

Story Words
chore
complete
effort
interest
invisible

1. **Make Connections** Imagine what the world would be like if Philo Farnsworth had never invented television. What would be different? Would this change be good or bad? Explain.

2. **Determine Author's Purpose** In your own words, explain the author's purpose for writing *The Boy Who Invented TV: The Story of Philo Farnsworth*. Use these questions and the notes on your author's purpose chart to help you.
   - Does the author try to get you to do or believe something, or does she teach you something with facts about Philo Farnsworth?
   - What is the most important idea the author wants you to know about Philo Farnsworth?
   - What are some details that support this idea?

3. **Determine Importance** In the book, you read about how Philo Farnsworth studied the lines he had plowed in his potato field. Why is this important?

4. BIG Question **Generalize** What did it take for Philo Farnsworth to get things done? What qualities did he have that helped him reach his goal?

COPY READY

COPY READY

Name ______________________ Date ____________

Discussion Guide

Connect Across Texts

Share the story words with your group. Then take notes as you listen to each summary.

All Aboard! Elijah McCoy's Steam Engine
Levi Strauss and Blue Jeans
Marvelous Mattie: How Margaret E. Knight Became an Inventor
The Boy Who Invented TV: The Story of Philo Farnsworth

Compare and contrast the books you have read. Discuss these questions with your group.

1. What did the people from your books do that changed the world?

2. What is the author's purpose for writing each of these books? What did they want us to learn about?

3. BIG Question The inventors in the books all found better ways to get things done. Why is it important to listen to new ideas? What else does it take to get things done?

Speaking and Listening Observation Log

As you monitor students in their small groups, put a check mark beside each behavior that you observe. Use conferences to coach students in developing speaking and listening skills.

Speaking and Listening Standards

Student Name																							
Comprehension and Collaboration **1.** Engage effectively in a range of collaborative discussions (one-on-one, in groups, and teacher-led) with diverse partners on *grade 3 topics and texts*, building on others' ideas and expressing their own clearly. CC.3.SL.1																							
a. Come to discussions prepared, having read or studied required material; explicitly draw on that preparation and other information known about the topic to explore ideas under discussion. CC.3.SL.1.a																							
b. Follow agreed upon rules for discussions (e.g., gaining the floor in respectful ways, listening to others with care, speaking one at a time about the topics and text under discussion). CC.3.SL.1.b																							
c. Ask questions to check understanding of information presented, stay on topic, and link their comments to the remarks of others. CC.3.SL.1.c																							
d. Explain their own ideas and understanding in light of the discussion. CC.3.SL.1.d																							
2. Determine the main ideas and supporting details of a text read aloud or information presented in diverse media and formats, including visually, quantitatively, and orally. CC.3.SL.2																							
3. Ask and answer questions about information from a speaker, offering appropriate elaboration and detail. CC.3.SL.3																							

COPY READY

COPY READY

Name ______________________ Date ______________________

Book Title ______________________ Pages ______________________

Reading Strategy Assessment

Check the reading strategies the student used and ask the questions that follow about how the student used the strategy. Use the rubric to help you determine how well the student used the strategy. Circle the student's score.

Ask: *What did you do while you were reading?*
Were there any parts of the book that confused you or were hard to follow?
What did you do to understand better?
How did it work?

Reading Strategy Rubrics			
	Plan and Monitor 4 3 2 1	**Ask Questions** 4 3 2 1	**Make Inferences** 4 3 2 1
	• *What did you do before you started reading the book?* • *When you were reading, did you go back and reread any part of the book for better understanding?* • *When you didn't understand, what did you do?* • *How did the meaning become clear to you?*	• *What questions did you have when you were reading?* • *Did you find answers to the questions?* • *Can you tell me some examples of these kinds of questions and what you learned?*	• *Did you infer, or figure out, something in the book that was not stated directly?* • *Were there details in the book that helped you figure this out?* • *What did you already know about those details that helped you make this inference?*
4	Consistently previews text and makes and confirms predictions. Monitors when comprehension breaks down and demonstrates ability to clarify text successfully.	Expands text meaning by asking questions that address large concepts and clarify confusion. Can provide relevant examples related to the book.	Makes inferences using examples from the text and background knowledge. Can use inferences to interpret the text.
3	Often previews text and makes and confirms predictions. Monitors comprehension, but cannot always clarify text independently.	Asks relevant questions and looks for answers to clarify confusion or understand the text.	Makes inferences that are consistent with the text or background knowledge. Cannot tell you how inference was made.
2	Sometimes previews and makes predictions, but may not confirm them. Can monitor when comprehension has broken down, but does not attempt to clarify text.	Asks only literal questions.	Makes inferences that are inaccurate or unsubstantiated.
1	Does not preview or make predictions. Is not aware of how to monitor comprehension or clarify meaning.	Does not ask questions or asks irrelevant questions.	Does not attempt to make inferences.

Name ______________________ Date ______________________

Book Title ______________________ Pages ______________________

Reading Strategy Assessment

Unit 4

Reading Strategy Rubrics				
	Determine Importance (Unit Focus) 4 3 2 1	**Make Connections** 4 3 2 1	**Visualize** 4 3 2 1	**Synthesize** 4 3 2 1
	• *What is an important idea in the book you chose?* • *Why do you think that is important?* • *How would you summarize this book for someone who has not read it?*	• *Did you read anything in the book that connects to your life? What was that, and how does it connect?* • *Did you read anything that reminded you of something else you read? What was that, and how does it connect?* • *Did you read anything you already knew about in the world around you? What was that, and how does it connect?*	• *Was there a part of the book that made you visualize (see pictures in your mind)?* • *How did this help you understand what you were reading?* • *Are there particular words that helped you visualize?*	• *Tell me about the book you read. What about the book can you generalize, or say is true most of the time?* • *What can you conclude from these parts?* • *Based on this book and what you know about (topic), what do you think is probably true about (topic)?*
4	Uses many parts of the text (pictures, title, words) to accurately identify an important idea, and summarizes the important ideas in the book.	Makes text-to-self, text-to-text, and/or text-to-world connections to enhance comprehension. Can explain how connections enrich understanding.	Describes multi-sensory mental images that go beyond the literal text. Explains how this helped understanding.	Synthesizes text accurately to draw conclusions and/or make generalizations. Can explain how synthesis helps comprehension.
3	Identifies and summarizes some important ideas from the text using a few parts of the text. Cannot explain importance.	Makes some type of relevant connection, but does not elaborate on how the connection helped understanding.	Describes multi-sensory mental images and goes beyond the literal text.	Combines some information from the text to draw basic conclusions or make limited generalizations.
2	Attempts to identify and summarize important ideas, but is inaccurate.	Attempts to make connections, but the connections are not relevant to understanding the text.	Describes few mental images directly related to text descriptions or pictures.	Attempts to synthesize, but synthesis is limited or leads to inaccurate conclusions or generalizations.
1	Cannot identify an important idea.	Does not make connections with the text.	Does not describe mental images related to the text.	Does not draw a conclusion or make a generalization about the text.

COPY READY

COPY READY

Name ____________________ Date ____________

Reader Reflection

Date	Title of Book	Author

Check all that apply.

1. Before I read this book, I:

- ☐ read the title.
- ☐ looked at the pictures.
- ☐ predicted what I would read about.
  I predicted: ____________________

2. If I didn't understand what I was reading, I:

- ☐ stopped to think about what I had just read.
- ☐ read it again.
- ☐ other (describe): ____________________

3. If I didn't understand a word while reading, I:

- ☐ stopped to think about its meaning.
- ☐ looked for clues to its meaning.
- ☐ checked in a dictionary or asked someone about the meaning of the word.
- ☐ other (describe): ____________________

4. This book reminded me of something I know or read already. It reminded me of:

____

This book was: ☐ easy ☐ about right ☐ hard

Rate this book! ☆ ☆ ☆ ☆ ☆

I would like to read other books: ☐ about this topic ☐ by this author

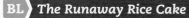

Practice Master SG4.2

Theme Chart Practice Master SG4.2

BL *The Runaway Rice Cake*

Clues from the Title:
The rice cake runs away.

Clues from the Characters:
The Chang family only has one rice cake for its holiday meal. The children are hungry. Crops have been bad, and they are poor.

Theme:
Giving leads to better things.

Clues from the Setting:
The family is preparing for the Chinese New Year.

Clues from the Events:
Because the family gives away their only rice cake, they get an even better celebration.

BL *Under the Lemon Moon*

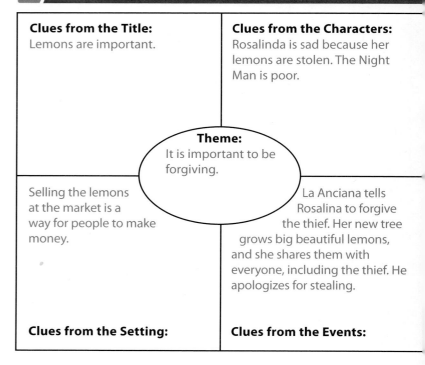

Clues from the Title:
Lemons are important.

Clues from the Characters:
Rosalinda is sad because her lemons are stolen. The Night Man is poor.

Theme:
It is important to be forgiving.

Clues from the Setting:
Selling the lemons at the market is a way for people to make money.

Clues from the Events:
La Anciana tells Rosalina to forgive the thief. Her new tree grows big beautiful lemons, and she shares them with everyone, including the thief. He apologizes for stealing.

OL *Four Feet, Two Sandals*

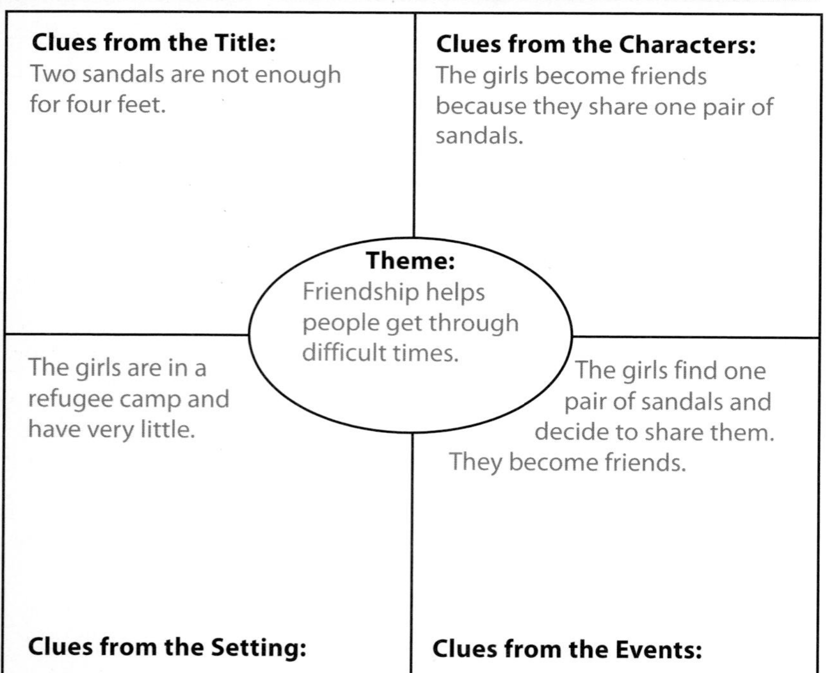

Clues from the Title:
Two sandals are not enough for four feet.

Clues from the Characters:
The girls become friends because they share one pair of sandals.

Theme:
Friendship helps people get through difficult times.

Clues from the Setting:
The girls are in a refugee camp and have very little.

Clues from the Events:
The girls find one pair of sandals and decide to share them. They become friends.

AL *Sadako and the Thousand Paper Cranes*

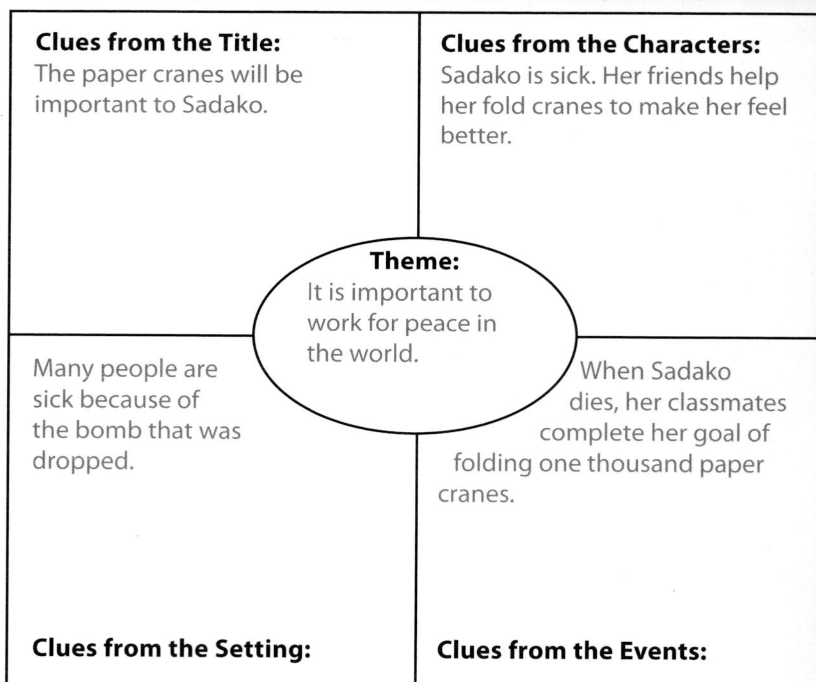

Clues from the Title:
The paper cranes will be important to Sadako.

Clues from the Characters:
Sadako is sick. Her friends help her fold cranes to make her feel better.

Theme:
It is important to work for peace in the world.

Clues from the Setting:
Many people are sick because of the bomb that was dropped.

Clues from the Events:
When Sadako dies, her classmates complete her goal of folding one thousand paper cranes.

Discussion Guides

Analyze Books

BL *The Runaway Rice Cake* Practice Master SG4.3

1. **Make Connections** (Students should tell what they would do in the Changs' situation and support their reasoning with details from the text and/or their own experiences.)
2. **Analyze Theme** When you are generous, others will be generous to you.
   - **Title** The rice cake is important.
   - **Characters** The children are hungry, and it is a holiday.
   - **Setting** Everyone is preparing the Chinese New Year. At celebrations, people often share special foods.
   - **Events** The Changs give their rice cake to an old woman. The villagers provide them with a wonderful celebration.
3. **Determine Importance** Without the rice cake, the Changs don't think they will have anything to eat for Chinese New Year. Because they were generous to the old woman, the villagers help them.
4. **Generalize** The community gives the Changs food, and the whole village celebrates together. They have the best Chinese New Year celebration ever.

BL *Under the Lemon Moon* Practice Master SG4.4

1. **Make Connections** (Students should tell what they would do in Rosalinda's situation and support their reasoning with details from the text and/or their own experiences.)
2. **Analyze Theme** Forgiving people is better than being angry.
   - **Title** The story will have something to do with lemons.
   - **Characters** Rosalinda has a nice home and family in a nice village. The Night Man and his family are very poor.
   - **Setting** He can sell the lemons at the market for money.
   - **Events** Rosalinda's lemons are stolen, which makes her angry. When she finds out the Night Man's family is poor and hungry, she is forgiving and helps him.
3. **Determine Importance** When Rosalinda sees the man, she is angry. When she realizes he needs the lemons to help his family, she wants to help him.
4. **Generalize** She wanted everyone to share her amazing lemons. She gives the Night Man a lemon so that he can plant the seeds and grow his own tree to sell the lemons. She gives so he won't have to steal.

OL *Four Feet, Two Sandals* Practice Master SG4.5

1. **Make Connections** (Students should tell what they would do in Lina's situation and support their reasoning with details from the text and/or their own experiences.)
2. **Analyze Theme** Friendship is important during difficult times.
   - **Title** There are not enough sandals.
   - **Characters** The girls become friends because they are sharing the one pair of sandals.
   - **Setting** Life is difficult. Many people have lost family members.
   - **Events** Lina is on the list to go to America. They each take a sandal to remember each other.
3. **Determine Importance** Sharing the sandals helps them become good friends.
4. **Generalize** Yes, they are each able to wear shoes some of the time, and they become friends, which makes camp life better.

AL *Sadako and the Thousand Paper Cranes* Practice Master SG4.6

1. **Make Connections** (Students should share other stories they have read, world events, or experiences, and tell how it reminds them of the story of Sadako.)
2. **Analyze Theme** It is important to work for peace.
   - **Title** The story will be about Sadako and paper cranes.
   - **Characters** She is sick because of a bomb that was dropped nine years earlier.
   - **Setting** A bomb had been dropped that continued to make people sick and die many years later.
   - **Events** She gets sick, but stays hopeful. She reminds people of how war can hurt people for a long time.
3. **Determine Importance** The cranes help give Sadako hope and later become a symbol of peace.
4. **Generalize** They finish her cranes and continue to place cranes at a statue of Sadako in the Hiroshima Peace Park.

Connect Across Texts Practice Master SG4.7

1. The Changs share their rice cake with the old woman. The Changs' neighbors all share food with them; Rosalinda shares her lemons with the community and helps the Night Man, instead of getting angry with him; Feroza and Lina share one pair of sandals; Sadako's classmates fold cranes for her to help her reach her goal after she dies. They also have a monument built in her name.
2. All the themes show why it is important to care about others. When people share and work together, there is always a better outcome.
3. Each book shows that life is better when people work together or help each other.

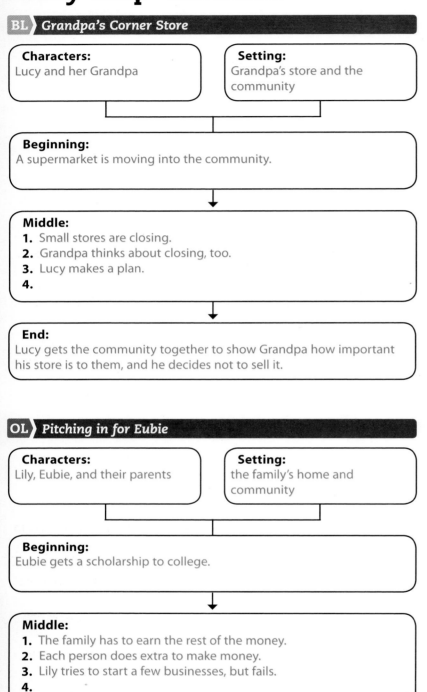

Practice Master SG4.9

Story Map Practice Master SG4.9

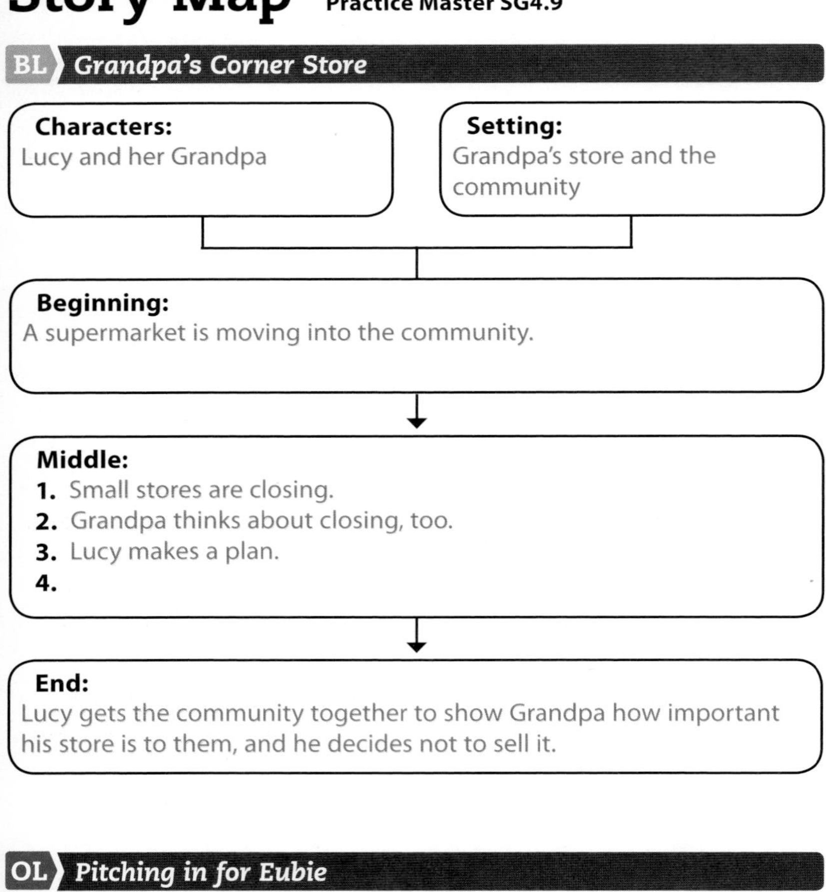

BL *Grandpa's Corner Store*

Characters:
Lucy and her Grandpa

Setting:
Grandpa's store and the community

Beginning:
A supermarket is moving into the community.

Middle:
1. Small stores are closing.
2. Grandpa thinks about closing, too.
3. Lucy makes a plan.
4.

End:
Lucy gets the community together to show Grandpa how important his store is to them, and he decides not to sell it.

BL *Uncle Willie and the Soup Kitchen*

Characters:
a boy and his Uncle Willie

Setting:
the community and the soup kitchen

Beginning:
The boy finds out about the soup kitchen and plans to go with Uncle Willie the next week.

Middle:
1. The boy goes with Uncle Willie to the soup kitchen.
2. He helps cook and set up for lunch.
3. He meets the people who come to eat.
4.

End:
The boy helps clean up and leaves the soup kitchen with Uncle Willie.

OL *Pitching in for Eubie*

Characters:
Lily, Eubie, and their parents

Setting:
the family's home and community

Beginning:
Eubie gets a scholarship to college.

Middle:
1. The family has to earn the rest of the money.
2. Each person does extra to make money.
3. Lily tries to start a few businesses, but fails.
4.

End:
Lily gets a job keeping an older woman company, and the family celebrates.

AL *My Rows and Piles of Coins*

Characters:
Saruni and his parents

Setting:
A village in Tanzania, the market

Beginning:
Saruni's mother gives him a few coins at the market.

Middle:
1. Saruni sees a bicycle.
2. He decides to save his coins to buy it.
3. He cannot save enough.
4.

End:
Saruni's father sells him his bicycle for the coins he has, and his mother gives the money back to him as a reward for being a good son.

Discussion Guides

Analyze Books

BL *Grandpa's Corner Store* — Practice Master SG4.10

1. **Character Motivation** He sees that his store is important to the community and that the supermarket can't give the community everything he can.
2. **Describe Story Elements**
   - **Characters** Lucy and Grandpa
   - **Setting** Grandpa's store and the community
   - **Beginning** There is a supermarket moving into the neighborhood.
   - **Middle** Her teacher talks about how a community is made up of people who live and work together.
   - **End** Grandpa decides to keep his store open because Lucy got the community together to show him how important the store is to them.
3. **Determine Importance** Because the supermarket is opening, small stores are closing. This makes Grandpa think he should sell his store, too.
4. **Generalize** People from the community get together at Grandpa's store to help clean it up and show him that they don't want him to sell it.

BL *Uncle Willie and the Soup Kitchen* — Practice Master SG4.11

1. **Character Motivation** He thinks it is important to help people.
2. **Describe Story Elements**
   - **Characters** the boy and Uncle Willie
   - **Setting** the community and the soup kitchen
   - **Beginning** He has the day off of school, and he wants to know what happens at a soup kitchen.
   - **Middle** He helps Uncle Willie pick up the food. Then he helps cut vegetables for the soup and gets the other food ready. He helps set the tables and greets people as they come in.
   - **End** He tells him that they fed one hundred and twenty-one people that day.
3. **Determine Importance** He feels sad when he sees her. He begins to wonder about the people who go to the soup kitchen and wants to know what it is like there.
4. **Generalize** An area market gives chickens for the soup. People from the community work there to cook, set tables, and clean up, so hungry people can have a nice meal.

OL *Pitching in for Eubie* — Practice Master SG4.12

1. **Character Motivation** She wants to help raise money so her sister can go to college.
2. **Describe Story Elements**
   - **Characters** Lily, Eubie, and their parents
   - **Setting** the family's home and community
   - **Beginning** Eubie has received a scholarship to college, but they will have to contribute three thousand dollars to her school fees.
   - **Middle** She tries selling iced tea, selling night crawlers, and taking care of people's pets.
   - **End** She gets a job keeping an elderly woman company. She will earn five dollars an hour, which is more than she expected. She feels like she is really pitching in for Eubie.
3. **Determine Importance** Her scholarship will not pay for all of her school fees. The rest of the story is about how Lily and her family try to help.
4. **Generalize** Everyone takes on extra work to earn money. They eat more leftovers for dinner, and don't eat together as often because everyone is working more.

AL *My Rows and Piles of Coins* — Practice Master SG4.13

1. **Character Motivation** He sees a bicycle he wants to buy, so he saves his coins so he'll have more money.
2. **Describe Story Elements**
   - **Characters** Saruni and his parents
   - **Setting** Tanzania and the village market. Saruni could use a bicycle to help his mother carry things to the market.
   - **Beginning** He saves them to buy a bicycle.
   - **Middle** He is told that he does not have enough money. He feels sad and disappointed.
   - **End** He makes a new goal of buying a cart to pull behind his bicycle so that he can help his mother even more.
3. **Determine Importance** The coins give him the idea to save money to buy a bicycle.
4. **Generalize** Saruni wants to buy a bicycle so he can help make his mother's work of going to the market easier. His parents help Saruni by giving him an old bicycle and letting him keep the money. He decides to save that money to buy a cart to help his mother even more.

Connect Across Texts — Practice Master SG4.14

1. Grandpa has a store, and Lucy helps him. Grandpa makes money by selling things; Uncle Willie works at a soup kitchen. He doesn't get paid; Lily tries many jobs and finally finds one that helps her earn money. Her family members all have paying jobs: Eubie babysits, her mother sews, her brother has a newspaper route and job at the gas station, and her father works in the fields; Saruni earns money by helping his mother at the market, doing house chores, and helping on the farm.
2. In all the books, the characters help each other for the good of the community or the family. People have jobs to help other people.
3. Each book gives an example of how people work together to reach a goal. They help save a store, feed the hungry, save money for college fees, and save money to buy a bicycle to help the family.

Week 3 Practice Master Answer Key
Nonfiction

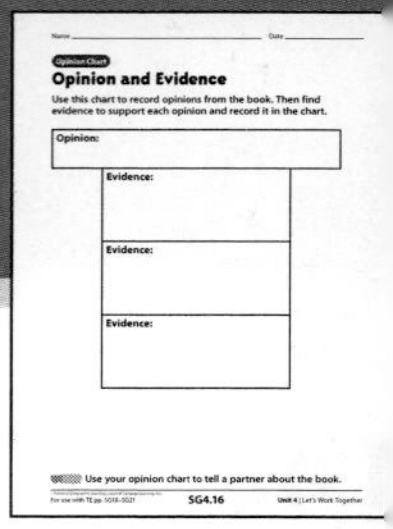

Practice Master SG4.16

Opinion Chart **Practice Master SG4.16**

BL *Making Water Clean*

Opinion:
Getting clean water to the faucet isn't as easy as it seems.

Evidence:
Water must be pumped many miles through pipes to water treatment plants.

Evidence:
Sediment must be removed using alum and filters. Then the water must be disinfected to remove bacteria.

Evidence:
Water is stored in large towers and pumped into homes through water mains.

BL *Farmers: Then and Now*

Opinion:
Farming became easier after the invention of farm machines.

Evidence:
Before machines, farmers had to do everything by hand.

Evidence:
Machines allow farmers to plant more land and grow more crops.

Evidence:
In 1830, it would take 300 hours to plant 100 bushels of wheat. In 1975, the same work took three or four hours because of machines.

OL *A Weed is a Flower*

Opinion:
George Washington Carver devoted his life to helping his people and the world around him.

Evidence:
He taught people about plants, even when he was a child.

Evidence:
He helped poor, black farmers grow more crops and make a better living.

Evidence:
He found many things could be made from peanuts and sweet potatoes.

AL *Ryan and Jimmy...*

Opinion:
One of the most serious problems in the world is the lack of safe drinking water.

Evidence:
People all over the world are dying without clean water.

Evidence:
In places like Jimmy's village, people have to walk miles every day to find water.

Evidence:
Much of the water is dirty. It makes people sick.

Discussion Guides

Analyze Books

BL Making Water Clean

Practice Master SG4.17

1. **Reread and Explain** During disinfection, chemicals are added to water to kill bacteria. Chlorine can be added to protect people from disease.
2. **Opinion and Evidence**
   - **Evidence** Water must be pumped many miles through pipes to water treatment plants.
   - **Evidence** The water must be treated to remove dirt and bacteria.
   - **Evidence** Water is stored in large towers and pumped into homes through water mains.
3. **Determine Importance: Summarize** Cities pump water into water treatment plants. Dirt is removed using filters and a powder called alum. Then water is disinfected to remove bacteria. Treating water is important because many water sources are polluted. Untreated water is full of dirt, particles, and bacteria that could make people sick.
4. **Generalize** Cities are responsible for making water clean by treating the water to remove dirt and bacteria. It is important to listen to new ideas because people need clean water, but it takes a lot of work. There might be an easier way to get clean water.

BL Farmers: Then and Now

Practice Master SG4.18

1. **Reread and Explain** We eat many things that come from a farm. Farmers work hard to grow the food we need to live.
2. **Opinion and Evidence**
   - **Evidence** Before machines, farmers had to do everything by hand.
   - **Evidence** Machines allow farmers to plant more land and grow more crops.
   - **Evidence** In 1830, it would take 300 hours to plant 100 bushels of wheat. In 1975, the same work took 3 or 4 hours because of machines.
3. **Determine Importance: Summarize** Before farming, people had to hunt and search for plants. They had to travel to find enough to eat. They were moving all the time. Once people started farming, they could stay in one place. This is important because it allowed people to build communities.
4. **Generalize** In the beginning, all farming was done by hand. Then machines were invented to make farming easier. New ways of watering and protecting crops were invented. Then farmers could grow more than they needed and sell the extra. New ideas help people get what they need and give them more free time to do other things.

OL A Weed is a Flower

Practice Master SG4.19

1. **Reread and Explain** Carver did not do all his work for money. He wanted to help people and did not ask for anything in return. Being at home and continuing to learn were the most important things to him.
2. **Opinion and Evidence**
   - **Evidence** He was called the Plant Doctor because he gave people advice about their plants.
   - **Evidence** He taught them to plant peanuts and sweet potatoes instead of just cotton.
   - **Evidence** He found hundreds of uses for sweet potatoes and peanuts, such as paper, ink, shaving cream, shampoo, and many kinds of food.
3. **Determine Importance: Summarize** His love for plants led him to make many important discoveries about farming and plant uses. This helped farmers improve their farming.
4. **Generalize** Carver never stopped wanting to learn and help his people. His ideas led to new discoveries about plants and farming.

AL Ryan and Jimmy...

Practice Master SG4.20

1. **Reread and Explain** They had to prove Jimmy's life would be in danger if he went back to Uganda. This meant Jimmy had to answer a judge's questions. Ryan's mom had to answer questions, too.
2. **Opinion and Evidence**
   - **Evidence** Hundreds of thousands of people are dying.
   - **Evidence** They had to walk up to 3 miles each way to find water and bring it back in jugs. Jimmy sometimes had to do that 3–4 times a day.
   - **Evidence** There isn't much water. People in Agweo are poor. They make their living by farming and don't have access to clean water.
3. **Determine Importance: Summarize** Ryan learned that many people in the world don't have clean water to drink. He wanted to raise money to build a well in Africa. He did chores to raise money. When people heard what he was doing, they sent him money. All his hard work paid off.
4. **Generalize** Ryan got other people involved. He worked hard to teach people about how many people did not have safe water to drink. He traveled around the world giving speeches to get support for the Ryan's Well Foundation.

Connect Across Texts **Practice Master SG4.21**

1. People need clean water. Sometimes cities clean the water for people. We can help people in the world who don't have clean water raise money to build wells. People need better ways of farming so they can produce more food. Tools make farming easier and faster. New uses for crops give farmers more options about useful things to grow.
2. (Students should explain why they know a statement is an opinion and provide adequate evidence from the text to support each opinion.)
3. Each book describes ways that people work to provide something that everyone needs to live, such as clean water and food.

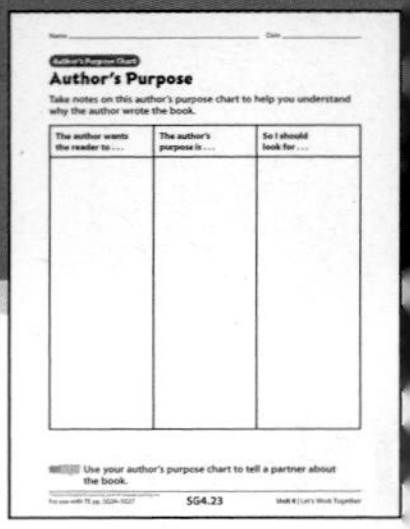

Practice Master SG4.23

Author's Purpose Chart Practice Master SG4.23

BL All Aboard! Elijah McCoy's Steam Engine

The author wants the reader to . . .	The author's purpose is . . .	So I should look for . . .
learn about Elijah McCoy and his invention.	to inform.	details about Elijah McCoy's life, such as what led him to inventing the oil cup for the steam locomotive, and why that was important.

BL Levi Strauss and Blue Jeans

The author wants the reader to . . .	The author's purpose is . . .	So I should look for . . .
learn about why and how Levi Strauss first made blue jeans.	to inform.	details about Levi Strauss's life, what led him to make blue jeans, and why that was important.

OL Marvelous Mattie

The author wants the reader to . . .	The author's purpose is . . .	So I should look for . . .
learn about Mattie Knight and her invention.	to inform.	details about Mattie Knight's life, what led her to inventing the machine that makes flat-bottomed paper bags, and why that was important.

AL The Boy Who Invented TV

The author wants the reader to . . .	The author's purpose is . . .	So I should look for . . .
learn about Philo Farnsworth and his invention.	to inform.	details about Philo Farnsworth's life, what led him to inventing the television, and why that was important.

Discussion Guides

Analyze Books

BL *All Aboard! Elijah McCoy's Steam Engine* Practice Master SG4.24

1. **Make Connections** (Students should name technologies, such as cell phones, computers, or video games, and describe improvements that have been or could be made.)
2. **Determine Author's Purpose** The author's purpose is to inform the reader about the life of Elijah McCoy, tell how he came to invent the oil cup for the steam locomotive, and explain how this invention changed travel by train.
   - The author teaches with facts.
   - Elijah McCoy's oil cup invention made travel by train safer and faster.
   - He saw a problem with how the train's engine worked. It had to be oiled many times in one trip, which took a lot of time. Oiling the engine was dangerous work.
3. **Determine Importance** Working on the steam locomotive, McCoy saw how dangerous and slow it was to oil an engine by hand. This led to him inventing a way for an engine to oil itself, so that it would be safer and faster.
4. **Generalize** McCoy saw that the way things were done wasn't working well. So, he figured out a better way to do it and convinced others to try it.

OL *Marvelous Mattie* Practice Master SG4.26

1. **Make Connections** (Students should recall specific or general incidents of gender discrimination that they have seen, heard, or read about.)
2. **Determine Author's Purpose** The author's purpose is to inform the reader about Knight, tell how she came to invent the machine to make flat-bottomed paper bags, and tell why this invention was important.
   - The author teaches with facts.
   - Mattie Knight worked hard to invent the machine that makes the flat-bottomed paper bags used today.
   - Bags didn't stand up or hold up well. She spent years trying to make a machine to make better bags. She went to court to protect her idea.
3. **Determine Importance** Working in the factory, Mattie learned that someone was trying to invent a machine to cut and glue square-bottomed paper bags. This led her to the invention of that machine.
4. **Generalize** She showed that working hard and not giving up is the best way to find a solution. People didn't take her seriously because she was a young girl. People tried to steal her invention. But, she didn't give up and eventually succeeded.

BL *Levi Strauss and Blue Jeans* Practice Master SG4.25

1. **Make Connections** (Students should speculate on how their clothing and those of others would be different without Strauss's invention and tell if and how it would inhibit their daily activities.)
2. **Determine Author's Purpose** The author's purpose is to inform the reader about the life of Levi Strauss; tell how he came to make blue jeans; and explain how this development helped workers, such as cowboys and farmers, and changed fashion.
   - The author teaches with facts.
   - Levi Strauss created blue jeans, which were durable, long-lasting clothes that changed fashion forever.
   - He saw a problem with the pants miners were wearing and wanted to make pants that would last. His denim jeans are still worn today.
3. **Determine Importance** This shows that there was a big need for goods in the West and led the way for Strauss to provide something that the miners needed.
4. **Generalize** Strauss showed that understanding what people need is a good way to start a successful business.

AL *The Boy Who Invented TV* Practice Master SG4.27

1. **Make Connections** (Students should speculate about what the world would be like without television and make a judgment about whether the change would be good or bad. Students should tell how it would affect how and what we learn about the world.)
2. **Determine Author's Purpose** The author's purpose is to inform the reader about the life of Philo Farnsworth, tell how he came to invent the television, and explain how this invention changed the world.
   - The author teaches with facts.
   - Philo Farnsworth invented the first television.
   - He got the idea for how to send images on television from looking at the rows of potatoes on his farm.
3. **Determine Importance** The parallel lines made him think about how parallel lines of light could be used to make a picture. This is important because it led him to his invention of the television.
4. **Generalize** Farnsworth came up with the idea because he was smart and curious about how things worked. He accomplished his goal because he was also patient and hardworking.

Connect Across Texts Practice Master SG4.28

1. McCoy invented something that changed the way people travel; Strauss invented something that changed the way people dress; Knight invented something that changed the way people carry their groceries; Farnsworth invented something that changed the way people are informed and entertained.
2. In all the books, the author's purpose is to inform the reader about an important inventor in history who created something that changed people's lives.
3. The books describe inventors who worked hard and didn't give up, even when others didn't believe in them. They paid attention to see what was wrong, and they used creativity to come up with new ideas.

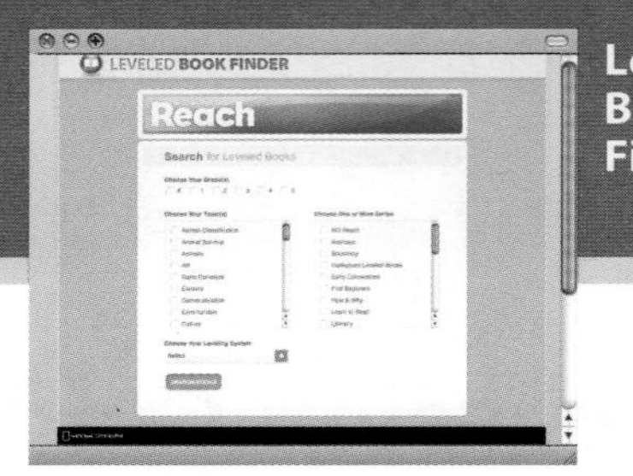

Leveled Book Finder

Recommended Books

	Fiction About Working Together	Nonfiction About Working Together
BL	Bunting, Eve. ***Flower Garden.*** Houghton Mifflin, 2000. Davis, Aubrey. ***Bone Button Borscht.*** Kids Can Press, 1996. Rylant, Cynthia. ***Poppleton and Friends.*** Scholastic Trade Books, 1998. Tolstoy, Alexi. ***The Enormous Turnip.*** Houghton Mifflin Harcourt, 2003.	Barton, Byron. ***Building a House.*** HarperCollins Publishers, 1990. Frost, Helen. ***Keeping Water Clean.*** Capstone Press, 2000. Levenson, Nancy S. ***Snowshoe Thompson.*** HarperCollins Publishers, 2000. Meiners, Cheri J. ***Reach Out and Give.*** Free Spirit Publishing, 2006.
BL	Fleischmann, Paul and David Roberts. ***The Dunderheads.*** Candlewick Press, 2009. McElligot, Matthew. ***The Lion's Share.*** Walker Publishing Company, 2009. Rylant, Cynthia. ***Poppleton Forever.*** Scholastic Trade Books, 1998. Seuss, Dr. ***Horton Hears a Who.*** Random House, Inc., 1954.	Deedy, Carmen Agra. ***14 Cows for America.*** Peachtree Publishing, 2009. COMMON CORE EXEMPLAR Dubowski, Mark, and Cathy East Dubowski. ***A Horse Named Seabiscuit.*** Penguin Young Readers Group, 2003. Raatma, Lucia. ***Consideration.*** Capstone Press, 2001. Ruffin, Frances E. ***Martin Luther King and the March on Washington.*** Penguin Young Readers Group, 2000. COMMON CORE EXEMPLAR
OL	Bowen, Fred. ***Dugout Rivals.*** Peachtree Publishers, 2010. Lionni, Leo. ***Swimmy.*** Random House, Inc., 1973. CALDECOTT HONOR BOOK Mohr, Nicholasa. ***Felita.*** Penguin Young Readers Group, 1999. Schotter, Roni. ***Nothing Ever Happens on 90th Street.*** Scholastic Trade Books, 1999.	Brallier, Jess. ***Who Was Albert Einstein?*** Penguin Young Readers Group, 2002. Fritz, Jean. ***What's the Big Idea, Ben Franklin?*** Penguin Young Readers Group, 1996. Hudson, Wade. ***Great Black Heroes: Five Notable Inventors.*** Scholastic Trade Books, 1995. Johnston, Johanna. ***They Led the Way: 14 American Women.*** Penguin Young Readers Group, 2004.
AL	Dahl, Roald. ***The Giraffe, the Pelly, and Me.*** Penguin Young Readers Group, 2009. Draper, Sharon M. ***The Backyard Animal Show.*** Simon & Schuster Children's Publishing, 2006. Mitchell, Margaret K. ***Uncle Jed's Barbershop.*** Simon & Schuster Children's Publishing, 1998. CORETTA SCOTT KING ILLUSTRATOR HONOR Woodson, Jacqueline. ***We Had a Picnic This Sunday Past.*** Disney Book Group, 2007.	Lewis, Barbara A. ***Kids with Courage: True Stories About Young People Making a Difference.*** Free Spirit Publishing, 1992. Old, Wendie. ***To Fly: The Story of the Wright Brothers.*** Houghton Mifflin Harcourt, 2002. St. George, Judith. ***So You Want to Be an Inventor?*** Penguin Young Readers Group, 2005. Winkler, Peter. ***Feeding the World.*** National Geographic, 2002.

Author Study: Grace Lin

Dim Sum for Everyone. Random House, Inc., 2003.

Fortune Cookie Fortunes. Random House, Inc., 2006.

Kite Flying. Random House, 2004.

Ling and Ting: Not Exactly the Same. Little, Brown and Company, 2009.

THEODOR SEUSS GEISEL HONOR BOOK

Contents at a Glance

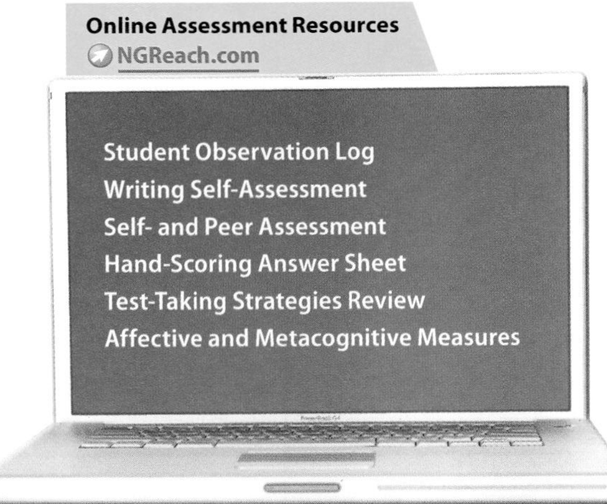

Online Assessment Resources
NGReach.com
Student Observation Log
Writing Self-Assessment
Self- and Peer Assessment
Hand-Scoring Answer Sheet
Test-Taking Strategies Review
Affective and Metacognitive Measures

Name ______________________ Date ______________________

Oral Reading Assessment

Unit 4

It was unusual for the quilting group to be this noisy. Usually, 12
people worked silently or talked in quiet voices. Today, everyone 22
was talking loudly and laughing. They were thinking about the 32
Volunteer Fire Department from the town. They wanted to 41
thank the volunteer firefighters by making a quilt for them. 51
They wanted to show them how much everyone in town 61
appreciated them. 63

The volunteer firefighters were just regular young people 71
everyone knew. They took their jobs seriously, though. They 80
were well trained and brave. Just last week, they had put out a 93
fire in the community center's kitchen. It was scary. But thanks 104
to them, no one was hurt. 110

It sounded like a party in the quilting room! The quilters were 122
grateful to the volunteer firefighters. Their warm feelings for the 132
firefighters were making the quilters lively as they stitched away. 142

The quilt was for the big Community Day celebration. It 152
would hang in the school gym. Each square showed something 162
important about one of the volunteers. Bonnie's square showed 171
how much she liked animals. It was filled with pictures of dogs 183
and cats stitched in colorful thread. Macon's square showed his 193
love of sports. It had a hockey stick, a basketball, and a football. 206
Karim's square had a stack of books, because Karim never 216
stopped reading. Terry's square had a picture of his truck, which 227
was his pride and joy. There were 20 squares for 20 brave young 240
people. Each square was quilted with love. 247

Name ______________________ Date ______________________

Oral Reading Assessment

Unit 4

2006 Hasbrouck & Tindal Oral Reading Fluency Data

Grade	Percentile	Fall WCPM	Winter WCPM	Spring WCPM
3	90	128	146	162
	75	99	120	137
	50	71	92	107
	25	44	62	78
	10	21	36	48

Accuracy and Rate

______ words attempted in one minute − ______ number of errors = ______ words correct per minute (wcpm)

Oral Reading Fluency Rubrics

Circle Score	Automaticity 4 3 2 1	Phrasing 4 3 2 1	Intonation 4 3 2 1	Expression 4 3 2 1
4	Reads smoothly and automatically. Pace is consistent.	Consistently pauses at all appropriate places in the text.	Changes pitch to match all of the content.	Reads with appropriate feeling for all content.
3	Reads most words automatically but still pauses to decode some words. Pace varies but is mostly consistent.	Frequently pauses at all appropriate places in the text.	Changes pitch to match some of the content.	Reads with appropriate feeling for most content.
2	Pauses to decode many words. Pace is slow with occasional stops and starts.	Occasionally pauses while reading the text.	Changes pitch, but does not match the content.	Reads with appropriate feeling for some content.
1	Can only read some high frequency words automatically. Pauses to decode all others or skips words. Pace is very slow and irregular with many stops and starts.	Rarely pauses while reading the text.	Does not change pitch.	Does not read with feeling.

Name ______________________________ Date ______________________________

Oral Reading Assessment

Retelling Rubric	
Circle Score	4 3 2 1
4	Student provides an accurate and complete retelling of the passage that includes the main idea and supporting details presented in a logical order.
3	Student's retelling is accurate and coherent but some elements and supporting details may be missing.
2	Student provides some details from the passage, but the retelling does not demonstrate understanding of the main idea and lacks coherence. Or, student may identify the topic without any elaboration.
1	Student is not able to retell the passage or retells it inaccurately.

Observations and Notes:

Oral Reading Assessment Wrap-up

- Ask the student about his or her reading. You can prompt the student with questions such as:

  Did you have any problems reading this passage?
  If yes: *What problems did you have?*
  What did you do when you didn't know a word?

- Share the positive things you noticed about the student's reading, for example:

  I noticed that you read with a lot of expression.
  Your reading is getting smoother. You don't stop as often as you used to.

- Make suggestions about what improvements are needed, for example:

  Try to read more smoothly without stopping between words.

- If you asked the student to retell the story, make notes about what the student needs to improve, e.g., distinguish the main idea from details, or present events in the proper sequence.

Name ______________________ Date ______________________

Reading Comprehension Test

Unit 4, Week 1

Directions: Read the story. Then answer the questions about the story.

Every summer, kids come to Myer Community Center from all over town. It's a fun place to play and learn.

Luisa works at the center and is getting it clean and ready for the summer program. The center will open in just two days. Luisa starts by sweeping the floor and wiping the tables, but she's worried. With so much work to do, she may not be able to finish on time.

Just then Luisa's friend Ken stops by the center. "I can help you," says Ken. Luisa is happy to have a helper and hands him a bucket of soapy water and a mop. Ken gets right to work mopping the floor.

Then Kate walks through the door. She calls some friends and tells them, "Luisa needs our help. Come and join the cleaning party." Kate begins to wash the windows. In no time at all, they are clear and sparkling clean.

Soon, many kids show up. Luisa smiles at what good friends she has. Myer Community Center will be ready for everyone, right on time!

GO ON

Name ________________________ Date ________________

Reading Comprehension Test

Unit 4, Week 1

1 Which of these happens first in the story?

Ⓐ Ken mops the floor.

Ⓑ Kate calls her friends.

Ⓒ Luisa sweeps the floor.

Ⓓ Kate washes windows.

2 What is the theme of the story?

Ⓐ Summer is a fun time to play.

Ⓑ It is important to have a good job.

Ⓒ Sometimes people work too much.

Ⓓ Work goes faster when more people help.

3 Which detail supports the theme?

Ⓐ Kids from all over town use the center.

Ⓑ Many kids come to the cleaning party.

Ⓒ Luisa works at Myer Community Center.

Ⓓ Myer Community Center is a fun place.

4 Which words from the story give details about how things look?

Ⓐ *ready for everyone*

Ⓑ *so much work to do*

Ⓒ *happy to have a helper*

Ⓓ *clear and sparkling clean*

COPY READY

Score
______/4

DONE!

ANSWER KEY: 1. C **2.** D **3.** B **4.** D

Name ____________________ Date ____________

Vocabulary Test

Unit 4, Week 1

Directions: Choose the answer that completes the sentence correctly.

1 He is a __________.

Ⓐ root

Ⓑ buyer

Ⓒ drought

Ⓓ solution

2 This is __________.

Ⓐ soil

Ⓑ nature

Ⓒ money

Ⓓ balance

3 This is a __________.

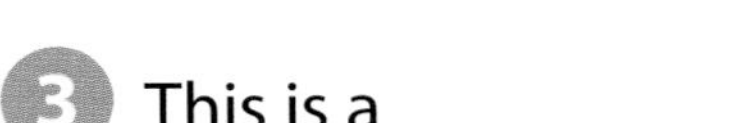

Ⓐ duty

Ⓑ weed

Ⓒ market

Ⓓ competition

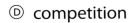

4 This is a __________.

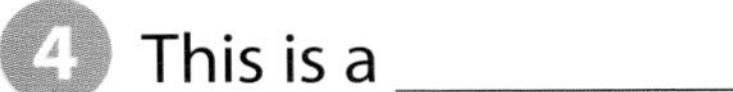

Ⓐ seller

Ⓑ desert

Ⓒ blossom

Ⓓ neighborhood

5 This is an __________.

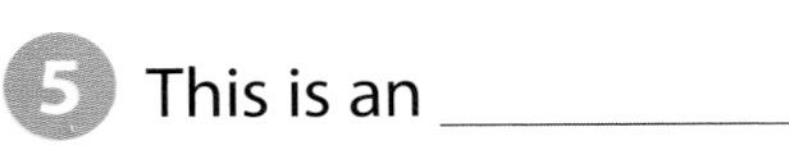

Ⓐ action

Ⓑ individual

Ⓒ ecosystem

Ⓓ advertisement

Apples

$ 1.00/lb

6 They __________ $6.00 for lunch.

Ⓐ pay

Ⓑ learn

Ⓒ improve

Ⓓ understand

GO ON

ANSWER KEY: 1. B 2. C 3. C 4. A 5. D 6. A

Name ______________________ Date ______________________

Vocabulary Test

Unit 4, Week 1

7 A __________ is a reason for doing something.

Ⓐ level

Ⓑ sprout

Ⓒ purpose

Ⓓ rainforest

8 __________ is when people work together.

Ⓐ Cooperation

Ⓑ Diversity

Ⓒ Impact

Ⓓ Nature

9 When you have __________ of something, you have a lot of it.

Ⓐ soil

Ⓑ plenty

Ⓒ conditions

Ⓓ competition

10 When you __________ something, you finish something that you want to do.

Ⓐ pay

Ⓑ protect

Ⓒ depend

Ⓓ accomplish

11 A __________ is a gift or prize for doing something well.

Ⓐ reward

Ⓑ market

Ⓒ characteristic

Ⓓ neighborhood

COPY READY

Score
______/11

DONE!

ANSWER KEY: **7.** C **8.** A **9.** B **10.** D **11.** A

COPY READY

Name ________________________ Date ________________

Writing, Revising, and Editing Test Unit 4, Week 1

Directions: Read the paragraph. Then answer the questions.

Our neighbor, Mrs. Martin, has a booth at the farmer's market. Each Saturday morning, she ___1___ the back of her truck full of lettuce, cabbage, and broccoli. Then she ___2___ to the market to sell her vegetables. Mrs. Martin's favorite customer is Mr. Toyama. When Mr. Toyama ___3___, he always ___4___ three cabbages and one head of broccoli. He ___5___ the vegetables together in a soup. Mrs. Martin ___6___ she would like to taste Mr. Toyama's soup someday.

---

1 Choose the answer that goes in Blank 1.

Ⓐ pack

Ⓑ packs

Ⓒ packes

2 Choose the answer that goes in Blank 2.

Ⓐ rush

Ⓑ rushs

Ⓒ rushes

3 Choose the answer that goes in Blank 3.

Ⓐ come

Ⓑ comes

Ⓒ comees

4 Choose the answer that goes in Blank 4.

Ⓐ buy

Ⓑ buys

Ⓒ buyes

GO ON

ANSWER KEY: 1. B 2. C 3. B 4. B

Name ______________________ Date ______________________

Writing, Revising, and Editing Test

Unit 4, Week 1

5 Choose the answer that goes in Blank 5.

Ⓐ mixes

Ⓑ mixs

Ⓒ mix

6 Choose the answer that goes in Blank 6.

Ⓐ sayes

Ⓑ says

Ⓒ say

---

7 Write a paragraph for your classmates about helping out in the classroom. The purpose of your paragraph may be to persuade, inform, entertain, or express an opinion. Choose a purpose, and make sure the purpose is clear in your paragraph.

Score
______/6 multiple-choice
______/4 writing

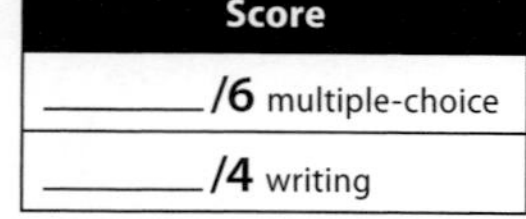

DONE!

COPY READY

ANSWER KEY: **5.** A **6.** B **7.** See Rubric

COPY READY

Name ______________________ Date ______________________

Reading Comprehension Test

Unit 4, Week 2

Directions: Read the story. Then answer the questions about the story.

Three Sisters: Storm Drains

"I've never seen it rain so hard!" Jennifer said. "I wonder why Samantha is outside."

Mom smiled. "You know your sister. She likes to splash around in puddles."

The front door opened and Samantha rushed in. She made no move to take off her dripping raincoat. "There's a pond out in the street!" Samantha exclaimed.

The three sisters crowded around a window. They saw that water was almost flooding over the curb. Cars had to drive through it very slowly.

"There's something wrong with the storm drain," said Mom.

Rachel put on her raincoat. "We'd better go fix it."

Moments later, the three girls were outside. "Leaves have probably plugged the drain," said Rachel. "Let's try raking the leaves off the drain." She hurried off to the garage and returned with some tools. Rachel tried to rake the leaves. It was difficult because they were heavy and wet. Once she managed to move them, the water just pushed them back.

"Try this," Samantha said. She handed Rachel a shovel.

GO ON

Name ______________________ Date ______________

Reading Comprehension Test

Unit 4, Week 2

Rachel pushed the shovel into the rushing water. Its flat blade fit through the grate's hole and pushed the sticks and leaves into the drain.

A whirlpool appeared and water sucked into the storm drain. The pond soon disappeared.

"We did it!" the girls shouted. Then Jennifer looked up the street. "Hang onto that shovel," she said. "More drains need to be fixed."

COPY READY

---

1. In the beginning of the story, Samantha wants to —
   - Ⓐ get tools from the garage.
   - Ⓑ splash in the puddles.
   - Ⓒ look out the window.
   - Ⓓ rake the leaves.

2. What happens in the middle of the story?
   - Ⓐ Jennifer wonders why Samantha is outside.
   - Ⓑ Rachel pushes the shovel into the water.
   - Ⓒ Samantha discovers a pond in the street.
   - Ⓓ The sisters decide to clean the storm drain.

3. What does the reader learn about Rachel?
   - Ⓐ She doesn't like rain.
   - Ⓑ She likes to tell jokes.
   - Ⓒ She works hard to fix things.
   - Ⓓ She doesn't get along with her sisters.

4. Which words from the story tell about the setting?
   - Ⓐ "I've never seen it rain so hard!"
   - Ⓑ "You know your sister."
   - Ⓒ "We'd better go fix it."
   - Ⓓ "We did it!"

GO ON

ANSWER KEY: **1.** B **2.** D **3.** C **4.** A

Name ____________________ Date ____________________

Reading Comprehension Test

Unit 4, Week 2

Directions: Read the story. Then answer the questions about the story.

Three Sisters: Speed Shopping

"Come on, girls," said Mom. "We're going grocery shopping at the new store that just opened."

When they stepped inside, all Samantha could say was, "Wow!"

"This place is huge!" Jennifer said. The back wall of the supermarket seemed very far away. Aisle after aisle stretched before them. "It's going to take forever to find what we need."

"Look up," said Mom, pointing overhead. "The big signs tell you where everything is."

"That makes it easy," said Rachel. "We can be out of here in 15 minutes if we shop as a team. Let's get some more shopping baskets."

Mom looked at her list. "We need cheese, butter, and milk. Does anybody see the dairy section?"

"It's over there," said Jennifer, pointing to the left. "I'll take care of that."

Mom nodded. "We also have to get bread and bagels."

"That's perfect for me," said Samantha. Her two sisters looked at her. "I'm the littlest one, so I should get the lightest groceries." Jennifer and Rachel laughed.

GO ON

Name ______________________ Date ______________________

Reading Comprehension Test

Unit 4, Week 2

"Then I'll take care of the fruits and vegetables," said Rachel.

"That's everything on the list," said Mom. "That gives me time to find some treats. If I ask you to do that, you'll fill a whole basket," she teased. "I'll meet you at the first checkout stand in 10 minutes."

Sure enough, 15 minutes later they were walking out the door with everything on the list—plus some treats.

---

5. Both stories have the same —
   - Ⓐ plot.
   - Ⓑ topic.
   - Ⓒ setting.
   - Ⓓ characters.

6. In both stories, the sisters —
   - Ⓐ take turns.
   - Ⓑ ask for help.
   - Ⓒ tease each other.
   - Ⓓ solve a problem.

7. The theme in both stories is about —
   - Ⓐ working together.
   - Ⓑ finishing on time.
   - Ⓒ making a choice.
   - Ⓓ taking a chance.

8. Which words from the second story help the reader understand the themes of the stories?
   - Ⓐ "The big signs tell you where everything is."
   - Ⓑ "If I ask you to do that, you'll fill a whole basket."
   - Ⓒ "We can be out of here in 15 minutes if we shop as a team."
   - Ⓓ "I'm the littlest one, so I should get the lightest groceries."

DONE!

Score
______/8

COPY READY

ANSWER KEY: **5.** D **6.** D **7.** A **8.** C

COPY READY

Name ______________________ Date ______________________

Vocabulary Test

Unit 4, Week 2

Directions: Read the question. Choose the correct answer.

1 What does untie mean?

I untie my shoelace.

Ⓐ tie again

Ⓑ tie before

Ⓒ opposite of tie

2 What does pretest mean?

We take a spelling pretest on Mondays.

Ⓐ test before

Ⓑ test again

Ⓒ large test

3 What does superpower mean?

The country is a superpower.

Ⓐ not a power

Ⓑ a large power

Ⓒ a power again

4 What does miscounted mean?

He miscounted his marbles.

Ⓐ did not count

Ⓑ counted again

Ⓒ counted incorrectly

Score
______/4

DONE!

ANSWER KEY: 1. C **2.** A **3.** B **4.** C

Name ______________________ Date ______________________

Writing, Revising, and Editing Test

Unit 4, Week 2

Directions: Read the paragraph. Then answer the questions.

My big sister ___1___ for a job in the newspaper. She ___2___ to an ad for a cat sitter. The people looking for a cat sitter are nice. They ___3___ my sister to a job interview. The people ___4___ her, "Do you ___5___ cats?" She answers, "Oh, yes! I ___6___ a lot of time with our cat every day."

---

1. Choose the answer that goes in Blank 1.
   - Ⓐ look
   - Ⓑ looks
   - Ⓒ lookes

2. Choose the answer that goes in Blank 2.
   - Ⓐ reply
   - Ⓑ replys
   - Ⓒ replies

3. Choose the answer that goes in Blank 3.
   - Ⓐ invite
   - Ⓑ invites
   - Ⓒ invities

4. Choose the answer that goes in Blank 4.
   - Ⓐ ask
   - Ⓑ asks
   - Ⓒ askes

COPY READY

GO ON

ANSWER KEY: **1.** B **2.** C **3.** A **4.** A

Name ______________________ Date ______________

Writing, Revising, and Editing Test

Unit 4, Week 2

5 Choose the answer that goes in Blank 5.

Ⓐ enjoies

Ⓑ enjoys

Ⓒ enjoy

6 Choose the answer that goes in Blank 6.

Ⓐ spendes

Ⓑ spends

Ⓒ spend

7 Write the first paragraph of a story about a class that is planning to clean up a park nearby. Use details to show what the characters are like. Underline the details that give clues about the characters.

Score
______/6 multiple-choice
______/4 writing

DONE!

COPY READY

ANSWER KEY: **5.** C **6.** C **7.** See Rubric

Name ______________________ Date ______________________

Reading Comprehension Test

Unit 4, Week 3

Directions: Read the passage. Then answer the questions about the passage.

Writing is more than just putting a pen to paper, or fingers to keyboard. It's one of the best tools you have to change the world. Whether you want to make big changes or small ones, try using the written word.

Do you want to make someone happy? Do you want to show someone that you care? Try writing a thank-you card. Maybe you have a friend who has been sick or in the hospital. A thoughtful note from you can make that person feel better.

Suppose that your school is raising money for a new soccer field. You can help by writing a catchy saying that gets people excited about giving. Imagine that trash is being dumped in a local creek. Write a letter to your newspaper. Explain that plants and animals depend on people to pick up after themselves. Your letter could lead to a creek cleanup.

Writing does two things. First, it lets you express yourself. Second, it gives you a chance to make a difference. Finally, when you write, you should never forget your most important reader. You! You can make a list of all the things you want to do, big and small. Writing a list helps you to plan and get things done.

GO ON

COPY READY

COPY READY

Name ____________________ Date ____________________

Reading Comprehension Test

Unit 4, Week 3

1. What is the most important idea in this passage?
   - Ⓐ Make a list of what you want to do.
   - Ⓑ Writing can help you get things done.
   - Ⓒ Plants and animals depend on people.
   - Ⓓ You can write a letter to the newspaper.

2. Which of these states an opinion?
   - Ⓐ Do you want to show someone that you care?
   - Ⓑ You should never forget your most important reader.
   - Ⓒ Maybe you have a friend who has been sick or in the hospital.
   - Ⓓ Suppose that your school is raising money for a new soccer field.

3. What evidence does the author give to support the opinion that writing can help raise money?
   - Ⓐ A list is one kind of writing.
   - Ⓑ A thoughtful card can show that you care.
   - Ⓒ A letter to the editor can explain a problem.
   - Ⓓ A catchy saying can make people want to help.

4. Which of these should be included in a summary of this passage?
   - Ⓐ Some changes are big and some are small.
   - Ⓑ Writing is more than putting pen to paper.
   - Ⓒ Writing can be a tool for change.
   - Ⓓ Some people feel better after getting a card.

Score
_______/4

DONE!

ANSWER KEY: **1.** B **2.** B **3.** D **4.** C

Name ____________________ Date ____________________

Vocabulary Test

Unit 4, Week 3

Directions: Choose the answer that completes the sentence correctly.

1 This is a __________.

Ⓐ gift

Ⓑ city

Ⓒ vine

Ⓓ field

2 This is a __________.

Ⓐ crop

Ⓑ seller

Ⓒ drought

Ⓓ solution

3 This is a __________.

Ⓐ seed

Ⓑ farmer

Ⓒ benefit

Ⓓ rain forest

4 They __________ their tomatoes.

Ⓐ pay

Ⓑ react

Ⓒ harvest

Ⓓ interact

5 __________ is the job of growing fruits and vegetables.

Ⓐ Kindness

Ⓑ Diversity

Ⓒ Agriculture

Ⓓ Competition

6 We __________ the land to plant corn.

Ⓐ value

Ⓑ plow

Ⓒ react

Ⓓ receive

GO ON

COPY READY

ANSWER KEY: **1.** D **2.** A **3.** B **4.** C **5.** C **6.** B

COPY READY

Name ______________________ Date ______________

Vocabulary Test

Unit 4, Week 3

7 The __________ is what will happen tomorrow or sometime after that.

Ⓐ sun

Ⓑ future

Ⓒ desert

Ⓓ rain forest

8 An __________ is another choice.

Ⓐ alternative

Ⓑ ecosystem

Ⓒ organism

Ⓓ amount

9 A __________ is a way of doing something.

Ⓐ balance

Ⓑ drought

Ⓒ method

Ⓓ level

10 __________ is the opposite of waste.

Ⓐ River

Ⓑ Blossom

Ⓒ Diversity

Ⓓ Conservation

11 When you __________ something, you keep it alive or in existence.

Ⓐ react

Ⓑ identify

Ⓒ sustain

Ⓓ decrease

Score
______/11

DONE!

ANSWER KEY: **7.** B **8.** A **9.** C **10.** D **11.** C

Name ______________________ Date ______________________

Writing, Revising, and Editing Test Unit 4, Week 3

Directions: Read the paragraph. Then answer the questions.

Some people think trash collectors have it easy. However, I know one who __1__ very hard. My uncle gets up very early in the morning. Then he __2__ heavy trash cans all day. I think he __3__ to bed earlier so he gets enough rest. I stay up reading on weekends, but I __4__ to sleep early during the week when I have school. My uncle says he knows he __5__ more sleep. He admits he is often tired and __6__ sleepy.

1 Choose the answer that goes in Blank 1.

Ⓐ do work

Ⓑ does work

Ⓒ does works

2 Choose the answer that goes in Blank 2.

Ⓐ should

Ⓑ must lift

Ⓒ lift could

3 Choose the answer that goes in Blank 3.

Ⓐ could

Ⓑ can goes

Ⓒ should go

4 Choose the answer that goes in Blank 4.

Ⓐ do go

Ⓑ does go

Ⓒ do goes

GO ON

COPY READY

ANSWER KEY: **1.** B **2.** B **3.** C **4.** A

Name ____________________ Date ____________________

Writing, Revising, and Editing Test

Unit 4, Week 3

5 Choose the answer that goes in Blank 5.

Ⓐ use must

Ⓑ must use

Ⓒ could use

6 Choose the answer that goes in Blank 6.

Ⓐ does feel

Ⓑ do feels

Ⓒ do feel

COPY READY

7 You are preparing to write a research report about public libraries. Read the two sources below about public libraries and evaluate them. Write several sentences to explain whether each source is good for research and why.

Source 1 – Newspaper Blog

www.TheTownHerald.com/readerblog
posted Sunday, November 6, 2004
thread: **shortening library hours**

I think it's a terrible idea to close the library on weeknights. I'm a student at Eastlake Elementary. My dad works until 5:30, so he can't take me to the library until after dinner. Sometimes I go there to do my homework away from my noisy little brother, or I just want to check out a book. If they need money, maybe they can sell candy like my school does. If they have to change their hours, they should close in the morning when most people are in school or at work.

Source 2 – Government Web Site

www.publicsvcs.gov
posted March 16, 2012
Topic: **Public Libraries**

Public libraries offer information and services to the public. The main purpose of libraries is to collect and save information. This information can be read by the public. Anybody in the community can borrow a book free of charge. Public libraries also offer other free services to the public. For example, most public libraries host book clubs and special book readings for children. Libraries also offer access to computers and the Internet.

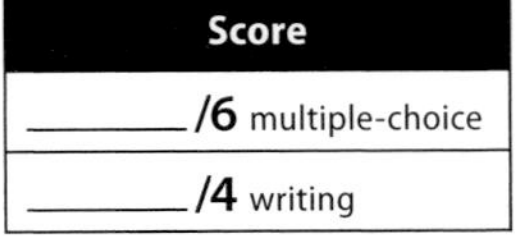

Score	
______/6	multiple-choice
______/4	writing

DONE!

ANSWER KEY: **5.** C **6.** A **7.** See Rubric

Name ________________________ Date ________________________

Reading Comprehension Test

Unit Test

Directions: Read the article. Then answer the questions about the article.

SPACE JUNK

The Problem with Space Junk

Back in 1957, a rocket was shot high in the air. After reaching outer space, it circled our planet. Since then, thousands of rockets and satellites have gone into outer space. Most of them are still up there, whizzing along at about 17,000 miles per hour. Some of them have broken into pieces. These old rocket parts are called "space junk."

There are more than 500,000 pieces of space junk. Most of them are very small. However, some are large enough to cause problems.

Some space junk leaves outer space and comes rushing toward Earth. Fortunately, most of it burns up long before hitting the ground. But sometimes really big pieces of space junk don't burn up completely. They crash into Earth. Usually they don't cause harm, but they certainly could.

There is a bigger problem, though. Space junk can hit satellites that we need for things such as tracking storms. The junk could also hit spacecraft or space stations with people in them. This could be very dangerous!

Solving the Problem

That's why Switzerland is building a satellite named CleanSpace One. Once it reaches outer space, it can grab pieces of space junk with giant claws. Then the satellite and the junk burn up as they fall back toward Earth.

The United States needs to clean up its own space junk. This will make Earth safer. This will also make things safer for astronauts. After all, we don't want them to be hit by space junk either.

That's why you should write to your government leaders. Explain that we should clean up the mess we've made in space. Everyone knows it's important not to litter. With space junk, littering is not just wrong. It's dangerous!

GO ON

COPY READY

Name ______________________ Date ______________________

Reading Comprehension Test

Unit Test

1 What is the author's purpose in the first part of the article, "The Problem with Space Junk?"

Ⓐ to teach a lesson about space junk

Ⓑ to inform the reader what space junk is

Ⓒ to explain how rockets are sent into space

Ⓓ to entertain the reader with a story about space junk

2 What is the author's purpose in the second part of the article, "Solving the Problem"?

Ⓐ to entertain the reader

Ⓑ to teach the reader a lesson

Ⓒ to persuade the reader to take action

3 Which of these is the most important idea in the article?

Ⓐ Space junk can be dangerous.

Ⓑ There are satellites in outer space.

Ⓒ Space junk usually doesn't hurt anybody.

Ⓓ Switzerland's satellite is named CleanSpace One.

4 Which of these is important to include in a summary of the article?

Ⓐ Satellites are used to track storms.

Ⓑ A rocket was shot into the air in 1957.

Ⓒ Rockets circle the Earth after they reach outer space.

Ⓓ Switzerland is building a satellite to clean up space junk.

5 Which of these gives an opinion?

Ⓐ Old rocket parts are called "space junk."

Ⓑ Most space junk burns up before it hits Earth.

Ⓒ The United States needs to clean up its own space junk.

Ⓓ There are more than 500,000 pieces of space junk in space.

6 What evidence does the author give for why we need to clean up space junk?

Ⓐ Space junk can harm people.

Ⓑ We use satellites to track storms.

Ⓒ We need to take space junk seriously.

Ⓓ Switzerland's satellite has claws.

GO ON

ANSWER KEY: **1.** B **2.** C **3.** A **4.** D **5.** C **6.** A

Name ______________________ Date ______________________

Reading Comprehension Test

Unit Test

Directions: Read the story. Then answer the questions about the story.

Yuri and His Big Brother

Yuri carried his math book down the hall and knocked on his older brother's door.

"Come in!" called Alex.

Yuri opened the door and peeked inside. "Hi," he said. "I was wondering if you could help me with my homework?"

"Sure thing," said Alex, moving things out of the way on his messy desk. "Let's see what you have."

Alex's room was one of Yuri's favorite places in the house. There was a big tree outside the window, and Alex had put lots of colorful posters on the walls. Best of all, Alex always made him feel welcome here.

After the homework was done, Alex pulled out a chessboard. "Are you in the mood to lose?" he asked.

Yuri laughed and nodded. He was actually a very good chess player. Ten minutes later, he proved it by capturing Alex's king.

"Checkmate," Yuri said.

Alex looked at the board in amazement. "I never should have taught you how to play this game," he joked.

That was when Yuri noticed a thick book on his brother's desk. It was a college catalog. Alex would be moving away to go to school in the fall. This made Yuri sad for a moment. It was hard for him to imagine a time when Alex wouldn't be here in this room.

GO ON

Name ______________________ Date ______________

Reading Comprehension Test

Unit Test

Alex looked up at Yuri and said, "Let's try just one more game."

The sadness passed. Alex was still here *now,* and Yuri wanted to enjoy every minute of their time together.

---

7. What makes Yuri sad?
   - Ⓐ He wants to play more chess.
   - Ⓑ He has too much math homework.
   - Ⓒ He thinks about Alex moving away.
   - Ⓓ He wants a room of his own like Alex.

8. At the end of the story, Yuri —
   - Ⓐ enjoys his time with Alex.
   - Ⓑ learns how to play chess.
   - Ⓒ looks at a college catalog.
   - Ⓓ asks Alex for help with his homework.

9. What is one way you can tell how Alex and Yuri feel about each other?
   - Ⓐ Alex is going to college.
   - Ⓑ Yuri beats Alex at chess.
   - Ⓒ Yuri needs help with his homework.
   - Ⓓ Alex always makes Yuri feel welcome.

10. The author's purpose for writing this story was to —
    - Ⓐ teach a lesson.
    - Ⓑ give an opinion.
    - Ⓒ entertain the reader.
    - Ⓓ persuade the reader to do something.

11. What is the theme of this story?
    - Ⓐ Enjoy the present instead of worrying about the future.
    - Ⓑ Big brothers should help younger brothers.
    - Ⓒ It is important to plan for the future.
    - Ⓓ You should always finish your work before playing games.

GO ON

COPY READY

ANSWER KEY: **7.** C **8.** A **9.** D **10.** C **11.** A

Name ______________________ Date ______________________

Reading Comprehension Test

Unit Test

Directions: Read the story. Then answer the questions about the story.

The house seemed different since Yuri's big brother, Alex, left for college last week. Yuri still had a younger brother and sister at home, but Alex was special. Alex had always been there to talk to and help Yuri with his homework. Yuri missed him already.

At dinner, the family talked about Alex. Then, Yuri's dad said, "Alex doesn't need his own room anymore. He can sleep in Yuri's room when he comes home on school breaks. So what should we do with Alex's room?"

Yuri had an idea right away. He wanted a quiet place with books and the computer. He knew, however, that his sister and brother would have ideas of their own. He guessed his sister wanted a place for her band to practice. His brother would probably want to turn it into a video game room. Yuri wanted to convince the others that his idea was the best.

After dinner, Yuri decided to write a list of reasons for his idea. A quiet room with books and the computer, away from the television, would be good for everyone. The family could read together, study, and work on the computer. It would be a place to help the children get ready for college, like Alex.

The next night, Yuri presented his list of reasons to the family. "That's a great idea," smiled Mom. To Yuri's surprise, everyone else nodded and agreed. It was settled!

GO ON

COPY READY

COPY READY

Name ______________________ Date ______________________

Reading Comprehension Test

Unit Test

12 Which word completes the sentence to state the theme for this story?

A good __________ can help everyone.

Ⓐ idea

Ⓑ book

Ⓒ college

Ⓓ computer

13 The author's purpose for writing this story was to —

Ⓐ explain.

Ⓑ inform.

Ⓒ entertain.

Ⓓ express feelings.

14 What is one way "Yuri's Idea" is different from "Yuri and His Big Brother"? In "Yuri's Idea," —

Ⓐ Alex has left for college.

Ⓑ Yuri asks his brother for help.

Ⓒ Alex and Yuri talk to each other.

Ⓓ Yuri spends time in Alex's room.

Score
_______/19

15 How does Yuri feel at the end of both stories?

Ⓐ tired

Ⓑ happy

Ⓒ angry

Ⓓ worried

16 Both of these stories are about —

Ⓐ getting ready to leave home.

Ⓑ spending time together with family.

Ⓒ learning how to do something new.

Ⓓ trying to make people like your idea.

17 Choose either "Yuri and His Big Brother" or "Yuri's Idea." Explain what Yuri's viewpoint is in the story you choose. Give at least one detail from the story that helped you figure out the viewpoint.

DONE!

ANSWER KEY: **12.** A **13.** C **14.** A **15.** B **16.** B **17.** See Rubric

Name ______________________ Date ______________________

Vocabulary Test

Unit Test

Directions: Read the question. Choose the correct answer.

1. For the topic animals, which word could be added to this group of words? cat, dog, ________

   Ⓐ car

   Ⓑ sock

   Ⓒ horse

2. For the topic sky, which word could be added to this group of words? sun, star, ________

   Ⓐ triangle

   Ⓑ moon

   Ⓒ river

3. For the topic family, which word could be added to this group of words? parent, sister, ________

   Ⓐ lunch

   Ⓑ uncle

   Ⓒ house

4. For the topic numbers, which word could be added to this group of words? two, four, ________

   Ⓐ six

   Ⓑ high

   Ⓒ count

5. What does reshape mean?

Marie wants to reshape her clay pot.

   Ⓐ shape again

   Ⓑ shape before

   Ⓒ shape very large

6. What does disappeared mean?

The clouds disappeared after the storm.

   Ⓐ appeared again

   Ⓑ appeared larger

   Ⓒ opposite of appeared

GO ON

COPY READY

ANSWER KEY: **1.** C **2.** B **3.** B **4.** A **5.** A **6.** C

COPY READY

Name ______________________ Date ______________________

Vocabulary Test

Unit Test

Directions: Choose the answer that completes the sentence correctly.

7. The __________ of corn was ready to pick in the summer.
   - Ⓐ crop
   - Ⓑ buyer
   - Ⓒ money
   - Ⓓ market

8. We __________ the corn when it is ready to eat.
   - Ⓐ pay
   - Ⓑ plow
   - Ⓒ sustain
   - Ⓓ harvest

9. She took the strawberries to the farmer's __________ to sell.
   - Ⓐ money
   - Ⓑ market
   - Ⓒ drought
   - Ⓓ agriculture

10. In the __________, there will be new ways to grow food.
    - Ⓐ future
    - Ⓑ reward
    - Ⓒ method
    - Ⓓ organism

11. Growing tomatoes in a greenhouse is an __________ to growing them outside.
    - Ⓐ address
    - Ⓑ agriculture
    - Ⓒ alternative
    - Ⓓ advertisement

12. Rain will __________ the plants during winter.
    - Ⓐ value
    - Ⓑ react
    - Ⓒ sustain
    - Ⓓ accomplish

Score
______/12

DONE!

ANSWER KEY: 7. A **8.** D **9.** B **10.** A **11.** C **12.** C

Name ______________________ Date ______________________

Writing, Revising, and Editing Test

Unit Test

Directions: Read the paragraph. Then answer the questions.

Meet Greg Campbell. He ___1___ a sheep farmer. Greg ___2___ about 30 sheep. His sheepdogs ___3___ helped with the sheep for years. When the dogs ___4___ puppies, they learn whistle commands. His dogs work together to gather the sheep!

COPY READY

1. Choose the answer that goes in Blank 1.
   - Ⓐ is
   - Ⓑ am
   - Ⓒ are

2. Choose the answer that goes in Blank 2.
   - Ⓐ have
   - Ⓑ has
   - Ⓒ is

3. Choose the answer that goes in Blank 3.
   - Ⓐ has
   - Ⓑ are
   - Ⓒ have

4. Choose the answer that goes in Blank 4.
   - Ⓐ is
   - Ⓑ am
   - Ⓒ are

GO ON

ANSWER KEY: 1. A **2.** B **3.** C **4.** C

COPY READY

Name ______________________ Date ______________________

Writing, Revising, and Editing Test

Unit Test

Directions: Read the paragraph. Then answer the questions.

> **(1)** Our garden are dry, and it needs a lot of water. **(2)** Our mom cannot find time to water it. **(3)** She do need some help. **(4)** So, my brother and I figured out what we do. **(5)** We has pricked holes in an old garden hose. **(6)** The hose circle the garden and drips into the soil. **(7)** Now, Mom can water the garden while she takes care of other things!

---

5 What is the correct way to write sentence 1?

- Ⓐ Our garden are dry and it needs a lot of water.
- Ⓑ Our garden are dry, and it need a lot of water.
- Ⓒ Our garden is dry, and it needs a lot of water.
- Ⓓ Correct as is

6 What is the correct way to write sentence 3?

- Ⓐ She does need some help.
- Ⓑ She do need some helps.
- Ⓒ She do needs some help.
- Ⓓ Correct as is

GO ON

ANSWER KEY: 5. C **6.** A

Name ______________________ Date ______________

Writing, Revising, and Editing Test

Unit Test

7 What is the correct way to write sentence 4?

Ⓐ So, my brother and me figured out what we do.

Ⓑ So, my brother and I figured out what we should do.

Ⓒ So, my brother and I figured out what we does.

Ⓓ Correct as is

8 What is the correct way to write sentence 5?

Ⓐ We has pricked holes in an old garden hoses.

Ⓑ We have pricked holes in an old garden hose.

Ⓒ We can has pricked holes in an old garden hose.

Ⓓ Correct as is

9 What is the correct way to write sentence 6?

Ⓐ The hose circles the garden and drips into the soil.

Ⓑ The hose circle the garden and drip into the soil.

Ⓒ The hose circle the garden and drips into the soils.

Ⓓ Correct as is

10 What is the correct way to write sentence 7?

Ⓐ Now, Mom can water the garden while she take care of other things!

Ⓑ Now, mom can water the garden while she takes care of other things!

Ⓒ Now, Mom can waters the garden while she takes care of other things!

Ⓓ Correct as is

GO ON

COPY READY

ANSWER KEY: 7. B 8. B 9. A 10. D

COPY READY

Name ______________________ Date ______________________

Writing, Revising, and Editing Test

Unit Test

11 Read the paragraph. There are six mistakes in grammar and usage, punctuation, or capitalization. Use the Editing and Proofreading Marks to correct each mistake.

(1) Ted, Andy, and Jorge is on the same baseball team. **(2)** If they want new uniforms, they need to raise money. **(3)** They does want new uniforms, so they decide to wash cars for money. **(4)** They will wash cars more quickly if they work together. **(5)** Each boy have a different job. **(6)** Ted am the one who holds the sign and takes the money. **(7)** Andy and Jorge washes the cars. **(8)** At the end of the day, the boys has raised a lot of money. **(9)** Now they can buy new uniforms.

Editing and Proofreading Marks

Mark	Meaning
^	Add.
(delete mark)	Take out.
(move mark)	Move to here.
^,	Add comma.
^⊙	Add period.

12 Write a persuasive essay to persuade your school principal to buy an innovation that will help the students. Be sure to tell what you think and back up your opinion with facts and examples. Your essay should have at least three paragraphs.

Score
______/10 multiple-choice
______/6 editing task
______/4 weekly writing skill
______/24 writing traits

DONE!

ANSWER KEY: **11.** See Rubric **12.** See Rubric

Name ______________________ Date ______________

Weekly and Unit Assessments

Unit 4

Enter the scores for the Oral Reading Assessment administered in this unit.

Oral Reading Assessment	wcpm	Oral Reading Fluency Rubrics				Retelling
		Automaticity	Phrasing	Intonation	Expression	
		____/4	____/4	____/4	____/4	____/4

Enter the scores from the Spelling Pre-Test and the End-of-Week Test in the table. Calculate the percent for each End-of-Week Test or use the conversion charts on page A4.44.

Spelling Tests	Week 1	Week 2	Week 3	Week 4
Pre-Test CC.3.Rfou.3, L.2, L.2.e, L.2.f	____/19	____/19	____/19	____/19
End-of-Week Test CC.3.Rfou.3, L.2, L.2.e, L.2.f	___/19 ___%	___/19 ___%	___/19 ___%	___/19 ___%

Circle the item number for each item answered correctly. Assign 1 point for each correct answer. For tests scored with rubrics, enter the student's rubric scores. Calculate the percent of the overall score or use the conversion charts on page A4.44.

Reading Comprehension Tests	Weekly Test Items			Unit Test Items Including Week 4	Totals Across Tests
	Week 1	Week 2	Week 3		
Central Message CC.3.Rlit.2	2 3			11 12	____/4
Compare Story Elements CC.3.Rlit.9, Rlit.5		5 6		14 15	____/4
Compare Themes CC.3.Rlit.9		7 8		16	____/3
Story Elements CC.3.Rlit.3, Rlit.5		1 2 3 4		7 8	____/6
Determine Importance CC.3.Rinf.2			1 4	3 4	____/4
Author's Use of Opinion and Evidence CC.3.Rinf.2			2 3	5 6	____/4
Author's Purpose CC.3.Rinf.10				1 2 10 13	____/4
Point of View CC.3.Rlit.6				9 17 (____/3)	____/4
Review Skill: Literature Text Structures CC.3.Rlit.5	1				____/1
Review Skill: Distinguish Literal and Nonliteral Language CC.3.Rlit.4	4				____/1
Total	___/4 ___%	___/8 ___%	___/4 ___%	___/19 ___%	

Vocabulary Tests	Weekly Test Items			Unit Test Items Including Week 4	Totals Across Tests
	Week 1	Week 2	Week 3		
Social Studies Vocabulary CC.3.L.6	1 2 3 4 5 6		1 2 3 4 5 6	7 8 9	____/15
Academic Vocabulary CC.3.L.6	7 8 9 10 11		7 8 9 10 11	10 11 12	____/13
Prefixes CC.3.L.4.b, Rfou.3.a, L.4.c		1 2 3 4		5 6	____/6
Classify Words CC.3.L.5, L.6				1 2 3 4	____/4
Total	___/11 ___%	___/4 ___%	___/11 ___%	___/12 ___%	

COPY READY

Name ______________________________ Date ______________________________

Weekly and Unit Assessments

Unit 4

Writing, Revising, and Editing Tests		Weekly Test Items: Week 1	Week 2	Week 3	Unit Test Items Including Week 4	Totals Across Tests
Revising and Editing	Subject-Verb Agreement CC.3.L.1.f, L.1.d, L.1.e, L.1.a, W.5	1 2 3 4 5 6	1 2 3 4 5 6		2 9 11c 11e	_____/16
	Helping Verbs CC.3.L.1.a, L.1.d, L.1.f, W.5			1 2 3 4 5 6	3 6 7 8 10 11b 11f	_____/13
	Linking Verbs CC.3.L.1.d, L.1.f, L.1.a, W.5				1 4 5 11a 11d	_____/5
	Subtotal	_____/6	_____/6	_____/6	_____/16	
Writing Skills	Establish and Follow a Purpose CC.3.W.10	_____/4				_____/4
	Introduce Characters CC.3.W.3.a		_____/4			_____/4
	Evaluate Information CC.3.W.8			_____/4		_____/4
	Link Opinions and Reasons CC.3.W.1.c, W.1.a, W.1.b				_____/4	_____/4
	Subtotal	_____/4	_____/4	_____/4	_____/4	
	Total	____/10 ____%	____/10 ____%	____/10 ____%	____/20 ____%	

Unit Test Writing Prompt—Traits CC.3.W.1.c, W.1.a, W.1.b	Ideas	Organization	Voice	Word Choice	Fluency	Conventions	Total
	_____/4	_____/4	_____/4	_____/4	_____/4	_____/4	_____/24

Fill in the strategy or the strategies used each week and enter the score.

Reading Strategy Assessments	Week 1	Week 2	Week 3	Week 4
	_____/4	_____/4	_____/4	_____/4
	_____/4	_____/4	_____/4	_____/4
	_____/4	_____/4	_____/4	_____/4
	_____/4	_____/4	_____/4	_____/4

Enter the score for each Weekly Project.

Weekly Projects	Week 1	Week 2	Week 3	Week 4
Writing or Research Project	_____/24	_____/24	_____/24	_____/24

Weekly and Unit Assessments

Unit 4

The Class Profile will help you group students for review and reteaching. Use the Student Profiles to complete this summary information for your class. Write a minus sign (–) if the student would benefit from review and reteaching.

	Student Name														
Reading Comprehension	Central Message CC.3.Rlit.2														
	Compare Story Elements CC.3.Rlit.9, Rlit.5														
	Compare Themes CC.3.Rlit.9														
	Story Elements CC.3.Rlit.3, Rlit.5														
	Determine Importance CC.3.Rinf.2														
	Author's Use of Opinion and Evidence CC.3.Rinf.2														
	Author's Purpose CC.3.Rlit.10														
	Point of View CC.3.Rlit.6														
	Review Skill: Literature Text Structures CC.3.Rlit.5														
	Review Skill: Distinguish Literal and Nonliteral Language CC.3.Rlit.4														
Writing, Revising, and Editing	Subject-Verb Agreement CC.3.L.1.f, L.1.d, L.1.e, L.1.a, W.5														
	Helping Verbs CC.3.L.1.a, L.1.d, L.1.f, W.5														
	Linking Verbs CC.3.L.1.d, L.1.f, L.1.a, W.5														
	Writing in Response to Prompt CC.3.W.10, W.3.a, W.8, W.1, W.1.a, W.1.b, W.1.c														
Vocabulary	Social Studies Vocabulary CC.3.L.6														
	Academic Vocabulary CC.3.L.6														
	Prefixes CC.3.L.4.b, Rfou.3.a, L.4.c														
	Classify Words CC.3.L.5, L.6														

COPY READY

Name ________________________ Date ________________

Strengths and Needs Summary

Use this chart to summarize the strengths and needs of individual students. This information will be helpful during student conferences and for instructional planning.

	Consistent Strengths	Some Successes	Greatest Needs
Reading Comprehension			
Oral Reading			
Vocabulary			
Spelling			
Grammar			
Written Composition			

Writing Rubric

Score Point	Ideas	Organization	Voice	Word Choice	Fluency	Conventions	Presentation
4	• The writing has a clear, focused message that keeps readers interested. • Details are accurate and relevant, showing in-depth knowledge of the topic.	• The writing has a clear structure throughout that suits the writer's audience and purpose. • All content flows smoothly and logically.	• The writing sounds genuine and unique. • The writer's tone is appropriate to the purpose and audience.	• Appropriate words were chosen to clearly convey the writer's message. • Language used throughout is appropriate for the audience and grabs readers' attention.	• All sentences are varied and effective and have appropriate transitions. • When read aloud, the writing sounds natural and rhythmic.	• The writing has only a few minor errors in spelling, punctuation, capitalization, grammar, usage, and paragraphing. • All the sentences are complete.	• The text is presented in an orderly way, significantly helping to convey the message. • Visuals are appropriate for the purpose and audience, and effectively support meaning.
3	• Most of the writing has a clear, focused message that keeps readers interested. • Most details are accurate and relevant, showing reasonable knowledge of the topic.	• Most of the writing has a clear structure that suits the writer's audience and purpose. • Most of the content flows smoothly and logically.	• Most of the writing sounds genuine and unique. • The writer's tone is mostly appropriate for the purpose and audience.	• Many appropriate words were chosen to clearly convey the writer's message. • Most language is appropriate for the audience and grabs readers' attention.	• Most sentences are varied and effective and have appropriate transitions. • When read aloud, most of the writing sounds natural and rhythmic.	• The writing has some errors in spelling, punctuation, capitalization, grammar, usage, and paragraphing. • Most of the sentences are complete.	• Most of the text is presented in an orderly way, generally helping to convey the message. • Most visuals are appropriate for the purpose and audience, and effectively support meaning.
2	• The writing has a fairly unclear and unfocused message, causing readers some confusion. • Some details are relevant and accurate, showing minimum knowledge of the topic.	• The writing does not have a structure that suits the writer's audience and purpose. • Some content flows smoothly and logically.	• Some of the writing sounds genuine and unique. • The writer's tone is somewhat inappropriate for the purpose and audience.	• Some appropriate words were chosen to clearly convey the writer's message. • Some language is appropriate for the audience and grabs readers' attention.	• Some sentences are varied and effective and have appropriate transitions. • When read aloud, some of the writing sounds natural and rhythmic.	• The writing has several errors in spelling, punctuation, capitalization, grammar, usage, and paragraphing. • Some of the sentences are complete.	• Some of the text is presented in an orderly way, but it is a little difficult to track and comprehend the message. • Some visuals are appropriate for the purpose and audience and support meaning.
1	• The writing does not have a clear, focused message, causing readers confusion. • Many details are irrelevant and inaccurate, indicating a lack of knowledge of the topic.	• The writing does not have a structure. • The content does not flow smoothly or logically.	• The writing does not sound genuine or unique. • The writer's tone is not appropriate for the purpose or audience.	• Few appropriate words were chosen to clearly convey the writer's message. • Language is dull, vague, and inappropriate for the audience, losing the readers' attention.	• Few or none of the sentences are varied or effective or have appropriate transitions. • When read aloud, the writing sounds unnatural.	• The writing has many errors in spelling, punctuation, capitalization, grammar, usage, and paragraphing. • Few sentences are complete.	• The text is not presented in an orderly way, making it very difficult to track and comprehend the message. • None of the visuals are appropriate for the purpose or audience, and do not support meaning.

COPY READY

Research Rubric

Unit 4, Week 3

Scale	Content	Speaking/Listening
4	• Research report contains strong facts from many different sources about how an area or the animals in an area were saved. • Student carefully evaluated information from print and digital sources and only used information that relates to the topic.	• Speaker reports on the topic with appropriate facts and relevant descriptive details. • Speaker speaks clearly and maintains eye contact with the audience throughout the presentation.
3	• Research report contains mostly strong facts from different sources about how an area or the animals in an area were saved. • Student evaluated information from print and digital sources and used information that mostly relates to the topic.	• Speaker reports on the topic with appropriate facts and relevant descriptive details most of the time. • Speaker speaks clearly and maintains eye contact with the audience most of the time during the presentation.
2	• Research report contains some strong facts from one or two sources about how an area or the animals in an area were saved. • Student did not adequately evaluate the information, so only some of what is included relates to the topic.	• Speaker inconsistently presents appropriate facts and relevant descriptive details. • Speaker speaks clearly only some of the time and struggles to make eye contact with the audience during the presentation.
1	• Research report does not contain strong facts, and only one source was used to find information about how an area or the animals in an area were saved. • Student did not evaluate the information, so much of what is included is unrelated to the topic.	• Speaker does not use appropriate facts and relevant descriptive details during the presentation. • Speaker fails to speak clearly or initiate eye contact during the presentation.

Name ______________________ Date ______________________

Unit Self-Assessment

Unit 4

Directions: Mark a ✔ in one box for each skill.

I can...	 I can do this and can tell others how to do it.	 I can do this by myself.	 I can do this if I have help or look at an example.
understand prefixes.			
classify words into different categories.			
determine what is an important idea when I read.			
understand the theme of a story.			
understand plot, characters, and setting in a story.			
compare stories.			
figure out what is an author's opinion and find evidence for that opinion.			
understand the author's purpose.			
understand the viewpoint of an author and the characters in a story.			
use present-tense action verbs correctly.			
use linking and helping verbs correctly.			

Of all the texts you read for Let's Work Together, which one was your favorite? ______________________

____

What did you like about it? ______________________

____

____

COPY READY

Answer Keys and Rubrics

COPY READY

Reading Comprehension

Week 1

Item	Key	Item Descriptor	CCSS Code
1	C	Plot	CC.3.Rlit.5
2	D	Theme	CC.3.Rlit.2
3	B	Support for Theme	CC.3.Rlit.2
4	D	Sensory Details	CC.3.Rlit.4

Week 2

Item	Key	Item Descriptor	CCSS Code
1	B	Story Elements: Plot	CC.3.Rlit.5
2	D	Story Elements: Plot	CC.3.Rlit.5
3	C	Story Elements: Characters	CC.3.Rlit.3
4	A	Story Elements: Setting	CC.3.Rlit.5
5	D	Compare Story Elements: Characters	CC.3.Rlit.9
6	D	Compare Story Elements: Characters	CC.3.Rlit.9
7	A	Compare Themes	CC.3.Rlit.9
8	C	Compare Themes	CC.3.Rlit.9

Week 3

Item	Key	Item Descriptor	CCSS Code
1	B	Determine Importance	CC.3.Rinf.2
2	B	Author's Use of Opinion and Evidence	CC.3.Rinf.2
3	D	Author's Use of Opinion and Evidence	CC.3.Rinf.2
4	C	Determine Importance	CC.3.Rinf.2

Unit Test (including Week 4)

Item	Key	Item Descriptor	CCSS Code
1	B	Author's Purpose	CC.3.Rinf.10
2	C	Author's Purpose	CC.3.Rinf.10
3	A	Determine Importance	CC.3.Rinf.2
4	D	Determine Importance	CC.3.Rinf.2
5	C	Author's Use of Opinion and Evidence	CC.3.Rinf.2
6	A	Author's Use of Opinion and Evidence	CC.3.Rinf.2
7	C	Story Elements: Characters	CC.3.Rlit.3
8	A	Story Elements: Characters	CC.3.Rlit.3
9	D	Analyze Viewpoint	CC.3.Rlit.6
10	C	Author's Purpose	CC.3.Rlit.10
11	A	Theme	CC.3.Rlit.2
12	A	Theme	CC.3.Rlit.2
13	C	Author's Purpose	CC.3.Rlit.10
14	A	Compare Story Elements: Characters	CC.3.Rlit.9
15	B	Compare Story Elements: Characters	CC.3.Rlit.9, Rlit.5
16	B	Compare Themes	CC.3.Rlit.9
17	Skill Rubric	Analyze Viewpoint	CC.3.Rlit.6

Vocabulary

Week 1 CC.3.L.6			Week 3 CC.3.L.6		
Item	Key	Word	Item	Key	Word
1	B	buyer	1	D	field
2	C	money	2	A	crop
3	C	market	3	B	farmer
4	A	seller	4	C	harvest
5	D	advertisement	5	C	Agriculture
6	A	pay	6	B	plow
7	C	purpose	7	B	future
8	A	Cooperation	8	A	alternative
9	B	plenty	9	C	method
10	D	accomplish	10	D	Conservation
11	A	reward	11	C	sustain

Week 2

Item	Key	Item Descriptor	CCSS Code
1	C	Prefixes	CC.3.L.4.b, Rfou.3.a, L.4.c
2	A	Prefixes	CC.3.L.4.b, Rfou.3.a, L.4.c
3	B	Prefixes	CC.3.L.4.b, Rfou.3.a, L.4.c
4	C	Prefixes	CC.3.L.4.b, Rfou.3.a, L.4.c

Unit Test (including Week 4)

Item	Key	Item Descriptor	CCSS Code
1	C	Classify Words	CC.3.L.5, L.6
2	B	Classify Words	CC.3.L.5, L.6
3	B	Classify Words	CC.3.L.5, L.6
4	A	Classify Words	CC.3.L.5, L.6
5	A	Prefixes	CC.3.L.4.b, Rfou.3.a, L.4.c
6	C	Prefixes	CC.3.L.4.b, Rfou.3.a, L.4.c
7	A	Social Studies Vocabulary	CC.3.L.6
8	D	Social Studies Vocabulary	CC.3.L.6
9	B	Social Studies Vocabulary	CC.3.L.6
10	A	Academic Vocabulary	CC.3.L.6
11	C	Academic Vocabulary	CC.3.L.6
12	C	Academic Vocabulary	CC.3.L.6

Answer Keys and Rubrics

Writing, Revising, and Editing

Week 1

Item	Key	Item Descriptor	CCSS Code
1	B	Present-Tense Action Verbs	CC.3.L.1.f, L.1.e, L.1.a
2	C	Present-Tense Action Verbs	CC.3.L.1.f, L.1.e, L.1.a
3	B	Present-Tense Action Verbs	CC.3.L.1.f, L.1.e, L.1.a
4	B	Present-Tense Action Verbs	CC.3.L.1.f, L.1.e, L.1.a
5	A	Present-Tense Action Verbs	CC.3.L.1.f, L.1.e, L.1.a
6	B	Present-Tense Action Verbs	CC.3.L.1.f, L.1.e, L.1.a
Prompt (7)	Skill Rubric	Establish and Follow a Purpose	CC.3.W.10

Week 2

Item	Key	Item Descriptor	CCSS Code
1	B	Present-Tense Action Verbs	CC.3.L.1.f, L.1.e, L.1.a
2	C	Present-Tense Action Verbs	CC.3.L.1.f, L.1.e, L.1.a
3	A	Present-Tense Action Verbs	CC.3.L.1.f, L.1.e, L.1.a
4	A	Present-Tense Action Verbs	CC.3.L.1.f, L.1.e, L.1.a
5	C	Present-Tense Action Verbs	CC.3.L.1.f, L.1.e, L.1.a
6	C	Present-Tense Action Verbs	CC.3.L.1.f, L.1.e, L.1.a
Prompt (7)	Skill Rubric	Introduce Characters	CC.3.W.3.a

Week 3

Item	Key	Item Descriptor	CCSS Code
1	B	Forms of *do*	CC.3.L.1.d, L.1.f, L.1.a
2	B	Helping Verbs (*must*)	CC.3.L.1.a
3	C	Helping Verbs (*should*)	CC.3.L.1.a
4	A	Forms of *do*	CC.3.L.1.d, L.1.f, L.1.a
5	C	Helping Verbs (*could*)	CC.3.L.1.a
6	A	Forms of *do*	CC.3.L.1.d, L.1.f, L.1.a
Prompt (7)	Skill Rubric	Evaluate Information	CC.3.W.8

Unit Test (including Week 4)

Item	Key	Item Descriptor	CCSS Code
1	A	Forms of *be*	CC.3.L.1.d, L.1.f, L.1.a
2	B	Forms of *have*	CC.3.L.1.d, L.1.f, L.1.a
3	C	Forms of *have*	CC.3.L.1.d, L.1.f, L.1.a
4	C	Forms of *be*	CC.3.L.1.d, L.1.f, L.1.a
5	C	Editing: Forms of *be*	CC.3.L.1.d, L.1.f, W.5
6	A	Editing: Forms of *do*	CC.3.L.1.d, L.1.f, W.5
7	B	Editing: Helping Verbs (*should*)	CC.3.L.1.a, W.5
8	B	Editing: Forms of *have*	CC.3.L.1.d, L.1.f, W.5
9	A	Editing: Present-Tense Action Verbs	CC.3.L.1.f, L.1.e, L.1.a
10	D	Editing: Helping Verbs (*can*)	CC.3.L.1.a, W.5
11a	Editing Rubric	Editing Task: Forms of *be*	CC.3.L.1.d, L.1.f, W.5
11b	Editing Rubric	Editing Task: Forms of *do*	CC.3.L.1.d, L.1.f, W.5
11c	Editing Rubric	Editing Task: Forms of *have*	CC.3.L.1.d, L.1.f, W.5
11d	Editing Rubric	Editing Task: Forms of *be*	CC.3.L.1.d, L.1.f, W.5
11e	Editing Rubric	Editing Task: Present-Tense Action Verbs	CC.3.L.1.d, L.1.f, W.5
11f	Editing Rubric	Editing Task: Forms of *have*	CC.3.L.1.d, L.1.f, W.5
Prompt (12)	Skill Rubric, Writing Rubric	Link Opinions and Reasons	CC.3.W.1.c, W.1.a, W.1.b

COPY READY

Answer Keys and Rubrics

Writing, Revising, and Editing

Week 1 Skill Rubric

Item 7 (Prompt) | Establish and Follow a Purpose

Student uses wording that conveys	
4 points	a strong and clear sense of purpose.
3 points	an adequate sense of purpose.
2 points	some sense of purpose.
1 point	a vague sense of purpose.

Week 2 Skill Rubric

Item 7 (Prompt) | Introduce Characters

Student writes introductory sentences that	
4 points	vividly introduce the character and the story.
3 points	adequately introduce the character and the story.
2 points	vaguely introduce the character and the story.
1 point	minimally introduce the character or the story.

Week 3 Skill Rubric

Item 7 (Prompt) | Evaluate Information

Student uses criteria of site type and purpose, author expertise, and date to write	
4 points	an appropriate and accurate evaluation of the sources.
3 points	a mostly accurate evaluation of the sources.
2 points	a somewhat accurate evaluation of the sources.
1 point	an inadequate evaluation of the sources.

Writing, Revising, and Editing

Unit Test Week 4 Skill Rubric

Item 12 (Prompt) | Link Opinions and Reasons

Student writes a persuasive essay that	
4 points	convincingly links opinion and reasons.
3 points	adequately links opinion and reasons.
2 points	somewhat links opinion and reasons.
1 point	minimally links opinion and reasons.

Use the Writing Rubric on page A4.39 to assess the writing traits of student responses for the Unit Test Writing Prompt.

Unit Test Editing Task Rubric

Item 11 | 1 point per correct response

11a	In sentence 1, change "is" to "are"
11b	In sentence 3, change "does" to "do"
11c	In sentence 5, change "have" to "has "
11d	In sentence 6, change "am" to "is"
11e	In sentence 7, change "washes" to "wash"
11f	In sentence 8, change "has" to "have"

Reading Comprehension

Unit Test Rubric

Item 17 | Analyze Viewpoint

3 points	Correctly describes the character's viewpoint and provides a supporting detail.
2 points	Correctly describes the character's viewpoint, but does not provide a supporting detail.
1 point	Does not correctly describe the character's viewpoint.

Scoring Note: Assign a score of zero for no response or an unscorable response.

Conversion Charts: Points Earned to Percent Scored

4 points

Points	1	2	3	4
%	25	50	75	100

8 points

Points	1	2	3	4	5	6	7	8
%	13	25	38	50	63	75	88	100

10 points

Points	1	2	3	4	5	6	7	8	9	10
%	10	20	30	40	50	60	70	80	90	100

11 points

Points	1	2	3	4	5	6	7	8	9	10	11
%	9	18	27	36	45	55	64	73	82	91	100

12 points

Points	1	2	3	4	5	6	7	8	9	10	11	12
%	8	17	25	33	42	50	58	67	75	83	92	100

18 points

Points	1	2	3	4	5	6	7	8	9	10	11	12	13	14	15	16	17	18
%	6	11	17	22	28	33	39	44	50	56	61	67	72	78	83	89	94	100

19 points

Points	1	2	3	4	5	6	7	8	9	10	11	12	13	14	15	16	17	18	19
%	5	11	16	21	26	32	37	42	47	53	58	63	68	74	79	84	89	95	100

20 points

Points	1	2	3	4	5	6	7	8	9	10	11	12	13	14	15	16	17	18	19	20
%	5	10	15	20	25	30	35	40	45	50	55	60	65	70	75	80	85	90	95	100

Name ______________________ Date ______________________

Theme

Reteach

Review the Rules

The theme is the main message of a story. Use what you know about the plot, setting, and characters in a story to figure out the theme.

Practice

Read "A Bad Day." Complete the theme chart. Then use the clues to write the story's theme.

A Bad Day

Ricky wanted to make a good impression at his new school, but nothing went right. In gym class, he tripped on his shoelace while running to first base. In the cafeteria, he dropped his lunch tray. Food went flying everywhere! He was so embarrassed, he wanted to cry.

"Hey, Ricky," said a girl as she walked toward him. "I'm Sophia. Want to sit outside and share my sandwich?" He nodded with relief.

On their way outside, Sophia ran smack into another student. Her lunch went flying all over the steps. She laughed. "I guess I'm having a bad day, too!" she said.

Theme Chart

Title	**Characters**
Setting	**Events**

Theme: ______________________

Apply

Tell a partner about a theme from one of your Small Group Reading books. Explain how you figured out the theme.

COPY READY

COPY READY

Name ______________________________ Date ______________

Determine Importance

Reteach

Review the Rules

When you decide what details you want to remember, y importance. As you read,

- **decide what you want to know about the topic**
- **look for important details that tell you more about w**

Practice

Read "The Plant House." Then complete the sentences.

The Plant House

Although it's new, The Plant House is already popular. It's in town. Emily Jax opened the store last week. Emily sells all kinds of plants and plant supplies. Some of the flowers she sells you can't find anywhere else. Olivia Golden lives in the apartment above The Plant House. She always sees happy customers come out of the shop. One day Olivia hopes she can work there!

1. The topic is ______________________________

____

2. I want to know ______________________________

____

3. The important details I'll remember are ______________________________

____

____

Apply

Determine the important details in one of your Small Group Reading books. Tell a partner what you'll remember about the topic.

Name ______________________ Date ______________________

Writing Trait: Fluency

Reteach

Review the Rules

Writing that is fluent has ideas that flow smoothly together. To make their writing fluent, writers use

- **some long and some short sentences**
- **different kinds of sentences**
- **transition words such as *first*, *then*, and *finally* to connect ideas.**

Practice

Read "Recycling Made Easy." Look at the underlined sentences.

Recycling Made Easy

Believe it or not, my neighbor did not know how to recycle! I showed her. I made a list. The list showed what could be recycled. The list included bottles. The list showed cans and cardboard. We found some boxes. We labeled the boxes. Finally, I showed her how to separate some old cans and bottles into the boxes. My neighbor was amazed at how easy it was to recycle!

Rewrite the paragraph. Change the underlined sentences and add transition words to make the writing fluent.

____

____

____

____

____

____

____

____

Apply

Write about something you showed someone else how to do. Use different kinds of sentences and lengths. Use transition words. Make your writing fluent.

COPY READY

COPY READY

Name ______________________ Date ______________

Story Elements

Reteach

Review the Rules

Stories have characters, settings, and plots. In many stories, the characters' actions

- **cause certain events to happen**
- **tell you what the characters are like.**

Practice

Read "The Dance." Then answer the questions.

The Dance

Chris and Elena waited for their turn to perform at the fair on Saturday. Finally, their names were called. But on their way up to the stage, Chris panicked.

"I forgot the CD," he whispered to Elena. "I'm so sorry. Now we can't perform," he said sadly.

"Wait," said Elena calmly. "I have another CD in my bag. It's not the same music, but we've practiced it before."

Elena grabbed the CD and put it in the player. "Relax and just have fun!" she told Chris.

Chris and Elena did have fun, and so did the audience. Almost everyone stood as they cheered for more!

1. Where does the story take place?

____

2. What causes Chris to panic?

____

3. What does Elena do when Chris panics?

____

4. What do Elena's actions and words show about her?

____

Apply

Talk with a partner about one of your Small Group Reading books. Describe the characters, setting, and events in the story.

Name ______________________ Date ______________

Determine Importance

Reteach

Review the Rules

When you decide what details you want to remember, you determine importance. As you read,

- **decide what you want to know about the topic**
- **look for important details that tell you more about what you want to know.**

Practice

Read "In the City." Then complete the sentences.

In the City

There are many ways to get around in the city. Some people need to get to work. Others want to see the sights. People can drive their own cars or ride in a bus. Some people prefer to ride in taxis because they want to avoid crowds. People who don't mind crowds at all can take the subway. The subway can be the fastest way to get somewhere. With sidewalks everywhere, people can walk, too!

1. The topic is ______________________

____

2. I want to know ______________________

____

3. The important details I'll remember are ______________________

____

____

Apply

Talk about one of your Small Group Reading books with a partner. Share the most important details you'll remember about the topic.

COPY READY

Name ______________________ Date ______________

Writing Trait: Voice

Reteach

Review the Rules

Writing that has a strong voice

- **sounds natural**
- **has dialogue that sounds like real people talk**
- **uses playful language for a humorous story.**

Practice

Read the two versions of "Talking to Ted." Circle the version that has the most natural voice.

Talking to Ted

"I would like to come to visit you," said Gina. "We could play with my new building set."

"I would like you to come," said Ted. "I would also like you to bring your new set."

"Let us make a plan for Saturday," said Gina.

Talking to Ted

"Can I come by some time soon?" asked Gina. "I've got a new building set and I think you'll love it."

"Great," said Ted. "I'd love to see you—and don't forget your building set."

"I'll stop by on Saturday then," said Gina. "Let's build some fun!"

Apply

Rewrite this conversation to make the voice sound natural.

"Let us go to the movies," said Mom. "What would you like to see?"

"I would like to see a movie that is funny," said Devin. "I think that would make me feel happy."

____

____

____

Name ______________________ Date ______________

Opinion and Evidence

Reteach

Review the Rules

An opinion is what someone believes or thinks about a topic.

- **An opinion often begins with *I think*, *I believe*, or *In my opinion*.**
- **To support an opinion, an author gives reasons, or evidence. Sometimes the evidence follows words such as *first*, *finally*, *because*, *since*, and *therefore*.**

Practice

Read "A True Survivor." Circle the author's opinion. Underline the evidence.

A True Survivor

You probably know that a scorpion has a poisonous stinger. But I think it has even more amazing survival abilities. First of all, a scorpion does not need a lot of oxygen or water, so it can slow down its body to save energy. Therefore, whenever prey comes its way a scorpion has the energy to deliver its quick, deadly strike. Secondly, a scorpion can survive in extreme environments. A group of scientists actually froze some scorpions, and then watched them thaw and walk away the next day! There's much more to a scorpion's survival than just a sting!

Apply

Tell a partner how an author uses reasons and evidence to support an opinion in one of your Small Group Reading books.

COPY READY

COPY READY

Name ______________________ Date ______________

Determine Importance

Reteach

Review the Rules

When you summarize, you talk about the most important ideas in something you've read.

- **Decide which details are more important than others.**
- **Use your own words to tell about the most important ideas in a sentence or two.**

Read the first paragraph of "Modern Pirates on the High Seas" and look at the underlined examples of important details.

Modern Pirates on the High Seas

Many people dream of finding a buried treasure. But some people make their living at it. These treasure hunters search land and sea to find a lost treasure. Then they sell it to make money.

Some experts feel that treasure hunting should be illegal. Treasure hunters destroy valuable pieces from our past. Experts could study these pieces for clues to the past. They believe that these pieces belong in museums. To them, treasure hunters rob the people from learning more about the world.

These are important details.

To summarize: Treasure hunters look for treasure to sell.

Practice

As you read the second paragraph, underline the important details. Then summarize the paragraph in one or two sentences.

____

____

____

____

Apply

Summarize a paragraph from one of your Small Group Reading books for a partner.

Name ______________________ Date ______________

Author's Purpose

Reteach

Review the Rules

Authors have different purposes for writing.

If the author wants the reader to	The author's purpose is
enjoy a story	to entertain
learn something	to inform, describe, or explain
know how he or she feels	to express feelings
believe or do something	to persuade

COPY READY

Practice

Read "Litter Solutions." Explain the author's purpose and why you chose it.

Litter Solutions

Many people are talking about the litter in our parks. There are food wrappers and soda cans all over. This makes enjoying the park hard for the public.

Some people want to put trash cans and recycling bins in the parks. They say this will stop others from throwing their trash on the ground. They feel clean parks are more enjoyable for everyone.

____

____

____

____

Apply

Share the author's purpose from one of your Small Group Reading books. Tell a partner why the author wrote the text.

COPY READY

Name ______________________ Date ______________

Viewpoints

Reteach

Review the Rules

A viewpoint is the way someone thinks or feels about something.

- **To find the narrator's viewpoint, look for what the narrator says about the characters and events.**
- **To find a character's viewpoint, look for what the character says, does, and feels. Look for how the character responds.**

Practice

Read "The Fox and the Crow." Look for words, actions, and dialogue that show the viewpoints of the narrator and the characters.

The Fox and the Crow

A crafty fox saw a crow fly to the top of a tree with a piece of cheese. The fox wanted that cheese. It had a plan to get it, too!

"Not only are crows ugly, but they are easy to trick," thought the fox. "They'll believe anything." So fox looked up at the crow and said, "What beautiful feathers you have. I'll bet that your singing is as fine as your feathers!"

The foolish crow was delighted by fox's words. It wanted to show the fox that, indeed, it could sing a sweet song.

"Tweet, tweet!" cawed the crow. As it did, the cheese fell right into the fox's mouth.

Complete the chart to describe the viewpoints in the story.

Narrator	**Fox**	**Crow**
The fox is __________. The crow is __________.	The crow is __________.	The fox is __________.

Apply

Talk with a partner about two or more of your Small Group Reading books. Describe the viewpoints of its characters and narrators.

Name ______________________________ Date ______________

Determine Importance

Reteach

Review the Rules

When you summarize, you tell the most important ideas in something you've read.

- **Decide which details are more important than others.**
- **Use your own words to retell the important ideas in a sentence or two.**

Read the first paragraph of "Amazing Ants." Look at the underlined details and sample summary.

Amazing Ants

Ants aren't always pests. Some kinds of ants can help keep nature balanced. In the jungle, for example, leafcutter ants recycle leaves. When the ants take the leaves, that helps the jungle from becoming overgrown.

Back in their nests, ants use the leaves to make their own food. They chop and smash the leaves into a paste. They wait until a fungus grows on the paste. Then they have a feast! The ants eat the fungus. When it is gone, they push the leaf paste out of their nest. The paste releases things into the soil that are good for plants.

These are important details.

To summarize:
Leafcutter ants help the jungle by recycling leaves.

Practice

Read the second paragraph. Underline the important details. Then summarize the paragraph in one or two sentences.

____

____

____

____

Apply

Choose a paragraph from one of your Small Group Reading books. Use the most important details to summarize the text for your partner.

COPY READY

COPY READY

Name ________________________ Date ____________

Writing Trait: Ideas

Reteach

Review the Rules

When you write, include enough information to make your message clear. State your opinions clearly, and use evidence to support your ideas.

Practice

Read "The Plastic Bag Problem." Circle the main idea. Underline the evidence.

The Plastic Bag Problem

Everyone should stop using plastic bags in grocery stores immediately. Americans use billions of plastic bags every year. Many of these bags get used only once. Afterward, they may end up in the ocean, causing harm to plants and animals there. Since shoppers can easily bring their own totes, we should stop using plastic bags now.

Read "Drinking Water." The ideas in the paragraph are not complete. Use the evidence to help you write a clear main idea to make the message clear.

Drinking Water

Did you know that tap water is as healthy as bottled water? Tap water also doesn't cause litter. Bottled water costs a lot. Drinking tap water is less expensive. Plastic bottles cause pollution. Tap water does not.

Apply

Talk with a partner about the ideas presented in one of your Small Group Reading books. Explain why you think the ideas are well-developed.

____

____

____

____

____

Reteaching Masters Answer Key

RT4.1 Theme

Title A Bad Day	Characters Ricky, Sophia
school cafeteria **Setting**	Ricky trips on his shoelace in gym class. He drops his tray at lunch. He meets Sophia. Sophia runs into another student. Sophia's lunch spills all over the steps. **Events**

Theme: Everyone has a bad day sometimes.

RT4.2 Determine Importance

Answers will vary, but should reflect the following.

1. The topic is a new store called The Plant House.
2. I want to know why The Plant House is popular.
3. The important details I'll remember are that it is the only plant store in town, it has a variety of plants and supplies, and it has some flowers you can't find anywhere else.

RT4.3 Writing Trait: Fluency

Possible response:

Recycling Made Easy

Believe it or not, my neighbor did not know how to recycle! So one day, I showed her how. First, I made a list of all the things that could be recycled. The list included bottles, cans, and cardboard. Then we found and labeled some boxes. Finally, I showed her how to separate some old cans and bottles into the boxes. My neighbor was amazed at how easy it was to recycle!

RT4.4 Story Elements

1. at a fair
2. He forgot the CD.
3. She finds a different CD and tells Chris to relax and have fun.
4. Elena is prepared, calm, and encouraging.

RT4.5 Determine Importance

Answers will vary, but should reflect the following.

1. The topic is ways to get around in the city.
2. I want to know the different ways you can get around in the city.
3. The important details I'll remember are that you can drive a car or ride in a bus, you can take a taxi or the subway, or you can walk.

RT4.6 Writing Trait: Voice

Students should circle the second version.

Apply

Possible response:

"Let's go to the movies," Mom suggested. "Anything you'd like to see?"

"I want to see a comedy," said Devin. "I could really use a laugh."

RT4.7 Opinion and Evidence

A True Survivor

You probably know that a scorpion has a poisonous stinger. But, I think it has even more amazing survival abilities. First of all, a scorpion does not need a lot of oxygen or water, so it can slow down its body to save energy. Therefore, whenever prey comes its way, a scorpion has the energy to deliver its quick, deadly strike. Secondly, a scorpion can survive in extreme environments. A group of scientists actually froze some scorpions, and then watched them thaw and walk away the next day! There's much more to a scorpion's survival than just a sting!

RT4.8 Determine Importance

Modern Pirates on the High Seas

Some experts feel that treasure hunting should be illegal. Treasure hunters destroy valuable pieces from our past. Experts could study these pieces for clues to the past. They believe that these pieces belong in museums. To them, treasure hunters rob the people from learning more about the world.

Possible response:

Some experts feel that treasure hunters destroy things that could tell us about our past.

RT4.9 Author's Purpose

Possible response:

The author's purpose is to describe. The author describes how people feel about litter in the park and what they think can be done about it.

RT4.10 Viewpoints

Narrator	Fox	Crow
The fox is smart and clever. The crow is not very smart and is easily fooled.	The crow is ugly, easy to trick, and stupid.	The fox is kind, nice, and likes beautiful things.

RT4.11 Determine Importance

Underlined important details:

Back in their nests, ants use the leaves to make their own food. They chop and smash the leaves into a paste. They wait until a fungus grows on the paste. Then they have a feast! The ants eat the fungus. When it is gone, they push the leaf paste out of their nest. The paste releases things into the soil that are good for plants.

Possible summary:

Leafcutter ants turn the leaves into a paste that is good for plants.

RT4.12 Writing Trait: Ideas

The Plastic Bag Problem

Everyone should stop using plastic bags in grocery stores immediately. Americans use billions of plastic bags every year. Many of these bags get used only once. Afterward, they may end up in the ocean, causing harm to plant and animals there. Since shoppers can easily bring their own totes, we should stop using plastic bags now.

Drinking Water

Possible response:

People should drink tap water instead of bottled water.

Contents

Reading Level Translation Key

Grade	Guided Reading	DRA	Lexile®	Reading Recovery	Grade
K	A	A–2		A–2	K
K	B	3		3	K
K	C			4	K
1	D	4		5	1
1				6	1
1	E	6		7	1
1	F	8		8	1
1			200L–400L	9	1
1	G	10		10	1
1	H			11	1
1	I	12		12	1
1	J	14		14	1
2				15	2
2		16	200L–400L		2
2	K				2
2	L–M	18–28	300L–500L	18–20	2
3	N–P	30–38	500L–700L	22–24	3
4	Q–R	40	650L–850L	26	4
5	S–U	44	750L–950L	28	5
6	V–W	50	850L–1000L		6

Reading levels are provided for each title in the ***National Geographic Reach for Reading*** Grade 1–2 Leveled Reading and Grades 3–5 Small Group Reading lessons. Please note that each leveling system is based on a different set of criteria. This may result in discrepancies when translating reading levels.

Grade 3 Unit 4 Cumulative Key Word List

accomplish (v)
achieve (v)
action (n)
advertisement (n)
agriculture (n)
alter (v)
alternative (n)
amount (n)
area (n)
artist (n)
balance (n)
behavior (n)
benefit (n)
blossom (n)
buyer (n)
carve (v)
category (n)
cause (n)
challenge (n)
character (n)
characteristic (n)
city (n)
clarify (v)
classify (v)
combine (v)
communicate (v)
compare (v)
comparison (n)
competition (n)
composition (n)
conclusion (n)
conditions (n)
connection (n)
conservation (n)
continent (n)
contrast (v)
control (v)
cooperation (n)
core (n)
create (v)
crop (n)
cycle (n)
decrease (v)
depend (v)
desert (n)
destination (n)
details (n)
determine (v)
develop (v)
difference (n)
direction (n)
discover (v)
distance (n)
diversity (n)
drought (n)
duty (n)
earthquake (n)
ecosystem (n)
effect (n)
endurance (n)
environment (n)
erupt (v)
estimate (v)
event (n)
evidence (n)
explore (v)
express (v)
farmer (n)
feelings (n)
feet (n)
field (n)
firm (adj)
flow (v)
food chain
force (n)
form (n)
freeze (v)
future (n)
generalization (n)
generation (n)
gift (n)
globe (n)
goal (n)
ground (n)
growth (n)
harvest (v)
heritage (n)
identify (v)
impact (n)
improve (v)
increase (v)
individual (n)
inference (n)
interact (v)
island (n)
journey (n)
kilometer (n)
kindness (n)
lava (n)
learn (v)
level (n)
liquid (n)
location (n)
magma (n)
main idea
market (n)
measurement (n)
melt (v)
meter (n)
method (n)
mixture (n)
money (n)
motive (n)
music (n)
narrator (n)
nature (n)
need (v)
negative (adj)
neighborhood (n)
occur (v)
ocean (n)
offer (v)
opinion (n)
order (n)
organism (n)
outcome (n)
paraphrase (v)
pay (v)
perform (v)
plate (n)
plenty (n)
plot (n)
plow (v)
point of view
popular (adj)
positive (adj)
power (n)
prediction (n)
prepare (v)
preservation (n)
pressure (n)
preview (v)
problem (n)
process (n)
produce (v)
protect (v)
purpose (n)
rainforest (n)
react (v)
receive (v)
region (n)
represent (v)
rescue (v)
resources (n)
reward (n)
rhythm (n)
river (n)
rock (n)
root (n)
sand (n)
scarce (adj)
scene (n)
seed (n)
seller (n)
sense (v)
sequence (n)
shore (n)
signal (n)
soil (n)
solid (n)
solution (n)
sprout (n)
stanza (n)
state (n)
storyteller (n)
strategy (n)
style (n)
substance (n)
summarize (v)
supply (n)
surface (n)
sustain (v)
tale (n)
temperature (n)
theme (n)
thermometer (n)
tradition (n)
trap (v)
tsunami (n)
understand (v)
unique (adj)
unit (n)
value (v)
vary (v)
vine (n)
visualize (v)
volcano (n)
volunteer (n)
want (v)
warn (v)
water (n)
wave (n)
weed (n)
wetland (n)
wood (n)

Words from Unit 4 appear in red type. For additional content words and story words, please see the Small Group Reading section.

Anthology Handbook

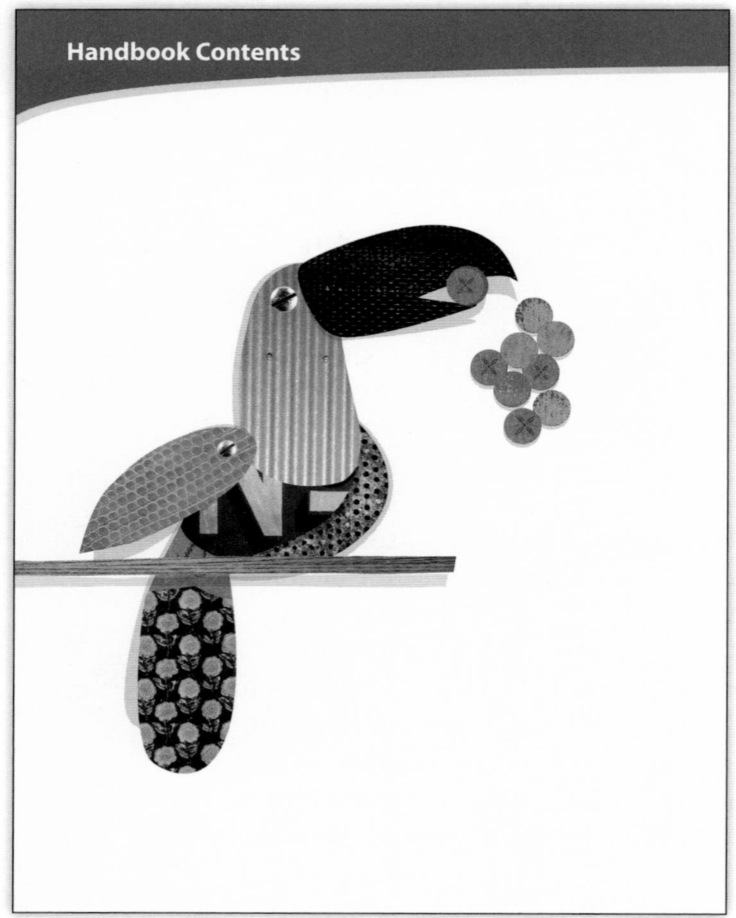

Handbook Contents

Page 554

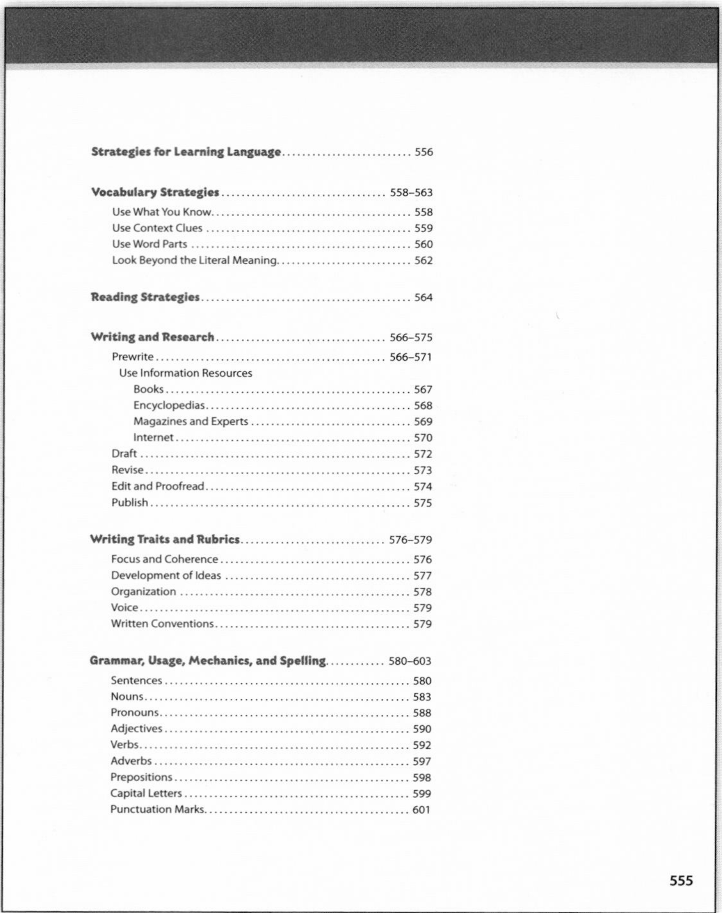

555

Page 555

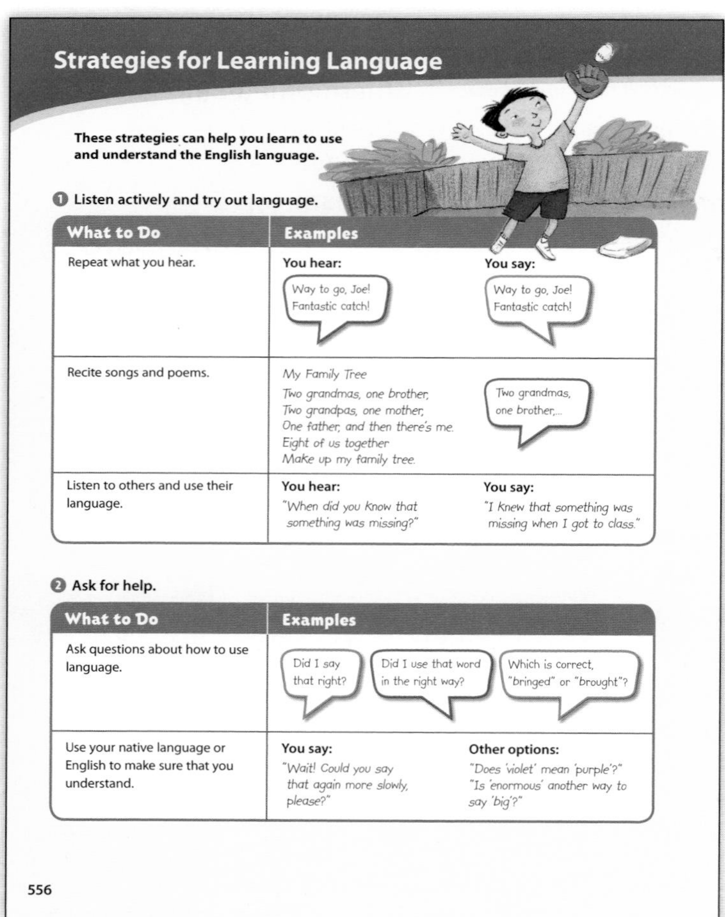

Strategies for Learning Language

These strategies can help you learn to use and understand the English language.

1 Listen actively and try out language.

What to Do	Examples	
Repeat what you hear.	**You hear:** *Way to go, Joe! Fantastic catch!*	**You say:** *Way to go, Joe! Fantastic catch!*
Recite songs and poems.	*My Family Tree* *Two grandmas, one brother,* *Two grandpas, one mother,* *One father, and then there's me.* *Eight of us together* *Make up my family tree.*	*Two grandmas, one brother,...*
Listen to others and use their language.	**You hear:** *"When did you know that something was missing?"*	**You say:** *"I knew that something was missing when I got to class."*

2 Ask for help.

What to Do	Examples		
Ask questions about how to use language.	*Did I say that right?*	*Did I use that word in the right way?*	*Which is correct, "bringed" or "brought"?*
Use your native language or English to make sure that you understand.	**You say:** *"Wait! Could you say that again more slowly, please?"*	**Other options:** *"Does 'violet' mean 'purple'?"* *"Is 'enormous' another way to say 'big'?"*	

556

Page 556

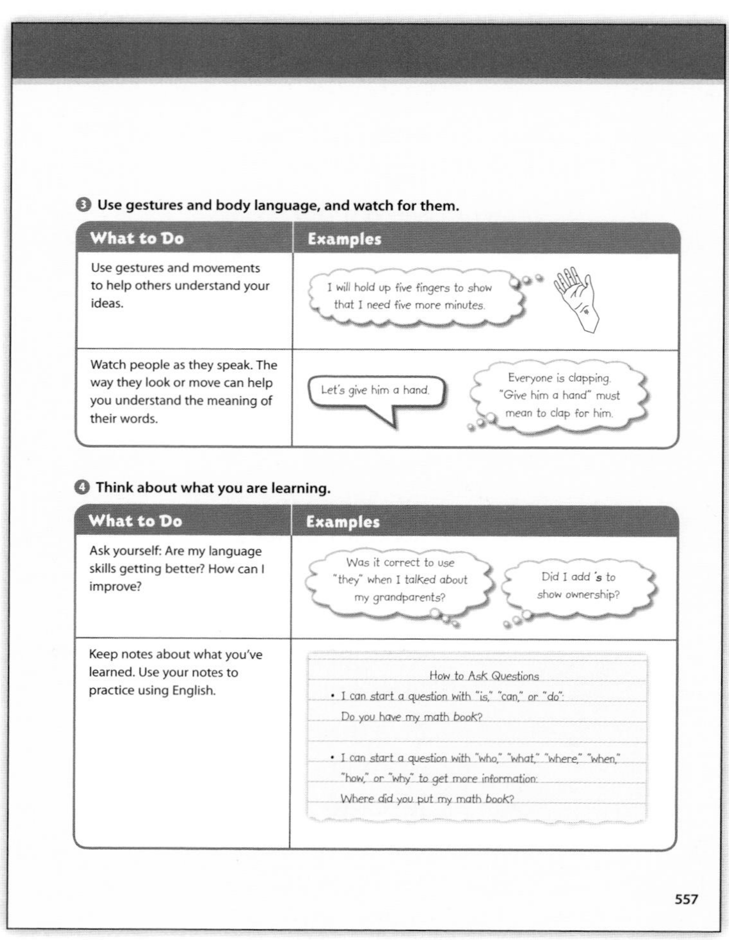

3 Use gestures and body language, and watch for them.

What to Do	Examples	
Use gestures and movements to help others understand your ideas.	*I will hold up five fingers to show that I need five more minutes.*	
Watch people as they speak. The way they look or move can help you understand the meaning of their words.	*Let's give him a hand.*	*Everyone is clapping. "Give him a hand" must mean to clap for him.*

4 Think about what you are learning.

What to Do	Examples	
Ask yourself: Are my language skills getting better? How can I improve?	*Was it correct to use "they" when I talked about my grandparents?*	*Did I add 's to show ownership?*
Keep notes about what you've learned. Use your notes to practice using English.	*How to Ask Questions* • *I can start a question with "is," "can," or "do":* *Do you have my math book?* • *I can start a question with "who," "what," "where," "when," "how," or "why" to get more information:* *Where did you put my math book?*	

557

Page 557

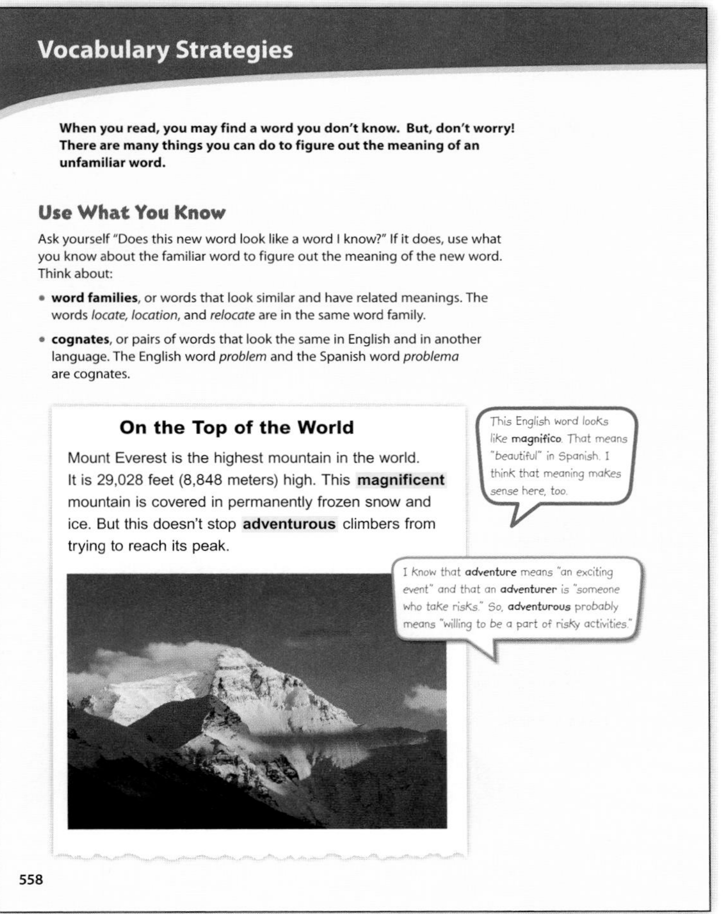

Vocabulary Strategies

When you read, you may find a word you don't know. But, don't worry! There are many things you can do to figure out the meaning of an unfamiliar word.

Use What You Know

Ask yourself "Does this new word look like a word I know?" If it does, use what you know about the familiar word to figure out the meaning of the new word. Think about:

- **word families**, or words that look similar and have related meanings. The words *locate, location,* and *relocate* are in the same word family.
- **cognates**, or pairs of words that look the same in English and in another language. The English word *problem* and the Spanish word *problema* are cognates.

On the Top of the World

Mount Everest is the highest mountain in the world. It is 29,028 feet (8,848 meters) high. This **magnificent** mountain is covered in permanently frozen snow and ice. But this doesn't stop **adventurous** climbers from trying to reach its peak.

This English word looks like **magnifico**. That means "beautiful" in Spanish. I think that meaning makes sense here, too.

I know that **adventure** means "an exciting event" and that an **adventurer** is "someone who take risks." So, **adventurous** probably means "willing to be a part of risky activities."

558

Page 558

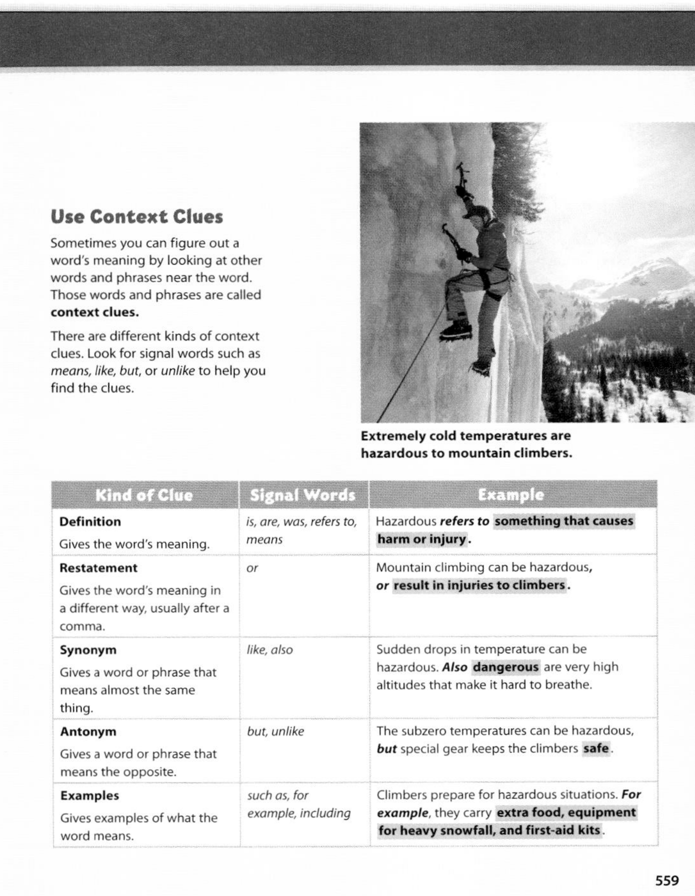

Use Context Clues

Sometimes you can figure out a word's meaning by looking at other words and phrases near the word. Those words and phrases are called **context clues.**

There are different kinds of context clues. Look for signal words such as *means, like, but,* or *unlike* to help you find the clues.

Extremely cold temperatures are hazardous to mountain climbers.

Kind of Clue	Signal Words	Example
Definition Gives the word's meaning.	*is, are, was, refers to, means*	Hazardous ***refers to*** **something that causes harm or injury**.
Restatement Gives the word's meaning in a different way, usually after a comma.	*or*	Mountain climbing can be hazardous, ***or*** **result in injuries to climbers**.
Synonym Gives a word or phrase that means almost the same thing.	*like, also*	Sudden drops in temperature can be hazardous. ***Also*** **dangerous** are very high altitudes that make it hard to breathe.
Antonym Gives a word or phrase that means the opposite.	*but, unlike*	The subzero temperatures can be hazardous, ***but*** special gear keeps the climbers **safe**.
Examples Gives examples of what the word means.	*such as, for example, including*	Climbers prepare for hazardous situations. ***For example***, they carry **extra food, equipment for heavy snowfall, and first-aid kits**.

559

Page 559

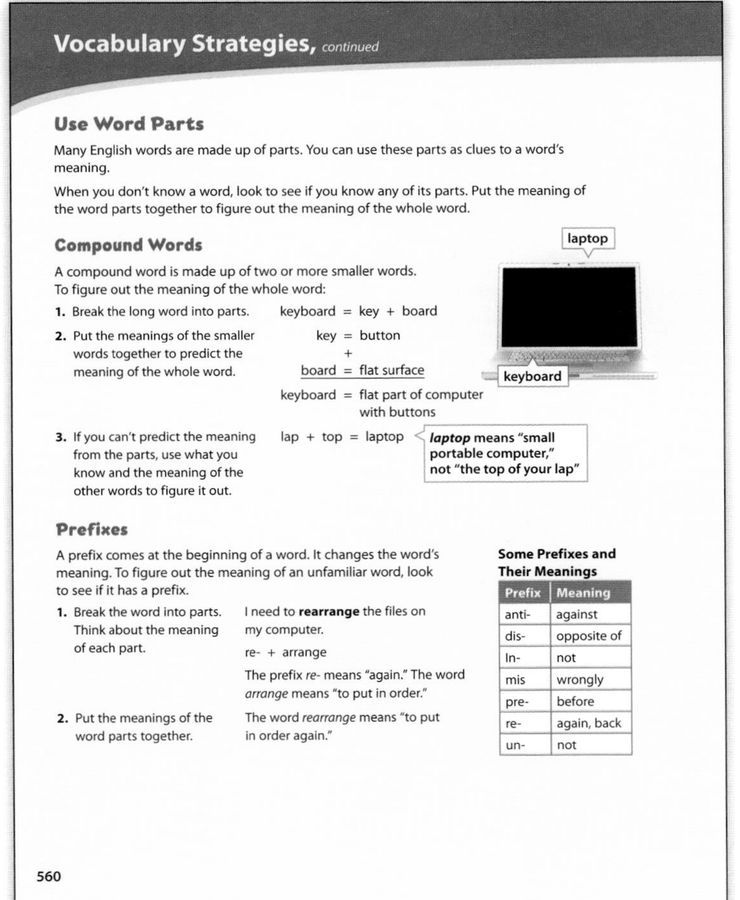

Vocabulary Strategies, *continued*

Use Word Parts

Many English words are made up of parts. You can use these parts as clues to a word's meaning.

When you don't know a word, look to see if you know any of its parts. Put the meaning of the word parts together to figure out the meaning of the whole word.

Compound Words

A compound word is made up of two or more smaller words. To figure out the meaning of the whole word:

1. Break the long word into parts. — keyboard = key + board
2. Put the meanings of the smaller words together to predict the meaning of the whole word. — key = button + board = flat surface; keyboard = flat part of computer with buttons
3. If you can't predict the meaning from the parts, use what you know and the meaning of the other words to figure it out. — lap + top = laptop — ***laptop*** **means "small portable computer," not "the top of your lap"**

laptop

keyboard

Prefixes

A prefix comes at the beginning of a word. It changes the word's meaning. To figure out the meaning of an unfamiliar word, look to see if it has a prefix.

1. Break the word into parts. Think about the meaning of each part. — I need to **rearrange** the files on my computer. re- + arrange. The prefix *re-* means "again." The word *arrange* means "to put in order."
2. Put the meanings of the word parts together. — The word *rearrange* means "to put in order again."

Some Prefixes and Their Meanings

Prefix	Meaning
anti-	against
dis-	opposite of
In-	not
mis	wrongly
pre-	before
re-	again, back
un-	not

560

Page 560

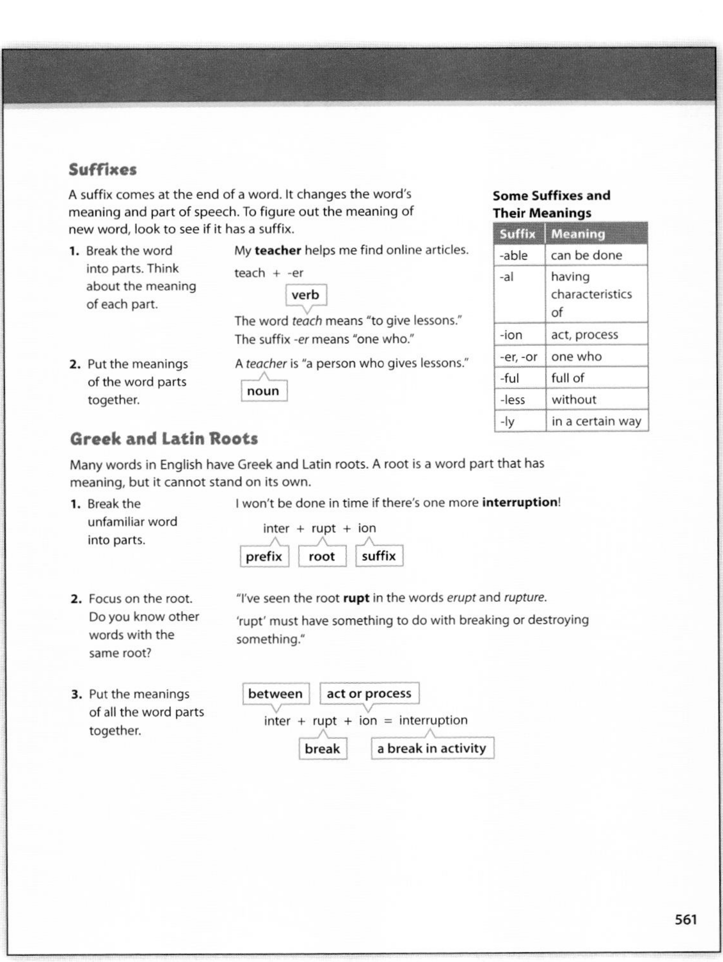

Suffixes

A suffix comes at the end of a word. It changes the word's meaning and part of speech. To figure out the meaning of a new word, look to see if it has a suffix.

1. Break the word into parts. Think about the meaning of each part. — My **teacher** helps me find online articles. teach + -er (verb). The word *teach* means "to give lessons." The suffix *-er* means "one who."
2. Put the meanings of the word parts together. — A *teacher* is "a person who gives lessons." (noun)

Some Suffixes and Their Meanings

Suffix	Meaning
-able	can be done
-al	having characteristics of
-ion	act, process
-er, -or	one who
-ful	full of
-less	without
-ly	in a certain way

Greek and Latin Roots

Many words in English have Greek and Latin roots. A root is a word part that has meaning, but it cannot stand on its own.

1. Break the unfamiliar word into parts. — I won't be done in time if there's one more **interruption**! inter + rupt + ion (prefix, root, suffix)
2. Focus on the root. Do you know other words with the same root? — "I've seen the root **rupt** in the words *erupt* and *rupture*. 'rupt' must have something to do with breaking or destroying something."
3. Put the meanings of all the word parts together. — inter (between) + rupt (break) + ion (act or process) = interruption (a break in activity)

561

Page 561

Vocabulary Strategies, *continued*

Look Beyond the Literal Meaning

Writers use colorful language to keep their readers interested. They use words and phrases that mean something different from their usual definitions. Figurative language and idioms are kinds of colorful language.

Figurative Language: Similes

A simile compares two things that are alike in some way. It uses the words *like* or *as* to make the comparison.

Simile	Things Compared	How They're Alike
Cory hiked across the desert **as sluggishly as a snail.**	Cory and a snail	They both move very slowly.
His skin was **like sheets of sandpaper.**	skin and sandpaper	They are both rough and very dry.

Figurative Language: Metaphors

A metaphor compares two things without using the words *like* or *as*.

Metaphor	Things Compared	Meaning
The **sun's rays were a thousand bee stings** on his face.	sun's rays and bee stings	The sun's rays blistered his face.
His only **companion was thirst.**	friend and thirst	His thirst was always there with him.

Figurative Language: Personification

When writers use personification they give human qualities to nonhuman things.

Personification	Object	Human Quality
The **angry sun** kept punishing him.	sun	has feelings
A **cactus reached out to** him.	cactus	is able to be friendly

562

Page 562

Idioms

An idiom is a special kind of phrase that means something different from what the words mean by themselves.

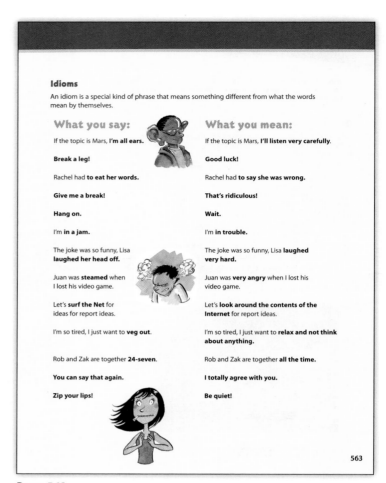

What you say:	What you mean:
If the topic is Mars, **I'm all ears.**	If the topic is Mars, **I'll listen very carefully.**
Break a leg!	**Good luck!**
Rachel had **to eat her words.**	Rachel had **to say she was wrong.**
Give me a break!	**That's ridiculous!**
Hang on.	**Wait.**
I'm **in a jam.**	I'm **in trouble.**
The joke was so funny, Lisa **laughed her head off.**	The joke was so funny, Lisa **laughed very hard.**
Juan was **steamed** when I lost his video game.	Juan was **very angry** when I lost his video game.
Let's **surf the Net** for ideas for report ideas.	Let's **look around the contents of the Internet** for report ideas.
I'm so tired, I just want to **veg out.**	I'm so tired, I just want to **relax and not think about anything.**
Rob and Zak are together **24-seven.**	Rob and Zak are together **all the time.**
You can say that again.	**I totally agree with you.**
Zip your lips!	**Be quiet!**

563

Page 563

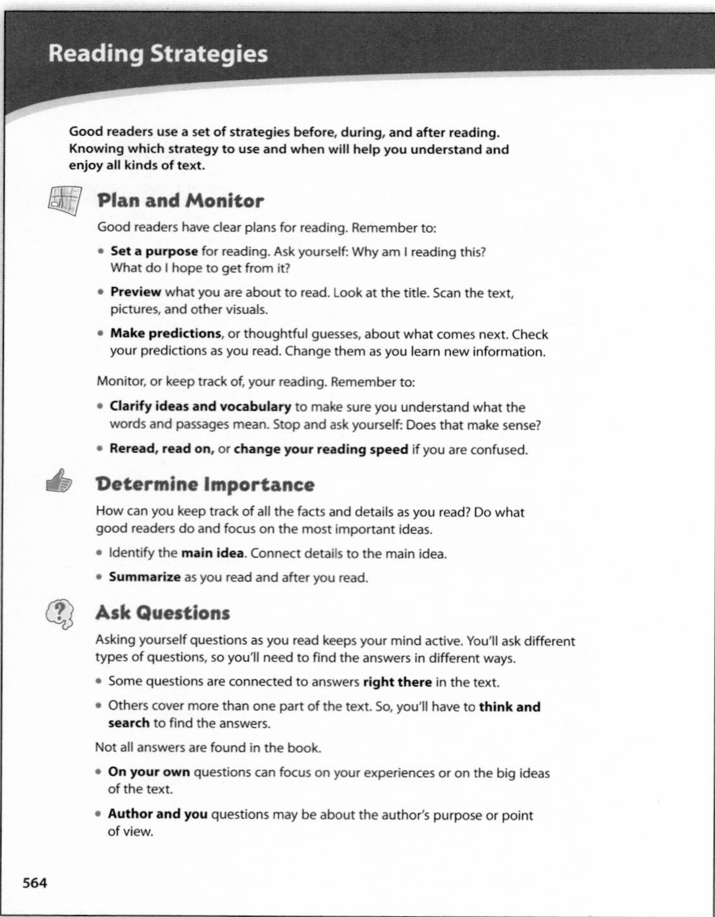

Reading Strategies

Good readers use a set of strategies before, during, and after reading. Knowing which strategy to use and when will help you understand and enjoy all kinds of text.

Plan and Monitor

Good readers have clear plans for reading. Remember to:

- **Set a purpose** for reading. Ask yourself: Why am I reading this? What do I hope to get from it?
- **Preview** what you are about to read. Look at the title. Scan the text, pictures, and other visuals.
- **Make predictions**, or thoughtful guesses, about what comes next. Check your predictions as you read. Change them as you learn new information.

Monitor, or keep track of, your reading. Remember to:

- **Clarify ideas and vocabulary** to make sure you understand what the words and passages mean. Stop and ask yourself: Does that make sense?
- **Reread, read on,** or **change your reading speed** if you are confused.

Determine Importance

How can you keep track of all the facts and details as you read? Do what good readers do and focus on the most important ideas.

- Identify the **main idea**. Connect details to the main idea.
- **Summarize** as you read and after you read.

Ask Questions

Asking yourself questions as you read keeps your mind active. You'll ask different types of questions, so you'll need to find the answers in different ways.

- Some questions are connected to answers **right there** in the text.
- Others cover more than one part of the text. So, you'll have to **think and search** to find the answers.

Not all answers are found in the book.

- **On your own** questions can focus on your experiences or on the big ideas of the text.
- **Author and you** questions may be about the author's purpose or point of view.

564

Page 564

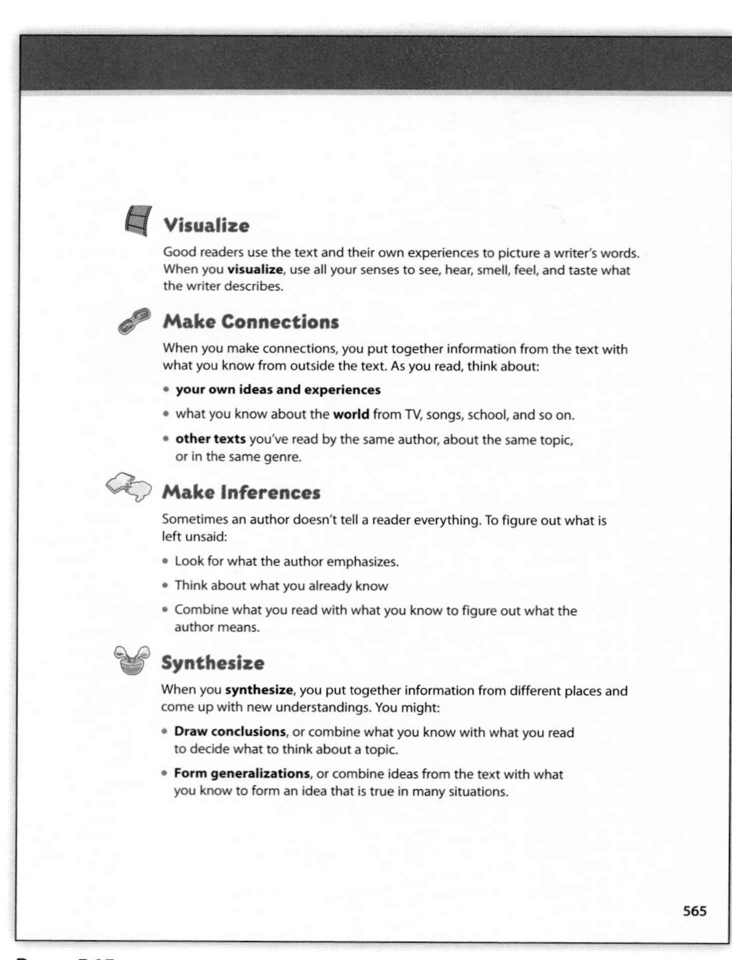

Visualize

Good readers use the text and their own experiences to picture a writer's words. When you **visualize**, use all your senses to see, hear, smell, feel, and taste what the writer describes.

Make Connections

When you make connections, you put together information from the text with what you know from outside the text. As you read, think about:

- **your own ideas and experiences**
- what you know about the **world** from TV, songs, school, and so on.
- **other texts** you've read by the same author, about the same topic, or in the same genre.

Make Inferences

Sometimes an author doesn't tell a reader everything. To figure out what is left unsaid:

- Look for what the author emphasizes.
- Think about what you already know
- Combine what you read with what you know to figure out what the author means.

Synthesize

When you **synthesize**, you put together information from different places and come up with new understandings. You might:

- **Draw conclusions**, or combine what you know with what you read to decide what to think about a topic.
- **Form generalizations**, or combine ideas from the text with what you know to form an idea that is true in many situations.

565

Page 565

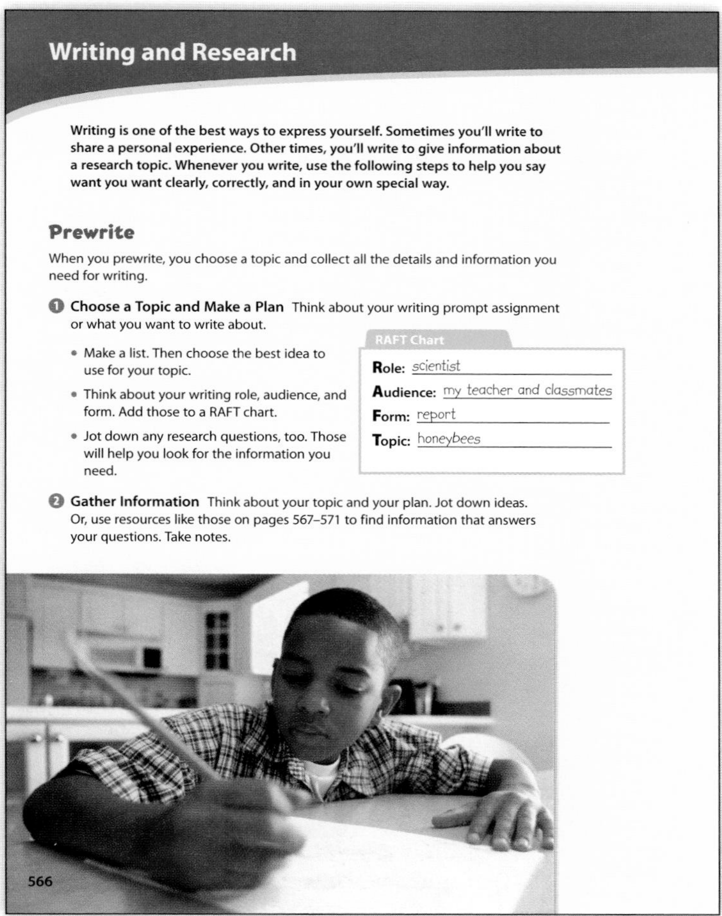

Writing and Research

Writing is one of the best ways to express yourself. Sometimes you'll write to share a personal experience. Other times, you'll write to give information about a research topic. Whenever you write, use the following steps to help you say want you want clearly, correctly, and in your own special way.

Prewrite

When you prewrite, you choose a topic and collect all the details and information you need for writing.

1. **Choose a Topic and Make a Plan** Think about your writing prompt assignment or what you want to write about.
   - Make a list. Then choose the best idea to use for your topic.
   - Think about your writing role, audience, and form. Add those to a RAFT chart.
   - Jot down any research questions, too. Those will help you look for the information you need.

RAFT Chart

Role: scientist
Audience: my teacher and classmates
Form: report
Topic: honeybees

2. **Gather Information** Think about your topic and your plan. Jot down ideas. Or, use resources like those on pages 567–571 to find information that answers your questions. Take notes.

566

Page 566

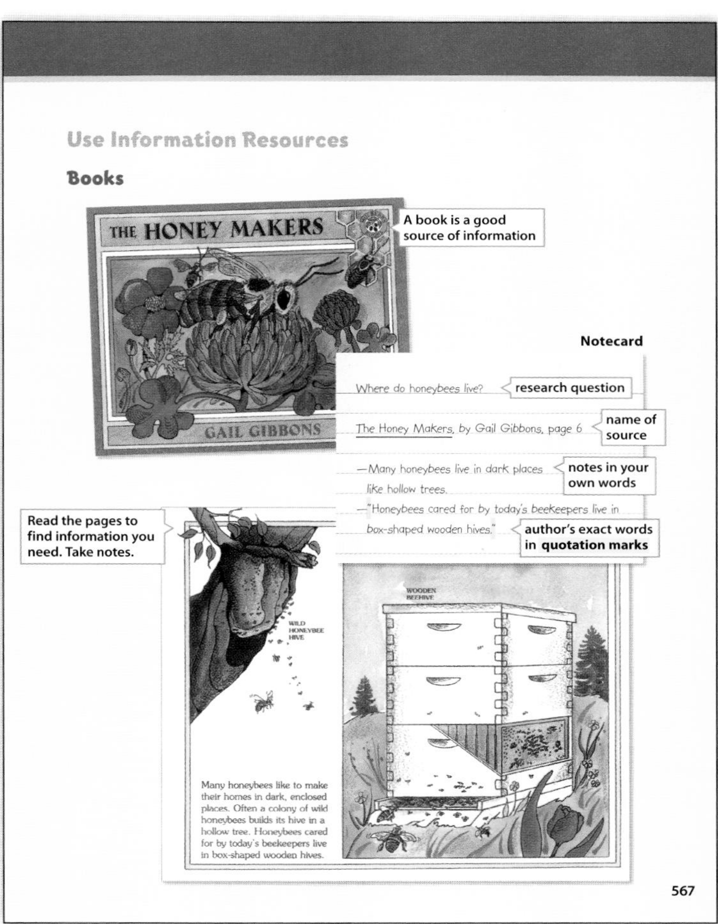

Use Information Resources

Books

THE HONEY MAKERS
GAIL GIBBONS
A book is a good source of information
Notecard
Where do honeybees live?
research question
The Honey Makers, by Gail Gibbons, page 6
name of source
—Many honeybees live in dark places like hollow trees.
notes in your own words
—"Honeybees cared for by today's beekeepers live in box-shaped wooden hives."
author's exact words in quotation marks
Read the pages to find information you need. Take notes.
WILD HONEYBEE HIVE
WOODEN BEEHIVE
Many honeybees like to make their homes in dark, enclosed places. Often a colony of wild honeybees builds its hive in a hollow tree. Honeybees cared for by today's beekeepers live in box-shaped wooden hives.

567

Page 567

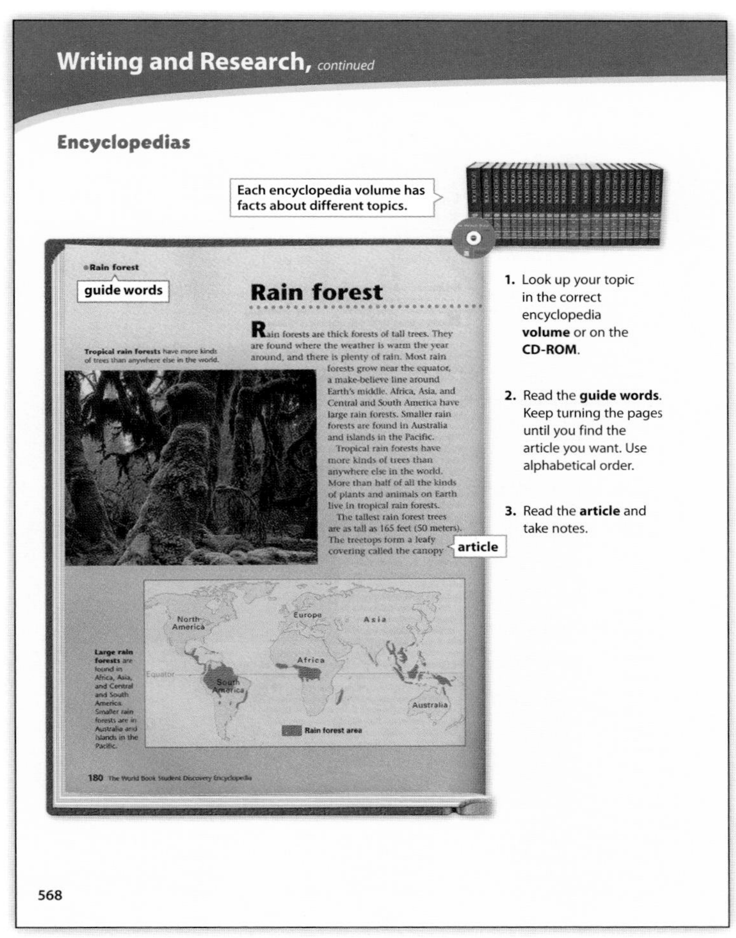

Writing and Research, *continued*

Encyclopedias

Each encyclopedia volume has facts about different topics.
Rain forest
guide words
Rain forest
Rain forests are thick forests of tall trees. They are found where the weather is warm the year around, and there is plenty of rain. Most rain forests grow near the equator, a make-believe line around Earth's middle. Africa, Asia, and Central and South America have large rain forests. Smaller rain forests are found in Australia and islands in the Pacific.
Tropical rain forests have more kinds of trees than anywhere else in the world. More than half of all the kinds of plants and animals on Earth live in tropical rain forests.
The tallest rain forest trees are as tall as 165 feet (50 meters). The treetops form a leafy covering called the canopy
article
Tropical rain forests have more kinds of trees than anywhere else in the world.
North America
Europe
Asia
Africa
Equator
South America
Australia
Rain forest area
Large rain forests are found in Africa, Asia, and Central and South America. Smaller rain forests are in Australia and islands in the Pacific.
180 The World Book Student Discovery Encyclopedia

1. Look up your topic in the correct encyclopedia **volume** or on the **CD-ROM**.
2. Read the **guide words**. Keep turning the pages until you find the article you want. Use alphabetical order.
3. Read the **article** and take notes.

568

Page 568

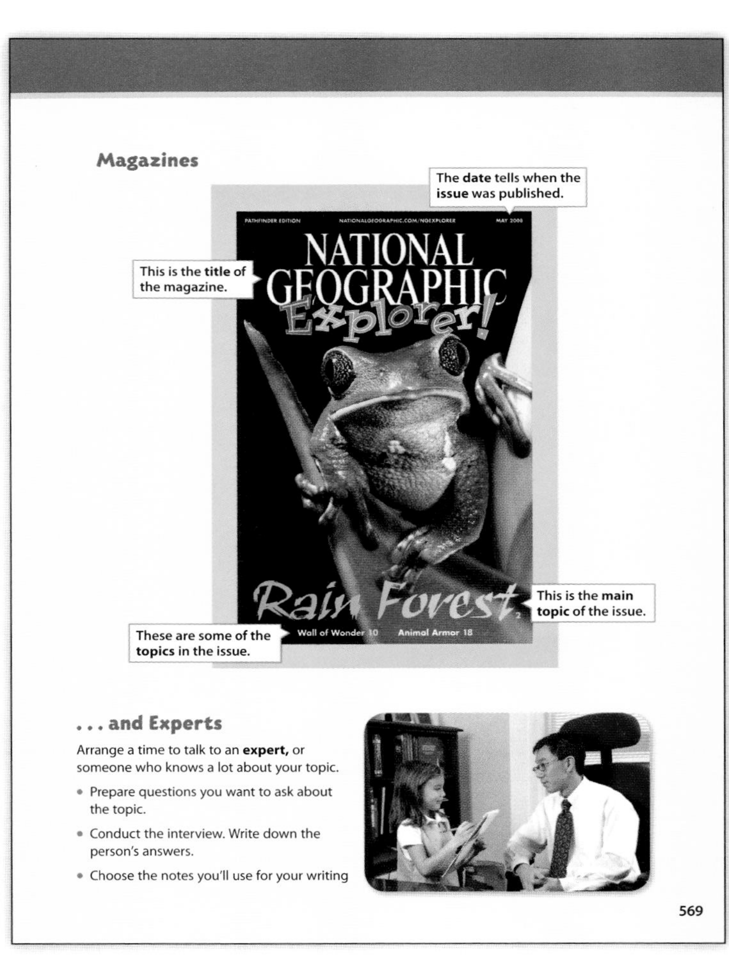

Magazines

The **date** tells when the issue was published.
This is the **title** of the magazine.
NATIONAL GEOGRAPHIC Explorer!
Rain Forest
This is the main **topic** of the issue.
These are some of the **topics** in the issue.
Wall of Wonder 10
Animal Armor 18

. . . and Experts

Arrange a time to talk to an **expert,** or someone who knows a lot about your topic.

- Prepare questions you want to ask about the topic.
- Conduct the interview. Write down the person's answers.
- Choose the notes you'll use for your writing

569

Page 569

Anthology Handbook, continued

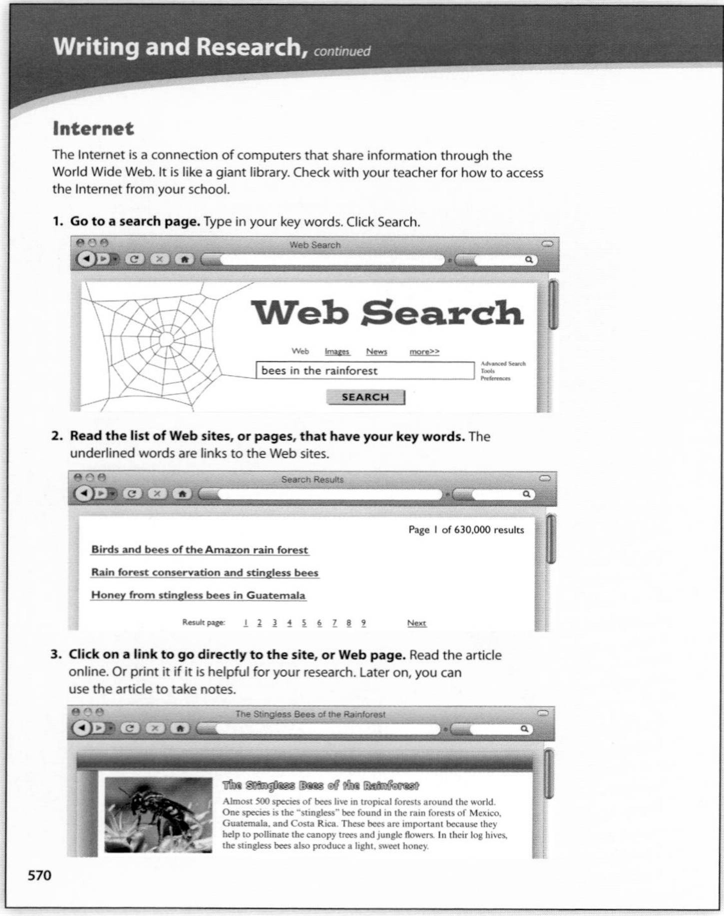

Writing and Research, *continued*

Internet

The Internet is a connection of computers that share information through the World Wide Web. It is like a giant library. Check with your teacher for how to access the Internet from your school.

1. **Go to a search page.** Type in your key words. Click Search.

2. **Read the list of Web sites, or pages, that have your key words.** The underlined words are links to the Web sites.

3. **Click on a link to go directly to the site, or Web page.** Read the article online. Or print it if it is helpful for your research. Later on, you can use the article to take notes.

570

Page 570

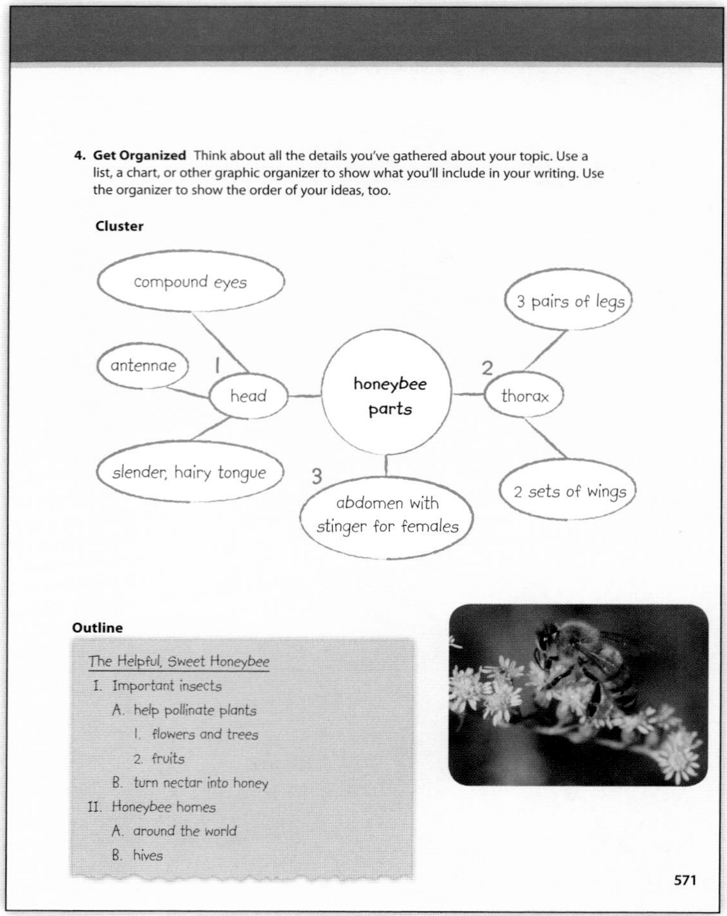

4. **Get Organized** Think about all the details you've gathered about your topic. Use a list, a chart, or other graphic organizer to show what you'll include in your writing. Use the organizer to show the order of your ideas, too.

Cluster

Outline

The Helpful, Sweet Honeybee
I. Important insects
A. help pollinate plants
1. flowers and trees
2. fruits
B. turn nectar into honey
II. Honeybee homes
A. around the world
B. hives

571

Page 571

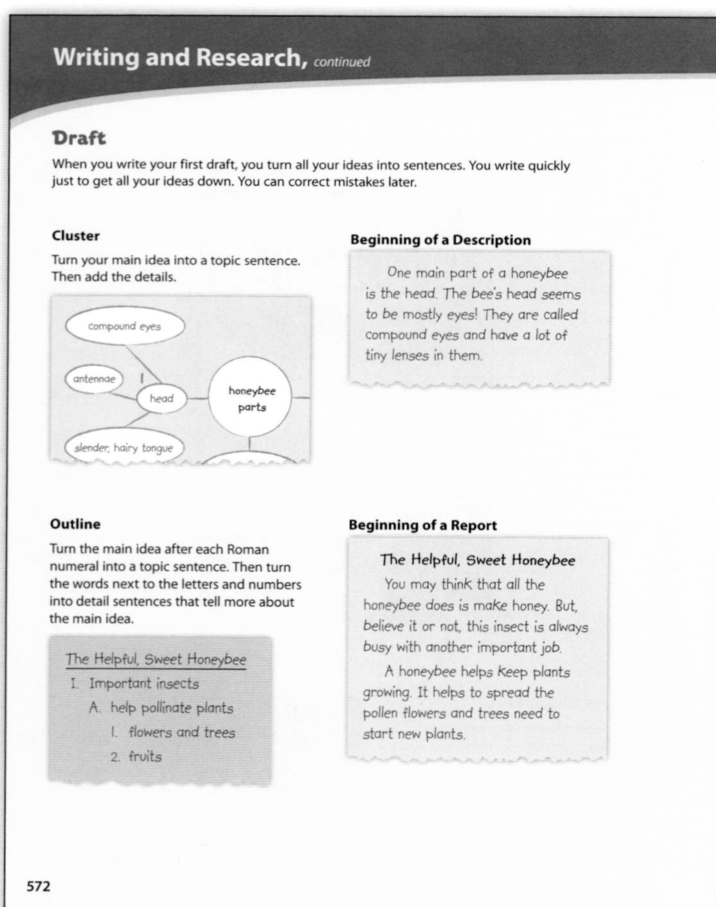

Writing and Research, *continued*

Draft

When you write your first draft, you turn all your ideas into sentences. You write quickly just to get all your ideas down. You can correct mistakes later.

Cluster

Turn your main idea into a topic sentence. Then add the details.

Beginning of a Description

One main part of a honeybee is the head. The bee's head seems to be mostly eyes! They are called compound eyes and have a lot of tiny lenses in them.

Outline

Turn the main idea after each Roman numeral into a topic sentence. Then turn the words next to the letters and numbers into detail sentences that tell more about the main idea.

The Helpful, Sweet Honeybee
I. Important insects
A. help pollinate plants
1. flowers and trees
2. fruits

Beginning of a Report

The Helpful, Sweet Honeybee

You may think that all the honeybee does is make honey. But, believe it or not, this insect is always busy with another important job.

A honeybee helps keep plants growing. It helps to spread the pollen flowers and trees need to start new plants.

572

Page 572

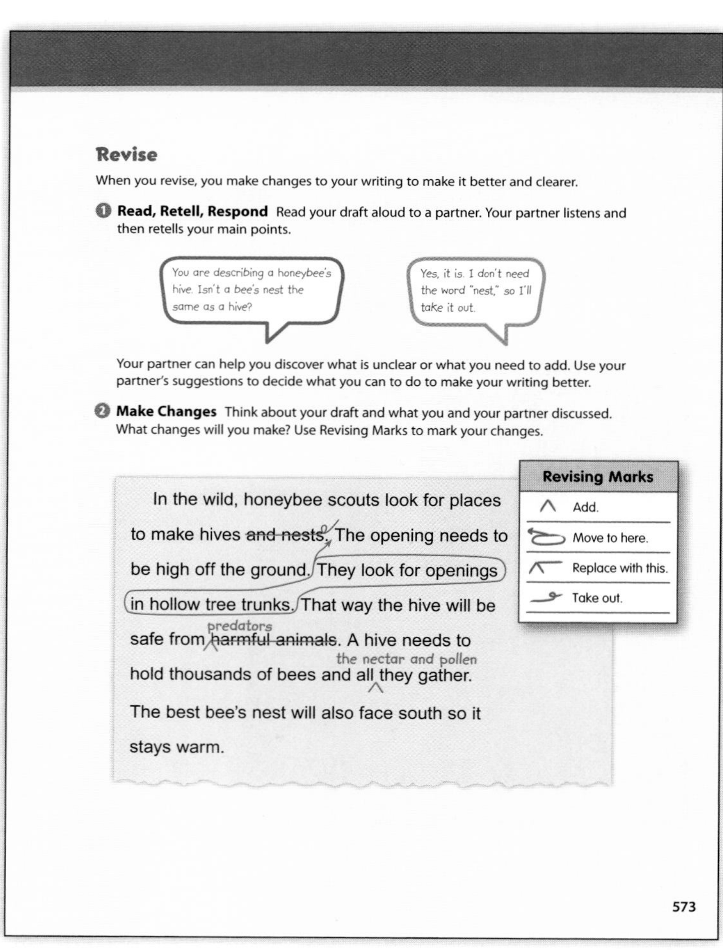

Revise

When you revise, you make changes to your writing to make it better and clearer.

1. **Read, Retell, Respond** Read your draft aloud to a partner. Your partner listens and then retells your main points.

Your partner can help you discover what is unclear or what you need to add. Use your partner's suggestions to decide what you can to do to make your writing better.

2. **Make Changes** Think about your draft and what you and your partner discussed. What changes will you make? Use Revising Marks to mark your changes.

In the wild, honeybee scouts look for places to make hives and nests. The opening needs to be high off the ground. They look for openings in hollow tree trunks. That way the hive will be safe from harmful animals. predators A hive needs to hold thousands of bees and all the nectar and pollen they gather.
The best bee's nest will also face south so it stays warm.
Revising Marks
Add.
Move to here.
Replace with this.
Take out.

573

Page 573

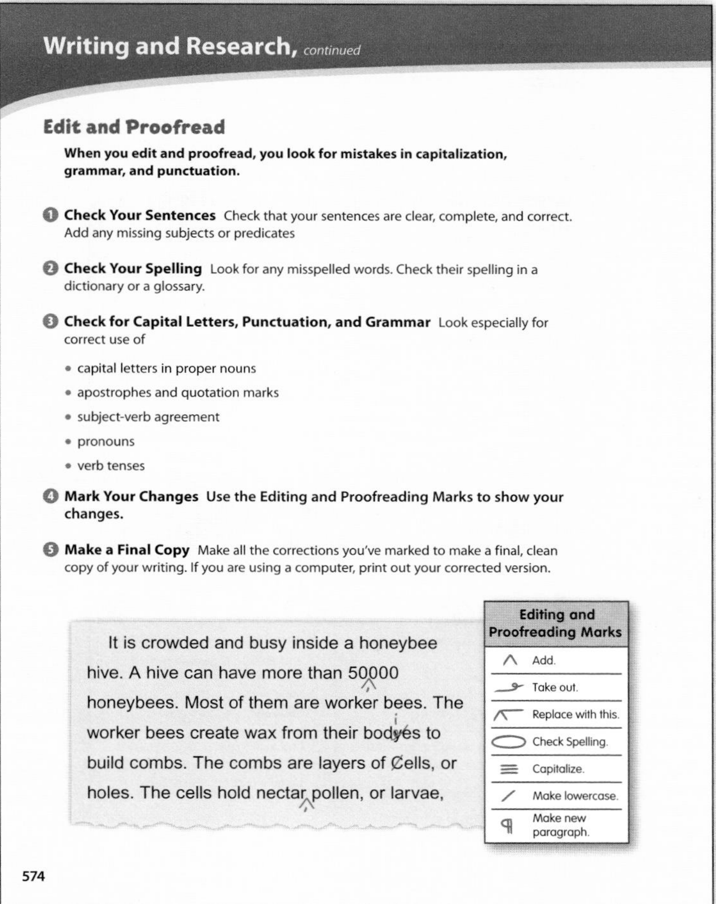

Writing and Research, *continued*

Edit and Proofread

When you edit and proofread, you look for mistakes in capitalization, grammar, and punctuation.

1. **Check Your Sentences** Check that your sentences are clear, complete, and correct. Add any missing subjects or predicates
2. **Check Your Spelling** Look for any misspelled words. Check their spelling in a dictionary or a glossary.
3. **Check for Capital Letters, Punctuation, and Grammar** Look especially for correct use of
   - capital letters in proper nouns
   - apostrophes and quotation marks
   - subject-verb agreement
   - pronouns
   - verb tenses
4. **Mark Your Changes** Use the Editing and Proofreading Marks to show your changes.
5. **Make a Final Copy** Make all the corrections you've marked to make a final, clean copy of your writing. If you are using a computer, print out your corrected version.

It is crowded and busy inside a honeybee hive. A hive can have more than 50000 honeybees. Most of them are worker bees. The worker bees create wax from their bodyes to build combs. The combs are layers of Cells, or holes. The cells hold nectar pollen, or larvae,

Editing and Proofreading Marks	
∧	Add.
⟶	Take out.
⌃	Replace with this.
◯	Check Spelling.
≡	Capitalize.
/	Make lowercase.
¶	Make new paragraph.

574

Page 574

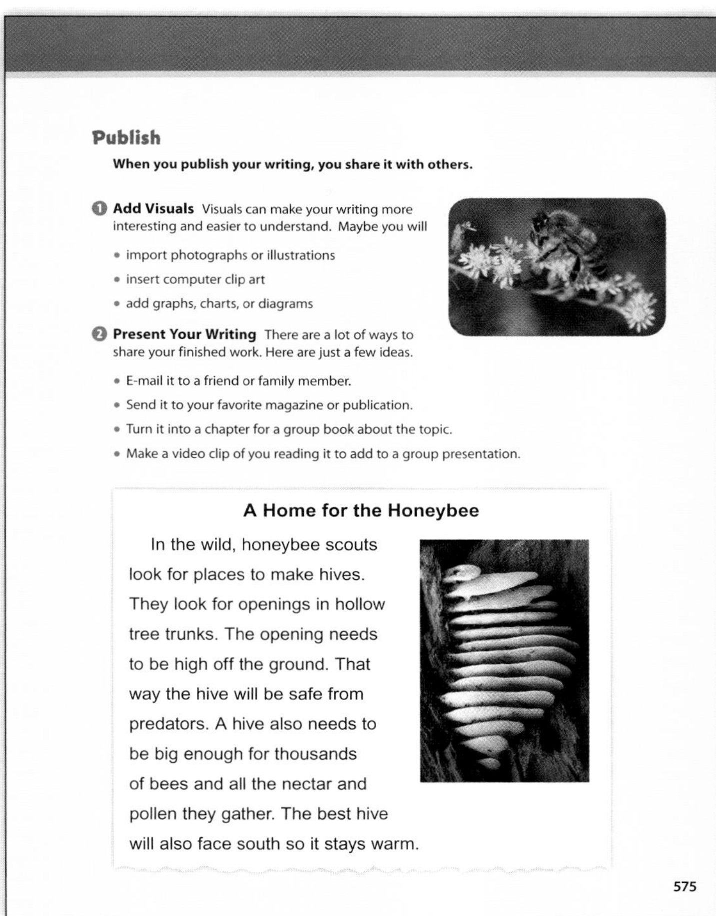

Publish

When you publish your writing, you share it with others.

1. **Add Visuals** Visuals can make your writing more interesting and easier to understand. Maybe you will
   - import photographs or illustrations
   - insert computer clip art
   - add graphs, charts, or diagrams
2. **Present Your Writing** There are a lot of ways to share your finished work. Here are just a few ideas.
   - E-mail it to a friend or family member.
   - Send it to your favorite magazine or publication.
   - Turn it into a chapter for a group book about the topic.
   - Make a video clip of you reading it to add to a group presentation.

A Home for the Honeybee

In the wild, honeybee scouts look for places to make hives. They look for openings in hollow tree trunks. The opening needs to be high off the ground. That way the hive will be safe from predators. A hive also needs to be big enough for thousands of bees and all the nectar and pollen they gather. The best hive will also face south so it stays warm.

575

Page 575

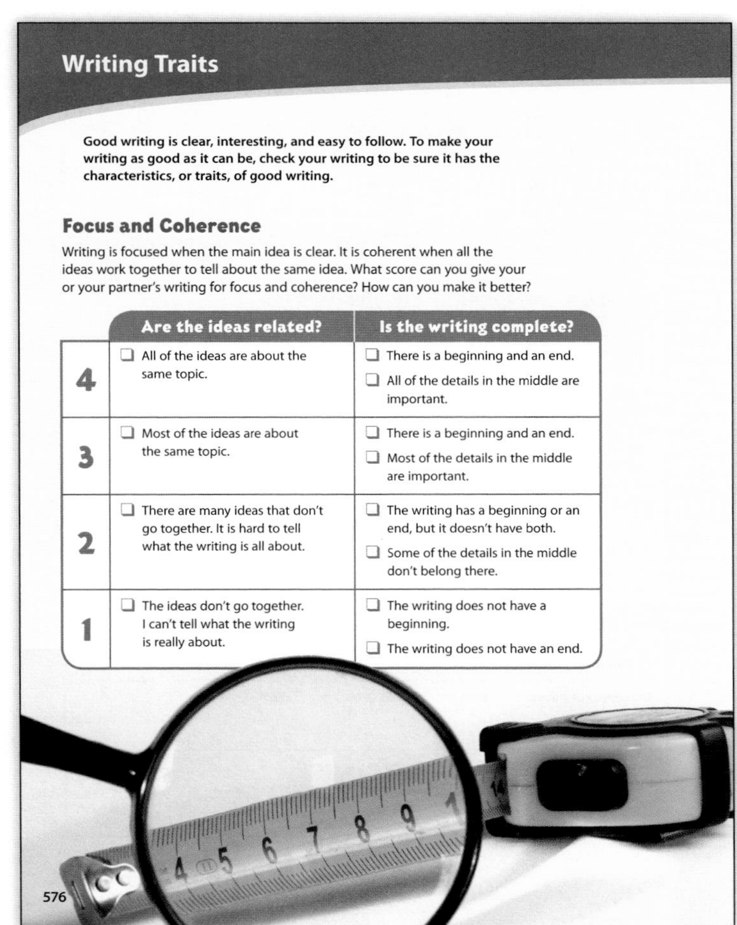

Writing Traits

Good writing is clear, interesting, and easy to follow. To make your writing as good as it can be, check your writing to be sure it has the characteristics, or traits, of good writing.

Focus and Coherence

Writing is focused when the main idea is clear. It is coherent when all the ideas work together to tell about the same idea. What score can you give your or your partner's writing for focus and coherence? How can you make it better?

	Are the ideas related?	Is the writing complete?
4	❑ All of the ideas are about the same topic.	❑ There is a beginning and an end. ❑ All of the details in the middle are important.
3	❑ Most of the ideas are about the same topic.	❑ There is a beginning and an end. ❑ Most of the details in the middle are important.
2	❑ There are many ideas that don't go together. It is hard to tell what the writing is all about.	❑ The writing has a beginning or an end, but it doesn't have both. ❑ Some of the details in the middle don't belong there.
1	❑ The ideas don't go together. I can't tell what the writing is really about.	❑ The writing does not have a beginning. ❑ The writing does not have an end.

576

Page 576

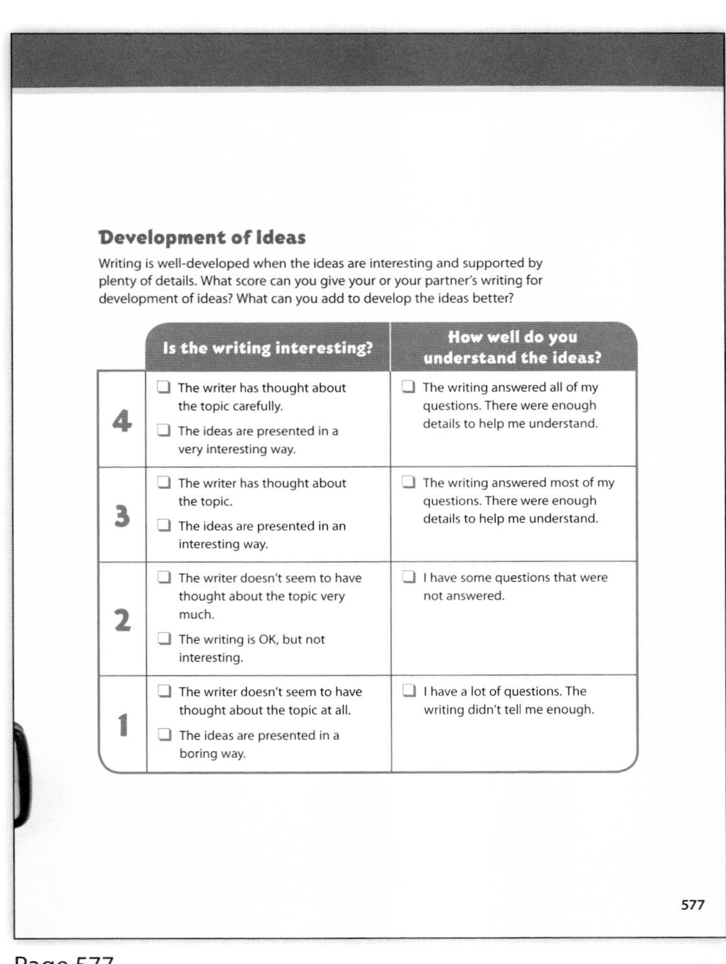

Development of Ideas

Writing is well-developed when the ideas are interesting and supported by plenty of details. What score can you give your or your partner's writing for development of ideas? What can you add to develop the ideas better?

	Is the writing interesting?	How well do you understand the ideas?
4	❑ The writer has thought about the topic carefully. ❑ The ideas are presented in a very interesting way.	❑ The writing answered all of my questions. There were enough details to help me understand.
3	❑ The writer has thought about the topic. ❑ The ideas are presented in an interesting way.	❑ The writing answered most of my questions. There were enough details to help me understand.
2	❑ The writer doesn't seem to have thought about the topic very much. ❑ The writing is OK, but not interesting.	❑ I have some questions that were not answered.
1	❑ The writer doesn't seem to have thought about the topic at all. ❑ The ideas are presented in a boring way.	❑ I have a lot of questions. The writing didn't tell me enough.

577

Page 577

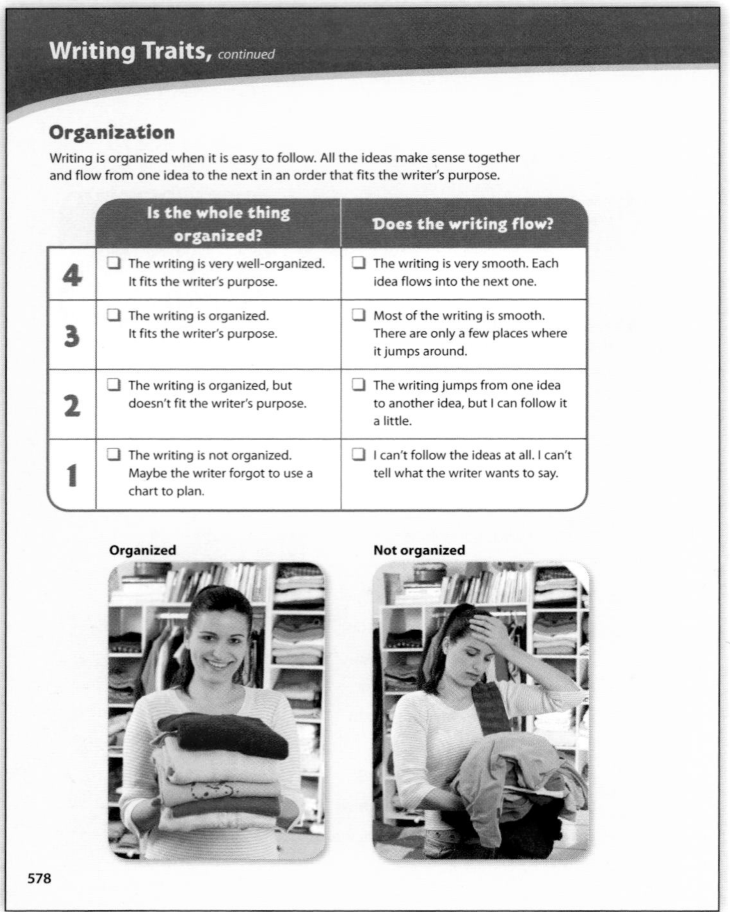

Writing Traits, *continued*

Organization

Writing is organized when it is easy to follow. All the ideas make sense together and flow from one idea to the next in an order that fits the writer's purpose.

	Is the whole thing organized?	Does the writing flow?
4	❑ The writing is very well-organized. It fits the writer's purpose.	❑ The writing is very smooth. Each idea flows into the next one.
3	❑ The writing is organized. It fits the writer's purpose.	❑ Most of the writing is smooth. There are only a few places where it jumps around.
2	❑ The writing is organized, but doesn't fit the writer's purpose.	❑ The writing jumps from one idea to another idea, but I can follow it a little.
1	❑ The writing is not organized. Maybe the writer forgot to use a chart to plan.	❑ I can't follow the ideas at all. I can't tell what the writer wants to say.

Organized

Not organized

578

Page 578

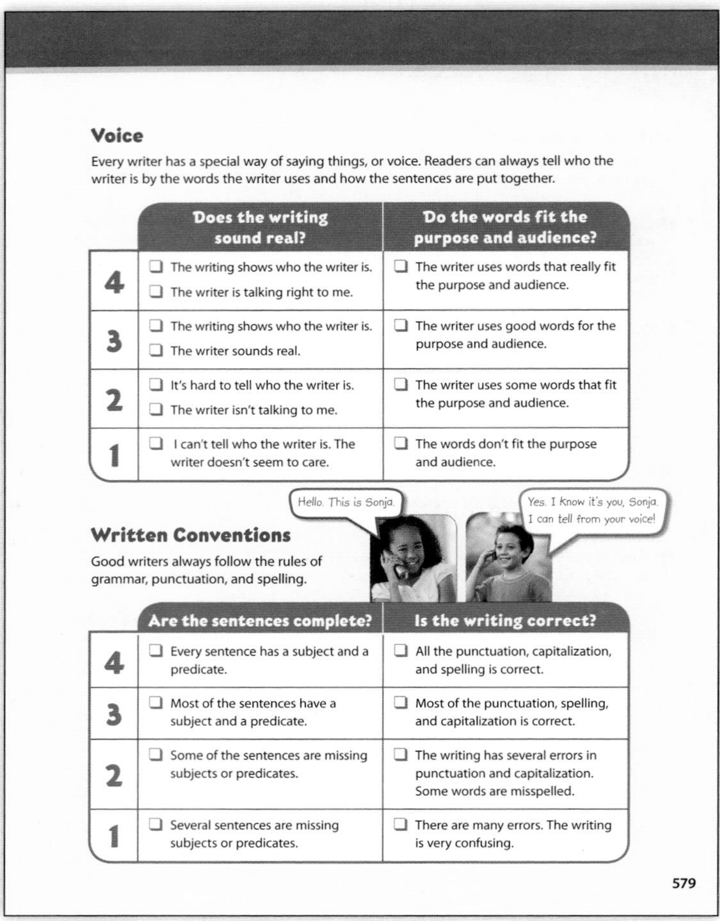

Voice

Every writer has a special way of saying things, or voice. Readers can always tell who the writer is by the words the writer uses and how the sentences are put together.

	Does the writing sound real?	Do the words fit the purpose and audience?
4	❑ The writing shows who the writer is. ❑ The writer is talking right to me.	❑ The writer uses words that really fit the purpose and audience.
3	❑ The writing shows who the writer is. ❑ The writer sounds real.	❑ The writer uses good words for the purpose and audience.
2	❑ It's hard to tell who the writer is. ❑ The writer isn't talking to me.	❑ The writer uses some words that fit the purpose and audience.
1	❑ I can't tell who the writer is. The writer doesn't seem to care.	❑ The words don't fit the purpose and audience.

Hello. This is Sonja.
Yes. I know it's you, Sonja. I can tell from your voice!

Written Conventions

Good writers always follow the rules of grammar, punctuation, and spelling.

	Are the sentences complete?	Is the writing correct?
4	❑ Every sentence has a subject and a predicate.	❑ All the punctuation, capitalization, and spelling is correct.
3	❑ Most of the sentences have a subject and a predicate.	❑ Most of the punctuation, spelling, and capitalization is correct.
2	❑ Some of the sentences are missing subjects or predicates.	❑ The writing has several errors in punctuation and capitalization. Some words are misspelled.
1	❑ Several sentences are missing subjects or predicates.	❑ There are many errors. The writing is very confusing.

579

Page 579

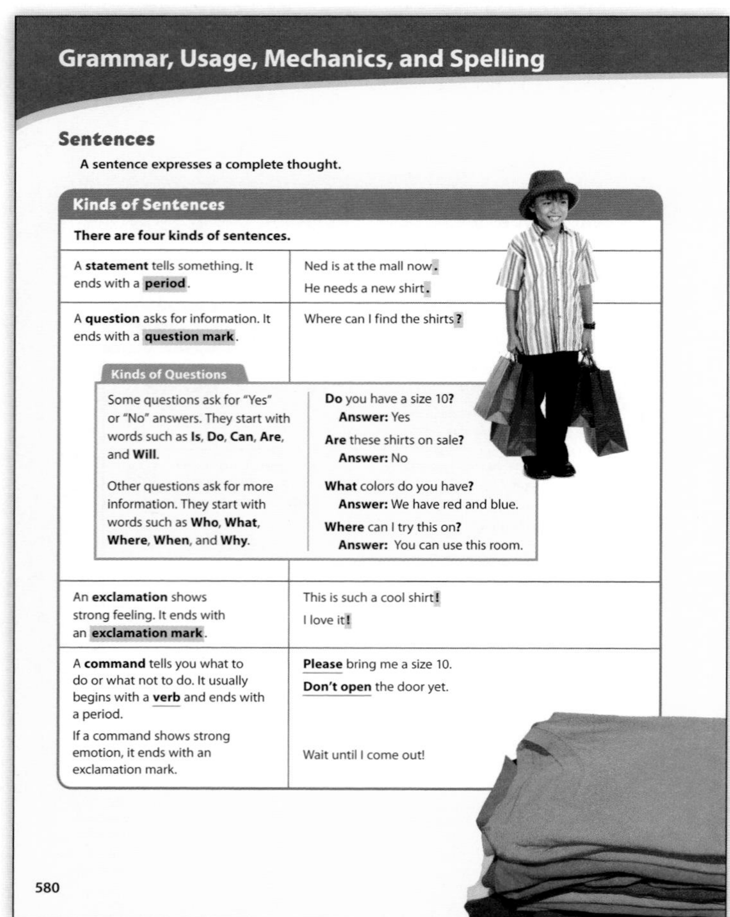

Grammar, Usage, Mechanics, and Spelling

Sentences

A sentence expresses a complete thought.

Kinds of Sentences

There are four kinds of sentences.	
A **statement** tells something. It ends with a **period**.	Ned is at the mall now. He needs a new shirt.
A **question** asks for information. It ends with a **question mark**.	Where can I find the shirts?

Kinds of Questions

Some questions ask for "Yes" or "No" answers. They start with words such as **Is**, **Do**, **Can**, **Are**, and **Will**.	**Do** you have a size 10? **Answer:** Yes **Are** these shirts on sale? **Answer:** No
Other questions ask for more information. They start with words such as **Who**, **What**, **Where**, **When**, and **Why**.	**What** colors do you have? **Answer:** We have red and blue. **Where** can I try this on? **Answer:** You can use this room.

An **exclamation** shows strong feeling. It ends with an **exclamation mark**.	This is such a cool shirt! I love it!
A **command** tells you what to do or what not to do. It usually begins with a **verb** and ends with a period. If a command shows strong emotion, it ends with an exclamation mark.	**Please** bring me a size 10. **Don't open** the door yet. Wait until I come out!

580

Page 580

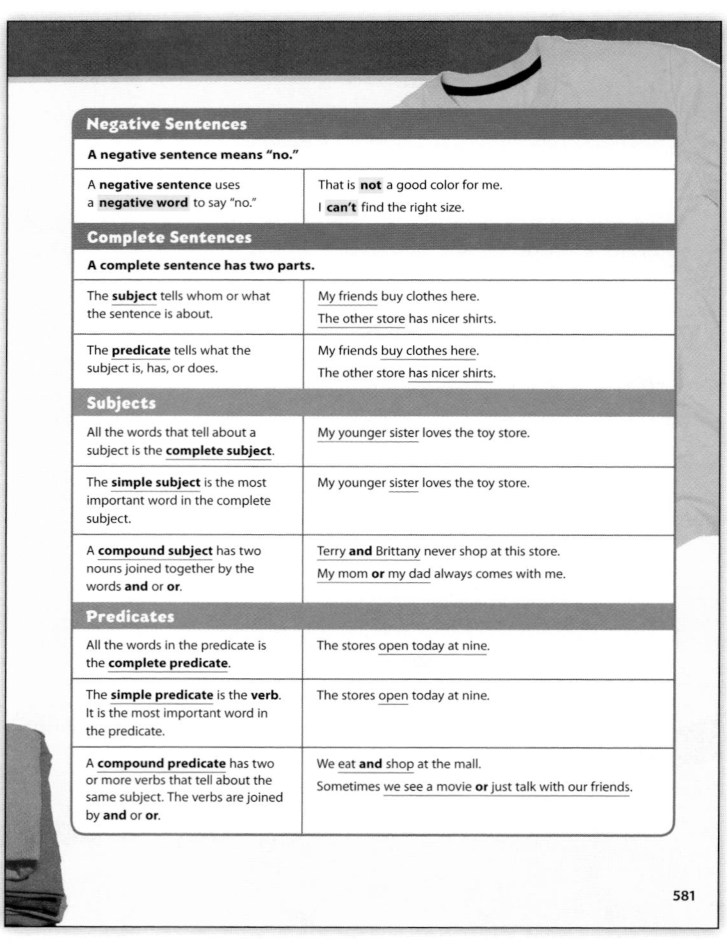

Negative Sentences	
A negative sentence means "no."	
A **negative sentence** uses a **negative word** to say "no."	That is **not** a good color for me. I **can't** find the right size.

Complete Sentences	
A complete sentence has two parts.	
The **subject** tells whom or what the sentence is about.	My friends buy clothes here. The other store has nicer shirts.
The **predicate** tells what the subject is, has, or does.	My friends buy clothes here. The other store has nicer shirts.

Subjects	
All the words that tell about a subject is the **complete subject**.	My younger sister loves the toy store.
The **simple subject** is the most important word in the complete subject.	My younger sister loves the toy store.
A **compound subject** has two nouns joined together by the words **and** or **or**.	Terry **and** Brittany never shop at this store. My mom **or** my dad always comes with me.

Predicates	
All the words in the predicate is the **complete predicate**.	The stores open today at nine.
The **simple predicate** is the **verb**. It is the most important word in the predicate.	The stores open today at nine.
A **compound predicate** has two or more verbs that tell about the same subject. The verbs are joined by **and** or **or**.	We eat **and** shop at the mall. Sometimes we see a movie **or** just talk with our friends.

581

Page 581

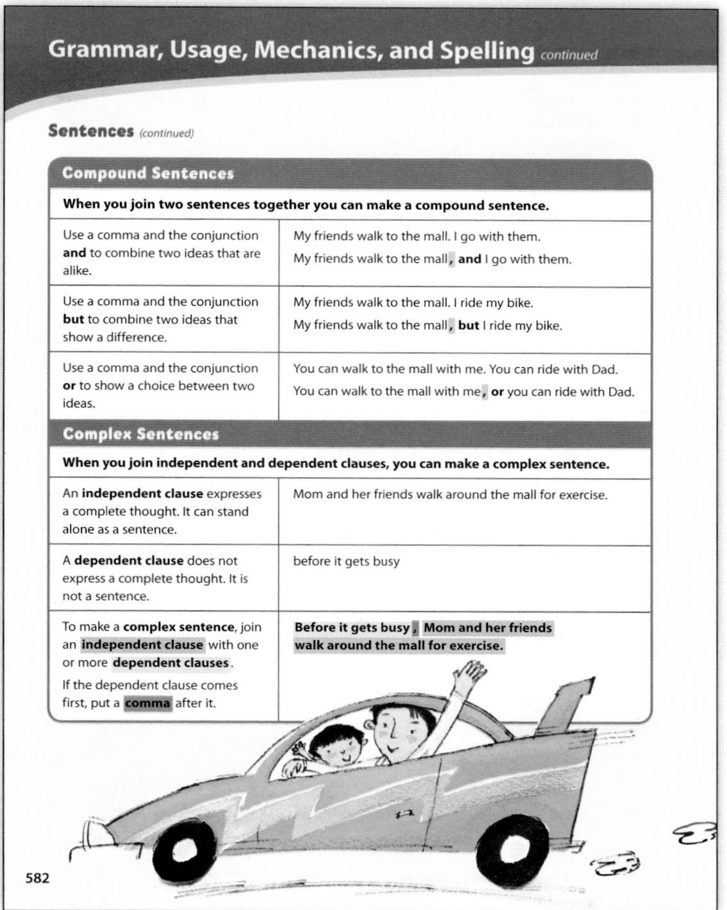

Grammar, Usage, Mechanics, and Spelling *continued*

Sentences *(continued)*

Compound Sentences

When you join two sentences together you can make a compound sentence.	
Use a comma and the conjunction **and** to combine two ideas that are alike.	My friends walk to the mall. I go with them. My friends walk to the mall**,** **and** I go with them.
Use a comma and the conjunction **but** to combine two ideas that show a difference.	My friends walk to the mall. I ride my bike. My friends walk to the mall**,** **but** I ride my bike.
Use a comma and the conjunction **or** to show a choice between two ideas.	You can walk to the mall with me. You can ride with Dad. You can walk to the mall with me**,** **or** you can ride with Dad.

Complex Sentences

When you join independent and dependent clauses, you can make a complex sentence.	
An **independent clause** expresses a complete thought. It can stand alone as a sentence.	Mom and her friends walk around the mall for exercise.
A **dependent clause** does not express a complete thought. It is not a sentence.	before it gets busy
To make a **complex sentence**, join an **independent clause** with one or more **dependent clauses**. If the dependent clause comes first, put a **comma** after it.	**Before it gets busy, Mom and her friends walk around the mall for exercise.**

582

Page 582

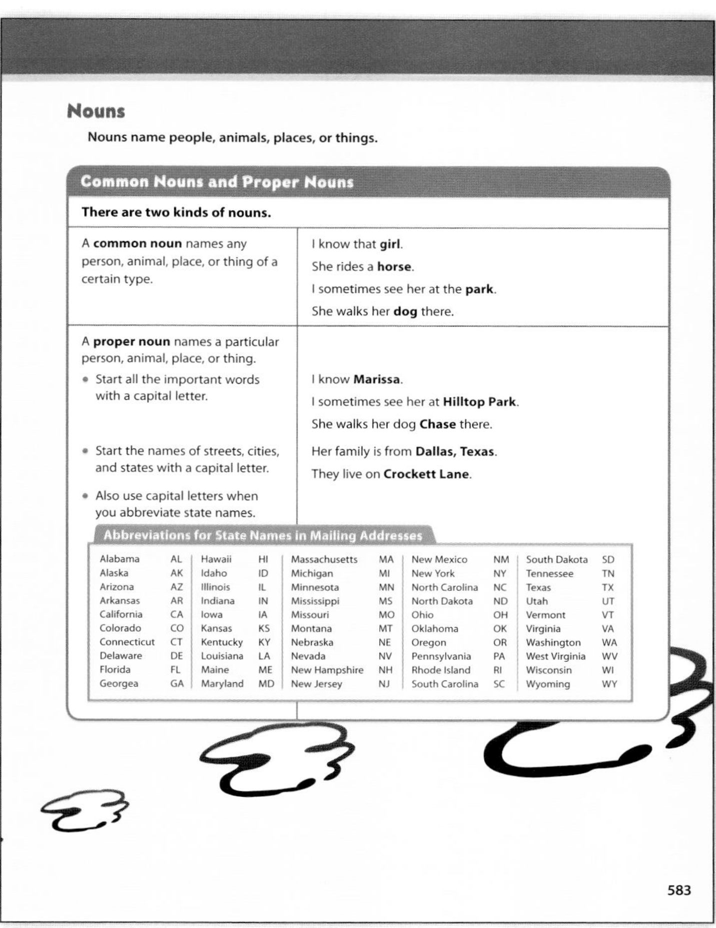

Nouns

Nouns name people, animals, places, or things.

Common Nouns and Proper Nouns

There are two kinds of nouns.	
A **common noun** names any person, animal, place, or thing of a certain type.	I know that **girl**. She rides a **horse**. I sometimes see her at the **park**. She walks her **dog** there.
A **proper noun** names a particular person, animal, place, or thing. • Start all the important words with a capital letter.	I know **Marissa**. I sometimes see her at **Hilltop Park**. She walks her dog **Chase** there.
• Start the names of streets, cities, and states with a capital letter.	Her family is from **Dallas, Texas**. They live on **Crockett Lane**.
• Also use capital letters when you abbreviate state names.	

Abbreviations for State Names in Mailing Addresses

Alabama	AL	Hawaii	HI	Massachusetts	MA	New Mexico	NM	South Dakota	SD
Alaska	AK	Idaho	ID	Michigan	MI	New York	NY	Tennessee	TN
Arizona	AZ	Illinois	IL	Minnesota	MN	North Carolina	NC	Texas	TX
Arkansas	AR	Indiana	IN	Mississippi	MS	North Dakota	ND	Utah	UT
California	CA	Iowa	IA	Missouri	MO	Ohio	OH	Vermont	VT
Colorado	CO	Kansas	KS	Montana	MT	Oklahoma	OK	Virginia	VA
Connecticut	CT	Kentucky	KY	Nebraska	NE	Oregon	OR	Washington	WA
Delaware	DE	Louisiana	LA	Nevada	NV	Pennsylvania	PA	West Virginia	WV
Florida	FL	Maine	ME	New Hampshire	NH	Rhode Island	RI	Wisconsin	WI
Georgea	GA	Maryland	MD	New Jersey	NJ	South Carolina	SC	Wyoming	WY

583

Page 583

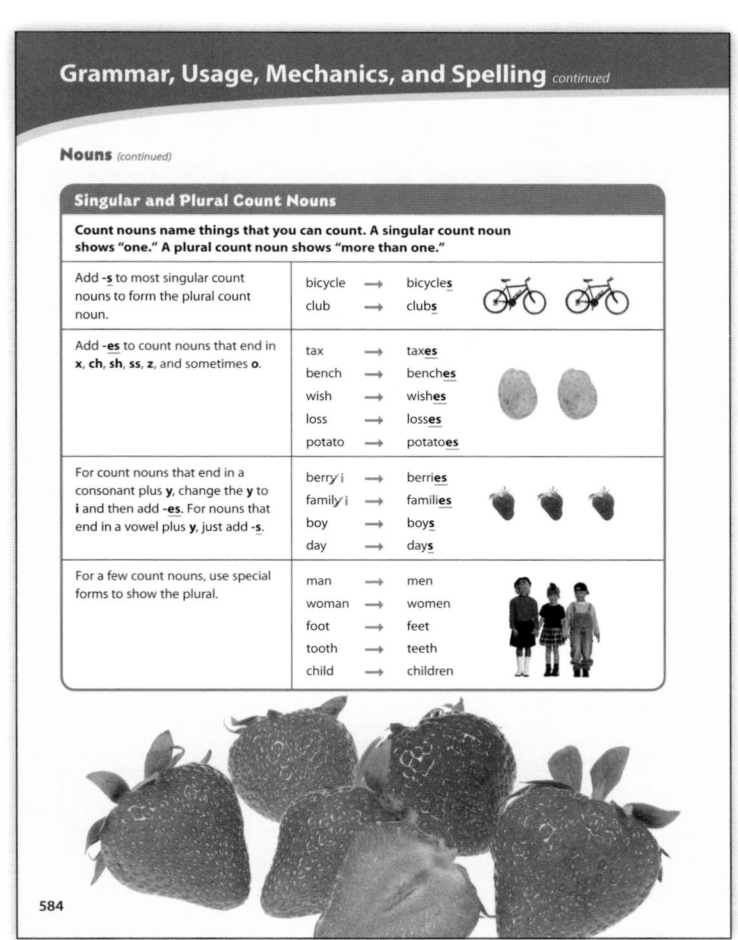

Grammar, Usage, Mechanics, and Spelling *continued*

Nouns *(continued)*

Singular and Plural Count Nouns

Count nouns name things that you can count. A singular count noun shows "one." A plural count noun shows "more than one."	
Add **-s** to most singular count nouns to form the plural count noun.	bicycle → bicycle**s** club → club**s**
Add **-es** to count nouns that end in **x**, **ch**, **sh**, **ss**, **z**, and sometimes **o**.	tax → tax**es** bench → bench**es** wish → wish**es** loss → loss**es** potato → potato**es**
For count nouns that end in a consonant plus **y**, change the **y** to **i** and then add **-es**. For nouns that end in a vowel plus **y**, just add **-s**.	berry → berr**ies** family → famil**ies** boy → boy**s** day → day**s**
For a few count nouns, use special forms to show the plural.	man → men woman → women foot → feet tooth → teeth child → children

584

Page 584

Noncount Nouns

Noncount nouns name things that you cannot count. Noncount nouns have one form for "one" and "more than one."	
Weather Words	fog heat lightning thunder rain **YES:** **Thunder** and **lightning** scare my dog. **NO:** Thunders and lightnings scare my dog.
Food Words Some food items can be counted by using a measurement word such as **cup**, **slice**, **glass**, or **head** plus the word **of**. To show the plural form, make the measurement word plural.	bread corn milk rice soup **YES:** I'm thirsty for **milk**. I want **two glasses of milk.** **NO:** I'm thirsty for milks. I want milks.
Ideas and Feelings	fun help honesty luck work **YES:** I need **help** to finish my homework. **NO:** I need helps to finish my homework.
Category Nouns	clothing equipment mail money time **YES:** My football **equipment** is in the car. **NO:** My football equipments is in the car.
Materials	air gold paper water wood **YES:** Is the **water** in this river clean? **NO:** Is the waters in this river clean?
Activities and Sports	baseball dancing golf singing soccer **YES:** I played **soccer** three times this week. **NO:** I played soccers three times this week.

585

Page 585

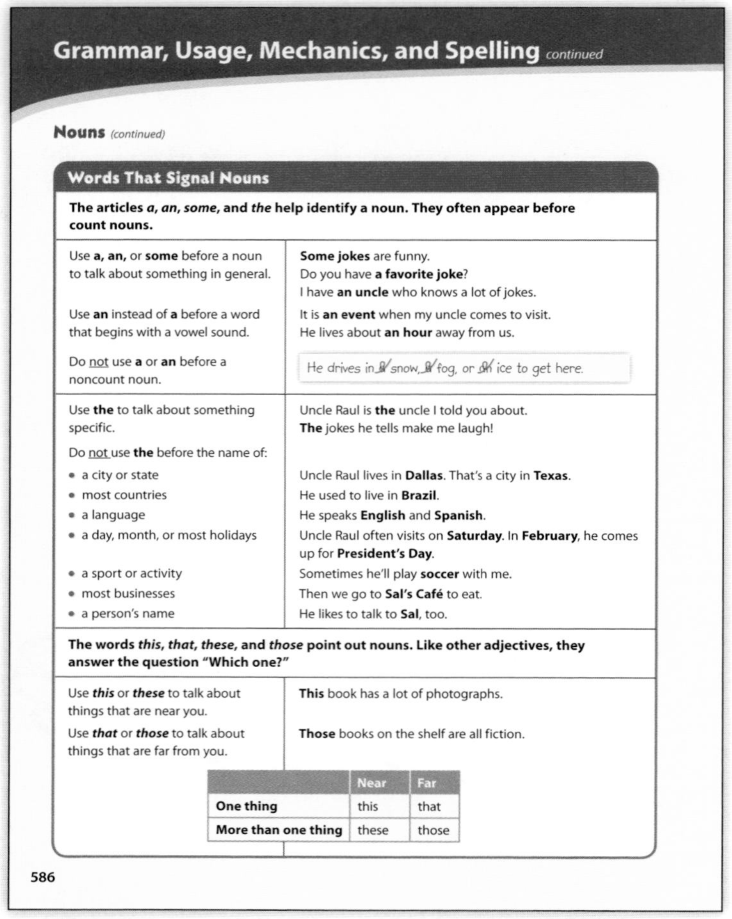

Grammar, Usage, Mechanics, and Spelling *continued*

Nouns *(continued)*

Words That Signal Nouns

The articles *a, an, some,* and *the* help identify a noun. They often appear before count nouns.

Use **a, an,** or **some** before a noun to talk about something in general.	**Some jokes** are funny. Do you have **a favorite joke**? I have **an uncle** who knows a lot of jokes.
Use **an** instead of **a** before a word that begins with a vowel sound.	It is **an event** when my uncle comes to visit. He lives about **an hour** away from us.
Do not use **a** or **an** before a noncount noun.	He drives in a snow, a fog, or an ice to get here.
Use **the** to talk about something specific.	Uncle Raul is **the** uncle I told you about. **The** jokes he tells make me laugh!
Do not use **the** before the name of: • a city or state • most countries • a language • a day, month, or most holidays • a sport or activity • most businesses • a person's name	Uncle Raul lives in **Dallas**. That's a city in **Texas**. He used to live in **Brazil**. He speaks **English** and **Spanish**. Uncle Raul often visits on **Saturday**. In **February**, he comes up for **President's Day**. Sometimes he'll play **soccer** with me. Then we go to **Sal's Café** to eat. He likes to talk to **Sal**, too.

The words *this, that, these,* and *those* point out nouns. Like other adjectives, they answer the question "Which one?"

Use ***this*** or ***these*** to talk about things that are near you.	**This** book has a lot of photographs.
Use ***that*** or ***those*** to talk about things that are far from you.	**Those** books on the shelf are all fiction.

	Near	Far
One thing	this	that
More than one thing	these	those

586

Page 586

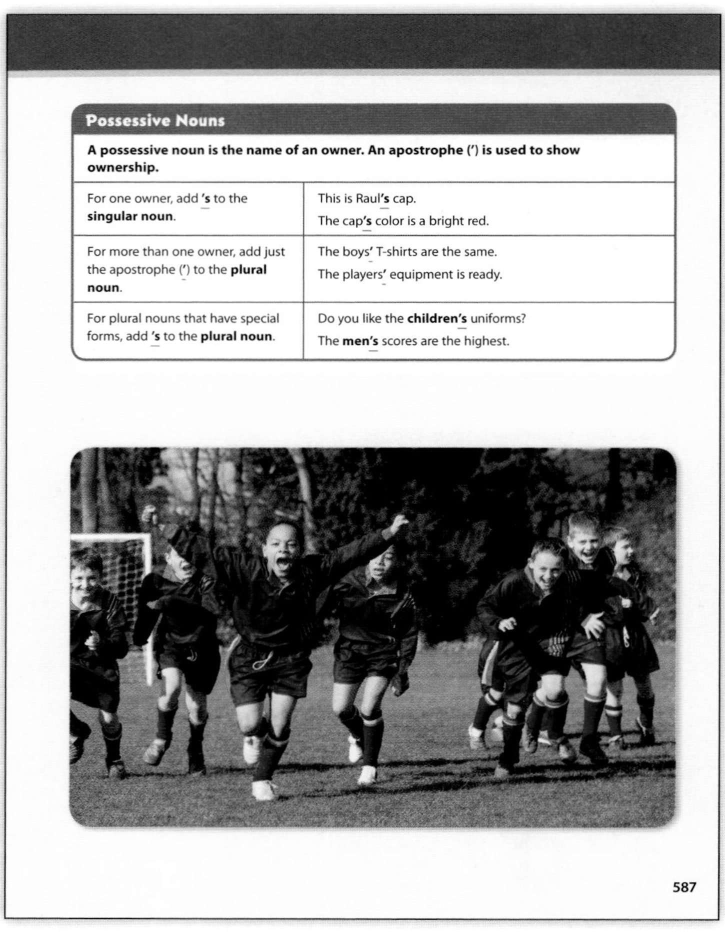

Possessive Nouns

A possessive noun is the name of an owner. An apostrophe (') is used to show ownership.

For one owner, add **'s** to the **singular noun**.	This is Raul**'s** cap. The cap**'s** color is a bright red.
For more than one owner, add just the apostrophe (') to the **plural noun**.	The boys**'** T-shirts are the same. The players**'** equipment is ready.
For plural nouns that have special forms, add **'s** to the **plural noun**.	Do you like the **children's** uniforms? The **men's** scores are the highest.

587

Page 587

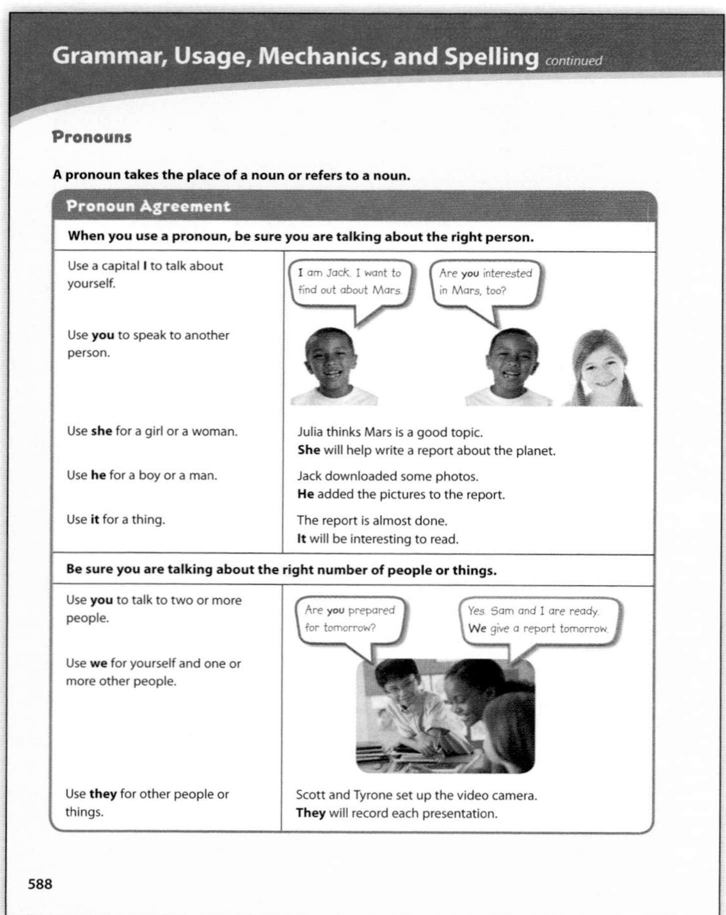

Grammar, Usage, Mechanics, and Spelling *continued*

Pronouns

A pronoun takes the place of a noun or refers to a noun.

Pronoun Agreement

When you use a pronoun, be sure you are talking about the right person.

Use a capital **I** to talk about yourself.	I am Jack. I want to find out about Mars.
Use **you** to speak to another person.	Are **you** interested in Mars, too?
Use **she** for a girl or a woman.	Julia thinks Mars is a good topic. **She** will help write a report about the planet.
Use **he** for a boy or a man.	Jack downloaded some photos. **He** added the pictures to the report.
Use **it** for a thing.	The report is almost done. **It** will be interesting to read.

Be sure you are talking about the right number of people or things.

Use **you** to talk to two or more people.	Are **you** prepared for tomorrow?
Use **we** for yourself and one or more other people.	Yes. Sam and I are ready. **We** give a report tomorrow.
Use **they** for other people or things.	Scott and Tyrone set up the video camera. **They** will record each presentation.

588

Page 588

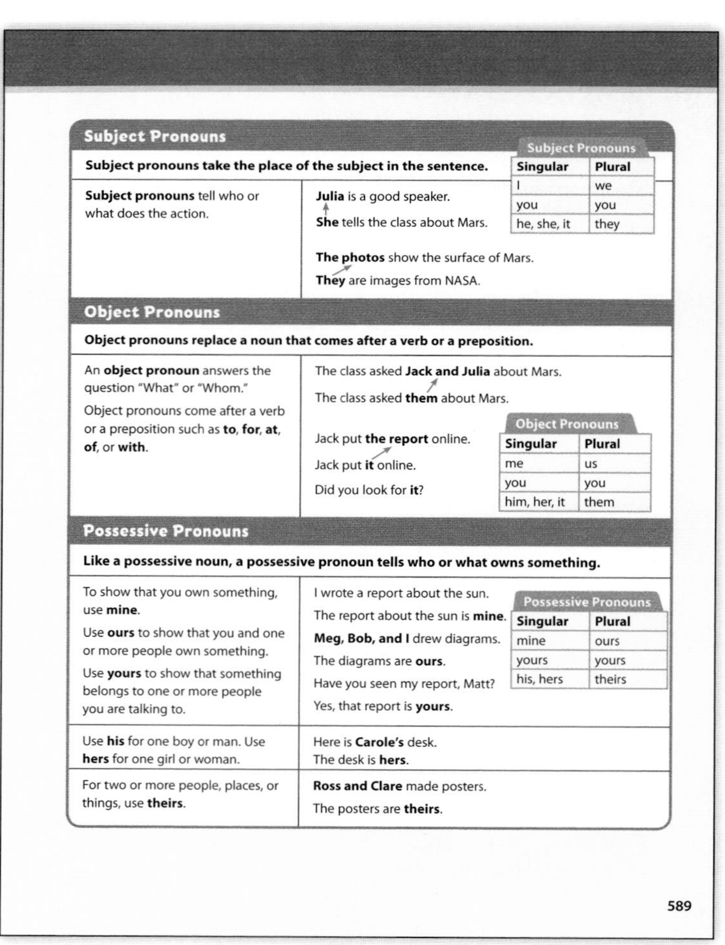

Subject Pronouns

Subject pronouns take the place of the subject in the sentence.

Subject pronouns tell who or what does the action.	**Julia** is a good speaker. **She** tells the class about Mars. **The photos** show the surface of Mars. **They** are images from NASA.

Subject Pronouns	
Singular	**Plural**
I	we
you	you
he, she, it	they

Object Pronouns

Object pronouns replace a noun that comes after a verb or a preposition.

An **object pronoun** answers the question "What" or "Whom." Object pronouns come after a verb or a preposition such as **to, for, at, of,** or **with**.	The class asked **Jack and Julia** about Mars. The class asked **them** about Mars. Jack put **the report** online. Jack put **it** online. Did you look for **it**?

Object Pronouns	
Singular	**Plural**
me	us
you	you
him, her, it	them

Possessive Pronouns

Like a possessive noun, a possessive pronoun tells who or what owns something.

To show that you own something, use **mine**. Use **ours** to show that you and one or more people own something. Use **yours** to show that something belongs to one or more people you are talking to.	I wrote a report about the sun. The report about the sun is **mine**. **Meg, Bob, and I** drew diagrams. The diagrams are **ours**. Have you seen my report, Matt? Yes, that report is **yours**.
Use **his** for one boy or man. Use **hers** for one girl or woman.	Here is **Carole's** desk. The desk is **hers**.
For two or more people, places, or things, use **theirs**.	**Ross and Clare** made posters. The posters are **theirs**.

Possessive Pronouns	
Singular	**Plural**
mine	ours
yours	yours
his, hers	theirs

589

Page 589

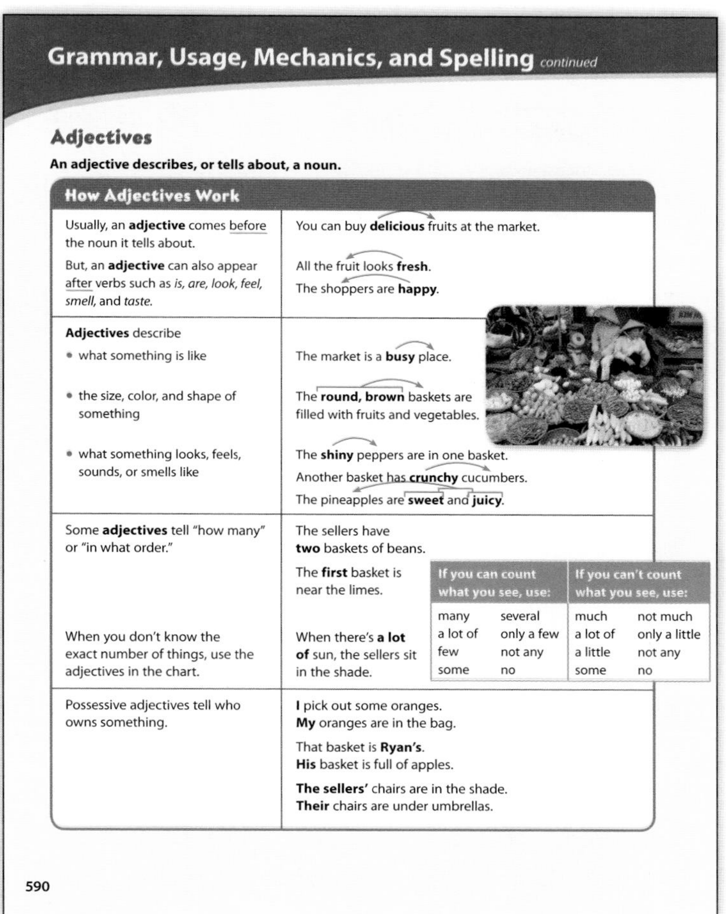

Adjectives

An adjective describes, or tells about, a noun.

How Adjectives Work

Usually, an **adjective** comes before the noun it tells about. But, an **adjective** can also appear after verbs such as *is, are, look, feel, smell,* and *taste.*	You can buy **delicious** fruits at the market. All the fruit looks **fresh**. The shoppers are **happy**.
Adjectives describe • what something is like • the size, color, and shape of something • what something looks, feels, sounds, or smells like	The market is a **busy** place. The **round, brown** baskets are filled with fruits and vegetables. The **shiny** peppers are in one basket. Another basket has **crunchy** cucumbers. The pineapples are **sweet** and **juicy**.
Some **adjectives** tell "how many" or "in what order." When you don't know the exact number of things, use the adjectives in the chart.	The sellers have **two** baskets of beans. The **first** basket is near the limes. When there's **a lot of** sun, the sellers sit in the shade.
Possessive adjectives tell who owns something.	**I** pick out some oranges. **My** oranges are in the bag. That basket is **Ryan's**. **His** basket is full of apples. **The sellers'** chairs are in the shade. **Their** chairs are under umbrellas.

If you can count what you see, use:		If you can't count what you see, use:	
many	several	much	not much
a lot of	only a few	a lot of	only a little
few	not any	a little	not any
some	no	some	no

Page 590

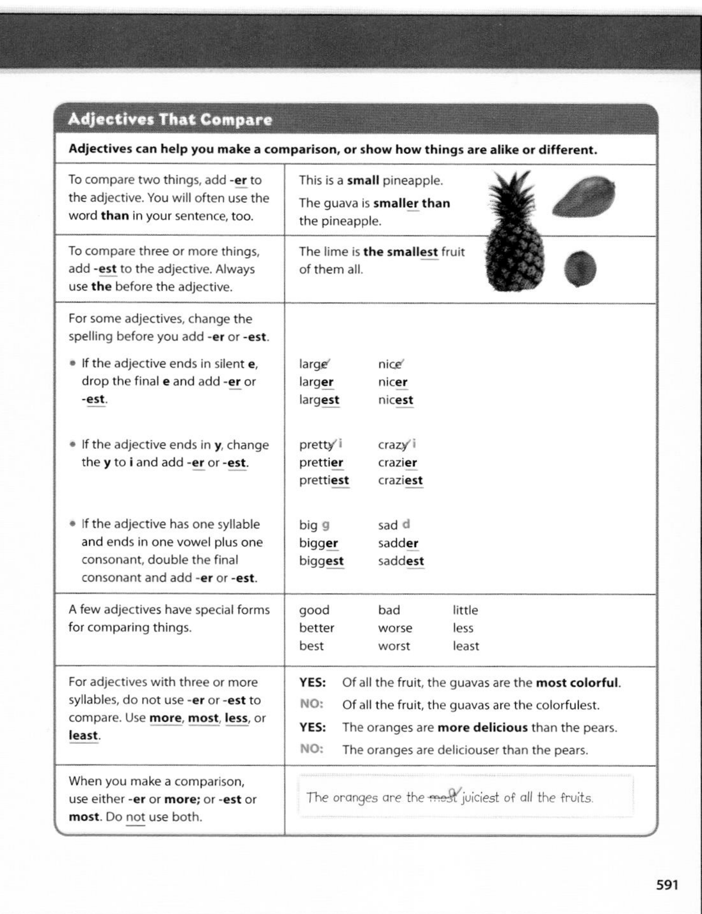

Adjectives That Compare

Adjectives can help you make a comparison, or show how things are alike or different.

To compare two things, add **-er** to the adjective. You will often use the word **than** in your sentence, too.	This is a **small** pineapple. The guava is **smaller than** the pineapple.
To compare three or more things, add **-est** to the adjective. Always use **the** before the adjective.	The lime is **the smallest** fruit of them all.
For some adjectives, change the spelling before you add **-er** or **-est**. • If the adjective ends in silent **e**, drop the final **e** and add **-er** or **-est**. • If the adjective ends in **y**, change the **y** to **i** and add **-er** or **-est**. • If the adjective has one syllable and ends in one vowel plus one consonant, double the final consonant and add **-er** or **-est**.	large, larg**er**, larg**est** — nice, nic**er**, nic**est** pretty, prett**ier**, prett**iest** — crazy, craz**ier**, craz**iest** big, bigg**er**, bigg**est** — sad, sadd**er**, sadd**est**
A few adjectives have special forms for comparing things.	good, better, best — bad, worse, worst — little, less, least
For adjectives with three or more syllables, do not use **-er** or **-est** to compare. Use **more**, **most**, **less**, or **least**.	**YES:** Of all the fruit, the guavas are the **most colorful**. **NO:** Of all the fruit, the guavas are the colorfulest. **YES:** The oranges are **more delicious** than the pears. **NO:** The oranges are deliciouser than the pears.
When you make a comparison, use either **-er** or **more;** or **-est** or **most**. Do not use both.	The oranges are the ~~most~~ juiciest of all the fruits.

Page 591

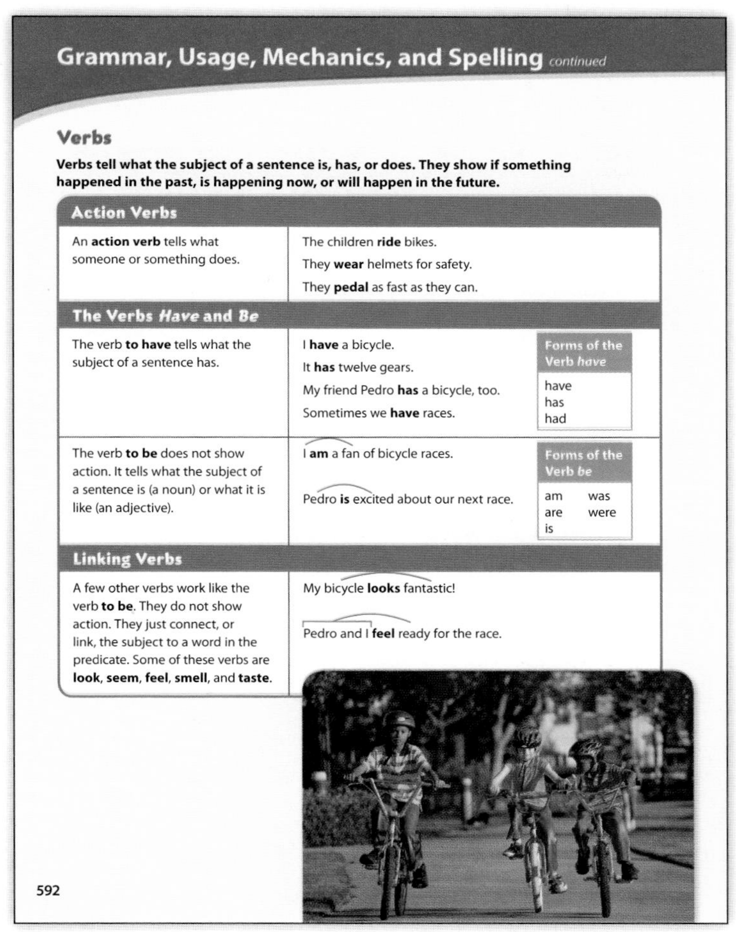

Verbs

Verbs tell what the subject of a sentence is, has, or does. They show if something happened in the past, is happening now, or will happen in the future.

Action Verbs

An **action verb** tells what someone or something does.	The children **ride** bikes. They **wear** helmets for safety. They **pedal** as fast as they can.

The Verbs *Have* and *Be*

The verb **to have** tells what the subject of a sentence has.	I **have** a bicycle. It **has** twelve gears. My friend Pedro **has** a bicycle, too. Sometimes we **have** races. Forms of the Verb *have*: have, has, had
The verb **to be** does not show action. It tells what the subject of a sentence is (a noun) or what it is like (an adjective).	I **am** a fan of bicycle races. Pedro **is** excited about our next race. Forms of the Verb *be*: am, are, is, was, were

Linking Verbs

A few other verbs work like the verb **to be**. They do not show action. They just connect, or link, the subject to a word in the predicate. Some of these verbs are **look**, **seem**, **feel**, **smell**, and **taste**.	My bicycle **looks** fantastic! Pedro and I **feel** ready for the race.

Page 592

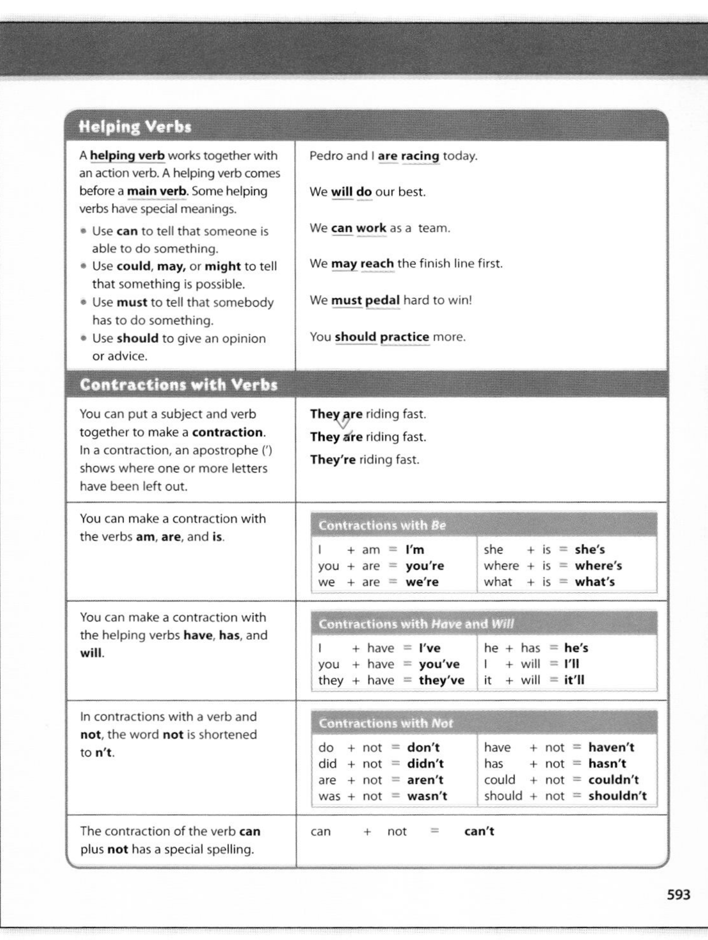

Helping Verbs

A **helping verb** works together with an action verb. A helping verb comes before a **main verb**. Some helping verbs have special meanings. • Use **can** to tell that someone is able to do something. • Use **could, may,** or **might** to tell that something is possible. • Use **must** to tell that somebody has to do something. • Use **should** to give an opinion or advice.	Pedro and I **are racing** today. We **will do** our best. We **can work** as a team. We **may reach** the finish line first. We **must pedal** hard to win! You **should practice** more.

Contractions with Verbs

You can put a subject and verb together to make a **contraction**. In a contraction, an apostrophe (') shows where one or more letters have been left out.	**They are** riding fast. **They are** riding fast. **They're** riding fast.
You can make a contraction with the verbs **am**, **are**, and **is**.	Contractions with *Be*: I + am = **I'm**; you + are = **you're**; we + are = **we're**; she + is = **she's**; where + is = **where's**; what + is = **what's**
You can make a contraction with the helping verbs **have**, **has**, and **will**.	Contractions with *Have* and *Will*: I + have = **I've**; you + have = **you've**; they + have = **they've**; he + has = **he's**; I + will = **I'll**; it + will = **it'll**
In contractions with a verb and **not**, the word **not** is shortened to **n't**.	Contractions with *Not*: do + not = **don't**; did + not = **didn't**; are + not = **aren't**; was + not = **wasn't**; have + not = **haven't**; has + not = **hasn't**; could + not = **couldn't**; should + not = **shouldn't**
The contraction of the verb **can** plus **not** has a special spelling.	can + not = **can't**

Page 593

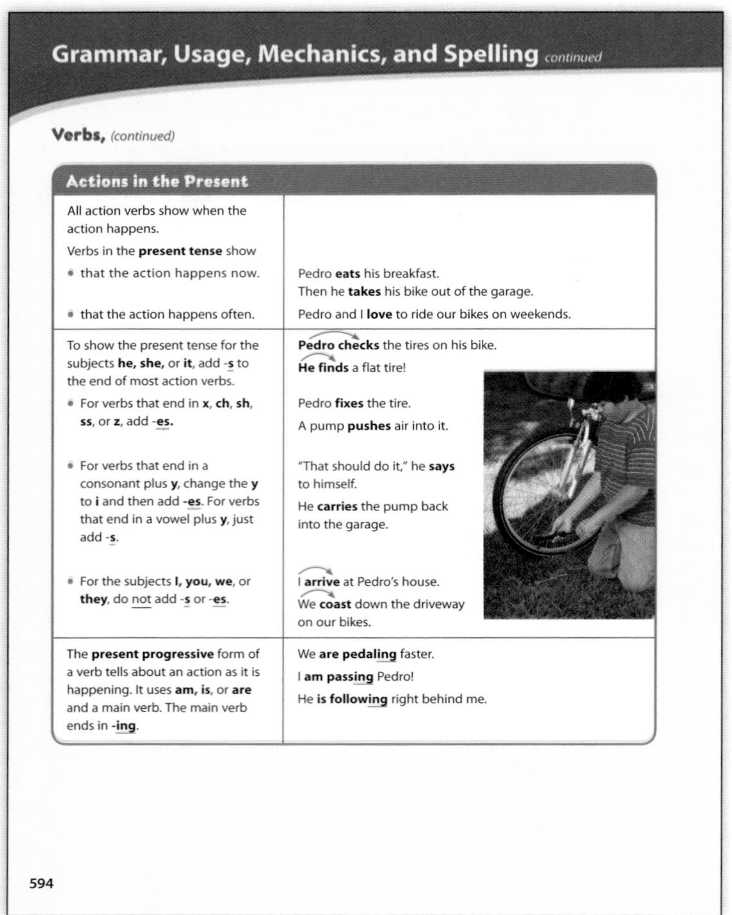

Grammar, Usage, Mechanics, and Spelling *continued*

Verbs, *(continued)*

Actions in the Present

All action verbs show when the action happens. Verbs in the **present tense** show • that the action happens now. • that the action happens often.	Pedro **eats** his breakfast. Then he **takes** his bike out of the garage. Pedro and I **love** to ride our bikes on weekends.
To show the present tense for the subjects **he, she,** or **it**, add **-s** to the end of most action verbs. • For verbs that end in **x**, **ch**, **sh**, **ss**, or **z**, add **-es**. • For verbs that end in a consonant plus **y**, change the **y** to **i** and then add **-es**. For verbs that end in a vowel plus **y**, just add **-s**. • For the subjects **I, you, we,** or **they**, do not add **-s** or **-es**.	**Pedro checks** the tires on his bike. **He finds** a flat tire! Pedro **fixes** the tire. A pump **pushes** air into it. "That should do it," he **says** to himself. He **carries** the pump back into the garage. I **arrive** at Pedro's house. We **coast** down the driveway on our bikes.
The **present progressive** form of a verb tells about an action as it is happening. It uses **am, is,** or **are** and a main verb. The main verb ends in **-ing**.	We **are pedaling** faster. I **am passing** Pedro! He **is following** right behind me.

594

Page 594

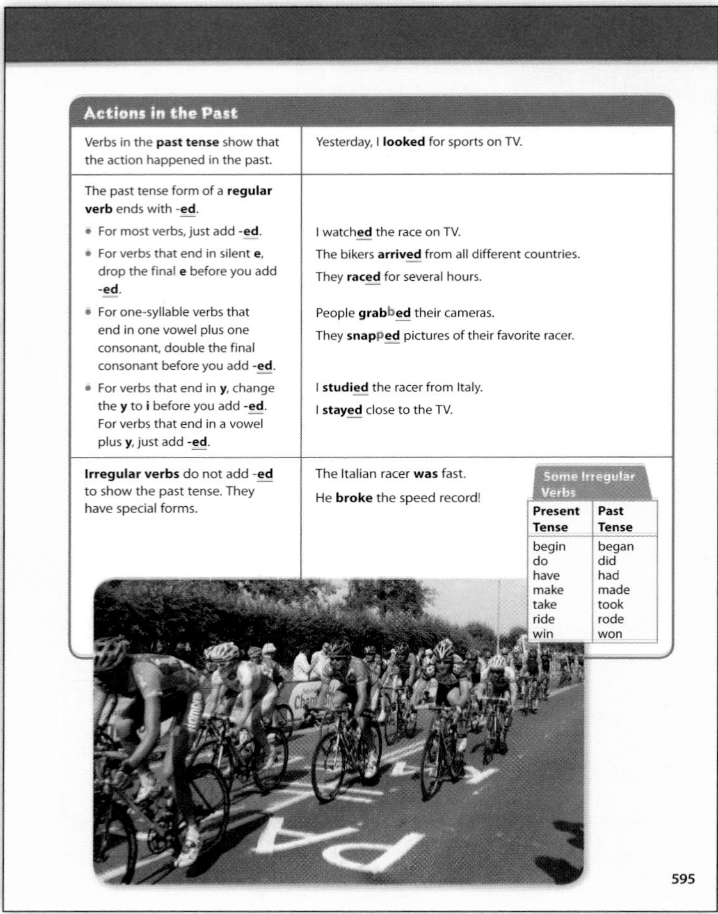

Actions in the Past

Verbs in the **past tense** show that the action happened in the past.	Yesterday, I **looked** for sports on TV.
The past tense form of a **regular verb** ends with **-ed**. • For most verbs, just add **-ed**. • For verbs that end in silent **e**, drop the final **e** before you add **-ed**. • For one-syllable verbs that end in one vowel plus one consonant, double the final consonant before you add **-ed**. • For verbs that end in **y**, change the **y** to **i** before you add **-ed**. For verbs that end in a vowel plus **y**, just add **-ed**.	I watch**ed** the race on TV. The bikers **arrived** from all different countries. They **raced** for several hours. People **grabbed** their cameras. They **snapped** pictures of their favorite racer. I **studied** the racer from Italy. I **stayed** close to the TV.
Irregular verbs do not add **-ed** to show the past tense. They have special forms.	The Italian racer **was** fast. He **broke** the speed record!

Some Irregular Verbs

Present Tense	Past Tense
begin	began
do	did
have	had
make	made
take	took
ride	rode
win	won

595

Page 595

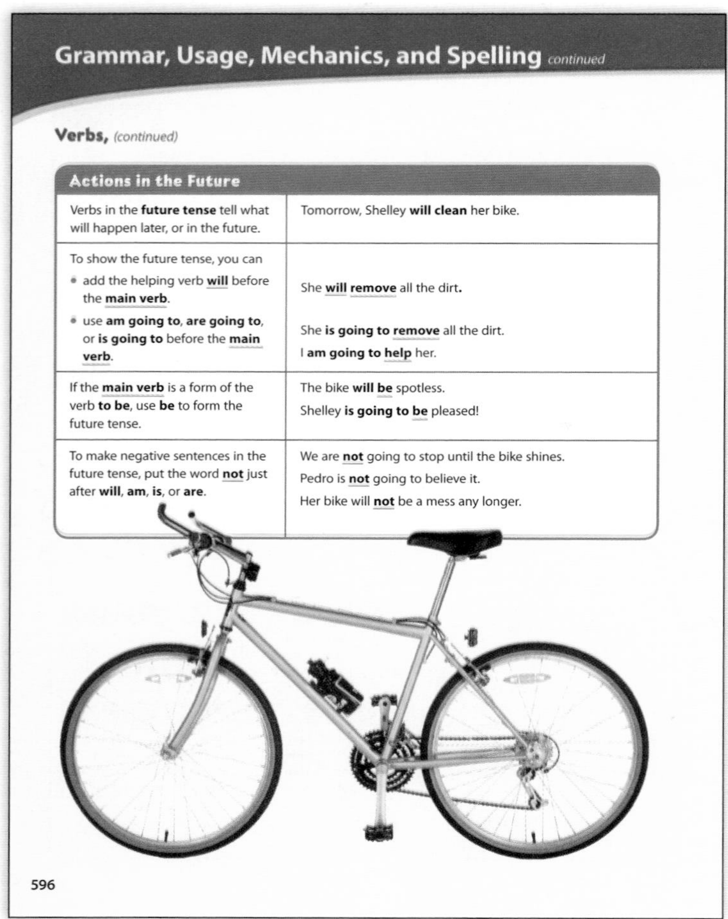

Grammar, Usage, Mechanics, and Spelling *continued*

Verbs, *(continued)*

Actions in the Future

Verbs in the **future tense** tell what will happen later, or in the future.	Tomorrow, Shelley **will clean** her bike.
To show the future tense, you can • add the helping verb **will** before the **main verb**. • use **am going to**, **are going to**, or **is going to** before the **main verb**.	She **will remove** all the dirt. She **is going to remove** all the dirt. I **am going to help** her.
If the **main verb** is a form of the verb **to be**, use **be** to form the future tense.	The bike **will be** spotless. Shelley **is going to be** pleased!
To make negative sentences in the future tense, put the word **not** just after **will**, **am**, **is**, or **are**.	We are **not** going to stop until the bike shines. Pedro is **not** going to believe it. Her bike will **not** be a mess any longer.

596

Page 596

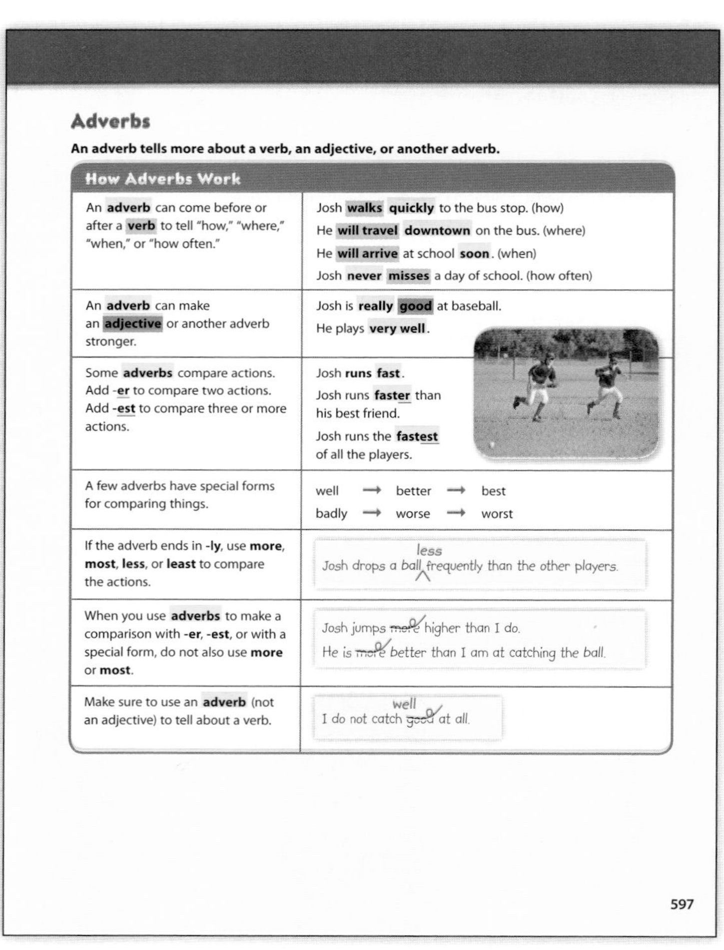

Adverbs

An adverb tells more about a verb, an adjective, or another adverb.

How Adverbs Work

An **adverb** can come before or after a **verb** to tell "how," "where," "when," or "how often."	Josh **walks quickly** to the bus stop. (how) He **will travel downtown** on the bus. (where) He **will arrive** at school **soon**. (when) Josh **never misses** a day of school. (how often)
An **adverb** can make an **adjective** or another adverb stronger.	Josh is **really good** at baseball. He plays **very well**.
Some **adverbs** compare actions. Add **-er** to compare two actions. Add **-est** to compare three or more actions.	Josh **runs fast**. Josh runs **faster** than his best friend. Josh runs the **fastest** of all the players.
A few adverbs have special forms for comparing things.	well → better → best badly → worse → worst
If the adverb ends in **-ly**, use **more**, **most**, **less**, or **least** to compare the actions.	*Josh drops a ball less frequently than the other players.*
When you use **adverbs** to make a comparison with **-er**, **-est**, or with a special form, do not also use **more** or **most**.	*Josh jumps ~~more~~ higher than I do.* *He is ~~more~~ better than I am at catching the ball.*
Make sure to use an **adverb** (not an adjective) to tell about a verb.	*I do not catch ~~good~~ well at all.*

597

Page 597

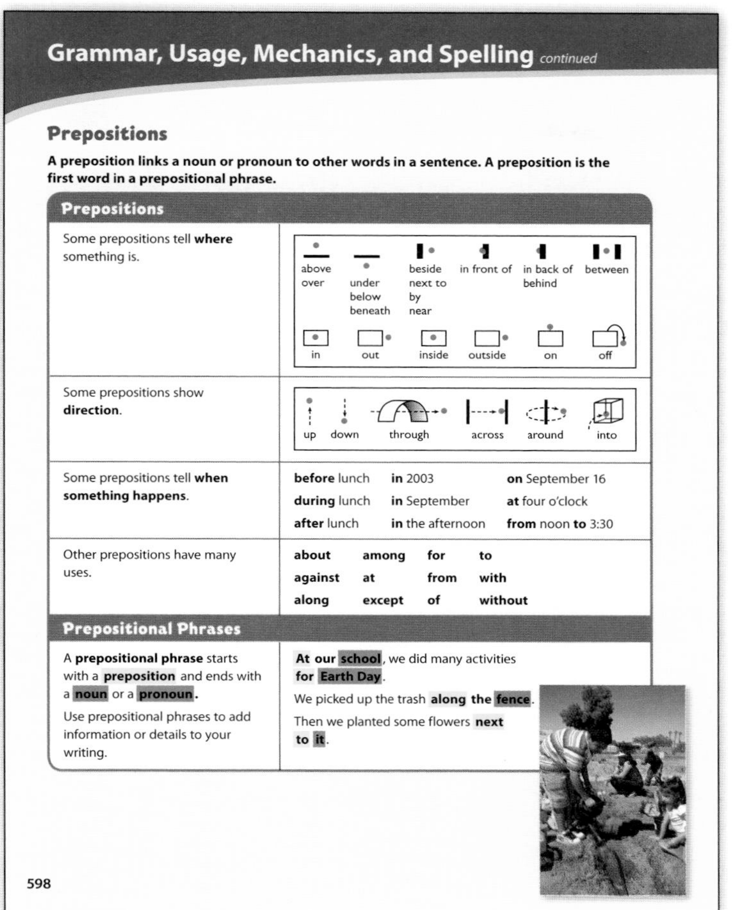

Grammar, Usage, Mechanics, and Spelling *continued*

Prepositions

A preposition links a noun or pronoun to other words in a sentence. A preposition is the first word in a prepositional phrase.

Prepositions	
Some prepositions tell **where** something is.	above, over; under, below, beneath; beside, next to, by, near; in front of; in back of, behind; between; in; out; inside; outside; on; off
Some prepositions show **direction**.	up; down; through; across; around; into
Some prepositions tell **when something happens**.	**before** lunch, **during** lunch, **after** lunch; **in** 2003, **in** September, **in** the afternoon; **on** September 16, **at** four o'clock, **from** noon **to** 3:30
Other prepositions have many uses.	**about, against, along, among, at, except, for, from, of, to, with, without**
Prepositional Phrases	
A **prepositional phrase** starts with a **preposition** and ends with a **noun** or a **pronoun**. Use prepositional phrases to add information or details to your writing.	**At our school**, we did many activities **for Earth Day**. We picked up the trash **along the fence**. Then we planted some flowers **next to it**.

598

Page 598

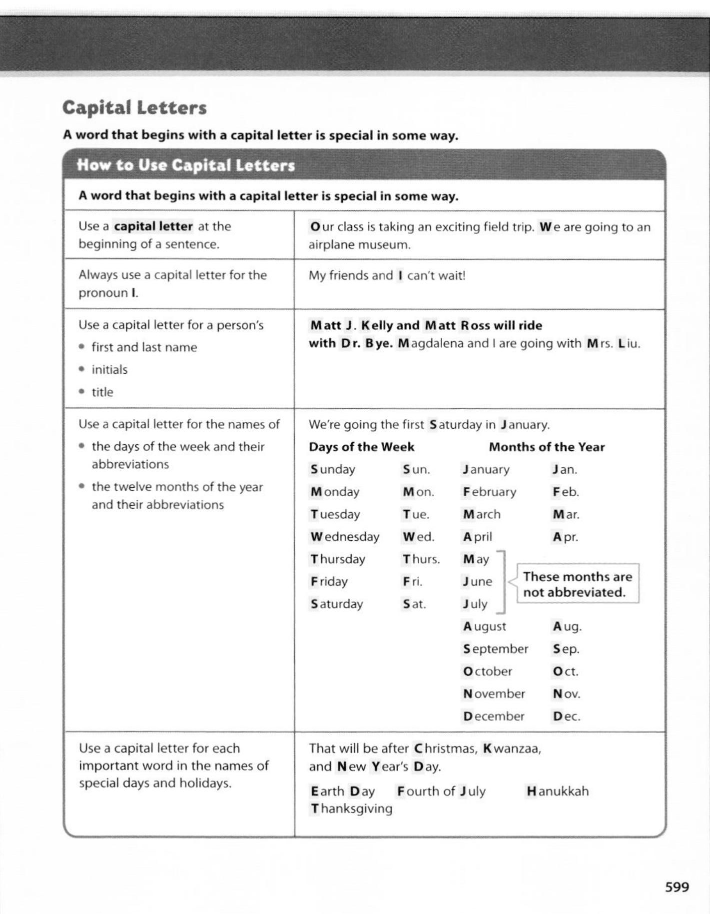

Capital Letters

A word that begins with a capital letter is special in some way.

How to Use Capital Letters	
A word that begins with a capital letter is special in some way.	
Use a **capital letter** at the beginning of a sentence.	**O**ur class is taking an exciting field trip. **W**e are going to an airplane museum.
Always use a capital letter for the pronoun **I**.	My friends and **I** can't wait!
Use a capital letter for a person's • first and last name • initials • title	**M**att **J**. **K**elly and **M**att **R**oss will ride with **D**r. **B**ye. **M**agdalena and I are going with **M**rs. **L**iu.
Use a capital letter for the names of • the days of the week and their abbreviations • the twelve months of the year and their abbreviations	We're going the first **S**aturday in **J**anuary. **Days of the Week:** **S**unday **S**un.; **M**onday **M**on.; **T**uesday **T**ue.; **W**ednesday **W**ed.; **T**hursday **T**hurs.; **F**riday **F**ri.; **S**aturday **S**at. **Months of the Year:** **J**anuary **J**an.; **F**ebruary **F**eb.; **M**arch **M**ar.; **A**pril **A**pr.; **M**ay, **J**une, **J**uly (These months are not abbreviated.); **A**ugust **A**ug.; **S**eptember **S**ep.; **O**ctober **O**ct.; **N**ovember **N**ov.; **D**ecember **D**ec.
Use a capital letter for each important word in the names of special days and holidays.	That will be after **C**hristmas, **K**wanzaa, and **N**ew **Y**ear's **D**ay. **E**arth **D**ay, **F**ourth of **J**uly, **H**anukkah, **T**hanksgiving

599

Page 599

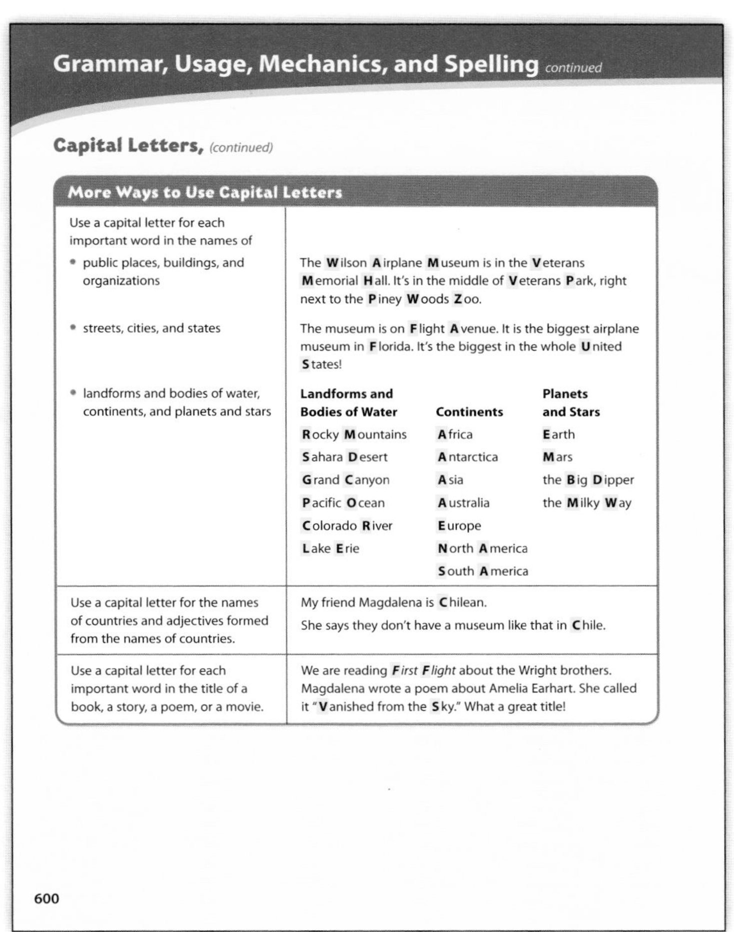

Grammar, Usage, Mechanics, and Spelling *continued*

Capital Letters, *(continued)*

More Ways to Use Capital Letters	
Use a capital letter for each important word in the names of • public places, buildings, and organizations	The **W**ilson **A**irplane **M**useum is in the **V**eterans **M**emorial **H**all. It's in the middle of **V**eterans **P**ark, right next to the **P**iney **W**oods **Z**oo.
• streets, cities, and states	The museum is on **F**light **A**venue. It is the biggest airplane museum in **F**lorida. It's the biggest in the whole **U**nited **S**tates!
• landforms and bodies of water, continents, and planets and stars	**Landforms and Bodies of Water:** **R**ocky **M**ountains, **S**ahara **D**esert, **G**rand **C**anyon, **P**acific **O**cean, **C**olorado **R**iver, Lake **E**rie **Continents:** **A**frica, **A**ntarctica, **A**sia, **A**ustralia, **E**urope, **N**orth **A**merica, **S**outh **A**merica **Planets and Stars:** **E**arth, **M**ars, the **B**ig **D**ipper, the **M**ilky **W**ay
Use a capital letter for the names of countries and adjectives formed from the names of countries.	My friend Magdalena is **C**hilean. She says they don't have a museum like that in **C**hile.
Use a capital letter for each important word in the title of a book, a story, a poem, or a movie.	We are reading ***F**irst **F**light* about the Wright brothers. Magdalena wrote a poem about Amelia Earhart. She called it "**V**anished from the **S**ky." What a great title!

600

Page 600

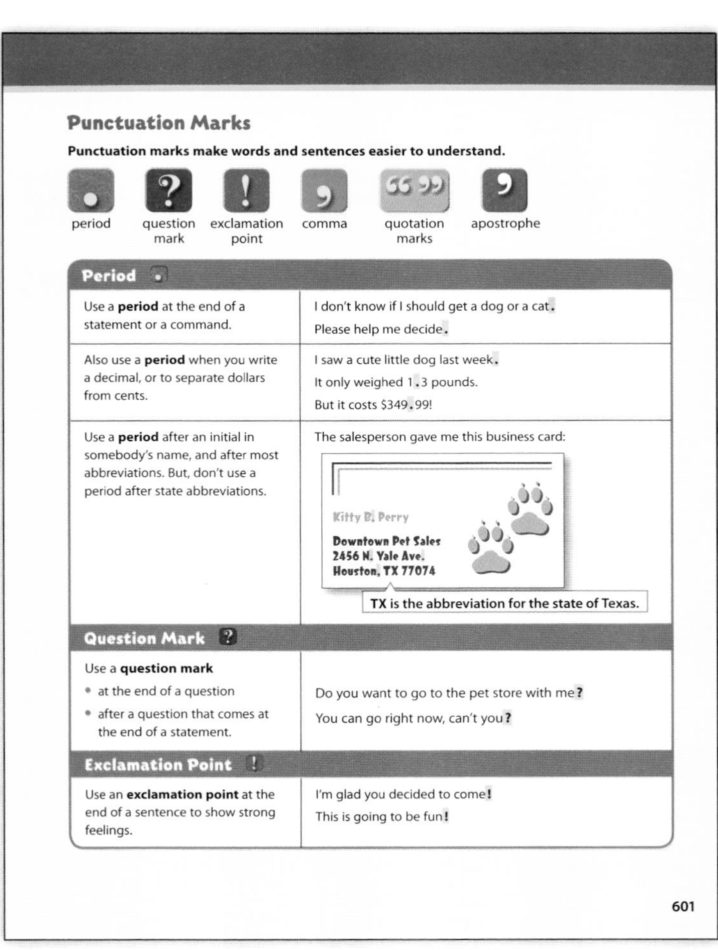

Punctuation Marks

Punctuation marks make words and sentences easier to understand.

period; question mark; exclamation point; comma; quotation marks; apostrophe

Period	
Use a **period** at the end of a statement or a command.	I don't know if I should get a dog or a cat. Please help me decide.
Also use a **period** when you write a decimal, or to separate dollars from cents.	I saw a cute little dog last week. It only weighed 1.3 pounds. But it costs $349.99!
Use a **period** after an initial in somebody's name, and after most abbreviations. But, don't use a period after state abbreviations.	The salesperson gave me this business card: Kitty D. Perry Downtown Pet Sales 2456 N. Yale Ave. Houston, TX 77074 TX is the abbreviation for the state of Texas.
Question Mark	
Use a **question mark** • at the end of a question • after a question that comes at the end of a statement.	Do you want to go to the pet store with me? You can go right now, can't you?
Exclamation Point	
Use an **exclamation point** at the end of a sentence to show strong feelings.	I'm glad you decided to come! This is going to be fun!

601

Page 601

Anthology Handbook, continued

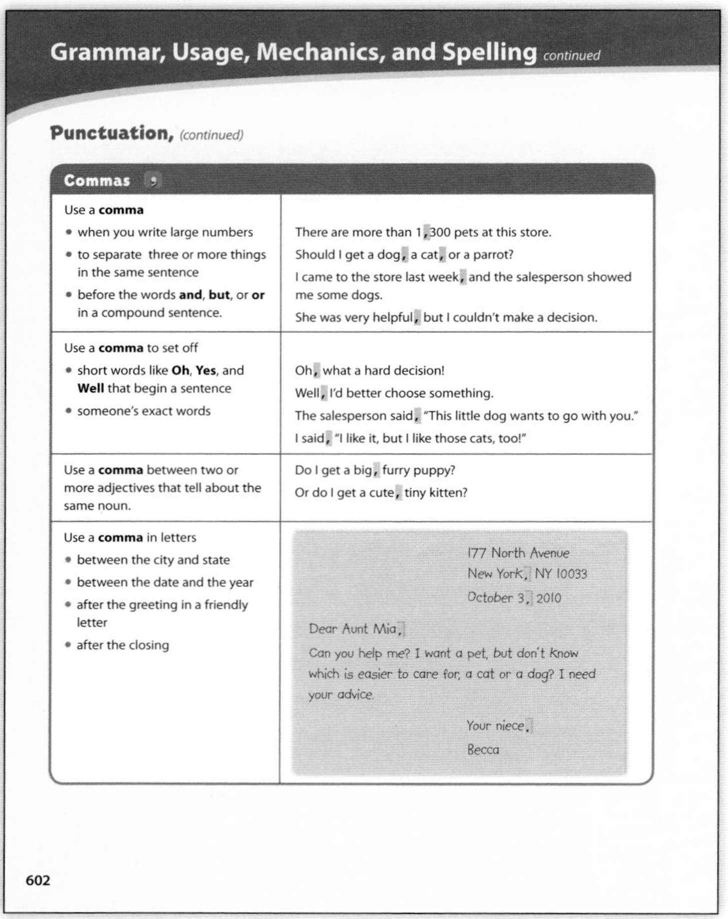

Grammar, Usage, Mechanics, and Spelling *continued*

Punctuation, *(continued)*

Commas	
Use a **comma** • when you write large numbers • to separate three or more things in the same sentence • before the words **and**, **but**, or **or** in a compound sentence.	There are more than 1,300 pets at this store. Should I get a dog, a cat, or a parrot? I came to the store last week, and the salesperson showed me some dogs. She was very helpful, but I couldn't make a decision.
Use a **comma** to set off • short words like **Oh**, **Yes**, and **Well** that begin a sentence • someone's exact words	Oh, what a hard decision! Well, I'd better choose something. The salesperson said, "This little dog wants to go with you." I said, "I like it, but I like those cats, too!"
Use a **comma** between two or more adjectives that tell about the same noun.	Do I get a big, furry puppy? Or do I get a cute, tiny kitten?
Use a **comma** in letters • between the city and state • between the date and the year • after the greeting in a friendly letter • after the closing	177 North Avenue New York, NY 10033 October 3, 2010 Dear Aunt Mia, Can you help me? I want a pet, but don't know which is easier to care for, a cat or a dog? I need your advice. Your niece, Becca

602

Page 602

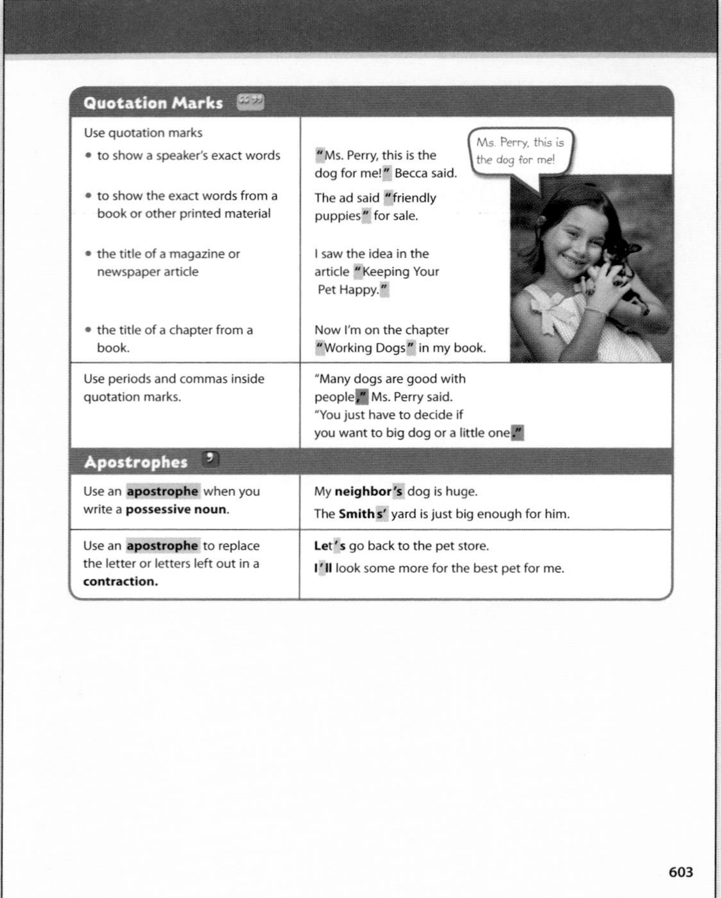

Quotation Marks	
Use quotation marks • to show a speaker's exact words	"Ms. Perry, this is the dog for me!" Becca said.
• to show the exact words from a book or other printed material	The ad said "friendly puppies" for sale.
• the title of a magazine or newspaper article	I saw the idea in the article "Keeping Your Pet Happy."
• the title of a chapter from a book.	Now I'm on the chapter "Working Dogs" in my book.
Use periods and commas inside quotation marks.	"Many dogs are good with people," Ms. Perry said. "You just have to decide if you want to big dog or a little one."

Apostrophes	
Use an **apostrophe** when you write a **possessive noun**.	My **neighbor's** dog is huge. The **Smiths'** yard is just big enough for him.
Use an **apostrophe** to replace the letter or letters left out in a **contraction.**	**Let's** go back to the pet store. **I'll** look some more for the best pet for me.

603

Page 603

Anthology Picture Dictionary

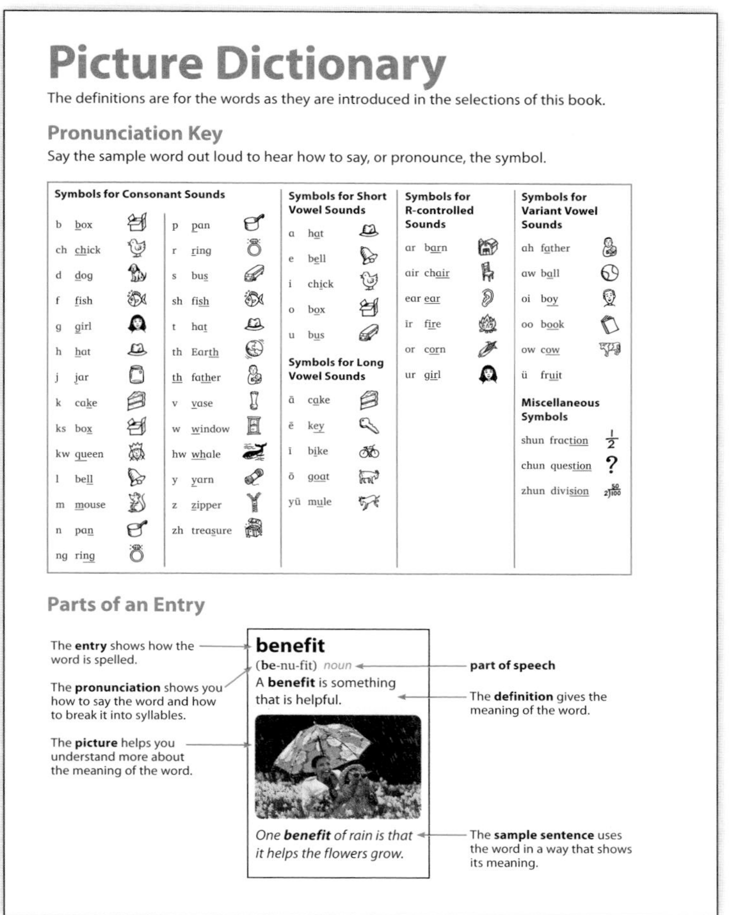

Picture Dictionary

The definitions are for the words as they are introduced in the selections of this book.

Pronunciation Key

Say the sample word out loud to hear how to say, or pronounce, the symbol.

Symbols for Consonant Sounds

b	box	p	pan
ch	chick	r	ring
d	dog	s	bus
f	fish	sh	fish
g	girl	t	hat
h	hat	th	Earth
j	jar	th	father
k	cake	v	vase
ks	box	w	window
kw	queen	hw	whale
l	bell	y	yarn
m	mouse	z	zipper
n	pan	zh	treasure
ng	ring		

Symbols for Short Vowel Sounds

a	hat
e	bell
i	chick
o	box
u	bus

Symbols for Long Vowel Sounds

ā	cake
ē	key
ī	bike
ō	goat
yū	mule

Symbols for R-controlled Sounds

ar	barn
air	chair
ear	ear
ir	fire
or	corn
ur	girl

Symbols for Variant Vowel Sounds

ah	father
aw	ball
oi	boy
oo	book
ow	cow
ü	fruit

Miscellaneous Symbols

shun	fraction
chun	question
zhun	division

Parts of an Entry

The **entry** shows how the word is spelled.

The **pronunciation** shows you how to say the word and how to break it into syllables.

The **picture** helps you understand more about the meaning of the word.

benefit
(be-nu-fit) *noun*
A **benefit** is something that is helpful.

*One **benefit** of rain is that it helps the flowers grow.*

part of speech

The **definition** gives the meaning of the word.

The **sample sentence** uses the word in a way that shows its meaning.

Page 604

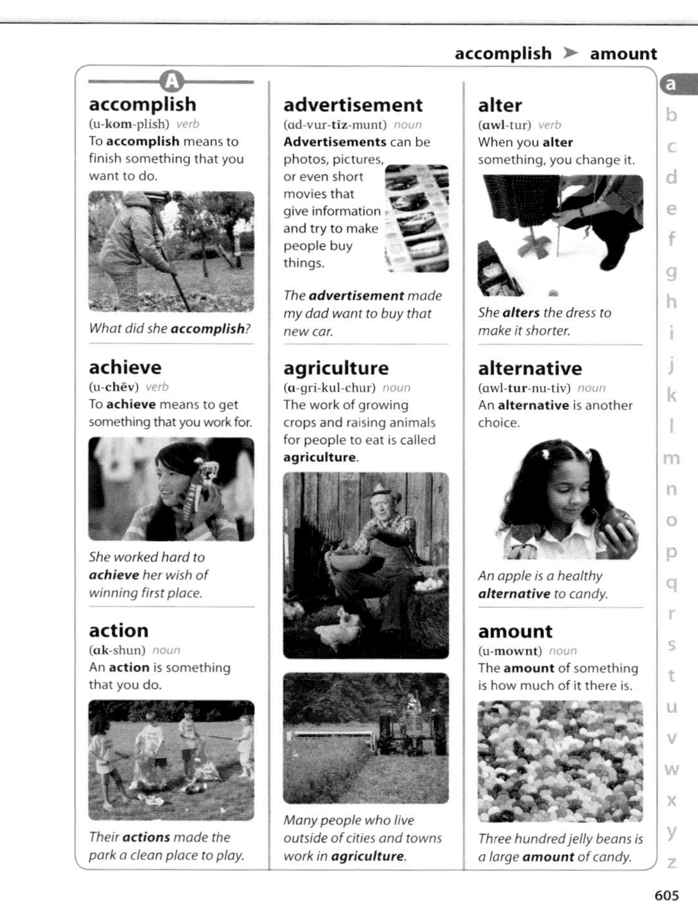

accomplish ➤ amount

A

accomplish
(u-kom-plish) *verb*
To **accomplish** means to finish something that you want to do.

*What did she **accomplish**?*

achieve
(u-chēv) *verb*
To **achieve** means to get something that you work for.

*She worked hard to **achieve** her wish of winning first place.*

action
(ak-shun) *noun*
An **action** is something that you do.

*Their **actions** made the park a clean place to play.*

advertisement
(ad-vur-tiz-munt) *noun*
Advertisements can be photos, pictures, or even short movies that give information and try to make people buy things.

*The **advertisement** made my dad want to buy that new car.*

agriculture
(a-gri-kul-chur) *noun*
The work of growing crops and raising animals for people to eat is called **agriculture**.

*Many people who live outside of cities and towns work in **agriculture**.*

alter
(awl-tur) *verb*
When you **alter** something, you change it.

*She **alters** the dress to make it shorter.*

alternative
(awl-tur-nu-tiv) *noun*
An **alternative** is another choice.

*An apple is a healthy **alternative** to candy.*

amount
(u-mownt) *noun*
The **amount** of something is how much of it there is.

*Three hundred jelly beans is a large **amount** of candy.*

a b c d e f g h i j k l m n o p q r s t u v w x y z

605

Page 605

area ➤ buyer

area
(air-ē-u) *noun*
An **area** is a part of a place.

*A classroom can have an **area** for reading.*

artist
(ar-tist) *noun*
An **artist** is someone who is skilled at drawing, painting, making things, or performing.

*This **artist** paints what she sees outdoors.*

B

balance
(ba-luns) *noun*
When things are in **balance**, they are even.

*The two sides of the scale are in **balance**.*

behavior
(bi-hā-vyur) *noun*
Behavior is what a person or animal does.

*Squirrels store nuts for the winter. It's part of their **behavior**.*

benefit
(be-nu-fit) *noun*
A **benefit** is something that is helpful.

*One **benefit** of rain is that it helps the flowers grow.*

blossom
(blah-sum) *noun*
A **blossom** is the flower of a seed plant.

*This **blossom** comes from an apple tree.*

buyer
(bi-ur) *noun*
A **buyer** is someone who gets something by paying money for it.

*He wants a **buyer** for his flowers.*

a b c d e f g h i j k l m n o p q r s t u v w x y z

606

Page 606

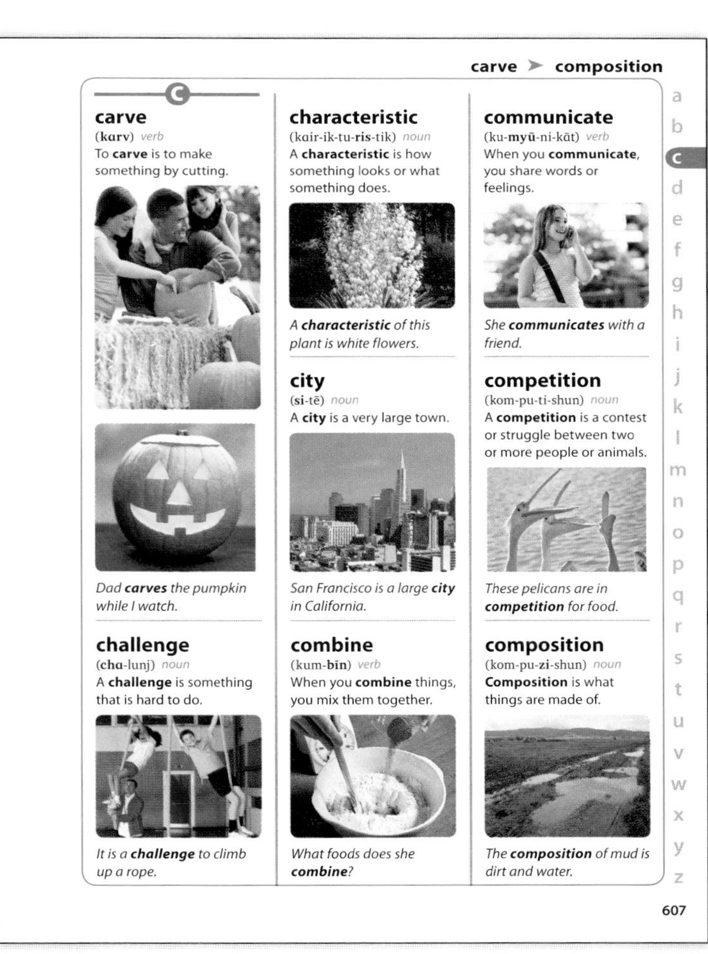

carve ➤ composition

C

carve
(karv) *verb*
To **carve** is to make something by cutting.

*Dad **carves** the pumpkin while I watch.*

challenge
(cha-lunj) *noun*
A **challenge** is something that is hard to do.

*It is a **challenge** to climb up a rope.*

characteristic
(kair-ik-tu-ris-tik) *noun*
A **characteristic** is how something looks or what something does.

*A **characteristic** of this plant is white flowers.*

city
(si-tē) *noun*
A **city** is a very large town.

*San Francisco is a large **city** in California.*

combine
(kum-bin) *verb*
When you **combine** things, you mix them together.

*What foods does she **combine**?*

communicate
(ku-myū-ni-kāt) *verb*
When you **communicate**, you share words or feelings.

*She **communicates** with a friend.*

competition
(kom-pu-ti-shun) *noun*
A **competition** is a contest or struggle between two or more people or animals.

*These pelicans are in **competition** for food.*

composition
(kom-pu-zi-shun) *noun*
Composition is what things are made of.

*The **composition** of mud is dirt and water.*

a b c d e f g h i j k l m n o p q r s t u v w x y z

607

Page 607

Anthology Picture Dictionary, continued

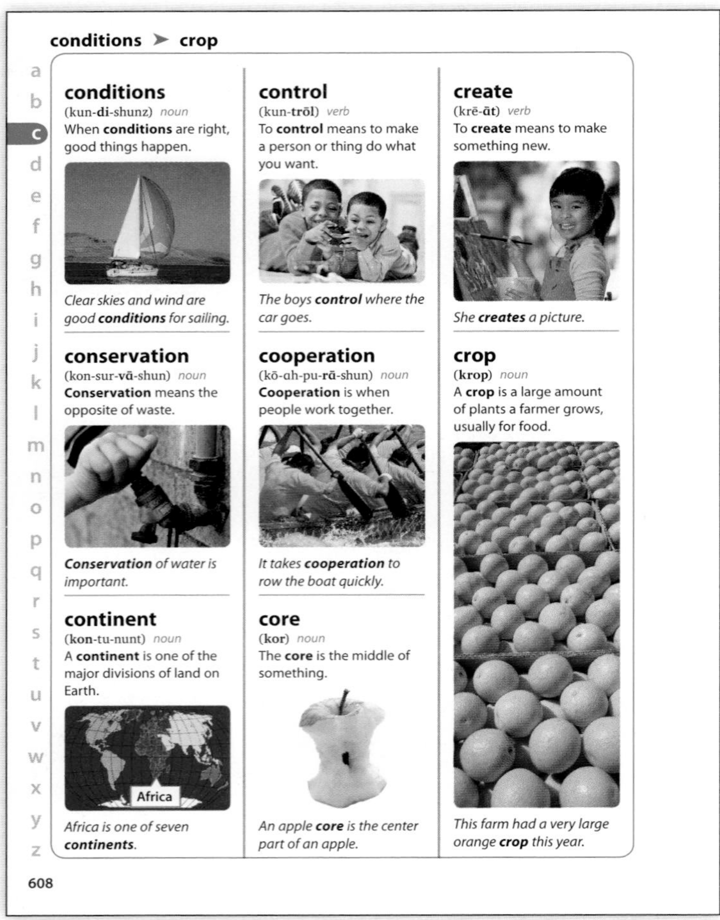

conditions ➤ crop

conditions
(**kun-di**-shunz) *noun*
When **conditions** are right, good things happen.

*Clear skies and wind are good **conditions** for sailing.*

control
(kun-**trōl**) *verb*
To **control** means to make a person or thing do what you want.

*The boys **control** where the car goes.*

create
(krē-**āt**) *verb*
To **create** means to make something new.

*She **creates** a picture.*

conservation
(kon-sur-**vā**-shun) *noun*
Conservation means the opposite of waste.

***Conservation** of water is important.*

cooperation
(kō-ah-pu-**rā**-shun) *noun*
Cooperation is when people work together.

*It takes **cooperation** to row the boat quickly.*

crop
(**krop**) *noun*
A **crop** is a large amount of plants a farmer grows, usually for food.

*This farm had a very large orange **crop** this year.*

continent
(**kon**-tu-nunt) *noun*
A **continent** is one of the major divisions of land on Earth.

*Africa is one of seven **continents**.*

core
(**kor**) *noun*
The **core** is the middle of something.

*An apple **core** is the center part of an apple.*

a b c d e f g h i j k l m n o p q r s t u v w x y z

608

Page 608

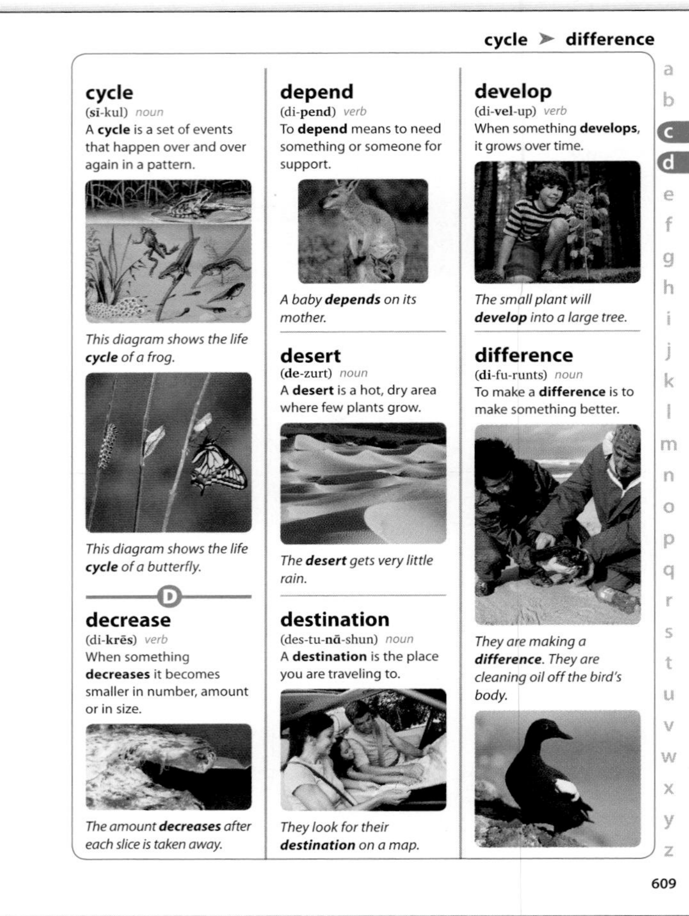

cycle ➤ difference

cycle
(**sī**-kul) *noun*
A **cycle** is a set of events that happen over and over again in a pattern.

*This diagram shows the life **cycle** of a frog.*

*This diagram shows the life **cycle** of a butterfly.*

depend
(di-**pend**) *verb*
To **depend** means to need something or someone for support.

*A baby **depends** on its mother.*

develop
(di-**vel**-up) *verb*
When something **develops**, it grows over time.

*The small plant will **develop** into a large tree.*

desert
(**de**-zurt) *noun*
A **desert** is a hot, dry area where few plants grow.

*The **desert** gets very little rain.*

difference
(**di**-fu-runts) *noun*
To make a **difference** is to make something better.

*They are making a **difference**. They are cleaning oil off the bird's body.*

D

decrease
(di-**krēs**) *verb*
When something **decreases** it becomes smaller in number, amount or in size.

*The amount **decreases** after each slice is taken away.*

destination
(des-tu-**nā**-shun) *noun*
A **destination** is the place you are traveling to.

*They look for their **destination** on a map.*

a b c d e f g h i j k l m n o p q r s t u v w x y z

609

Page 609

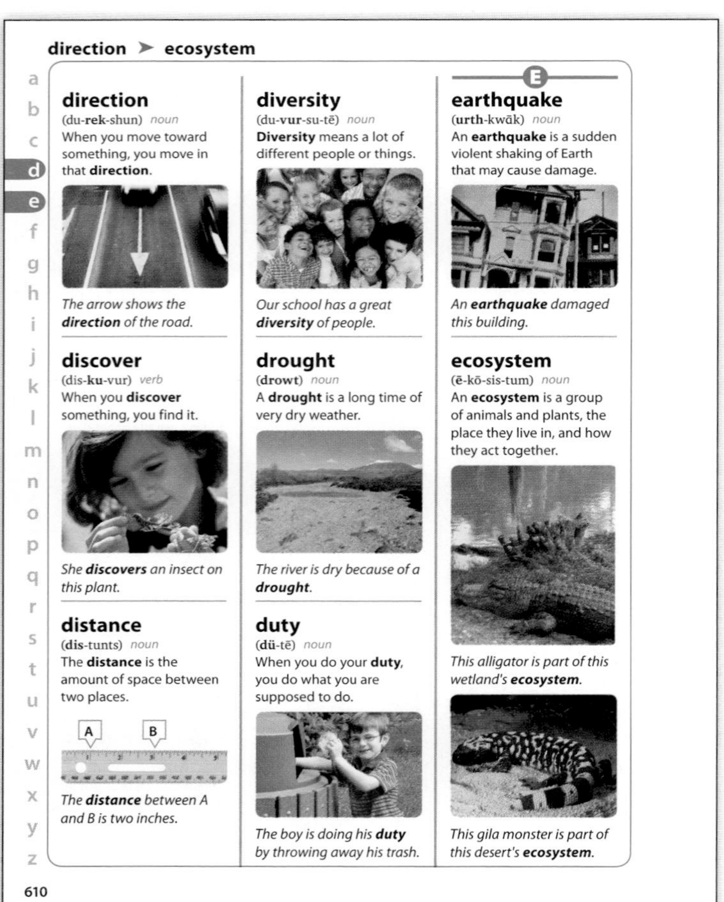

direction ➤ ecosystem

direction
(du-**rek**-shun) *noun*
When you move toward something, you move in that **direction**.

*The arrow shows the **direction** of the road.*

diversity
(du-**vur**-su-tē) *noun*
Diversity means a lot of different people or things.

*Our school has a great **diversity** of people.*

E

earthquake
(**urth**-kwāk) *noun*
An **earthquake** is a sudden violent shaking of Earth that may cause damage.

*An **earthquake** damaged this building.*

discover
(dis-**ku**-vur) *verb*
When you **discover** something, you find it.

*She **discovers** an insect on this plant.*

drought
(**drowt**) *noun*
A **drought** is a long time of very dry weather.

*The river is dry because of a **drought**.*

ecosystem
(**ē**-kō-sis-tum) *noun*
An **ecosystem** is a group of animals and plants, the place they live in, and how they act together.

*This alligator is part of this wetland's **ecosystem**.*

*This gila monster is part of this desert's **ecosystem**.*

distance
(**dis**-tunts) *noun*
The **distance** is the amount of space between two places.

*The **distance** between A and B is two inches.*

duty
(**dü**-tē) *noun*
When you do your **duty**, you do what you are supposed to do.

*The boy is doing his **duty** by throwing away his trash.*

a b c d e f g h i j k l m n o p q r s t u v w x y z

610

Page 610

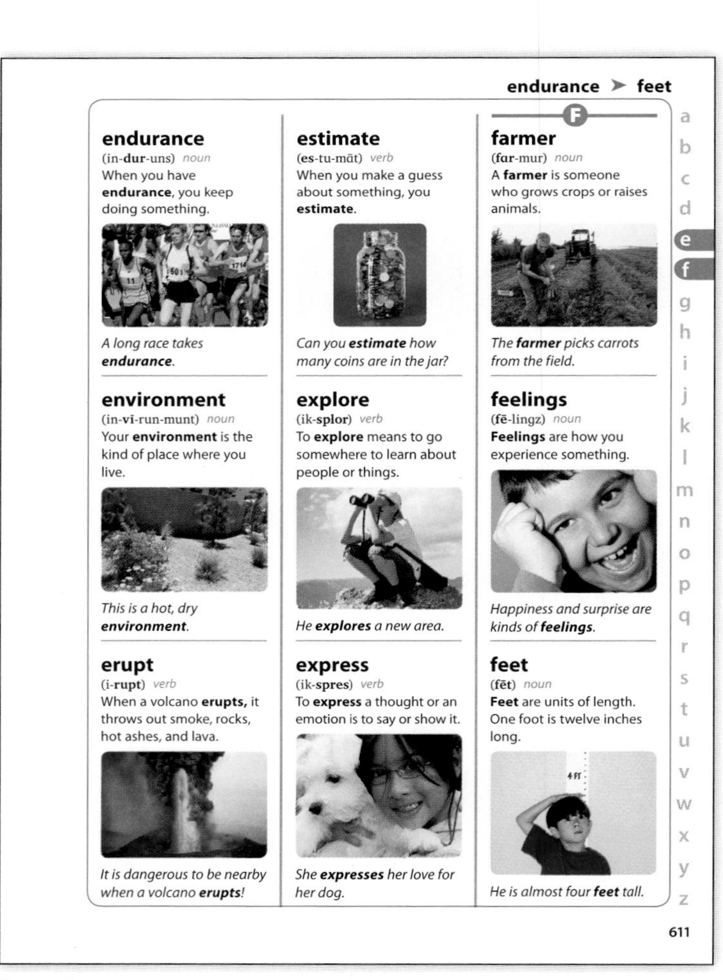

endurance ➤ feet

endurance
(in-**dur**-uns) *noun*
When you have **endurance**, you keep doing something.

*A long race takes **endurance**.*

estimate
(**es**-tu-māt) *verb*
When you make a guess about something, you **estimate**.

*Can you **estimate** how many coins are in the jar?*

F

farmer
(**far**-mur) *noun*
A **farmer** is someone who grows crops or raises animals.

*The **farmer** picks carrots from the field.*

environment
(in-**vī**-run-munt) *noun*
Your **environment** is the kind of place where you live.

*This is a hot, dry **environment**.*

explore
(ik-**splor**) *verb*
To **explore** means to go somewhere to learn about people or things.

*He **explores** a new area.*

feelings
(**fē**-lingz) *noun*
Feelings are how you experience something.

*Happiness and surprise are kinds of **feelings**.*

erupt
(i-**rupt**) *verb*
When a volcano **erupts**, it throws out smoke, rocks, hot ashes, and lava.

*It is dangerous to be nearby when a volcano **erupts**!*

express
(ik-**spres**) *verb*
To **express** a thought or an emotion is to say or show it.

*She **expresses** her love for her dog.*

feet
(**fēt**) *noun*
Feet are units of length. One foot is twelve inches long.

*He is almost four **feet** tall.*

a b c d e f g h i j k l m n o p q r s t u v w x y z

611

Page 611

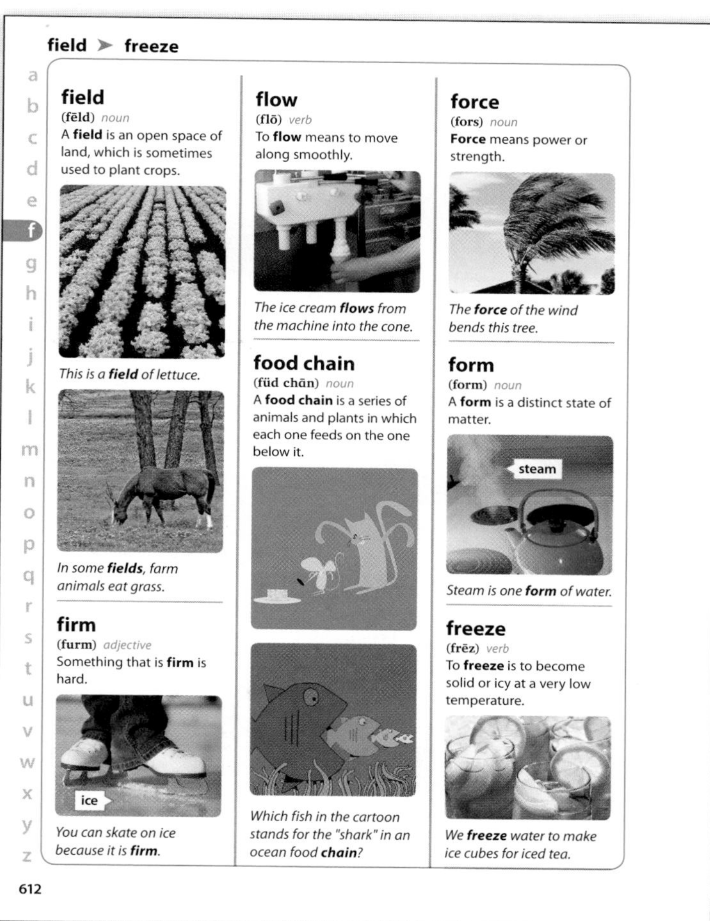

field
(fēld) *noun*
A **field** is an open space of land, which is sometimes used to plant crops.

*This is a **field** of lettuce.*

*In some **fields**, farm animals eat grass.*

firm
(furm) *adjective*
Something that is **firm** is hard.

*You can skate on ice because it is **firm**.*

flow
(flō) *verb*
To **flow** means to move along smoothly.

*The ice cream **flows** from the machine into the cone.*

food chain
(fūd chān) *noun*
A **food chain** is a series of animals and plants in which each one feeds on the one below it.

*Which fish in the cartoon stands for the "shark" in an ocean food **chain**?*

force
(fors) *noun*
Force means power or strength.

*The **force** of the wind bends this tree.*

form
(form) *noun*
A **form** is a distinct state of matter.

*Steam is one **form** of water.*

freeze
(frēz) *verb*
To **freeze** is to become solid or icy at a very low temperature.

*We **freeze** water to make ice cubes for iced tea.*

Page 612

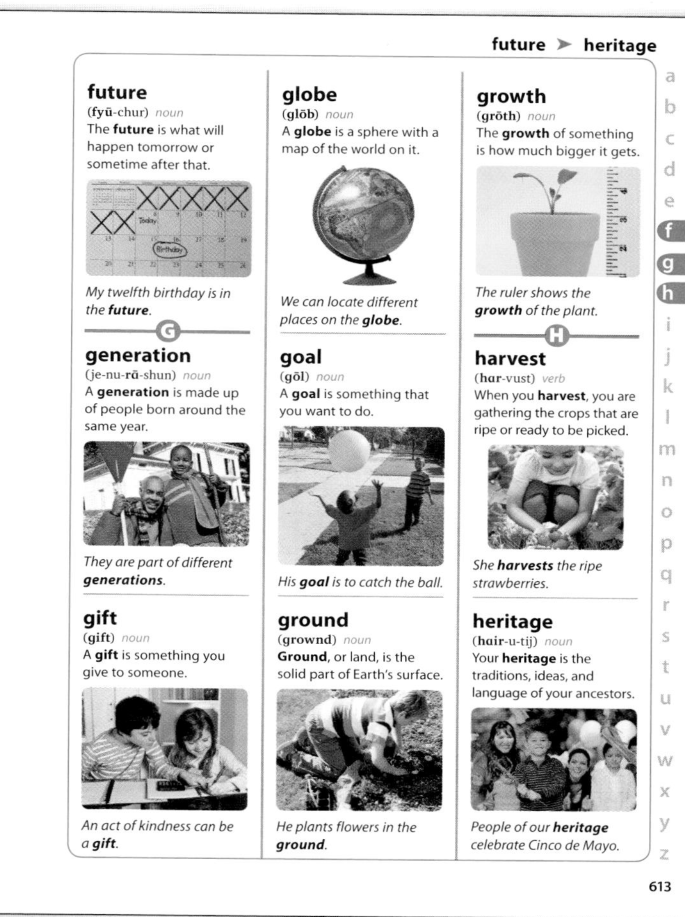

future
(fyū-chur) *noun*
The **future** is what will happen tomorrow or sometime after that.

*My twelfth birthday is in the **future**.*

G

generation
(je-nu-rā-shun) *noun*
A **generation** is made up of people born around the same year.

*They are part of different **generations**.*

gift
(gift) *noun*
A **gift** is something you give to someone.

*An act of kindness can be a **gift**.*

globe
(glōb) *noun*
A **globe** is a sphere with a map of the world on it.

*We can locate different places on the **globe**.*

goal
(gōl) *noun*
A **goal** is something that you want to do.

*His **goal** is to catch the ball.*

ground
(grownd) *noun*
Ground, or land, is the solid part of Earth's surface.

*He plants flowers in the **ground**.*

growth
(grōth) *noun*
The **growth** of something is how much bigger it gets.

*The ruler shows the **growth** of the plant.*

H

harvest
(har-vust) *verb*
When you **harvest**, you are gathering the crops that are ripe or ready to be picked.

*She **harvests** the ripe strawberries.*

heritage
(hair-u-tij) *noun*
Your **heritage** is the traditions, ideas, and language of your ancestors.

*People of our **heritage** celebrate Cinco de Mayo.*

Page 613

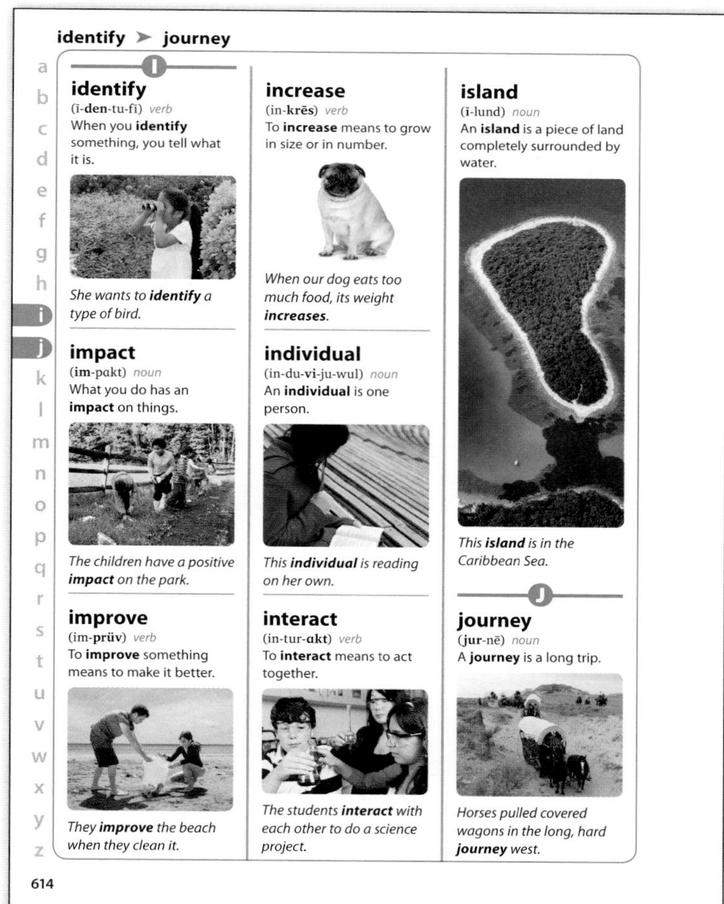

I

identify
(i-den-tu-fī) *verb*
When you **identify** something, you tell what it is.

*She wants to **identify** a type of bird.*

impact
(im-pakt) *noun*
What you do has an **impact** on things.

*The children have a positive **impact** on the park.*

improve
(im-prūv) *verb*
To **improve** something means to make it better.

*They **improve** the beach when they clean it.*

increase
(in-krēs) *verb*
To **increase** means to grow in size or in number.

*When our dog eats too much food, its weight **increases**.*

individual
(in-du-vi-ju-wul) *noun*
An **individual** is one person.

*This **individual** is reading on her own.*

interact
(in-tur-akt) *verb*
To **interact** means to act together.

*The students **interact** with each other to do a science project.*

island
(ī-lund) *noun*
An **island** is a piece of land completely surrounded by water.

*This **island** is in the Caribbean Sea.*

J

journey
(jur-nē) *noun*
A **journey** is a long trip.

*Horses pulled covered wagons in the long, hard **journey** west.*

Page 614

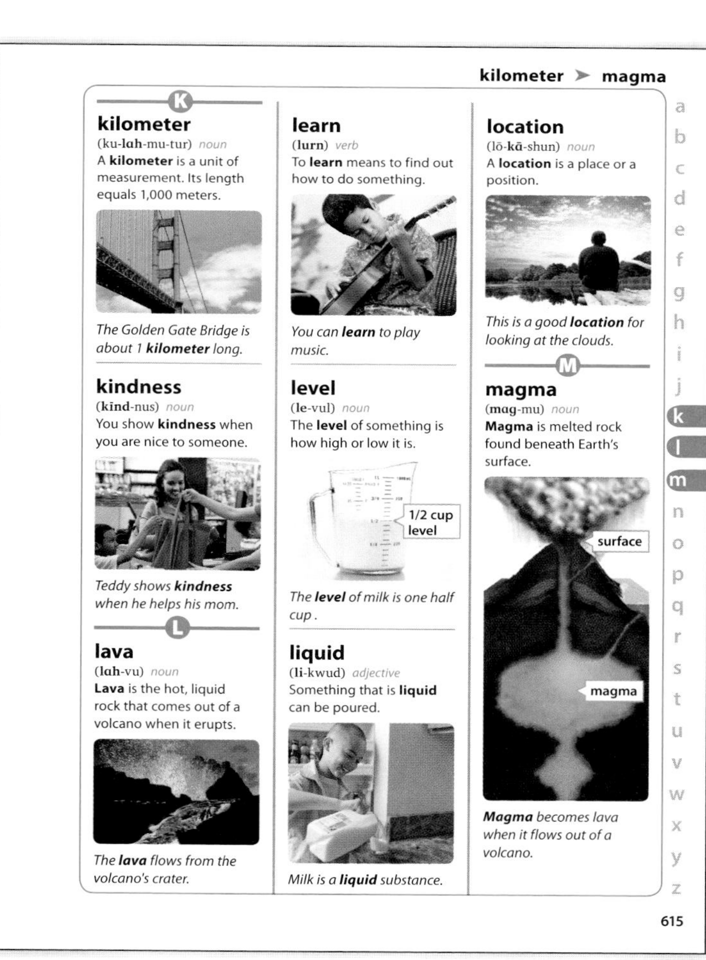

K

kilometer
(ku-lah-mu-tur) *noun*
A **kilometer** is a unit of measurement. Its length equals 1,000 meters.

*The Golden Gate Bridge is about 1 **kilometer** long.*

kindness
(kind-nus) *noun*
You show **kindness** when you are nice to someone.

*Teddy shows **kindness** when he helps his mom.*

L

lava
(lah-vu) *noun*
Lava is the hot, liquid rock that comes out of a volcano when it erupts.

*The **lava** flows from the volcano's crater.*

learn
(lurn) *verb*
To **learn** means to find out how to do something.

*You can **learn** to play music.*

level
(le-vul) *noun*
The **level** of something is how high or low it is.

*The **level** of milk is one half cup .*

liquid
(li-kwud) *adjective*
Something that is **liquid** can be poured.

*Milk is a **liquid** substance.*

location
(lō-kā-shun) *noun*
A **location** is a place or a position.

*This is a good **location** for looking at the clouds.*

M

magma
(mag-mu) *noun*
Magma is melted rock found beneath Earth's surface.

***Magma** becomes lava when it flows out of a volcano.*

Page 615

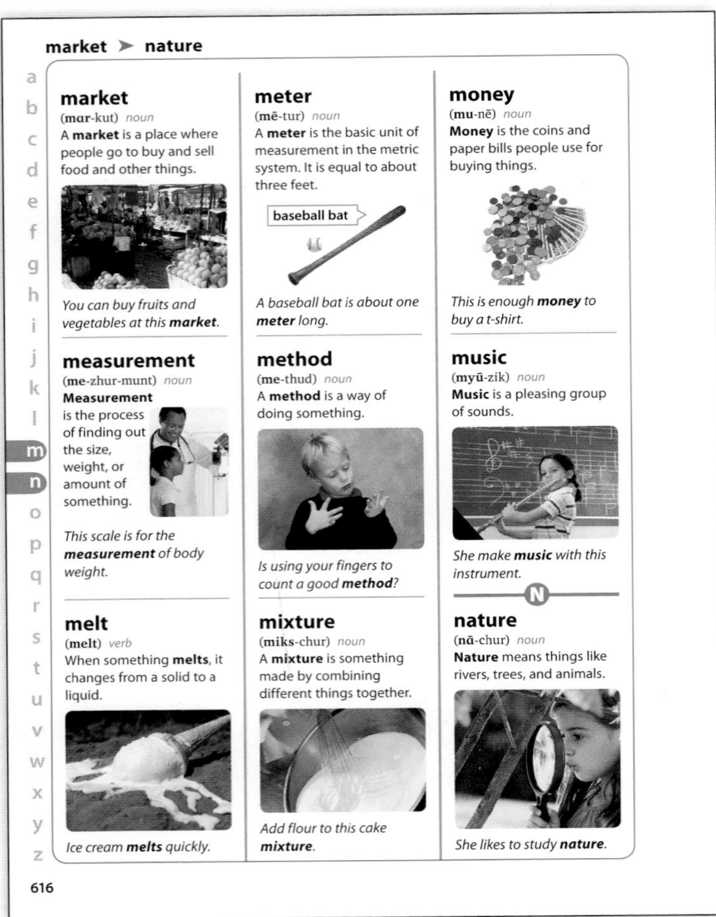

market
(mar-kut) *noun*
A **market** is a place where people go to buy and sell food and other things.

*You can buy fruits and vegetables at this **market**.*

measurement
(me-zhur-munt) *noun*
Measurement is the process of finding out the size, weight, or amount of something.

*This scale is for the **measurement** of body weight.*

melt
(melt) *verb*
When something **melts**, it changes from a solid to a liquid.

*Ice cream **melts** quickly.*

meter
(mē-tur) *noun*
A **meter** is the basic unit of measurement in the metric system. It is equal to about three feet.

*A baseball bat is about one **meter** long.*

method
(me-thud) *noun*
A **method** is a way of doing something.

*Is using your fingers to count a good **method**?*

mixture
(miks-chur) *noun*
A **mixture** is something made by combining different things together.

*Add flour to this cake **mixture**.*

money
(mu-nē) *noun*
Money is the coins and paper bills people use for buying things.

*This is enough **money** to buy a t-shirt.*

music
(myū-zik) *noun*
Music is a pleasing group of sounds.

*She make **music** with this instrument.*

N

nature
(nā-chur) *noun*
Nature means things like rivers, trees, and animals.

*She likes to study **nature**.*

Page 616

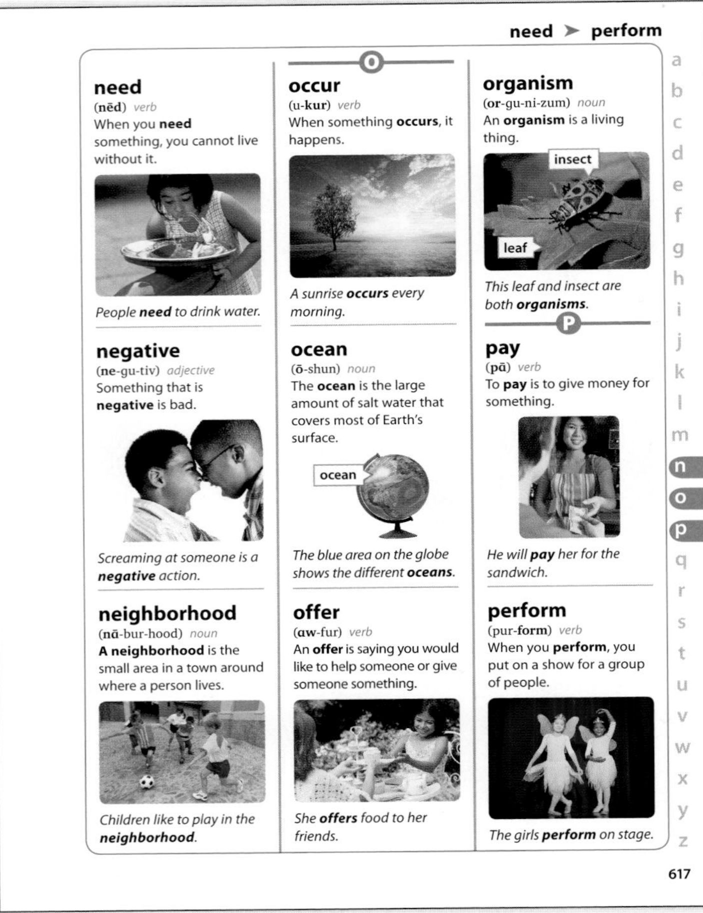

need
(nēd) *verb*
When you **need** something, you cannot live without it.

*People **need** to drink water.*

negative
(ne-gu-tiv) *adjective*
Something that is **negative** is bad.

*Screaming at someone is a **negative** action.*

neighborhood
(nā-bur-hood) *noun*
A **neighborhood** is the small area in a town around where a person lives.

*Children like to play in the **neighborhood**.*

O

occur
(u-kur) *verb*
When something **occurs**, it happens.

*A sunrise **occurs** every morning.*

ocean
(ō-shun) *noun*
The **ocean** is the large amount of salt water that covers most of Earth's surface.

*The blue area on the globe shows the different **oceans**.*

offer
(aw-fur) *verb*
An **offer** is saying you would like to help someone or give someone something.

*She **offers** food to her friends.*

organism
(or-gu-ni-zum) *noun*
An **organism** is a living thing.

*This leaf and insect are both **organisms**.*

P

pay
(pā) *verb*
To **pay** is to give money for something.

*He will **pay** her for the sandwich.*

perform
(pur-form) *verb*
When you **perform**, you put on a show for a group of people.

*The girls **perform** on stage.*

Page 617

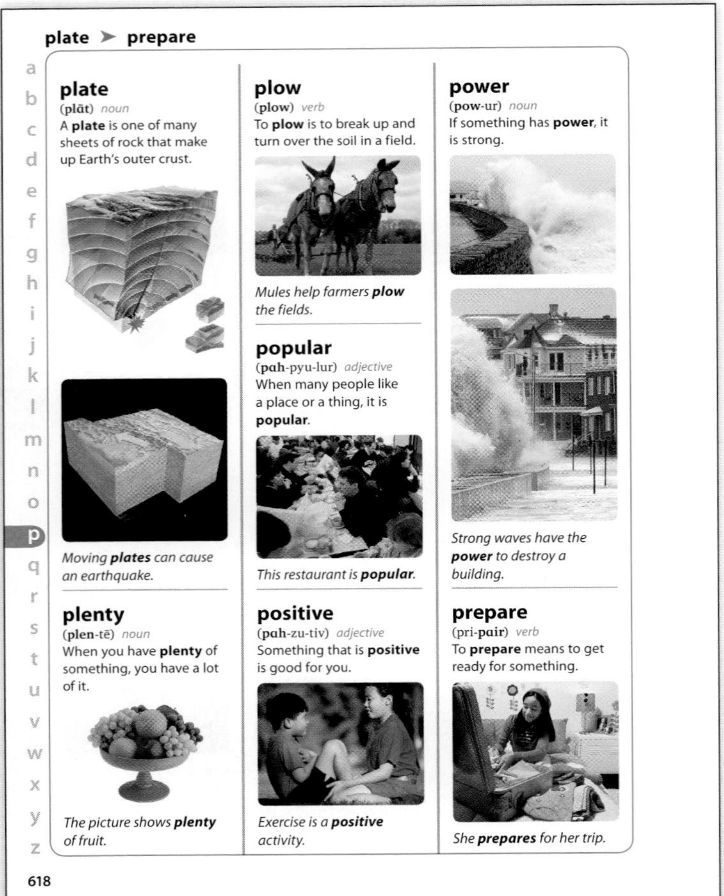

plate
(plāt) *noun*
A **plate** is one of many sheets of rock that make up Earth's outer crust.

*Moving **plates** can cause an earthquake.*

plenty
(plen-tē) *noun*
When you have **plenty** of something, you have a lot of it.

*The picture shows **plenty** of fruit.*

plow
(plow) *verb*
To **plow** is to break up and turn over the soil in a field.

*Mules help farmers **plow** the fields.*

popular
(pah-pyu-lur) *adjective*
When many people like a place or a thing, it is **popular**.

*This restaurant is **popular**.*

positive
(pah-zu-tiv) *adjective*
Something that is **positive** is good for you.

*Exercise is a **positive** activity.*

power
(pow-ur) *noun*
If something has **power**, it is strong.

*Strong waves have the **power** to destroy a building.*

prepare
(pri-pair) *verb*
To **prepare** means to get ready for something.

*She **prepares** for her trip.*

Page 618

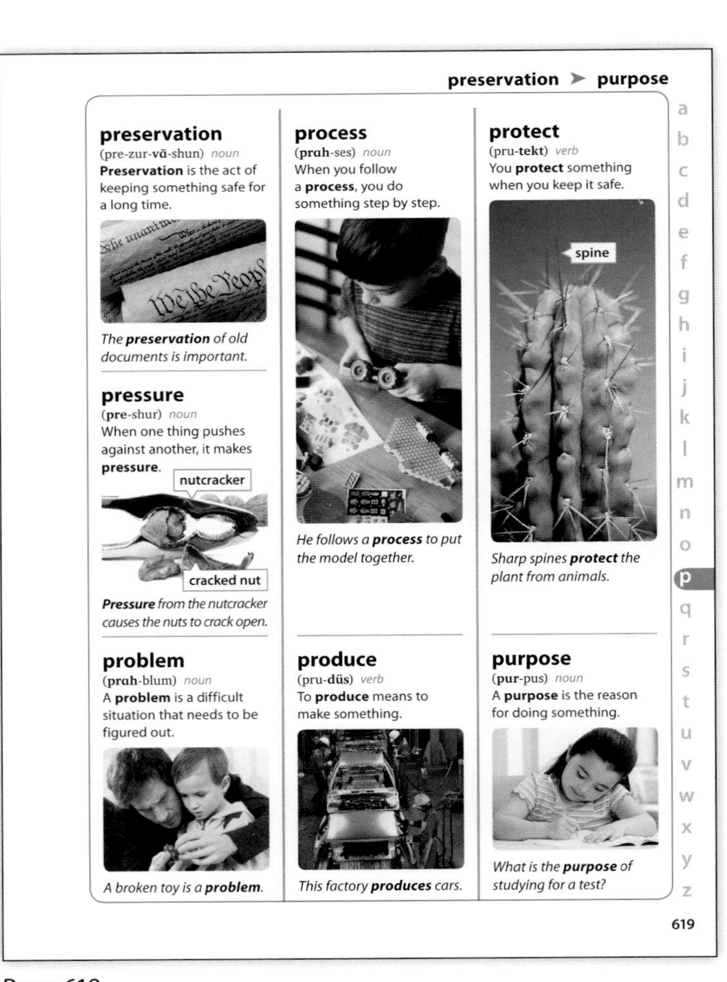

preservation
(pre-zur-vā-shun) *noun*
Preservation is the act of keeping something safe for a long time.

*The **preservation** of old documents is important.*

pressure
(pre-shur) *noun*
When one thing pushes against another, it makes **pressure**.

***Pressure** from the nutcracker causes the nuts to crack open.*

problem
(prah-blum) *noun*
A **problem** is a difficult situation that needs to be figured out.

*A broken toy is a **problem**.*

process
(prah-ses) *noun*
When you follow a **process**, you do something step by step.

*He follows a **process** to put the model together.*

produce
(pru-dūs) *verb*
To **produce** means to make something.

*This factory **produces** cars.*

protect
(pru-tekt) *verb*
You **protect** something when you keep it safe.

*Sharp spines **protect** the plant from animals.*

purpose
(pur-pus) *noun*
A **purpose** is the reason for doing something.

*What is the **purpose** of studying for a test?*

Page 619

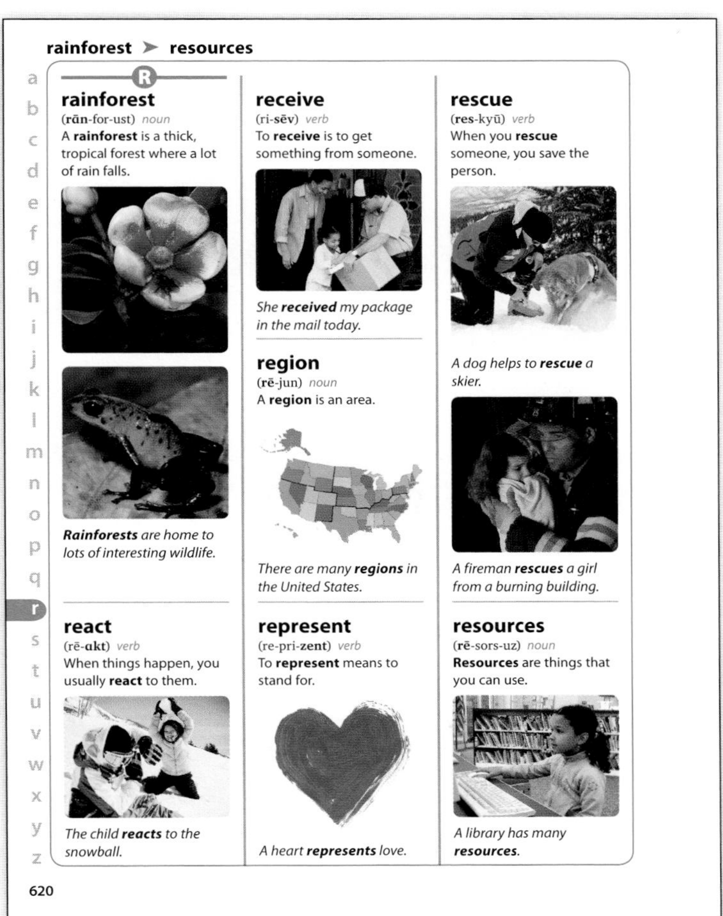

R

rainforest
(rān-for-ust) *noun*
A **rainforest** is a thick, tropical forest where a lot of rain falls.

Rainforests are home to lots of interesting wildlife.

receive
(ri-sēv) *verb*
To **receive** is to get something from someone.

*She **received** my package in the mail today.*

rescue
(res-kyū) *verb*
When you **rescue** someone, you save the person.

*A dog helps to **rescue** a skier.*

*A fireman **rescues** a girl from a burning building.*

region
(rē-jun) *noun*
A **region** is an area.

*There are many **regions** in the United States.*

react
(rē-akt) *verb*
When things happen, you usually **react** to them.

*The child **reacts** to the snowball.*

represent
(re-pri-zent) *verb*
To **represent** means to stand for.

*A heart **represents** love.*

resources
(rē-sors-uz) *noun*
Resources are things that you can use.

*A library has many **resources**.*

Page 620

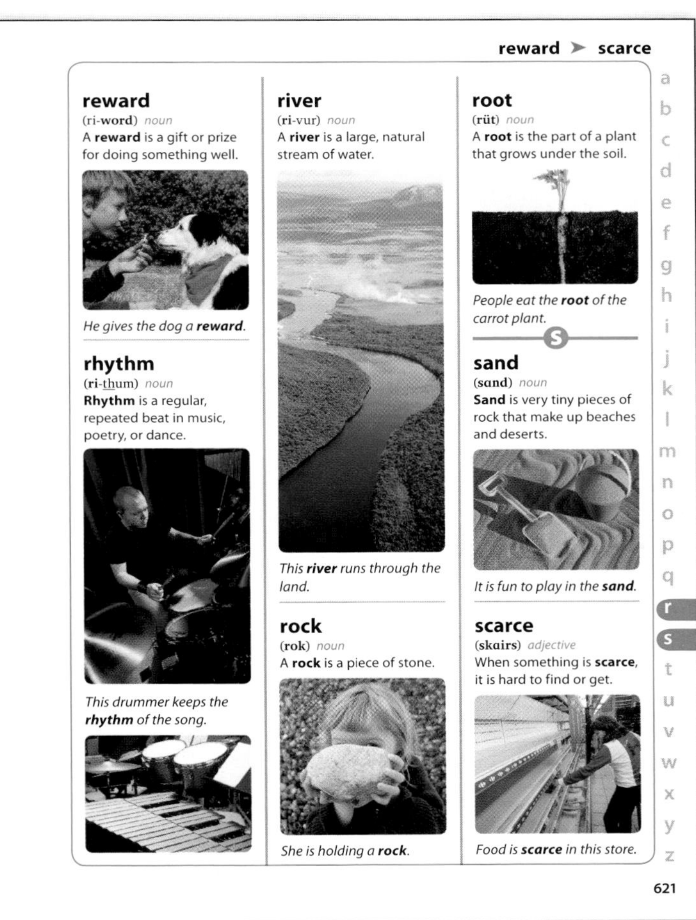

reward
(ri-word) *noun*
A **reward** is a gift or prize for doing something well.

*He gives the dog a **reward**.*

rhythm
(ri-thum) *noun*
Rhythm is a regular, repeated beat in music, poetry, or dance.

*This drummer keeps the **rhythm** of the song.*

river
(ri-vur) *noun*
A **river** is a large, natural stream of water.

*This **river** runs through the land.*

rock
(rok) *noun*
A **rock** is a piece of stone.

*She is holding a **rock**.*

root
(rüt) *noun*
A **root** is the part of a plant that grows under the soil.

*People eat the **root** of the carrot plant.*

S

sand
(sand) *noun*
Sand is very tiny pieces of rock that make up beaches and deserts.

*It is fun to play in the **sand**.*

scarce
(skairs) *adjective*
When something is **scarce**, it is hard to find or get.

*Food is **scarce** in this store.*

Page 621

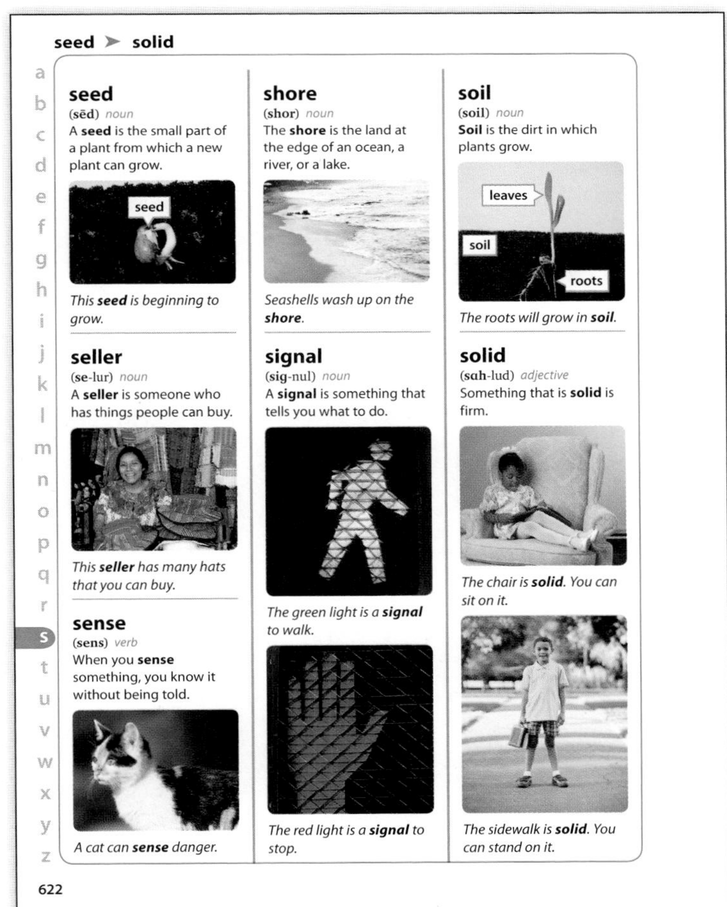

seed
(sēd) *noun*
A **seed** is the small part of a plant from which a new plant can grow.

*This **seed** is beginning to grow.*

seller
(se-lur) *noun*
A **seller** is someone who has things people can buy.

*This **seller** has many hats that you can buy.*

sense
(sens) *verb*
When you **sense** something, you know it without being told.

*A cat can **sense** danger.*

shore
(shor) *noun*
The **shore** is the land at the edge of an ocean, a river, or a lake.

*Seashells wash up on the **shore**.*

signal
(sig-nul) *noun*
A **signal** is something that tells you what to do.

*The green light is a **signal** to walk.*

*The red light is a **signal** to stop.*

soil
(soil) *noun*
Soil is the dirt in which plants grow.

*The roots will grow in **soil**.*

solid
(sah-lud) *adjective*
Something that is **solid** is firm.

*The chair is **solid**. You can sit on it.*

*The sidewalk is **solid**. You can stand on it.*

Page 622

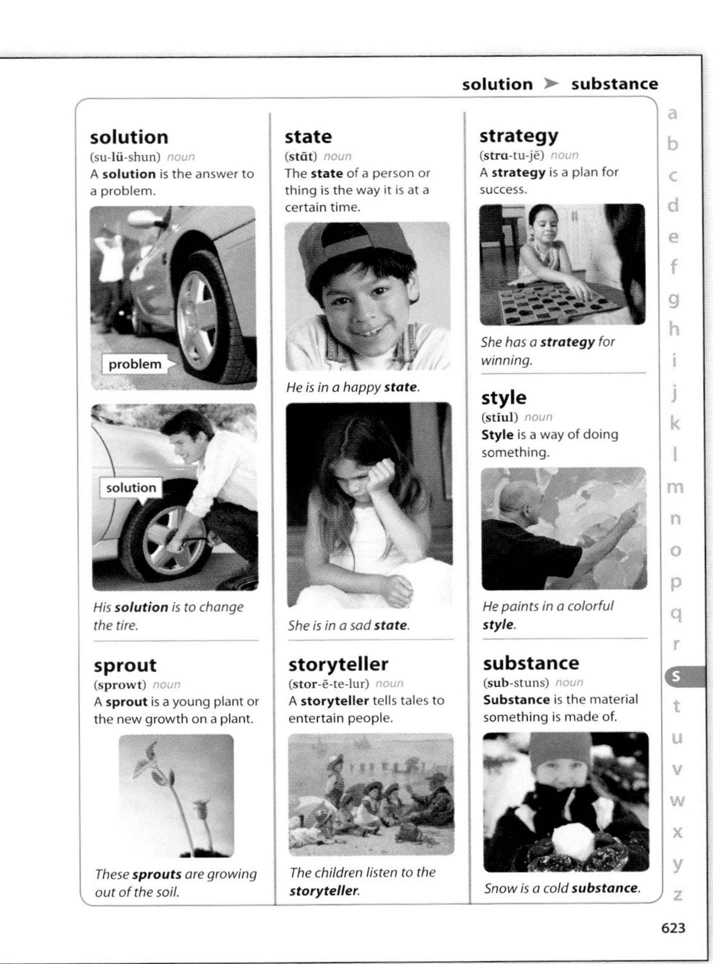

solution
(su-lü-shun) *noun*
A **solution** is the answer to a problem.

*His **solution** is to change the tire.*

sprout
(sprout) *noun*
A **sprout** is a young plant or the new growth on a plant.

*These **sprouts** are growing out of the soil.*

state
(stāt) *noun*
The **state** of a person or thing is the way it is at a certain time.

*He is in a happy **state**.*

*She is in a sad **state**.*

storyteller
(stor-ē-te-lur) *noun*
A **storyteller** tells tales to entertain people.

*The children listen to the **storyteller**.*

strategy
(stra-tu-jē) *noun*
A **strategy** is a plan for success.

*She has a **strategy** for winning.*

style
(stiul) *noun*
Style is a way of doing something.

*He paints in a colorful **style**.*

substance
(sub-stuns) *noun*
Substance is the material something is made of.

*Snow is a cold **substance**.*

Page 623

Anthology Picture Dictionary, continued

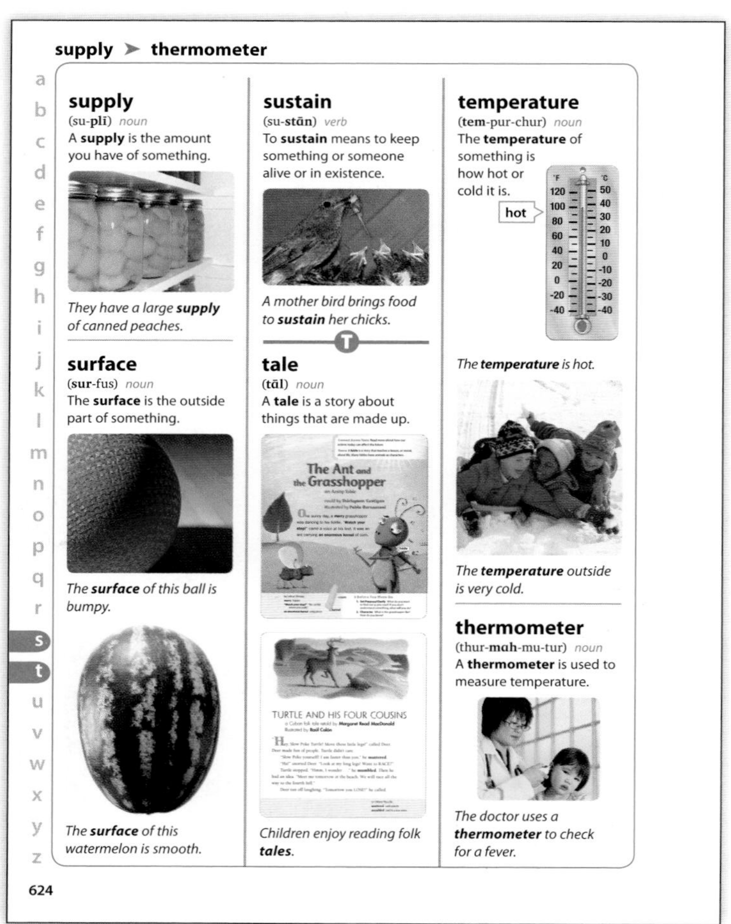

supply
(su-plī) *noun*
A **supply** is the amount you have of something.

*They have a large **supply** of canned peaches.*

surface
(sur-fus) *noun*
The **surface** is the outside part of something.

*The **surface** of this ball is bumpy.*

*The **surface** of this watermelon is smooth.*

sustain
(su-stān) *verb*
To **sustain** means to keep something or someone alive or in existence.

*A mother bird brings food to **sustain** her chicks.*

T

tale
(tāl) *noun*
A **tale** is a story about things that are made up.

*Children enjoy reading folk **tales**.*

temperature
(tem-pur-chur) *noun*
The **temperature** of something is how hot or cold it is.

*The **temperature** is hot.*

*The **temperature** outside is very cold.*

thermometer
(thur-mah-mu-tur) *noun*
A **thermometer** is used to measure temperature.

*The doctor uses a **thermometer** to check for a fever.*

Page 624

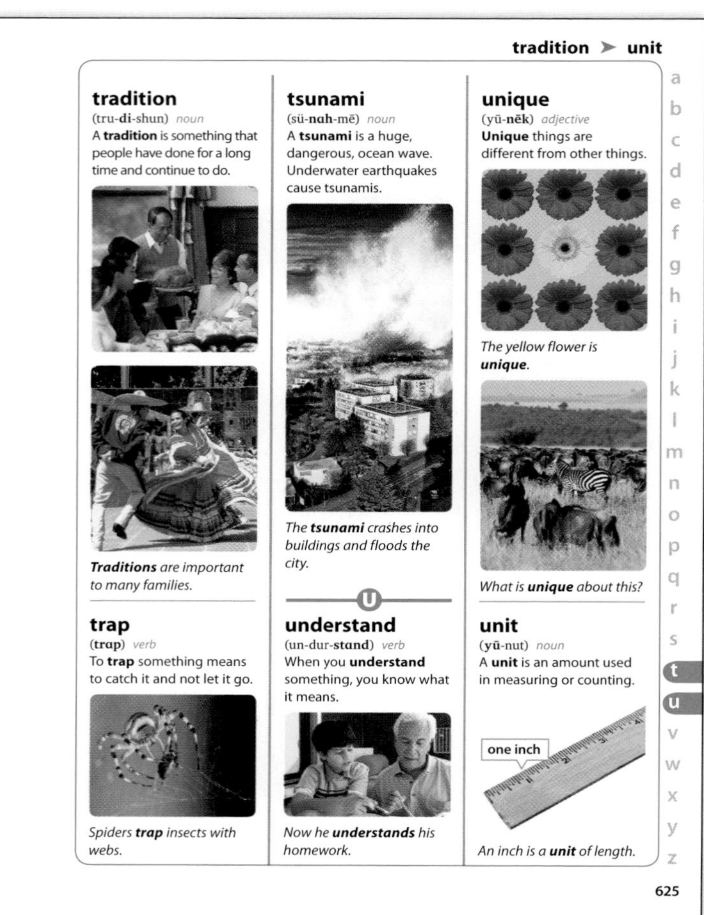

tradition
(tru-di-shun) *noun*
A **tradition** is something that people have done for a long time and continue to do.

***Traditions** are important to many families.*

trap
(trap) *verb*
To **trap** something means to catch it and not let it go.

*Spiders **trap** insects with webs.*

tsunami
(sü-nah-mē) *noun*
A **tsunami** is a huge, dangerous, ocean wave. Underwater earthquakes cause tsunamis.

*The **tsunami** crashes into buildings and floods the city.*

U

understand
(un-dur-stand) *verb*
When you **understand** something, you know what it means.

*Now he **understands** his homework.*

unique
(yū-nēk) *adjective*
Unique things are different from other things.

*The yellow flower is **unique**.*

*What is **unique** about this?*

unit
(yū-nut) *noun*
A **unit** is an amount used in measuring or counting.

*An inch is a **unit** of length.*

Page 625

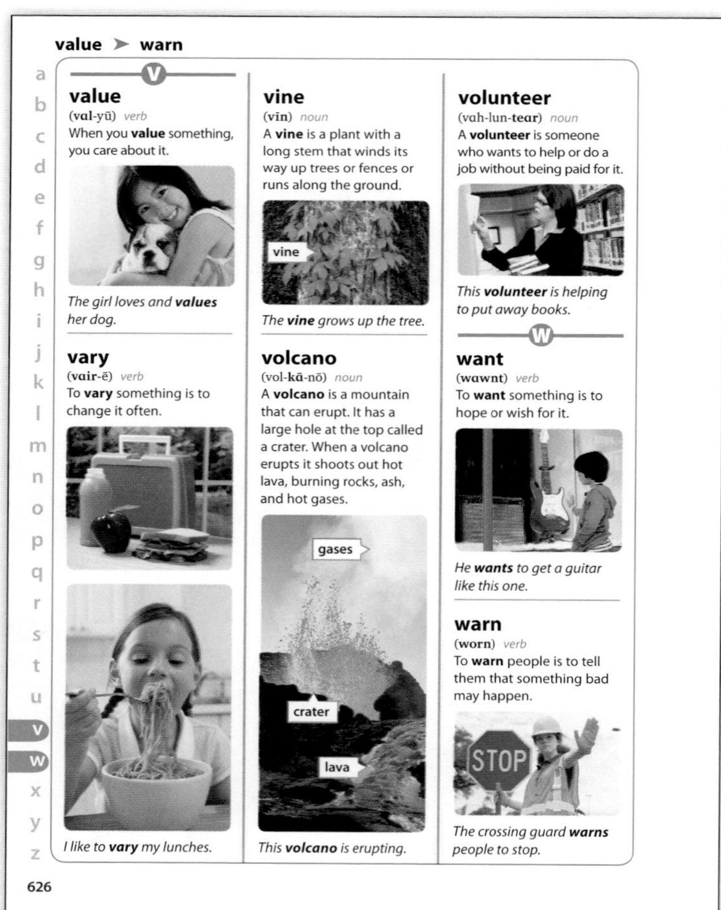

V

value
(val-yū) *verb*
When you **value** something, you care about it.

*The girl loves and **values** her dog.*

vary
(vair-ē) *verb*
To **vary** something is to change it often.

*I like to **vary** my lunches.*

vine
(vīn) *noun*
A **vine** is a plant with a long stem that winds its way up trees or fences or runs along the ground.

*The **vine** grows up the tree.*

volcano
(vol-kā-nō) *noun*
A **volcano** is a mountain that can erupt. It has a large hole at the top called a crater. When a volcano erupts it shoots out hot lava, burning rocks, ash, and hot gases.

*This **volcano** is erupting.*

volunteer
(vah-lun-tear) *noun*
A **volunteer** is someone who wants to help or do a job without being paid for it.

*This **volunteer** is helping to put away books.*

W

want
(wawnt) *verb*
To **want** something is to hope or wish for it.

*He **wants** to get a guitar like this one.*

warn
(worn) *verb*
To **warn** people is to tell them that something bad may happen.

*The crossing guard **warns** people to stop.*

Page 626

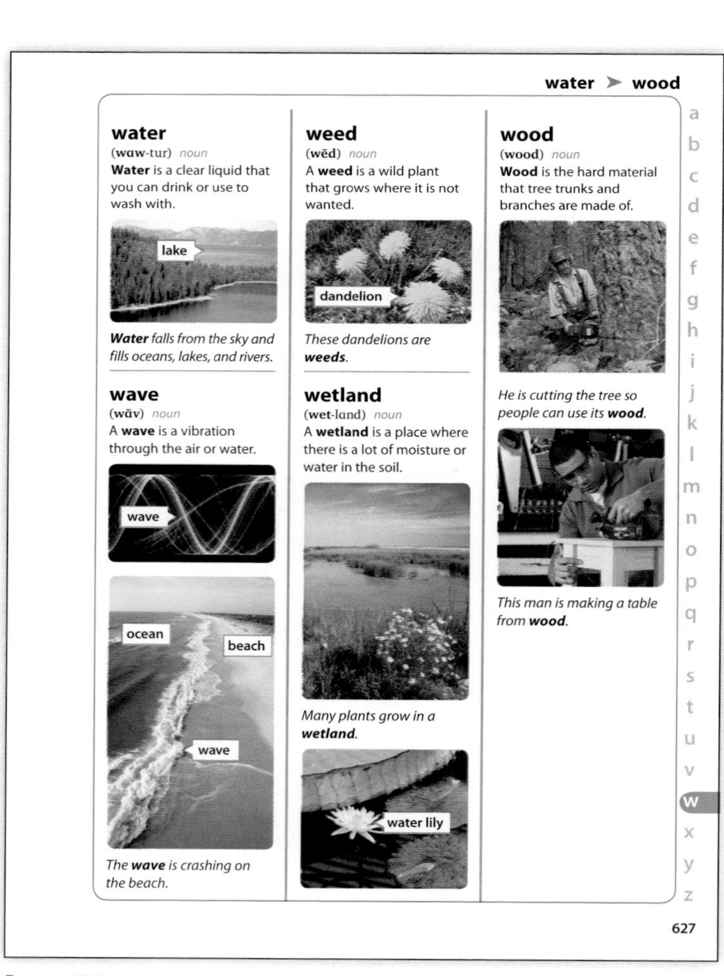

water
(waw-tur) *noun*
Water is a clear liquid that you can drink or use to wash with.

***Water** falls from the sky and fills oceans, lakes, and rivers.*

wave
(wāv) *noun*
A **wave** is a vibration through the air or water.

*The **wave** is crashing on the beach.*

weed
(wēd) *noun*
A **weed** is a wild plant that grows where it is not wanted.

*These dandelions are **weeds**.*

wetland
(wet-land) *noun*
A **wetland** is a place where there is a lot of moisture or water in the soil.

*Many plants grow in a **wetland**.*

wood
(wood) *noun*
Wood is the hard material that tree trunks and branches are made of.

*He is cutting the tree so people can use its **wood**.*

*This man is making a table from **wood**.*

Page 627

Anthology Index

Index

Page 628

Page 629

Index, continued

Page 630

Page 631

Page 632

Page 633

Page 634

Page 635

Index, continued

Index, continued

Page 640

Index of Authors

Index of Illustrators

Page 641

Research Base and Bibliography

Language and Literacy

Asher, J., & Price, B. (1967). The learning strategy of total physical response: Some age differences. *Child Development*, 38, 1219–1227.

Asher, J. (1969). The total physical response approach to second language learning. The Modern Language Journal, 53, 1.

Au, K. (2006). *Multicultural issues and literacy achievement.* Mahwah, NJ: Lawrence Erlbaum.

August, D., & Hakuta, K. (1998). *Educating language-minority children.* Washington, DC: National Research Council.

August, D., & Shanahan, T. (Eds.). (2006). *Developing literacy in second-language learners: Report of the National Literacy Panel on Language-Minority Children and Youth.* Mahwah, NJ: Erlbaum.

August, D. L., & Shanahan, T. (2006). Synthesis: Instruction and professional development. In D. L. August & T. Shanahan (Eds.), *Developing literacy in a second language: Report of the National Literacy Panel.* Mahwah, NJ: Lawrence Erlbaum Associates.

Bailey, A. (Ed.). (2006). *The language demands of school: Putting academic English to the test.* New Haven, CT: Yale University Press.

Bauman, J. F., Russell, N.S., & Jones, L. A. (1992). Effects of think-aloud instruction on elementary students' comprehension abilities. *Journal of Reading Behavior*, 24 (2), 143–172.

Berg, C. (1999). The effects of trained peer response on esl students' revision types and writing quality. *Journal of Second Language Writing,* 8 (3), 215–241.

Bicais, J., & Correira, M. G. (2008). Peer-learning spaces: A staple in the English learner's tool kit for developing language and literacy. *Journal of Research in Childhood Education,* 22(4), 363–375.

Biemiller, A. (1999). *Language and reading success.* Newton Upper Falls, MA: Brookline Books.

Blum-Kulka, S., & Snow, C. E. (2004). Introduction: The potential of peer talk. *Discourse Studies,* 6(3), 291–306.

Brice, A., & Roseberry-McKibben, C. (1999). Turning frustration into success for English language learners. *Educational Leadership,* 56(7), 53–55.

Brown, A., Campoine, J., and Day, J. (1981). Learning to learn: On training students to learn from texts. *Educational Researcher,* 10, 14–24.

Bruner, J., Goodnow, J, & Austin, G. A. (1967). *A study of thinking.* New York: Science Editions.

Callow, J. (2008, May). Show me: principles for assessing students' visual literacy. *The Reading Teacher,* 61(8), 616–626.

Celce-Murcia, M., Brinton, D., & Goodwin, J. (1996). *Teaching pronunciation: A reference for teachers of English to speakers of other languages.* Cambridge: Cambridge University Press.

Chamot, A. U., & O'Malley, J. M. (1994) *The calla handbook: implementing the cognitive academic language learning approach.* White Plains, NY: Addison Wesley Longman.

Collier, V. P. (1995). *Promoting academic success for ESL students: Understanding second language acquisition for school.* Elizabeth, NJ: New Jersey Teachers of English to Speakers of Other Languages-Bilingual Educators.

Collier, V. P., & Thomas, W. P. (1989). How quickly can immigrants become proficient in school English? *Journal of Educational Issues of Language Minority Students,* 5, 26–38.

Crandall, J. (Ed.). 1987. *ESL through content area instruction: mathematics, science, social studies.* Englewood Cliffs, NJ: Prentice Hall.

Cummins, J. (2000). *Language, power and pedagogy: Bilingual children in the crossfire.* Buffalo, NY: Multilingual Matters.

Cunningham-Flores, M. (1998). *Improving adult esl learners' pronunciation skills.* National Center for ESL Literacy Education.

Day, J. P. (2002). We learn from each other: Collaboration and community in a bilingual classroom. In R. Allington & P. H. Johnston (Eds.), *Reading to learn: Lessons learned from exemplary fourth-grade classrooms* (pp. 99–122). New York: Guildford Press.

Diaz-Rico, L. T., & Weed, K. Z. (2002). *The crosscultural, language, and academic development handbook: A complete K–12 reference guide.* Boston, MA: Allyn & Bacon.

Dickinson, D. K., & Tabors, P. (Eds.). (2001). *Beginning literacy with language.* Baltimore: Brookes.

Dong, Y. R. (2006/2007). Learning to think in English. *Educational Leadership, Best of 2006–2007,* 9–13.

Dressler, C. (2006). First and second-language literacy. In D. L. August & T. Shanahan (Eds.), *Developing literacy in a second language: Report of the National Literacy Panel.* Mahwah, NJ: Lawrence Erlbaum Associates.

Droop, M., & Verhoeven, L. (2003). Language proficiency and reading ability in first- and second-language learners. *Reading Research Quarterly,* 38(1), 78–103.

Dutro, S., & Moran, C. (2002), Rethinking English language instruction: An architectural approach. In G. Garcia (Ed.), *English learners reading at the highest level of English literacy.* Newark, DE: International Reading Association.

Echevarria, J., Short, D., & Vogt, M. (2008). *Making content comprehensible. The sheltered instruction observation protocol.* Boston, MA: Pearson.

Echevarria, J., Vogt, M. A., & Short, D. J. (2004). *Making content comprehensible for English learners: The SIOP model* (2nd ed.). Boston, MA: Allyn & Bacon.

Feldman, K., & Kinsella, K. (2005). *Create an active participation classroom. The CORE Reading Expert.* Retrieved from www.corelearn.com/pdfs/Newsletters/CORE%202005%20Spring%20Newsletter.pdf.

Fillmore, L. W. (2004). *The role of language in academic development.* In Excerpts from a presentation by Lily Wong Fillmore at the Closing the Achievement Gap for EL Students conference. Santa Rosa: CA: Sonoma County Office of Education. Retrieved from www.scoe.k12.ca.us/aiming_high/docs/AH_language.pdf.

Fitzgerald, J. (1995). English-as-a-second-language learners' cognitive reading processes: A review of research in the United States. *Review of Educational Research,* 65, 145–190.

Fitzgerald, J. (1993). Literacy and students who are learning English as a second language. *The Reading Teacher,* 46, 638–647.

Francis, D., Lesaux, N., & August, D. (2006). Language instruction. In D. August & T. Shanahan (Eds.), *Developing literacy in second-language learners: Report of the National Literacy Panel on Language-Minority Children and Youth* (pp. 365–413). Mahwah, NJ: Erlbaum.

Francis, D. J., Rivera, M., Lesaux, N., Kieffer, M., & Rivera, H. (2006). *Practical guidelines for the education of English language learners: Research-based recommendations for instruction and academic interventions.* Retrieved from www.centeroninstruction.org/files/ELL1-Interventions.pdf.

Gambrell, L. B., Morrow, L. M., & Pressley, M. (Eds.). (2007) *Best Practices in Literacy Instruction.* New York: Guilford.

Garcia, G., & Beltran, D. (2005) Revisioning the blueprint: Building for the academic success of English learners. In G. Garcia (Ed.). *English learners: Reaching the highest levels of English literacy.* Newark: DE: International Reading Association.

Genesee, F., Lindholm-Leary, K., Saunders, W., & Christian, D. (2006). *Educating English language learners: A synthesis of research evidence.* New York: Cambridge University Press.

Genesee, F. & Geva, E. (2006). Cross-linguistic relationships in working memory, phonological processes, and oral language. In D. L. August & T. Shanahan (Eds.), *Developing literacy in a second language: Report of the National Literacy Panel.* Mahwah, NJ: Lawrence Erlbaum Associates.

Gersten, R., & Baker, S. (2000). What we know about effective instructional practices for English-language learners. *Exceptional Children,* 66, 454–470.

Gibbons, P. (2002). *Scaffolding language, scaffolding learning: Teaching second language learners in the mainstream classroom.* Portsmouth, NH: Heinemann.

Girard, V. (2005). English learners and the language arts. In V. Girard (Ed.), *Schools moving up: A WestEd initiative.* Retrieved November 8, 2006, from www.schoolsmovingup.net/cs/wested/view/e/140

Goldenberg, C. (2006). *Improving achievement for English learners: Conclusions from 2 research reviews.* Retrieved from www.colorincolorado.org/article/12918

Goldenberg, C. (2004). *Successful school change: Creating settings to improve teaching and learning.* New York: Teachers College Press.

Goldenberg, C. (1992–1993). Instructional conversations: promoting comprehension through discussion, *The Reading Teacher,* 46 (4), 316–326.

Goldenberg, C., Rueda, R., & August, D. (2006). Sociocultural influences on the literacy attainment of language-minority children and youth. In D. August & T. Shanahan (Eds.), *Developing literacy in second-language learners: Report of the National Literacy Panel on Language-Minority Children and Youth* (pp. 269–318). Mahwah, NJ: Erlbaum.

High, J. (1993). *Second language learning through cooperative learning.* San Clemente, CA: Kagan Publishing.

Hill, J., & Flynn, K. (2006). *Classroom instruction that works with English language learners.* Alexandria, VA: Association for Supervision and Curriculum Development.

Johnson, D., & Johnson, R. (1995). *Creative controversy: Intellectual challenge in the classroom* (3rd ed.). Edina, MN: Interaction Book Company.

Kagan, S. (1990). Cooperative learning for students limited in language proficiency. In M. Brubacker, R. Payne & K. Rickett (Eds.), *Perspectives on small group learning.* Oakville, Ontario, Canada.

Kagan, S. (1992). *Cooperative learning.* San Juan Capistrano, CA: Kagan Cooperative Learning.

Kim, Y., & Turner, J. D. (2006). Creating literacy communities in multicultural and multilingual classrooms: Lessons learned from two European American elementary teachers. In R.T. Jimenez & V.O. Pang (Eds.), *Race, Ethnicity, and Education Volume 2: Language and Literacy in Schools* (pp.219–236). Westport, CT: Praeger Publishing Group.

Kirschner, P. A., Sweller, J., and Clark, R. E. (2006). Why minimal guidance during instruction does not work: An analysis of the failure of constructivist, discovery, problem-based, experiential, and inquiry-based teaching. *Educational Psychologist,* 41, 75–86.

Krashen, S. (1987). *Principles and practices in second language acquisition.* New York: Prentice-Hall.

Leeman, J. (2003). Recasts and second language development: Beyond negative evidence. *Studies in Second Language Acquisition*, 25, 37–63.

Lesaux, N. K. (2006). Development of literacy of language minority learners. In D. L. August & T. Shanahan (Eds.), *Developing literacy in a second language: Report of the National Literacy Panel.* Mahwah, NJ: Lawrence Erlbaum Associates.

Lesaux, N., & Siegel, L. (2003). The development of reading in children who speak English as a second language. *Developmental Psychology,* 39, 1005–1019.

Lesaux, N. K., Lipka, O., & Siegel, L.S. (2006). Investigating cognitive and linguistic abilities that influence the reading comprehension skills of children from diverse linguistic backgrounds. *Reading and Writing: An Interdisciplinary Journal,* 19(1), 99–131.

Lesaux, N. K. & Crosson, A.C. (2005). Addressing variability and vulnerability: Promoting the academic achievement of English learners in San Diego. In R. Hess (Ed.),*Urban reform: Lessons from San Diego*(pp. 263–281). Cambridge, MA: Harvard Education Press.

Lyman, F. T. (1981). The responsive classroom discussion: The inclusion of all students. In A. Anderson (Ed.), *Mainstreaming Digest* (pp. 109–113). College Park: University of Maryland Press.

Marzano, R. J., Pickering, D. J., & Pollock, J. E. (2001). *Classroom instruction that works: Research-based strategies for increasing student achievement.* Alexandria, VA: Association for Supervision and Curriculum Development.

Marzano, R. (2004). *Building academic background.* Alexandria, VA: MCREL, ASCD.

Mayer, R. (2003). *Learning and instruction.* New Jersey: Pearson Education, Inc.

Medina-Jerez, W., Clark, D.B., Medina, A., & Ramirez-Marin, F. (2007). Science for ELLs: Rethinking our approach. *The Science Teacher, 74*, 52–56.

Miller, J. F., Heilmann, J., Nockerts, A., Iglesias, A., Fabiano, L., & Francis, D. J. (2006). Oral language and reading in bilingual children. *Learning Disabilities Research & Practice,* 21, 30–43.

Morrison Institute for Public Policy. (2006). *Why some schools with Latino children beat the odds and others don't.* Tempe, AZ: Author.

National Research Council. (2000). *How people learn: Brain, mind, experience, and school.* Washington, DC: National Academies Press.

Novak, J. D. (1995). Concept mapping: a strategy for organizing knowledge. In S. M. Glynn & R. Duit (eds.), *Learning Science in the Schools: Research Reforming Practice.* Mahwah, NJ: Lawrence Erlbaum Associates.

Pearson, P. D., & Gallagher, G. (1983). The gradual release of responsibility model of instruction. *Contemporary Educational Psychology, 8*, 112–123.

Powell, M. (1996). *Presenting in English.* Hove: Language Teaching Publications.

Saenz, L. M., Fuchs, L. S., & Fuchs, D. (2005). Peer-assisted learning strategies for English language learners with learning disabilities. *Exceptional Children,* 71, 231–247.

Rousculp, E. E., & Maring, G. H. (1992). Portfolios for a community of learners. *Journal of Reading, 35*, 378–385.

Samway K., & McKeon, D. (2007). *Myths and realities: best practices for English language learners.* Portsmouth NH: Heineman.

Saunders, W. M., & Goldenberg, C. (1999). Effects of instructional conversations and literature logs on limited- and fluent-English proficient students' story comprehension and thematic understanding. *Elementary School Journal,* 99(4), 277–301.

Saunders, W. M., Foorman, B. P., & Carlson, C. D. (2006). Do we need a separate block of time for oral English language development in programs for English learners? *The Elementary School Journal,* 107, 181–198.

Scarcella, R. (2003). *Academic English: A conceptual framework.* Los Angeles: Language Minority Research Institute.

Scarcella, R. (2003). *Accelerating academic English: A focus on the English learner.* Oakland, CA: Regents of the University of California.

Schleppegrell, M. J. (2001). Linguistic features of the language of schooling. *Linguistics and Education,* 12, 431–459.

Schleppegrell, M. J. (2004). *The language of schooling: A functional linguistics perspective.* Mahwah, NJ: Erlbaum.

Seidlitz, J. (2008) *Navigating the ELPS: Using the new standards to improve instruction for English language learners.* San Antonio, TX: Canter Press.

Seidlitz, J. & Perryman, B., (2008) *Seven steps to building an interactive classroom: Engaging all students in academic conversation.* San Antonio TX: Canter Press.

Shanahan, T. & Beck, I.L. (2006). Effective literacy teaching for English-language learners. In D. L. August & T. Shanahan (Eds.), *Developing literacy in a second language: Report of the National Literacy Panel.* Mahwah, NJ: Lawrence Erlbaum Associates.

Snow, C. E., & Fillmore, L. W. (2000). *Clearinghouse on languages and linguistics.* Retrieved from www.cal.org/ericcll/teachers/teacher.pdf.

Tabors, P., Paez, M., & Lopez, L. (2003). Dual language abilities of bilingual four- year olds: Initial findings from the Early Childhood Study of language and literacy development of Spanish-speaking children. *NABE Journal of Research and Practice,* 1(1), 70–91.

Taba, H. (1962). *Curriculum development: Theory and practice.* New York: Harcourt Brace & World.

Thornburry, S. (2005). *How to teach speaking.* Essex, England: Pearson.

Turner, J. D., & Kim, Y. (2005). Learning about building literacy communities in multicultural and multilingual communities from effective elementary teachers. *Literacy Teaching and Learning, 10*, 21–42.

Turner, J. (2007). Beyond cultural awareness: Prospective teachers' visions of culturally responsive teaching. *Action in Teacher Education, 29*(3), 12–24.

Uchikoshi, Y. (2005). Narrative development in bilingual kindergarteners: Can Arthur help? Developmental Psychology, 41, 464–478.

Vail, N. J. and Papenfuss, J. (1993). *Daily oral language plus.* Evanston, IL: McDougal, Littell.

Vaughn, S., Cirino, P. T., Linan- Thompson, S., Mathes, P. G., Carlson, C. D., Cardenas-Hagan, E., et al. (2006). Effectiveness of a Spanish intervention and an English intervention for English language learners at risk for reading problems. *American Educational Research Journal,* 43, 449–487.

Weaver, C. (1996). *Teaching grammar in context.* Portsmouth, NH: Boynton, Cook Publishers.

Wennerstrom, A. (1993). Content-based pronunciation. *TESOL Journal,* 1(3), 15–18.

Wong-Fillmore, L. & Snow, C. (2000). *What teachers need to know about language.* Washington, DC: ERIC Clearinghouse on Languages and Linguistics.

Zwiers, J. (2008). *Building Academic Language.* Newark, DE: Jossey-Bass/International Reading Association.

Vocabulary

August, D., Carlo, M., Dressler, C., & Snow, C. (2005). The critical role of vocabulary development for English language learners. *Learning Disabilities Research and Practice,* 20, 50–57.

Bauman, J. F., & E. Kame'enui (Eds.). (2004). *Vocabulary Instruction: Research to Practice.* New York: Guilford.

Bear, D. R., Invernizzi, M., Templeton, S., & Johnson, F. (2004). *Words their way: Word study for phonics, vocabulary, and spelling instruction (2nd Ed.).* Upper Saddle River, NJ: Merrill Prentice Hall.

Beck, I. L., McKeown, M.G., & Kucan, L. (2002). *Bringing words to life.* New York: The Guilford Press.

Beck, I. L., & McKeown, M. G. (1991). Conditions of vocabulary acquisition. In R. Barr, M. L. Kamil, P. B. Mosenthal, & P. D. Pearson (Eds.), *Handbook of reading research* (Vol. 2, pp. 789–814). White Plains, NY: Longman.

Beck, I. L., McKeown, M. G., & Omanson, R. C. (1987). The effects and uses of diverse vocabulary instructional techniques. In M.G. McKeown & M.E. Curtis (Eds.), *The nature of vocabulary acquisition* (pp.147–163). Mahwah, NJ: Lawrence Erlbaum Associates.

Biemiller, A. (2004). Teaching vocabulary in the primary grades: Vocabulary instruction needed. In J.F. Baumann & E. Kame'enui (Eds.), *Vocabulary instruction: Bringing research to practice* (pp.209–242). Mahwah, NJ: Lawrence Erlbaum Associates.

Blachowicz, C. L. Z., & Fisher, P. J. L. (2000). Vocabulary instruction. In M. L. Kamil, P. B. Mosenthal, P. D. Pearson, & R. Barr (Eds.), *Handbook of reading research* (Vol. 3, pp. 503–523). White Plains, NY: Longman.

Blachowicz, C. L. Z., Fisher, P. J. L., Ogle D., & Watts-Taffe, S. (2006). Vocabulary: Questions from the classroom. *Reading Research Quarterly,* 41, 524–539.

Carlo, M. S., August, D., McLaughlin, B., Snow, C. E., Dressler, C., Lippman, D. N., Lively, T. J., & White, C. E. (2004). Closing the gap: Addressing the vocabulary needs of English-language learners in bilingual and mainstream classrooms. *Reading Research Quarterly,* 39, 188–215.

Carlo, M. S., August, D., & Snow, C. E. (2005). Sustained vocabulary-learning strategies for English language learners. In E. H. Hiebert & M. Kamil (Eds.), *Teaching and learning vocabulary: Bringing research to practice* (pp.137–153). Mahwah, NJ: Lawrence Erlbaum Associates.

Coxhead, A. (2000). A new Academic Word List. *TESOL Quarterly,* 34(2): 213–238.

Eyraud, K., Giles, G., Koenig, S., & Stoller, F. (2000). The word wall approach: Promoting L2 vocabulary learning. *English Teaching Forum,* 38, pp. 2–11.

Graves, M. F. (2006). *The vocabulary book: Learning and instruction.* New York: Teacher's College Press.

Harrington, M. J. (1996). Basic instruction in word analysis skills to improve spelling competence. *Education,* 117, 22. Available at: www.questia.com.

Kieffer, M. J., & Lesaux, N. K. (in press). Breaking down words to build meaning: Morphology, vocabulary, and reading comprehension in the urban classroom. *The Reading Teacher.*

Lehr, F., Osborn, J., & Hiebert, E. H. (2004). *A focus on vocabulary.* Honolulu, HI: Pacific Regional Educational Laboratory. Available at: www.prel.org/programs/rel/vocabularyforum.asp.

Nagy, W. E., & Scott, J. A. (2000). Vocabulary processes. In R. Barr, M. L. Kamil, P. Mosenthal, & P. D. Pearson (Eds.), *Handbook of reading research: Vol. 3* (pp. 269–284). New York: Longman.

Nagy, W. E., & Stahl, S. A. (2006). *Teaching word meanings.* Mahwah, NJ: Lawrence Erlbaum Associates.

Roser, N., & Juel, C. (1982). Effects of vocabulary instruction on reading comprehension. In J.A. Niles & L.A. Harris (Eds.), *Yearbook of the National Reading Conference: Vol. 31. New inquiries in reading research and Instruction* (pp. 110–118). Rochester, NY: National Reading Conference.

Ruddell, M. R., & Shearer, B. A. (2002). "Extraordinary," "tremendous," exhilarating," "magnificient": Middle school at-risk students become avid word learners with the vocabulary-self collection strategy (VSS). *Journal of Adolescent and Adult Literacy,* 45(4), 352–363.

Stahl, S. A. (1999). *Vocabulary development.* Cambridge, MA: Brookline Books.

Stahl, S. A., & Nagy, W. E. (2006). *Teaching word meanings.* Mahwah, NJ: Lawrence Erlbaum Associates.

White, T., Sowell, J., & Yanagihara, A. (1989). Teaching elementary students to use word-part clues. *The Reading Teacher,* 42, 302–308.

Wixson, K. K. (1986). Vocabulary instruction and children's comprehension of basal stories. *Reading Research Quarterly,* 21(3) 317–329.

Reading

Allington, R. L. (2001). *What really matters for struggling readers: Designing research-based programs.* New York, NY: Addison Wesley Educational Publishers Inc.

Baker, L. (2004). Reading comprehension and science inquiry: Metacognitive connections. In E.W. Saul (Ed.), *Crossing borders in literacy and science instruction: Perspectives on theory and practice.* Newark, DE: International Reading Association; Arlington, VA: National Science Teachers Association (NSTA) Press.

Beck, I. L. (2006). *Making sense of phonics: The hows and whys.* New York: Guilford Press.

Beck, I. L., & McKeown, M. G., (2001). Inviting students into the pursuit of meaning. *Educational Psychology Review,* 13(3), 225–241.

Beck, I. L., McKeown, M. G., Hamilton, R. L., and Kucan, L. (1997). *Questioning the Author: An approach for enhancing student engagement with text.* Delaware: International Reading Association.

Boulware, B. J., & Crow, M. (2008, March). Using the concept attainment strategy to enhance reading comprehension. *The Reading Teacher,* 61(6), 491–495.

Cain, K. & Oakhill, J. (1998). Comprehension skill and inference-making ability: Issues and causality. In C. Hulme and R.M. Joshi (Eds.), *Reading and spelling: Development and disorders.* London: Lawrence Erlbaum.

Cain, K. & Oakhill, J. (2000). Inference making ability and its relation to comprehension failure in young children. *Reading and Writing: An Interdisciplinary Journal,* 11,489–503.

Calhoon, M. B., Al Otaiba, S., Cihak, D., King, A., & Avalos, A. C. (2006). *Effects of a peer-mediated program on reading skill acquisition for two-way bilingual first grade classrooms.* Manuscript submitted for publication.

Cirino, P. T., Vaughn, S., Linan-Thompson, S., Cardenas-Hagan, E., Fletcher, J. M., & Francis, D. J. (2007). *One year follow-up outcomes of Spanish and English interventions for English language learners at-risk for reading problems.* Manuscript submitted for publication.

Crawford, E. C., & Torgesen, J. K. (2006). *Teaching all students to read: Practices from Reading First schools with strong intervention outcomes.* Tallahassee, FL: Florida Center for Reading Research. Available at: www.fcrr.org.

Cunningham, A. E., & Stanovich, K. (1998). *What reading does to the mind.* American Educator, 22 (1), 8–15.

Denton, C. A., Anthony, J. L., Parker, R., & Hasbrouck, J. E. (2004). Effects of two tutoring programs on the English reading development of Spanish-English bilingual students. *The Elementary School Journal,* 104, 289–305.

Dole, J., Duffy, G., Roehler, L., & Pearson, P. (1991). Moving from the old to the new: Research in reading comprehension instruction. *Review of Educational Research,* 61, 239–264.

Duke, N. K., & Pearson, P. D. (2002). Effective practices for developing reading comprehension. In A. E. Farstrup & S. J. Samuels (Eds.), *What research has to say about reading instruction* (3rd ed.) (pp. 205–242). Newark, DE: International Reading Association.

Fielding, L., Kerr, N., & Rosier, P. (2007). *Annual growth for all students, catch-up growth for those who are behind.* Kennewick, WA: The New Foundation Press.

Garcia, G. E. (2000). Bilingual children's reading. In M. L. Kamil, P. B. Mosenthal, P. D. Pearson, & R. Barr (Eds.), *Handbook of reading research: Volume III* (pp. 813–834). Mahwah, NJ: Lawrence Erlbaum Associates.

Gerber, M., Jimenez, T., Leafstedt, J., Villaruz, J., Richards, C., & English, J. (2004). English reading effects of small-group intensive instruction in Spanish for K–1 English learners. *Learning Disabilities Research & Practice,* 19(4), 239–251.

Head, M., & Readence, J. (1986). Anticipation guides: Meaning through prediction. In E. Dishner, T. Bean, J. Readence, & D. Moore (Eds.), *Reading in the Content Areas,* Dubuque, IA: Kendall/Hunt.

Kosanovich, M., Ladinsky, K., Nelson, L., & Torgesen, J. (2006). *Differentiated reading instruction: Small group lesson structures for all students.* Tallahassee, FL: Florida Center for Reading Research. Available at: www.fcrr.org.

Lehr, F. & Osborne, J. (2006). *Focus on comprehension.* Honolulu, HI: Pacific Regional Educational Laboratory. Available at: www.prel.org/programs/rel/comprehensionforum.asp.

Lesaux, N. K., & Kieffer, M. J. (in press). Sources of reading comprehension difficulties for language minority learners and their classmates in early adolescence. *American Educational Research Journal.*

Lesaux, N. K., & Siegel, L. S. (2003). The development of reading in children who speak English as a second language. *Developmental Psychology,* 39(6), 1005–1019.

Lesaux, N. K., Lipka, O., & Siegel, L. S. (2006). Investigating cognitive and linguistic abilities that influence the reading comprehension skills of children from diverse linguistic backgrounds. *Reading and Writing: An Interdisciplinary Journal,* 19, 99–131.

Linan-Thompson, S., & Hickman-Davis, P. (2002). Supplemental reading instruction for students at risk for reading disabilities: Improve reading 30 minutes at a time. *Learning Disabilities Research and Practice,* 17(4), 242–251.

Linan-Thompson, S., Vaughn, S., Hickman-Davis, P., & Kouzekanani, K. (2003). Effectiveness of supplemental reading instruction for second-grade English language learners with reading difficulties. *The Elementary School Journal,* 103(3), 221–238.

McMaster, K. L., Kung, H., Han, I., & Cao, M. (in press). Peer-assisted learning strategies: A "tier 1" approach to promoting responsiveness to beginning reading instruction for English learners. *Exceptional Children.*

McKeown, M. G., Beck, I. L., & Worthy, M. J. (1993). Grappling with text ideas: Questioning the author. *Reading Teacher,* 46, 560–66.

National Reading Panel. (2000). *Report of the National Reading Panel: Teaching children to read.* Bethesda, MD: National Institute of Child Health and Human Development.

Ogle, D. S. (1986). K-W-L group instructional strategy. In A. S. Palincsar, D. S. Ogle, B. F. Jones, & E. G. Carr (Eds.), *Teaching reading as thinking.* Alexandria, VA: Association for Supervision and Curriculum Development.

Palincsar, A. S., & Brown, A. L. (1985). Reciprocal teaching: Activities to promote reading with your mind. In T. L. Harris & E. J. Cooper (Eds.), *Reading thinking and concept development: Strategies for the classroom.* New York: The College Board.

Pressley, M. (2000). What should comprehension instruction be the instruction of? In M. Kamil, P. B. Mosenthal, P. D. Pearson, & R. Barr (Eds.), *Handbook of Reading Research: Vol. 3* (pp. 545–561). Mahwah, NJ: Lawrence Erlbaum Associates.

Pressley, M., & Afflerbach, P. (1995). *Verbal protocols of reading: The nature of constructively responsive reading.* Hillsdale, NJ: Erlbaum.

Proctor, C. P., Carlo, M., August, D., & Snow, C. (2005). Native Spanish-speaking children reading in English: Toward a model of comprehension. *Journal of Educational Psychology,* 97, 246–256.

Quiroga, T., Lemos-Britton, Z., Mostafapour, E., Abbott, R. D., & Berninger, V. W. (2002). Phonological awareness and beginning reading in Spanish-speaking ESL first graders: Research into practice. *Journal of School Psychology,* 40, 85–111.

Riedel, B. W. (2007). The relation between DIBELS, reading comprehension, and vocabulary in urban, first grade students. *Reading Research Quarterly,* 42, 460–466.

Saunders, W. M., & Goldenberg, C. (1999). Effects of instructional conversations and literature logs on limited- and fluent- English-proficient students' story comprehension and thematic understanding. *Elementary School Journal,* 99, 277–301.

Schlick Noe, K., & Johnson, N. (1999). *Getting started with literature circles.* Norwood, MA: Christopher-Gordon Publishers, Inc.

Slavin, R., & Cheung, A. (2005). A synthesis of research on language of reading instruction for English language learners. *Review of Educational Research,* 75, 247–284.

Snow, C. E., Burns, M. S., & Griffin, P. (Eds.). (1998). *Preventing reading difficulties in young children.* Washington, DC: National Academy Press.

Swanson, H. L., Sáez, L., & Gerber, M. (2004). Do phonological and executive processes in English learners at risk for reading disabilities in grade 1 predict performance in grade 2? *Learning Disabilities Research & Practice,* 19, 225–238.

Taylor, W. (1953). Cloze procedure a new tool for measuring readability. *Journalism Quarterly,* 30, 415–433.

Torgesen, J. K. (2006). *A principal's guide to intensive reading interventions for struggling readers in early elementary school.* Portsmouth, NH: RMC Research Corporation, Center on Instruction. Available at: www.centeroninstruction.org.

Tumner, J., & Chapman, J. (1995). Context use in early reading development: Premature exclusion of a source or individual differences? *Issues in Education*,1, 97–100.

Vaughn, S., Cirino, P. T., Linan-Thompson, S., Mathes, P. G., Carlson, C. D., Cardenas-Hagan, E., et al. (2006). Effectiveness of a Spanish intervention and an English intervention for English language learners at risk for reading problems. *American Educational Research Journal,* 43, 449–487.

Vaughn, S., Mathes, P., Linan-Thompson, S., Cirino, P., Carlson, C., Pollard-Durodola, S., et al. (2006). Effectiveness of an English intervention for first-grade English language learners at risk for reading problems. *Elementary School Journal,* 107, 153–180.

Vaughn, S., Linan-Thompson, S., & Hickman-Davis, P. (2003). Response to treatment as a means for identifying students with reading/learning disabilities. *Exceptional Children,* 69, 391–410.

Vaughn, S., Mathes, P., Linan-Thompson, S., & Francis, D. (2005). Teaching English language learners at risk for reading disabilities to read: Putting research into practice. *Learning Disabilities Research and Practice,* 20(1), 58–67.

Verhoeven, L. (1990). Acquisition of reading in a second language. *Reading Research Quarterly,* 25, 90–114.

Verhoeven, L. T. (2000). Components in early second language reading and spelling. *Scientific Studies of Reading,* 4, 313–330.

Willhelm, J. (2002). *Action strategies for deepening comprehension*. New York: Scholastic.

Writing

Britton, J. (1983). Writing and the story of the world. In B. Kroll & E. Wells (Eds.), *Explorations in the development of writing theory, research, and practice* (p. 3–30). New York: Wiley.

Calderón, M., Hertz-Lazarowitz, R., & Slavin, R. (1998). Effects of bilingual cooperative integrated reading and composition on students transitioning from Spanish to English reading. *Elementary School Journal,* 99, 153–165.

Celce-Murcia, M. (2002). On the use of selected grammatical features in academic writing. In M. C. Colombi & M. J. Schleppegrell (Eds.), *Developing advanced literacy in first and second languages* (pp. 143–158). Mahwah, NJ: Erlbaum.

Cunningham, P., & Allington, R. (2003). *Classrooms that work.* New York: Pearson Education, Inc.

Dyson, A. H. (1989). *Multiple worlds of child writers: Friends learning to write.* New York: Teachers College Press.

Elbow, P. (1998). *Writing with power.* Oxford: Oxford University Press.

Fisher, D., & Frey, N. (2008). Releasing responsibility. *Educational Leadership, 66*(3), 32–37.

Fisher, D., & Frey, N. (2007). *Scaffolded writing instruction: Teaching with a gradual-release framework.* New York: Scholastic.

Fisher, D., Frey, N., & Rothenberg, C., (2008). *Content area conversations: How to plan discussion-based lessons for diverse language learners.* Alexandria, VA: Association for Supervision and Curriculum Development.

Fearn, L., & Farnan, N. (2001). *Interactions: Teaching writing and the language arts.* Boston: Houghton Mifflin.

Kirby, D., Kirby, D. L., & Liner, T. (2004). *Inside out: Strategies for teaching writing.* Portsmouth, NH: Heinemann.

McCarrier, A., Pinnell, G. S., & Fountas, I. C. (2000). *Interactive writing: How language and literacy come together, K–2.* Portsmouth, NH: Heinemann.

Samway, K. (2006). *When English language learners write: connecting research to practice.* Portsmouth: Heineman.

Schleppegrell, M. J., & Go, A. L. (2007). Analyzing the writing of English learners: A functional approach. *Language Arts, 84*(6), 529–538.

Strong, W. (2001). Coaching writing: *The power of guided practice.* Portsmouth, NH: Heinemann-Boynton/Cook.

Fluency

Breznitz, Z. (2006). *Fluency in reading.* Mahwah, NJ: Lawrence Erlbaum Associates.

Crosson, A. C., & Lesaux, N. K. (in press). Revisiting assumptions about the relationship of fluent reading to comprehension: Spanish-speakers' text-reading fluency in English. *Reading and Writing: An Interdisciplinary Journal.*

Dowhower, S. L. (1987). Effects of repeated reading on second grade transitional readers' fluency and comprehension. *Reading Research Quarterly,* 22(4), 389–406.

Geva, E., & Yaghoub-Zadeh, Z. (2006). Reading efficiency in native English-speaking and English-as-a-second-language children: The role of oral proficiency and underlying cognitive-linguistic processes. *Scientific Studies of Reading,* 10, 31–57.

Kuhn, M. R. (2005). Helping students become accurate, expressive readers: Fluency instruction for small groups. *The Reading Teacher,* 58, 338–344.

Kung, S. H. (2009). *Predicting the success on a state standards test for culturally and linguistically diverse students using curriculum-based oral reading measures.* Unpublished doctoral dissertation, University of Minnesota.

LaBerge, D., & Samuels, S. J. (1974). Toward a theory of automatic information processing in reading. *Cognitive Psychology,* 6, 293–323.

Maurice, K. (1983). The fluency workshop. *TESOL Newsletter,* 17, 4.

Osborn, J., Lehr, F., & Hiebert, E. H. (2003). *A Focus on Fluency.* Honolulu, HI: Pacific Resources for Education and Learning. Available at www.prel.org/programs/rel/rel.asp.

Pikulski, J., & Chard, D. (2005). Fluency: the bridge between decoding and reading comprehension. *The Reading Teacher,* 58, 510–521.

Samuels, S. J., & Farstrup, A. E. (2006). *What research has to say about fluency instruction.* Newark, DE: International Reading Association.

Schilling, S. G., Carlisle, J. F., Scott, S. E., & Zeng, J. (2007). Are fluency measures accurate predictors of reading achievement? *The Elementary School Journal,* 107, 429–448.

Vaughn, S., Chard, D. J., Bryant, D. P., Coleman, M., Tyler, B. J., Linan-Thompson, S., & Kouzekanani, K. (2000). Fluency and comprehension interventions for third-grade students. *Remedial and Special Education,* 21(6), 325–335.

Technology

Fisher, D., & Frey, N. (in press). *Literacy 2.0: Language, literacy and learning in a new century* [working title]. Bloomington, IN: Solution Tree.

Gee, J. P. (2007). *What video games have to teach us about learning and literacy.* New York: Palgrave Macmillan.

International Reading Association. (May 2009). *New literacies and 21st century technologies: A position statement of the International Reading Association.* Newark, DE: Author. Used with permission.

Leu, D. J., O'Byrne, W. I., Zawilinski, L., McVerry, J. G., & Everett-Cacopardo, H. (2009). Expanding the new literacies conversation. *Educational Researcher,* 38(4), 264–269.

Mayer, R. E. (2001). Multimedia learning. New York: Cambridge University Press. Partnership for 21st Century Skills. (2009). Framework for 21st century learning. Retrieved from www.21stcenturyskills.org/index.php?option=com_content&task=view&id=254&Itemid=120.

Ybarra, R. & Green, T. (2003). Using technology to teach ESL/EFL students to develop language skills. *The Internet TESL Journal, 9,* n.p.

Assessment

Afflerbach, P. (2007). *Understanding and using reading assessment K–12.* Newark, DE: International Reading Association.

Carpenter, S. K., Pashler, H., Cepeda, N. J., and Alvarez, D. (2007). Applying the principles of testing and spacing to classroom learning. In D. S. McNamara and J. G. Trafton (Eds.), *Proceedings of the 29th Annual Cognitive Science Society* (p. 19). Nashville, TN: Cognitive Science Society.

Carpenter, S. K., Pashler, H., Wixted, J. T., and Vul, E. (in press). The effects of tests on learning and forgetting. *Memory & Cognition.*

Dempster, F. N., & Perkins, P. G. (1993). Revitalizing classroom assessment: Using tests to promote learning. *Journal of Instructional Psychology,* 20, 197–203.

Dominguez de Ramirez, R., & Shapiro, E. S. (2006). Curriculum-based measurement and the evaluation of reading skills of Spanish-speaking English language learners in bilingual education classrooms. *School Psychology Review,* 35, 356–369.

Edwards, P., Turner, J. D., & Mokhtari, K. (2008). Balancing the assessment of and the assessment for learning in support of student literacy achievement. *Reading Teacher,* 61, 682–684.

Fisher, D., & Frey, N. (2007). *Checking for understanding: Formative assessment techniques for your classroom.* Alexandria, VA: Association for Supervision and Curriculum Development.

Frey, N., & Heibert, E. (2002). Teacher-based assessment of literacy learning. In J. Flood, D. Lapp, J. R. Squire, & J. M. Jensen (Eds.). *Handbook of Research on the Teaching of English Language Arts* (2nd ed.), pp.608–618. Mahwah, NJ: Lawrence Erlbaum.

Gersten, R., Dimino, J., & Jayanthi, M. (in press). Development of a classroom observational system. In B. Taylor & J. Ysseldyke (Eds.), *Reading instruction for English language learners: The Bond symposium.* New York: Teachers College.

Goodman, Y. (2002). Informal methods of evaluation. In J. Flood, D. Lapp, J. R. Squire, & J. M. Jensen (Eds.). *Handbook of Research on the Teaching of English Language Arts* (2nd ed.), pp. 600–607. Mahwah, NJ: Lawrence Erlbaum.

Johnston, P. (2005). Literacy assessment and the future. *The Reading Teacher,* 58(7), 684–686.

Limbos, M. (2006). Early identification of second language students at risk for reading disability. *Dissertation Abstracts International,* 66 (10-A), 3566A.

Schumm, J. S. & Arguelles, M. E. (2006). No two learners are alike: The importance of assessment and differentiated instruction. In J. S. Schumm (Ed.), *Reading assessment and instruction for all learners.* New York: Guilford Press.

Torgesen, J. K. (2006). *A comprehensive K–3 reading assessment plan: Guidance for school leaders.* Portsmouth, NH: RMC Research Corporation, Center on Instruction. Available at: www.centeroninstruction.org.

Townsend, D., Lee, E., & Chiappe, P. (2006). *English or Spanish? The efficacy of assessing Latino/a children in Spanish for risk of reading disabilities.* Paper presented at the meeting of the Society for the Scientific Study of Reading, Vancouver, BC, Canada.

Wiley, H. I., & Deno, S. L. (2005). Oral reading and maze measures as predictors of success for English learners on a state standards assessment. *Remedial and Special Education,* 26, 207–214.

Scope and Sequence

Reading

	Grade					
	K	1	2	3	4	5
LITERATURE						
Key Ideas and Details						
Retell or Explain a Story	•	•	•	•	•	•
Analyze Story Elements	•	•	•	•	•	•
Plot	•	•	•	•	•	•
Characters	•	•	•	•	•	•
Setting	•	•	•	•	•	•
Theme, Lesson, or Moral		•	•	•	•	•
Use Reading Strategies	•	•	•	•	•	•
Preview and Make Predictions	•	•	•	•	•	•
Monitor Understanding	•	•	•	•	•	•
Ask and Answer Questions	•	•	•	•	•	•
Summarize Texts	•	•	•	•	•	•
Make Inferences	•	•	•	•	•	•
Visualize	•	•	•	•	•	•
Make Connections	•	•	•	•	•	•
Synthesize: Draw Conclusions			•	•	•	•
Synthesize: Draw Generalizations			•	•	•	•
Relate Ideas	•	•	•	•	•	•
Chronology	•	•	•	•	•	•
Comparison	•	•	•	•	•	•
Cause/Effect		•	•	•	•	•
Goal/Outcome				•	•	•
Problem/Solution					•	•
Craft and Structure						
Determine the Meaning of Words and Phrases in a Text	•	•	•	•	•	•
Identify Elements of Genre	•	•	•	•	•	•
Describe Structure of Stories, Dramas, and Poems			•	•	•	•
Identify Introduction and Conclusion			•	•	•	•
Identify Text Segments: Chapter, Scene, Stanza				•	•	•
Identify Elements of Poetry: Rhyme, Rhythm	•	•	•	•	•	•
Identify Elements of Poetry: Verse, Meter, Line Breaks					•	•
Identify Elements of Drama: List of Characters, Dialogue, Stage Directions					•	•
Compare Drama and Prose			•	•	•	•
Compare Poetry and Prose			•	•	•	•
Identify Author and Illustrator	•	•	•	•	•	•
Identify Narrator		•	•	•	•	•
Identify and Distinguish Points of View			•	•	•	•

Grade

Reading, continued	K	1	2	3	4	5
Integration of Knowledge and Ideas						
Analyze Text Elements	●	●	●	●	●	●
Use Information in Illustrations	●	●	●	●	●	●
Connect Text and Oral or Visual Presentation of Story or Versions of a Story	●	●	●	●	●	●
Analyze Visual or Multimedia Elements in a Text		●	●	●	●	●
Compare Ideas or Texts	●	●	●	●	●	●
Compare Fiction and Nonfiction	●	●	●	●	●	●
Compare Characters	●	●	●	●	●	●
Compare Settings	●	●	●	●	●	●
Compare Events	●	●	●	●	●	●
Compare Topics	●	●	●	●	●	●
Compare Themes				●	●	●
Range of Reading and Level of Text Complexity						
Read and Comprehend Literature at and Above Grade Level Complexity	●	●	●	●	●	●
Participate in Shared Reading	●	●	●	●	●	●
Read Independently	●	●	●	●	●	●

INFORMATIONAL TEXT	K	1	2	3	4	5
Key Ideas and Details						
Retell or Explain a Text	●	●	●	●	●	●
Use Reading Strategies	●	●	●	●	●	●
Preview and Make Predictions	●	●	●	●	●	●
Monitor Understanding	●	●	●	●	●	●
Ask and Answer Questions	●	●	●	●	●	●
Determine Importance: Identify the Topic, Main Idea, and Key Details	●	●	●	●	●	●
Determine Importance: Summarize		●	●	●	●	●
Make Inferences	●	●	●	●	●	●
Visualize	●	●	●	●	●	●
Make Connections	●	●	●	●	●	●
Synthesize: Draw Conclusions			●	●	●	●
Synthesize: Make Generalizations			●	●	●	●
Relate Ideas and Describe Text Structure	●	●	●	●	●	●
Logical Order	●	●	●	●	●	●
Chronology	●	●	●	●	●	●
Comparison		●	●	●	●	●
Cause/Effect		●	●	●	●	●
Problem/Solution, Goal/Outcome		●	●	●	●	●
Compare Text Structure					●	●

Scope and Sequence, continued

Reading, continued	Grade K	1	2	3	4	5
Craft and Structure						
Determine the Meaning of Words and Phrases in a Text	•	•	•	•	•	•
Identify and Use Text Features	•	•	•	•	•	•
Covers and Title Page	•	•	•	•	•	•
Table of Contents or Electronic Menus	•	•	•		•	
Headings and Subheadings		•	•	•	•	•
Topic Sentence			•	•	•	•
Glossaries and Indexes		•	•	•	•	•
Captions, Labels, Icons, Hyperlinks and Callouts		•	•		•	•
Graphs, Diagrams, Tables, and Maps		•	•		•	•
Sidebars				•	•	•
Distinguish Between Information in Illustrations and Information in Text	•	•	•	•	•	•
Identify Author and Illustrator	•	•	•		•	•
Identify Author's Purpose		•	•		•	•
Distinguish Points of View or Accounts				•	•	•
Integration of Knowledge and Ideas						
Use Information in Illustrations and Media	•	•	•	•	•	•
Interpret Information Presented in Multiple Formats					•	•
Identify and Distinguish Facts and Opinions		•	•	•	•	•
Identify Author's Reasons and Evidence	•	•	•	•	•	•
Explain Connections Within a Text		•	•	•	•	•
Compare Texts	•	•	•	•	•	•
Range of Reading and Level of Text Complexity						
Read and Comprehend Text at and above Grade Level Complexity		•	•	•	•	•
Participate in Shared Reading	•	•	•	•	•	•
Read Independently	•	•	•	•	•	•

Reading, continued	K	1	2	3	4	5
FOUNDATIONAL SKILLS						
Print Concepts						
Understand Directionality of Text	•	•	•			
Recognize the Relationship of Letters and Words to Speech	•	•				
Recognize and Name Alphabet Letters	•	•				
Know the Order of the Alphabet	•	•				
Identify Letters	•	•	•			
Match Uppercase and Lowercase Letters	•	•	•			
Identify a Word	•	•	•			
Identify End Punctuation	•	•	•			
Identify Title	•	•	•			
Hold a Book and Turn the Pages	•	•	•			
Identify Sentence Capitalization	•	•	•			
Use Page Numbers	•	•	•			
Identify Dialogue			•			
Identify Indentions of Paragraphs			•			
Phonological Awareness						
Distinguish Long and Short Vowel Sounds	•	•	•			
Isolate Words in a Sentence	•	•	•			
Identify Syllables	•	•	•			
Blend Syllables to Form a Word	•	•	•			
Segment a Word into Syllables	•	•	•			
Identify Rhyming Words	•	•	•			
Generate Rhyming Words	•	•	•			
Match Initial, Medial, and Final Sounds	•	•	•			
Identify and Isolate Initial, Medial, and Final Sounds	•	•	•			
Blend Onset and Rime	•	•	•			
Blend Sounds to Form a Word	•	•	•			
Segment a Word into Sounds	•	•	•			
Manipulate Sounds in Words (Add, Delete, Substitute)	•	•	•			

Use **Reach into Phonics** to provide intervention for foundational reading skills in grades 3–5.

Reading, continued	K	1	2	3	4	5
Phonics and Word Recognition						
Identify Letter/Sounds and Read Words	●	●	●			
Consonants	●	●	●			
Short Vowels	●	●	●			
Long Vowels	●	●	●			
Consonant Blends and Digraphs	●	●	●			
Vowel Digraphs: *ai, ay, ee, ea, ie, igh, oa, ow, oo, ou, ui*	●	●	●			
r-Controlled Vowels: *ar, or, -ore, er, ir, ur, air, -are, eer, ear*		●	●			
Sounds for *-y:* /ē/, /ī/	●	●	●			
Diphthongs: *oi, oy, ou, ow*	●	●	●			
Variant Vowels: *aw, au, al, all, oo, ew, ea*	●	●				
Vowel Patterns: *-igh, -old, -alk*	●	●	●			
Vowel Patterns: *o, i, -ight*			●			
Schwa			●			
Soft *c*	●	●	●			
Soft *g*	●	●	●			
Silent Consonants *kn, wr, gn, mb*	●	●	●			
Plurals *-s, -es, -ies*		●	●			
Read Words with Spelling Patterns		●	●			
CVC*e* Word Patterns with *a, i, o, u, e*	●	●	●			
CV Word Patterns with *o, e*	●	●	●			
Short and Long Vowels in CVC and CVC*e* Word Patterns	●	●	●			
CVVC Word Patterns		●	●			
Read Multisyllabic Words		●	●			
Compound Words		●	●			
VCCV Syllable Division (bas/ket, kit/ten)		●	●			
VCCCV Syllable Division (hun/dred)		●	●			
VCV Syllable Division (mu/sic, cab/in)		●	●			
Words with Consonant + *le*		●	●			
Suffixes		●	●			
Prefixes		●	●			
Inflected Forms		●	●			
Syllable Types: *r*-Controlled, Consonant + *le*, Vowel Team, Vowel + Silent *e*		●	●			
Final Syllables with *-tion, -ture, -ent, -ant*			●			

Use **Reach into Phonics** to provide intervention for foundational reading skills in grades 3–5.

Reading, continued

	Grade K	1	2	3	4	5
Phonics and Word Recognition, continued						
Use Decoding Strategies	•	•	•			
Blend Sounds to Decode Words						
Recognize Word Families and Similarly-Spelled Words	•	•	•			
Use Structural Clues		•	•			
Identify Syllable Types		•	•			
Recognize High Frequency Words	•	•	•			
Distinguish Between Similarly-Spelled Words	•	•	•			
Read Irregularly-Spelled Words	•	•	•			
Fluency						
Read with Purpose and Understanding	•	•	•	•	•	•
Read with Accuracy and Appropriate Rate	•	•	•	•	•	•
Use Phrasing		•	•	•	•	•
Read with Expression		•	•	•	•	•
Read with Correct Intonation		•	•	•	•	•
Read Instructional Level Materials Fluently	•	•	•	•	•	•
Use Context to Support Decoding	•	•	•	•	•	•

Writing

	K	1	2	3	4	5
Text Types and Purposes						
Opinion Pieces	•	•	•	•	•	•
Informative/Explanatory Text	•	•	•	•	•	•
Interview			•	•	•	•
Letter or Email		•	•	•	•	•
Report			•	•	•	•
Persuasive Essay				•	•	•
Procedural Text		•	•	•	•	•
Explanatory Text		•	•	•	•	•
Narratives	•	•	•	•	•	•
Story or Account	•	•	•	•	•	•
Character Sketch				•	•	•
Poem		•	•	•	•	•
Tall Tale/Myth/Trickster Tale/Folk Tale			•	•	•	•
Science Fiction Story					•	•
Response Text	•	•	•	•	•	•
Write to Demonstrate Comprehension	•	•	•	•	•	•

Writing, continued	K	1	2	3	4	5
Writing Skills						
Organization and Purpose	•	•	•	•	•	•
Introduce a Topic	•	•	•	•	•	•
Write a Conclusion	•	•	•	•	•	•
Establish and Follow a Purpose	•	•	•	•	•	•
Identify Context for Formal and Informal English	•	•	•	•	•	•
State Main Ideas and Support with Details		•	•	•	•	•
Introduce and State an Opinion	•	•	•	•	•	•
Supply Reasons and Evidence		•	•	•	•	•
Write Facts, Definitions, and Details	•	•	•	•	•	•
Maintain Point of View					•	•
Use Persuasive Techniques or Language		•	•	•	•	•
Organize Writing	•	•	•	•	•	•
Sequence Events	•	•	•	•	•	•
Fiction			•	•	•	•
Include Dialogue					•	•
Tell About Events and Details	•	•	•	•	•	•
Introduce Characters or a Narrator				•	•	•
Word Choice	•	•	•	•	•	•
Use Signal Words		•	•	•	•	•
Use Concrete Words and Phrases		•	•	•	•	•
Use Sensory Words and Phrases		•	•	•	•	•
Use Figurative Language					•	•
Use Colorful Details to Elaborate				•	•	•
Use Linking Words		•	•	•	•	•
Use Quotations		•	•	•	•	•
Use Precise Language and Vocabulary				•	•	•
Use Your Own Words	•	•	•	•	•	•
Sentence Fluency	•	•	•	•	•	
Connect Ideas				•	•	•
Break Up Long Sentences				•	•	•
Combine Sentences				•	•	•
Vary Sentences		•	•	•	•	•
Production and Distribution of Writing						
Produce Writing for Specific Tasks, Purposes, and Audiences	•	•	•	•	•	•
Prewrite		•	•	•	•	•
Analyze a Model		•	•	•	•	•
Determine the Role, Audience, Form, and Topic		•	•	•	•	•
Organize Ideas		•	•	•	•	•

Writing, continued	K	1	2	3	4	5
	Grade					
Production and Distribution of Writing, continued						
Draft	●	●	●	●	●	●
Use Appropriate Development and Organization		●	●	●	●	●
Use Technology to Produce Writing	●	●	●	●	●	●
Demonstrate Keyboarding Skills					●	●
Revise	●	●	●	●	●	●
Respond to Peer Suggestions	●	●	●	●	●	●
Add, Combine, or Delete Details	●	●	●	●	●	●
Edit and Proofread		●	●	●	●	●
Publish and Present	●	●	●	●	●	●
Use Visuals or Multimedia to Enhance Meaning		●	●	●	●	●
Keep a Portfolio	●	●	●	●	●	●
Writing Traits						
Ideas		●	●	●	●	●
Organization		●	●	●	●	●
Voice		●	●	●	●	●
Word Choice		●	●	●	●	●
Sentence Fluency		●	●	●	●	●
Conventions		●	●	●	●	●
Presentation		●	●	●	●	●
Research to Build and Present Knowledge						
Create Research and Writing Projects	●	●	●	●	●	●
Recall or Gather Information	●	●	●	●	●	●
Choose and Focus a Topic	●	●	●	●	●	●
Develop Research Questions					●	●
Locate Sources of Information		●	●	●	●	●
Evaluate Information					●	●
Find Information in Sources			●	●	●	●
Take and Sort Notes			●	●	●	●
Distinguish Plagiarism from Quoting or Paraphrasing					●	●
Distinguish Relevant from Irrelevant Information		●	●	●	●	●
Integrate Information from Multiple Sources				●	●	●
Provide a List of Sources				●	●	●
Draw Evidence from Text to Support Analysis, Reflection, and Research				●	●	●
Range of Writing						
Write Routinely for a Variety of Tasks, Purposes, and Audiences	●	●	●	●	●	●

Scope and Sequence, continued

Speaking and Listening	Grade K	1	2	3	4	5
Comprehension and Collaboration						
Engage in Collaborative Discussions	•	•	•	•	•	•
Follow Agreed-Upon Rules	•	•	•	•	•	•
Build on and Connect Others' Ideas	•	•	•	•	•	•
Ask for Clarification	•	•	•	•	•	•
Come to Discussions Prepared	•	•	•	•	•	•
Explain and Review Ideas and Understanding	•	•	•	•	•	•
Restate Ideas	•	•	•	•	•	•
Elaborate	•	•	•	•	•	•
Evaluate Information Presented in Diverse Media and Formats	•	•	•	•	•	•
Analyze the Message			•	•	•	•
Identify or Describe Media Elements including Visual, Functional and Auditory Details		•	•	•	•	•
Ask and Answer Questions for Information, Clarification, or Understanding	•	•	•	•	•	•
Identify a Speaker's Reasons and Evidence					•	•
Presentation of Knowledge and Ideas						
Describe with Facts and Details	•	•	•	•	•	•
Tell a Story	•	•	•	•	•	•
Recount an Experience	•	•	•	•	•	•
Report on a Text or Topic	•	•	•	•	•	•
Present an Opinion					•	•
Speak Clearly, at an Appropriate Pace	•	•	•	•	•	•
Organize Ideas					•	•
Add Visual, Audio, or Multimedia Support	•	•	•	•	•	•
Produce Complete Sentences	•	•	•	•	•	•
Adapt Speech to the Context and Task	•	•	•	•	•	•

Language

Language	K	1	2	3	4	5
Conventions of Standard English						
Print Upper and Lower Case Letters	•	•				
Sentences	•	•	•	•	•	•
Statements, Questions, Exclamations, and Commands	•	•	•	•	•	•
Negative Sentences	•	•	•	•	•	•
Compound Sentences		•	•	•	•	•
Complex Sentences				•	•	•
Complete Subject	•	•	•	•	•	•
Simple Subject	•	•	•	•	•	•
Compound Subject		•	•	•	•	•

Language, continued

	Grade					
	K	1	2	3	4	5
Conventions of Standard English, continued						
Complete Predicate	•	•	•	•	•	•
Simple Predicate	•	•	•	•	•	•
Compound Predicate		•	•	•	•	•
Complete Sentences	•	•	•	•	•	•
Fragment/Dependent Clause					•	•
Independent Clause			•	•	•	•
Participial Phrases						•
Run-On Sentences			•	•	•	•
Subject-Verb Agreement	•	•	•		•	•
Parts of Speech	•	•	•	•	•	•
Nouns	•	•	•	•	•	•
Common and Proper		•	•	•	•	•
Count and Noncount		•	•	•	•	•
Plurals	•	•	•	•	•	•
Possessive		•	•	•	•	•
Abstract				•		
Articles/Determiners		•	•	•	•	•
Pronouns		•	•	•	•	•
Subject	•	•	•	•	•	•
Object	•	•	•	•	•	•
Demonstrative			•	•	•	•
Indefinite		•	•	•	•	•
Reflexive			•	•	•	•
Relative					•	
Possessive		•	•	•	•	•
Pronoun Agreement	•	•	•	•	•	•
Adjectives	•	•	•	•	•	•
Comparative and Superlative			•	•	•	•
Relative					•	
Demonstrative	•	•	•	•	•	•
Predicate					•	•
Possessive		•	•	•	•	•
Indefinite		•	•	•	•	
Proper						•
Order within Sentences					•	•

Language, continued	Grade K	1	2	3	4	5
Conventions of Standard English, continued						
Verbs	●	●	●	●	●	●
Action	●	●	●	●	●	●
Transitive/Intransitive	●	●	●	●	●	●
Linking			●	●	●	●
Modals			●	●	●	●
Helping			●	●	●	●
Present Tense	●	●	●	●	●	●
Past Tense (Regular and Irregular)		●	●	●	●	●
Future Tense		●	●	●	●	●
Present-Perfect Tense						●
Past-Perfect Tense						●
Future-Perfect Tense						●
Progressive Forms		●	●	●	●	●
Contractions		●	●	●	●	●
Adverbs		●	●	●	●	●
Comparative and Superlative			●	●	●	●
Relative					●	●
Adverbial Clauses					●	●
Prepositions	●	●	●	●	●	●
Prepositional Phrases			●	●	●	●
Conjunctions	●	●	●	●	●	●
Coordinating		●	●	●	●	●
Subordinating		●	●	●	●	●
Correlative						●
Interjections						●
Mechanics	●	●	●	●	●	●
Capitalization	●	●	●	●	●	●
End Punctuation	●	●	●	●	●	●
Abbreviations			●	●	●	●
Comma		●	●	●	●	●
Apostrophe			●	●	●	●
Quotation Marks				●	●	●
Underlining or Italics						●
Spelling	●	●	●	●	●	●
High Frequency Words	●	●	●	Use **Reach into Phonics** for foundational spelling skills in G3–5		
Use Phonetic Knowledge to Spell	●	●	●			
Consult Reference Materials to Check Spelling		●	●	●	●	●
Use Spelling Patterns	●	●	●	●	●	●

Language, continued	Grade K	1	2	3	4	5
Knowledge of Language						
Compare Formal and Informal Uses of English	●	●	●		●	●
Recognize the Difference Between Spoken and Written English	●	●	●	●	●	
Choose Words and Phrases or Punctuation for Effect				●	●	●
Vary Sentences for Meaning, Interest, and Style		●	●	●	●	●
Vocabulary Acquisition and Use						
Determine Meanings of Unfamiliar and Multiple-Meaning Words	●	●	●	●	●	●
Acquire and Use Academic Vocabulary	●	●	●	●	●	●
Acquire and Use Domain-Specific Vocabulary	●	●	●	●	●	●
Use Inflections and Affixes	●	●	●	●	●	●
Use Context	●	●	●	●	●	●
Use Root Words		●	●	●	●	●
Use Prefixes and Suffixes		●	●	●	●	●
Use Individual Words Within Compound Words		●	●	●	●	●
Use a Glossary, Dictionary, and Thesaurus		●	●	●	●	●
Explore Word Relationships	●	●	●	●	●	●
Categorize Words	●	●	●	●	●	●
Identify Antonyms	●	●	●	●	●	●
Identify Synonyms	●	●	●	●	●	●
Identify Homographs					●	●
Identify Homophones					●	●
Connect Between Words and Their Uses	●	●	●	●	●	●
Distinguish Shades of Meaning	●	●	●	●	●	●
Identify Feeling Words and Sensory Words	●	●	●		●	●
Distinguish Literal from Nonliteral Meanings				●	●	●
Use Analogies					●	●
Figurative and Literary Language					●	●
Explain Similes and Metaphors					●	●
Identify Personification					●	●
Interpret Idioms, Expressions, Dialect, Adages, Proverbs, and Sayings					●	●

Grade 3 Common Core Standards

Reading

Strand	Code	Standards Text	Grade 3 Units 1–8 Standards Correlations
Literature			
Key Ideas and Details	**CC.3.Rlit.1**	**(1)** Ask and answer questions to demonstrate understanding of a text, referring explicitly to the text as the basis for the answers.	**Unit 2:** T76, T80–81, T82–83, T84–85, T89, T90–91, T94, T98, T100, SG8, SG9; **Unit 4:** T237a; **Unit 7:** T452–453, T457, T459, T460–461, T464
	CC.3.Rlit.2	**(2)** Recount stories, including fables, folktales, and myths from diverse cultures; determine the central message, lesson, or moral and explain how it is conveyed through key details in the text.	**Unit 1:** T12–13, T20, T22, SG8, SG9, SG15; **Unit 2:** SG8, SG9; **Unit 3:** T152–153, T154–155, T158, T162, T164a, SG9, SG15; **Unit 4:** T211a, T222, T227, T230, T232a, T236, T261, T262–263, T264–265, T267d, SG8; **Unit 6:** T396a, T396b, T402, T403a, T404, T405f, T405g, SG26, SG27; **Unit 7:** T430, T456, T462; **Unit 8:** T498, T506a, T508a, T517a, SG15
	CC.3.Rlit.3	**(3)** Describe characters in a story (e.g., their traits, motivations, or feelings) and explain how their actions contribute to the sequence of events.	**Unit 1:** T12–13, T14–15, T16–17, T18–19, T20, T23, T24, T25, T30, T33f, T33g, T33r; **Unit 2:** T94a; **Unit 3:** T141i, T154–155, T156, T162, SG10, SG11; Unit 4: T222, T223, T225, T227, T232a, T234a, T234b, T236, T237, T237a, T239a, T239b, T239d, T262–263, SG14, SG15; **Unit 5:** T277a, T286–287, T288–289, T293, T294–295, T296, T298, T298a; **Unit 8:** T496, T497, T502–503, T504, T506, T506a, T508a, T508b, T510–511, T512–513, T514–515, T519a, T519b, SG14
Craft and Structure	**CC.3.Rlit.4**	**(4)** Determine the meaning of words and phrases as they are used in a text, distinguishing literal from non-literal language.	**Unit 2:** T96a, T96b, T97, T98, T100, T101a, T103a, T103b, T103d; **Unit 3:** T160–161, T166a; **Unit 4:** T210, T211, T240, T241; **Unit 5:** T296; **Unit 6:** T359; **Unit 7:** T415a, T426–427, T432, T440; **Unit 8:** T494–495, T520, T521
	CC.3.Rlit.5	**(5)** Refer to parts of stories, dramas, and poems when writing or speaking about a text, using terms such as chapter, scene, and stanza; describe how each successive part builds on earlier sections.	**Unit 1:** T4, T5a, T20, T22, T24, T26, T26a, T28a, T28b, T29, T30, T31a, T32, T33a, T33b, SG8, SG9; **Unit 2:** T103f, T103g; **Unit 3:** T154–155, T156, T158, T159, T162, T164a, T166a, T166b, T167, T171a; **Unit 4:** T232a, T234a, T234b, T239a, T239b, SG14; **Unit 5:** T282, T284–285, T286–287, T292, T293, T298, T298a; **Unit 6:** T364, T364a, T400–401; **Unit 7:** T424–425, T426–427, T431, T432, T434a, T443o, T445a, T446, T464a; **Unit 8:** T506a, T517a, T519f, T519g
	CC.3.Rlit.6	**(6)** Distinguish their own point of view from that of the narrator or those of the characters.	**Unit 3:** T162; **Unit 4:** T217, T226, T228–229, T235, T267a, T267b, T267f, T267g; **Unit 7:** T464; **Unit 8:** T519a, T519b, T519d
Integration of Knowledge and Ideas	**CC.3.Rlit.7**	**(7)** Explain how specific aspects of a text's illustrations contribute to what is conveyed by the words in a story (e.g., create mood, emphasize aspects of a character or setting).	**Unit 2:** T97, T99; **Unit 6:** T354–355, T359, T392, T396c, T405a, T405b, T405d; **Unit 7:** T426–427, T450, T458, T463a; **Unit 8:** T500
	CC.3.Rlit.9	**(9)** Compare and contrast the themes, settings, and plots of stories written by the same author about the same or similar characters (e.g., in books from a series).	**Unit 2:** T69j; **Unit 4:** T233j, T239a, T239b, T239f, T239g, T267g; **Unit 5:** T273j; **Unit 7:** T411j; **Unit 8:** T507i
Range and Level of Complexity	**CC.3.Rlit.10**	**(10)** By the end of the year, read and comprehend literature, including stories, dramas, and poetry, at the high end of the grades 2–3 text complexity band independently and proficiently.	**Unit 1:** T1i, T8, T11, T12–13, T14–15, T16–17, T18–19, T20, T23, T24, T26a, T27j, T29, T31a, T32, T33a, T33f, T33r, SG8, SG9, SG14, SG15; **Unit 2:** T69j, T73a, T76, T79, T80–81, T82–83, T84–85, T89, T90–91, T94a, T95j, T96a, T96b, T97c, T98, T99, T100, T101, T101a, T103a, T103b, T103f, T103g, SG8, SG9; **Unit 3:** T141j, T145a, T146, T148, T149, T151, T152–153, T154–155, T156, T157, T158, T159, T160–161, T162, T163, T164, T164a, T166a, T166b, T167, T168–169, T170–171, T171a, T173r, SG8, SG9, SG14, SG15; **Unit 4:** T207j, T217, T218–219, T220–221, T222, T225, T226, T227, T228–229, T230, T231, T232a, T233j, T235, T236, T237a, T239a, T239b, T239f, T239r, T260a, T260b, T261, T262–263, T265a, T267a, T267b, T267f, T267g, SG8, SG9, SG14, SG15; **Unit 5:** T273j, T280, T281, SG8, SG9; **Unit 6:** T341j, T373r, T400–401, T402, SG8, SG9, SG20, SG26, SG27; **Unit 7:** T411j, T415a, T421, T422-423, T424–425, T426–427, T431, T432, T434a, T443p, T445a, T452–453, T454–455, T457, T458, T459, T460–461, T462, T463, T464a, T465, SG20, SG21; **Unit 8:** T481j, T485a, T491, T492–493, T494–495, T496, T499, T500, T501, T502–503, T504, T505, T507j, T509, T510–511, T512–513, T514–515, SG8, SG9, SG14, SG15

Search for activities that meet each **Common Core Standard.** NGReach.com

Strand	Code	Standards Text	Grade 3 Units 1–8 Standards Correlations
Informational Text			
Key Ideas and Details	**CC.3.Rinf.1**	**(1)** Ask and answer questions to demonstrate understanding of a text, referring explicitly to the text as the basis for the answers.	**Unit 2:** T108, T109, T112–113, T116–117, T122–123, T130–131, SG14, SG15, SG20, SG21, SG26, SG27; **Unit 6:** SG16, SG17; **Unit 7:** T437, T438, T439, T440, T467, T469, T470; **Unit 8:** SG10, SG11, SG16, SG17
	CC.3.Rinf.2	**(2)** Determine the main idea of a text; recount the key details and explain how they support the main idea.	**Unit 1:** T27j, T58–59, SG4, SG5, SG10, SG11; **Unit 2:** T128a, T128b, T129, T130–131, T135a, T135b, SG4, SG5, SG10, SG11, SG14, SG26; **Unit 3:** T175a, T176, T182–183, T184–185, T186, T188, T189, T191, T192, T193, T194a, T201f, T201g, SG4, SG5, SG20; **Unit 4:** T244, T248–249, T252, T255, T256, SG10, SG11; **Unit 5:** T307d, T324, SG14, SG16, SG17; **Unit 6:** T368, T390, SG10, SG11; **Unit 7:** T465j, T466a, T466b, T469, T470, SG26; **Unit 8:** T521a, T522, T530, T533, T534–535, T538a, T541, SG20
	CC.3.Rinf.3	**(3)** Describe the relationship between a series of historical events, scientific ideas or concepts, or steps in technical procedures in a text, using language that pertains to time, sequence, and cause/effect.	**Unit 2:** T105a, T112–113, T114–115, T116–117, T118–119, T121, T122–123, T126a, T133a, SG20, SG21, SG22, SG23; **Unit 3:** T173a, T173b, T173d, T173f, T173g, T173h, T190, T194, T194a, T198, SG10, SG11; **Unit 4:** SG22, SG23; **Unit 5:** T309a, T316–317, T321, T323, T324, T326a, T335a, T335b, SG4, SG5, SG20; **Unit 6:** T375a, T384–385, T386–387, T392, T394a, SG22, SG23; **Unit 7:** T435j, T436a, T436b, T438, T440, T443a, T443b, T443f; **Unit 8:** T521a, T532, T538a, T540a, T540b, T545a, T547a, T547b, SG4, SG5, SG20, SG26
Craft and Structure	**CC.3.Rinf.4**	**(4)** Determine the meaning of general academic and domain-specific words and phrases in a text relevant to a grade 3 topic or subject area.	**Unit 5:** SG22, SG23; **Unit 7:** T473c, T473e
	CC.3.Rinf.5	**(5)** Use text features and search tools (e.g., key words, sidebars, hyperlinks) to locate information relevant to a given topic efficiently.	**Unit 1:** T55h, T57; **Unit 2:** T103y, T103z, T114–115, T116–117, T121, T122–123, T127a, T129; **Unit 3:** T165i, T181, T182–183, T184–185, T189, T191, T196a, T196b, T197, T198, T199a, T201a, T201b, T201d, SG22, SG23, SG26; **Unit 4:** T246, T247, T250–251, T252; **Unit 5:** T303, T307a, T307b, T314, T315, T322, T328a, T328b, T330, T331, T332, T333a, T335f, T335g, SG10, SG11, SG26; **Unit 6:** T380, T381, T382–383, T384–385, T386–387, T388–389; **Unit 7:** T443p, T467, T468; **Unit 8:** T526, T527, T528, T531
	CC.3.Rinf.6	**(6)** Distinguish their own point of view from that of the author of a text.	**Unit 1:** T41, T48, T53a, T56a, T56b, T57, T58–59; **Unit 2:** T135f, T135g; **Unit 4:** T250–251, T257, SG16, SG17; **Unit 5:** T330, T331; **Unit 8:** T547f, T547g
Integration of Knowledge and Ideas	**CC.3.Rinf.7**	**(7)** Use information gained from illustrations (e.g., maps, photographs) and the words in a text to demonstrate understanding of the text (e.g., where, when, why, and how key events occur).	**Unit 3:** T196a, T196b, T198, SG26; **Unit 4:** SG4, SG5; **Unit 5:** T314, T315, T321, T322, T323; **Unit 6:** T366a, T366b, T366c, T369, T370, T371a, T373a, T373b, T373g, T394, SG14; **Unit 7:** T466c, T468, SG4, SG5, SG10, SG11; **Unit 8:** T540c, SG22, SG23
	CC.3.Rinf.8	**(8)** Describe the logical connection between particular sentences and paragraphs in a text (e.g., comparison, cause/effect, first/second/third in a sequence).	**Unit 1:** T42–43, T52, T54a, T55, SG20, SG21, SG22, SG23, SG26; **Unit 2:** T126a; **Unit 3:** T173a, T173b, T190, T198, SG16, SG17; **Unit 4:** SG22, SG23; **Unit 5:** SG20; **Unit 6:** SG4, SG5, SG20; **Unit 7:** T416a, T418, T443f, T443g, SG14, SG22, SG23; **Unit 8:** T521a
	CC.3.Rinf.9	**(9)** Compare and contrast the most important points and key details presented in two texts on the same topic.	**Unit 1:** T61a, T63f, T63g, SG16, SG17; **Unit 2:** T133a, SG16, SG17; **Unit 3:** T173g, T173h, T201g; **Unit 5:** T300a, T300b, T303, T304, T305a, T307f, T307g, SG14; **Unit 7:** T435q, T435r, T441a, T442, T443g, T443h, T443p, T471a, T472, T473g, T473h, SG16, SG17; **Unit 8:** T545a
Range and Level of Text Complexity	**CC.3.Rinf.10**	**(10)** By the end of the year, read and comprehend informational texts, including history/social studies, science, and technical texts, at the high end of the grades 2–3 text complexity band independently and proficiently**.**	**Unit 1:** T1i, T27j, T33r, T38, T41, T42–43, T47, T48, T49, T50–51, T52, T53, T53a, T54a, T55h, T56a, T56b, T57, T61a, T63a, T63f, SG5, SG11, SG17, SG20, SG21, SG23, SG26, SG27; **Unit 2:** T95j, T103r, T108, T111, T112–113, T114–115, T116–117, T121, T122–123, T126a, T127h, T128a, T128b, T129, T130–131, T133a, T135a, T135b, T135f, T135g, SG5, SG11, SG14, SG15, SG17, SG20, SG21, SG23, SG26, SG27; **Unit 3:** T141j, T165j, T173a, T173b, T173f, T173r, T178, T181, T182–T183, T184–185, T186, T189, T190, T191, T192, T194a, T195h, T196a, T196b, T197, T198, T199a, SG5, SG11, SG17, SG20, SG21, SG23, SG26, SG27; **Unit 4:** T207j, T233j, T239r, T241a, T259h, T260a, T260b, SG5, SG11, SG17, SG20, SG21, SG23, SG26, SG27; **Unit 5:** T273j, T299j, T307r, T312, T315, T316–317, T326a, T327, T327h, SG5, SG11, SG14, SG15, SG17, SG20, SG21, SG23, SG26, SG27; **Unit 6:** T341j, T348, T365j, T373g, T373r, T378, T395h, T397, T398–399, SG5, SG11, SG14, SG15, SG17, SG20, SG23; **Unit 7:** T418, T436a, T437, T438, T439, T440, T441a, T443a, T443b, T443f, T443g, T448, T465j, T466a, T466b, T467, T468, T469, T470, T471a, T473a, T473b, T473f, T473g, SG5, SG11, SG14, SG15, SG17, SG23, SG26, SG27; **Unit 8:** T481j, T488, T507j, T519r, T524, T527, T528, T529, T530, T531, T533, T534–535, T539h, T541, T542–543, T547a, T547b, T547f, T547g, SG5, SG11, SG17, SG20, SG21, SG23, SG26, SG27

Grade 3 Common Core Standards

Reading, continued

Strand	Code	Standards Text	Grade 3 Units 1–8 Standards Correlations
Foundational Skills			
Phonics and Word Recognition	**CC.3.Rfou.3**	**(3)** Know and apply grade-level phonics and word analysis skills in decoding words.	**Unit 1:** T1i, T1l, T1m, T27j, T27m, T27n, T33r, T33u, T33v, T55h, T55k, T55l; **Unit 2:** T69j, T69k, T69l, T69m, T69n, T95j, T95k, T95l, T95m, T95n, T96, T96c, T103c, T103e, T103r, T103s, T103t, T103u, T103v, T127h, T127l, T127q, T128, T128c, T135c, T135e; **Unit 3:** T141j, T141m, T141n, T165j, T165m, T166c, T173r, T173u, T173v, T195h, T195k, T195l, T196, T196c, T201c, T201e; **Unit 4:** T207j, T207k, T207l, T207m, T207n, T233j, T233k, T233l, T233m, T239r, T239s, T239t, T259h, T259i, T259j; **Unit 5:** T273j, T273k, T273l, T273m, T273n, T299j, T299k, T299l, T299m, T299n, T307r, T307s, T307t, T307u, T307v, T327h, T327i, T327j, T327k, T327l; **Unit 6:** T341j, T341k, T341l, T341n, T365j, T365k, T365l, T365m, T365n, T373r, T373s, T373t, T373u, T373v, T395h, T395i, T395j, T395k, T395l; **Unit 7:** T411j, T411k, T411l, T411m, T411n, T435j, T435m, T435n, T443p, T443s, T443t, T465j, T465m, T465s, T466, T466c; **Unit 8:** T481j, T481k, T481l, T481n, T507i, T507j, T507k, T507l, T507n, T519r, T519u, T519v, T539h, T539k
	CC.3.Rfou.3.a	**(a)** Identify and know the meaning of the most common prefixes and derivational suffixes.	**Unit 3:** T196, T196c, T201c, T201e; **Unit 4:** T233s, T234, T234c, T239c, T239e; **Unit 8:** T481m, T481n, T507m, T507n
	CC.3.Rfou.3.b	**(b)** Decode words with common Latin suffixes.	**Unit 8:** T481l, T507k, T507l, T519t, T539j
	CC.3.Rfou.3.c	**(c)** Decode multi-syllable words.	**Unit 2:** T127q, T128, T128c, T135c, T135e; **Unit 3:** T165k, T165l; **Unit 4:** T207m, T207n, T233k, T233l, T233m; **Unit 5:** T273m, T299n, T307v, T327k; **Unit 6:** T341k, T341l, T341m, T365n, T373u, T395l; **Unit 7:** T443q, T443r, T465i, T465k, T465l, T465s, T466, T466c, T473c; **Unit 8:** T481m, T481n, T507m, T507n, T519s, T519t, T519u, T539j, T539k, T539l
	CC.3.Rfou.3.d	**(d)** Read grade-appropriate irregularly spelled words.	**Unit 1:** T1j, T1k, T33s, T33t, T55i, T55j; **Unit 2:** T69k, T69l, T95k, T95l, T103s, T103t, T127i, T127j; **Unit 3:** T141k, T141l, T165k, T165l, T173s, T173t, T195i, T195j; **Unit 4:** T207k, T207l, T239s, T239t, T259i, T259j; **Unit 5:** T273k, T273l, T299k, T299l, T307s, T307t, T327i, T327j; **Unit 6:** T341k, T341l, T365k, T365l, T373s, T373t, T395i, T396j; **Unit 7:** T411k, T411l, T435k, T435l, T443q, T443r, T465k, T465l; **Unit 8:** T481k, T481l, T507k, T507l, T519s, T519t, T539j
Fluency	**CC.3.Rfou.4**	**(4)** Read with sufficient accuracy and fluency to support comprehension.	**Unit 1:** T5a, T8, T12–13, T28a, T29, T31a, T33b, T35a, T38, T42–43, T56a, T57, T62, T63b; **Unit 2:** T73a, T76, T80–81, T96a, T97, T101a, T103b, T105a, T108, T112–113, T128a, T129, T134, T135b; **Unit 3:** T145a, T148, T152–153, T166a, T167, T172, T173b, T175a, T178, T182–183, T196a, T197, T200, T201b; **Unit 4:** T211a, T214, T218–219, T234a, T235, T238, T239b, T241a, T244, T248–249, T260a, T261, T266, T267b; **Unit 5:** T277a, T280, T286–287, T300a, T301, T306, T307b, T309a, T312, T316–317, T328a, T329, T334, T335b; **Unit 6:** T345a, T348, T352–353, T366a, T367, T372, T373b, T375a, T378, T382–383, T396a, T397, T404, T405b; **Unit 7:** T415a, T418, T422–423, T432, T436a, T437, T442, T443b, T445a, T448, T452–453, T457, T465, T466a, T467, T471a, T473b; **Unit 8:** T485a, T488, T494–495, T508a, T509, T518, T519b, T521a, T524, T528, T533, T539, T540a, T541, T546, T547b
	CC.3.Rfou.4.a	**(a)** Read on-level text with purpose and understanding.	**Unit 1:** T12–13, T23, T42–43, T47; **Unit 4:** T214, SG8, SG9, SG14, SG15; **Unit 6:** T397; **Unit 7:** T437, T452–453, T457, T467; **Unit 8:** T541, T547b
	CC.3.Rfou.4.b	**(b)** Read on-level prose and poetry orally with accuracy, appropriate rate, and expression on successive readings.	**Unit 1:** T1i, T12–13, T23, T27, T27i, T28a, T29, T31a, T33b, T33d, T33l, T33r, T42–43, T47, T54a; **Unit 2:** T69j, T80–81, T89, T95, T103r, T112–113, T121, T127; **Unit 3:** T141i, T141j, T152–153, T159, T164a, T165, T166a, T167, T172, T173b, T173r, T182–183, T189, T195; **Unit 4:** T207j, T218–219, T225, T233, T234a, T235, T238, T239b, T239r, T248–249, T255, T258a, T259h; **Unit 5:** T273j, T286–287, T293, T299, T307r, T316–317, T321, T326a; **Unit 6:** T341j, T352–353, T357, T365, T366a, T367, T372, T373r, T382–383, T391, T395; **Unit 7:** T411j, T422–423, T435, T436a, T437, T442, T443b, T443o, T443p, T466a, T467, T471a, T473b; **Unit 8:** T481j, T494–495, T499, T507, T507i, T508a, T509, T518, T519b, T519r, T540a, T541, T546, T547b
	CC.3.Rfou.4.c	**(c)** Use context to confirm or self-correct word recognition and understanding, rereading as necessary.	**Unit 6:** T405e; **Unit 8:** T539q, T540, T540c, T547c, T547e

Writing

Strand	Code	Standards Text	Grade 3 Units 1–8 Standards Correlations
Text Types and Purposes	**CC.3.W.1**	**(1)** Write opinion pieces on topics or texts, supporting a point of view with reasons.	**Unit 4:** T233b, T233c, T258, T259g, T259o, T259p, T268, T269, T270, T273; **Unit 5:** T327o, T327p, T337, T338, T339; **Unit 6:** T341i, T373g, T388–389, T403; **Unit 7:** T434, T471; **Unit 8:** T481q, T481r, T507b, T507c, T516–517, T547d
	CC.3.W.1.a	**(a)** Introduce the topic or text they are writing about, state an opinion, and create an organizational structure that lists reasons.	**Unit 4:** T259o, T259p, T268, T269, T270; **Unit 5:** T327o, T327p, T337, T338, T339; **Unit 8:** T507b
	CC.3.W.1.b	**(b)** Provide reasons that support the opinion.	**Unit 4:** T233b, T233c, T259g, T259o, T259p, T268, T269, T270, T273; **Unit 5:** T337, T338; **Unit 6:** T373g, T388–389, T403; **Unit 7:** T434; **Unit 8:** T481q, T481r
	CC.3.W.1.c	**(c)** Use linking words and phrases (e.g., because, therefore, since, for example) to connect opinion and reasons.	**Unit 4:** T242, T259o, T259p, T268, T269, T270; **Unit 5:** T337, T338; **Unit 6:** T341i; **Unit 7:** T471; **Unit 8:** T481q, T481r, T516–517
	CC.3.W.1.d	**(d)** Provide a concluding statement or section.	**Unit 5:** T327p, T337, T338; **Unit 8:** T507b, T507c
	CC.3.W.2	**(2)** Write informative/explanatory texts to examine a topic and convey ideas and information clearly.	**Unit 1:** T55g, T68, T69; **Unit 2:** T69i, T103q, T127g, T137, T138; **Unit 3:** T141i, T165j, T173q, T195g, T195h, T195o, T195p, T202, T203, T204, T205; **Unit 4:** T207j, T259h; **Unit 5:** T273j, T299q, T299r, T307i, T307j, T307k, T307l, T307q, T307r, T327g; **Unit 6:** T373j, T373k, T373l, T395h; **Unit 7:** T465i, T465q, T465r, T478; **Unit 8:** T481i, T507i, T507j, T519q
	CC.3.W.2.a	**(a)** Introduce a topic and group related information together; include illustrations when useful to aiding comprehension.	**Unit 2:** T69i, T103r, T127g, T137, T138; **Unit 3:** T141j, T165j, T173r, T195o, T195p, T202, T203; **Unit 4:** T233i, T259g; **Unit 5:** T273j, T299q, T299r, T307j, T327g; **Unit 6:** T395o, T395p, T406, T407; **Unit 7:** T435q, T435r, T465q, T465r, T478; **Unit 8:** T481i, T519q, T539a, T539b, T553
	CC.3.W.2.b	**(b)** Develop the topic with facts, definitions, and details.	**Unit 2:** T127o, T127p, T137, T138; **Unit 3:** T203, T204; **Unit 5:** T307j, T307k, T307q; **Unit 7:** T465q, T465r, T476, T476a, T478
	CC.3.W.2.c	**(c)** Use linking words and phrases (e.g., also, another, and, more, but) to connect ideas within categories of information.	**Unit 3:** T141q, T141r; **Unit 7:** T436b, T443d, T465q, T465r
	CC.3.W.2.d	**(d)** Provide a concluding statement or section.	**Unit 6:** T373k
	CC.3.W.3	**(3)** Write narratives to develop real or imagined experiences or events using effective technique, descriptive details, and clear event sequences.	**Unit 1:** T1h, T27b, T27c, T65, T66; **Unit 2:** T95b, T95c, T103q; **Unit 3:** T141q, T141r, T165a, T165b, T165c, T165d, T165q, T165r; **Unit 5:** T307q, T341; **Unit 6:** T373q, T395g; **Unit 7:** T411i, T416, T465b; **Unit 8:** T481i, T519j, T519k, T519q, T548, T549, T550
	CC.3.W.3.a	**(a)** Establish a situation and introduce a narrator and/or characters; organize an event sequence that unfolds naturally.	**Unit 1:** T1p, T1q, T27a, T27b, T27c, T55b, T65, T66; **Unit 2:** T103q; **Unit 4:** T233q, T233r, T239j, T239k; **Unit 5:** T307q; **Unit 7:** T465b; **Unit 8:** T507i, T507q, T507r, T519j, T519k, T548, T549, T550
	CC.3.W.3.b	**(b)** Use dialogue and descriptions of actions, thoughts, and feelings to develop experiences and events or show the response of characters to situations.	**Unit 1:** T27c, T27q, T27r, T33i, T33j, T33k, T55b, T65, T66; **Unit 2:** T95b, T95c, T141; **Unit 4:** T231a, T273; **Unit 5:** T273i, T273q, T273r, T290–291, T297a, T299a, T299b, T299c, T299d, T299i; **Unit 7:** T443w, T443x, T454–455, T465b, T465c; **Unit 8:** T505a, T507i, T507q, T507r
	CC.3.W.3.c	**(c)** Use temporal words and phrases to signal event order.	**Unit 1:** T1q, T55b
	CC.3.W.3.d	**(d)** Provide a sense of closure.	**Unit 1:** T1q, T66; **Unit 8:** T539o, T539p
Production and Distribution of Writing	**CC.3.W.4**	**(4)** With guidance and support from adults, produce writing in which the development and organization are appropriate to task and purpose. (Grade-specific expectations for writing types are defined in standards 1–3 above.)	**Unit 1:** T33i, T33j, T33k; **Unit 2:** T95i, T103i, T103j, T103k; **Unit 3:** T165a, T165b, T165c, T165d, T173i, T173j, T173k, T173l; **Unit 4:** T259g; **Unit 6:** T341q, T341r, T365b, T365q, T365r, T373i, T373j, T373k, T373l, T411; **Unit 7:** T435a, T435b, T435c, T435d, T465b, T465c, T474–475, T476, T476a, T477, T478
	CC.3.W.5	**(5)** With guidance and support from peers and adults, develop and strengthen writing as needed by planning, revising, and editing. (Editing for conventions should demonstrate command of Language standards 1–3 up to and including grade 3 on pages 28 and 29.)	**Unit 1:** T1o, T27a, T27b, T27c, T27d, T27p, T33i, T33j, T33k, T33l, T33x, T55n, T64, T65, T66; **Unit 2:** T69p, T95a, T95b, T95c, T95d, T95i, T95p, T103i, T103j, T103k, T103l, T103x, T127n, T136, T137, T138; **Unit 3:** T141i, T141p, T165a, T165b, T165c, T165d, T165p, T173i, T173j, T173k, T173l, T173x, T195n, T202, T203, T204, T205; **Unit 4:** T207p, T233a, T233b, T233c, T233d, T233p, T239i, T239j, T239k, T239l, T239x, T259n, T268, T269, T270; **Unit 5:** T273p, T299a, T299b, T299c, T299d, T299p, T307i, T307j, T307k, T307l, T307x, T327m, T336, T337, T338, T339; **Unit 6:** T341p, T365a, T365b, T365c, T365d, T365p, T373i, T373j, T373k, T373l, T373x, T395n, T406, T407, T408, T409; **Unit 7:** T411p, T435b, T435c, T435d, T435p, T465a, T465b, T465c, T465d, T465p, T476, T476a, T477, T478, T479; **Unit 8:** T481p, T507a, T507b, T507c, T507d, T507p, T519i, T519j, T519k, T519l, T519x, T539n, T548, T549, T550
	CC.3.W.6	**(6)** With guidance and support from adults, use technology to produce and publish writing (using keyboarding skills) as well as to interact and collaborate with others.	**Unit 2:** T95j, T127b; **Unit 3:** T165a, T165b, T165c, T165d, T173i, T173j, T173k, T173l, T195b, T195g, T195o, T195p; **Unit 4:** T239y, T239z; **Unit 6:** T365b, T365c, T365d, T373j, T373k, T373l; **Unit 7:** T465b, T465c, T465d

Grade 3 Common Core Standards

Writing, continued

Strand	Code	Standards Text	Grade 3 Units 1–8 Standards Correlations
Research to Build and Present Knowledge	**CC.3.W.7**	**(7)** Conduct short research projects that build knowledge about a topic.	**Unit 1:** T33q, T33z, T55a; **Unit 2:** T103y, T103z; **Unit 3:** T173q, T173y, T173z, T195a, T195b, T195h, T202; **Unit 4:** T207j, T239y, T239z, T259a; **Unit 5:** T327a, T327b; **Unit 6:** T373i, T373j; **Unit 7:** T411j, T435i, T435q, T443i, T476, T476a; **Unit 8:** T539a, T539b
	CC.3.W.8	**(8)** Recall information from experiences or gather information from print and digital sources; take brief notes on sources and sort evidence into provided categories.	**Unit 1:** T1i, T33q, T33z, T55a, T55h; **Unit 2:** T69j, T103r, T127a, T127b; **Unit 3:** T141i, T141j, T165i, T165j, T173q, T173r, T173y, T173z, T195a, T195b, T195h, T202, T203; **Unit 4:** T259a, T259b; **Unit 5:** T299i, T299j, T307y, T307z, T327a, T327b; **Unit 6:** T341j, T373i, T373j, T373y, T373z, T395a, T395b, T395g; **Unit 7:** T411j, T435i, T435q, T435r, T443i, T443j, T443p, T465i, T476a, T477, T478; **Unit 8:** T519y, T519z, T539a, T539b
Range of Writing	**CC.3.W.10**	**(10)** Write routinely over extended time frames (time for research, reflection, and revision) and shorter time frames (a single sitting or a day or two) for a range of discipline-specific tasks, purposes, and audiences.	**Unit 1:** T1h, T6, T8, T9, T21, T25, T26, T27b, T27c, T27i, T27s, T31, T31a, T33d, T33g, T33j, T33k, T33q, T34, T36, T38, T39, T44–45, T53a, T54, T55g, T56b, T60–61, T61a, T63d, T63g, T65, T66, SG8, SG9, SG14, SG15, SG20, SG21, SG26, SG27; **Unit 2:** T69i, T69q, T69r, T74, T76, T77, T86–87, T92–93, T94, T95i, T95j, T95q, T95r, T96b, T100, T101, T101a, T103d, T103g, T103i, T103j, T103k, T103l, T106, T108, T118–119, T124–125, T126, T127g, T128b, T132–133, T133a, T135d, T135g, T140, SG8, SG9, SG14, SG15, SG20, SG21, SG26, SG27; **Unit 3:** T146, T148, T149, T157, T163a, T164, T165a, T165b, T165c, T165d, T165i, T166b, T170–171, T171a, T173d, T173g, T173i, T173j, T173k, T173l, T176, T178, T179, T187, T193, T194, T195g, T195q, T196b, T199, T199a, T201d, T201g, T202, T203, T204, T205, T206, T207, SG8, SG9, SG14, SG15, SG20, SG21, SG26, SG27; **Unit 4:** T207i, T207q, T207r, T212, T214, T215, T223, T224, T233b, T233c, T233i, T234b, T237, T237a, T239d, T239g, T239j, T239k, T239q, T239r, T242, T244, T245, T253, T257, T258, T260b, T264–265, T265a, T267d, T267g, T268, T269, T270, T272, T273, SG8, SG9, SG14, SG15, SG20, SG21, SG26, SG27; **Unit 5:** T273i, T278, T280, T281, T282, T292, T298, T299a, T299b, T299c, T299d, T299i, T300b, T305, T305a, T307d, T307g, T307i, T307j, T307k, T307l, T310, T312, T313, T318–319, T325, T326, T328b, T333, T333a, T335d, T335g, T336, T337, T338, T339, T340, T341, SG8, SG9, SG14, SG15, SG20, SG21, SG26, SG27; **Unit 6:** T341i, T346, T348, T349, T354–355, T363a, T364, T365a, T365b, T365c, T365d, T365i, T365j, T366b, T371, T371a, T373a, T373e, T373i, T373j, T373k, T373l, T373q, T376, T378, T379, T380, T393, T394, T396b, T403, T403a, T405d, T405g, T406, T407, T408, T409, T410, T411, SG8, SG9, SG14, SG15, SG20, SG21, SG26, SG27; **Unit 7:** T418, T428–429, T433, T433a, T436b, T441, T441a, T443d, T443g, T443i, T443j, T443o, T446, T448, T449, T454–455, T463a, T464, T466b, T466c, T471a, T473d, T473g, T480, T481, SG8, SG9, SG14, SG15, SG20, SG21, SG26, SG27; **Unit 8:** T486, T488, T489, T497, T505a, T506, T507b, T507c, T508b, T508c, T517a, T519d, T519g, T519j, T519k, T522, T524, T525, T531, T536–537, T538, T539g, T540b, T544–545, T545a, T547d, T547g, T548, T549, T550, T552, T553, SG8, SG9, SG14, SG15, SG20, SG21, SG26, SG27

Speaking and Listening

Strand	Code	Standards Text	Grade 3 Units 1–8 Standards Correlations
Comprehension and Collaboration	**CC.3.SL.1**	**(1)** Engage effectively in a range of collaborative discussions (one-on-one, in groups, and teacher-led) with diverse partners on grade 3 topics and texts, building on others' ideas and expressing their own clearly.	**Unit 1:** T1h, T10, T26, T27i, T27s, T28c, T32, T33h, T33r, T36a, T46, T55g, T55q, T56c, T62, T63h; **Unit 2:** T69i, T88, T102, T103h, T106a, T107, T110, T120, T128c, T134, T135h, T141; **Unit 3:** T141i, T150, T165i, T165j, T166c, T172, T173q, T180, T194, T195g, T195h, T195q, T196c, T200, T201, T201d, T201h; **Unit 4:** T210, T216, T224, T232, T233, T233i, T234c, T239d, T239h, T242a, T254, T258, T259, T259g, T259q, T260c, T266, T267h, T273; **Unit 5:** T273i, T276, T277, T282, T292, T298, T299, T299i, T299j, T299s, T300c, T306, T314, T320, T326, T327, T327g, T327h, T327q, T328c, T334; **Unit 6:** T341i, T350, T356, T365s, T372, T373r, T380, T394, T395h, T396c, T404, T405d; **Unit 7:** T420, T435i, T436c, T446a, T464, T465i, T465j; **Unit 8:** T481i, T481j, T490, T506, T507s, T508c, T518, T519q, T519r, T520, T526, T539g, T539q, T540c, T546
	CC.3.SL.1.a	**(a)** Come to discussions prepared, having read or studied required material; explicitly draw on that preparation and other information known about the topic to explore ideas under discussion.	**Unit 1:** T63d, SG8, SG9, SG14, SG15, SG20, SG21, SG26, SG27; **Unit 2:** T96c, T106a, T127h, T140, T141, SG8, SG9, SG14, SG15, SG20, SG21, SG26, SG27; **Unit 3:** T164, T165, T165i, T173q, T201d, T201h, T206, SG8, SG9, SG14, SG15, SG20, SG21, SG26, SG27; **Unit 4:** T232, T239d, T258, T259, T266, T272, SG8, SG9, SG14, SG15, SG20, SG21, SG26, SG27; **Unit 5:** T273i, T299i, T307h, T335h, T340, T341, SG8, SG9, SG14, SG15, SG20, SG21, SG26, SG27; **Unit 6:** T373h, T395q, T405h, T410, SG8, SG9, SG14, SG15, SG20, SG21, SG26, SG27; **Unit 7:** T412, T434, T443h, T465j, T473h, T480, T481, SG8, SG9, SG14, SG15, SG20, SG21, SG26, SG27; **Unit 8:** T517a, T519h, T547h, T552, T553, SG8, SG9, SG14, SG15, SG20, SG21, SG26, SG27
	CC.3.SL.1.b	**(b)** Follow agreed-upon rules for discussions (e.g., gaining the floor in respectful ways, listening to others with care, speaking one at a time about the topics and texts under discussion).	**Unit 1:** T27s, T36a, T55q; **Unit 3:** T195q; **Unit 4:** T238, T239h, T267h; **Unit 5:** T327q; **Unit 7:** T411i
	CC.3.SL.1.c	**(c)** Ask questions to check understanding of information presented, stay on topic, and link their comments to the remarks of others.	**Unit 1:** T27s, T33z; **Unit 2:** T69i, T72, T95i, T106a, T127q, T135h; **Unit 3:** T145, T146a, T147, T165s, T207; **Unit 4:** T273; **Unit 5:** T278a; **Unit 6:** T350, T365s, T409, T410, T411; **Unit 7:** T443d; **Unit 8:** T552, T553
	CC.3.SL.1.d	**(d)** Explain their own ideas and understanding in light of the discussion.	**Unit 1:** T26, T40, T54; **Unit 2:** T69i, T95i, T126, T127q; **Unit 3:** T141i, T146a, T165i, T173q, T176a, T195g; **Unit 4:** T210, T240, T241, T242a, T254, T258, T259, T266; **Unit 5:** T299s, T306, T334; **Unit 6:** T372; **Unit 7:** T416a, T435s, T444, T445, T465s; **Unit 8:** T486a, T518
	CC.3.SL.2	**(2)** Determine the main ideas and supporting details of a text read aloud or information presented in diverse media and formats, including visually, quantitatively, and orally.	**Unit 1:** T2, T36a; **Unit 2:** T70, T127g, T135a, T135b, T135d; **Unit 3:** T142; **Unit 4:** T207i, T208, T233j, T239q, T259g; **Unit 5:** T307d; **Unit 6:** T342, T346a, T373d, T373q, T405d, T410, T411; **Unit 7:** T411i, T435j, T443p, T465i, T473d; **Unit 8:** T482, T538, T539g
	CC.3.SL.3	**(3)** Ask and answer questions about information from a speaker, offering appropriate elaboration and detail.	**Unit 1:** T33q, T33z, T55b, T55g, T68, T69; **Unit 2:** T127g; **Unit 3:** T145, T146a, T174; **Unit 4:** T239q, T240, T273; **Unit 5:** T307q, T310a, T327b; **Unit 6:** T341i, T344, T345, T346a, T364, T365, T365i, T395g; **Unit 7:** T465i; **Unit 8:** T481i, T484, T485, T519q, T522a
Presentation of Knowledge and Ideas	**CC.3.SL.4**	**(4)** Report on a topic or text, tell a story, or recount an experience with appropriate facts and relevant, descriptive details, speaking clearly at an understandable pace.	**Unit 1:** T1h, T4, T5, T6a, T22, T26, T33q, T34, T55b, T55g, T69; **Unit 2:** T74a, T94, T95s, T126; **Unit 3:** T158, T162, T173d, T173h, T173r, T195b; **Unit 4:** T207i, T207j, T212a, T233i, T233s, T259b, T267d; **Unit 5:** T306, T307q, T308, T327b, T327g, T334, T341; **Unit 6:** T341j, T356, T365s, T373q, T395b, T395g, T405d; **Unit 7:** T414, T415, T435j, T443j, T443p, T465j, T472; **Unit 8:** T507d, T507s, T519d, T532, T539b, T539h, T547d
	CC.3.SL.5	**(5)** Create engaging audio recordings of stories or poems that demonstrate fluid reading at an understandable pace; add visual displays when appropriate to emphasize or enhance certain facts or details.	**Unit 1:** T1h, T27i, T33l, T55b; **Unit 2:** T127b, T141; **Unit 3:** T195b; **Unit 4:** T207i, T239l; **Unit 5:** T273i, T299, T307r; **Unit 6:** T365d, T365i, T373q, T395b; **Unit 7:** T435j, T465j, T479, T481; **Unit 8:** T507i, T519l, T519q, T539h, T551
	CC.3.SL.6	**(6)** Speak in complete sentences when appropriate to task and situation in order to provide requested detail or clarification. (See grade 3 Language standards 1 and 3 on pages 28 and 29 for specific expectations.)	**Unit 2:** T78, T95i, T103q, T104, T126, T127g; **Unit 7:** T435i; **Unit 8:** T520

Grade 3 Common Core Standards

Language

Strand	Code	Standards Text	Grade 3 Units 1–8 Standards Correlations
Conventions of Standard English	**CC.3.L.1**	**(1)** Demonstrate command of the conventions of standard English grammar and usage when writing or speaking.	**Unit 1:** T1n, T1o, T27d, T27o, T27p, T32a, T33, T33l, T33w, T33x, T55m, T55n, T55o, T55p, T62a, T63, T66; **Unit 2:** T95d, T102a, T103, T103q, T103w, T103x, T127m, T127n, T134a, T135, T138; **Unit 3:** T141o, T141p, T165d, T165o, T165p, T172a, T173, T173l, T173u, T173w, T173x, T195m, T195n, T200a, T201, T204, T207; **Unit 4:** T207o, T207p, T233d, T233o, T233p, T238a, T239, T239l, T239w, T239x, T259m, T259n, T266a, T267, T270; **Unit 5:** T273o, T273p, T299c, T299o, T299p, T306a, T307, T307l, T307w, T307x, T327m, T327n, T334a, T335, T338; **Unit 6:** T341o, T341p, T365d, T365o, T365p, T372a, T373, T373l, T373w, T373x, T395m, T395n, T404a, T405, T408; **Unit 7:** T411o, T411p, T433, T434, T435o, T435p, T442a, T443, T443u, T443v, T465o, T465p, T472a, T473; **Unit 8:** T481o, T481p, T507d, T507o, T507p, T518a, T519, T519w, T519x, T539m, T539n, T546a, T547, T550
	CC.3.L.1.a	**(a)** Explain the function of nouns, pronouns, verbs, adjectives, and adverbs in general and their functions in particular sentences.	**Unit 1:** T1n, T1o, T27d, T27o, T27p, T33l, T33w, T33x; **Unit 3:** T173l, T204; **Unit 4:** T207o, T207p, T239w, T239x, T259m, T259n; **Unit 5:** T273o, T273p, T299o, T299p, T306a, T307w, T307x; **Unit 6:** T341o, T341p, T365o, T365p, T373l, T373w, T373x, T395m, T395n, T404a, T405; **Unit 7:** T411o, T411p, T416, T419, T435o, T435p, T442a, T443u, T443v; **Unit 8:** T481o, T481p, T539m, T539n
	CC.3.L.1.b	**(b)** Form and use regular and irregular plural nouns.	**Unit 3:** T165o, T165p, T172a, T173, T173l, T173w, T173x, T195n, T200a, T201, T204
	CC.3.L.1.c	**(c)** Use abstract nouns (e.g., childhood).	**Unit 1:** T1o
	CC.3.L.1.d	**(d)** Form and use regular and irregular verbs.	**Unit 4:** T233d, T239l, T239w, T239x, T259m, T259n, T266a, T267, T270; **Unit 8:** T481o, T481p, T507d, T507o, T507p, T518a, T519, T519l, T519w, T519x, T550
	CC.3.L.1.e	**(e)** Form and use the simple (e.g., I walked; I walk; I will walk) verb tenses.	**Unit 4:** T207o, T207p, T233o, T233p, T238a, T239, T239u, T239v, T259k, T259l; **Unit 8:** T481o, T481p, T507d, T507o, T507p, T518a, T519, T519l, T519w, T519x, T539m, T539n, T546a, T547, T550
	CC.3.L.1.f	**(f)** Ensure subject-verb and pronoun-antecedent agreement.	**Unit 1:** T55m, T55n, T62a, T63, T66; **Unit 4:** T207o, T207p, T233o, T233p, T238a, T259m, T259n, T266a, T267; **Unit 6:** T341o, T341p, T365d, T408; **Unit 8:** T519w
	CC.3.L.1.g	**(g)** Form and use comparative and superlative adjectives and adverbs, and choose between them depending on what is to be modified.	**Unit 5:** T273o, T273p, T299g, T299o, T299p, T306a, T307, T307l; **Unit 7:** T411p, T435d, T435o, T435p, T442a, T443, T443u, T443v
	CC.3.L.1.h	**(h)** Use coordinating and subordinating conjunctions.	**Unit 1:** T55m; **Unit 2:** T127m, T127n, T134a, T135; **Unit 3:** T141o, T141p
	CC.3.L.1.i	**(i)** Produce simple, compound, and complex sentences.	**Unit 2:** T95i, T103w, T103x, T127m, T127n, T134a, T135, T138; **Unit 3:** T141o, T141p, T165d; **Unit 4:** T234c; **Unit 6:** T365q, T365r
	CC.3.L.2	**(2)** Demonstrate command of the conventions of standard English capitalization, punctuation, and spelling when writing.	**Unit 1:** T1l, T1m, T1n, T1o, T27m, T27n, T27p, T33u, T55k; **Unit 2:** T69m, T69n, T69o, T69p, T95m, T95o, T95p, T102a, T103, T103l, T103v, T103w, T103x, T127l, T127m, T127n, T134a, T135; **Unit 3:** T141m, T141o, T141p, T165d, T165n, T165o, T165p, T172a, T173, T173l, T173u, T173v, T173w, T173x, T195l, T195n, T200a, T201; **Unit 4:** T207m, T207n, T207p, T233m, T233n, T233o, T233p, T238a, T239s, T239t, T239v, T259k, T259l; **Unit 5:** T273m, T273n, T307v, T327k, T327l, T327m, T327n; **Unit 6:** T341m, T365n, T373v, T395k, T395l; **Unit 7:** T411m, T435n, T443t, T454–455, T465m, T465n; **Unit 8:** T481m, T481n, T481o, T481p, T507d, T507m, T507n, T507o, T507p, T518a, T519, T519u, T539k, T539l
	CC.3.L.2.a	**(a)** Capitalize appropriate words in titles.	**Unit 2:** T69o, T69p
	CC.3.L.2.b	**(b)** Use commas in addresses.	**Unit 2:** T69o, T69p
	CC.3.L.2.c	**(c)** Use commas and quotation marks in dialogue.	**Unit 2:** T69p, T95d, T141; **Unit 4:** T273; **Unit 7:** T443w, T443x, T465c
	CC.3.L.2.d	**(d)** Form and use possessives.	**Unit 5:** T327m, T327n, T334a, T335, T338; **Unit 6:** T408
	CC.3.L.2.e	**(e)** Use conventional spelling for high-frequency and other studied words and for adding suffixes to base words (e.g., sitting, smiled, cries, happiness).	**Unit 1:** T1j, T1k, T1m, T27k, T27l, T27n, T33s, T33t, T33v, T55i, T55j, T55l; **Unit 2:** T69k, T69l, T69n, T95k, T95l, T95n, T103s, T103t, T103v, T127i, T127j, T127k, T127l; **Unit 3:** T141k, T141l, T141n, T165k, T165l, T165m, T165n, T173s, T173t, T173v, T195i, T195j, T195k; **Unit 4:** T207k, T207l, T207n, T233k, T233l, T233n, T239s, T239t, T239u, T239v, T259i, T259j, T259l; **Unit 5:** T273k, T273l, T273n, T299k, T299l, T299m, T299n, T307s, T307t, T307v, T327i, T327j, T327l; **Unit 6:** T341k, T341l, T341n, T365k, T365l, T365m, T373s, T373t, T373u, T373v, T395i, T395j, T395l; **Unit 7:** T411k, T411l, T411m, T411n, T435k, T435l, T435n, T443r, T443t, T465l, T465n; **Unit 8:** T481k, T481l, T481n, T507k, T507l, T507n, T519s, T519t, T519v, T539j, T539l
	CC.3.L.2.f	**(f)** Use spelling patterns and generalizations (e.g., word families, position-based spellings, syllable patterns, ending rules, meaningful word parts) in writing words.	**Unit 1:** T1j, T1k, T1l, T1m, T27k, T27l, T27m, T33s, T33t, T33u, T33v, T55i, T55j, T55l; **Unit 2:** T69k, T69l, T69m, T95k, T95l, T95n, T103s, T103t, T103u, T103v, T127i, T127j, T127k, T127l; **Unit 3:** T141k, T141l, T141m, T141n, T165k, T165l, T165m, T173s, T173t, T173u, T173v, T195i, T195j, T195k, T195l; **Unit 4:** T207k, T207l, T207n, T233k, T233l, T233n, T239s, T239t, T239u, T259i, T259j, T259k; **Unit 5:** T273k, T273l, T273m, T299k, T299l, T299n, T307s, T307t, T327i, T327j; **Unit 6:** T341k, T341l, T341m, T341n, T365k, T365l, T365m, T373s, T373t, T373u, T395i, T395j, T395l; **Unit 7:** T411k, T411l, T411m, T411n, T435k, T435l, T435m, T443r, T443s, T443t, T465l, T465m, T465n; **Unit 8:** T481k, T481l, T507k, T507l, T519s, T519t, T519u, T539i, T539j
	CC.3.L.2.g	**(g)** Consult reference materials, including beginning dictionaries, as needed to check and correct spellings.	**Unit 1:** T27n; **Unit 2:** T127l; **Unit 4:** T259l; **Unit 5:** T307v; **Unit 7:** T443t; **Unit 8:** T519u , T539k

Language, continued

Strand	Code	Standards Text	Grade 3 Units 1–8 Standards Correlations
Knowledge of Language	**CC.3.L.3**	**(3)** Use knowledge of language and its conventions when writing, speaking, reading, or listening.	**Unit 1:** T27d, T27q, T27r, T32a, T33, T33l, T62a, T63, T66, T68, T69; **Unit 2:** T95d, T95q, T95r, T102a, T103, T103l, T134a, T135, T138; **Unit 3:** T165d, T172a, T173, T173l, T200a, T201, T204; **Unit 4:** T233d, T238a, T239, T239l, T266a, T267, T270; **Unit 5:** T299d, T302, T306a, T307, T307l, T334a, T335, T338; **Unit 6:** T341q, T341r, T345a, T352–353, T359, T362, T363a, T363b, T364, T364a, T365d, T372a, T373, T373a, T373b, T373c, T373d, T373l, T404a, T405, T408, T410, T411, SG6, SG7, SG24, SG25; **Unit 7:** T411i, T411q, T411r, T435c, T435d, T442a, T443, T472a, T473; **Unit 8:** T507d, T518a, T519, T519l, T546a, T547, T550
	CC.3.L.3.a	**(a)** Choose words and phrases for effect.	**Unit 1:** T27q, T27r, T28b, T33d, T69; **Unit 2:** T95q, T95r, T103i, T103j, T103k, T141; **Unit 3:** T165q, T165r; **Unit 5:** T273i, T335e; **Unit 6:** T341q, T341r, T365a, T365b, T365c, T373a, T373b, T373c, T373d, T411; **Unit 7:** T411i, T411q, T411r, T435a, T435b, T435c
	CC.3.L.3.b	**(b)** Recognize and observe differences between the conventions of spoken and written standard English.	**Unit 1:** T55o, T55p; **Unit 3:** T206; **Unit 4:** T273; **Unit 7:** T443o, T443w, T443x, T481
Vocabulary Acquisition and Use	**CC.3.L.4**	**(4)** Determine or clarify the meaning of unknown and multiple-meaning words and phrases based on grade 3 reading and content, choosing flexibly from a range of strategies.	**Unit 1:** T4, T5, T6a, T7, T33a, T34, T35, T36a, T37, T55q, T56, T56c, T63c, T63e; **Unit 2:** T74a, T75, T95i, T95j, T97, T103q, T106a, T107; **Unit 3:** T146a, T147, T165s, T166, T166c, T173c, T173e, T176a, T177; **Unit 4:** T212a, T213, T231b, T232, T242a, T243; **Unit 5:** T278a, T279, T310a, T311, T328c; **Unit 6:** T346a, T347, T376a, T377; **Unit 7:** T417, T435s, T436, T436c, T443c, T443e, T444, T445, T465s, T466, T466c, T473c, T473e; **Unit 8:** T486a, T487, T522a, T523
	CC.3.L.4.a	**(a)** Use sentence-level context as a clue to the meaning of a word or phrase.	**Unit 3:** T165s, T166, T166c, T173c, T173e; **Unit 5:** T327q, T328
	CC.3.L.4.b	**(b)** Determine the meaning of the new word formed when a known affix is added to a known word (e.g., agreeable/disagreeable, comfortable/uncomfortable, care/careless, heat/preheat).	**Unit 3:** T195g, T195q, T195r, T196c, T201c, T201e; **Unit 4:** T233s, T234, T234c, T239c, T239e
	CC.3.L.4.c	**(c)** Use a known root word as a clue to the meaning of an unknown word with the same root (e.g., company, companion).	**Unit 4:** T233s, T234, T234c, T239c, T239e; **Unit 7:** T435s, T436, T436c, T443c, T443e
	CC.3.L.4.d	**(d)** Use glossaries or beginning dictionaries, both print and digital, to determine or clarify the precise meaning of key words and phrases.	**Unit 1:** T1l, T33v, T55l, T55q, T56, T56c, T63c, T63e; **Unit 2:** T69n, T95n, T103q; **Unit 3:** T141n, T165n, T173v, T195l; **Unit 4:** T207m, T207n, T233n; **Unit 5:** T273n, T327k, T307c, T307e; **Unit 6:** T365i, T395g; **Unit 7:** T435n, T465n; **Unit 8:** T481g, T507m, T519e, T540c
	CC.3.L.5	**(5)** Demonstrate understanding of word relationships and nuances in word meanings.	**Unit 3:** T166b; **Unit 4:** T259q, T260, T260c, T267c, T267e; **Unit 5:** T299s, T300, T300c, T307c, T307e, T327g, T327q, T328, T328c, T335c, T335e; **Unit 6:** T348, T349, T395q, T396, T396c; **Unit 7:** T411i, T411q, T411r, T435c, T465s, T466, T466c, T473c, T473e; **Unit 8:** T507s, T508, T508c, T519c, T519e
	CC.3.L.5.a	**(a)** Distinguish the literal and non-literal meanings of words and phrases in context (e.g., take steps).	**Unit 2:** T141; **Unit 6:** T365s, T366, T366a, T366b, T366c, T368, T370, T373a, T373c, T373e
	CC.3.L.5.b	**(b)** Identify real-life connections between words and their use (e.g., describe people who are friendly or helpful).	**Unit 6:** T345a, T358, T363a, T364a
	CC.3.L.5.c	**(c)** Distinguish shades of meaning among related words that describe states of mind or degrees of certainty (e.g., knew, believed, suspected, heard, wondered).	**Unit 5:** T328, T328c, T335c, T335d; **Unit 8:** T508c, T519c, T519e
	CC.3.L.6	**(6)** Acquire and use accurately grade-appropriate conversational, general academic, and domain specific words and phrases, including those that signal spatial and temporal relationships (e.g., After dinner that night we went looking for them).	**Unit 1:** T1h, T4, T5, T6a, T7, T10, T22, T25a, T27i, T31a, T33q, T34, T35, T36a, T37, T40, T46, T53b, T55g, T55q, T56, T56c, T61a, T63c, T63e, SG5, SG6, SG7, SG11, SG12, SG13, SG17, SG18, SG19, SG23, SG24, SG25; **Unit 2:** T69i, T72, T73, T74a, T75, T78, T88, T93a, T95i, T101a, T103q, T104, T105, T106a, T107, T110, T120, T125a, T127g, T133a, SG5, SG6, SG7, SG11, SG12, SG13, SG17, SG18, SG19, SG23, SG24, SG25; **Unit 3:** T141i, T144, T145, T146a, T147, T150, T158, T163b, T165i, T165s, T166, T171a, T173q, T174, T175, T176a, T177, T180, T188, T193a, T195g, T199a, SG5, SG6, SG7, SG11, SG12, SG13, SG17, SG18, SG19, SG23, SG24, SG25; **Unit 4:** T207i, T210, T211, T212a, T213, T216, T224, T231b, T233i, T237a, T239q, T240, T241, T242a, T243, T246, T254, T257a, T259g, T259q, T260, T260c, T265a, T267c, T267e, SG5, SG6, SG7, SG11, SG12, SG13, SG17, SG18, SG19, SG23, SG24, SG25; **Unit 5:** T273i, T276, T277, T278a, T279, T282, T292, T297b, T299i, T299s, T305a, T307q, T308, T309, T310a, T311, T314, T320, T325a, T326, T327g, T333a, SG5, SG6, SG7, SG11, SG12, SG13, SG17, SG18, SG19, SG23, SG24, SG25; **Unit 6:** T341i, T344, T345, T346a, T347, T350, T356, T363b, T365i, T366c, T371a, T373q, T374, T375, T376a, T377, T380, T390, T393a, T394, T395g, T395q, T403a, T410, T411, SG5, SG6, SG7, SG11, SG12, SG13, SG17, SG18, SG19, SG23, SG24, SG25; **Unit 7:** T411i, T414, T415, T415a, T416a, T417, T420, T430, T433a, T435i, T435j, T441a, T443o, T444, T445, T446a, T447, T450, T456, T463b, T465i, T471a, SG5, SG6, SG7, SG11, SG12, SG13, SG17, SG18, SG19, SG23, SG24, SG25; **Unit 8:** T481i, T484, T485, T486a, T487, T490, T498, T505b, T507i, T507s, T508, T517a, T519q, T520, T521, T522a, T523, T526, T532, T537a, T539g, T539q, T540, T545a, SG5, SG6, SG7, SG11, SG12, SG13, SG17, SG18, SG19, SG23, SG24, SG25

Program Features and Resources Index

I

L

M

N

O

P

R

S

T

Skills Index

Note: Page numbers in bold indicate main discussion.

A

B

C

N

O

P

Q

R

T

U

V

W

Index of Authors

Index of Illustrators/ Photographers

cknowledgements

Acknowledgments, continued

Text Credits

Unit One

Candlewick Press: Excerpt from *Those Shoes* by Maribeth Boelts, illustrated by Noah Z. Jones. Text copyright © 2007 by Maribeth Boelts. Illustrations © 2007 by Noah Z. Jones. Reproduced by permission of the publisher, Candlewick Press, Sommerville, Mass.

Children's Book Press: "Guardian Angel," by Francisco X. Alarcon, from *Angels Ride Bikes*, Copyright © 1999 by Francisco X. Alarcon. Reprinted by permission of the publisher, Childrenís Book Press, San Francisco, Calif., www.childrensbookpress.org.

Highlights for Children: Excerpt from "The World's Greatest Underachiever" by Henry Winkler from *Highlights for Children*, March 2005. Copyright © 2005 by Highlights for Children. Reprinted by permission of Highlights for Children, Inc.

Unit Two

Penguin Group (USA) Inc.: Excerpt from *When the Pigs Took Over* by Arthur Dorros, illustrated by Diane Greenseid. Text copyright © 2002 by Arthur Dorros. Illustrations © 2002 by Diane Greenseid. Used by permission of Dutton Children's Books, a Division of Penguin Young Readers Group, a Member of Penguin Group (USA) Inc., 345 Hudson Street, New York, NY 10014. All rights reserved.

Walker & Company: Excerpt from *When the Wolves Returned* by Dorothy Hinshaw Patent. Text copyright © 2008 by Dorothy Hinshaw Patent. Photographs © 2008 by Dan Hartman and Cassie Hartman. Reprinted by permission of Walker & Company. All rights reserved.

Unit Three

Random House Children's Books: Excerpt from *Two Old Potatoes and Me* by John Coy, illustrated by Carolyn Fisher. Text copyright © 2009 by John Coy. Illustrations © 2009 by Carolyn Fisher. Reprinted by permission of Random House Children's Books.

Lee & Low Books: "Papaya", "Potato," and "Corn" from *Yum! ¡Mm Mm! ¡Qué rico! Americasí Sproutings* by Pat Mora. Text copyright © 2007 by Pat Mora. Illustrations © 2007 by Rafael López. Reprinted by permission of Lee & Low Books, Inc., New York, NY 10016.

Unit Four

Barefoot Books: Excerpt from *Mama Panya's Pancakes* by Mary and Rich Chamberlin. Text copyright © 2005 by Mary and Rich Chamberlin. Illustrations © 2005 by Julie Cairns. Reprinted by permission of Barefoot Books.

Unit Five

Cengage Learning, Inc.: Excerpt from *Quicksand* by Kris Hirschmann. Copyright © 2002 by Gale. Reprinted by permission of Cengage Learning, Inc., www.cengage.com/permissions.

Unit Six

Henry Holt and Company LLC: Excerpt from *Oye, Celia! A Song for Celia Cruz* by Katie Sciurba, illustrated by Edel Rodriguez. Text copyright © 2007 by Katherina Sciurba. Illustrations © 2007 by Edel Rodriguez. Reprinted by arrangement of Henry Holt and Company LLC.

Highlights for Children, Inc.: Excerpt from "Carving Stones in Cedar" by Kristine F. Anderson from *Highlights for Children*, November 2007. Copyright © 2007 by Highlights for Children. Reprinted by permission of Highlights for Children, Inc.

Unit Seven

HarperCollins Publishers: Excerpt from *An Island Grows* by Lola M. Schaefer, Illustrated by Cathie Felstead. Text copyright © 2006 by Lola M. Schaefer. Illustrations © 2006 by Cathie Felstead. Reprinted by permission of HarperCollins Children's Books.

Shen's Books: Excerpt from *Selvakumar Knew Better* by Virginia Kroll, illustrated by Xiaojun Li. Text copyright © 2009 by Virginia Kroll. Illustrations © 2009 by Xiaogun Li. Reprinted by permission of Shen's Books.

Unit Eight

Evans Brothers Ltd.: Excerpt from *Running Shoes* by Frederick Lipp, illustrated by Jason Gaillard. Text copyright © 2007 by Frederick Lipp. Illustrations © 2007 by Jason Gaillard. First published by Zero to Ten Limited (a member of the Evans Publishing Group). Text and illustrations reproduced with kind permission of Evans Brothers Ltd., 2A Portman Mansions, Chiltern Street, London, W1U 6NR.

NATIONAL GEOGRAPHIC SCHOOL PUBLISHING

National Geographic School Publishing gratefully acknowledges the contributions of the following National Geographic Explorers to our program and to our planet:

Joseph Lekuton, 2006 National Geographic Emerging Explorer
Zeb Hogan, 2004 National Geographic Emerging Explorer
Cornielle Ewango, 2007 National Geographic Emerging Explorer
Cid Simoes and Paola Segura, 2008 National Geographic Emerging Explorers
Maycira Costa, National Geographic grantee
Elizabeth Kapu'uwailani Lindsey, National Geographic Fellow
Carsten Peter, National Geographic Contributing Photographer
Constanza Ceruti, 2005 National Geographic Emerging Explorer

Photographic Credits

iv (tl) Gideon Mendel/Corbis. v (tl) Mak Remissa/epa/Corbis. vi (tr) Eric Loddé/UNESCO - World Heritage Centre. vii (tr) Carlos Nascimento/Earth University. viii (tr) Emielke van Wyk/Gallo Images/Getty Images. ix (tl) Dinodia/Stock Connection. x (tl) Carsten Peter/National Geographic Image Collection. xi (tl) photo courtesy of Constanza Ceruti/copyright Constanza Ceruti. xv (br) Picture Contact/Alamy Images. 2-3 (UnitOp) Tim Pannell/Ivy/Corbis. 7 (bl) Don Mason/Blend Images/Getty Images. (br) James Woodson/Photodisc/Getty Images. (tc) Robert Brenner/PhotoEdit. (tl) Ariel Skelley/Blend Images/age fotostock. (tr) Hola Images/Corbis. 28 (b) DigitalStock/Corbis. (c) anna1311/Shutterstock. (t) RonTech2000/iStockphoto. 35 (b) Ted Foxx/Alamy Images. (tl, tr) Tim Pannell/Corbis. 37 (bl) Leland Bobbé/Corbis. (br) Stephen Simpson/Taxi/Getty Images. (tc) charlybutcher/iStockphoto. (tl) Ariel Skelley/Blend Images/Getty Images. (tr) Shaun Egan/Photodisc/Getty Images. 40-41 H. Armstrong Roberts/Getty Images. 42 (l, r) Henry Winkler. 43 ICM (International Creative Management). 46 Courtesy of Tom Mela. 50 Hampton-Brown/National Geographic School Publishing. 51 Paramount/Everett Collection. 52 (b) Stefan Rousseau/PA Wire/AP Images. (t) Lincoln Journal Star, Robert Becker/AP Images. 53 Fred Duval/FilmMagic/Getty Images. 57 (bg) Curt Wiler/Alamy Images. (inset) Suzannah Weiss. 58 (b) Carl & Ann Purcell/Corbis. (t) SV Photography/Alamy Images. 59 Courtesy of Joseph Lekuton. 60 Picture Contact/Alamy Images. 61 Gideon Mendel/Corbis. 62 (l) H. Armstrong Roberts/Getty Images. (r) Suzannah Weiss. 64 Myrleen Pearson/The Image Works, Inc. 68 Tim Pannell/Ivy/Corbis. 69 Ed Bock/Corbis. 70 (UnitOp) Michael Nichols/National Geographic Image Collection. 75 (bl) quavondo/iStockphoto. (br) Samuel Aranda/Stringer/Getty Images. (tc) Andersen Ross/Blend Images/Getty Images. (tl) Jozsef Szasz-Fabian/iStockphoto. (tr) Arthur Kwiatkowski/iStockphoto. 97 DigitalStock/Corbis. 98 PhotoDisc/Getty Images. 99 Jim Brandenburg/Minden Pictures/National Geographic Image Collection. 100 Digital Vision/Getty Images. (inset) PhotoDisc/Getty Images. 101 Jeff Schultes/Shutterstock. 105 (b) Tim Graham/Getty Images. (t) Alaska Stock. 106 (l) Dave Logan/iStockphoto. (r) bierchen/Shutterstock. 107 (bl) PhotoDisc/Getty Images. (br) Rob Marmion/Shutterstock. (tc) Judy Barranco/iStockphoto. (tl) ampower/Shutterstock. (tr) Tanya Constantine/Getty Images. 108 Justin Guariglia/National Geographic Image Collection. 109 Natalia Bratslavsky/iStockphoto. 110 (inset) Dan & Cassie Hartman. 110-111 (bg) Dan & Cassie Hartman. 112 (l, r) Dan & Cassie Hartman. 113 Dan & Cassie Hartman. 114 (b, bg, t) Dan & Cassie Hartman. 116 Dan & Cassie Hartman. 117 (b) Dan & Cassie Hartman. (inset) Dan & Cassie Hartman. 118 Dan & Cassie Hartman. 119 Dan & Cassie Hartman. 120 (inset) Dan & Cassie Hartman. 120-121 (bg) Dan & Cassie Hartman. 122 Dan & Cassie Hartman. 122-123 Dan & Cassie Hartman. 124 (l, r) Dan & Cassie Hartman. 125 Dan & Cassie Hartman. 126 Dan & Cassie Hartman. 129 (bg) Asia Images/Masterfile. (inset) Apichart Weerawong/AP Images. 130 (bc) Zeb Hogan/AP Images. (bl) Richard Vogel/AP Images. (br) Andy Eames/AP Images. 130-131 (t) Lou Oates/Shutterstock. 131 (l) Mak Remissa/epa/Corbis. 132 (l) Robert Nickelsberg/Time Life Pictures/Getty Images. (r) Bruno Morandi/age fotostock. 132-133 (t) Lou Oates/Shutterstock. 133 Apichart Weerawong/AP Images. 136 Dan & Cassie Hartman. 140 Michael Nichols/National Geographic Image Collection. 141 Hnin Khine/iStockphoto. 142-143 (UnitOp) Scott Sinklier/AgStock Images/Corbis. 145 (bl) Per Makitalo/Getty Images. (br) VikaValter/iStockphoto. (cl) Artville. (cr, t) Barry Runk/Grant Heilman Photography. 147 (bl) Walter B. McKenzie/Getty Images. (br) Sandro Tucci/Time & Life Pictures/Getty Images. (tc) Teodor Ostojic/Shutterstock. (tl) Geoff Kidd/Oxford Scientific (OSF)/Photolibrary. (tr) Theo Allofs/Corbis. 166 (l) Brandon Blinkenberg/Shutterstock. (r) Jiang Dao Hua/Shutterstock. 173 (bcl, bcr, bl) ranplett/iStockphoto. (tc, tl, tr)

ge 642

Dean Turner/iStockphoto. 174 (bl) PhotoDisc/Getty Images. (br) Tim Fitzharris/Minden Pictures/National Geographic Image Collection. (cl, cr, l, tr) Hampton-Brown/National Geographic School Publishing. (r) Michael and Patricia Fogden/Minden Pictures/National Geographic Image Collection. 175 (bl) Image Source Pink/Alamy Images. (r) David Messent/Photolibrary. (tl) Helmut Meyer zur Capellen/Corbis. 176 (l) PhotoDisc/Getty Images. (r) Tim Fitzharris/Minden Pictures/National Geographic Image Collection. 177 (bl) BananaStock/Jupiterimages. (br) Radius Images/Jupiterimages. (tc) wonderlandstock/Alamy Images. (tl) Kevin Dodge/Photolibrary. (tr) Polka Dot Images/age fotostock. 178 Darlyne A. Murawski/National Geographic Image Collection. 179 DigitalStock/Corbis. 180 (l) Bruce Davidson/Nature Picture Library. 180-181 (bg) Eric Loddé/UNESCO - World Heritage Centre. 182-183 Bruce Davidson/Nature Picture Library. 186 (b) Reto Kuster. (tl) James H Robinson/Oxford Scientific (OSF)/Photolibrary. (tr) Bruce Davidson/Nature Picture Library. 187 Bruce Davidson/Nature Picture Library. 192 Randy Olson/National Geographic Image Collection. 193 (b, t) Photo courtesy of Goldman Environmental Prize. 194 (b) Eric Loddé/UNESCO - World Heritage Centre. (t) Bruce Davidson/Nature Picture Library. 196 Beyza Sultan Durna/iStockphoto. 197 (bg) John Foxx Images/Imagestate. (inset) Eric Loddé/UNESCO - World Heritage Centre. 198 (l, r) White Oak Conservation Center. 198-199 (bg) John Foxx Images/Imagestate. 199 (inset) Randy Olson/National Geographic Image Collection. 200 Bruce Davidson/Nature Picture Library. 202 Finnbarr Webster/Alamy Images. 206 Scott Sinklier/AgStock Images/Corbis. 207 Adrian Grosu/Shutterstock. 208 (UnitOp) Blend Images/Veer/Corbis. 211 Bill Aron/PhotoEdit. 213 (bl) Jose Luis Pelaez Inc/Blend Images/Getty Images. (br) Annette Wiechmann/iStockphoto. (tc) Jong Kiam Soon/Shutterstock. (tl) Inc/Alamy Images. (tr) Artville. 224 (b) Rafael Pesquera/iStockphoto. 229 (br) MetaTools. 230 (b) C Squared Studios/Photodisc/Getty Images. 234 Norman Chan/Shutterstock. 241 (bl) Siegfried Layda/Getty Images. (br) James P. Blair/National Geographic Image Collection. (tl) Bryan Alldredge/iStockphoto. (tr) Galushko Sergey/Shutterstock. 243 (bl) PhotoDisc/Getty Images. (br) Lucie Danninger/Shutterstock. (tc) Jacobus verhagen/iStockphoto. (tl) Rob Marmion/Shutterstock. (tr) Eyewire/Getty Images. 246-247 Kevin R. Morris/Bohemian Nomad Picturemakers/Corbis. 249 Rhett A. Butler/Mongabay.com. 250 Rebecca Hale/National Geographic Image Collection. 251 (bg) Ligia Botero/The Image Bank/Getty Images. (inset) Carlos Nascimento/Earth University. 252 (l) Norman Chan/iStockphoto. (r) imagebroker/Alamy Images. 253 (l, r) Rebecca Hale/National Geographic Image Collection. 254 (r) Lamberto Scipioni/Keystone RM/age fotostock. 255 (b) Mark Moffett/Minden Pictures. (t) SambaPhoto/Silvestre Silva/Getty Images. 256 Noah Addis/Corbis. 257 (b) SambaPhoto/Silvestre Silva/Getty Images. (t) Fernanda Preto/Alamy Images. 258 (b) Rebecca Hale/National Geographic Image Collection. 260 Aron Brand/Shutterstock. 261 (b) Stockbyte/Getty Images. 268 Tony Anderson/Getty Images. 272 (t) Blend Images/Veer/Corbis/Corbis. 273 (b) Algecireño/Shutterstock. (t) Michael DeLeon/iStockphoto. 274 (UnitOp) Colin Brynn/Getty Images. 279 (bl) Elena Elisseeva/Shutterstock. (br) Lion Hijmans/iStockphoto. (tc) Iakov Kalinin/iStockphoto. (tl) Comstock/Jupiterimages. (tl) Ugurhan Betin/iStockphoto. 297 Marisa Montes. 301 (bg) Arne Hodalic/Corbis. (inset) International Mammoth Committee/National Geographic Image Collection. 302-303 (bg) DigitalStock/Corbis. 303 (b) NTV, Russian Television Channel/AP Images. 304 (inset) International Mammoth Committee/National Geographic Image Collection. 304-305 (bg) DigitalStock/Corbis. 305 (b, t) International Mammoth Committee/National Geographic Image Collection. 311 (bl) Rich Legg/iStockphoto. (br) Thomas Northcut/Photodisc/Getty Images. (tc) Don Bayley/iStockphoto. (tl) Ryan McVay/Photodisc/Getty Images. (tr) aniad/Shutterstock. 312 Joseph Devenney/Getty Images. 314-315 Roland Liptak/Alamy Images. 316 (l) Bettmann/Corbis. (r) Everett Collection. 317 James Smedley/Alamy Images. 318 Emielke van Wyk/Gallo Images/Getty Images. 319 (l) Harald Sund/Getty Images. (r) Alexander Walter/Digital Vision/Getty Images. 320 Comstock Images/Jupiterimages/Getty Images. 322 Winfield Parks/National Geographic Image Collection. 323 Giorgio Fochesato/Digital Vision/Getty Images. 324-325 (bg) Jeff D. Burgess/J.D. Burgess Online. 326 Bettmann/Corbis. 328 Mike Clarke/iStockphoto. 329 Jim Zuckerman/Corbis. (inset) Maycira Costa. 330 (bc-inset) Michael Nichols/National Geographic Image Collection. (b-inset) Panoramic Stock Images/National Geographic Image Collection. (t) Joseph H. Bailey/National Geographic Image Collection. (tc-inset) James P. Blair/National Geographic Image Collection. (t-inset) Macduff Everton/Corbis. 330-331 (bg) Panoramic Stock Images/National Geographic Image Collection. 331 (bc-inset) Bates Littlehales/National Geographic Image Collection. (b-inset) Gerry Ellis/Minden Pictures/National Geographic Image Collection. (tc-inset) Maycira Costa. (t-inset) Luciano Candisani/Minden Pictures/National Geographic Image Collection. 332 (b-inset) Maycira Costa. (c-inset) Earth Imaging/Getty Images. 332-333 (bg) Joel Sartore/National Geographic Image Collection. 333 (b-inset) Jim Sugar/Corbis. 340 Colin Brynn/Getty Images. 341 (tr) Eyewire. 342-343 (UnitOp) Abraham Nowitz/National Geographic Image Collection. 345 (b) Bob Krist/Corbis. (tl) Alija/iStockphoto. (tr) William Albert Allard/National Geographic Image Collection. 346 (r) Jeremy Woodhouse/Blend Images/Getty Images. 347 (bl) Jan Halaska/Index Stock Imagery RF/Photolibrary. (br) Sami Sarkis/Getty Images. (tc) Andres Peiro Palmer/iStockphoto. (tl) Paolo Florendo/iStockphoto. (tr) John-Francis Bourke/Getty Images. 353 (b) C Squared Studios/Photodisc/Getty Images. 363 (l) Reuters/Corbis. (r) Roey Ahram/Katie Sciurba. 367 (b) Hulton Archive/Getty Images. (t) Artville. 368 (inset) The Granger Collection, New York. 368-369 Border (top) Artville. 369 (inset) Bradley Smith/Corbis. 370 (l) Chicago Defender. (r) Colin Underhill/Alamy Images. 370-371 Border (top) Artville. 371 (c) Redferns/Getty Images. (l) WireImage/Getty Images. (r) Jon Super/Redferns/Getty Images. 377 (bl) Corbis Premium RF/Alamy Images. (br) Dmitriy Shironosov/Shutterstock. (tc, tl) BananaStock/Jupiterimages. (tr) Bonnie Jacobs/iStockphoto. 380 (inset-bg) University of Washington - Libraries Digital Collections. (inset-r) Dinodia/Stock Connection. 380-381 (bg) University of Washington - Libraries Digital Collections. 381 (r) Dinodia/Stock Connection. 382-383 (bg) Joseph Sohm/amanaimages/Corbis. 383 (r) DreamPictures/Photodisc/Getty Images. 384 Shotridge Studios. 385 (border-b) Joseph Sohm/amanaimages/Corbis. (bl, br, tr) Shotridge Studios. 386 (bg) Akira Kaede/Photodisc/Getty Images. (bl) Shotridge Studios. (inset) Highlights for Children. 387 (br, tl, tr) Shotridge Studios. 388 Melissa Farlow/National Geographic Image Collection. 389 (bl) Melissa Farlow/National Geographic Image Collection. (t) Marilyn Angel Wynn/Nativestock Pictures. 390 Shotridge Studios. 392 (b) Digital Vision/Getty Images. 394 (b) Shotridge Studios. 397 (b) Kauila Barber/Elizabeth Lindsey. (t) Dorling Kindersley/Getty Images. 398 (b) Adam Jones/Visuals Unlimited. (t) Diane Cook and Len Jenshel/National Geographic Image Collection. 399 (t) Nick Kato/Elizabeth Lindsey. 405 (l) Jupiterimages. (r) BananaStock/Jupiterimages. 406 Beth Schlanker/AP Images. 410 (t) Abraham Nowitz/National Geographic Image Collection. 412 (UnitOp) Tom Pfeiffer/VolcanoDiscovery/Getty Images. 415 (r) Philippe Bourseiller/Getty Images. 417 (bl) Corbis/Jupiterimages. (br) Martin Wagner/iStockphoto. (tc) Blend Images. (tl) FoodCollection/StockFood America. (tr) Stuart O'Sullivan/Taxi/Getty Images. 418 mikeuk/iStockphoto. 425 (b) A.T. White/Getty Images. 437 Carsten Peter/National Geographic Image Collection. 438-439 (bg) Carsten Peter/National Geographic Image Collection. 439 (l) Carsten Peter/National Geographic Image Collection. (r) Carsten Peter/National Geographic Image Collection. 440 (inset) Carsten Peter/National Geographic Image Collection. 440-441 (bg) Carsten Peter/National Geographic Image Collection. 441 (inset) Carsten Peter/National Geographic Image Collection. 447 (bl) John Foxx Images/Imagestate. (br) Sharon Dominick/iStockphoto. (tc) Mark Rose/iStockphoto. (tl) Michael Dwyer/AP Images. (tr) Image Source/Corbis. 448 China Daily/Reuters. 463 (l) Chris Tomlinson/AP Images. (r) Xiaojun Li. 466 (l) Warren Faidley/Oxford Scientific (OSF)/Photolibrary. (r) DigitalStock/Corbis. 467 (bg, inset) DigitalStock/Corbis. 468-469 (bg) DigitalStock/Corbis. 469 (b) Bettmann/Corbis. 470 (inset) Marco Garcia/Getty Images. (t) DigitalStock/Corbis. 470-471 (bg) DigitalStock/Corbis. 474 (t) Corbis. 476 (t) Carsten Peter/National Geographic Image Collection. 480 (b) Brand X/Jupiterimages/Alamy Images. (t) Tom Pfeiffer/VolcanoDiscovery/Getty Images. 482-483 (UnitOp) Pauline St Denis/Fancy/Photolibrary. 485 Lawrence Wee/Shutterstock. 487 (bl) Jupiterimages. (br) Somos/Veer/Getty Images. (tc) Maciek Zawada/National Geographic Image Collection. (tl) Bruce Dale/National Geographic Image Collection. (tr) Kate Mathis/Photodisc/Getty Images. 492 (b) maxstockphoto/Shutterstock. 499 (b) Jasmin Awad/iStockphoto. 505 Hilary Downie. 521 Brian Hagiwara/Brand X Pictures/Getty Images. 523 (bl) Pavel Semenov/Shutterstock. (br) Eric Raptosh Photography/Brand X Pictures/Getty Images. (tc) Angelo Cavalli/Stockbyte/Getty Images. (tl) Richard Lewisohn/Getty Images. (tr) Foto011/Shutterstock. 525 (b) John Foxx Images/Imagestate. (c) Rudi Von Briel/Index Stock/age fotostock. (t) Donald R. Swartz/Shutterstock. 526-527 (bg) Douglas Gilmour. 527 (r) Brian Smale. 528 Erden Eruç/Around-n-Over. 529 (b) Galyna Andrushko/Shutterstock. (c) Gary S Chapman/Photographer's Choice RF/Getty Images. (t) SteveStone/iStockphoto. 530 Erden Eruç/Around-n-Over. 532 Terry Schmitt. 534 (bl) Terry Schmitt/Terry Schmitt. (c) Erden Eruç/Around-n-Over. (tr) Around-n-Over. 535 (b) zts/iStockphoto. (t) Erden Eruç/Around-n-Over. 536 Erden Eruç/Around-n-Over. 537 Erden Eruç/Around-n-Over. 538 Erden Eruç/Around-n-Over. 540 (l) Mark Hatfield/

Page 643

iStockphoto. (r) DAJ/Getty Images. 541 photo courtesy of Constanza Ceruti/copyright Constanza Ceruti. 542 (b) photo courtesy of Constanza Ceruti/copyright Constanza Ceruti. 543 (bl, br, cc, cl, cr, t) Maria Stenzel/National Geographic Image Collection. 544 Photo courtesy of Constanza Ceruti/copyright Constanza Ceruti. 545 Maria Stenzel/National Geographic Image Collection. 548 Matthew Cole/Shutterstock. 552 Pauline St Denis/Fancy/Photolibrary. 558 Warren Morgan/Corbis. 559 Jupiterimages/Comstock Images/Getty Images. 560 Yuri Arcurs/Shutterstock. 566 Andersen Ross/Blend Images/Getty Images. 569 David Young-Wolff/PhotoEdit. 570 Anthony Bannister/Gallo Images/Getty Images. 571 Andrew Tichovolsky/Shutterstock. 572 Andrew Tichovolsky/Shutterstock. 575 (b) Pete Oxford/Minden Pictures/National Geographic Image Collection. (t) Andrew Tichovolsky/Shutterstock. 576 Semisatch/Shutterstock. 578 (l, r) icyimage/Shutterstock. 579 (l) Monkey Business Images/Shutterstock. (r) Russell Glenister/image100/Corbis. 580 (b) Graça Victoria/Shutterstock. (t) Stuart Miles/Shutterstock. 581 jocicalek/Shutterstock. 584 (b) LianeM/Shutterstock. (cb) Comstock/Jupiterimages. (cc, cl, cr) FoodCollection/StockFood America. (tcl, tcr, tl, tr) Stockbyte/Getty Images. 587 Image Source/Photolibrary. 588 (b) Comstock Images/Getty Images. (tc, tl) Jani Bryson/iStockphoto. (tr) Nathan Blaney/Photodisc/Getty Images. 589 Digital Vision/Getty Images. 590 PCL/Alamy Images. 591 (tc) Goodshoot/Jupiterimages. (tcr) Stockbyte/Getty Images. (tr) Medioimages/Photodisc/Getty Images. 592 Myrleen Pearson/Alamy Images. 594 David Young-Wolff/PhotoEdit. 595 Simone van den Berg/Shutterstock. 596 Dave King/Dorling Kindersley/Getty Images. 597 sonya etchison/Shutterstock. 598 Jim West/Alamy Images. 603 Judy Kennamer/iStockphoto. 604 Ariel Skelley/Blend Images/Getty Images. 605 (bc) Digital Vision/Getty Images. (bl) Leland Bobbe/Getty Images. (br) Brad Wynnyk/Shutterstock. (cc) PhotoDisc/Getty Images. (cl) Bruce Dale/National Geographic Image Collection. (cr) Rob Marmion/Shutterstock. (tc) Eden Studio Photo/Stock Image/Getty Images. (tl) Inc/Alamy Images. (tr) Ugurhan Betin/iStockphoto. 606 (bc) Ariel Skelley/Blend Images/Getty Images. (bl) Jozsef Szasz-Fabian/iStockphoto. (br) PhotoDisc/Getty Images. (cc) Kim Taylor/Dorling Kindersley/Getty Images. (cl) Chris Noble/Digital Vision/Getty Images. (cr) John Foxx Images/Imagestate. (tc) Chris Johns/National Geographic Image Collection. (tl) Ryan McVay/Photodisc/Getty Images. (tr) Dariusz Majgier/Shutterstock. 607 (bc) Don Bayley/iStockphoto. (bl) Richard Lewisohn/Getty Images. (br) aniad/Shutterstock. (cc) John Wang/Photodisc/Getty Images. (cl) Steve Baxter/Digital Vision/Getty Images. (cr) ampower/Shutterstock. (tc) Geoff Kidd/Oxford Scientific (OSF)/Photolibrary. (tl) Jupiterimages/Brand X Pictures/Getty Images. (tr) BananaStock/Jupiterimages. 608 (bc) FoodCollection/StockFood America. (bl) A. Huber/U. Starke/Corbis. (br) Digital Vision/Getty Images. (cc) Jong Kiam Soon/Shutterstock. (cl) Jacobus verhagen/iStockphoto. (tc) Andersen Ross/Blend Images/Getty Images. (tl) Teodor Ostojic/Shutterstock. (tr) Blend Images. 609 (bc) Andersen Ross/Getty Images. (bl) PhotoDisc/Getty Images. (br) Tim Fitzharris/Minden Pictures/National Geographic Image Collection. (cc) PhotoDisc/Getty Images. (cl) Ralph A. Clevenger/Corbis. (cr) Xulio Villarino/Hulton Archive/Getty Images. (tc) Theo Allofs/Corbis. (tl) De Agostini Picture Library/Getty Images. (tr) Stuart O'Sullivan/Taxi/Getty Images. 610 (bc) Paolo Florendo/iStockphoto. (bc) charlybutcher/iStockphoto. (bl) Getty Images. (bl) Westend61/Masterfile. (br) Jim Merli/Visuals Unlimited/Getty Images. (cc) Michael Bradley/Getty Images. (cc) Pavel Semenov/Shutterstock. (cl) Angelo Cavalli/Stockbyte/Getty Images. (cl) wonderlandstock/Alamy Images. (cr) Heidi & Hans-Juergen Koch/Minden Pictures. (tc) Kate Mathis/Photodisc/Getty Images. (tc) Kevin Dodge/Photolibrary. (tl) Maciek Zawada/National Geographic Image Collection. (tr) SuperStock. 611 (br) Randy Faris/Flirt Collection/Photolibrary. (cr) Andres Peiro Palmer/iStockphoto. (tl) Foto011/Shutterstock. (tr) Cultura Limited/SuperStock. 612 (bc) Masterfile. (bl) Rich Legg/iStockphoto. (br) Hannamariah/Shutterstock. (cc) Lara Gardarsdottir/iStockphoto. (cl) Jeff R Clow/Flickr/Getty Images. (cr) Marvin Dembinsky Photo Associates/Alamy Images. (tc) Joe Raedle/Getty Images. (tl) Fancy Collection/SuperStock. (tr) Corbis/Jupiterimages. 613 (bc) SuperStock. (bl) Anyka/Alamy Images. (br) Blend Images/SuperStock. (cc) Jupiterimages. (cl) BananaStock/Jupiterimages. (cr) FoodCollection/SuperStock. (tc) Ingram Publishing/Superstock. (tr) Walter B. McKenzie/Getty Images. 614 (bc) Arthur Kwiatkowski/iStockphoto. (bl) cultura/Corbis. (br) James L. Amos/Corbis. (cc) Mehmet Yunus/Shutterstock. (cl) Leland Bobbé/Corbis. (tc) Eric Isselée/Shutterstock. (tl) Shaun Egan/Photodisc/Getty Images. (tr) Drazen Vukelic/iStockphoto. 615 (bc) Uppercut Images/SuperStock. (bl) juliengrondin/Shutterstock. (br) BSIP/Photo Researchers, Inc. (cc) David Arky/Flame/Corbis. (cl) Ariel Skelley/Blend Images/age fotostock. (tc) Stephen Simpson/Taxi/Getty Images. (tl) Shutterstock. (tr) Galyna Andrushko/Shutterstock. 616 (bc) PhotoDisc/Getty Images. (bl) Moira Lovell/Alamy Images. (br) Judy Barranco/iStockphoto. (cc) PhotoDisc/Getty Images. (cl) Corbis. (cr) Digital Vision/Getty Images. (tc) Photodisc/Getty Images. (tl) Alberto Coto/Getty Images. (tr) Robert Gebbie Photography/Shutterstock. 617 (bc) Masterfile. (bl) Enrico Calderoni/Aflo Foto Agency/Photolibrary. (br) John-Francis Bourke/Getty Images. (cc) Ingram Publishing/Superstock. (cl) Tanya Constantine/Getty Images. (cr) SuperStock. (tc) Iakov Kalinin/iStockphoto. (tl) Robert Brenner/PhotoEdit. (tr) Polka Dot Images/age fotostock. 618 (bc) PhotoDisc/Getty Images. (bl) Artville. (br) Eric Raptosh Photography/Brand X Pictures/Getty Images. (cc) Jan Halaska/Index Stock Imagery RF/Photolibrary. (cl) Gary Hincks/Photo Researchers, Inc. (cr) Michael Dwyer/AP Images. (tc) Susan Van Etten/PhotoEdit. (tl) Richard Leech/National Geographic Image Collection. (tr) Xie Mingfei/ChinaFotoPress/Getty Images. 619 (bc) Sandro Tucci/Time & Life Pictures/Getty Images. (bl) Westend61/age fotostock. (br) Jose Luis Pelaez Inc/Blend Images/Getty Images. (cl) Martin Wagner/iStockphoto. (tc) Corbis Premium RF/Alamy Images. (tl) Bonnie Jacobs/iStockphoto. (tr) BananaStock/Jupiterimages. 620 (bc) Dmitriy Shironosov/Shutterstock. (bl) quavondo/iStockphoto. (br) Rob Marmion/Shutterstock. (cc) More Similar Images/Shutterstock. (cl) M.P.L. Fogden/Photoshot. (cr) JGI/Getty Images. (tc) Tom & Dee Ann McCarthy/Corbis. (tl) Mark Moffett/Minden Pictures. (tr) Mark Rose/iStockphoto. 621 (bc) age fotostock/SuperStock. (bl) Nancy Brammer/iStockphoto. (br) Samuel Aranda/Stringer/Getty Images. (cl) Photodisc/age fotostock. (cr) MetaTools. (tc) Janne Hämäläinen/Shutterstock. (tl) Annette Wiechmann/iStockphoto. (tr) Fancy/Corbis. 622 (bc) Image Source/Getty Images. (bl) Image Source/Corbis. (br) Paul Simcock/Photodisc/Getty Images. (cc) John Foxx Images/Imagestate. (cl) Michel Renaudeau/age fotostock. (cr) DigitalStock/Corbis. (tc) michaeljung/Shutterstock. (tl, tr) Nigel Cattlin/Visuals Unlimited. 623 (bc) Mary Evans Picture Library/The Image Works, Inc. (bl) Johanna Doorenbosch/iStockphoto. (br) Elena Elisseeva/Shutterstock. (cc) REB Images/Blend Images/Getty Images. (cl) SuperStock. (cr) Sami Sarkis/Getty Images. (tc) Comstock/Jupiterimages. (tl) Stockbyte/Getty Images. (tr) Somos/Veer/Getty Images. 624 (bl) FoodCollection/StockFood America. (br) Peter Dazeley/Photographer's Choice/Getty Images. (cl) Thomas Northcut/Photodisc/Getty Images. (cr) Steve Skjold/Alamy Images. (tc) Lucie Danninger/Shutterstock. (tl) Tamy Nichole Thomason/Shutterstock. 625 (bc) Hola Images/Corbis. (bl) Lion Hijmans/iStockphoto. (br) Rob Byron/Shutterstock. (cl) David Young-Wolff/PhotoEdit. (cr) Daryl Balfour/ The Image Bank/Getty Images. (tc) Fouquin Christophe/Panther Media/age fotostock. (tl) Ariel Skelley/Blend Images/Corbis. (tr) Radius Images/Jupiterimages. 626 (bc) juliengrondin/Shutterstock. (bl) Comstock Images/Getty Images. (br) Lisa F. Young/iStockphoto. (cl) PhotoDisc/Getty Images. (cr) James Woodson/Photodisc/Getty Images. (tc) Panoramic Images/Getty Images. (tl) Don Mason/Blend Images/Getty Images. (tr) Masterfile. 627 (bc) Neil Juggins/Alamy Images. (bl) Ingram Publishing/SuperStock. (cc) Fred Leonero/Shutterstock. (cl) Buslik/Shutterstock. (cr) Tetra Images/age fotostock. (tc) Frank Krahmer/Masterfile. (tl) Photodisc/Medioimages/Getty Images. (tr) Ingram Publishing/SuperStock.

Illustrator Credits

Cover Joel Sotelo, Visual Asylum. xii Amanda Hall. 3–6, 8–9 TSI Graphics. 29–31 Josée Masse. 34, 36, 38 TSI Graphics. 41–51 Chris MacNeil. 57 Mapping Specialists. 63, 67–69 TSI Graphics. 71–74, 76–77, 97–101 ("Animals, More or Less") Jared Lee. 104 TSI Graphics. 112 (map) Mapping Specialists. 130 (map and globe) Mapping Specialists. 139–141 TSI Graphics. 143–144, 146, 148, 206–207 Eileen Hine. 182 (map and globe) Mapping Specialists. 209–212, 214–215 TSI Graphics. 235–237 ("Ba's Business") Grace Lin. 240, 242, 244 TSI Graphics. 248 Chris Vallo. 250 (globe) Mapping Specialists. 261–265 ("The Ant and the Grasshopper") Pablo Bernasconi. 271–272 TSI Graphics. 275–278, 280 Chris Vallo. 282–297 Brian Ajhar. 300 Chris Vallo. 303 Mapping Specialists. 307–308 Chris Vallo. 309 John Kurtz. 310 Chris Vallo. 314, 321 Stephen Durke. 324–325 Norm Bendell. 331 Mapping Specialists. 336, 340–341 Chris Vallo. 343–344, 348 TSI Graphics. 352 Mapping Specialists. 374, 376, 378–379 TSI Graphics. 382 Mapping Specialists. 391–393 Amanda Hall. 396 TSI Graphics. 400–403 Belle Yang. 409–411 TSI Graphics. 413–414 Chris Vallo. 415 John Kurtz. 416, 444 Chris Vallo. 445 John Kurtz. 446 Chris Vallo. 468 Alain Cree. 469 Mapping Specialists. 471 Alain Cree. 473, 479–481 Chris Vallo. 483–484, 486, 488–489, 520, 522, 524 Chris Vallo. 526, 531, 533 (maps) Mapping Specialists. 542 (globe) Mapping Specialists. 551–553 Chris Vallo. 509–517 ("Two Clever Plans") Raúl Colón.

ge 644

Acknowledgements, continued

Mark-Up Models

Illustrations: 4.1 S1-S2 Grace Lin; 4.2 S1-S3 Chi Chung.

Cross Curricular Teamwork

Photographs: 22 Stephen Aaron Rees/Shutterstock. 33 lemonlight features/Alamy. 38 (tl) STILLFX/Shutterstock, (tr) fotosav/iStockphotoChristopher. 47 Andres Peiro Palmer/iStockphoto.

Language Builder Picture Cards

Photographs: D1 PhotoDisc/Getty Images. D2 Blend Images/Alamy Images. D3 ThinkStock/SuperStock. D4 Monkey Business Images/Shutterstock. D5 The Daily Oklahoman, Paul Southerland/AP Images. D6 Andersen Ross/Blend Images/Corbis. D7 Ed Bock/Corbis. D8 Scott J. Ferrell/Congressional Quarterly/Getty Images. D9 Nic Bothma/epa Nic Bothma/Corbis. D10 Thinkstock/Getty Images. D11 Richar Nowitz/National Geographic Image Collection. D12 Top-Pics TBK/Alamy Images. D13 StockStill/Alamy Images. D14 Emory Kristof/National Geographic Image Collection. D15 Sharpenson Ltd/Photo Researchers, Inc. D16 Bates Littlehales/Animals Animals. D17 Richard Day/Animals Animals. D18 Michael Nichols/National Geographic Image Collection. D19 Wes C. Skiles/National Geographic Image Collection. D20 Michael S. Quinton/National Geographic Image Collection. D21 Laura Romin & Larry Dalton/Alamy Images. D22 William Leaman/Alamy Images. D23 R. Andrew Odum/Peter Arnold, Inc. D24 George F. Mobley/National Geographic Image Collection. D25 John Foxx Images/Imagestate. D26 Gavin Thorn/Alamy Images. D27 yxowert/Shutterstock. D28 David R. Frazier Photolibrary, Inc./Alamy Images. D29 Pinchuk Alexey/Shutterstock. D30 David Thyberg/Shutterstock. D31 Arvind Balaraman/Shutterstock. D32 Inta Eihmane/Shutterstock. D33 Chris Curtis/Shutterstock. D34 thumb/Shutterstock. D35 John A. Anderson/Shutterstock. D36 Igor Plotnikov/Shutterstock. D37 Pixtal/SuperStock. D38 John Fortunato Photography/Corbis. D39 Michael Newman/PhotoEdit. D40 Corbis. D41 Brand X Pictures/PunchStock. D42 PhotoDisc/Getty Images. D43 H. Edward Kim/National Geographic Image Collection. D44 Hulton Archive/Getty Images. D45 Monty Rakusen/Jupiterimages. D46 dbimages/Alamy Images. D47 Jupiterimages. D48 Philip and Karen Smith/Jupiterimages. D49-D50 Michael Newman/PhotoEdit. D51 Peter Cade/Stone/Getty Images. D52 Sebastian Duda/Shutterstock. D53 Stocksearch/Alamy Images. D54 WitR/Shutterstock. D55 Susan Fox/Shutterstock. D56 Claudio Baldini/Shutterstock. D57 Kevin Britland/Shutterstock. D58 John Foxx Images/Imagestate. D59 Robert Kyllo/Shutterstock. D60 Jim Richardson/National Geographic Image Collection. D61 Bailey-Cooper Photography 4/Alamy Images. D62 Rich Reid/Animals Animals. D63 Stuart Walker/Alamy Images. D64 PearlBucknall/Alamy Images. D65 Artville. D66 Layland Masuda/Shutterstock. D67 Jorge R. Gonzalez/Shutterstock. D68 Premier Edition Image Library/Superstock. D69 Ingram Publishing/Superstock. D70 Corbis. D71 Marco Andras/age footstock. D72 Clive Chilvers/Shutterstock. D73 Michael Newman/PhotoEdit. D74 Cosmo Condina North America/Alamy Images. D75 Sergio Pitamitz/Alamy Images. D76 Bettina Strenske/Alamy Images. D77 Alaska Stock Images/National Geographic Image Collection. D78 juliengrondin/Shutterstock. D79 Karen Kasmauski/National Geographic Image Collection. D80 Carsten Peter/National Geographic Image Collection. D81 Simon Fraser/Photo Researchers, Inc. D82 Creatas/Jupiterimages. D83 Patrick Koster/Alamy Images. D84 imagebroker/Alamy Images. D85 Freddy Eliasson/Shutterstock. D86 Interfoto/Alamy Images. D87 Phil Degginger/Alamy Images. D88 Emmanuel Lattes/Alamy Images. D89 James L. Stanfield/National Geographic Image Collection. D90 Jo Kearney/Alamy Images. D91 John Scofield/National Geographic Image Collection. D92 Tibor BOGNAR/Photononstop/Photolibrary. D93 Richard Powers/Corbis. D94 Ingram Publishing (Superstock Limited)/Alamy Images. D95 Jenny Acheson/Lifesize/Getty Images. D96 Colin Underhill/Alamy Images. D97 PhotoDisc/Getty Images. D98 Frank Siteman/PhotoEdit. D99 FancyVeerSet16/Alamy Images. D100 Neil Holmes Freelance Digital/Alamy Images. D101 PhotoDisc/Getty Images. D102 foto-zone/Alamy Images. D103 Andrew Twort/Alamy Images. D104 Tony Freeman/PhotoEdit.

Language and Literacy Teamwork

Photographs: 5 Scott Peterson/Getty Images. 20 Creatas/Jupiterimages. 22 Tui De Roy/Minden Pictures/National Geographic Image Collection. 27 Chris Lyon/Getty Images. 31 Jonathan Blair/Corbis. 36 Artville.